POINT
COUNTERPOINT

eight cases for composition

Thayle K. Anderson
Murray State University

Kent Forrester
Murray State University

Harcourt Brace Jovanovich, Publishers

San Diego   New York   Chicago   Austin   Washington, D.C.
London   Sydney   Tokyo   Toronto

For our parents

Mark Kermit Anderson
Gwen Morrill Anderson

George Washington Forrester
Fern Milner Forrester

Preface

Although the almost 100 essays in *Point Counterpoint: Eight Cases for Composition* can serve to inspire and generate all kinds of writing assignments, they should serve particularly well as sources for research papers and argumentation essays. In fact, this book contains almost everything the instructor needs for courses in which students write papers that incorporate the ideas of others.

Chapter 1, for example, includes information on how to analyze the argument in a published essay as well as directions for the beginning writer who must write an argument or documented report. Chapter 10 contains a brief handbook on the research paper that reviews problem areas such as introducing quotations, handling paraphrases, and constructing summaries. The concluding chapter also includes instruction on the correct format for the research paper, the use of footnotes, and proper bibliographic style.

Each of the other eight chapters of *Point Counterpoint* contains thematically grouped reading selections that are so closely related that students will be able to write well-developed research papers without going beyond the material in that chapter. All the readings have been chosen both for their general appeal and for their specific reference to issues across the college curriculum.

The material in the middle eight chapters can, of course, be used in a variety of ways. For example, students can be asked to read the essays in a given chapter, choose a side, and then write a documented research paper in which they state a position and support it with material from the book. Or students may be asked to write a research essay in which they analyze and summarize the many different views presented on a particular subject. Reading just a few essays in a given chapter should provide enough information for students to write a comparison/contrast paper or an informed personal essay.

Each chapter begins with a short introduction to the issue at hand and ends with a list of suggestions for writing. To assist the process of documentation, we have placed a note at the bottom of the page on which each selection begins. These notes include bibliographical details. In addition, they often include descriptions of the periodical in which the selection appeared and remarks about the author. We have not, however, included the original page numbers of these selections. Thus, students, in their citations, will have to use the page numbers of this book as if they were the page numbers of the original sources.

We would like to thank a number of people who helped us put this book together. Four of our colleagues at Murray State University—John Adams, Mike Cohen, Fred Cornelius, and Jerry Herndon—read Chapter 1 and showed us ways to improve it. John Snapper of Grossmont College read the complete manuscript and offered suggestions and encouragement. Finally, we want to thank our editors: Paul Nockleby, whose suggestions during the early stages of the book were invaluable; Eleanor Garner, whose friendly advice and research acumen made gathering copyright permissions a whole lot easier than it otherwise would have been; Rick Roehrich and Janice Anderson, whose careful attention to details saved us from seeing our errors in print.

Contents

· 1 ·

Taking It Apart: Reading an Argument (and Hints for Writing One)   1

· 2 ·

The Wilderness: Leave It Alone?   15

·3·

Abortion: Under What Circumstances?   77

·4·

Advertising: Is It More Than Harmless Puffery?   129

· 5 ·

Sex Differences: Innate or Acquired?   179

·6·

Bilingual Education: Does It Work?   227

·7·

Fairy Tales: Benign or Pernicious?   275

·8·

Obscenity: To Censor or Not? 321

·9·

Japanese Internment: Wartime Necessity or Tragic Error? 395

· 10 ·

Putting It Together: A Research Writer's Handbook   473

· 1 ·

Taking It Apart: Reading an Argument (And Hints for Writing One)

Preachers argue that we'd best change our ways if we want to get into Heaven. Advertisers argue that we ought to buy more widgets. Environmentalists argue that we ought to stop buying those abominable widgets. Ardent poets try to reason their coy mistresses into bed. Coy mistresses argue that there is world enough and time for *that*. As children, we argue that time will never pass and we'd better open the Christmas presents now. As old people, perhaps we'll argue, as Goethe did on his deathbed, that time passes *too* quickly and we need more time and light. W.C. Fields argued on his gravestone that he'd be better off in Philadelphia.

This book is also full of arguments. We think they'll challenge your mind. We're sure that some of them will stir your blood. You may want to jump in, for instance, and argue along with some of the writers in Chapter 2 that we ought to ban automobiles and convenience stores from our national parks. Or you may be eager to test your arguments against those of the writers in Chapter 3 who claim that it's morally right to terminate the life of a fetus through abortion. Or you may even want to pick a few nits with those in Chapter 8 who argue that fairy tales are a terrible influence on kids.

There's nothing like a good argument to warm the heart and engage the ego. Economics bores most people to tears. But give them a side to argue—let's say, John

1

Maynard Keynes's ideas on deficit spending—and suddenly Keynesian theory is the most wonderful and interesting thing in the world, quite obviously the best of the economic theories, and soon these brand-new Keynesians are saying bah! to the anti-Keynesians, neo-Keynesians, pseudo-Keynesians, and crypto-Keynesians. It's also a practical thing to be able to construct good arguments. It sometimes seems as though arguments, not love, make the world go round. We're always trying to persuade someone of something. Here's why you ought to marry me. Here's why you ought to hire me. Here's why you ought to promote me.

It's important to be able to tell when someone is blowing smoke rather than making a sound argument. Too much credulity, and we're off buying flimsy toys and flimsy politics. These are reasons enough to learn more about how to read and how to write arguments.

FROM THE READER'S VIEW: THINKING ABOUT THE WRITER'S AUDIENCE

The audience influences the way a writer or speaker communicates. When Samuel Johnson heard that there was a woman preaching the gospel in eighteenth-century London, he huffed to his drinking companions, "Sir, a woman preaching is like a dog's walking on his hind legs. It is not done well; but you are surprised to find it done at all."

You women out there! How do *you* like Johnson's argument? It's quite sound, don't you think? No? You mean to say that a woman preacher is not like a dog walking on its hind legs? You think Johnson's argument facile, his sentiments sexist, his analogy false? How can that be? His argument went over quite well indeed when he first uttered it to a bunch of like-minded eighteenth-century gentlemen, all of whom thought it splendid reasoning, unassailable really, and quite the best thing on the subject that they'd heard in a fortnight. We suspect, however, that if Johnson had been arguing with a group of eighteenth-century ladies, he probably would have constructed his argument somewhat differently, perhaps with polite deference to his listeners.

Writers who argue well keep their audience in mind. In an essay in *Christianity Today*, John Stott argues that the fetus is very much a human being. He then goes on to quote the New Testament, which states that an expectant mother is a "woman with child" ("Does Life Begin before Birth?" p. 106). That biblical quotation no doubt worked well in *Christianity Today*, a magazine for readers who have a special interest in reading articles from a Christian viewpoint. Stott rightly assumed that Biblical quotations would give a special kind of authority to his argument.

That same biblical quotation wouldn't have worked as well in *Harper's*, a general interest magazine. *Harper's* no doubt has Christian readers. But *Harper's* also has readers who are atheists, Buddhists, agnostics, Jews, and Druids. Because each special-interest group forms only a small part of the total audience, *Harper's* writers can't afford to make a special appeal to any single segment.

Now for a suggestion: before you read an article in this text, it's a good idea to read the footnote to discover the periodical in which the article originally appeared.

If you find a general-interest periodical there—*Newsweek, Atlantic, Saturday Review*—the writer's audience was the "common reader." "Common" readers, of course, include cat fanciers, joggers, recluses, high school graduates, Ph.D.s, and vegetarians, as well as people with every other interest and appetite. But they don't come to a general-interest periodical to satisfy their special interest or political predilections. They go, for example, to *Vegetarian Weekly* or the *Village Voice* for those things.

If you find a specialized periodical in that footnote—*Christian Century, Commonweal, Ms., National Review,* and the like—you will probably notice a more personal tone, allusions to common beliefs, scorn for common enemies, easy generalizations. When writers know that their readers already agree with their position, they don't feel as much pressure to construct a heavily reasoned, fact-filled argument with every generalization qualified and validated. In fact, they sometimes write merely to stir up the troops.

We're not saying that you should dismiss the arguments in these specialized journals, but we do suggest that you keep in mind the audience for which they were originally created. That's part of judging an argument. Keep a grain of salt handy— that is, read with your critical intelligence functioning.

WRITING HINTS: TAKING ACCOUNT OF YOUR AUDIENCE

1. Write for the common reader. Like the writer for *Newsweek,* your audience will likely be—unless your instructor tells you otherwise—that ill-defined, amorphous "common reader." (Actually, of course, you're writing for your English teacher. But your instructor is no doubt common enough to use as a representative specimen.) You can't count on your common readers' knowledge of technical matters, but you can count on their knowledge of matters of general interest. They read the newspapers and a few magazines and books. See those people waiting at the bus stop? They're your audience.

Of course, they're ready to be interested in coins, cats, coffins, or arguments about birth control or euthanasia—if you can present the information in an interesting way. And if you're fair enough and persuasive enough, you might even get them to change their minds.

2. Imagine an individual. Even though a picture of this "common reader" is hazy, that doesn't mean you can't have someone in particular in mind as you write. Indeed, you might imagine yourself talking to a friend. Look your friend in the face. Now try to clarify a point. Try to be persuasive. Anticipate your friend's objections and reactions to what you're saying. Your writing will probably be clearer and fresher if you can do this.

3. Stop to explain. Because you have this generalized audience in mind (even when represented by a single person), your discussion can't be too technical— unless, of course, you stop to explain or define. What you stop for, of course, is a matter of judgment. You'll probably need to stop and explain what a double helix is, but you won't want to stop and explain what an electron microscope is. Once again, picture your friend. You would probably need to explain to that person, for instance, why stylites had to get up on the right side of the bed. But for most references, you will have to use your best judgment. Would you need to describe a *danse macabre*? a snorkle? the Snorkles? endorphins? Margaret Sanger? *Candide*? Dopey and Doc? C. S. Lewis? symbolism? satire? future shock? Think of your reader before making your decisions. Definitions clog the flow of writing, so don't stop to define too often. Often the context of the reference will make it understandable.

Of course, when a definition lies at the heart of your argument, take all the time you need to explain it clearly. If you were writing on abortion, for instance, you would want to make absolutely clear to your readers the distinction between an embryo and a fetus. You don't have to do this formally: "We had better define our terms before we begin. . . ." Nothing smothers a paper more thoroughly than beginning with a formal definition. But somewhere in your essay—probably early, perhaps even in a note—you'll have to make important distinctions clear.

When in doubt about whether to explain a reference, our advice is to assume your readers know more than they do. It's better to flatter your readers by assuming they recognize a reference rather than patronize them by assuming they don't.

4. Don't antagonize your readers needlessly. If you were writing for an audience that shared your quirks and politics, your writing would be shaped by that specialized audience. For instance, if you were writing for the *New Republic*, you might drop a snide remark about Richard Nixon. Your audience, composed of passionate liberals, would no doubt enjoy your good taste and wit.

However, if you were to drop that same snide remark on your common reader, you'd likely turn off a whole pack of them. There are a lot of staunch Republicans, Whittier College alumni, and just plain folks out there who think that Richard Nixon is one heck of a guy. So if you're really trying to persuade your readers rather than just blowing smoke, you'll have to keep your political passions and snide remarks in check. Save them for discussions with like-minded friends.

5. Take care when writing against the grain. When you're writing against the grain—arguing on the unpopular side of an issue—your job is even more difficult. They're out there, you know, all those people who disagree with your position, waiting to pounce on your argument and reveal it for the flimsy thing it is.

Because of those disapproving hordes out there, it's important for you to spell out each step of your argument and to identify underlying assumptions. You might even want to begin further back than you normally would. For instance, if you were writing a defense of an unpopular position—let's say a defense of the manipulative language of advertising—you might have to begin by discussing why advertising language needs defending. Later on, you may want to bring up (so you can dissect and discard) the opposing arguments—the ones that will spring so easily to the minds of that hostile audience out there. (If you've noticed, it's infinitely easier to spot the logical flaws in an argument we don't agree with than in one we are fond of.)

6. Work hard to hold the common reader's attention. You'll have to work harder to capture the interest of a general audience than you would for a specialized audience. If you were writing for *Cat World*, a discussion of the relative merits of the brands of kitty litter may very well freeze your readers to their seats and leave them panting for more. But when you're writing for a general audience, most of what you say about cats is boring—unless you make those cats come alive and leap off the page.

Fortunately, a good controversy, like the ones that many of you will be writing, usually produces lively prose. Just don't let your paper become too theory-laden. Stay close to earth. Be specific and concrete. Fill your paper with examples, case histories, and real people.

FROM THE READER'S VIEW: ANALYZING A WRITER'S REASONING

A writer's reasoning, his or her "pure" argument, is sometimes obscured by the mass of words that twist and turn their way down the page. By the time readers get to the end of the essay, having taken a few detours and double-backs along the way, they aren't quite sure how they got there.

Good readers learn to distinguish between the main road of the writer's argument and the meandering sideroads. They can then see more clearly the writer's bare argument. Let's look at an excerpt from one of the most famous arguments in recent history, Winston Churchill's speech to the House of Commons in 1940, just before the Battle of Britain:

> The whole fury and might of the enemy must very soon be turned on us. Hitler knows that he will have to break us in this island or lose the war. If we can stand up to him, all Europe may be free and the life of the world may move forward into broad, sunlit uplands. But if we fail, then the whole world, including the United States, . . . will sink into the abyss of a new Dark Age made more sinister . . . by the lights of perverted science. Let us therefore brace ourselves to our duties, and so bear ourselves that, if the British Empire and its Commonwealth last for a thousand years, men will still say, "This was their finest hour."

Now let's break it down to its bare argument:

Premise: If we win the coming battle, the world will flourish.
Premise: If we lose the coming battle, the world will decline.
Conclusion: Therefore, we must win.

That's all there is to it. As you read the essays in this book, you will discover that the arguments can almost always be reduced to a few simple premises (reasons) that support the writer's conclusion. Of course, in an essay the conclusion will usually be stated first, in the writer's introduction. Then as the essay proceeds, the writer will present his or her reasons, or premises, for having come to that conclusion. At any rate, if you want to see the writer's reasoning, first clear away the undergrowth to make the writer's premises stand up straight and tall.

WRITING HINTS: YOUR REASONING

1. Before you begin writing, break down your argument to its simplest form. Write your conclusion first. (That, of course, will be your thesis statement, which will most likely appear in the first paragraph of your paper.) Then underneath that conclusion, list the reasons that led you to that conclusion. These are the topic sentences that support your thesis. You have just written a simple outline.

2. Don't overgeneralize. On the street, our sweeping generalizations usually go unchallenged: "My mom is the best cook in the world."; "The Republicans are trying to ruin the country." Fortunately, words that come from our mouths are as ephemeral as wisps of smoke, and listeners don't expect us to scrupulously support our generalizations. But they expect much more from us when we write.

Naturally, you don't have to qualify every generalization. Writers who do that sound pompous. But you do need to qualify those general statements that are conspicuously false, or those that are central to your argument. If you were to begin your paper with "Music is vital to everyone," your reader might very well respond, in his or her mind, with, "Oh really? It's not to me." Here's that same statement, now qualified a number of ways:

Music is vital to *most* people.
Music is vital to *many* people.
Music is vital to *some* people.
Music is vital to a *few* people.
Music is vital *to me.*

The point is this: know when you're making a generalization and ask yourself if it might strike your reader as a statement that needs to be qualified.

3. Don't reduce complicated problems to a single cause. For instance, if you blame the ban on school prayer for poor discipline in schools, you have oversimplified the causes. If you blame television for poor reading skills, you have oversimplified the causes. These are complicated matters that shouldn't be reduced to single causes. Of course, if you want to discuss only one cause, you can begin your argument by saying, "There are various reasons for poor reading skills today—simplified textbooks, poor reading instruction, the pace of modern life, and so on—but I want to discuss what I feel is the most important reason: too much television watching."

FROM THE READER'S VIEW: ANALYZING A WRITER'S SOURCES

Reasons are airy things that are apt to float away unless they're tied down and supported. Good writers frequently support their reasons by giving examples and by citing statistics. They also borrow other writers' ideas. Here are three reasons why a writer borrows:

1. To support an opinion. In Russell Kirk's essay, "Children and the Lex Talionis" (p. 303), the author asserts that fairy tales are good for children. To support his opinion, Kirk calls up an idea by Bruno Bettelheim, an "eminent" (Kirk's word) psychologist. According to Kirk, Bettelheim believes that a fairy tale "satisfies the child's yearning for order and justice." Quite obviously, it's a good idea to have experts like Bruno Bettelheim agree with you.

Of course, it's all a bit more complicated than we have let on. In questions having to do with aesthetics and ethics, the experts' opinions are often little more than educated guesses. Bettelheim the psychologist may be wrong about fairy tales, and your Aunt Matilda, who believes that fairy tales warp a kid's sense of justice, may be right. But for all that, it's still better to use Bettelheim as your authority than your Aunt Matilda.

Now for a pop quiz to end this discussion: Is a literature professor's opinion of whether a book is pornographic more valid than that of a gamekeeper? If it is, why is it? If it is not, why would a writer want to support his own opinion with a literature professor's opinion?

2. To clarify or support a technical point. When an argument turns on technical matters, writers call on experts. Obviously, a writer who is arguing that Pascal is a better computer language than BASIC is better off quoting a computer programmer than a carpenter. Experts can't settle ethical matters—no one can "settle" an ethical matter—but they can sometimes settle technical questions around which an ethical argument revolves. For instance, when arguing that capital punishment is a deterrent to violent crime, an author might very well call on the writings of a research criminologist who has studied the issue of deterrency. That would not settle the question of whether the state should execute criminals—that's an ethical consideration—but it can lend weight to one of the writer's premises.

Here's the kind of thing we're talking about: Jo Durden-Smith and Diane deSimone ("The Perils of Paul, the Pangs of Pauline," p. 201) support their argument that males have a "math gene" by bringing up a study by two Johns Hopkins professors, Camilla Benbow and Julian Stanley, who had concluded that there is likely a "biological basis" for the difference between males and females in mathematical reasoning. Simple enough: Benbow and Stanley, the experts, are being used to support an argument by Durden-Smith and deSimone. Remember, though, Benbow and Stanley's findings don't settle an ethical question, such as whether we should encourage females to take math classes. That is a question of values. Experts can only testify on their expertise.

In fact, Benbow and Stanley's conclusion doesn't even really *settle* the question of whether males are biologically programmed to perform better at math. Research findings on educational matters (in particular those on the nature/nurture issue) are difficult to interpret and never as definitive as the answer to a laboratory finding— whether, for instance, an amoeba shuns light. Be modest in what you claim for your experts.

3. To represent the other side. To clarify their own positions, writers have to tell their readers what the other side thinks. As Sidney Harris of the *Chicago Sun-Times* once wrote, "The stone of opposition sharpens ideas." Watch how Charles Hartshorne, arguing for abortion ("Concerning Abortion: Attempt at a Rational View," p. 112), first summarizes one of his opponents:

> One theologian who writes on the subject—Paul Ramsey—thinks that a human egg cell becomes a human individual with a moral claim to survive if it has been fertilized.

Now that Hartshorne has summarized his opponent's idea, he argues with the summary:

> Yet this egg cell has none of the qualities that we have in mind when we proclaim our superior worth to the chimpanzees or dolphins. It cannot speak, reason, or judge between right and wrong.

Easy enough. Writers clarify their own positions by paraphrasing or quoting their opponents.

WRITING HINTS: YOUR USE OF SOURCES

Naturally, you will be using sources for the same reasons that the professional writers do—to support an opinion, to clarify a technical point, to bring up the opposition's words to argue with. But there are other matters to think about when you use sources.

1. Paraphrase your source until there is something pungent to quote. Most of your borrowings will be composed of paraphrases, not quotations. In fact, you should have a reason for quoting. Don't "ride" your source. Wait until the author says something flavorfully or poignantly or starkly; then stop and quote your source. Otherwise, paraphrase.

2. Keep your quotations short. Even when you do have a good reason for quoting rather than paraphrasing, keep the quotation short. There is rarely a good reason to quote an entire paragraph. Quote a word, a phrase, a sentence. If you quote more than a few sentences, you're probably quoting too much.

3. When your source's background is such that it might lend some credibility to the author's words, don't fail to mention it. In fact, unless your source is so famous that no introduction is needed, you should identify the author's occupation or special expertise: "As the Nobel Prize winning physicist, Susan Harcourt says, . . ."

4. Don't hesitate to cite a staff writer for *Newsweek* or the *Atlantic* or some other national magazine. You needn't apologize. Some of the most thoughtful writing nowadays comes from essays that appear in weekly newsmagazines. Besides, there are few "experts" in morality outside of Mother Teresa. If the *Newsweek* author is anonymous, merely write, "In a *Newsweek* article, the author claims that. . . ." If the article is signed, you might mention the reporter's name and introduce the quotation something like this: "Jim Massey, a *Newsweek* correspondent, concludes that. . . ."

5. Don't claim too much merely because your authority is famous. For one thing, the reputation of your famous authority may have declined over the years. Freud's idea that there is a sexual basis for almost all mental illness has been discredited. Marx's theories about the inevitable decline of capitalism have been challenged by most economists. Christopher Wren's ideas about the use of pillars in architecture are outdated. Joshua Reynold's ideas about art are no longer valid for most artists. Just because you've found a famous "expert," don't assume that you've clinched your case.

6. If the author or the periodical in which the essay appears has a strong and well-known bias, treat it with care. Because you're writing for a general audience, you'd better not crow too loudly that you have borrowed from *Rolling Stone* or *National Review*. This is not to say that you can't borrow words from an author writing for *Rolling Stone*. You might just have to handle it differently. For one thing, if you think that the periodical might turn off readers, there's no sense in going out of your way to call attention to it by mentioning its name in the introduction to your quotation. If you want to mention it, you might anticipate, and therefore defuse, your readers' objections by calling attention to the source's partisan slant. You could, for instance, write, "Although it's true that *Soldier of Fortune* tends to romanticize war, Lance Hearty's argument in that magazine in favor of the citizen's right to own tactical nuclear weapons remains cogent and clear-eyed."

FROM THE READER'S VIEW: ANALYZING A WRITER'S EXAMPLES

Writers also support their reasons by using examples. Naturally, an example or two never "proves" anything. Writers use them mainly to give their airy reasons a bit of life and substance. In a *Time* article, "The Weaker Sex? Hah!" (p. 181), for instance, the writer shows us that even pregnancy should not deter the athletic woman. He cites the example of Wendy Boglioli, who competed in the national

A.A.U. 100-yard-freestyle swimming competition when she was 5 months pregnant. An example can be a powerful persuader—as long as it doesn't stick out as the kind of thing that happens too rarely to worry about.

WRITING HINTS: YOUR USE OF EXAMPLES

1. Choose your examples from a large and representative barrel of apples. If you pick a crispy apple from a barrel and then conclude that the rest of the apples are also crispy, you have jumped to a hasty conclusion. You should have examined several apples from all levels of the barrel.

Of course, it's hard to say how many examples you will need. Sometimes a single representative example will suffice; at other times you will need to follow a point with many examples. We know that's not very helpful advice, but the situations that can arise are too varied to allow us to offer anything more specific.

2. Look for gut-wrenching examples. Describe the festering resentment of Japanese Americans whose rights were abridged in World War II "relocation" camps; detail a fetus's movements as it is being aborted; show the trash-strewn grounds and air pollution of Yellowstone Park. Don't flinch at the real world that lies behind your bloodless abstractions.

FROM THE READER'S VIEW: ANALYZING A WRITER'S USE OF PERSONAL EXPERIENCES

Writers who strive for a tone of objectivity avoid supporting their argument with personal experiences. Of course, some writers are willing to trade that objectivity for the credibility and tone of "authenticity" that personal examples give to an argument.

Professionals writing within their expertise often mix personal experiences with more conventional argumentative devices. In "Why I Favor Liberalized Abortion" (p. 92), Dr. Alan Guttmacher begins one paragraph with these words: "The second person I ever saw die was a Mrs. K, the mother of four children, who succumbed to the effects of an illegal, probably self-induced abortion." That is an effective use of a personal experience.

And of course no one can describe the feelings of someone as well as the person who felt it. In "Outcast Americans" (p. 407), William Robinson describes his feelings when his gardener's Japanese American daughter, whom he had known since her birth, was picked up early in World War II by War Relocation officials. First he quotes the young girl's parting words: "I hope you will think of me. I shall think of you." Then Robinson describes, in an effectively understated way, his own thoughts: "The door closed and she was gone. I don't know where she is now."

WRITING HINTS: YOUR USE OF PERSONAL EXPERIENCES

1. Certain kinds of arguments almost forbid the use of personal experiences. If you were writing a paper for your astronomy professor on the chemical makeup of the gas in stellar clouds, you wouldn't want to insert yourself too obtrusively into the article: "Then I looked into the telescope and discovered, my goodness, the prettiest colors I'd ever seen. . . ." Or if you were writing a literary paper showing that the apple in *Snow White* is a symbol of seduction, you wouldn't want to describe your experiences with apples.

2. Don't let your argument hinge on personal experiences. You might, however, offer them up in your introduction or conclusion. If, for instance, you were writing about increasing the penalty for drunken driving, you might begin by recounting the accident you had when a drunken driver slammed into the side of your car. Or you might offer up a personal experience to lend additonal weight to the authorities you've already used.

But don't let your argument depend too heavily on personal experiences. Focus your reader's attention on the thing you are discussing, not on your reaction to (or personal experiences with) the thing.

FROM THE READER'S VIEW: ANALYZING A WRITER'S ANALOGIES

An analogy is a tricky thing. A dying person, in many ways, is *like* a falling leaf. A hospital room, in some ways, is *like* a prison. Snowmobile tracks in a wilderness area, in some way, are *like* the desecration of a church. But you see the problem, don't you? In each case there are some obvious and significant differences between the two things that are being compared.

The reader may find herself saying, "Wait a minute, a patient in a hospital is not like a criminal in a prison. The patient in a hospital room is there voluntarily; a criminal in a prison is there involuntarily." Once the reader begins arguing with a writer's analogies, the writer has lost the argument.

WRITING HINTS: YOUR USE OF ANALOGIES

1. Don't let your argument rest on an analogy. Analogies can be persuasive and suggestive, but it's foolhardy to let a point rest on one. The easiest way out of this problem is to be modest about the purpose of your analogy. You could, for instance, introduce your analogy with, "In one important way, reading a book is like taking a trip." Now you can go on to develop your analogy without worry.

2. Think your analogies through carefully. Let's say that you are arguing that the state has every right to execute criminals. To support that argument, you use this analogy: "Just as the farmer has a right to protect his sheep by shooting hungry wolves, the state has the right to protect its citizens from dangerous criminals by executing them." But analogies can be the Achilles' heel of an argument. That analogy between the wolves and the criminals, for instance, would probably prompt your reader to say, "We shouldn't treat humans in the same way that we treat wolves. Besides, a farmer doesn't have to consider constitutional safeguards as he blasts away at marauding wolves."

If you use an analogy, think it through first. There should be no crucial differences between the two things being compared.

FROM THE READER'S VIEW: ANALYZING A WRITER'S USE OF STATISTICS

In the kinds of arguments that the writers are making in this book, statistics lend credibility, but not proof. Let's see why. Here's part of the opening paragraph of an anti-abortion argument by John Stott ("Does Life Begin Before Birth?" p. 106):

> In England and Wales, since David Steel's 1967 Abortion Act, although illegal abortions have not decreased, the annual average of legal abortions has increased from 10 to more than 100,000. For every five babies born alive, one is now aborted. A human fetus is being destroyed every five minutes.

Those statistics—100,000 fetuses destroyed each year—are troubling. But in fact those statistics have little to do with the "pure" part of the author's argument against abortion, which comes later in his essay. His statistics only prove that legal abortions have increased since abortions became legal. A supporter of legal abortions might very well use the same statistics to buttress the argument that legal abortions have prevented untold suffering because now women are having abortions in the clean, safe environs of a hospital rather than in the rat-infested backrooms of illegal storefront abortionists.

The point is this: when a writer uses statistics, you should think about them carefully. What are they doing there? In what way, if in any way, do they support the writer's argument? What is their purpose?

WRITING HINTS: YOUR USE OF STATISTICS

1. One of the best places to use statistics, especially if they are interesting or startling, is in your introduction. Here's the kind of thing we mean. In an argument that women are catching up with men in athletic achievement ("In Sports, 'Lions' vs. 'Tigers,'" p. 194), Eric Gelman tells us that Don Schollander set an Olympic and world record in the 400-meter freestyle in 4 minutes, 12.2 seconds in 1964. If he had clocked the same time in the women's 400-meter freestyle in the 1980 Olympics, he would have placed fifth.

When you have eye-opening statistics, begin your paper with them. However, make sure they're eye-opening. The usual dull statistics make terrible openings.

2. Don't claim too much for your statistics. When Dr. Stott brings up that troubling statistic, 100,000 abortions a year, his only claim—and it is only implied—is that there is a problem. Only later does he argue. Statistics usually only point out a problem; they are not used as a part of the reasoning process.

FROM THE READER'S VIEW: ANALYZING A WRITER'S STYLE AND TONE

A writer's style and tone have to fit the circumstances. It would be fatal for a writer to be too casual and flippant in an article for *Sunnyside and Casket*, a magazine for morticians. It would be fatal for a writer to use a stiff formal style in a piece about Bozo the Clown.

For most situations, writers use the "middle" style—clear, unpretentious, sometimes ironic, relatively unadorned. There is, of course, a great deal of latitude within that middle style, as you will see in the articles in this book.

And most writers try to give their essays the appearance of fair-mindedness and tolerance. In fact, those two qualities probably do more for their argument than a hundred examples and the most refined logic. Lewis Smedes builds almost his whole article ("The Arguments in Favor of Abortion Are Strong . . . ," p. 122) around the arguments the other side makes. Here's how his article begins:

> Sometimes I like to list the strongest arguments I can find to support a point of view I think is wrong.

He then goes on to list each of his opponent's arguments, in turn, and he treats each with respect. In fact, he agrees with all of them except the last—the question of the "humanness" of the fetus. I think you'll see that Smedes's argument against abortion is helped immensely by his fair-minded and tolerant tone.

WRITING HINTS: MANAGING YOUR STYLE AND TONE

Ethical questions of the kind that you'll be arguing in your papers can't be proved. Whether we *can* keep patients alive after their hearts have stopped is a matter that can be settled. But whether we *should* keep them alive—an ethical question—is arguable. Reasonable people can differ.

That is why all of us should be modest, tolerant, honest, and fair-minded. We should argue vigorously, but we should also be virtuous by arguing fairly.

1. Develop a tolerant tone. Truth, after all, comes in many forms and is usually found wavering somewhere on a line between two extremes. Under these circumstances, the best you can do is find your position on that line and then do the best and fairest job you can of persuading others that the place you've chosen is reasonable.

If you're cocksure and intolerant, you'll get the expected knee-jerk reaction from those who already agree with you, but you'll antagonize those who are ready to be persuaded. Bring up the opposing arguments and treat them with respect. Go ahead and admit, if you can stand it, that the other side of the argument is not *pure* nonsense. That admission won't kill you. In fact, it might even leave your reader with the impression that you're a person who listens to all sides of the argument before making up your mind.

2. Develop a reasoned tone. Give your reader the impression that you're after the truth, not just a strong argument. If your source is contradicted by another source, comment on that fact. If the facts in the case are ambiguous, inform your reader of that ambiguity. You're a searcher after truth, wherever it lies. And avoid the word "prove." Begin your contentions with words like "These arguments suggest that . . .," "These examples make it easy to believe that . . .," "Thus, there is good reason to believe that. . . ."

3. Use the middle style when writing for the common reader. Avoid the low. Avoid words that smack of hipness, like "unreal" and "gross." If you feel proud about how hip or streetwise one of your words is, it's probably too low for your paper.

Avoid the high. Let your writing speak simply, directly, honestly. Don't be afraid to let your personality come through. And don't be inhibited by counterfeit rules of grammar. You can begin sentences with coordinating conjunctions; you can end sentences with prepositions; and you can use contractions. Professional writers writing at all levels have never paid attention to these supposed rules.

Don't be afraid to sprinkle short, pithy sentences throughout your writing. Don't be too stiff or formal by stringing long, noun-laden, abstract sentences together. That makes your prose unreadable and pompous. If you've used a word in a sentence that you don't ordinarily use in daily conversation, be suspicious of it. Roll it around in your mouth. If it doesn't feel quite right, spit it out.

Try this: read your prose aloud to someone. If you find yourself stumbling over words, it's likely that your writing at that point is stiff and deserves revision. Loosen up. You'll do fine.

· 2 ·

The Wilderness:
Leave It Alone?

"Conservation" and "preservation" may strike you as being synonymous, but don't tell that to a conservationist or a preservationist. They face one another—indeed, they often glare at one another—from the opposite sides of an ideological fence.

The issue centers on the huge real-estate holdings of the U.S. government, which owns over 720 million acres (including over half of several Western states and three-fourths of Alaska). The conservationists and the preservationists have different ideas about how this land should be used.

The conservationists say that public land should serve many of the competing needs of our society; it should serve the needs of the backpacker and the naturalist, but it should also serve the needs of industry and of society at large.

The preservationists claim that these public lands should remain protected enclaves. Indeed, some of the preservationists see nature as a value independent of other human concerns—independent of humans themselves. To the preservationists, as to Ralph Waldo Emerson, "Beauty is its own excuse for being."

The ranks of the preservationists have grown through the twentieth century, and by the 1960s such groups as the Sierra Club and the Wilderness Society had become a powerful lobbying force. Their cause was fueled by the national concern over the vanishing resources and ecological balance of "Island Earth." Small wonder, then, that preservationists were largely responsible for the landmark Wilderness Preservation Act of 1964—and its rhetoric—in which Congress defined "wilderness" as "an area where the earth and its community of life are untrammeled by man, where man himself is a visitor but does not remain."

15

That act set aside 80 million acres where almost everything that would facilitate anything but the briefest of human habitation is prohibited. It also provided for vast tracts of additional land to be withheld from multiple uses until the time when Congress could determine whether those "probationary" lands should be added to the wilderness preserves. These wilderness areas do not include the federal wildlife preserves, which now total nearly 145 million acres.

In recent years preservationists have also begun to worry about our heavily visited national parks. Convinced that the population density at national recreation areas may soon result in Winnebagos outnumbering trees, preservationists have tried to influence the National Park Service to limit public access by prohibiting convenience stores, asphalt parking lots, recreational vehicles, and, in some cases, even automobiles.

The ideological gains scored by the preservationists over the past two decades, however, have hardly driven the conservationists underground. And they too have called up the same image of Island Earth to support their claims. Our energy resources may be limited, they say, and thinking small may be the order of the day, but there are very real limits about how small an industrial society of more than 230 million people can afford to think. Regardless of how successful our efforts to conserve our energy resources become, they say, our energy needs will remain immense, and we have yet to free ourselves from a heavy dependence on foreign sources for energy. We thus need to begin to develop those energy resources that lie in the federally owned parts of the West and Alaska.

The conservationists often describe the preservationists as elitists. The federal government merely has stewardship over public lands, the conservationists say; its function is *not* to deny access to everyone who can't backpack into a rugged wilderness area. Like the preservationists, the conservationists don't want to see Yosemite turned into Cleveland, but they contend that some compromise must be made if Yosemite is to remain more than a source for inspiration for backpackers. Middle-class families in Winnebagos also enjoy beauty.

According to both sides in the debate, the stakes are high: our future depends on which of the two sides dominates national policy.

WILDERNESS
Aldo Leopold

Wilderness is the raw material out of which man has hammered the artifact called civilization.

Wilderness was never a homogeneous raw material. It was very diverse, and the resulting artifacts are very diverse. These differences in the end-product are known as cultures. The rich diversity of the world's cultures reflects a corresponding diversity in the wilds that gave them birth.

For the first time in the history of the human species, two changes are now impending. One is the exhaustion of wilderness in the more habitable portions of the globe. The other is the world-wide hybridization of cultures through modern transport and industrialization. Neither can be prevented, and perhaps should not be, but the question arises whether, by some slight amelioration of the impending changes, certain values can be preserved that would otherwise be lost.

To the laborer in the sweat of his labor, the raw stuff on his anvil is an adversary to be conquered. So was wilderness an adversary to the pioneer.

But to the laborer in repose, able for the moment to cast a philosophical eye on his world, that same raw stuff is something to be loved and cherished, because it gives definition and meaning to his life. This is a plea for the preservation of some tag-ends of wilderness, as museum pieces, for the edification of those who may one day wish to see, feel, or study the origins of their cultural inheritance.

THE REMNANTS

Many of the diverse wildernesses out of which we have hammered America are already gone; hence in any practical program the unit areas to be preserved must vary greatly in size and in degree of wildness.

No living man will see again the long-grass prairie, where a sea of prairie flowers lapped at the stirrups of the pioneer. We shall do well to find a forty here and there on which the prairie plants can be kept alive as species. There were a hundred such plants, many of exceptional beauty. Most of them are quite unknown to those who have inherited their domain.

But the short-grass prairie, where Cabeza de Vaca saw the horizon under the bellies of the buffalo, is still extant in a few spots of 10,000-acre size, albeit severely chewed up by sheep, cattle, and dry-farmers. If the forty-niners are worth commemorating on the walls of state capitols, is not the scene of their mighty hegira worth commemorating in several national prairie reservations?

No living man will see again the virgin pineries of the Lake States, or the flatwoods of the coastal plain, or the giant hardwoods; of these, samples of a few acres each will have to suffice. But there are still several blocks of maple-hemlock of thousand-acre size; there are similar blocks of Appalachian hardwoods, of southern

Aldo Leopold, "Wilderness," in *A Sand County Almanac* (New York: Oxford University Press, 1966). Leopold helped establish the first federally reserved wilderness area, the Gila National Forest, in 1924. *A Sand County Almanac* was first published in 1948 shortly after Leopold's death.

hardwood swamp, of cypress swamp, and of Adirondack spruce. Few of these tag-ends are secure from prospective cuttings, and fewer still from prospective tourist roads.

One of the fastest-shrinking categories of wilderness is coastlines. Cottages and tourist roads have all but annihilated wild coasts on both oceans, and Lake Superior is now losing the last large remnant of wild shoreline on the Great Lakes. No single kind of wilderness is more intimately interwoven with history, and none nearer the point of complete disappearance.

In all of North America east of the Rockies, there is only one large area formally reserved as a wilderness: the Quetico-Superior International Park in Minnesota and Ontario. This magnificent block of canoe-country, a mosaic of lakes and rivers, lies mostly in Canada, and can be about as large as Canada chooses to make it, but its integrity is threatened by two recent developments: the growth of fishing resorts served by pontoon-equipped airplanes, and a jurisdictional dispute whether the Minnesota end of the area shall be all National Forest, or partly State Forest. The whole region is in danger of power impoundments, and this regrettable cleavage among proponents of wilderness may end in giving power the whiphand.

In the Rocky Mountain states, a score of areas in the National Forests, varying in size from a hundred thousand to half a million acres, are withdrawn as wilderness, and closed to roads, hotels, and other inimical uses. In the National Parks the same principle is recognized, but no specific boundaries are delimited. Collectively, these federal areas are the backbone of the wilderness program, but they are not so secure as the paper record might lead one to believe. Local pressures for new tourist roads knock off a chip here and a slab there. There is perennial pressure for extension of roads for forest-fire control, and these, by slow degrees, become public highways. Idle CCC camps presented a widespread temptation to build new and often needless roads. Lumber shortages during the war gave the impetus of military necessity to many road extensions, legitimate and otherwise. At the present moment, ski-tows and ski-hotels are being promoted in many mountain areas, often without regard to their prior designation as wilderness.

One of the most insidious invasions of wilderness is via predator control. It works thus: wolves and lions are cleaned out of a wilderness area in the interest of big-game management. The big-game herds (usually deer or elk) then increase to the point of overbrowsing the range. Hunters must then be encouraged to harvest the surplus, but modern hunters refuse to operate far from a car; hence a road must be built to provide access to the surplus game. Again and again, wilderness areas have been split by this process, but it still continues.

The Rocky Mountain system of wilderness areas covers a wide gamut of forest types, from the juniper breaks of the Southwest to the 'illimitable woods where rolls the Oregon.' It is lacking, however, in desert areas, probably because of that under-aged brand of esthetics which limits the definition of 'scenery' to lakes and pine trees.

In Canada and Alaska there are still large expanses of virgin country

> Where nameless men by nameless rivers wander
> and in strange valleys die strange deaths alone.

A representative series of these areas can, and should, be kept. Many are of negligible or negative value for economic use. It will be contended, of course, that no deliberate planning to this end is necessary; that adequate areas will survive anyhow. All recent history belies so comforting an assumption. Even if wild spots do survive, what of their fauna? The woodland caribou, the several races of mountain sheep, the pure form of woods buffalo, the barren ground grizzly, the freshwater seals, and the whales are even now threatened. Of what use are wild areas destitute of their distinctive faunas? There are now organizations and development groups actively embarked on the industrialization of the Arctic wastes, and plans even larger are actively being pressed. The wilderness of the Far North as yet has no formal protection and though still extensive, is beginning to dwindle.

To what extent Canada and Alaska will be able to see and grasp their opportunities is anybody's guess. Pioneers usually scoff at any effort to perpetuate pioneering.

WILDERNESS FOR RECREATION

Physical combat for the means of subsistence was, for unnumbered centuries, an economic fact. When it disappeared as such, a sound instinct led us to preserve it in the form of athletic sports and games.

Physical combat between men and beasts was, in like manner, an economic fact, now preserved as hunting and fishing for sport.

Public wilderness areas are, first of all, a means of perpetuating, in sport form, the more virile and primitive skills in pioneering travel and subsistence.

Some of these skills are of generalized distribution; the details have been adapted to the American scene, but the skill is world-wide. Hunting, fishing, and foot travel by pack are examples.

Two of them, however, are as American as a hickory tree; they have been copied elsewhere, but they were developed to their full perfection only on this continent. One of these is canoe travel, and the other is travel by pack-train. Both are shrinking rapidly. Your Hudson Bay Indian now has a put-put, and your mountaineer a Ford. If I had to make a living by canoe or packhorse, I should likely do likewise, for both are grueling labor. But we who seek wilderness travel for sport are foiled when we are forced to compete with mechanized substitutes. It is bootless to execute a portage to the tune of motor launches, or to turn out your bell-mare in the pasture of a summer hotel. It is better to stay home.

Wilderness areas are first of all a series of sanctuaries for the primitive arts of wilderness travel, especially canoeing and packing.

I suppose some will wish to debate whether it is important to keep these primitive arts alive. I shall not debate it. Either you know it in your bones, or you are very, very old.

European hunting and fishing are largely devoid of the thing that wilderness areas might be the means of preserving in this country. Europeans do not camp, cook, or do their own work in the woods if they can avoid doing so. Work chores are delegated to beaters and servants, and a hunt carries the atmosphere of a picnic, rather than of pioneering. The test of skill is confined largely to the actual taking of game or fish.

There are those who decry wilderness sports as 'undemocratic' because the recreational carrying capacity of a wilderness is small, as compared with a golf links or
a tourist camp. The basic error in such argument is that it applies the philosophy of
mass-production to what is intended to counteract mass-production. The value of
recreation is not a matter of ciphers. Recreation is valuable in proportion to the
intensity of its experiences, and to the degree to which it *differs from* and *contrasts
with* workaday life. By these criteria, mechanized outings are at best a milk-and-
water affair.

Mechanized recreation already has seized nine-tenths of the woods and mountains; a decent respect for minorities should dedicate the other tenth to wilderness.

WILDERNESS FOR SCIENCE

The most important characteristic of an organism is that capacity for internal
self-renewal known as health.

There are two organisms whose processes of self-renewal have been subjected to
human interference and control. One of these is man himself (medicine and public
health). The other is land (agriculture and conservation).

The effort to control the health of land has not been very successful. It is now
generally understood that when soil loses fertility, or washes away faster than it
forms, and when water systems exhibit abnormal floods and shortages, the land
is sick.

Other derangements are known as facts, but are not yet thought of as symptoms
of land sickness. The disappearance of plants and animal species without visible
cause, despite efforts to protect them, and the irruption of others as pests despite
efforts to control them, must, in the absence of simpler explanations, be regarded
as symptoms of sickness in the land organism. Both are occurring too frequently to
be dismissed as normal evolutionary events.

The status of thought on these ailments of the land is reflected in the fact that
our treatments for them are still prevailingly local. Thus when a soil loses fertility
we pour on fertilizer, or at best alter its tame flora and fauna, without considering
the fact that its wild flora and fauna, which built the soil to begin with, may likewise
be important to its maintenance. It was recently discovered, for example, that good
tobacco crops depend, for some unknown reason, on the preconditioning of the soil
by wild ragweed. It does not occur to us that such unexpected chains of dependency
may have wide prevalence in nature.

When prairie dogs, ground squirrels, or mice increase to pest levels we poison
them, but we do not look beyond the animal to find the cause of the irruption. We
assume that animal troubles must have animal causes. The latest scientific evidence
points to derangements of the *plant* community as the real seat of rodent irruptions,
but few explorations of this clue are being made.

Many forest plantations are producing one-log or two-log trees on soil which
originally grew three-log and four-log trees. Why? Thinking foresters know that the
cause probably lies not in the tree, but in the micro-flora of the soil, and that it may
take more years to restore the soil flora than it took to destroy it.

Many conservation treatments are obviously superficial. Flood-control dams have
no relation to the cause of floods. Check dams and terraces do not touch the cause

of erosion. Refuges and hatcheries to maintain the supply of game and fish do not explain why the supply fails to maintain itself.

In general, the trend of the evidence indicates that in land, just as in the human body, the symptoms may lie in one organ and the cause in another. The practices we now call conservation are, to a large extent, local alleviations of biotic pain. They are necessary, but they must not be confused with cures. The art of land doctoring is being practiced with vigor, but the science of land health is yet to be born.

A science of land health needs, first of all, a base datum of normality, a picture of how healthy land maintains itself as an organism.

We have two available norms. One is found where land physiology remains largely normal despite centuries of human occupation. I know of only one such place: northeastern Europe. It is not likely that we shall fail to study it.

The other and most perfect norm is wilderness. Paleontology offers abundant evidence that wilderness maintained itself for immensely long periods; that its component species were rarely lost, neither did they get out of hand; that weather and water built soil as fast or faster than it was carried away. Wilderness, then, assumes unexpected importance as a laboratory for the study of land-health.

One cannot study the physiology of Montana in the Amazon; each biotic province needs its own wilderness for comparative studies of used and unused land. It is of course too late to salvage more than a lopsided system of wilderness study areas, and most of these remnants are far too small to retain their normality in all respects. Even the National Parks, which run up to a million acres each in size, have not been large enough to retain their natural predators, or to exclude animal diseases carried by livestock. Thus the Yellowstone has lost its wolves and cougars, with the result that elk are ruining the flora, particularly on the winter range. At the same time the grizzly bear and the mountain sheep are shrinking, the latter by reason of disease.

While even the largest wilderness areas become partially deranged, it required only a few wild acres for J.E. Weaver to discover why the prairie flora is more drouth-resistant than the agronomic flora which has supplanted it. Weaver found that the prairie species practice 'team work' underground by distributing their root-systems to cover all levels, whereas the species comprising the agronomic rotation overdraw one level and neglect another, thus building up cumulative deficits. An important agronomic principle emerged from Weaver's researches.

Again, it required only a few wild acres for Togrediak to discover why pines on old fields never achieve the size or wind-firmness of pines on uncleared forest soils. In the latter case, the roots follow old root channels, and thus strike deeper.

In many cases we literally do not know how good a performance to expect of healthy land unless we have a wild area for comparison with sick ones. Thus most of the early travelers in the Southwest describe the mountain rivers as originally clear, but a doubt remains, for they may, by accident, have seen them at favorable seasons. Erosion engineers had no base datum until it was discovered that exactly similar rivers in the Sierra Madre of Chihuahua, never grazed or used for fear of Indians, show at their worst a milky hue, not too cloudy for a trout fly. Moss grows to the water's edge on their banks. Most of the corresponding rivers in Arizona and

New Mexico are ribbons of boulders, mossless, soil-less, and all but treeless. The preservation and study of the Sierra Madre wilderness by an international experiment station, as a norm for the cure of sick land on both sides of the border, would be a good-neighbor enterprise well worthy of consideration.

In short all available wild areas, large or small, are likely to have value as norms for land science. Recreation is not their only, or even their principal, utility.

WILDERNESS FOR WILDLIFE

The National Parks do not suffice as a means of perpetuating the larger carnivores; witness the precarious status of the grizzly bear, and the fact that the park system is already wolfless. Neither do they suffice for mountain sheep; most sheep herds are shrinking.

The reasons for this are clear in some cases and obscure in others. The parks are certainly too small for such a far-ranging species as the wolf. Many animal species, for reasons unknown, do not seem to thrive as detached islands of population.

The most feasible way to enlarge the area available for wilderness fauna is for the wilder parts of the National Forests, which usually surround the Parks, to function as parks in respect to threatened species. That they have not so functioned is tragically illustrated in the case of the grizzly bear.

In 1909, when I first saw the West, there were grizzlies in every major mountain mass, but you could travel for months without meeting a conservation officer. Today there is some kind of conservation officer 'behind every bush,' yet as wildlife bureaus grow, our most magnificent mammal retreats steadily toward the Canadian border. Of the 6,000 grizzlies officially reported as remaining in areas owned by the United States, 5,000 are in Alaska. Only five states have any at all. There seems to be a tacit assumption that if grizzlies survive in Canada and Alaska, that is good enough. It is not good enough for me. The Alaskan bears are a distinct species. Relegating grizzlies to Alaska is about like relegating happiness to heaven; one may never get there.

Saving the grizzly requires a series of large areas from which roads and livestock are excluded, or in which livestock damage is compensated. Buying out scattered livestock ranches is the only way to create such areas, but despite large authority to buy and exchange lands, the conservation bureaus have accomplished virtually nothing toward this end. The Forest Service has established a grizzly range in Montana, but I know of a mountain range in Utah in which the Forest Service actually promoted a sheep industry, despite the fact that it harbored the sole remnant of grizzlies in that state.

Permanent grizzly ranges and permanent wilderness areas are of course two names for one problem. Enthusiasm about either requires a long view of conservation, and a historical perspective. Only those able to see the pageant of evolution can be expected to value its theater, the wilderness, or its outstanding achievement, the grizzly. But if education really educates, there will, in time, be more and more citizens who understand that relics of the old West add meaning and value to the new. Youth yet unborn will pole up the Missouri with Lewis and Clark, or climb the Sierras with James Capen Adams, and each generation in turn will ask: Where is the big white bear? It will be a sorry answer to say he went under while conservationists weren't looking.

DEFENDERS OF WILDERNESS

Wilderness is a resource which can shrink but not grow. Invasions can be arrested or modified in a manner to keep an area usable either for recreation, or for science, or for wildlife, but the creation of new wilderness in the full sense of the word is impossible.

It follows, then, that any wilderness program is a rearguard action, through which retreats are reduced to a minimum. The Wilderness Society was organized in 1935 'for the one purpose of saving the wilderness remnants in America.' The Sierra Club is doing yeoman work toward the same end.

It does not suffice, however, to have a few such societies, nor can one be content that Congress has enacted a bill aimed at wilderness preservation. Unless there be wilderness-minded men scattered through all the conservation bureaus, the societies may never learn of new invasions until the time for action has passed. Furthermore, a militant minority of wilderness-minded citizens must be on watch throughout the nation and vigilantly available for action.

In Europe, where wilderness has now retreated to the Carpathians and Siberia, every thinking conservationist bemoans its loss. Even in Britain, which has less room for land-luxuries than almost any other civilized country, there is a vigorous if belated movement for saving a few small spots of semi-wild land.

Ability to see the cultural value of wilderness boils down, in the last analysis, to a question of intellectual humility. The shallow-minded modern who has lost his rootage in the land assumes that he has already discovered what is important; it is such who prate of empires, political or economic, that will last a thousand years. It is only the scholar who appreciates that all history consists of successive excursions from a single starting-point, to which man returns again and again to organize yet another search for a durable scale of values. It is only the scholar who understands why the raw wilderness gives definition and meaning to the human enterprise.

WILDERNESS LETTER
Wallace Stegner

Los Altos, Calif.
Dec. 3, 1960

David E. Pesonen
Wildland Research Center
Agricultural Experiment Station
243 Mulford Hall
University of California
Berkeley 4, Calif.

Dear Mr. Pesonen:

I believe that you are working on the wilderness portion of the Outdoor Recreation Resources Review Commission's report. If I may, I should like to urge some arguments for wilderness preservation that involve recreation, as it is ordinarily conceived, hardly at all. Hunting, fishing, hiking, mountain-climbing, camping, photography, and the enjoyment of natural scenery will all, surely, figure in your report. So will the wilderness as a genetic reserve, a scientific yardstick by which we may measure the world in its natural balance against the world in its man-made imbalance. What I want to speak for is not so much the wilderness uses, valuable as those are, but the wilderness *idea*, which is a resource in itself. Being an intangible and spiritual resource, it will seem mystical to the practical-minded—but then anything that cannot be moved by a bulldozer is likely to seem mystical to them.

I want to speak for the wilderness idea as something that has helped form our character and that has certainly shaped our history as a people. It has no more to do with recreation than churches have to do with recreation, or than the strenuousness and optimism and expansiveness of what historians call the "American Dream" have to do with recreation. Nevertheless, since it is only in this recreation survey that the values of wilderness are being compiled, I hope you will permit me to insert this idea between the leaves, as it were, of the recreation report.

Something will have gone out of us as a people if we ever let the remaining wilderness be destroyed; if we permit the last virgin forests to be turned into comic books and plastic cigarette cases; if we drive the few remaining members of the wild species into zoos or to extinction; if we pollute the last clear air and dirty the last clean streams and push out paved roads through the last of the silence, so that never again will Americans be free in their own country from the noise, the exhausts, the stinks of human and automotive waste. And so that never again can we have the chance to see ourselves single, separate, vertical and individual in the world, part of the environment of trees and rocks and soil, brother to the other animals, part of

Wallace Stegner, "Wilderness Letter," in *The Sound of Mountain Water* (Garden City, New York: Doubleday, 1969). Stegner, a former Director of Creative Writing at Stanford University, is the author of numerous works of nonfiction and fiction. His fiction includes a Pulitzer Prize winning novel, *Angle of Repose* (1973), and a National Book award winner, *The Spectator Bird* (1976).

the natural world and competent to belong in it. Without any remaining wilderness we are committed wholly, without chance for even momentary reflection and rest, to a headlong drive into our technological termite-life, the Brave New World of a completely man-controlled environment. We need wilderness preserved—as much of it as is still left, and as many kinds—because it was the challenge against which our character as a people was formed. The reminder and the reassurance that it is still there is good for our spiritual health even if we never once in ten years set foot in it. It is good for us when we are young, because of the incomparable sanity it can bring briefly, as vacation and rest, into our insane lives. It is important to us when we are old simply because it is there—important, that is, simply as idea.

We are a wild species, as Darwin pointed out. Nobody ever tamed or domesticated or scientifically bred us. But for at least three millennia we have been engaged in a cumulative and ambitious race to modify and gain control of our environment, and in the process we have come close to domesticating ourselves. Not many people are likely, any more, to look upon what we call "progress" as an unmixed blessing. Just as surely as it has brought us increased comfort and more material goods, it has brought us spiritual losses, and it threatens now to become the Frankenstein that will destroy us. One means of sanity is to retain a hold on the natural world, to remain, insofar as we can, good animals. Americans still have that chance, more than many peoples; for while we were demonstrating ourselves the most efficient and ruthless environment-busters in history, and slashing and burning and cutting our way through a wilderness continent, the wilderness was working on us. It remains in us as surely as Indian names remain on the land. If the abstract dream of human liberty and human dignity became, in America, something more than an abstract dream, mark it down at least partially to the fact that we were in subtle ways subdued by what we conquered.

The Connecticut Yankee, sending likely candidates from King Arthur's unjust kingdom to his Man Factory for rehabilitation, was over-optimistic, as he later admitted. These things cannot be forced, they have to grow. To make such a man, such a democrat, such a believer in human individual dignity, as Mark Twain himself, the frontier was necessary, Hannibal and the Mississippi and Virginia City, and reaching out from those the wilderness; the wilderness as opportunity and as idea, the thing that has helped to make an American different from and, until we forget it in the roar of our industrial cities, more fortunate than other men. For an American, insofar as he is new and different at all, is a civilized man who has renewed himself in the wild. The American experience has been the confrontation by old peoples and cultures of a world as new as if it had just risen from the sea. That gave us our hope and our excitement, and the hope and excitement can be passed on to newer Americans, Americans who never saw any phase of the frontier. But only so long as we keep the remainder of our wild as a reserve and a promise—a sort of wilderness bank.

As a novelist, I may perhaps be forgiven for taking literature as a reflection, indirect but profoundly true, of our national consciousness. And our literature, as perhaps you are aware, is sick, embittered, losing its mind, losing its faith. Our novelists are the declared enemies of their society. There has hardly been a serious or important novel in this century that did not repudiate in part or in whole

American technological culture for its commercialism, its vulgarity, and the way in which it has dirtied a clean continent and a clean dream. I do not expect that the preservation of our remaining wilderness is going to cure this condition. But the mere example that we can as a nation apply some other criteria than commercial and exploitative considerations would be heartening to many Americans, novelists or otherwise. We need to demonstrate our acceptance of the natural world, including ourselves; we need the spiritual refreshment that being natural can produce. And one of the best places for us to get that is in the wilderness where the fun houses, the bulldozers, and the pavements of our civilization are shut out.

Sherwood Anderson, in a letter to Waldo Frank in the 1920's, said it better than I can. "Is it not likely that when the country was new and men were often alone in the fields and the forest they got a sense of bigness outside themselves that has now in some way been lost . . . Mystery whispered in the grass, played in the branches of trees overhead, was caught up and blown across the American line in clouds of dust at evening on the prairies . . . I am old enough to remember tales that strengthen my belief in a deep semi-religious influence that was formerly at work among our people. The flavor of it hangs over the best work of Mark Twain . . . I can remember old fellows in my home town speaking feelingly of an evening spent on the big empty plains. It had taken the shrillness out of them. They had learned the trick of quiet . . ."

We could learn it too, even yet; even our children and grandchildren could learn it. But only if we save, for just such absolutely non-recreational, impractical, and mystical uses as this, all the wild that still remains to us.

It seems to me significant that the distinct downturn in our literature from hope to bitterness took place almost at the precise time when the frontier officially came to an end, in 1890, and when the American way of life had begun to turn strongly urban and industrial. The more urban it has become, and the more frantic with technological change, the sicker and more embittered our literature, and I believe our people, have become. For myself, I grew up on the empty plains of Saskatchewan and Montana and in the mountains of Utah, and I put a very high valuation on what those places gave me. And if I had not been able periodically to renew myself in the mountains and deserts of western America I would be very nearly bughouse. Even when I can't get to the back country, the thought of the colored deserts of southern Utah, or the reassurance that there are still stretches of prairie where the world can be instantaneously perceived as disk and bowl, and where the little but intensely important human being is exposed to the five directions and the thirty-six winds, is a positive consolation. The idea alone can sustain me. But as the wilderness areas are progressively exploited or "improved," as the jeep and bulldozers of uranium prospectors scar up the deserts and the roads are cut into the alpine timberlands, and as the remnants of the unspoiled and natural world are progressively eroded, every such loss is a little death in me. In us.

I am not moved by the argument that those wilderness areas which have already been exposed to grazing or mining are already deflowered, and so might as well be "harvested." For mining I cannot say much good except that its operations are generally short-lived. The extractable wealth is taken and the shafts, the tailings, and the ruins left, and in a dry country such as the American West the wounds men make in the earth do not quickly heal. Still, they are only wounds; they aren't absolutely mortal. Better a wounded wilderness than none at all. And as for grazing, if it is strictly controlled so that it does not destroy the ground cover, damage the ecology, or compete with the wildlife it is in itself nothing that need conflict with the wilderness feeling or the validity of the wilderness experience. I have known enough range cattle to recognize them as wild animals; and the people who herd them have, in the wilderness context, the dignity of rareness; they belong on the frontier, moreover, and have a look of rightness. The invasion they make on the virgin country is a sort of invasion that is as old as Neolithic man, and they can, in moderation, even emphasize a man's feelings of belonging to the natural world. Under surveillance, they can belong; under control, they need not deface or mar. I do not believe that in wilderness areas where grazing has never been permitted, it should be permitted; but I do not believe either that an otherwise untouched wilderness should be eliminated from the preservation plan because of limited existing uses such as grazing which are in consonance with the frontier condition and image.

Let me say something on the subject of the kinds of wilderness worth preserving. Most of those areas contemplated are in the national forests and in high mountain country. For all the usual recreational purposes, the alpine and forest wildernesses are obviously the most important, both as genetic banks and as beauty spots. But for the spiritual renewal, the recognition of identity, the birth of awe, other kinds will serve every bit as well. Perhaps, because they are less friendly to life, more abstractly nonhuman, they will serve even better. On our Saskatchewan prairie, the nearest neighbor was four miles away, and at night we saw only two lights on all the dark rounding earth. The earth was full of animals—field mice, ground squirrels, weasels, ferrets, badgers, coyotes, burrowing owls, snakes. I knew them as my little brothers, as fellow creatures, and I have never been able to look upon animals in any other way since. The sky in that country came clear down to the ground on every side, and it was full of great weathers, and clouds, and winds, and hawks. I hope I learned something from knowing intimately the creatures of the earth; I hope I learned something from looking a long way, from looking up, from being much alone. A prairie like that, one big enough to carry the eye clear to the sinking, rounding horizon, can be as lonely and grand and simple in its forms as the sea. It is as good a place as any for the wilderness experience to happen; the vanishing prairie is as worth preserving for the wilderness idea as the alpine forests.

So are great reaches of our western deserts, scarred somewhat by prospectors but otherwise open, beautiful, waiting, close to whatever God you want to see in them. Just as a sample, let me suggest the Robbers' Roost country in Wayne County, Utah, near the Capitol Reef National Monument. In that desert climate the dozer and jeep tracks will not soon melt back into the earth, but the country has a way of making the scars insignificant. It is a lovely and terrible wilderness, such a wilderness as Christ and the prophets went out into; harshly and beautiful colored, broken and worn until its bones are exposed, its great sky without a smudge or taint from Technocracy, and in hidden corners and pockets under its cliffs the sudden poetry of springs. Save a piece of country like that intact, and it does not matter in the slightest that only a few people every year will go into it. That is precisely its value.

Roads would be a desecration, crowds would ruin it. But those who haven't the strength or youth to go into it and live can simply sit and look. They can look two hundred miles, clear into Colorado; and looking down over the cliffs and canyons of the San Rafael Swell and the Robbers' Roost they can also look as deeply into themselves as anywhere I know. And if they can't even get to the places on the Aquarius Plateau where the present roads will carry them, they can simply contemplate the *idea*, take pleasure in the fact that such a timeless and uncontrolled part of earth is still there.

These are some of the things wilderness can do for us. That is the reason we need to put into effect, for its preservation, some other principle than the principles of exploitation or "usefulness" or even recreation. We simply need that wild country available to us, even if we never do more than drive to its edge and look in. For it can be a means of reassuring ourselves of our sanity as creatures, a part of the geography of hope.

LET'S OPEN UP OUR WILDERNESS AREAS
Eric Julber

The prevailing philosophy with regard to the use of some 40 million acres of America's magnificent wilderness has become what I term "purist-conservationist." The purist is, generally speaking, against everything. He is against roads, campgrounds, ski lifts and restaurants. He has very strong ideas about who deserves to enjoy natural beauty and, ideally, would reserve beauty for those who are willing and able to hike, climb, crawl or cliffhang to achieve it. The purist believes that those who do not agree with him desire to "rape the landscape."

The purist standards were embodied in the Wilderness Act of 1964, which provides that in such areas there shall be "no permanent road . . . no temporary road . . . no mechanical transport and no structure or installation." The practical effect of this philosophy, thus frozen into federal law, has been to make many of the most beautiful areas of the United States "off limits" to anyone who is not willing and able to backpack into them. Statistics show that this means 99 *percent* of Americans.

In 1965, there were 1,475,000 visitors to the Wilderness areas. In 1970, the number of visitors had increased only to 1,543,000. This represents use by less than one percent of our population. Moreover, a survey on behalf of the President's Outdoor Recreation Resources Review Commission (ORRRC) showed, by statistical analysis, that the users are the intellectual and financial elite of our nation.

Reports the ORRRC: "In the sample of Wilderness users interviewed, more than 75 percent had at least a college degree, and a high proportion have done postgraduate work or hold advanced degrees. . . . Wilderness users are disproportionately drawn from the higher income levels. Professional and semiprofessional people, and those in white-collar occupations, account for approximately three quarters of those interviewed."

And what of ordinary Americans, those whose favorite recreations are driving, sightseeing, easy walking and camping? What of the too-old, the too-young, the timid, the inexperienced, the frail, the hurried, the out-of-shape or the just-plain-lazy, all of whose taxes acquired and maintain the Wilderness areas?

For this group—99 percent of the American population—federal agencies provide 73,700 acres of campgrounds and 39,100 acres of picnic sites: a total of 112,800 acres. And I believe that the areas provided to the common American are not the prime scenic areas; they are the fringes, the leftovers, the secondary scenic areas.

I feel I can speak with some authority as to purist philosophy, because I was once a purist myself. I have carried many a 50-pound pack; I've hiked to the top of Mt. Whitney, there to think beautiful thoughts; I've hiked the 200-mile length of California's John Muir Trail, running from Yosemite to Sequoia. And even in later years, when the press of law practice kept me physically away from the wilderness, in spirit I remained a purist. Keep those roads and crowds out, I said!

Eric Julber, "Let's Open Up Our Wilderness Areas," *Reader's Digest* May 1972. Julber, an ardent hiker and nature photographer, is a Los Angeles attorney who specializes in maritime law.

But no more. Recently I paid a visit to Switzerland. What I saw there made a non-purist out of me. Switzerland has, within the boundaries of a country half as large as South Carolina, one of the most astonishing concentrations of natural beauty on the face of the earth. Not only was I overwhelmed by Switzerland's beauty, but I was amazed to find that virtually every part of it was accessible and thoroughly used by people of all shapes and ages. It was, in fact, exploited to the ultimate—crisscrossed with roads, its mountain valleys heavily grazed and farmed, hotels and restaurants everywhere. Where the automobile cannot go, railroads take you; and when the going gets too steep for cogwheel trains, you catch an aerial tramway.

The most remarkable viewpoints in the country have been deliberately made accessible by some kind of comfortable transportation. People from all over Europe sit on Switzerland's restaurant patios, 10,000 feet high, admiring the magnificent views—views that in America would be excluded from 99 percent of our population without days of the most arduous struggle.

The Swiss philosophy says: Invite people in; the more the better. The purist says: Keep people out. The Swiss say: Let the strong climb if they choose (and many of them do), but let the children, the aged, the hurried or just-plain-lazy ride.

I, who have now done it both ways, say: My thoughts were just as beautiful on top of Switzerland's Schilthorn—9,757 feet up; restaurant lunch of fondue, wine, strawberry pastry and coffee; reached by 30-minute tram ride—as they were on top of Mt. Lyell in America's Yosemite—13,095 feet up; lunch of peanut-butter sandwich; reached by two-day hike. I conclude that the purist philosophy which keeps Americans out of their own land is an unwise misuse of our wilderness resources.

Let me propose an alternative philosophy. For want of a better term, call it an "access" philosophy. Consider as an example Muir Trail in California, with its magnificent Wilderness scenery—peaks, meadows, hundreds of lakes, streams, even glaciers. Its southern end is 212 miles from Los Angeles, its northern end 215 miles from San Francisco. Under present purist conditions, the Muir Trail is inaccessible to all except the hardiest, for only two roads touch it between its two ends. To reach its most beautiful parts you have to hike over mountain passes averaging 10,000 feet in height, packing supplies on your back.

Under the "access" philosophy, I would install aerial tramways at three or four locations within easy driving distance of Los Angeles. These tramways would have large gondola cars suspended from cables between towers that can be up to a mile apart; the cars would move silently high above the landscape. At the terminal of each tramway—after, say, an hour's ride—there would be restaurant facilities, picnic areas, observation points. A family could stay for a few hours or camp for weeks. General access would be year-round, as compared to the present 90-day, snow-free period.

Why not also put a tramway in Grand Canyon?

The visitor now cannot get from the South Rim to the North Rim (a distance of from 8 to 18 miles) without driving 217 miles around, and he cannot get to the bottom of the canyon (the most interesting part) except on foot or muleback. I would install an aerial tramway in an inconspicuous fold of the canyon, so that visitors could ride from the South Rim to the bottom, and from the bottom to the North Rim, thus getting a feel for its immense depths.

That brings up the ultimate argument that purists always fall back on: that the Swiss can do such things with taste, judgment and reverence for the landscape; that we Americans would botch it up. This is neither altogether true nor altogether false. We are capable of abominations, but we are just as capable of tasteful building as Europeans. Witness the beautiful aerial tramway at Palm Springs, Calif., which carries visitors to the slopes of Mt. San Jacinto. Built in 1963, after 15 years of battle with purists, this tramway has taken 2.5 million people to a lovely area which before was a full day's arduous climb away.

Surprisingly, the litter problem is often least great in precisely those areas where access is provided to beautiful spots. The Palm Springs aerial tramway, for instance, and Glacier Point in Yosemite are remarkably free of litter despite heavy visitation. This, I think, is because people will not litter when they feel others are watching; and also because purchasing a ticket on a tramway gives one a proprietary interest in keeping the premises clean.

It is my firm belief that if Americans were permitted access to Wilderness areas in the manner I have suggested, we would soon create a generation of avid nature lovers. Americans would cease to be "alienated" from their landscape, and would mend their littering tendencies. If you question any purist or wilderness buff, you will find that what initially "turned him on," in almost every case, was an experience in which he was provided access to natural beauty—be it in Glacier Park, Yellowstone, Grand Canyon or Yosemite (as in my own case)—by roads, bus or other similar non-purist means. Yet, if purists had had the influence 100 years ago that they have today, there would be no roads or other facilities in Yosemite Valley, and the strong probability is that neither I nor millions of other Americans would ever have seen its beauties, except on postcards.

I believe that the purist philosophy is unfair and undemocratic, and that an alternate philosophy, one of enlightened, carefully controlled "access," is more desirable and also ecologically sound. If the Swiss can do it, why can't we?

CONSERVATION AND THE ENVIRONMENTAL CRISIS
Charles F. Park, Jr.

Everyone sees the renewable resources of the earth, the flora and fauna, and most people are concerned about the preservation of scenery, primitive areas, and wildlife. Management of the large public domain is a fascinating, growing science. Seldom, however, until they are faced with shortages, problems of pollution, or unsightly change, do people think of conservation as applying to the other category of the earth's natural resources, those that are nonrenewable. Not often do they realize that renewable and nonrenewable resources are interrelated when it comes to conservation.

WHAT IS CONSERVATION?

Everyone expresses approval of the principle, but rarely do two people mean quite the same thing by *conservation*. To many people the word means *preservation* of the renewable resources—how to save lovely landscapes, how to prevent destruction and further reduction of the areas relatively unspoiled by our forefathers, how to maintain clean air and water, or how to protect or restore a diminishing wildlife species. The United States National Park Service considers itself an organization of conservationists. It encourages the preservation of large areas of unique public lands and natural wonders for recreation. No removal of or damage to vegetation or natural object is permitted, no privately owned mechanical equipment or industry (other than tourist facilities) is allowed to be installed within park boundaries.

The United States Forest Service also considers itself devoted to conservation. But conservation to the Forest Service, except in its mandated administration of the recently created Wilderness areas where entry is allowed only on foot, means *multiple use* of the land. It will permit within the national forests lumbering, grazing, mining, oil field development, hunting, and the leasing of summer home sites to the public.

Thus conservation means preservation to some, but multiple use to others, or something in between to still other groups. Peter Ellis says, "One sees in conservation what one wants to see." The subject is highly emotional; discussions about conservation are almost always lacking in objectivity. Opinions are stated with insufficient knowledge of the facts, which results in strongly biased viewpoints. Advocates of the preservationist point of view label anyone who uses the land in any way contrary to the preservationist belief as a destroyer of the wild and a killer of flora and fauna; extremists of the other side call these preservationists impractical dreamers, unfamiliar with the real world and willing to exaggerate conditions in order to create public sentiments favorable to their cause.

Charles F. Park, Jr., "Conservation and the Environmental Crisis," in *Earthbound: Minerals, Energy, and Man's Future* (San Francisco: Freeman, Cooper and Co., 1975). Park, dean of the School of Mineral Science at Stanford University, is the author of *Affluence in Jeopardy: Minerals and the Political Economy* (1968).

Like many extreme positions, that of the preservationists in some ways implies a lack of knowledge. For instance, opposition to fires in the wild, a part of the point of view of the strict conservationist, seems reasonable unless one knows that fire is a normal facet of the environment. Without fire to clear the land and provide a propitious environment, the reproduction of the California giant redwood is inhib-ited. The animals of the African plains could hardly maintain their life cycle without the fires that frequently sweep over grasslands and permit new grass to grow unimpeded.

The fervor of the preservationist attitude was well expressed by Ehrlich and Ehrlich when they said, "Each gain is temporary, but each loss is permanent. Species cannot be resurrected; places cannot be restored to their primitive state. Conse-quently, even if the conservationists were evenly matched against the destroyers, the battle would probably remain a losing one."

Who are these destroyers? Anyone who uses a sheet of paper, who drives an automobile, who has a telephone, a radio, a refrigerator. Anyone who owns a television set or uses artificial light. Anyone who heats a home, who applies paint, hammers a nail, or flushes a toilet. Even the staunchest of preservationists is such a destroyer. How can the preservationists expect their battle not to remain a losing one when those they are fighting include themselves? As Pogo put it, "We have met the enemy and he is us."

The problem of conservation stems directly from the pressure of growing numbers of people and the progressive reduction of amount of wild open space. This is recognized by everyone interested in maintaining an acceptable standard of living, clean air and water, a generally clean environment, and some regions of unspoiled wilderness. It is useless, however, to attempt to divorce man and his works from the rest of the environment because man is an integral part of the ecological system; he can no longer consider it something that exists only to serve him. "We abuse land because we regard it as a commodity belonging to us," said Aldo Leopold. "When we see land as a community to which we belong, we may begin to use it with love and respect."

Clearly man influences and changes the environment, but so does nature; oth-erwise the hairy mammoth and the dinosaurs would still be with us. Changes are inherent in nature, a fact well expressed by DuBridge: "The environment of this planet earth has been under continuous change for about 4.5 billion years. The earth never was in a stable state, for it has changed and evolved continually and radically through these many eons. In fact nature seems to abhor stability and to be in love with change."

Change cannot be avoided, although much of it can be directed. It is unrealistic to expect any family willingly to forgo the modern conveniences of life. It is unrea-sonable to expect people not to use deposits of needed minerals such as copper when the deposits are close at hand and their products help to lighten the burden of work. Civilized people want and must have raw materials, especially energy, at moderate prices; nations have gone to the extreme of war to obtain them. For this reason, if for no other, those who advocate the preservation of large wilderness areas known to contain valuable and necessary raw materials are not going to prevail. Actually, the minerals industries use a very small percentage of the land surface, and this use is temporary. Mineral extraction does not of necessity destroy the usefulness of land or its beauty, and many wilderness areas do not contain ore deposits or oil fields.

Here we use the term *conservation* as defined by Peter Ellis in a penetrating discussion: "Conservation is the effort to insure to society the maximum present and future benefit from the use of natural resources." We take conservation to mean, not the indefinite preservation of numerous large areas of unusable and inaccessible wilderness, to be visited only by the hardiest hikers, but maximum use for the benefit of the most people. This is not to say that primitive wilderness areas should not be established; they should be. But not all public land should be wilderness, any more than it should all be given over to mining. Either wilderness or mineral extraction represents only one use of the land. Conservation should mean its multiple use. . . .

EFFECTS OF THE EXTRACTIVE INDUSTRIES ON THE ENVIRONMENT

If land is to provide for society the maximum present and future benefit, no single use can be allowed to spoil it for other uses. Many examples can be cited of abandoned mining areas that have become unsightly, barren dumps, dusty tailing piles, heaps of rusty equipment, and dilapidated buildings. These places are ruined for recreation and esthetic enjoyment, and sometimes for wildlife. People say, bitterly, "This is what mining does to a lovely countryside."

Not all of these examples are old mines, unfortunately; a few have been abandoned recently. Also, all too often one sees ugly bulldozer cuts and unnecessary roads marring a landscape where mining is currently in progress. Legislation to prevent this type of destruction is overdue; proper regulation of industry, particularly on public lands, is a recognized and necessary function of government. If regulatory laws do not exist, they should be passed and enforced, even though such legislation may be difficult to formulate because frequently the destruction occurs on private property and takes place with the consent of the owner. Over twenty years ago Aldo Leopold pointed out a fact that is still too true: "When the private landowner is asked to perform some unprofitable act for the good of the community, he today assents only with outstretched palm." Ideally man should respect his environment to such an extent that he accepts personal responsibility for its care, instead of having responsibility forced on him by law.

In recent years the extractive industries have spent many millions of dollars in attempts to maintain an acceptable environment. In order to survive, they must cooperate with reasonable conservational and environmental objectives. All but a very few know this and have accepted these objectives as their own. Now is the time for closer cooperation between conservationists and industry, cooperation which could yield results that would be approved by all except the most extreme preservationist and the most shortsighted businessman. The goals of thinking people on both sides are now really not far apart.

Situations where the extractive industries have harmed the environment are for the most part in the past. However, situations where organizations devoted to the thesis of no further mineral development on public lands have caused the delay, for a time at least, or even the prevention of the development of mineral deposits are all in the present. These include the phosphate deposits along the shores near Savannah, Georgia; the molybdenum deposits at White Cloud, Idaho; the copper deposits on Plummer Mountain near Glacier Peak, Washington; and the chromium, nickel, and copper deposits of the Stillwater Basin in Montana. There are many others. One of the most interesting is a large copper deposit in Puerto Rico, where opposition to development has been organized by the Episcopal clergy in New York City, with the theme of preserving the culture of the poor, semiprimitive people in that part of the island. If this deposit were mined with careful protection of its environment, the culture of the local people would be changed by the addition of jobs and the improvement of their standard of living. Furthermore, the dependence of the United States upon foreign supplies would be decreased, as would inflation because of the beneficial effect on the balance of payments. Some people have suggested that the problem should be solved by pretending that the deposits do not exist, a desperate form of self-deception that would accomplish as much as a frightened ostrich does by burying its head in the sand. There must be a policy. What can it be except multiple use?

Approximately one third of the land area of the United States, most of it in Alaska, is owned by the federal government. The administration of this tremendous area is under the direction of various federal bureaus, such as the Bureau of Land Management, the National Park Service, the United States Forest Service, and the Department of Defense. To a lesser extent, overlapping control is exerted by others such as Fish and Wildlife, the Bureau of Indian Affairs, the Reclamation Service, the Bureau of Mines, and the Geological Survey. Some government bureaus are able to enforce regulations, others are not. The Forest Service can control the location of access roads and the cutting of timber; the Bureau of Land Management can prevent road building.

Additional amounts of land are owned by individual states and administered by various state bureaus.

Proper land management is a complex and enormous job. The conflicting goals of the many agencies and the needs of the public must all be taken into account. Maximum use of land for the most people cannot be achieved efficiently, and probably cannot be achieved at all, while numerous agencies with overlapping jurisdictions exercise varying amounts of control.

LAWS GOVERNING MINERAL RESOURCES ON PUBLIC LANDS

Laws governing mineral resources on public lands in the United States are highly complicated and variable. For oil, gas, and many of the nonmetallic minerals such as potash, a system of bidding and leasing is employed. For most metal deposits in solid rock, a system of mineral claims, based upon the land laws of 1872, is still in use. These mining claims have a maximum size of six hundred feet wide by fifteen hundred feet long. For *placers* (stream gravels and beach sands containing economic minerals) or gravel deposits, the claims contain up to a maximum of twenty acres.

Mineral land laws have been changed but little in recent years and many proposed changes have been vigorously opposed by most mining industrialists. They claim that the present system has been eminently workable, though they will admit to some abuses that need correction. Complete rewriting of the old law of 1872 has been advocated by others, who would like to extend the leasing system to cover all nonrenewable resources.

The leasing system has its drawbacks, particularly in the way it favors the larger operations and is apt to limit healthy competition. However, the leasing system is operating successfully in Australia, South Africa, Ireland, and elsewhere.

Four concepts are basic to any realistic and effective mining law:

- Prospecting for minerals should be encouraged by allowing individuals and companies maximum but nonexclusive access to public lands to search for ore deposits.
- A prospector or company having found evidence of the probable presence of a mineral deposit should be given exclusive exploration rights for a limited area for a limited time while he is focusing his exploratory activity on it.
- A person or corporation having discovered a valuable mineral deposit should have an exclusive right to develop and mine it, including the right to defer such development for a reasonable period of years until economic or technological conditions justify production.
- The law must provide the person or corporation with tenure for the duration of mining, on reasonable terms set in advance.

THE FUTURE

If one could foretell the future status of conservation of the environment, one would know the future of the human race. What we have to conserve is not one but all of our requirements of space, energy, and minerals. The environment we must protect is the entire earth, including its air and water. The awesome aspect of the situation is its magnitude, the interrelationship of its components, and the fact that it demands from man almost immediate action, objectivity, knowledge, wisdom, and cooperation. The hopeful aspect is that man has shown forethought about his future and is already trying to do something about the conservation of his environment.

NEW ENVIRONMENTAL FIGHT LOOMS OVER DEVELOPING COAL-RICH UTAH AREA
Molly Ivins

What may be the largest energy project since the Alaska pipeline is threatening to bring on Round Two of a fierce fight over the Kaiparowits Plateau in southern Utah.

At issue is one of the nation's largest undeveloped bodies of high-quality coal, lying underneath the plateau. The coal also lies at the center of what environmentalists call a "golden circle" of national parks, national forests, wilderness areas, Indian reservations and archeological sites in ecologically fragile high desert country.

Three years ago a consortium of utility companies ended Round One by canceling plans to build a mammoth, coal-fired electrical plant on the Kaiparowits Plateau.

"The environmentalists didn't kill that Kaiparowits project," said Calvin Rampton, who was Governor of Utah during that round. "It was killed by inflation. But anything that contributed to delay, contributed to inflation." Environmentalists certainly contributed to the delay.

Mr. Rampton, a lawyer, has been retained to sound out the "political feasibility" of another Kaiparowits project. A new consortium with some familiar members is once again planning to deep-mine Kaiparowits coal. But instead of burning it in a power plant on the plateau—the Round One plan that stirred up so much dust over potential damage to air quality—the consortium plans to build a 237-mile railroad to ship the coal to southern California. The estimated cost of the new railroad is $350 million, making it the largest new railroad project in 50 years.

The Interior Department, which owns about two-thirds of the land through which the new railroad would pass, will ultimately decide the fate of the project.

The consortium has not yet made a final decision on whether to try for the "California Coal Connection," according to Barry Combs, head of public relations for Union Pacific Railroad, which would build the new tracks. No decision is expected before this summer. The consortium is studying three elements in the project: The environmental and political considerations, engineering considerations—just how difficult and how expensive will it be to build a new track in the rough country—and "whether the market is there," said Mr. Combs.

A study by the Stanford Research Institute of California indicates that the market is there. The 1978 Energy Act encourages the use of coal in new electric plants. California, the most populous state in the nation, now gets only 6 percent of its electricity from coal, as against 45 percent for the nation as a whole. And California voters have so far halted construction of new nuclear plants in the state.

Molly Ivins, "New Environmental Fight Looms over Developing Coal-Rich Utah Area," *New York Times* 12 March 1979, sec. A.

In addition to energy companies such as Peabody Coal Company, Consolidated Coal and El Paso Natural Gas Company, a consortium of utilities also holds coal leases in the plateau—Arizona Public Service Company, Southern California Edison Company and San Diego Gas & Electric Company. If the California connection is developed, Southern California Edison would be able to buy coal from itself. A spokesman for that company said that the arrangement would offer customers the best possible deal, since the company would buy the coal at cost.

Another potential market is Japan, which now gets most of its coal from Australia and has started to buy Chinese coal. Mr. Rampton feels that, given this country's serious trade deficit with Japan, selling the Japanese 10 to 15 million tons of coal a year would be an advantage. However, some experts believe that Utah coal would prove too expensive for the Japanese.

To environmentalists, the idea of ripping up Kaiparowits for coal not even needed in this country is an abomination. Already a coalition of environmental groups, most of which were involved with the struggle to stop the first Kaiparowits project, has started action to stop the second.

Friends of the Earth, the Audubon Society, Environmental Defense Fund, Sierra Club, American Wilderness Alliance, Wilderness Society, and the Public Lands Institute, among others, have sent out a "Kaiparowits Coal Alert" to their members. "This is a national issue," said Ronald Rudolph, energy coordinator of Friends of the Earth. "This project would drive a spike through the heartlands of our national parks."

According to the environmentalists, the project does not make economic sense. They estimate that initial capital investment for the total project, including the railroad and the deep mines, would be $1.7 billion. "These huge capital outlays would result in long-term prices for Kaiparowits coal rail-delivered to California averaging more than $10 per ton more than comparable coal supplies shipped from other, already developed underground Western sources," said the "Alert" bulletin.

There are two separate routes under study for the proposed rail line. It would run from the heart of the plateau to East Chance Creek to connect with existing lines at either Cedar City or Marysville. It would take three years to construct and cost more than $1 million a mile. Union Pacific estimates that to recover its cost it would have to transport between 40 and 50 million tons of coal a year. The plateau, which has been thoroughly surveyed, is estimated to contain more than four billion tons of low-sulfur coal.

The environmental impact of such a project is as open to different interpretations as is the economic effect. Although the railroad project would not do the obvious damage to air quality that the power plant would have done, environmentalists still expect the railroad project to have enormous impact. Some of the mining operations would be visible from national parks and possibly would topple fragile, eroded rock spires.

Aside from the project's effect on specific protected wilderness areas, there is a larger question of whether the fragile desert ecology can stand much development or the boom that will come with the mines.

Kane and Garfield counties now have a scattered rural population of 7,000. Environmentalists estimated that 10,000 miners would move in by 1990 if the project went through.

Water is always a problem in the arid West. Since the Interior Department no longer allows inter-basin water transfers, the water table would likely drop significantly, as it has already done under the impact of development in northern Arizona. According to an Interior Department environmental impact study of another smaller proposed coal development in southern Utah, the effect on everything from wildlife to vegetation to air quality to the social fabric of the area would be deleterious.

In some parts of the West, there is a standard line used to express resentment of energy resources: "They steal our water and pollute our air so they can run their hair dryers in Los Angeles." But . . . the majority of local people favored the first Kaiparowits project, believing it would bring jobs and prosperity to the economically stagnant area. That support is expected to be there for the new project as well.

IS NATURE TOO GOOD FOR US?
William Tucker

Probably nothing has been more central to the environmental movement than the concept of wilderness. "In wildness is the preservation of the world," wrote Thoreau, and environmental writers and speakers have intoned his message repeatedly. Wilderness, in the environmental pantheon, represents a particular kind of sanctuary in which all true values—that is, all nonhuman values—are reposited. Wildernesses are often described as "temples," "churches," and "sacred ground"— refuges for the proposed "new religion" based on environmental consciousness. Carrying the religious metaphor to the extreme, one of the most famous essays of the environmental era holds the Judeo-Christian religon responsible for "ecological crisis."

The wilderness issue also has a political edge. Since 1964, long-standing preservation groups like the Wilderness Society and the Sierra Club have been pressuring conservation agencies like the National Forest Service and the Bureau of Land Management to put large tracts of their holdings into permanent "wilderness designations," countering the "multiple use" concept that was one of the cornerstones of the Conservation Era of the early 1900s.

Preservation and conservation groups have been at odds since the end of the last century, and the rift between them has been a major controversy of environmentalism. The leaders of the Conservation Movement—most notably Theodore Roosevelt, Gifford Pinchot, and John Wesley Powell—called for rational, efficient development of land and other natural resources: multiple use, or reconciling competing uses of land, and also "highest use," or forfeiting more immediate profits from land development for more lasting gains. Preservationists, on the other hand, the followers of California woodsman John Muir, have advocated protecting land in its natural state, setting aside tracts and keeping them inviolate. "Wilderness area" battles have become one of the hottest political issues of the day, especially in western states—the current "Sagebrush Revolt" comes to mind—where large quantities of potentially commercially usable land are at stake.

The term "wilderness" generally connotes mountains, trees, clear streams, rushing waterfalls, grasslands, or parched deserts, but the concept has been institutionalized and has a careful legal definition as well. The one given by the 1964 Wilderness Act, and that most environmentalists favor, is that wilderness is an area "where man is a visitor but does not remain." People do not "leave footprints there," wilderness exponents often say. Wildernesses are, most importantly, areas in which *evidence of human activity is excluded*; they need not have any particular scenic, aesthetic, or recreational value. The values, as environmentalists usually say, are "ecological"—which means, roughly translated, that natural systems are allowed to operate as free from human interference as possible.

William Tucker, "Is Nature Too Good for Us?" *Harper's* March 1982.

The concept of excluding human activity is not to be taken lightly. One of the major issues in wilderness areas has been whether or not federal agencies should fight forest fires. The general decision has been that they should not, except in cases where other lands are threatened. The federal agencies also do not fight the fires with motorized vehicles, which are prohibited in wilderness areas except in extreme emergencies. Thus in recent years both the National Forest Service and the National Park Service have taken to letting forest fires burn unchecked, to the frequent alarm of tourists. The defense is that many forests require periodic leveling by fire in order to make room for new growth. There are some pine trees, for instance, whose cones will break open and scatter their seeds only when burned. This theoretical justification has won some converts, but very few in the timber companies, which bridle at watching millions of board-feet go up in smoke when their own "harvesting" of mature forests has the same effect in clearing the way for new growth and does less damage to forest soils.

The effort to set aside permanent wilderness areas on federal lands began with the National Forest Service in the 1920s. The first permanent reservation was in the Gila National Forest in New Mexico. It was set aside by a young Forest Service officer named Aldo Leopold, who was later to write *A Sand County Almanac*, which has become one of the bibles of the wilderness movement. Robert Marshall, another Forest Service officer, continued the program, and by the 1950s nearly 14 million of the National Forest System's 186 million acres had been administratively designated wilderness preserves.

Leopold and Marshall had been disillusioned by one of the first great efforts at "game management" under the National Forest Service, carried out in the Kaibab Plateau, just north of the Grand Canyon. As early as 1906 federal officials began a program of "predator control" to increase the deer population in the area. Mountain lions, wolves, coyotes, and bobcats were systematically hunted and trapped by game officials. By 1920, the program appeared to be spectacularly successful. The deer population, formerly numbering 4,000, had grown to almost 100,000. But it was realized too late that it was the range's limited food resources that would threaten the deer's existence. During two severe winters, in 1924–26, 60 percent of the herd died, and by 1939 the population had shrunk to only 10,000. Deer populations (unlike human populations) were found to have no way of putting limits on their own reproduction. The case is still cited as the classic example of the "boom and bust" disequilibrium that comes from thoughtless intervention in an ecological system.

The idea of setting aside as wilderness areas larger and larger segments of federally controlled lands began to gain more support from the old preservation groups. In part, this came from preservationists' growing realization, during the 1950s, that they had not won the battle during the Conservation Era, and that the national forests were not parks that would be protected forever from commercial activity.

Pinchot's plan for practicing "conservation" in the western forests was to encourage a partnership between the government and large industry. In order to discourage overcutting and destructive competition, he formulated a plan that would promote conservation activities among the larger timber companies while placing large segments of the western forests under federal control. It was a classic case of "market restriction," carried out by the joint efforts of larger businesses and government. Only the larger companies, Pinchot reasoned, could generate the profits that would allow them to cut their forest holdings *slowly* so that the trees would have time to grow back. In order to ensure these profit margins, the National Forest Service would hold most of its timber lands out of the market for some time. This would hold up the price of timber and prevent a rampage through the forests by smaller companies trying to beat small profit margins by cutting everything in sight. Then, in later years, the federal lands would gradually be worked into the "sustained yield" cycles, and timber rights put up for sale. It was when the national forests finally came up for cutting in the 1950s that the old preservation groups began to react.

The battle was fought in Congress. The 1960 Multiple Use and Sustained Yield Act tried to reaffirm the principles of the Conservation Movement. But the wilderness groups had their day in 1964 with the passing of the Wilderness Act. The law required all the federal land-management agencies—the National Forest Service, the National Park Service, and the Fish and Wildlife Service—to review all their holdings, keeping in mind that "wilderness" now constituted a valid alternative in the "multiple use" concept—even though the concept of wilderness is essentially a rejection of the idea of multiple use. The Forest Service, with 190 million acres, and the Park Service and Fish and Wildlife Service, each with about 35 million acres, were all given twenty years to start designating wilderness areas. At the time, only 14.5 million acres of National Forest System land were in wilderness designations.

The results have been mixed. The wilderness concept appears valid if it is recognized for what it is—an attempt to create what are essentially "ecological museums" in scenic and biologically significant areas of these lands. But "wilderness," in the hands of environmentalists, has become an all-purpose tool for stopping economic activity as well. This is particularly crucial now because of the many mineral and energy resources available on western lands that environmentalists are trying to push through as wilderness designations. The original legislation specified that lands were to be surveyed for valuable mineral resources before they were put into wilderness preservation. Yet with so much land being reviewed at once, these inventories have been sketchy at best. And once land is locked up as wilderness, it becomes illegal even to explore it for mineral or energy resources.

Thus the situation in western states—where the federal government still owns 68 percent of the land, counting Alaska—has in recent years become a race between mining companies trying to prospect under severely restricted conditions, and environmental groups trying to lock the doors to resource development for good. This kind of permanent preservation—the antithesis of conservation—will probably have enormous effects on our future international trade in energy and mineral resources.

At stake in both the national forests and the Bureau of Land Management holdings are what are called the "roadless areas." Environmentalists call these lands "de facto wilderness," and say that because they have not yet been explored or developed for resources they should not be explored and developed in the future. The Forest Service began its Roadless Area Resources Evaluation (RARE) in 1972, while the Bureau of Land Management began four years later in 1976, after Congress brought its 174 million acres under jurisdiction of the 1964 act. The Forest Service is studying 62 million roadless acres, while the BLM is reviewing 24 million.

In 1974 the Forest Service recommended that 15 million of the 50 million acres then under study be designated as permanent wilderness. Environmental groups, which wanted much more set aside, immediately challenged the decision in court. Naturally, they had no trouble finding flaws in a study intended to cover such a huge amount of land, and in 1977 the Carter administration decided to start over with a "RARE II" study, completed in 1979. This has also been challenged by a consortium of environmental groups that include the Sierra Club, the Wilderness Society, the National Wildlife Federation, and the Natural Resources Defense Council. The RARE II report also recommended putting about 15 million acres in permanent wilderness, with 36 million released for development and 11 million held for further study. The Bureau of Land Management is not scheduled to complete the study of its 24 million acres until 1991.

The effects of this campaign against resource development have been powerful. From 1972 to 1980, the price of a Douglas fir in Oregon increased 500 percent, largely due to the delays in timber sales from the national forests because of the battles over wilderness areas. Over the decade, timber production from the national forests declined slightly, putting far more pressure on the timber industry's own lands. The nation has now become an importer of logs, despite the vast resources on federal lands. In 1979, environmentalists succeeded in pressuring Congress into setting aside 750,000 acres in Idaho as the Sawtooth Wilderness and National Recreational Area. A resource survey, which was not completed until *after* the congressional action, showed that the area contained an estimated billion dollars' worth of molybdenum, zinc, silver, and gold. The same tract also contained a potential source of cobalt, an important mineral for which we are now dependent on foreign sources for 97 percent of what we use.

Perhaps most fiercely contested are the energy supplies believed to be lying under the geological strata running through Colorado, Wyoming, and Montana just east of the Rockies, called the Overthrust Belt. Much of this land is still administered by the Bureau of Land Management for multiple usage. But with the prospect of energy development, environmental groups have been rushing to try to have these high-plains areas designated as wilderness areas as well (cattle grazing is still allowed in wilderness tracts). On those lands permanently withdrawn from commercial use, mineral exploration will be allowed to continue until 1983. Any mines begun by then can continue on a very restricted basis. But the exploration in "roadless areas" is severely limited, in that in most cases there can be no roads constructed (and no use of off-roads vehicles) while exploration is going on. Environmentalists have argued that wells can still be drilled and test mines explored using helicopters. But any such exploration is likely to be extraordinarily expensive and ineffective. Wilderness restrictions are now being drawn so tightly that people on the site are not allowed to leave their excrement in the area.

What is the purpose of all this? The standard environmental argument is that we have to "preserve these last few wild places before they all disappear." Yet it is obvious that something more is at stake. What is being purveyed is a view of the world in which human activity is defined as "bad" and natural conditions are defined as "good." What is being preserved is evidently much more than "ecosystems." What is being preserved is an *image* of wilderness as a semisacred place beyond humanity's intrusion.

It is instructive to consider how environmentalists themselves define the wilderness. David Brower, former director of the Sierra Club, wrote in his introduction to Paul Ehrlich's *The Population Bomb* (1968):

> Whatever resources the wilderness still held would not sustain [man] in his old habits of growing and reaching without limits. Wilderness could, however, provide answers for questions he had not yet learned how to ask. He could predict that the day of creation was not over, that there would be wiser men, and they would thank him for leaving the source of those answers. Wilderness would remain part of his geography of hope, as Wallace Stegner put it, and could, merely because wilderness endured on the planet, prevent man's world from becoming a cage.

The wilderness, he suggested, is a source of peace and freedom. Yet setting wilderness aside for the purposes of solitude doesn't always work very well. Environmentalists have discovered this over and over again, much to their chagrin. Every time a new "untouched paradise" is discovered, the first thing everyone wants to do is visit it. By their united enthusiasm to find these "sanctuaries," people bring the "cage" of society with them. Very quickly it becomes necessary to erect bars to keep people *out*—which is exactly what most of the "wilderness" legislation has been all about.

In 1964, for example, the Sierra Club published a book on the relatively "undiscovered" paradise of Kauai, the second most westerly island in the Hawaiian chain. It wasn't long before the island had been overrun with tourists. When *Time* magazine ran a feature on Kauai in 1979, one unhappy island resident wrote in to convey this telling sentiment: "We're hoping the shortages of jet fuel will stay around and keep people away from here." The age of environmentalism has also been marked by the near overrunning of popular national parks like Yosemite (which now has a full-time jail), intense pressure on woodland recreational areas, full bookings two and three years in advance for raft trips through the Grand Canyon, and dozens of other spectacles of people crowding into isolated areas to get away from it all. Environmentalists are often critical of these inundations, but they must recognize that they have at least contributed to them.

I am not arguing against wild things, scenic beauty, pristine landscapes, and scenic preservation. What I am questioning is the argument that wilderness is a value against which every other human activity must be judged, and that human beings are somehow unworthy of the landscape. The wilderness has been equated with freedom, but there are many different ideas about what constitutes freedom. In the Middle Ages, the saying was that "city air makes a man free," meaning that the harsh social burdens of medieval fuedalism vanished once a person escaped into the heady anonymity of a metropolitan community. When city planner Jane Jacobs, author of *The Death and Life of Great American Cities,* was asked by an interviewer if "overpopulation" and "crowding into large cities" weren't making social prisoners of us all, her simple reply was: "Have you ever lived in a small town?"

It may seem unfair to itemize the personal idiosyncrasies of people who feel comfortable only in wilderness, but it must be remembered that the environmental movement has been shaped by many people who literally spent years of their lives living in isolation. John Muir, the founder of the National Parks movement and the Sierra Club, spent almost ten years living alone in the Sierra Mountains while learning to be a trail guide. David Brower, who headed the Sierra Club for over a decade and later broke with it to found the Friends of the Earth, also spent years as a mountaineer. Gary Snyder, the poet laureate of the environmental movement, has lived much of his life in wilderness isolation and has also spent several years in a Zen monastery. All these people far outdid Thoreau in their desire to get a little perspective on the world. There is nothing reprehensible in this, and the literature and philosophy that emerge from such experiences are often admirable. But it seems questionable to me that the ethic that comes out of this wilderness isolation—and the sense of ownership of natural landscapes that inevitably follows—can serve as the basis for a useful national philosophy.

The American frontier is generally agreed to have closed down physically in 1890, the year the last Indian Territory of Oklahoma was opened for settlement. After that, the Conservation Movement arose quickly to protect the remaining resources and wilderness from heedless stripping and development. Along with this came a significant psychological change in the national character, as the "frontier spirit" diminished and social issues attracted greater attention. The Progressive Movement, the Social Gospel among religious groups, Populism, and Conservation all arose in quick succession immediately after the "closing of the frontier." It seems fair to say that it was only after the frontier had been settled and the sense of endless possibilities that came with open spaces had been constricted in the national consciousness that the country started "growing up."

Does this mean the new environmental consciousness has arisen because we are once again "running out of space"? I doubt it. Anyone taking an airplane across almost any part of the country is inevitably struck by how much greenery and open territory remain, and how little room our towns and cities really occupy. The amount of standing forest in the country, for example, has not diminished appreciably over the last fifty years, and is 75 percent of what it was in 1620. In addition, as environmentalists constantly remind us, trees are "renewable resources." If they continue to be handled intelligently, the forests will always grow back. As farming has moved out to the Great Plains of the Middle West, many eastern areas that were once farmed have reverted back to trees. Though mining operations can permanently scar hillsides and plains, they are usually very limited in scope (and as often as not, it is the roads leading to these mines that environmentalists find most objectionable).

It seems to me that the wilderness ethic has actually represented an attempt psychologically to reopen the American frontier. We have been desperate to maintain belief in unlimited, uncharted vistas within our borders, a preoccupation that has eclipsed the permanent shrinking of the rest of the world outside. Why else would it be so necessary to preserve such huge tracts of "roadless territory" simply because they are now roadless, regardless of their scenic, recreational, or aesthetic values? The environmental movement, among other things, has been a rather backward-looking effort to recapture America's lost innocence.

The central figure in this effort has been the backpacker. The backpacker is a young, unprepossessing person (inevitably white and upper middle class) who journeys into the wilderness as a passive observer. He or she brings his or her own food, treads softly, leaves no litter, and has no need to make use of any of the resources at hand. Backpackers bring all the necessary accouterments of civilization with them. All their needs have been met by the society from which they seek temporary release. The backpacker is freed from the need to support himself in order to enjoy the aesthetic and spiritual values that are made available by this temporary *removal* from the demands of nature. Many dangers—raging rivers or precipitous cliffs, for instance—become sought-out adventures.

Yet once the backpacker runs out of supplies and starts using resources around him—cutting trees for firewood, putting up a shelter against the rain—he is violating some aspect of the federal Wilderness Act. For example, one of the issues fought in the national forests revolves around tying one's horse to a tree. Purists claim the practice should be forbidden, since it may leave a trodden ring around the tree. They say horses should be hobbled and allowed to graze instead. In recent years, the National Forest Service has come under pressure from environmental groups to enforce this restriction.

Wildernesses, then, are essentially parks for the upper middle class. They are vacation reserves for people who want to rough it—with the assurance that few other people will have the time, energy, or means to follow them into the solitude. This is dramatically highlighted in one Sierra Club book that shows a picture of a professorial sort of individual backpacking off into the woods. The ironic caption is a quote from Julius Viancour, an official of the Western Council of Lumber and Sawmill Workers: "The inaccessible wilderness and primitive areas are off limits to most laboring people. We must have access. . . ." The implication for Sierra Club readers is: "What do these beer-drinking, gun-toting, working people want to do in *our* woods?"

This class-oriented vision of wilderness as an upper-middle-class preserve is further illustrated by the fact that most of the opposition to wilderness designations comes not from industry but from owners of off-road vehicles. In most northern rural areas, snowmobiles are now regarded as the greatest invention since the automobile, and people are ready to fight rather than stay cooped up all winter in their houses. It seems ludicrous to them that snowmobiles (which can't be said even to endanger the ground) should be restricted from vast tracts of land so that the occasional city visitor can have solitude while hiking past on snowshoes.

The recent Boundary Waters Canoe Area controversy in northern Minnesota is an excellent example of the conflict. When the tract was first designated as wilderness in 1964, Congress included a special provision that allowed motorboats into the entire area. By the mid-1970s, outboards and inboards were roaming all over the wilderness, and environmental groups began asking that certain portions of the million-acre preserve be set aside exclusively for canoes. Local residents protested vigorously, arguing that fishing expeditions, via motorboats, contributed to their own recreation. Nevertheless, Congress eventually excluded motorboats from 670,000 acres to the north.

A more even split would seem fairer. It should certainly be possible to accommodate both forms of recreation in the area, and there is as much to be said for canoeing in solitude as there is for making rapid expeditions by powerboat. The natural landscape is not likely to suffer very much from either form of recreation. It is not absolute "ecological" values that are really at stake, but simply different tastes in recreation.

At bottom, then, the mystique of the wilderness has been little more than a revival of Rousseau's Romanticism about the "state of nature." The notion that "only in wilderness are human beings truly free," a credo of environmentalists, is merely a variation on Rousseau's dictum that "man is born free, and everywhere he is in chains." According to Rousseau, only society could enslave people, and only in the "state of nature" was the "noble savage"—the preoccupation of so many early explorers—a fulfilled human being.

The "noble savage" and other indigenous peoples, however, have been carefully excised from the environmentalists' vision. Where environmental efforts have encountered primitive peoples, these indigenous residents have often proved one of the biggest problems. One of the most bitter issues in Alaska is the efforts by environmental groups to restrict Indians in their hunting practices.

At the same time, few modern wilderness enthusiasts could imagine, for example, the experience of the nineteenth-century artist J. Ross Browne, who wrote in *Harper's New Monthly Magazine* after visiting the Arizona territories in 1864:

Sketching in Arizona is . . . rather a ticklish pursuit. . . . I never before traveled through a country in which I was compelled to pursue the fine arts with a revolver strapped around my body, a double-barreled shot-gun lying across my knees, and half a dozen soldiers armed with Sharpe's carbines keeping guard in the distance. Even with all the safeguards . . . I am free to admit that on occasions of this kind I frequently looked behind to see how the country appeared in its rear aspect. An artist with an arrow in his back may be a very picturesque object . . . but I would rather draw him on paper than sit for the portrait myself.

Wilderness today means the land *after* the Indians have been cleared away but *before* the settlers have arrived. It represents an attempt to hold that particular moment forever frozen in time, that moment when the visionary American settler looked out on the land and imagined it as an empty paradise, waiting to be molded to our vision.

In the absence of the noble savage, the environmentalist substitutes himself. The wilderness, while free of human dangers, becomes a kind of basic-training ground for upper-middle-class values. Hence the rise of "survival" groups, where college kids are taken out into the woods for a week or two and let loose to prove their survival instincts. No risks are spared on these expeditions. Several people have died on them, and a string of lawsuits has already been launched by parents and survivors who didn't realize how seriously these survival courses were being taken.

The ultimate aim of these efforts is to test upper-middle-class values against the natural environment. "Survival" candidates cannot hunt, kill, or use much of the natural resources available. The true test is whether their zero-degree sleeping bags and dried-food kits prove equal to the hazards of the tasks. What happens is not necessarily related to nature. One could as easily test survival skills by turning a person loose without money or means in New York City for three days.

I do not mean to imply that these efforts do not require enormous amounts of courage and daring—"survival skills." I am only suggesting that what the back-packer or survival hiker encounters is not entirely "nature," and that the effort to go "back to nature" is one that is carefully circumscribed by the most intensely civilized artifacts. Irving Babbitt, the early twentieth-century critic of Rousseau's Romanticism, is particularly vigorous in his dissent from the idea of civilized people going "back to nature." This type, he says, is actually "the least primitive of all beings":

> We have seen that the special form of unreality encouraged by the aesthetic romanticism of Rousseau is the dream of the simple life, the return to a nature that never existed, and that this dream made its special appeal to an age that was suffering from an excess of artificiality and conventionalism.

Babbitt notes shrewdly that our concept of the "state of nature" is actually one of the most sophisticated productions of civilization. Most primitive peoples, who live much closer to the soil than we do, are repelled by wilderness. The American colonists, when they first encountered the unspoiled landscape, saw nothing but a horrible desert, filled with savages.

What we really encounter when we talk about "wilderness," then, is one of the highest products of civilization. It is a reserve set up to keep people *out*, rather than a "state of nature" in which the inhabitants are "truly free." The only thing that makes people "free" in such a reservation is that they can leave so much behind when they enter. Those who try to stay too long find out how spurious this "freedom" is. After spending a year in a cabin in the north Canadian woods, Elizabeth Arthur wrote in *Island Sojourn:* "I never felt so completely tied to *objects*, resources, and the tools to shape them with."

What we are witnessing in the environmental movement's obsession with purified wilderness is what has often been called the "pastoral impulse." The image of nature as unspoiled, unspotted wilderness where we can go to learn the lessons of ecology is both a product of a complex, technological society and an escape from it. It is this undeniable paradox that forms the real problem of setting up "wildernesses." Only when we have created a society that gives us the leisure to appreciate it can we go out and experience what we imagine to be untrammeled nature. Yet if we lock up too much of our land in these reserves, we are cutting into our resources and endangering the very leisure that allows us to enjoy nature.

The answer is, of course, that we cannot simply let nature "take over" and assume that because we have kept roads and people out of huge tracts of land, then we have absolved ourselves of a national guilt. The concept of stewardship means taking responsibility, not simply letting nature take its course. Where tracts can be set aside from commercialism at no great cost, they should be. Where primitive hiking and recreation areas are appealing, they should be maintained. But if we think we are somehow appeasing the gods by *not* developing resources where they exist, then we are being very shortsighted. Conservation, not preservation, is once again the best guiding principle.

WHERE NATURE AND INDUSTRY COLLIDE

Ruth Kern understands all too well the conflict between energy and environment.

When she drives from her A-frame house south of Jackson to her job in a downtown gift shop, she is surrounded by mountains, trees and rivers that comprise some of the most spectacular scenery in North America. And she makes the 13-mile trip in a big four-wheel-drive station wagon that gets about 10 miles per gallon.

Like most residents of Jackson, Kern needs her gas-guzzler to traverse a rugged countryside that is snowbound much of the winter. "Our way of life requires lots of energy," she notes, "but we don't want to destroy the beauty that makes this such a nice place to live."

The conflict between fuel and nature is a topic of intense debate these days in Jackson, a town of 5,000 located in Jackson Hole, a broad valley at the foot of the snow-capped Grand Teton mountains.

The mountains, teeming wildlife and proximity to Yellowstone and Grand Teton national parks and several national forests make Jackson a mecca for thousands of tourists, hunters, skiers and campers each year.

Catering to these visitors is the city's most lucrative business.

But a new industry has arrived on the scene, promising even greater economic benefits. Jackson sits at the edge of the oil-and-gas-rich Rocky Mountain Overthrust Belt. Drilling rigs are probing the Teton foothills and gullies near town, and rumors of big natural-gas discoveries are making the rounds in local cafés and bars.

Environmental and citizen groups that oppose drilling in Jackson Hole and surrounding national forests and wilderness areas have won some early skirmishes. An oil company abandoned an effort to drill along Cache Creek after petitions and public meetings indicated widespread opposition. "Cache Creek is almost like a city park for Jackson," explains Donald MacLeod, a retired doctor who has lived in Jackson for 45 years.

Interior Secretary James Watt's decision to ban mineral exploration in wilderness areas until the year 2000 should slow the drilling activity to some extent. But oil companies already hold leases on most of the private land in Jackson Hole and are filing applications to explore in nearby national forests and proposed wilderness areas.

Some Jackson residents welcome the economic riches promised by the oil industry, but most are alarmed that Jackson might become another Western boom town like Evanston or Rock Springs, two Wyoming cities that have experienced dramatic growth as a result of nearby oil and gas discoveries.

Rip Woodin, editor of the *Jackson Hole Guide*, sums up the debate this way: "People don't come here to see oil wells. They come to see mountains, streams,

"Where Nature and Industry Collide," *U.S. News and World Report* 8 March 1982.

forest and wildlife. But we are a very poor area. We have to struggle to build schools, and income from oil and gas would certainly help."

An oil-company official says that Jackson's ambivalence is not unusual. "Like most Americans," he says, "they know the country needs the energy to keep running. They just don't want it produced in their back yards."

BATTLE OVER THE WILDERNESS
Melinda Beck

Roland Falcioni scans the scores of campers and trailers lining the beach at the Cape Cod National Seashore and wonders how long it will be before the environmentalists evict them. The National Park Service has already taken steps to protect the fragile dunes from the ravages of human feet and tire treads. But three environmental groups have sued, demanding a ban on off-road vehicles. Falcioni's group, the Massachusetts Beach Buggy Association, has joined the fray and negotiations between the two sides have broken down. "It seems like every year they come up with more ways to deprive people of recreational activities," says Mary-Jo Avellar, chairman of the Provincetown Board of Selectmen. "You can't take your dog out there, you can't pick the flowers. What are the dunes for? You can't admire them if you can't get on them."

Woody Guthrie got it right when he wrote "This land is your land, this land is my land." That's just the problem: the federal government owns one-third of America, and citizens are battling over virtually every acre from California to the New York island. The disputes are older than the range wars and as basic as preservation versus development. The extremes among partisans range from Earth First!, the radical environmental group that tolerates sabotage in the cause of preservation, to conservative think tanks that view public ownership of land as nothing short of socialism.

But even Americans who simply want to get away from it all this summer are fighting among themselves over who gets to use Uncle Sam's land—and how. There is now a 10-year waiting list to float a private raft down the Colorado River. Ticketron is handling scarce camping reservations, and "backcountry permits" have been sewn up for months at some of the most isolated spots. The bitterest battles are raging over the right to love nature in different ways. One hiker in the Pecos Wilderness near Santa Fe became so incensed when he encountered another walking his dog on a trail that he slit the puppy's throat. At the nearby Rio Grande Wild and Scenic River, fist fights have broken out over the right to eat lunch on a limited number of sandbars.

At the center of the storm is Interior Secretary James Watt, who, as one of his first acts in office, symbolically turned the bison on the department's seal to face right instead of left. Since then, environmentalists say Watt has freed more federal acreage for oil, gas, coal and geothermal exploration than any interior secretary in history. He has also relaxed strip-mining controls, streamlined rules requiring environmental-impact statements and virtually halted national-park acquisitions in favor of restoring man-made facilities. Last year Congress thwarted his plan to open wilderness areas to oil and gas development, but a federal court has upheld his proposal to release the entire U. S. outer continental shelf to offshore oil drilling. Watt's latest gambit—a call for increased development on wildlife refuges—so

Melinda Beck, "Battle over the Wilderness," *Newsweek* 25 July 1983.

incensed Rep. John Dingell of Michigan that this week Dingell plans to call for an investigation by the General Accounting Office.

Watt argues that it is his job to administer public lands for diverse interests and not just for the sector of society represented by environmental groups. He also says that the nation's public lands are in far better condition as a result of his steward-ship—and that he plans to acquire more—and blames much of the furor on partisan politics. But increasingly, animosity toward the outspoken secretary cuts across party lines. Democratic pollster Peter Hart warns that opposition to Watt is so strong in the West that some traditionally Republican states might swing Democratic in 1984. Ronald Reagan himself consistently claims to be an environmentalist, but after meeting with the president earlier this month, photographer and wilderness enthu-siast Ansel Adams told reporters: "This administration places emphasis on use and exploitation without any regard for the future. For the past 60 years, things have never been this polarized."

The controversies over public lands go far deeper, however, than one interior secretary or one administration, raising questions that go to the very heart of de-mocracy and the national character. How much access should the people have to their land? What if one man's recreation is another's noisy interruption? Should a government dedicated to the principle of private property own more than half of Utah, Idaho, Oregon and Nevada and nearly 75 percent of Alaska? In addition to splendid forests and awesome canyons, federal lands contain 40 percent of the nation's salable timber, 50 percent of its coal, 80 percent of its shale oil and most of its copper, silver, asbestos, lead, berylium, molybdenum, phosphate and potash. How much land should be put into commercial production? How much should be saved for future generations or preserved just as it is?

The debate is complicated by the bureaucratic wilderness of federal agencies that have jurisdiction over the lands—including the Bureau of Land Management, the National Park Service, the U.S. Fish and Wildlife Service and the Forest Service, an agency of the Department of Agriculture. The departments of Defense, Energy and Transportation also have small tracts, as do NASA and the Army Corps of Engineers. There is a Talmudic tangle of separate land classifications such as Wil-derness Areas, National Trails, Grasslands, Seashores, Lakeshores, Monuments, Battlefields, Historical Sites, Wild and Scenic Rivers and Recreation Areas—some of whose boundaries overlap. And the laws governing the lands are sometimes contradictory. The National Park Service, for example, is charged with protecting the natural resources *and* serving the public on its 79 million acres. Much of the remaining land is held by law for "multiple use"—a somewhat implausible doctrine that requires federal land managers to juggle hunting, fishing, timbering, grazing, oil, gas and mineral development, watershed protection, wildlife preservation and recreation on the same lands.

The needs of still other government agencies affect public holdings. The Depart-ment of Energy, for example, is considering building a high-level radioactive waste dump within viewing distance of the Canyonlands National Park in southeastern Utah. Many communities and special-interest groups in the West hate the Bureau of Reclamation, the nation's dam operator—and some blame it for mismanaging the flood of the Colorado River in recent weeks. (When not in flood stage, the mighty Colorado, which carved the Grand Canyon over 200 million years, is controlled these days by a computer in Montrose, Calif., which regulates its flow according to the electricity needs of bustling Western cities.) Last year the House of Representatives passed a bill that would require Interior to consider the impact of other federal-agency actions on adjacent parklands. But Interior officials oppose the measure, claiming it would foster still more paperwork—and more lawsuits—over public-land policies.

Given the vast range of competing interests they must serve, many beleaguered federal land managers figure that if everyone is mad at them, they must be doing something right. Aside from the major philosophical disputes, they also have to contend with such minor annoyances as pot hunters who illegally forage for ancient artifacts; pot *growers*, who use national forests to raise marijuana crops; cactus rustlers feeding a chic new market in Southwestern landscaping; "survivalists," who occasionally hold paramilitary maneuvers on federal lands—and even Satanists seeking a bit of isolation like everybody else. "It's real life in the parks," marvels Walter Herriman, superintendent of New Mexico's Chaco Culture National Historical Park, where one ranger was shot at while confronting a pot hunter last summer.

Twenty years ago, residents near Moab, Utah, decided that the spectacular array of needles, arches, mesas and basins carved by the confluence of the Green and Colorado rivers was so dramatic that it ought to be a national park. Town fathers went to Washington to press the idea. Congress accepted and in 1962, Park Service drew up a proposal envisioning a road, an observation area and tasteful motel accommodations. Today there is no observation area and no motel, and the road dead-ends four miles from the river confluence. Park officials are managing most of Canyonlands National Park as a de facto "wilderness area," accessible only to those with Jeeps or the stamina to hike hours into the desert.

"We created a monster," laments Ray Tibbetts, former chairman of the Grand County Commissioners. "Now we know how the Indians feel about broken promises from the federal government," agrees another leader, Cal Black. Locals are so furious that several years ago, when the BLM was considering other nearby parcels for wilderness designation, county commissioners ordered roads cut in the land in hopes of disqualifying it and organized a picnic to watch.

Of all the concepts in federal land-management policy, none arouses more passion than "wilderness." Technically, the term applies only to 80 million federal acres designated by Congress since 1964 to remain in their most pristine, natural state, "where man is a visitor who does not remain." In theory, that means no roads, no cabins, no water systems, no toilet facilities, no mining, no drilling, no timber harvesting and no mechanized anything. There are inevitable exceptions, but the law is quite serious. The Forest Service cannot use chain saws to cut trees that fall on trails in wilderness areas. When a service helicopter crashed in a wilderness area several years ago, rescue workers had to take it apart and carry it out on foot.

Environmentalists see wilderness as the last refuge against man's ravages—a place that has "answers to questions we haven't learned how to ask yet," says Richard Beamish of the National Audubon Society—and in the environmental heyday of the 1960s and '70s, there was a rush to designate new areas. But the pace has slowed in recent years, in part because of local opposition. "A lot of people who hike up here are not very experienced," says Reuben Rajala, a trail supervisor for the Appalachian Mountain Club, which is leery of more wilderness designations in New Hampshire's White Mountains. "They may not want a Howard Johnson's, but they want toilet facilities and water." In northern California, where the timber industry says a proposed 2.4 million-acre wilderness would cost the local economy 1,300 logging and sawmilling jobs, one popular bumper sticker reads: "Sierra Club—Kiss My Axe."

Many local battles are in legal limbo now, since Watt and Assistant Agriculture Secretary John B. Crowell, who presides over the Forest Service, announced that millions of acres set aside for wilderness consideration under previous administrations would be released or re-examined. That, in turn, has sparked a new round of lawsuits and charges that the Reagan administration is "waging a war on wilderness."

As contentious as designating wilderness areas is, the question of managing the nation's wildlands is worse, and the problem applies not only to official wilderness areas, but to "backcountry" sections of national parks as well. Ever since a 1963 report by biologist A. Starker Leopold recommended that national parks be run as "vignettes of primitive America," many park officials have stopped interfering in natural cycles, even letting some forest fires burn. But man's efforts to erase his own imprint have sometimes proved futile—and often controversial. As rangers in Yellowstone closed down the garbage dumps that fed grizzly bears for decades, the hungry grizzlies started foraging in campsites and off park boundaries where they sometimes maul humans and end up being shot. Last year, to the horror of locals, Yellowstone officials allowed some of the park's magnificent bighorn sheep to walk off cliffs to their death rather than treat an infection of pinkeye that was blinding the herd.

Managing people in wilderness is even more troublesome—in no small part because of the growing enthusiasm for isolated areas. "We're in danger of loving wilderness to death," warns preservationist author Roderick Nash, who admits that environmentalists have been their own worst enemies. "Sierra Club calendars have done for wilderness what Playboy did for women," Nash says. As New Mexico BLM official Forrest (Frosty) Littrell puts it, designating an area wilderness sometimes has a "neon-sign effect": suddenly, everyone wants to see it. To maintain some semblance of solitude in such areas, many national parks have had to limit access to backcountry areas—a seeming contradiction that troubles some wilderness enthusiasts. "'Wilderness' is unrestrained freedom—and that doesn't jive with regulations," says Michael Scott of the Wilderness Society in Denver. "But unrestrained freedom will destroy the area. What do you do?"

Many backcountry managers learned the need for such limits from experience. At Grand Canyon National Park, the epiphany came on a fateful Easter weekend in 1971 when nearly 1,000 people showed up at Bright Angel Campground, a narrow strip of campsites at the base of the canyon designed to accommodate fewer than 100 campers. "These people hadn't escaped from anything," recalls canyon District Ranger Larry Van Slyke. "The very thing they had hiked down to avoid was confronting them." Since then, canyon officials have required permits for overnight camping in the canyon, and beginning in October, they will go further, assigning campers to one of 78 separate "zones" in the backcountry based on their equipment and experience. Far from resenting the hassle, most hikers appreciate the system. "It's sort of like buying tickets for a rock concert," shrugged Robert Bachmann of California, one of dozens of people standing in a predawn line outside the Grand Canyon's "Backcountry Reservations Office" for a chance at a permit cancellation. "If you want to go bad enough, you'll do just about anything."

Nash would go still further. He has advocated dividing public wildlands into five categories—from well-developed areas with clearly marked trails, to the most remote Alaskan mountainscapes—and requiring visitors to qualify for licenses by demonstrating their wilderness skills. (No humans at all would be allowed in "Class Five" lands, which would be left undisturbed as a genetic pool for the future of the earth.) "You wouldn't allow an untrained person to examine a rare piece of art," Nash argues. "When you have increasingly rare environments, you don't want to turn people indiscriminately loose in them."

To more populist nature lovers, Nash's scheme conjures up the specter of "vacation police," and many argue that even now, wilderness is an elitist notion that discriminates in favor of the healthy, wealthy and fit. Even there, however, there is widespread disagreement. "Those who say wilderness is only for the young, wealthy elite are wrong," says "W" Mitchell, former mayor of Crested Butte, Colo., who has run five different wild rivers despite being confined to a wheelchair. "I don't need my $20,000 mobile home, my $10,000 four-wheel drive or my $5,000 dirt bike to enjoy wilderness. It's the great equalizer."

While some long-running disputes over recreational rights have been settled, others are just beginning. Last year Grand Canyon officials ended their 10-year motorboat-versus-oars battle with a compromise (Sept. 16 to Dec. 15 it's "oars only" on the Colorado River). But they have yet to take on the 40-odd companies that operate scenic flights over the canyon, disturbing the "natural quiet" for hikers. Whose interests take precedence is often a matter of political clout or just plain tradition. "The hikers were there first, and that's all they have going for them," says Andy Lundstrom, who has been apprehended three times for running the Yellowstone River in his kayak against park regulations. "We could claim we don't like to see them hiking along with their aluminum and nylon backpacks and digging up the trails with their shoes."

By 1984, visitors to the Grand Canyon will not even need to venture into the park to "experience" its splendors. At a $5 million complex going up less than a mile from the park boundary, they can view a 30-minute film of the canyon's four seasons in a 100-foot-high theater. Next door, 32 tourists at a time can brave a five-minute simulated raft ride through four feet of artificially swooshed waters, riding rafts just like the ones real river runners use. "We'll show [visitors] what they can't see by standing on the rim and looking in," says Toby Rowe, a spokesman for FORMA Properties, which is planning similar thrill centers outside Yosemite and Yellowstone.

Indeed, the debate over backcountry usage is lost on the vast majority of national park and forest visitors, to many of whom a "wilderness experience" means bad TV reception in a park lodge or campground Winnebago. "Wilderness is largely a state of mind," says National Park Service Director Russell Dickenson. "A lot of people enjoy a 'windshield vacation,' driving through the park and stopping at the overlooks. Who's to say that's better or worse than a canoe trip in 50 miles of isolation?"

But catering to the "windshield visitors" (also known as the "Winnebago tribe" or the "subspecies *touristica*") presents its own set of dilemmas. Tourist facilities in most national parks reflect the recreational tastes of past generations, and some park planners are trying to introduce a more natural, 1980s element. In Yellowstone the Hamilton Store at Old Faithful long ago stopped serving "geyser-water coffee"—made from water pumped in, naturally hot, from the geyser basin—and the bathhouses that once stood over the hot springs have been removed. At Yosemite, after receiving comments from 63,000 individuals and groups, park planners decided to reduce the number of parking spaces, banking and postal services and overnight accommodations. Auto repairs and car rentals are no longer available in Yosemite Valley. "The feeling was that if you wanted a resort atmosphere, you could go somewhere else," says Park Service official John Adams. (The swimming pool will remain by popular demand, however, as will the beauty shop at the Awanhee Hotel.) In parts of many national parks, private automobiles have been banned in favor of free shuttle buses. "Instead of people problems, we have auto problems," says Dickenson.

Reeking of pot, swarming with humanity and rocking to the beat of countless oversize radios, Gateway National Recreation Area is the electric Kool-Aid acid test of federal land policy. Sprawling over 26,000 patchwork acres of Brooklyn, Queens, Staten Island and New Jersey, the park boasts such unnatural wonders as an abandoned airport, a nudist colony, a video-game arcade and a bay polluted with toxic wastes. On weekends, 50 U.S. Park Police come up from Washington to help keep order, and an average of 30 arrests are made. Many park-service veterans think Gateway shouldn't be a national park in the company of Yellowstone and Yosemite. But Gateway rangers say this park is important for different reasons. For city kids, Gateway provides a first campout under scraggly pines, a first glimpse of open sea and a chance to learn, as ranger Patricia Resignio puts it, that "all vegetables don't come from cans."

While some conservatives think the federal government owns too much of America, conservationists point to the growing crowds and say more land is needed—

particularly for the newest "urban parks." But the pendulum has swung away from park acquisitions since the mid-1970s, when the late Rep. Phil Burton of California pushed a "park-a-month" plan through Congress, a measure fondly dubbed "park-barrelling." Watt has argued that the parks should fix up the facilities they have before acquiring new lands, and some groups applaud his five-year, $1 billion reha-bilitation program. But others charge that he has tied up acquisition funds approved by Congress and warn that some choice land parcels—such as those around the Santa Monica Mountains National Recreation Area in Los Angeles—may be lost to development or rising prices if not purchased quickly.

Another argument for acquiring more federal lands is the need to protect fragile ecosystems on existing public holdings. Booming oil, gas, timber, housing and geothermal developments in the region around Jackson, Wyo., for example, threaten five national forests, two national parks, a wildlife refuge, elk migrations and even Yellowstone's geysers. Jackson residents worry about the menaces to the region's natural beauty but county officials cannot legally deny subdivision applica-tions on environmental grounds. Federal officials, meanwhile, throw up their hands at the notion of "buffer" acquisitions. "Where does the buffer end?" asks Assistant Interior Secretary Ray Arnett. "Does it stretch from the Atlantic to the Pacific?"

Additional land purchases would not solve many of the environmental problems public lands are facing. Resource specialists at the Grand Canyon, for example, can do little about the smog from Los Angeles that is reducing visibility, one of the park's most critical features. Other park officials have made progress through simple cooperation. When rangers at Montana's Glacier National Park noticed high levels of fluoride in park flora and fauna, they notified a nearby Arco plant, which volun-tarily installed smokestack scrubbers and launched a monitoring program. But a nascent cooperative effort may come too late to save the Everglades National Park. Used for decades as a "pumping station" for South Florida's urban and agricultural needs, the fragile water system that is home to many threatened wildlife species "is sick and dying with a limited prognosis," says former Assistant Interior Secretary Nathaniel Reed.

When Bernard Vandewater of Quinault Lake, Wash., says "this land is my land," he can show you the actual deed. One of perhaps 1 million "inholders" who live or own property inside national-park boundaries, Vandewater personifies perhaps the thorniest public-land problem of all. According to Charles Cushman, director of the National Inholders Associ-ation, more than 70,000 Americans have lost their homes to National Park Service "land grabs" since 1966. (Park Service officials say that most inholders have been offered generous settlements or "easements," and that actual condemnations are rare.) For his part, Vandewater says he's not budging. He and other inholders at Olympic National Park have signed a pact not to sell and are working instead to have Quinault Lake deleted from the park.

While inholders struggle to keep their land from Uncle Sam, proposals to sell public lands also spark uproars. Earlier this year, when the Reagan administration proposed to sell several million acres of federal land to help reduce the national debt, there were coast-to-coast protests as citizens realized that private ownership might shut them out. Some feared that religious cults or foreign speculators would buy the properties; ranchers worried about higher grazing fees. "I know of no other issue in the last year and a half that has drawn more controversy, concern or misunderstanding," says Rep. Larry Craig, Republican of Idaho. Some administration officials still favor the idea, but even Watt recently pronounced the plan "stupid," and some experts believe it is dead.

If the federal government is so intent on raising revenues from its land, why doesn't it charge more for the oil, gas, timber, coal and other resources it sells and leases? Grazing fees on federal rangelands are only about one-fourth of those charged by private range owners. The Forest Service *spends* more money building roads and administering logging operations than it takes in from timber sales, according to some calculations. (It may be illegal, but Steven Hanke, an economist with the conservative Heritage Foundation, says that marijuana is the biggest revenue generator on Western forestland.) "Any resemblance between federal resources management and market value is pure coincidence," says Pat Parentau of the National Wildlife Federation. If the government exploits the nation's resources at the expense of wildlife and wilderness, it should at least insure that taxpayers get their money's worth, environmentalists insist.

Critics are particularly incensed that the Reagan administration is increasing oil, gas, coal and timber sales at a time when there are surpluses of those commodities. The prices they fetch amount to little more than fire sales: the GAO estimates that Watt's controversial coal lease in the Powder River Basin cost the federal government $100 million in lost revenues. Watt plans additional major coal leases from environmentally sensitive areas, even though experts say enough coal has already been mined to satisfy U.S. needs for the rest of the century. Agriculture's Crowell plans to double timber sales from U.S. Forest Service land, even though there is a three-year backlog of timber lying sold, but uncut, because of the housing slump. "These are supposed to be people who know about supply and demand!" marvels National Audubon Society president Russell Peterson. "The lasting legacy of this administration will be a large-scale transfer of publicly owned lands to private hands at below-market rates in a short period of time," agrees Geoffrey Webb of Friends of the Earth.

Crowell insists that the housing slump is temporary and says that there are other considerations besides maximizing profits. "Sustaining a local or regional economy may mean encouraging production in areas that are not . . . economical," he says. Watt maintains that he has received higher prices for coal leases than the Carter administration did and claims Congress, not Interior, sets royalties and other fees for public-land leasing. Assistant Interior Secretary Garrey Carruthers says that total revenues from "multiple use" lands exceed the cost of managing them and that when recreational activities are figured in, "Americans are getting a number of uses at a pretty good price." Critics are unconvinced. If the federal government were a corporation that had to answer to stockholders, says Hanke, they would vote it out of business.

Could private business manage the lands any better? Some critics think so. "A private owner has incentive to take care of the land," argues Hanke, who says that public lands aren't really controlled by the public, but by politicians, bureaucrats and special interests. That "tragedy of commons" notion is echoed at the Center for Political Economy and Natural Resources in Montana, where a small group of scholars thinks that government's need to balance competing interests virtually guarantees mismanagement. Even wilderness would fare better in the free market, the group maintains: without government subsidies, only profitable forests would be harvested and the rest would be left alone. "The history of private ownership of forests has been 'cut out and get out,'" counters Rupert Cutler, John Crowell's predecessor under Jimmy Carter and now a National Audubon Society vice president. "That's why the Forest Service was established."

Curiously, much of the land now owned by the federal government is land nobody wanted. Through America's first two centuries, Uncle Sam gave land away, through homesteading, deeds to states and grants to railroads as an incentive to move westward. To the first settlers, wilderness was an evil that had to be tamed. It was only after the 1890 census, when historian Frederick Jackson Turner declared the frontier closed, that many Americans began to view wilderness as a treasure to be protected.

Even today it is hard for most Americans flying, driving or hiking across the country to believe there is a shortage of wilderness, so much of the land looks empty. Indeed, according to Frank Popper of Resources for the Future, 383 million acres of Western land—17 percent of the country—have never been surveyed. There is enough frontier left, he notes, that great wonders like Leviathan Cave in eastern Nevada and Indian rock carvings in Lassen County, Calif., were discovered just in the last two decades.

Will there still be wondrous surprises from the land in the decades to come? Will Yellowstone someday be seen as America's Acropolis—or will future generations wonder why we saved it? If there is any consensus in the current wilderness wars, it is that this land is *their* land and that the decisions made now will affect it profoundly.

THE DAMNATION OF A CANYON
Edward Abbey

There was a time when, in my search for essences, I concluded that the canyon-land country has no heart. I was wrong. The canyonlands did have a heart, a living heart, and that heart was Glen Canyon and the golden, flowing Colorado River.

In the summer of 1959 a friend and I made a float trip in little rubber rafts down through the length of Glen Canyon, starting at Hite and getting off the river near Gunsight Butte—The Crossing of the Fathers. In this voyage of some 150 miles and ten days our only motive power, and all that we needed, was the current of the Colorado River.

In the summer and fall of 1967 I worked as a seasonal park ranger at the new Glen Canyon National Recreation Area. During my five-month tour of duty I worked at the main marina and headquarters area called Wahweap, at Bullfrog Basin toward the upper end of the reservoir, and finally at Lee's Ferry downriver from Glen Canyon Dam. In a number of powerboat tours I was privileged to see almost all of our nation's newest, biggest and most impressive "recreational facility."

Having thus seen Glen Canyon both before and after what we may fairly call its damnation, I feel that I am in a position to evaluate the transformation of the region caused by construction of the dam. I have had the unique opportunity to observe first-hand some of the differences between the environment of a free river and a power-plant reservoir.

One should admit at the outset to a certain bias. Indeed I am a "butterfly chaser, googly eyed bleeding heart and wild conservative." I take a dim view of dams; I find it hard to learn to love cement; I am poorly impressed by concrete aggregates and statistics in the cubic tons. But in this weakness I am not alone, for I belong to that ever-growing number of Americans, probably a good majority now, who have become aware that a fully industrialized, thoroughly urbanized, elegantly computerized social system is not suitable for human habitation. Great for machines, yes. But unfit for people.

Lake Powell, formed by Glen Canyon Dam, is not a lake. It is a reservoir, with a constantly fluctuating water level—more like a bathtub that is never drained than a true lake. As at Hoover (or Boulder) Dam, the sole practical function of this impounded water is to drive the turbines that generate electricity in the powerhouse at the base of the dam. Recreational benefits were of secondary importance in the minds of those who conceived and built this dam. As a result the volume of water in the reservoir is continually being increased or decreased according to the requirements of the Basin States Compact and the power-grid system of which Glen Canyon Dam is a component.

Edward Abbey, "The Damnation of a Canyon," in *Beyond the Wall* (New York: Holt, Rinehart and Winston, 1984). Abbey's fifteen years as a park ranger for the National Park Service in the American West have provided the basis for many of his essays on wilderness areas. He is widely known for his lively, sometimes bitter and irreverent, defense of the world's wilderness areas. His books include *Fire on the Mountain* (1962), *Desert Solitaire* (1968), and *Good News* (1980).

The rising and falling water level entails various consequences. One of the most obvious, well known to all who have seen Lake Mead, is the "bathtub ring" left on the canyon walls after each drawdown of water, or what rangers at Glen Canyon call the Bathtub Formation. This phenomenon is perhaps of no more than aesthetic importance; yet it is sufficient to dispel any illusion one might have, in contemplating the scene, that you are looking upon a natural lake.

Of much more significance is the fact that plant life, because of the unstable water line, cannot establish itself on the shores of the reservoir. When the water is low, plant life dies of thirst; when high, it is drowned. Much of the shoreline of the reservoir consists of near-perpendicular sandstone bluffs, where very little flora ever did or ever could subsist, but the remainder includes bays, coves, sloping hills and the many side canyons, where the original plant life has been drowned and new plant life cannot get a foothold. And of course where there is little or no plant life there is little or no animal life.

The utter barrenness of the reservoir shoreline recalls by contrast the aspect of things before the dam, when Glen Canyon formed the course of the untamed Colorado. Then we had a wild and flowing river lined by boulder-strewn shores, sandy beaches, thickets of tamarisk and willow, and glades of cottonwoods.

The thickets teemed with songbirds: vireos, warblers, mockingbirds and thrushes. On the open beaches were killdeer, sandpipers, herons, ibises, egrets. Living in grottoes in the canyon walls were swallows, swifts, hawks, wrens and owls. Beaver were common if not abundant: not an evening would pass, in drifting down the river, that we did not see them or at least hear the whack of their flat tails on the water. Above the river shores were the great recessed alcoves where water seeped from the sandstone, nourishing the semitropical hanging gardens of orchid, ivy and columbine, with their associated swarms of insects and birdlife.

Up most of the side canyons, before damnation, there were springs, sometimes flowing streams, waterfalls and plunge pools—the kind of marvels you can now find only in such small-scale remnants of Glen Canyon as the Escalante area. In the rich flora of these laterals the larger mammals—mule deer, coyote, bobcat, ring-tailed cat, gray fox, kit fox, skunk, badger and others—found a home. When the river was dammed almost all of these things were lost. Crowded out—or drowned and buried under mud.

The difference between the present reservoir, with its silent sterile shores and debris-choked side canyons, and the original Glen Canyon, is the difference between death and life. Glen Canyon was alive. Lake Powell is a graveyard.

For those who may think I exaggerate the contrast between the former river canyon and the present man-made impoundment, I suggest a trip on Lake Powell followed immediately by another boat trip on the river below the dam. Take a boat from Lee's Ferry up the river to within sight of the dam, then shut off the motor and allow yourself the rare delight of a quiet, effortless drifting down the stream. In that twelve-mile stretch of living green, singing birds, flowing water and untarnished canyon walls—sights and sounds a million years older and infinitely lovelier than the roar of motorboats—you will rediscover a small and imperfect sampling of the kind of experience that was taken away from everybody when the oligarchs and politicians condemned our river for purposes of their own.

The effects of Glen Canyon Dam also extend downstream, causing changes in the character and ecology of Marble Gorge and Grand Canyon. Because the annual spring floods are now a thing of the past, the shores are becoming overgrown with brush, the rapids are getting worse where the river no longer has enough force to carry away the boulders washed down from the lateral canyons, and the beaches are disappearing, losing sand that is not replaced.

Lake Powell, though not a lake, may well be as its defenders assert the most beautiful reservoir in the world. Certainly it has a photogenic backdrop of buttes and mesas projecting above the expansive surface of stagnant waters where the speedboats, houseboats and cabin cruisers ply. But it is no longer a wilderness. It is no longer a place of natural life. It is no longer Glen Canyon.

The defenders of the dam argue that the recreational benefits available on the surface of the reservoir outweigh the loss of Indian ruins, historical sites, wildlife and wilderness adventure. Relying on the familiar quantitative logic of business and bureaucracy, they assert that whereas only a few thousand citizens ever ventured down the river through Glen Canyon, now millions can—or will—enjoy the motorized boating and hatchery fishing available on the reservoir. They will also argue that the rising waters behind the dam have made such places as Rainbow Bridge accessible by powerboat. Formerly you could get there only by walking (six miles).

This argument appeals to the wheelchair ethos of the wealthy, upper-middle-class American slob. If Rainbow Bridge is worth seeing at all, then by God it should be easily, readily, immediately available to everybody with the money to buy a big powerboat. Why should a trip to such a place be the privilege only of those who are willing to walk six miles? Or if Pikes Peak is worth getting to, then why not build a highway to the top of it so that anyone can get there? Anytime? Without effort? Or as my old man would say, "By Christ, one man's just as good as another—if not a damn sight better."

Or as ex-Commissioner Floyd Dominy of the U.S. Bureau of Reclamation pointed out poetically in his handsomely engraved and illustrated brochure *Lake Powell: Jewel of the Colorado* (produced by the U.S. Government Printing Office at our expense): "There's something about a lake which brings us a littler closer to God." In this case, Lake Powell, about five hundred feet closer. Eh, Floyd?

It is quite true that the flooding of Glen Canyon has opened up to the motorboat explorer parts of side canyons that formerly could be reached only by people able to walk. But the sum total of terrain visible to the eye and touchable by hand and foot has been greatly diminished, not increased. Because of the dam the river is gone, the inner canyon is gone, the best parts of the numerous side canyons are gone—all hidden beneath hundreds of feet of polluted water, accumulating silt, and mounting tons of trash. This portion of Glen Canyon—and who can estimate how many cubic miles were lost?—*is no longer accessible to anybody.* (Except scuba divers.) And this, do not forget, was the most valuable part of Glen Canyon, richest in scenery, archaeology, history, flora and fauna.

Not only has the heart of Glen Canyon been buried, but many of the side canyons above the fluctuating waterline are now rendered more difficult, not easier, to get into. This because the debris brought down into them by desert storms, no longer carried away by the river, must unavoidably build up in the area where flood meets reservoir. Narrow Canyon, for example, at the head of the impounded waters, is already beginning to silt up and to amass huge quantities of driftwood, some of it floating on the surface, some of it half afloat beneath the surface. Anyone who has tried to pilot a motorboat through a raft of half-sunken logs and bloated dead cows will have his own thoughts on the accessibility of these waters.

Hite Marina, at the mouth of Narrow Canyon, will probably have to be abandoned within twenty or thirty years. After that it will be the turn of Bullfrog Marina. And then Rainbow Bridge Marina. And eventually, inevitably, whether it takes ten centuries or only one, Wahweap. Lake Powell, like Lake Mead, is foredoomed sooner or later to become a solid mass of mud, and its dam a waterfall. Assuming, of course, that either one stands that long.

Second, the question of costs. It is often stated that the dam and its reservoir have opened up to the many what was formerly restricted to the few, implying in this case that what was once expensive has now been made cheap. Exactly the opposite is true.

Before the dam, a float trip down the river through Glen Canyon would cost you a minimum of seven days' time, well within anyone's vacation allotment, and a capital outlay of about forty dollars—the prevailing price of a two-man rubber boat with oars, available at any army-navy surplus store. A life jacket might be useful but not required, for there were no dangerous rapids in the 150 miles of Glen Canyon. As the name implies, this stretch of the river was in fact so easy and gentle that the trip could be and was made by all sorts of amateurs: by Boy Scouts, Camp Fire Girls, stenographers, schoolteachers, students, little old ladies in inner tubes. Guides, professional boatmen, giant pontoons, outboard motors, radios, rescue equipment were not needed. The Glen Canyon float trip was an adventure anyone could enjoy, on his own, for a cost less than that of spending two days and nights in a Page motel. Even food was there, in the water: the channel catfish were easier to catch and a lot better eating than the striped bass and rainbow trout dumped by the ton into the reservoir these days. And one other thing: at the end of the float trip you still owned your boat, usable for many more such casual and carefree expeditions.

What is the situation now? Float trips are no longer possible. The only way left for the exploration of the reservoir and what remains of Glen Canyon demands the use of a powerboat. Here you have three options: (1) buy your own boat and engine, the necessary auxiliary equipment, the fuel to keep it moving, the parts and repairs to keep it running, the permits and licenses required for legal operation, the trailer to transport it; (2) rent a boat; or (3) go on a commercial excursion boat, packed in with other sightseers, following a preplanned itinerary. This kind of play is only for the affluent.

The inescapable conclusion is that no matter how one attempts to calculate the cost in dollars and cents, a float trip down Glen Canyon was much cheaper than a powerboat tour of the reservoir. Being less expensive, as well as safer and easier, the float trip was an adventure open to far more people than will ever be able to afford motorboat excursions in the area now.

What about the "human impact" of motorized use of the Glen Canyon impoundment? We can visualize the floor of the reservoir gradually accumulating not only silt, mud, waterlogged trees and drowned cattle but also the usual debris that is left behind when the urban, industrial style of recreation is carried into the open country. There is also the problem of human wastes. The waters of the wild river were good to drink, but nobody in his senses would drink from Lake Powell. Eventually, as is already sometimes the case at Lake Mead, the stagnant waters will become too foul even for swimming. The trouble is that while some boats have what are called "self-contained" heads, the majority do not; most sewage is disposed of by simply pumping it into the water. It will take a while, but long before it becomes a solid mass of mud Lake Powell ("Jewel of the Colorado") will enjoy a passing fame as the biggest sewage lagoon in the American Southwest. Most tourists will never be able to afford a boat trip on this reservoir, but everybody within fifty miles will be able to smell it.

All of the foregoing would be nothing but a futile exercise in nostalgia (so much water over the dam) if I had nothing constructive and concrete to offer. But I do. As alternate methods of power generation are developed, such as solar, and as the nation establishes a way of life adapted to actual resources and basic needs, so that the demand for electrical power begins to diminish, we can shut down the Glen Canyon power plant, open the diversion tunnels, and drain the reservoir.

This will no doubt expose a drear and hideous scene: immense mud flats and whole plateaus of sodden garbage strewn with dead trees, sunken boats, the skeletons of long-forgotten, decomposing water-skiers. But to those who find the prospect too appalling, I say give nature a little time. In five years, at most in ten, the sun and wind and storms will cleanse and sterilize the repellent mess. The inevitable floods will soon remove all that does not belong within the canyons. Fresh green willow, box elder and redbud will reappear; and the ancient drowned cottonwoods (noble monuments to themselves) will be replaced by young of their own kind. With the renewal of plant life will come the insects, the birds, the lizards and snakes, the mammals. Within a generation—thirty years—I predict the river and canyons will bear a decent resemblance to their former selves. Within the lifetime of our children Glen Canyon and the living river, heart of the canyonlands, will be restored to us. The wilderness will again belong to God, the people and the wild things that call it home.

"BOOMERS" VS. "SNIFFERS"
Richard Sandza

Billie Sheldon kills the outboard and lets his splintered rowboat drift into the weeds as his three-year-old grandson hangs over the gunwales. "Big *Sii Lik, Ta Ta*," says the child, pointing at the net. It is filled with dozens of fish, most of them northern pike—Sii Lik, in Eskimo. Grandpa (Ta Ta) Sheldon quickly harvests the catch, tossing it into an old oil drum. If half an hour he has gathered nearly 100 pike, sheefish and whitefish.

Sheldon is a full-blooded Inupiat Eskimo who has subsisted on hunting and fishing near his home in Noorvik, Alaska, for most of his 65 years. In December 1980 Jimmy Carter signed the Alaska National Interest Land Conservation Act (ANILCA), which turned Sheldon's hunting grounds into Selawik National Wildlife Refuge. Because of a special ANILCA provision, subsistence hunters like Sheldon are allowed to fish and hunt within the federal parklands. But hardly anyone else can do so, and that—like many other ANILCA provisions strictly governing the use of about one-third of the state—has set off bitter protests. In fact, Alaska raises the incredible possibility that a state twice the size of Texas—spanning four time zones and two hemispheres—may not have enough land for a population the size of Oklahoma City's.

For years, the state has been abroil with a fight between those who want to exploit the state's oil, gas and minerals ("the boomers") and those who don't ("the posy-sniffers"). But despite the infighting in the 49th state, Alaskans are nearly unanimous in their contempt for Washington, which has carved up the state's lands and restricted the sale of its resources. Visitors can get a feel for the sensitivity of the issue by bringing up the subject over dinner in a rural restaurant. Suddenly, everybody falls silent and listens—just like a commercial for E.F. Hutton. Soon, everyone from construction workers to the waitress lets loose with complaints about ANILCA.

ANILCA is a compromise that makes no one happy—a law designed to settle the various land disputes that arose from the Alaska Statehood Act of 1958. Alaskans supported statehood to get more control over Alaska land and its extraordinary riches, from wildlife (the state is home to 30,000 American bald eagles, 20 times the number in the lower 48, and grizzly bears are so abundant that the state permits hunting them) to natural resources (it contains world-class deposits of timber, oil and other minerals). But 25 years later the federal government still controls 75 percent of the state's area. Through ANILCA, Congress has imposed federal control in perpetuity—and Alaskans don't like it. Alaskans for Independence, founded in 1973, is a group dedicated to being left alone by the rest of the nation. "This land was put here by God Almighty for people to use," says chairman Joe Vogler. "It wasn't put here for planners to restrict or for the state to own."

Richard Sandza, " 'Boomers' vs. 'Sniffers,' " *Newsweek* 25 July 1983.

Some Alaskans are trying to bargain. The Arctic Slope Regional Corp., one of 13 native-owned corporations endowed with about 44 million acres under the Native Claims Settlement Act, has offered the federal government 92,000 acres adjacent to Gates of the Arctic National Park in exchange for oil-exploration areas inside the Arctic National Wildlife Refuge. The Cook Inlet Regional Corp. has proposed swapping 12,000 acres of mainland waterfowl nesting area for 4,200 acres of wildlife refuge on St. Matthew Island in the Bering Sea. The corporations want to lease the land to oil companies as a staging base for offshore drilling 400 miles from the mainland.

James Watt appears to support such swaps. The administration also supports a bill, sponsored by Alaska Sen. Ted Stevens, that would redesignate about 12 million acres of ANILCA parkland as "preserve," giving sportsmen the same access as subsistence hunters. It is, argues Republican Stevens, "a simple matter of justice." Meanwhile, conservationists—who argue that both arrangements contravene Congress's intent in enacting ANILCA—are doing their best to stall. Their main hope is that Reagan and Watt won't survive the 1984 election—and that a new administration will be on their side in the fight over the greatest of all American wildlands.

ACCESS TO PUBLIC LANDS:
A NATIONAL NECESSITY
Cynthia Riggs

Quick! Name America's largest landowner. No, not the King Ranch. No, not the Bank of America. No, Exxon isn't even in the running. The answer is the federal government. Of America's 2,271 million acres, 720 million belong to Uncle Sam. Add another 966 million underwater acres of the country's continental shelf, and you've got an impressive bit of real estate there.

In terms of the nation's resources, that vast range of public property represents enormous volumes of timber, grass, and minerals. Copper, zinc, gold, vanadium, tantalum, iron, and silver are among dozens of metallic minerals mined on federal lands. In energy minerals alone, government land may contain more than half the nation's remaining resources. According to the Department of Energy, this includes 85 percent of the nation's crude oil, 40 percent of natural gas, 40 percent of uranium, 35 percent of coal, 80 percent of oil shale, 85 percent of tar sands, and 50 percent of geothermal resources.

What does this mean to those of us who don't even own a 50- by 100-foot lot? Like others who visit national parks and camp in national forests and photograph national monuments, we consider these lands our heritage. Divide it among us, and we'd each have something like three acres apiece. Like all landowners, we'd like those three acres cared for, protected, preserved. It's nice to be a landowner. But there's the rub. Each of us also needs farmland for crops, rangeland for grazing, timber for homes, metals for machines, and energy for heat and fuel. For these, we must turn increasingly to those same public lands of ours where such resources are still to be found.

"No one can feel happy about intrusion upon the wilderness," writes Dr. Charles F. Park, professor of geology at Stanford University, in his book, *Earthbound.* "It is justified only by the urgency of the need."

The need is urgent, and getting more so. Yet tens of millions of acres of public lands have been closed to mineral development by law or administrative actions. As of early 1983 only 162 million acres of federal onshore land and 13 million acres of offshore land were under lease for oil and natural gas exploration and production.

And the trend is away from development and toward preservation. In many cases the economic uses of land is prohibited in favor of a single-purpose use, such as preserving an area where a species of bird may nest, setting aside territory for grizzly bears, reestablishing a prairie ecosystem, or saving a historic site. From this clear need to protect a specific site, the drive for preservation has overwhelmed the concept of multiple use until today vast acreages of federal lands are permanently closed without reason or need, often without an evaluation of the land's aesthetic,

Cynthia Riggs, "Access to Public Lands: A National Necessity," *Exxon USA* (second quarter 1984). Riggs, a geologist, is a former writer for the American Petroleum Institute.

biological, recreational, and economic resources. Would-be users—miners, skiers, cattle and sheep ranchers, farmers, campers, timber harvesters, energy firms— are affected.

Groups opposed to the multiple use of federal lands defend their stand in strong language: ". . . the industrial juggernaut must not further degrade the environment . . ." says an official of the Wilderness Society. Authors of the original law governing mineral extraction on federal lands are called a "rapacious gaggle of politicos" motivated by "cupidity and corruption." Under the appealing slogan, "Preserve the Wilderness," the society fights to keep federal lands out of the hands of the "destroyers."

Who are the destroyers?

"Anyone who uses a sheet of paper, who drives an automobile, who has a telephone, a radio, a refrigerator," Dr. Park says. "Anyone who owns a television set or uses artificial light. Anyone who heats a home, who applies paint, hammers a nail, or flushes a toilet. Even the staunchest of preservationists is such a destroyer."

Are environmentalists hypocritical, then?

Not really. Most hold their convictions with the best of intentions and genuine good will. They fear that without the strongest of safeguards, all public lands would be subject to indiscriminate development. They see bulldozers coming over every horizon. Yet most federal lands have no potential for mining or oil. Mineral lodes and oil- and gas-bearing structures are not common. Their very rarity is what gives their development such high priority. The U.S. Geological Survey has identified 260 million of its onshore acres in the lower 48 states as worth exploring for petroleum, which is a small percentage of the total acreage of federal lands. Of that, oil or gas deposits might lie beneath no more than one out of 10 of those acres. Were oil exploration encouraged to the fullest, few Americans would ever see signs of it. Nor would development, as conducted under today's environmental regulations, result in more than temporary change to the land.

Nonetheless, some environmental professionals continue to insist that more land should be set aside as wilderness. Robert Cahn, Washington editor for *Audubon Magazine*, writing of land within Alaska Wildlife Refuges, says that "the national interest might be served better by wilderness than by development." Cahn praises the Alaska National Interest Lands Conservation Act (which added 10 new national parks, 44 million acres to the National Park, and 56 million acres to the National Wilderness Preservation System) as "the greatest land-protection law in modern history."

And so it is. Yet land withdrawals of such magnitude must inevitably have serious implications for the American economy. "Civilized people want and must have raw materials, especially energy, at moderate prices," emphasizes Dr. Parks. "Nations have gone to the extreme of war to obtain them. For this reason, if for no other, those who advocate the preservation of large wilderness areas known to contain valuable and necessary raw materials are not going to prevail."

Other scientists confirm this view. Dr. William Conway, director of the New York Zoological Society and Bronx Zoo, advises, "It is absolutely impractical to imagine that the human race will not develop the undeveloped lands that remain on this earth." And he calls for a collaborative effort for development and conservation.

Similarly, public officials worried for America's welfare deplore extremes in the name of the environment. John B. Crowell, Jr., Assistant Secretary of Agriculture for Natural Resources and Environment, speaking at an Audubon Society meeting on pressures on the land, told his audience, "We are concerned that additions to the wilderness system be made with careful consideration of the costs . . . of foregoing the long-term availability of resources such as timber, minerals, oil and gas, geothermal power, developed recreation, and forest production."

The wilderness of which he speaks is one of several categories of the federal land system, which includes national parks and national monuments. The former now encompasses 68 million acres of land of exceptional natural, historic, or recreational value; the latter, a much smaller volume, covering the smallest area compatible with proper care or management. National monuments may be single buildings, such as Ford's Theatre in Washington, D.C. or an area of special geologic interest such as the 211,000-acre Dinosaur National Monument in Utah and Colorado.

Mineral extraction is prohibited in national parks and national monuments.

Wildlife preserves account for almost 90 million acres of federal lands. Almost 54 million acres were added in 1980, all in Alaska. Petroleum exploration and production is permitted by law on wildlife refuges, provided proper environmental precautions are taken. In practice, however, few leases have been granted for such activities in these areas.

Wild and scenic rivers comprise another one million acres in the 49 states other than Alaska, and five million acres in Alaska. This relatively small percentage of federal lands has a large impact on energy development because it limits access to other lands. Seismic or exploration crews cannot work across or near scenic rivers, and pipeline rights of way are restricted. Another federal land designation that limits economic use is that of National Grasslands and Wetlands. Petroleum operations are permitted legally, but administrative delays in granting leases drag on for months and even years. Military reservations make up another 30 million acres, and on these lands, public use of all kinds is tightly restricted. Indian lands generally have not presented an access problem, and tribal councils have worked with oil companies to make oil exploration and production compatible with Indian use— and economically desirable.

Two land programs particularly inhibiting to economic development are the Wilderness Preservation System, set up in 1964, and the Endangered Species Act. Together, these programs present a tangle of confusing and sometimes contradictory regulations.

The Wilderness Act defines wilderness as "an area where the earth and its community of life are untrammeled by man, where man himself is a visitor who does not remain." A wilderness area must be at least 5,000 acres in area, roadless, and unimproved. The wilderness program has grown from nine million acres to 80 million acres. If land now under study is added to the system, the wilderness area could be doubled to 167 million acres. The wilderness designation puts land off limits to all but a few users, such as backpackers. Motorized vehicles are prohibited, and road and permanent facilities are not allowed.

Some groups feel this is the way it should be. "Just because (land) is there, it's important, whether you or I or anyone else can get at it or not," says Stephen Chapman, of Minnesota's Clean Air, Clean Water Unlimited. "Perhaps (the land) is even better because we can't get to it."

Of wilderness, an article in *Harper's* magazine explains that "The wilderness concept appears valid if it is recognized for what it is—an attempt to create what are essentially 'ecological museums' in scenic and biologically significant areas of the lands. But 'wilderness' in the hands of environmentalists has become an all-purpose tool for stopping economic activity as well."

Conveniently ignored in all of this is the fact that most government land is not suitable for the "wilderness" category proposed for it. It has little aesthetic or recreational value. It has nothing in common with those spectacular parks such as Yellowstone, Yosemite, the Grand Canyon, or the Grand Teton. When land of scientific and recreational value is subtracted from the total, hundreds of millions of acres remain that can and should contribute to the national welfare through practical use. Its value as a source of raw materials far exceeds its value for recreation or science. Yet these lands, too, are often locked up with the rest.

Ignored, too, is the fact that the environmental impact of such economic activities as oil and gas extraction is slight, temporary, and carried out under strict guidelines that allow the land to revert eventually to its natural state. Yet it continues to be an article of faith among environmental activists that oil and gas activities equate with wholesale and permanent destruction which can be prevented only by prohibiting access to areas where the presence of hydrocarbons is suspected.

The Endangered Species Act is another law that has been widely used to stop economic activity. The story of the snail darter is well known. This small, minnow-sized fish, found in an area about to be inundated by construction of the Tellico Dam, a part of the TVA system, was pronounced an endangered species. As a result, construction of the multimillion-dollar dam was delayed for years at immense cost while scientists studied the possibility of relocating the fish to a new habitat. Eventually, it was discovered that snail darters are not all that uncommon, and the species was removed from the endangered list. But not until millions of dollars and valuable time had been lost.

Even private land is not exempt from the government's land policies. According to the Chase Manhattan Bank, about 30 percent of private land in the lower 48 states "has been effectively withdrawn by the need to comply with mind-boggling environmental laws and regulations. All this without any explicit analysis of the energy loss associated with alternate land uses."

Should Americans worry about the loss of energy resources? Some say no. We have enough oil and gas now, goes the argument. Let's lock up the land until we need its raw materials.

Yet the argument collapses in the face of the facts:

- America imports one-third of its oil at a cost of $50 billion a year.
- America consumes two barrels of oil from its reserves for each barrel of new oil found.
- On today's oil search, tomorrow's energy security depends.

Oil development is a long-range proposition. From the time a decision is made to prospect for oil, some 10 years may be needed to go through the lengthy process of looking for, finding, testing, developing, and producing oil into the nation's supply system. If the oil search is not pressed today, there won't be enough to go around tomorrow.

This reality lends a sense of urgency to the need to resolve a growing impasse over access to public lands. Arbitrary barriers to exploration and development of minerals on most public lands are neither wise nor necessary. A policy of careful, orderly, and steady development is preferable to one of nothing today followed by a crash program tomorrow when the awful truth sinks in.

Isn't that what you would prefer for your three acres? Should you be among the few to claim three acres in the Grand Canyon, you would certainly vote to protect it. But if you are among the many with three parched acres of sagebrush, tumbleweed, and alkali dust in Nevada's Basin and Range Province, or in the frozen bleak and barren tundra of North Alaska, your decision might well be, "Let's see if there isn't some badly needed oil under that land."

A FOREST OF MANMADE THREATS DESCENDS ON YELLOWSTONE PARK
James Coates

INSPIRATION POINT, Wyo.—Millions of Americans have come here to gaze in awe over the rim of the Yellowstone Canyon at the pencil-thin green strand at the bottom of the abyss that is, in fact, the 75-foot-wide Yellowstone River.

From there, their eyes travel up past towering cliffs of yellow and red rock pocked with steam-belching geysers to the thundering Yellowstone Falls, where white water churns off a 308-foot precipice.

As chief administrator of Yellowstone National Park, Robert Barbee looks at that stunning scene each day and becomes troubled about ever-more-vexing signs that modern society is slowly—but most measurably—ruining one of its few remaining natural treasures.

Copper foundries 900 miles away in Arizona and even across the border in Mexico send chemicals into the air, which come out of the skies as acid rain over Yellowstone Lake, which feeds the falls.

Barbee said a recent rainfall acidity pH reading of 4.4 was similar "to the worst" recorded in Canada when many lakes were said to have "died" because they turned acid.

"We don't view this as at the crisis stage, at least not yet," Barbee said. "But it's something we are watching very closely."

"We're watching a lot of things closely, it seems," he added ruefully.

A private group, the Greater Yellowstone Coalition, has outlined 88 threats to Yellowstone that its experts warn could mean the loss of many of the natural wonders that still are commonplace here in America's first national park.

Among these threats are:

- Oil companies pressuring to drill gas wells just across the park's boundaries in areas where grizzly bears feed when their food in the park gives out. The bears will not seek food so close to humans, and the result could be eradication of the park's estimated 350 grizzlies.

- Developers planning to build a ski resort called Ski Yellowstone just across the park's border at West Yellowstone, Mont., in the path of major elk and bear migration routes.

- Cattle and sheep ranchers who graze their animals in national forests alongside the park demand that buffalo be shot when they wander outside the park. Last winter 88 bison were shot by the Montana Department of Game and Fish near Gardiner, Mont.

James Coates, "A Forest of Manmade Threats Descends on Yellowstone Park," *The Chicago Tribune* 19 May 1985, sec. 1.

- Korean businessmen hire American poachers to sneak into the park and shoot bear for their gall bladders and elk for their antlers, both of which are sold for high profits as aphrodisiacs in Korea and China.

- Timber companies have obtained permits to clear cut logs in watersheds that environmentalists warn will ruin fly fishing by causing mud to collect in the waters of the awesome Yellowstone, Madison and Henry's Fork Rivers.

- Several state and federal dam projects near the park's boundaries pose similar threats to fly fishing because the projects will stem the migration of fish.

As park officials put the finishing touches on plans to handle the annual influx of tourists, Barbee noted that virtually every well-known aspect of Yellowstone appears threatened by the ever-more-populous world that presses in from every direction.

Last year, for example, there were more incidents in which human beings ran afoul of grizzly bears in the park than ever before.

One tourist, Britt Fredenhagen, 25, was killed by a grizzly and a dozen people were mauled with varying degrees of severity. There had been only three previous cases of bears killing humans in the park since 1916.

"We just have ever more people who want to enjoy the same country where the bears range, and that means more contacts and more problems," the park chief said.

After the attacks began last summer, the Montana Game and Fish Department suggested opening a limited hunting season for grizzlies but abandoned the idea, at least temporarily, after protests from environmentalists.

"I think we could solve our grizzly bear problem if we could hunt two or three a year," Don Bianchi, public information officer for the department, said at the time.

But, Barbee noted, the idea of shooting bison when they cross the park boundary remains "an active one because the animals carry a disease called brucellosis, which causes ranchers' cows to abort their calves.

"There is brucellosis all over the place besides from buffalo," he said. "Elk carry it. So do rodents and even some insects."

Montana's shooting of the 88 bison that wandered outside the park last winter created controversy when it was learned that because of a bureaucratic snafu the carcasses were allowed to rot in a warehouse instead of being used for food, as the state had planned.

Barbee noted that there even has been speculation—which he discounts—that oil and gas wells near the park have tapped into thermal areas, throwing Old Faithful's schedule of eruptions off by 10 minutes and causing other geysers to stop erupting altogether.

A major study by biologists, chemists, geologists and other experts with the Greater Yellowstone Coalition concluded that unexpected pressures on the national forests, mountains and farm and ranch country that surround the 2 million-acre national park are threatening to change park conditions that are close to the way they were before the first settler—white or Indian—arrived.

Bob Anderson, executive director of the coalition, said in an interview: "We look at many projects or policies and we see great danger from their cumulative effects.

"Any one of them could be tolerated, but taken together, they will destroy this national treasure."

SUGGESTIONS FOR WRITING

Informal Essays

1. Using a personal experience and a passage or two from one of the essays in this chapter, argue that we should or should not deny access to automobiles in a national park of your choice.
2. After reading a few selections in this chapter, write a personal essay on the value that you derive from your favorite natural setting.
3. Write a personal essay in which you show why you prefer the "unnatural" environment of towns and cities over the "natural" environment of rocks and trees. Approach the topic ironically or humorously if you wish.

Short Documented Papers

1. Contrast two or three of the strongest arguments on each side of the issue concerning access to national parks.
2. Contrast one or two of the strongest points on both sides of the issue concerning the use of federal lands for oil and mineral exploitation.
3. Develop two or three of the arguments of either the preservationist's or the conservationist's side of the issue of wilderness use.

Longer Documented Papers

1. Write a research report in which you describe three or four of the strongest points made by the opposing sides in the controversy.
2. Write a research argument in which you take a side in the controversy. As you argue, don't fail to take the other side's argument into account.
3. Make the complete case for limiting or expanding access to national parks.

· 3 ·

Abortion:
Under What
Circumstances?

As dismayed politicians keep rediscovering, the abortion controversy simply won't go away.

The issue began in earnest in the mid-1960s, when an increasing number of Americans began to view death or injury resulting from illegal abortions as a serious social problem. That emerging concern, reflected in the increasingly permissive attitude toward abortion and fueled by the women's liberation and population-control movements, led to the founding of groups such as the National Association for the Repeal of Abortion Laws. It also eventually prompted 17 state legislatures to pass laws that allowed abortions under certain circumstances (such as cases in which the woman is raped or when a birth might endanger the woman's life). Many of those laws limited abortions to the first three months of pregnancy.

In 1973 the controversy reached a rolling boil when the Supreme Court decided (in *Roe* v *Wade*) by a five to four majority that states no longer had the right to deny a woman an abortion during the first three months of her pregnancy. That same ruling permitted states to totally prohibit abortions only during the last three months of a woman's pregnancy when the woman's health was not endangered. Moreover, the Supreme Court defined the word "health" to include a woman's mental as well as her physical condition. If a state legislature chose to do nothing, the Supreme Court ruling, in effect, permitted abortion on demand.

In the past, the stamp of legality has gradually conferred legitimacy and propriety on a controversial position. That has not happened in the case of the Supreme

Court's 1973 position on abortion. Although the number of abortions has soared since 1973, opposition to abortion remains widespread and heated. Several large national organizations, such as the National Right to Life Committee, have sprung up since the Supreme Court's ruling.

The major goal of the anti-abortion groups has been to reverse the Supreme Court's decision in *Roe v Wade*, either through congressional legislation or through a constitutional convention. To date, this goal has eluded the movement, but it continues, nevertheless, to wield considerable political clout. Indeed, in the 1984 elections, 11 years after *Roe v Wade*, Walter Mondale, Geraldine Ferraro, and scores of other politicians discovered that there is but one political issue for tens of thousands of voters.

As you will soon discover in this chapter's readings, the labels that the pro-abortion and the anti-abortion advocates have conferred on their respective causes reveal the premises from which each group argues. Members of the "pro-choice" movement ground their argument on the relationship between the individual and the state. A democratic state, they contend, has no right to impose its will on the private morality of the individual. They also view the right of a woman to control the functions of her own body to be absolute and sacrosanct. Contending, moreover, that women have always sought abortions, regardless of the legality of such a pursuit, pro-choicers say that prohibiting abortions merely imperils the lives of many women who inevitably seek the services of "back alley" abortionists operating outside the law.

The "pro-life" forces, on the other hand, center their argument on a definition of what constitutes human life—or at what point it begins. The humanness of the embryo, they say, begins at conception, or at the latest, very early in the embryonic stage. Thus, to the pro-life advocates, abortion is nothing less than murder.

Naturally, many of those engaged in the controversy share at least an island or two of common ground with their opponents. Many pro-lifers, for example, concede that abortion should not necessarily be prohibited in cases that involve rape or danger to the mother's life; and many pro-choicers concede that abortion should only be a measure of last resort, that it should be sought only after sober, moral reflection.

A DEFENSE OF ABORTION
Judith Jarvis Thomson

Most opposition to abortion relies on the premise that the fetus is a human being, a person, from the moment of conception. The premise is argued for, but, as I think, not well. Take, for example, the most common argument. We are asked to notice that the development of a human being from conception through birth into child-hood is continuous; then it is said that to draw a line, to choose a point in this development and say "before this point the thing is not a person, after this point it is a person" is to make an arbitrary choice, a choice for which in the nature of things no good reason can be given. It is concluded that the fetus is, or anyway that we had better say it is, a person from the moment of conception. But this conclusion does not follow. Similar things might be said about the development of an acorn into an oak tree, and it does not follow that acorns are oak trees, or that we had better say they are. Arguments of this form are sometimes called "slippery slope arguments"—the phrase is perhaps self-explanatory—and it is dismaying that opponents of abortion rely on them so heavily and uncritically.

I am inclined to agree, however, that the prospects for "drawing a line" in the development of the fetus look dim. I am inclined to think also that we shall probably have to agree that the fetus has already become a human person well before birth. Indeed, it comes as a surprise when one first learns how early in its life it begins to acquire human characteristics. By the tenth week, for example, it already has a face, arms and legs, fingers and toes; it has internal organs, and brain activity is detecta-ble. On the other hand, I think that the premise is false, that the fetus is not a person from the moment of conception. A newly fertilized ovum, a newly implanted clump of cells, is no more a person than an acorn is an oak tree. But I shall not discuss any of this. For it seems to me to be of great interest to ask what happens if, for the sake of argument, we allow the premise. How, precisely, are we supposed to get from there to the conclusion that abortion is morally impermissible? Opponents of abortion commonly spend most of their time establishing that the fetus is a person, and hardly any time explaining the step from there to the impermissibility of abortion. Perhaps they think the step too simple and obvious to require much comment. Or perhaps instead they are simply being economical in argument. Many of those who defend abortion rely on the premise that the fetus is not a person, but only a bit of tissue that will become a person at birth, and why pay out more arguments than you have to? Whatever the explanation, I suggest that the step they take is neither easy nor obvious, that it calls for closer examination than it is commonly given, and that when we do give it this closer examination we shall feel inclined to reject it.

I propose, then, that we grant that the fetus is a person from the moment of conception. How does the argument go from here? Something like this, I take it. Every person has a right to life. So the fetus has a right to life. No doubt the mother

Judith Jarvis Thomson, "A Defense of Abortion," *Philosophy and Public Affairs* 1 (1971). Thomson is a professor of philosophy at the Massachusetts Institute of Technology.

has a right to decide what shall happen in and to her body; everyone would grant that. But surely a person's right to life is stronger and more stringent than the mother's right to decide what happens in and to her body, and so outweighs it. So the fetus may not be killed; an abortion may not be performed.

It sounds plausible. But now let me ask you to imagine this. You wake up in the morning and find yourself back to back in bed with an unconscious violinist. A famous unconscious violinist. He has been found to have a fatal kidney ailment, and the Society of Music Lovers has canvassed all the available medical records and found that you alone have the right blood type to help. They have therefore kidnapped you, and last night the violinist's circulatory system was plugged into yours, so that your kidneys can be used to extract poisons from his blood as well as your own. The director of the hospital now tells you, "Look, we're sorry the Society of Music Lovers did this to you—we would never have permitted it if we had known. But still, they did it, and the violinist now is plugged into you. To unplug you would be to kill him. But never mind, it's only for nine months. By then he will have recovered from his ailment, and can safely be unplugged from you." Is it morally incumbent on you to accede to this situation? No doubt it would be very nice of you if you did, a great kindness. But do you *have* to accede to it? What if it were not nine months, but nine years? Or longer still? What if the director of the hospital says, "Tough luck, I agree, but you've now got to stay in bed, with the violinist plugged into you, for the rest of your life. Because remember this. All persons have a right to life, and violinists are persons. Granted you have a right to decide what happens in and to your body, but a person's right to life outweighs your right to decide what happens in and to your body. So you cannot ever be unplugged from him." I imagine you would regard this as outrageous, which suggests that something really is wrong with that plausible-sounding argument I mentioned a moment ago.

In this case, of course, you were kidnapped, you didn't volunteer for the operation that plugged the violinist into your kidneys. Can those who oppose abortion on the ground I mentioned make an exception for a pregnancy due to rape? Certainly. They can say that persons have a right to life only if they didn't come into existence because of rape; or they can say that all persons have a right to life, but that some have less of a right to life than others, in particular, that those who came into existence because of rape have less. But these statements have a rather unpleasant sound. Surely the question of whether you have a right to life at all, or how much of it you have, shouldn't turn on the question of whether or not you are the product of a rape. And in fact the people who oppose abortion on the ground I mentioned do not make this distinction, and hence do not make an exception in case of rape.

Nor do they make an exception for a case in which the mother has to spend the nine months of her pregnancy in bed. They would agree that would be a great pity, and hard on the mother; but all the same, all persons have a right to life, the fetus is a person, and so on. I suspect, in fact, that they would not make an exception for a case in which, miraculously enough, the pregnancy went on for nine years, or even the rest of the mother's life.

Some won't even make an exception for a case in which continuation of the pregnancy is likely to shorten the mother's life; they regard abortion as impermissible

even to save the mother's life. Such cases are nowadays very rare, and many opponents of abortion do not accept this extreme view. All the same, it is a good place
to begin: a number of points of interest come out in respect to it.

1. Let us call the view that abortion is impermissible even to save the mother's
life "the extreme view." I want to suggest first that it does not issue from the
argument I mentioned earlier without the addition of some fairly powerful premises.
Suppose a woman has become pregnant, and now learns that she has a cardiac
condition such that she will die if she carries the baby to term. What may be done
for her? The fetus, being a person, has a right to life, but as the mother is a person
too, so has she a right to life. Presumably they have an equal right to life. How is it
supposed to come out that an abortion may not be performed? If mother and child
have an equal right to life, shouldn't we perhaps flip a coin? Or should we add to
the mother's right to life her right to decide what happens in and to her body, which
everybody seems to be ready to grant—the sum of her rights now outweighing the
fetus' right to life?

The most familiar argument here is the following. We are told that performing
the abortion would be directly killing the child, whereas doing nothing would not
be killing the mother, but only letting her die. Moreover, in killing the child, one
would be killing an innocent person, for the child has committed no crime, and is
not aiming at his mother's death. And then there are a variety of ways in which this
might be continued. (1) But as directly killing an innocent person is always and
absolutely impermissible, an abortion may not be performed. Or, (2) as directly
killing an innocent person is murder, and murder is always and absolutely impermissible, an abortion may not be performed. Or, (3) as one's duty to refrain from directly
killing an innocent person is more stringent than one's duty to keep a person from
dying, an abortion may not be performed. Or, (4) if one's only options are directly
killing an innocent person or letting a person die, one must prefer letting the person
die, and thus an abortion may not be performed.

Some people seem to have thought that these are not further premises which
must be added if the conclusion is to be reached, but that they follow from the very
fact that an innocent person has a right to life. But this seems to me to be a mistake,
and perhaps the simplest way to show this is to bring out that while we must certainly
grant that innocent persons have a right to life, the theses in (1) through (4) are all
false. Take (2), for example. If directly killing an innocent person is murder, and
thus is impermissible, then the mother's directly killing the innocent person inside
her is murder, and thus is impermissible. But it cannot seriously be thought to be
murder if the mother performs an abortion on herself to save her life. It cannot
seriously be said that she *must* refrain, that she *must* sit passively by and wait for her
death. Let us look again at the case of you and the violinist. There you are, in bed
with the violinist, and the director of the hospital says to you, "It's all most distress-
ing, and I deeply sympathize, but you see this is putting an additional strain on your
kidneys, and you'll be dead within the month. But you *have* to stay where you are
all the same. Because unplugging you would be directly killing an innocent violinist,
and that's murder, and that's impermissible." If anything in the world is true, it is
that you do not commit murder, you do not do what is impermissible, if you reach
around to your back and unplug yourself from that violinist to save your life.

The main focus of attention in writings on abortion has been on what a third party may or may not do in answer to a request from a woman for an abortion. This is in a way understandable. Things being as they are, there isn't much a woman can safely do to abort herself. So the question asked is what a third party may do, and what the mother may do, if it is mentioned at all, is deduced, almost as an after-thought, from what it is concluded that third parties may do. But it seems to me that to treat the matter in this way is to refuse to grant to the mother that very status of person which is so firmly insisted on for the fetus. For we cannot simply read off what a person may do from what a third party may do. Suppose you find yourself trapped in a tiny house with a growing child. I mean a very tiny house, and a rapidly growing child—you are already up against the wall of the house and in a few minutes you'll be crushed to death. The child on the other hand won't be crushed to death; if nothing is done to stop him from growing he'll be hurt, but in the end he'll simply burst open the house and walk out a free man. Now I could well understand it if a bystander were to say, "There's nothing we can do for you. We cannot choose between your life and his, we cannot be the ones to decide who is to live, we cannot intervene." But it cannot be concluded that you too can do nothing, that you cannot attack it to save your life. However innocent the child may be, you do not have to wait passively while it crushes you to death. Perhaps a pregnant woman is vaguely felt to have the status of house, to which we don't allow the right of self-defense. But if the woman houses the child, it should be remembered that she is a person who houses it.

I should perhaps stop to say explicitly that I am not claiming that people have a right to do anything whatever to save their lives. I think, rather, that there are drastic limits to the right of self-defense. If someone threatens you with death unless you torture someone else to death, I think you have not the right, even to save your life, to do so. But the case under consideration here is very different. In our case there are only two people involved, one whose life is threatened, and one who threatens it. Both are innocent: the one who is threatened is not threatened because of any fault, the one who threatens does not threaten because of any fault. For this reason we may feel that we bystanders cannot intervene. But the person threat-ened can.

In sum, a woman surely can defend her life against the threat to it posed by the unborn child, even if doing so involves its death. And this shows not merely that the theses in (1) through (4) are false; it shows also that the extreme view of abortion is false, and so we need not canvass any other possible ways of arriving at it from the argument I mentioned at the outset.

2. The extreme view could of course be weakened to say that while abortion is permissible to save the mother's life, it may not be performed by a third party, but only by the mother herself. But this cannot be right either. For what we have to keep in mind is that the mother and the unborn child are not like two tenants in a small house which has, by an unfortunate mistake, been rented to both: the mother *owns* the house. The fact that she does adds to the offensiveness of deducing that the mother can do nothing from the supposition that third parties can do nothing. But it does more than this: it casts a bright light on the supposition that third parties can do nothing. Certainly it lets us see that a third party who says "I cannot choose

between you" is fooling himself if he thinks this is impartiality. If Jones has found and fastened on a certain coat, which he needs to keep him from freezing, but which Smith also needs to keep him from freezing, then it is not impartiality that says "I cannot choose between you" when Smith owns the coat. Women have said again and again "This body is *my* body!" and they have reason to feel angry, reason to feel that it has been like shouting into the wind. Smith, after all, is hardly likely to bless us if we say to him, "Of course it's your coat, anybody would grant that it is. But no one may choose between you and Jones who is to have it."

We should really ask what it is that says "no one may choose" in the face of the fact that the body that houses the child is the mother's body. It may be simply a failure to appreciate this fact. But it may be something more interesting, namely the sense that one has a right to refuse to lay hands on people, even where it would be just and fair to do so, even where justice seems to require that somebody do so. Thus justice might call for somebody to get Smith's coat back from Jones, and yet you have a right to refuse to be the one to lay hands on Jones, a right to refuse to do physical violence to him. This, I think, must be granted. But then what should be said is not "no one may choose," but only "*I* cannot choose," and indeed not even this, but "*I* will not *act*," leaving it open that somebody else can or should, and in particular that anyone in a position of authority, with the job of securing people's rights, both can and should. So this is no difficulty. I have not been arguing that any given third party must accede to the mother's request that he perform an abortion to save her life, but only that he may.

I suppose that in some views of human life the mother's body is only on loan to her, the loan not being one which gives her any prior claim to it. One who held this view might well think it impartiality to say "I cannot choose." But I shall simply ignore this possibility. My own view is that if a human being has any just, prior claim to anything at all, he has a just, prior claim to his own body. And perhaps this needn't be argued for here anyway, since, as I mentioned, the arguments against abortion we are looking at do grant that the woman has a right to decide what happens in and to her body.

But although they do grant it, I have tried to show that they do not take seriously what is done in granting it. I suggest the same thing will reappear even more clearly when we turn away from cases in which the mother's life is at stake, and attend, as I propose we now do, to the vastly more common cases in which a woman wants an abortion for some less weighty reason than preserving her own life.

3. Where the mother's life is not at stake, the argument I mentioned at the outset seems to have a much stronger pull. "Everyone has a right to life, so the unborn person has a right to life." And isn't the child's right to life weightier than anything other than the mother's own right to life, which she might put forward as ground for an abortion?

This argument treats the right to life as if it were unproblematic. It is not, and this seems to me to be precisely the source of the mistake.

For we should now, at long last, ask what it comes to, to have a right to life. In some views having a right to life includes having a right to be given at least the bare minimum one needs for continued life. But suppose that what in fact *is* the bare minimum a man needs for continued life is something he has no right at all to be given? If I am sick unto death, and the only thing that will save my life is the touch of Henry Fonda's cool hand on my fevered brow, then all the same, I have no right to be given the touch of Henry Fonda's cool hand on my fevered brow. It would be frightfully nice of him to fly in from the West Coast to provide it. It would be less nice, though no doubt well meant, if my friends flew out to the West Coast and carried Henry Fonda back with them. But I have no right at all against anybody that he should do this for me. Or again, to return to the story I told earlier, the fact that for continued life that violinist needs the continued use of your kidneys does not establish that he has a right to be given the continued use of your kidneys. He certainly has no right against you that *you* should give him continued use of your kidneys. For nobody has any right to use your kidneys unless you give him such a right; and nobody has the right against you that you shall give him this right—if you do allow him to go on using your kidneys, this is a kindness on your part, and not something he can claim from you as his due. Nor has he any right against anybody else that *they* should give him continued use of your kidneys. Certainly he had no right against the Society of Music Lovers that they should plug him into you in the first place. And if you now start to unplug yourself, having learned that you will otherwise have to spend nine years in bed with him, there is nobody in the world who must try to prevent you, in order to see to it that he is given something he has a right to be given.

Some people are rather stricter about the right to life. In their view, it does not include the right to be given anything, but amounts to, and only to, the right not to be killed by anybody. But here a related difficulty arises. If everybody is to refrain from killing that violinist, then everybody must refrain from doing a great many different sorts of things. Everybody must refrain from slitting his throat, everybody must refrain from shooting him—and everybody must refrain from unplugging you from him. But does he have a right against everybody that they shall refrain from unplugging you from him? To refrain from doing this is to allow him to continue to use your kidneys. It could be argued that he has a right against us that *we* should allow him to continue to use your kidneys. That is, while he had no right against us that we should give him the use of your kidneys, it might be argued that he anyway has a right against us that we shall not now intervene and deprive him of the use of your kidneys. I shall come back to third-party interventions later. But certainly the violinist has no right against you that *you* shall allow him to continue to use your kidneys. As I said, if you do allow him to use them, it is a kindness on your part, and not something you owe him.

The difficulty I point to here is not peculiar to the right of life. It reappears in connection with all the other natural rights; and it is something which an adequate account of rights must deal with. For present purposes it is enough just to draw attention to it. But I would stress that I am not arguing that people do not have a right to life—quite to the contrary, it seems to me that the primary control we must place on the acceptability of an account of rights is that it should turn out in that account to be a truth that all persons have a right to life. I am arguing only that having a right to life does not guarantee having either a right to be given the use of or a right to be allowed continued use of another person's body—even if one needs it for life itself. So the right to life will not serve the opponents of abortion in the very simple and clear way in which they seem to have thought it would.

4. There is another way to bring out the difficulty. In the most ordinary sort of case, to deprive someone of what he has a right to is to treat him unjustly. Suppose a boy and his small brother are jointly given a box of chocolates for Christmas. If the older boy takes the box and refuses to give his brother any of the chocolates, he is unjust to him, for the brother has been given a right to half of them. But suppose that, having learned that otherwise it means nine years in bed with that violinist, you unplug yourself from him. You surely are not being unjust to him for you gave him no right to use your kidneys, and no one else can have given him any such right. But we have to notice that in unplugging yourself, you are killing him, and violinists, like everybody else, have a right to life, and thus in the view we were considering just now, the right not to be killed. So here you do what he supposedly has a right you shall not do, but you do not act unjustly to him in doing it.

The emendation which may be made at this point is this: the right to life consists not in the right not to be killed, but rather in the right not to be killed unjustly. This runs a risk of circularity, but never mind: it would enable us to square the fact that the violinist has a right to life with the fact that you do not act unjustly toward him in unplugging yourself, thereby killing him. For if you do not kill him unjustly, you do not violate his right to life, and so it is no wonder you do him no injustice.

But if this emendation is accepted, the gap in the argument against abortion stares us plainly in the face: it is by no means enough to show that the fetus is a person, and to remind us that all persons have a right to life—we need to be shown also that killing the fetus violates its right to life, i.e., that abortion is unjust killing. And is it?

I suppose we may take it as a datum that in a case of pregnancy due to rape the mother has not given the unborn person a right to the use of her body for food and shelter. Indeed, in what pregnancy could it be supposed that the mother has given the unborn person such a right? It is not as if there were unborn persons drifting about the world, to whom a woman who wants a child says "I invite you in."

But it might be argued that there are other ways one can have acquired a right to the use of another person's body than by having been invited to use it by that person. Suppose a woman voluntarily indulges in intercourse, knowing of the chance it will issue in pregnancy, and then she does become pregnant; is she not in part responsible for the presence, in fact the very existence, of the unborn person inside? No doubt she did not invite it in. But doesn't her partial responsibility for its being there itself give it a right to the use of her body? If so, then her aborting it would be more like the boy's taking away the chocolates, and less like your unplugging yourself from the violinist—doing so would be depriving it of what it does have a right to, and thus would be doing it an injustice.

And then, too, it might be asked whether or not she can kill it even to save her own life: If she voluntarily called it into existence, how can she now kill it, even in self-defense?

The first thing to be said about this is that it is something new. Opponents of abortion have been so concerned to make out the independence of the fetus, in order to establish that it has a right to life, just as its mother does, that they have tended to overlook the possible support they might gain from making out that the fetus is *dependent* on the mother, in order to establish that she has a special kind of responsibility for it, a responsibility that gives it rights against her which are not possessed by any independent person—such as an ailing violinist who is a stranger to her.

On the other hand, this argument would give the unborn person a right to its mother's body only if her pregnancy resulted from a voluntary act, undertaken in full knowledge of the chance a pregnancy might result from it. It would leave out entirely the unborn person whose existence is due to rape. Pending the availability of some further argument, then, we would be left with the conclusion that unborn persons whose existence is due to rape have no right to the use of their mothers' bodies, and thus that aborting them is not depriving them of anything they have a right to and hence is not unjust killing.

And we should also notice that it is not at all plain that this argument really does go even as far as it purports to. For there are cases and cases, and the details make a difference. If the room is stuffy, and I therefore open a window to air it, and a burglar climbs in, it would be absurd to say, "Ah, now he can stay, she's given him a right to the use of her house—for she is partially responsible for his presence there, having voluntarily done what enabled him to get in, in full knowledge that there are such things as burglars, and that burglars burgle." It would be still more absurd to say this if I had had bars installed outside my windows, precisely to prevent burglars from getting in, and a burglar got in only because of a defect in the bars. It remains equally absurd if we imagine it is not a burglar who climbs in, but an innocent person who blunders or falls in. Again, suppose it were like this: people-seeds drift about in the air like pollen, and if you open your windows, one may drift in and take root in your carpets or upholstery. You don't want children, so you fix up your windows with fine mesh screens, the very best you can buy. As can happen, however, and on very, very rare occasions does happen, one of the screens is defective; and a seed drifts in and takes root. Does the person-plant who now develops have a right to the use of your house? Surely not—despite the fact that you voluntarily opened your windows, you knowingly kept carpets and upholstered furniture, and you knew that screens were sometimes defective. Someone may argue that you are responsible for its rooting, that it does have a right to your house, because after all you *could* have lived out your life with bare floors and furniture, or with sealed windows and doors. But this won't do—for by the same token anyone can avoid a pregnancy due to rape by having a hysterectomy, or anyway by never leaving home without a (reliable!) army.

It seems to me that the argument we are looking at can establish at most that there are *some* cases in which the unborn person has a right to the use of its mother's body, and therefore *some* cases in which abortion is unjust killing. There is room for much discussion and argument as to precisely which, if any. But I think we should sidestep this issue and leave it open, for at any rate the argument certainly does not establish that all abortion is unjust killing.

5. There is room for yet another argument here, however. We surely must all grant that there may be cases in which it would be morally indecent to detach a

person from your body at the cost of his life. Suppose you learn that what the violinist needs is not nine years of your life, but only one hour: all you need do to save his life is to spend one hour in that bed with him. Suppose also that letting him use your kidneys for that one hour would not affect your health in the slightest. Admittedly you were kidnapped. Admittedly you did not give anyone permission to plug him into you. Nevertheless it seems to me plain you *ought* to allow him to use your kidneys for that one hour—it would be indecent to refuse.

Again, suppose pregnancy lasted only an hour, and constituted no threat to life or health. And suppose that a woman becomes pregnant as a result of rape. Admittedly she did not voluntarily do anything to bring about the existence of a child. Admittedly she did nothing at all which would give the unborn person a right to the use of her body. All the same it might well be said, as in the newly emended violinist story, that she *ought* to allow it to remain for that hour—that it would be indecent in her to refuse.

Now some people are inclined to use the term "right" in such a way that it follows from the fact that you ought to allow a person to use your body for the hour he needs, that he has a right to use your body for the hour he needs, even though he has not been given that right by any person or act. They may say that it follows also that if you refuse, you act unjustly toward him. This use of the term is perhaps so common that it cannot be called wrong; nevertheless it seems to me to be an unfortunate loosening of what we would do better to keep a tight rein on. Suppose that box of chocolates I mentioned earlier had not been given to both boys jointly, but was given only to the older boy. There he sits, stolidly eating his way through the box, his small brother watching enviously. Here we are likely to say "You ought not to be so mean. You ought to give your brother some of those chocolates." My own view is that it just does not follow from the truth of this that the brother has any right to any of the chocolates. If the boy refuses to give his brother any, he is greedy, stingy, callous—but not unjust. I suppose that the people I have in mind will say it does follow that the brother has a right to some of the chocolates, and thus that the boy does act unjustly if he refuses to give his brother any. But the effect of saying this is to obscure what we should keep distinct, namely the difference between the boy's refusal in this case and the boy's refusal in the earlier case, in which the box was given to both boys jointly, and in which the small brother thus had what was from any point of view clear title to half.

A further objection to so using the term "right" that from the fact that A ought to do a thing for B, it follows that B has a right against A that A do it for him, is that it is going to make the question of whether or not a man has a right to a thing turn on how easy it is to provide him with it; and it seems not merely unfortunate, but morally unacceptable. Take the case of Henry Fonda again. I said earlier that I had no right to the touch of his cool hand on my fevered brow, even though I needed it to save my life. I said it would be frightfully nice of him to fly in from the West Coast to provide me with it, but that I had no right against him that he should do so. But suppose he isn't on the West Coast. Suppose he has only to walk across the room, place a hand briefly on my brow—and lo, my life is saved. Then surely he ought to do it, it would be indecent to refuse. Is it to be said "Ah, well, it follows that in this case she has a right to the touch of his hand on her brow, and so it would be an injustice in him to refuse"? So that I have a right to it when it is easy for him to provide it, though no right when it's hard? It's rather a shocking idea that anyone's rights should fade away and disappear as it gets harder and harder to accord them to him.

So my own view is that even though you ought to let the violinist use your kidneys for the one hour he needs, we should not conclude that he has a right to do so—we should say that if you refuse, you are, like the boy who owns all the chocolates and will give none away, self-centered and callous, indecent in fact, but not unjust. And similarly, that even supposing a case in which a woman pregnant due to rape ought to allow the unborn person to use her body for the hour he needs, we should not conclude that he has a right to do so; we should conclude that she is self-centered, callous, indecent, but not unjust, if she refuses. The complaints are no less grave; they are just different. However, there is no need to insist on this point. If anyone does wish to deduce "he has a right" from "you ought," then all the same he must surely grant that there are cases in which it is not morally required of you that you allow that violinist to use your kidneys, and in which he does not have a right to use them, and in which you do not do him an injustice if you refuse. And so also for mother and unborn child. Except in such cases as the unborn person has a right to demand it—and we were leaving open the possibility that there may be such cases—nobody is morally *required* to make large sacrifices, of health, of all other interests and concerns, of all other duties and commitments, for nine years, or even for nine months, in order to keep another person alive.

6. We have in fact to distinguish between two kinds of Samaritan: the Good Samaritan and what we might call the Minimally Decent Samaritan. The story of the Good Samaritan, you will remember, goes like this:

> A certain man went down from Jerusalem to Jericho, and fell among thieves, which stripped him of his raiment, and wounded him, and departed, leaving him half dead.
>
> And by chance there came down a certain priest that way; and when he saw him, he passed by on the other side.
>
> And likewise a Levite, when he was at the place, came and looked on him, and passed by on the other side.
>
> But a certain Samaritan, as he journeyed, came where he was; and when he saw him he had compassion on him.
>
> And went to him, and bound up his wounds, pouring in oil and wine, and set him on his own beast, and brought him to an inn, and took care of him.
>
> And on the morrow, when he departed, he took out two pence, and gave them to the host, and said unto him, "Take care of him; and whatsoever thou spendest more, when I come again, I will repay thee." (Luke 10:30–35)

The Good Samaritan went out of his way, at some cost to himself, to help one in need of it. We are not told what the options were, that is, whether or not the priest and the Levite could have helped by doing less than the Good Samaritan did, but assuming they could have, then the fact they did nothing at all shows they were not even Minimally Decent Samaritans, not because they were not Samaritans, but because they were not even minimally decent.

These things are a matter of degree, of course, but there is a difference, and it comes out perhaps most clearly in the story of Kitty Genovese, who, as you will remember, was murdered while thirty-eight people watched or listened, and did nothing at all to help her. A Good Samaritan would have rushed out to give direct assistance against the murderer. Or perhaps we had better allow that it would have been a Splendid Samaritan who did this, on the ground that it would have involved a risk of death for himself. But the thirty-eight not only did not do this, they did not even trouble to pick up a phone to call the police. Minimally Decent Samaritanism would call for doing at least that, and their not having done it was monstrous.

After telling the story of the Good Samaritan, Jesus said "Go and do thou likewise." Perhaps he meant that we are morally required to act as the Good Samaritan did. Perhaps he was urging people to do more than is morally required of them. At all events it seems plain that it was not morally required of any of the thirty-eight that he rush out to give direct assistance at the risk of his own life, and that it is not morally required of anyone that he give long stretches of his life—nine years or nine months—to sustaining the life of a person who has no special right (we are leaving open the possibility of this) to demand it.

Indeed, with one rather striking class of exceptions, no one in any country in the world is *legally* required to do anywhere near as much as this for anyone else. The class of exceptions is obvious. My main concern here is not the state of the law in respect to abortion, but it is worth drawing attention to the fact that in no state in this country is any man compelled by law to be even a Minimally Decent Samaritan to any person; there is no law under which charges could be brought against the thirty-eight who stood by while Kitty Genovese died. By contrast, in most states in this country women are compelled by law to be not merely Minimally Decent Samaritans, but Good Samaritans to unborn persons inside them. This doesn't by itself settle anything one way or the other, because it may well be argued that there should be laws in this country—as there are in many European countries—compelling at least Minimally Decent Samaritanism. But it does show that there is a gross injustice in the existing state of the law. And it shows also that the groups currently working against liberalization of abortion laws, in fact working toward having it declared unconstitutional for a state to permit abortion, had better start working for the adoption of Good Samaritan laws generally, or earn the charge that they are acting in bad faith.

I should think, myself, that Minimally Decent Samaritan laws would be one thing, Good Samaritan laws quite another, and in fact highly improper. But we are not here concerned with the law. What we should ask is not whether anybody should be compelled by law to be a Good Samaritan, but whether we must accede to a situation in which somebody is being compelled—by nature, perhaps—to be a Good Samaritan. We have, in other words, to look now at third-party interventions. I have been arguing that no person is morally required to make large sacrifices to sustain the life of another who has no right to demand them, and this even where the sacrifices do not include life itself; we are not morally required to be Good Samaritans or anyway Very Good Samaritans to one another. But what if a man cannot extricate himself from such a situation? What if he appeals to us to extricate him? It seems to me plain that there are cases in which we can, cases in which a

Good Samaritan would extricate him. There you are, you were kidnapped, and nine years in bed with that violinist lie ahead of you. You have your own life to lead. You are sorry, but you simply cannot see giving up so much of your life to the sustaining of his. You cannot extricate yourself, and ask us to do so. I should have thought that—in light of his having no right to the use of your body—it was obvious that we do not have to accede to your being forced to give up so much. We can do what you ask. There is no injustice to the violinist in our doing so.

7. Following the lead of the opponents of abortion, I have throughout been speaking of the fetus merely as a person, and what I have been asking is whether or not the argument we began with, which proceeds only from the fetus' being a person, really does establish its conclusion. I have argued that it does not.

But of course there are arguments and arguments, and it may be said that I have simply fastened on the wrong one. It may be said that what is important is not merely the fact that the fetus is a person, but that it is a person for whom the woman has a special kind of responsibility issuing from the fact that she is its mother. And it might be argued that all my analogies are therefore irrelevant—for you do not have that special kind of responsibility for that violinist, Henry Fonda does not have that special kind of responsibility for me. And our attention might be drawn to the fact that men and woman both *are* compelled by law to provide support for their children.

I have in effect dealt (briefly) with this argument in section 4 above; but a (still briefer) recapitulation now may be in order. Surely we do not have any such "special responsibility" for a person unless we have assumed it, explicitly or implicitly. If a set of parents do not try to prevent pregnancy, do not obtain an abortion, but rather take it home with them, then they have assumed responsibility for it, they have given it rights, and they cannot *now* withdraw support from it at the cost of its life because they now find it difficult to go on providing for it. But if they have taken all reasonable precautions against having a child, they do not simply by virtue of their biological relationship to the child who comes into existence have a special responsibility for it. They may wish to assume responsibility for it, or they may not wish to. And I am suggesting that if assuming responsibility for it would require large sacrifices, then they may refuse. A Good Samaritan would not refuse—or anyway, a Splendid Samaritan, if the sacrifices that had to be made were enormous. But then so would a Good Samaritan assume responsibility for that violinist; so would Henry Fonda, if he is a Good Samaritan, fly in from the West Coast and assume responsibility for me.

8. My argument will be found unsatisfactory on two counts by many of those who want to regard abortion as morally permissible. First, while I do argue that abortion is not impermissible, I do not agree that it is always permissible. There may well be cases in which carrying the child to term requires only Minimally Decent Samaritanism of the mother, and this is a standard we must not fall below. I am inclined to think it a merit of my account precisely that it does *not* give a general yes or a general no. It allows for and supports our sense that, for example, a sick and desperately frightened fourteen-year-old schoolgirl, pregnant due to rape, may of *course* choose abortion, and that any law which rules this out is an insane law. And it also allows for and supports our sense that in other cases resort to abortion is even

positively indecent. It would be indecent in the woman to request an abortion, and indecent in a doctor to perform it, if she is in her seventh month, and wants the abortion just to avoid the nuisance of postponing a trip abroad. The very fact that the arguments I have been drawing attention to treat all cases of abortion, or even all cases of abortion in which the mother's life is not at stake, as morally on a par ought to have made them suspect at the outset.

Secondly, while I am arguing for the permissibility of abortion in some cases, I am not arguing for the right to secure the death of the unborn child. It is easy to confuse these two things in that up to a certain point in the life of the fetus it is not able to survive outside the mother's body; hence removing it from her body guarantees its death. But they are importantly different. I have argued that you are not morally required to spend nine months in bed, sustaining the life of that violinist; but to say this is by no means to say that if, when you unplug yourself, there is a miracle and he survives, you then have a right to turn round and slit his throat. You may detach yourself even if this costs him his life; you have no right to be guaranteed his death, by some other means, if unplugging yourself does not kill him. There are some people who will feel dissatisfied by this feature of my argument. A woman may be utterly devastated by the thought of a child, a bit of herself, put out for adoption and never seen or heard of again. She may therefore want not merely that the child be detached from her, but more, that it die. Some opponents of abortion are inclined to regard this as beneath contempt—thereby showing insensitivity to what is surely a powerful source of despair. All the same, I agree that the desire for the child's death is not one which anybody may gratify, should it turn out to be possible to detach the child alive.

At this place, however, it should be remembered that we have only been pretending throughout that the fetus is a human being from the moment of conception. A very early abortion is surely not the killing of a person, and so is not dealt with by anything I have said here.

WHY I FAVOR LIBERALIZED ABORTION
Alan F. Guttmacher

A straggly line of young people bearing placards, some also with babies and children, partially blocked the entrance to the Peter Bent Brigham Hospital in Boston as I went there to speak not long ago. One youth wore a white surgeon's gown spattered with red paint, and carried a sign that cried "Murderer"; across his chest was the identification, "Dr. Guttmacher."

My reaction was one of sadness. For much of my life, I have been subjected to similar denunciation. Until recent years, its focus was my stand in favor of birth control. Now that contraception is applauded, and used by virtually all Americans, I am condemned for my liberal stand on abortion.

The ironic fact is that those who oppose and those who favor legalization of abortion share a common goal—the elimination of *all* abortions. The difference is that while anti-abortionists believe this can be accomplished by tough, punitive statutes, the abortion-law reformers point to evidence showing that these laws have never worked in the past and never will. In the years preceding liberalization of abortion laws in this country, for example, a conservative estimate is that at least one million illegal operations were being performed annually. Those who favor liberalization want to substitute safe abortion for the dangerous, clandestine variety, until contraception is so widely practiced that unwanted pregnancy—and therefore the need for abortion—disappears.

The debate over abortion has been raging for years but, as the political reality of liberalization has come into sharper focus, the dispute has grown more intense. Whenever a bill is introduced to modify an abortion statute, state legislators are assaulted with arguments and pressures from each side. The basic anti-abortion argument is that respect for life demands protection of the fetus. The basic pro-abortion argument is that the decision to remain pregnant is a highly personal one, to be made only by the woman involved and with full freedom of choice. The proabortionists respect life, too, but they argue that every child should be given the invaluable birthright of being born *wanted*.

Beginning in 1967, 12 states partially, and four almost fully, liberalized their abortion laws. Meanwhile, in order to decide the issue on a national level, the Supreme Court agreed to determine the constitutionality of the abortion laws of two states, Texas and Georgia. The Texas law permitted abortion only to preserve the life of the mother. The Georgia law was more liberal, but required that abortion be performed in an accredited hospital, that it be approved by a hospital committee and that the pregnant woman be a Georgia resident.

Alan F. Guttmacher, "Why I Favor Liberalized Abortion," *Reader's Digest* November 1973. Dr. Guttmacher, president of the Planned Parenthood Federation, is the former chief of obstetrics and gynecology at Mt. Sinai Hospital in New York City. He is also the author of several books, including *Pregnancy, Birth, and Family Planning* (1973).

Last January, the Court declared—by identical 7-to-2 margins—that both statutes were unconstitutional on the ground of interference with the right of privacy guaranteed by the Constitution. They ruled that a fetus has no legal rights, since the Constitution makes it clear that a fetus is not a person until birth, and constitutional rights are guaranteed only to *persons*.

The Court further ruled that it was illegal for a state to place *any* restrictions on abortion, except that it be performed by a licensed doctor during the first three months of pregnancy. During the second three months, regulations could be imposed to protect the patient (for example, requiring that abortions be performed in a hospital only). But such regulations could not interfere with the ready availability of abortion to any woman desiring it.

The wide sweep of the Court's decisions surprised and pleased protagonists and agonized antagonists. Some states are accepting the inevitable, while others continue to interpose roadblocks which eventually will be crumbled by the courts. For now, it is clear that the only way to negate the Court's judgment is via a constitutional amendment—a tortuous process requiring approval by Congress and then by three quarters of the 50 state legislatures.

As must be clear from the foregoing, I am a long-time advocate of liberalized abortion and thus hardly qualify as a neutral discussant. I do believe, however, that my many years in private and hospital practice, and in the arena of public debate, give me a special vantage point to try to put this difficult subject in perspective.

To understand my thinking, one must first understand how and why I became convinced that abortion should be made legal. Justice Harry Blackmun, in his preface to the majority opinion of the Supreme Court, wrote: "One's philosophy, one's experiences, one's exposure to the raw edges of human existence . . . and the moral standards one establishes and seeks to observe, are all likely to influence and to color one's thinking and conclusions about abortion." His words concisely explain the basis for my own change in attitude, from one of firm opposition to abortion, except in cases of great medical need, to one which would allow a woman free choice.

When I was introduced to obstetrics in 1922 as a third-year medical student, there was general acceptance of the highly restrictive abortion laws then in force. None of my teachers at the Johns Hopkins Medical School in Baltimore appeared to question the propriety of the Maryland statute, which permitted abortion only when no other therapeutic measure would "secure the safety of the mother." Nor did I. Indeed, I graduated from medical school firm in the belief that abortion was a simple, straightforward matter: bad guys did it; good guys did not.

However, four years of hospital residency, and several experiences during my early years of practice, radically changed my attitude.

The second person I ever saw die was a Mrs. K, the mother of four children, who succumbed to the effects of an illegal, probably self-induced abortion. Unlike most who die, Mrs. K was not granted the blessing of coma, but remained conscious to the moment of death, screaming vainly for life.

Only a few months later, a mature-looking 15-year-old girl was brought to our surgical floor mortally ill from a bungled abortion. The senior staff was asked to consult to decide whether the child's slim chance for recovery would be helped by surgery, or by simply marking time. After a half-hour, it was decided to operate. The child died four hours later.

There are many other tragedies on the roster of illegal-abortion deaths I have witnessed. Many examples also cross my mind of the psychological destruction that enforced continuation of pregnancy sometimes causes. The common denominator in all these cases is that the victims came from "the wrong side of the railroad tracks." During my early years as a doctor in Baltimore, the city had two physician-abortionists, who practiced virtually unmolested. I knew them both. They did creditable work for a high fee—a fee unavailable to most who came from the wrong side of the tracks.

Lacking the fee, the poor could take their chances with Mary S, an ill-trained, granny-type midwife, or with Bill T, an operating-room orderly who had surreptitiously filched instruments from the hospital and set up an abortion shop. Or they could perform an abortion on themselves. All manner of articles were used for this: hatpins, clothes hangers, pencils, pens, slippery-elm bark—even, on one occasion, a goose quill. The sharp object was introduced through the cervix into the uterus, rupturing the fetal sac to bring on miscarriage—and often dangerous infection at the same time.

All these exposures "to the raw edges of human existence" influenced and colored my "thinking and conclusions about abortion" in the early '30s. Today I believe that my long advocacy of liberalization has been fully justified by the extraordinary results achieved wherever liberalization has taken place—and especially in New York City during the first 24 months under New York State's recently changed law. Results from California, Hawaii and Washington State have been equally satisfactory, although not as fully recorded.

I believe that three criteria enable one to judge the success or failure of legal abortion. First: Does the law promote reduction in abortion deaths and abortion-connected illness? Second: Does it largely eliminate ethnic and economic discrimination? Third: Does it curtail the number of illegal abortions?

During the first two years (July 1, 1970, to June 30, 1972) under New York's liberal statute, deaths from illegal abortion in New York City declined from an average of 23 to an average of 7 per year, while admissions to ten city hospitals for infected abortions declined dramatically. At the same time, the number of pregnancy and delivery fatalities unassociated with abortion fell from 35 to 27 per 100,000 births. This was so probably because there were fewer high-risk mothers—mothers less than 17 and more than 35 years of age, and mothers coming from the most impoverished segment of the community—giving birth. For the first time, safe abortion was available to them, and they have used it.

Prior to 1970 the relatively few legal abortions performed in New York City were done primarily for affluent white women. The ratio of white to nonwhite was more than 5 to 1, and of white to Puerto Rican 26 to 1. Recent data on the city's residents reveal a striking change in this ethnic mix. Forty-seven percent of abortions during the second year of the liberalized law were performed on black women, 42 percent on whites, and 11 percent on Puerto Ricans.

It is difficult to assess the true impact on the prevalence of illegal abortion of the removal of abortion from the criminal code. Deaths and illness from illegal abortion in New York City have declined sharply, which is a pretty good index. In addition, it has been calculated that 70 percent of New York's legal abortions were substitutes for those which would have been done illegally under a restrictive statute. In other words, legalizing abortion does not increase the number of abortions so much as it provides a safe substitute for illegal procedures.

Indeed, the number of legal operations performed in New York City seems already to have leveled off. During the first year under the new law, 174,000 legal procedures took place. During the second year, the total climbed to 228,000. But during the last year (from July 1972 through June 1973), the total dropped to 197,000. According to Dr. Christopher Tietze, a leading statistician in the abortion field who works for the Population Council, that figure should continue to decline until it levels off, some years from now, at around 100,000. Similar stabilization has occurred in Eastern Europe and Japan, following liberalization.

At this point, a word of caution is in order: Abortion should never be used casually, or as a substitute for mass contraception. From observation as a physician, and as president of Planned Parenthood, I decry the necessity for so large a number of abortions, for each abortion bespeaks medical or social failure. If every act of intercourse in which pregnancy is not the desired result were protected by effective contraception, few abortions would be performed. The first line of defense against unwanted conception must be contraception, which is both medically safer and socially preferable. Legal abortion can only be justified as the second line.

I realize that the subject of abortion is deeply divisive, with reaction felt more in the emotions than in the mind. For this reason, dispassionate factual discussions are more beneficial than the tossing about of violent slogans. I also realize that legalized abortion is far from the ideal solution to unwanted conception. Yet a lifetime of work in the field has convinced me that liberalized abortion is an absolutely essential tool to ease the lot of many women and families in a tough, tough world.

DEEPER INTO ABORTION
Bernard N. Nathanson

In early 1969 I and a group of equally concerned and indignant citizens who had been outspoken on the subject of legalized abortion, organized a political action unit known as NARAL—then standing for National Association for Repeal of Abortion Laws, now known as the National Abortion Rights Action League. We were outspokenly militant on this matter and enlisted the women's movement and the Protestant clergy into our ranks. We used every device available to political-action groups such as pamphleteering, public demonstrations, exploitation of the media and lobbying in the appropriate legislative chambers. In late 1969 we mounted a demonstration outside one of the major university hospitals in New York City that had refused to perform even therapeutic abortions. My wife was on that picket line, and my three-year old son proudly carried a placard urging legalized abortion for all. Largely as a result of the efforts of this and a few similar groups, the monumental New York State Abortion Statute of 1970 was passed and signed into law by Governor Nelson Rockefeller. Our next goal was to assure ourselves that low cost, safe and humane abortions were available to all, and to that end we established the Center for Reproductive and Sexual Health, which was the first—and largest—abortion clinic in the Western world. Its record was detailed in these pages in February, 1972.

Some time ago—after a tenure of a year and a half—I resigned as director of the Center for Reproductive and Sexual Health. The Center had performed 60,000 abortions with no maternal deaths—an outstanding record of which we are proud. However, I am deeply troubled by my own increasing certainty that I had in fact presided over 60,000 deaths.

There is no longer serious doubt in my mind that human life exists within the womb from the very onset of pregnancy, despite the fact that the nature of the intrauterine life has been the subject of considerable dispute in the past. Electrocardiographic evidence of heart function has been established in embryos as early as six weeks. Electroencephalographic recordings of human brain activity have been noted in embryos at eight weeks. Our capacity to measure signs of life is daily becoming more sophisticated, and as time goes by, we will doubtless be able to isolate life signs at earlier and earlier stages in fetal development.

The Harvard Criteria for the pronouncement of death assert that if the subject is unresponsive to external stimuli, (e.g., pain), if the deep reflexes are absent, if there are no spontaneous movements or respiratory efforts, if the electroencephalogram reveals no activity of the brain, one may conclude that the patient is dead. If any or all of these criteria are absent—and the fetus does respond to pain, makes respiratory

Bernard N. Nathanson, "Deeper into Abortion," *The New England Journal of Medicine* 291 (1974). Nathanson, a gynecologist, was formerly the medical chairman of the National Association for Repeal of Abortion Laws, and he was also the former Director of the Center for Reproductive and Sexual Health in New York City, the busiest licensed abortion facility in the U.S. during the early 1970s.

efforts, moves spontaneously, and has electroencephalographic activity—life must be present.

To those who cry that nothing can be human life that cannot exist independently, I ask if the patient totally dependent for his life on treatments by the artificial kidney twice weekly is alive? Is the person with chronic cardiac disease, solely dependent for his life on the tiny batteries on his pacemaker, alive? Would my life be safe in this city without my eyeglasses?

Life is an interdependent phenomenon for us all. It is a continuous spectrum that begins in utero and ends at death—the bands of the spectrum are designated by words such as fetus, infant, child, adolescent, and adult.

We must courageously face the fact—finally—that human life of a special order is being taken. And since the vast majority of pregnancies are carried successfully to term, abortion must be seen as the interruption of a process that would otherwise have produced a citizen of the world. Denial of this reality is the crassest kind of moral evasiveness.

The fierce militants of the Woman's Liberation evade this issue and assert that the woman's right to bear or not to bear children is her absolute right. On the other hand the ferocious Right-to-Life legions proclaim no rights for the woman and absolute rights for the fetus.

But these "rights" that are held to be so obvious and so undeniable are highly suspect. None of us have "rights" that go beyond the inter-related life that is our common heritage on this planet. Our "rights" exist only because others around us care enough about us to see to it that we have them. They have no other source. They result from no other cause.

Somewhere in the vast philosophic plateau between the two implacably opposed camps—past the slogans, past the pamphlets, past even the demonstrations and the legislative threats—lies the infinitely agonizing truth. We are taking life, and the deliberate taking of life, even of a special order and under special circumstances, is an inexpressibly serious matter.

Somehow, we must not deny the pervasive sense of loss that should accompany abortion and its most unfortunate interruption of life. We must not coarsen our sensitivities through common practice and brute denial.

I offer no panacea. Certainly, the medical profession itself cannot shoulder the burden of this matter. The phrase "between a woman and her physician" is an empty one since the physician is only the instrument of her decision, and has no special knowledge of the moral dilemma or the ethical agony involved in the decision. Furthermore, there are seldom any purely medical indications for abortion. The decision is the most serious responsibility a woman can experience in her lifetime, and at present it is hers alone.

Can there be no help for the pregnant woman bearing the incalculable weight of this moral tension? Perhaps we could make available to her—though it should by no means be mandatory—a consultative body of unique design, much like Saint-Simon's Council of Newton. To meet the new moral challenges of the abortion decision, we may very well need specialists, some of new kinds, to serve on such a body—a psychohistorian, a human ecologist, a medical philosopher, an urbanologist-clergyman. The counseling that such a body could offer a pregnant woman would be designed to bring the whole sweep of human experience to bear on the decision—not just the narrow partisanship of committed young women who have had abortions and who typically staff the counselor ranks of hospitals and clinics now.

My concern is increased by the fact that the sloganeers, with their righteous pontifications and their undisguised desires to assert power over others, have polarized American reactions into dimly understood but tenaciously held positions. The din that has arisen in our land has already created an atmosphere in which it is difficult, if not impossible, for the individual to see the issues clearly and to reach an understanding free from the taint of the last shibboleth that was screamed in her ear.

Our sense of values has always placed the greatest importance upon the value of life itself. With a completely permissive legal climate for abortion (and I believe that we must have such a climate—that abortion must be unregulated by law) there is a danger that society will lose a certain moral tension that has been a vital part of its fabric. In pursuing a course of unlimited and uncontrolled abortion over future years, we must not permit ourselves to sink to a debased level of utilitarian semi-consciousness.

I plead for an honest, clear-eyed consideration of the abortion dilemma—an end to blind polarity. We have had enough screaming placards and mindless marches. The issue is human life, and it deserves the reverent stillness and ineffably grave thought appropriate to it.

We must work together to create a moral climate rich enough to provide for abortion, but sensitive enough to life to accommodate a profound sense of loss.

OF TWO MINDS ABOUT ABORTION
Andrew Hacker

If opponents of abortion had their way, 1.3 million more babies would be born this year, for that is how many pregnancies are being artificially ended. If supporters of abortion had their way, there would be one million fewer births this year, for that is how many additional abortions could be performed were resources fully available.

Abortion has become the hardy perennial of our politics. It is a controversy with a life of its own, demanding a place on the public agenda no matter what other questions plague us. Of course there have been similar issues before, but none—not even Prohibition—has stirred so much soul-searching or ambiguity of feeling.

Not the least cause of confusion is that those most passionately embroiled in the struggle have defined the terms of debate. Thus we are asked to accept "Right to Life" and "Freedom of Choice" as the chief opposing principles. These slogans have been heard so often they need no rehearsing. ("A woman has the right to control her own body." "But not at the price of another life.") Yet being caught in a crossfire can help to clear the mind. One might wonder if more is at stake than either side will admit. As it happens, that suspicion is correct.

In fact, abortion conceals a basic social conflict, but one we are not prepared to discuss. The subject, of course, is sexual intercourse. But not in terms of attitudes or abstractions. At issue, rather, is the importance sexual pleasure is granted in our lives. For a growing number of Americans, full and frequent sexual activity is a vital source of enjoyment. Others see this development as endangering moral character and the survival of society. It is only in such a context that arguments over abortion become clear.

For this reason, it should be added that abortion is not the province of any single religion. Though the majority of opponents are indeed Roman Catholic, many Protestants and Jews join in the outcry, and women of every religious background have availed themselves of abortions. Catholic tenets may be congruent with "the right to life," but the anti-abortion movement has less to do with doctrinal scruples than with the sensibility of a class and a generation.

Of the 5 million pregnancies that occurred last year, 3.3 million resulted in live births, 1.3 million ended with abortions, and the remaining 400,000 were miscarriages or stillbirths. Supporters of abortion not only defend the 1.3 million terminations but would push the percentage higher. A recent study released by the Alan Guttmacher Institute—the main statistical source in this area—estimates that almost 600,000 women who wanted abortions last year were unable to obtain them because their region either lacked facilities or set onerous restrictions.

Some supporters go further. They claim that with suitable counseling, many women now disposed to bearing their babies would come to change their minds.

Andrew Hacker, "Of Two Minds about Abortion," *Harper's* September 1979. Hacker was a professor of political science at Queens College, New York, when he wrote this article. His books include *The End of the American Era* (1970) and *Free Enterprise in America* (1977).

Even with abortion available, each year almost 250,000 teenage women have out-of-wedlock births. Unintended pregnancies precipitate many marriages. More than 300,000 teenage brides are pregnant at their weddings. Those who favor abortion feel more can and should be done to convince these women that having their babies would be a mistake. And were this goal attained, the number of abortions in the United States would match the number of annual births. Japan has already struck that balance. The Soviet Union even tips it on the side of abortion.

Of course, it is difficult to imagine a person who is literally "pro-abortion." It is still a surgical procedure, requiring professional attention. Hence those who support abortion as an option speak of it as a last resort. Birth control, they say, is best. Abortion should be a recourse if contraception fails, or was never used at all.

Yet if this recourse has become increasingly necessary, the reasons are not always the ones we hear. By and large, youth, poverty, ignorance are cited as the causes of unplanned pregnancies. While these are obviously part of the explanation, statistics suggest other provocations as well.

Two-thirds of all abortions are performed on women over the age of twenty. Many are well-informed, middle-class persons, quite familiar with contraceptive methods. Nor is unreliable equipment often the cause. A significant reason women become unwillingly pregnant is that even the best-educated bring mixed motives to bed.

Ambiguous feelings about conceiving come with the condition of being a woman. To want and not want a baby at one and the same time is an emotion most women have experienced or certainly understand. Hence the high incidence of women reporting to their doctors that they had simply "forgotten" to take a pill or put a diaphragm in place, or had been certain that the "safe period" before ovulation had another day or so to run. Thus far, researchers have avoided this subject, which is probably just as well. We are dealing with sentiments even women themselves find it difficult to articulate. To call such behavior illogical, as men are apt to do, shows a failure of sympathy and imagination. Intercourse is not an act in which one is always in control or certain of one's intent. Repeated insistence on women's right to control their own bodies may itself be evidence of the ambivalence that attends surrender to sexual pleasure, aside from the public and political content of this phrase.

A woman can toy with the idea of becoming pregnant, without wishing to see the pregnancy through to term. This is especially so with younger women, curious about their capacities. Not only "Can I do it?" but "What will be its effect on me?" are things every woman wonders. No matter what else she does with her life—she can head a huge corporation—having achieved conception is still part of being a woman. And once that state has been attained, even if only for a fortnight, she may reconsider where it will lead. Or tell herself having a baby is fine; now is just not the time.

There are other forces at work. Women tend more than men to link intercourse with romance. The more one plans precautions, the less sublime it seems. Among women who do not have a steady sexual partner, few use the pill on a regular basis or wear an intrauterine device. Such ongoing protection is still relatively rare, even in our liberated age. Even today, most women still like to believe that intercourse requires the man's initiative. Not being prepared helps affirm that posture and adds to the spontaneity. It is only after a month or so has passed that the consequences must be faced.

There are instances where women obtain abortions to punish the father, their parents, themselves. But here I find myself intruding on territory I have no right or wish to enter. For whatever reason, it is nonetheless a fact that many "unwanted" pregnancies were either desired in a halfhearted way or resulted from knowingly taking chances. Such conceptions are as common among worldly women as among ingenuous girls in their teens.

The struggle to legalize abortion was conducted in the name of married women. The typical plaintiff ("Mrs. Roe") already had more children than the family budget could support. If allowed this one abortion, she would presumably ensure that it wouldn't happen again.

However, the chief clients for abortion have not been Mrs. Roe. Only one in six abortions is performed on women over thirty. And fewer than one in twelve is performed on mothers with more than three children. Fully 75 percent of all abortions are performed on unmarried women. A third of these women are still in their teens, and another third in their early twenties. In other words, the rising demand for abortion has attended the spread of youthful sexual activity. In fact, episodes of premarital intercourse were more common in the past than people admitted. What has changed is that once young people are initiated, they persist, usually with a steady partner.

A Guttmacher Institute survey of unmarried teenagers revealed that fewer than one in five of those deemed "sexually active" made consistent use of contraceptives. Fewer than half had protected themselves the last time they had intercourse, and only half of those used certifiably reliable methods. Moreover, some young women make pregnancy their goal. It is seen as a way of entering adulthood, of relieving an aimless life, of restoring self-esteem. Still, most teenagers are not equipped to be parents, and they have second thoughts when confronted with that fact of life. If they are not to be driven to abortion—as 400,000 annually are—then something must be done. But what?

Perhaps the most commonly heard solution is sex education in the schools. Supporters of abortion invariably invoke such programs in any remarks they make. The only problem is that "sex education" has become a vague and evasive symbol. Few who employ it have any idea what actually happens in the classroom, nor are they disposed to find out. Better to assume that experts know how to handle the niceties, as happens in driver training.

In fact, even the most liberal school districts allow little serious discussion of birth control. Teachers may mention various methods, but the descriptions are fairly summary. Not one school in a thousand will permit a diaphragm to be passed around, let alone give lessons on how to unroll a condom. On a purely verbal level it can be said that some teenagers acquire "information." It is at the next step, where information becomes instruction and practice, that the schools abdicate.

While boys can buy condoms at a drugstore, it is a rare mid-teen girl who will approach a gynecologist on her own. Birth-control services are increasingly available, especially on college campuses. The problem is reaching those who start sexual activity in their sophomore year of high school. What passes for sex education will not prevent premarital pregnancies until schools shepherd groups of pupils over to nearby clinics, with or without parental permission. Even progressive-minded parents draw the line at such proposals. The idea persists that equipping an adolescent can only encourage promiscuity. Once armored, she will indulge in indiscriminate sex with an endless array of partners. This fear may be universal, but it runs especially deep among parents of teenage daughters. They prefer to hope their children will use good sense about sex, whatever that may mean.

What emerges is that for young people abortion is not a "last resort" at all. Rather, it is the first intervention of adult society. We are told it must be available lest hundreds of thousands of young women be hobbled by early motherhood. Due to our chariness about sex education, we are asked to accept a quick, surgical remedy rather than face our own misgivings about providing preventive measures. It is only after a teenager has had an abortion that we feel we can give her the equipment she clearly needed earlier. At this point it should be admitted that abortion has become a major mode of birth control. And it will continue to be one until adults resolve their own dilemmas about teenage sexual experience.

With the advent of the abortion debate, a new word has entered common usage. While people always knew what "fetus" meant, it was not a term heard much in public. It belonged to biological science, denoting animals in gestation. But now we hear it all the time, at least among advocates of abortion. What is removed from a woman's womb is invariably called a "fetus." Or occasionally an embryo. Or even a fertilized egg. But never, of course, a baby.

The reasons, while hardly mysterious, deserve explicit discussion. Those who have had abortions are rarely unburdened of guilt. Even active lobbyists have lingering feelings that their advocacy is wrong. (The mention that someone has had, say, three abortions causes some discomfort, even in sophisticated circles.) Sometimes this guilt is labeled "ungrounded," an irrational emotion to be alleviated by therapy. Yet regard for human life is considered a test of civilization. These doubts have not been resolved, nor are they likely to be. Rather they are screened from immediate consciousness by calling whatever it is a "fetus." This is clearly a blindered solution, if it is any solution at all.

"Fetus" has another, more practical, use. It denotes something disposable, akin to an animal embryo discarded after a laboratory experiment. Here a "fetus" is construed as a growth within oneself, one of several inconveniences that can arise from sexual activity. And like those other annoyances, it has a prescribed mode of treatment.

Support for abortion comes primarily from men and women who admit to enjoying sexual activity and want safeguards for that pleasure. They have attained new realms of experience, which they have no wish to abandon. Apart from a small minority, they are not swingers or spouse-swappers or even necessarily unfaithful.

They compose a new class of Americans, for whom intercouse is an important leisure pursuit. But it is also an activity that needs abortion as a backup.

And what of the babies who are aborted? Even fervent supporters of abortion cannot claim to know which particular children would be better off unborn. Only in rare instances do we say of certain persons—those who have suffered greatly or inflicted suffering on others—that it would have been preferable for everyone had they never lived at all. One knows of babies who were initially unwanted, yet brought joy to their parents' lives. There are infants who came perilously close to abortion, but went on to lives of real distinction. This is too tangled a subject for dispassionate analysis. Those who favor abortion prefer to avoid the issue by focusing on how a birth may affect the mother. Opponents resolve the dilemma by demanding that everyone be born.

Opponents of abortion base their case on principle, which allows for no exceptions. An abortion is a planned assault on life, a murder with no extenuating circumstances. Thus far the majority of Americans have not accepted this view. Victims of incest or rape enjoy special sympathy, as do women certain to deliver babies that will be deformed. For this reason, opponents have settled for restrictions rather than abolition.

Thus one national Right to Life campaign resulted in Congress's adoption of the Hyde Amendment, named for its sponsor, Henry Hyde, an Illinois Representative. Beginning in the summer of 1977, no further Medicaid funds could be spent on abortions unless childbirth risked the mother's life. In the previous year, 295,000 women with low incomes had abortions paid for with federal funds. The Hyde ban has proved all but total. In the twelve-month period following its passage, fewer than 3,000 women qualified for Medicaid abortions.

While individual states can still pay the bills, only nine now do so fully. Most of the rest accept the Hyde Amendment's limitations. Some go further. Massachusetts, for example, has removed abortion from the health coverage of employees on its payroll and their spouses.

At this writing, figures are not yet available on how many abortions will be blocked by the states' restrictions. Even women able to pay are subject to hardship. Some states now require hospitalization, which easily doubles the cost. Louisiana requires a court order for women under eighteen. It also makes physicians remind potential patients that "the unborn child is a human life," and then offer a graphic description of its "tactile sensitivity." This law, considered a model by abortion opponents, passed the Louisiana legislature by a 123–1 margin. Now a constitutional amendment is pending that would make it a federal crime to end any unborn life.

What makes opponents of abortion insist that every pregnant woman be made to bear her baby? Their own answer is well-known: that child has a right to experience whatever its life may hold in store. This would suggest that opponents care deeply about the children they wish to save. Yet the record offers little concrete evidence of that professed concern.

This country has never claimed to offer equal opportunities to all its children. Those with privileged upbringings always stand a better chance than others. Still, with public education and a tolerance for talent, it could be argued that the odds allowed most youngsters hope for a decent start in life. However, recent years have seen the emergence of a generation of Americans who seem denied that hope, and destined by a host of disadvantages to careers of unfulfilled capacities. One of those disadvantages is early pregnancy, which writes a fairly predictable script for both mothers and children. Poor teenage girls who become pregnant generally quit school before they have the basic skills required for steady employment. Close to nine in ten keep their babies and enter the welfare rolls, where they remain as more children are born. Their infants begin with lower birth-weights and greater vulnerability to disease. In short, the children begin in settings similar to those where they were conceived.

To be sure, no one really knows to what degree society's intervention might improve their circumstances. Some very expensive programs (job training, for example) have had minimal effect. Still, there has been success in some cities. One program offers hostels for mothers while they finish high school, and day care for their children. Another adds to this counseling with job placement and frequent follow-ups. Needless to say, the high ratios needed of staff to constituency make these ventures very costly. Outlays can total five figures for each participant. Perhaps ultimately such services will be paid back, if mothers and their offspring become assets to society, but no one really knows.

What can be shown is that opponents of abortion have been conspicuously silent about services of this kind, particularly those funded by taxes. At best, they will point to a few homes for unwed mothers as a testament to their good will, and to services established to convince unmarried women that they ought to bear their babies. But as far as abortion opponents are concerned, once a child has been given its life it is on its own.

There is another reason for compelling the birth of a baby. It is a way to punish the mother. Chastening is what she deserves. She has had her hours of pleasure, and should be made to take the consequences, especially if those idylls were illicit. A baby as a burden sets limits on one's life, and one woman's forfeiture of freedom will be an example to others. When moral arguments go unheeded, motherhood remains a final threat.

Certainly, opponents of abortion want to see an end to youthful sexual intimacy. They make no pleas for birth-control instruction or providing contraceptives. Such safeguards will encourage the very acts they hope to halt. The aim is abstinence, at least until a couple has been married. Although these restraints are congruent with Catholic morals, the authority of the church alone does not seem to account for their persuasive power.

Nor is it only teenagers who require this stern attention. Too many older women who should know better are casual about intercourse and seek to avoid its responsibilities. Almost a quarter of all abortions are being performed on women who have had one before. This, plus eagerness for a "morning-after" pill, shows a penchant for pleasure devoid of moral sense. Only if abortion is no longer an option will these women come to realize that bedding down is something to think about twice.

Opponents of abortion see the pursuit of pleasure as contaminating our age. This view echoes a puritan as well as a Catholic heritage, which says enjoyments should be earned. And even those who earn them should take a slender ration. Needless to say, opponents of abortion do not say they are opposed to sexual activity, only that it must be enjoyed in marriage, and best on the sparing side.

People who oppose abortion see themselves as citizens who have paid their dues. They have not only accepted parenthood, but have kept their lusts in check. And they know—even envy—what they have missed. The evidence is all around them, not least on prime-time television. At this point, the tensions take on social contours. Below them they see the poor, engaging in carefree sex and then getting free abortions. Above them stands a modish middle class, enjoying an array of partners and putting abortions on credit cards. How can one keep one's own children moral with so many examples around to the contrary?

Feminists argue that opposition to abortion reflects hostility to women. Yet it happens that women—especially those married with several children—are abortion's most active adversaries. There is, in fact, a social division among women themselves. On one side are those accustomed to frequent sexual enjoyment; on the other, those unsettled by the notion of such indulgence. Were women alone to vote on abortion, the tally would still be close.

I feel I should end on a personal note. For my own part, I favor making abortion available, on an unrestricted basis. My reasons are those customarily given, and I have no new arguments to add. At the same time, I am far from happy finding myself in this position.

Abortion is a taking of human life. No legal or scientific theorizing can change that basic fact. My fear is that sanctioning abortion will direct our sensibilities from moral principles to pragmatic matters of cost and inconvenience. That aspect of abortion concerns me as much as anything else.

Moreover, I find I have sympathy for those on the other side. Far from being fanatics, they conceive of a social and moral order where citizenship has its duties and passions are held in check. They believe strongly in the family. Theirs may be a stern, even punitive, ethic, but they are people who have contributed their share to society, at no small cost to themselves.

I am not convinced that those supporting abortion have a parallel vision. Theirs is a highly personal outlook, stressing freedom and choice and pleasure. What is lacking is any sign of concern over the society we will have, and the people we will be, once their ends are attained. A fully active sexual life may be fine. But we should consider where it can take us. Opponents of abortion have done just that. Its supporters prefer to avoid such questions.

DOES LIFE BEGIN BEFORE BIRTH?
John R. Stott

In both the United States and the United Kingdom the recent liberalization of abortion laws has become for Christians a major moral issue. In England and Wales, since David Steel's 1967 Abortion Act, although illegal abortions have not decreased, the annual average of legal abortions has increased from 10 to more than 100,000. For every five babies born alive, one is now aborted. A human fetus is being destroyed every five minutes.

What is the issue? Proabortionists begin with the rights of the mother (especially her right to choose) and see abortion as little more than a retroactive contraceptive. Antiabortionists begin with the rights of the unborn child (especially his or her right to live) and see abortion as little less than prenatal infanticide. The former appeal particularly to compassion, and cite situations in which the mother and/or her family would suffer intolerable strain if the unwanted pregnancy were allowed to come to term. The latter appeal particularly to justice, and stress the need to defend the rights of an unborn child who cannot defend himself. But we must not set compassion and justice in opposition to one another. Compassion needs moral guidelines; without the ingredient of justice it is bound to go astray.

The moral question concerns the nature and status of the human fetus. If "it" were only a lump of jelly or blob of tissue, then of course it could be removed without qualms. But "it" is actually a "he" or "she," an unborn child. What is the evidence for this assertion?

We begin (as we always must) with the Bible. The author of Psalm 139 looks back to the antenatal stage of his existence. Three words sum up what he affirms. First, *creation*. He seems to liken God both to a potter who "formed" his inmost being and to a weaver who "knit him together" in his mother's womb (v. 13). Although the Bible makes no claim to be a textbook of embryology, here is a plain affirmation that the growth of the fetus is neither haphazard nor automatic but a divine work of creative skill.

The second word is *continuity*. The psalmist surveys his life in four stages: past (v. 1), present (vv. 2–6), future (vv. 7–12), and before birth (vv. 13–16), and in all four refers to himself as "I." He who is writing as a full-grown man has the same personal identity as the fetus in his mother's womb. He affirms a direct continuity between his antenatal and postnatal being.

The third word is *communion*, or relationship. Psalm 139 is arguably the most radical statement in the Old Testament of God's personal relationship to the individual. Personal pronouns and possessives occur in the first person (I, me, my) 46 times and in the second person (you, yours) 32 times. Further, the basis on which God knows us intimately (vv. 1–7) and attaches himself to us so that we cannot

John R. Stott, "Does Life Begin Before Birth?" *Christianity Today* 5 September 1980. Stott is rector emeritus of All Souls Church, London. In 1959 he was honorary chaplain to Her Majesty, Elizabeth II. His books include *Understanding the Bible* (1972) and *Focus on Christ* (1979).

escape from him (vv. 7–12) is that he formed us in the womb and established his relationship with us then (vv. 13–16).

These three words supply us with the essential biblical perspective in which to think. The fetus is not a growth in the mother's body (which can be removed as readily as her tonsils or appendix), nor even a potential human being, but a human life who, though not yet mature, has the potentiality to grow into the fullness of the humanity he already possesses. We cannot fix criteria of humanness (like self-consciousness, reason, independence, speech, moral choice, or responsive love) and then conclude that, lacking these, the fetus is not human. The newborn child and the senile old person lack these also. Nor can we draw a line at any point and say that after it the child is human and before it, not. There is no "decisive moment of humanization," subsequent to conception, whether implantation, or "animation" (when some early fathers, building on Aristotle, supposed that the fetus receives a rational soul, a boy at about one month and a girl at about two), or "quickening" (a purely subjective notion, when the mother first feels the fetus move), or viability (which is getting earlier and earlier), or birth (when the child takes his first independent breath). All these are stages in the continuous process by which an individual human life is developing into mature human personhood. From fusion onwards the fetus is an "unborn child."

The rest of Scripture endorses this perspective. An expectant mother is a "woman with child." When the pregnant Elizabeth (carying John the Baptist) was visited by the pregnant Mary (carrying Jesus) and heard her greeting, "the babe leaped in her womb for joy" (Luke 1:41,44). The same truth is confessed in the creed, since he who "was conceived by the Holy Spirit, born of the Virgin Mary, suffered under Pontius Pilate" was throughout—from conception to death—one and the same "Jesus Christ, God's only Son, our Lord."

This biblical evaluation of the humanness of the fetus is confirmed by modern medical science. In the 1960s the genetic code was unraveled. We now know that from the moment the ovum is fertilized by the penetration of the sperm, the zygote has a unique genotype distinct from both parents. The 23 pairs of chromosomes are complete. The sex, size, and shape, the color of skin, hair, and eyes, the intelligence and temperament of the child are already determined. At 3 to 3½ weeks the tiny heart begins to beat. At 4 weeks, although the embryo is only a quarter of an inch long, the head and body are distinguishable, as are also rudimentary eyes, ears, and mouth. At 6 to 7 weeks brain function can be detected, at 8 every limb has begun to appear, including fingers and toes, and at 9 to 10 weeks the child can use his hands to grasp and his mouth to suck his thumb. By 13 weeks, when the pregnancy is only one-third through—and when abortions usually begin—the embryo is completely organized, and a miniature baby lies in his mother's womb. He can alter his position, respond to pain, noise, and light, and have an attack of hiccups. Even his fingerprint is already unique. From then on he merely develops in size and strength.

If, then, the life of the fetus is a human life, with the full potentiality of growing into an adult human person, we have to think of mother and unborn child as two human beings at different stages of maturity. Doctors have to consider that they have two patients, not one, and seek the well-being of both. Lawyers and politicians have to think similarly, in accordance with the United Nations Declaration of the Rights of the Child (1959), that children need "special safeguards and care, including appropriate legal protection, *before as well as after birth.*" Christians will want to demand "extra" safeguards and care before birth because at this stage the child is helpless to protect himself, and the God of the Bible defends the powerless.

So "we have to assert as normative the general inviolability of the fetus" (Archbishop Michael Ramsey in 1967). Most Protestant theologians go on to say that, in certain extreme cases of urgent necessity, when the continuance of the pregnancy treatens to kill the mother, or drive her to suicide, or render her a complete "physical or mental wreck" (the McNaughten judgment in 1938) and so significantly shorten her life, it would be morally justifiable to sacrifice her unborn child in order to spare her. But in such circumstances death in some form is already present; "the doctor has not introduced death into the case" (Oliver O'Donovan in *The Christian and the Unborn Child,* 1973). The Christian conscience rebels against the notion that an unborn child may be destroyed because his birth would be a "burden" to the mother or her family. This argument could equally justify the destruction of a newborn child, the comatose victim of a car crash, or an imbecile. Yet such merciless "mercy killing" is totally unacceptable in a civilized community, as Dr. Francis Schaeffer and Dr. Everett Koop have powerfully argued in *Whatever Happened to the Human Race?*

If we Christians campaign for a stricter abortion policy, as we should, we must both back it up with an educational program to reduce unwanted pregnancies and also accept full responsibility for its social effects and ensure that mothers receive the personal, social, medical, and financial support they need. Louise Summerhill, the founder of *Birthright,* rightly said, "We help rather than abort. We believe in making a better world for babies to come into, rather than killing them."

THE ULTIMATE INVASION OF PRIVACY
Gloria Steinem

I remember the fear. Just out of school, working as a waitress in a London coffee shop, I searched naïvely and secretly through magazines and library shelves for a way to get my life, my self, my future back. With all my heart, I did not want to be pregnant. The years ahead seemed blocked by a brick wall.

Those three desperate winter months have always stayed fresh in some cell of my mind. I remember chemists who sold me bitter powders that did not work. I remember that, to my surprise (and uniquely in my life), I thought there was no way out. Yes, I finally found a kindly doctor who was willing to sign the complicated legal permission still necessary in England then. He sent me to a woman gynecologist who took most of my scholarship money for the next year—but who set me free. Even so, I told no one for years; not until the end of the sixties when women here began supporting each other by breaking our silence.

I soon learned that many women's experience was far, far more humiliating and dangerous than my own:

- The mother of six children who went to Puerto Rico for a semilegal abortion on borrowed money, and had to work a second job, as well as supporting her children, in order to pay the punishing amount of money back.

- The countless women whose frightening experience of abortion was accompanied by the humiliation of being made to submit sexually to the "doctor" first.

- The young black secretary who tried to get a legal abortion from a hospital, and found she was bargained with: yes, she could have a safe and legal abortion—but only if she agreed to be sterilized.

- The teenage prep school student from a rich New England family who paid heavily to a reliable abortion ring employing interns, but who had a hysterectomy because of a resulting infection she was too scared to confess.

- The granddaughter of a suburban housewife who died from a self-induced abortion, leaving a large Catholic family with a rage against church-induced guilt that had kept her from confiding in them, and a mourning for her loved and loving presence, that remains with them to this day.

- The woman for whom one doctor-prescribed method of contraception was dangerous and another failed, leaving her with a pregnancy that the doctor himself said he could do nothing about. "Try the street," he recommended cheerfully, and offered to "clean up the mess" after an illegal abortion.

- The teacher from the South who lost her job when she had to travel to a faraway state to have an abortion, and who lost her recommendations

Gloria Steinem, "The Ultimate Invasion of Privacy" (Ms. February 1981). Steinem is the founder and editor of Ms. magazine, and a national spokeswoman for the women's liberation movement.

for any other job when she explained to the principal what her trip had been for.

- The girl who was raped by her stepfather just a month after she was old enough to get pregnant at all, and whose mother feared his threats of violence too much to disclose rape and incest as a reason for getting her daughter a legal abortion. Thus, a child was forced to give birth to another child, and a hated man's punishment of two women continues for life.

The pain and rage and irreparable loss in these stories would have to be multiplied over and over again, and spread throughout this big country, to begin to resemble the truth. *In the single year before 1973 when the Supreme Court declared the choice of abortion to be part of the Constitutionally guaranteed right to privacy, for instance, more than one million women had abortions; almost all of them "criminal" and therefore profiteering and dangerous. Among the total population, even before legality, at least one in four adult American women had had an abortion. That's a conservative estimate.* There is no estimate at all of the injuries and deaths that resulted from these statistics in some direct or indirect way.

Even now, it would be difficult to find any family or group of more than a few people who were not touched by the insanity of searching for, fearing the need of, or having a dangerous illegal abortion.

"It was our Vietnam," as one feminist said looking back on the sixties and before. "At least as many women were killed or injured in the battle for control of our own bodies. But it happened to us with no support, no pay, no benefits—and the war was every year."

These are only a few of the visceral, real-life reasons why the feminist truth-telling of the sixties and early seventies spread quickly into a national and ever-growing majority consensus: abortion *must* be a safe and legal choice for a woman and her doctor. More than 70 percent of all Americans—including more than 60 percent of Catholic Americans—now agree with that general principle.

It's true that the question of federal or state funding for abortion was muddied in recent years by the ultraright wing's insistence on such funding as a sinful luxury at the taxpayers' expense; as if women would choose a surgical procedure if they did not have to. When prochoice groups refuted the expense argument by pointing out that the costs of unwanted pregnancies, much less unwanted children, were astronomically greater, the right wing hypocritically accused prochoice advocates of being interested in cost, not life. Antiabortion publicists also made the authoritarian argument that, even in this pluralistic society, every taxpayer can and must agree with every purpose for which tax dollars are spent; a suggestion that the same groups did not make on spending for the military.

In fact, the poor phrasing of abortion-funding questions in public opinion polls still allows such misconceptions to prevail. Nonetheless, there is an increased understanding that funding one alternative and not another—whether it's sterilization and not abortion, or pregnancy and not abortion—creates a whole class of Americans who are coerced out of their basic right to privacy and reproductive freedom; a class that could include any one of us at any time that we happen to be out of a job.

It is precisely the overwhelming, populist, majority support for the right of the individual to decide whether and when to have children, without government control or coercion, that has brought about the current, well-organized authoritarian backlash by the ultraright wing. After all, if the patriarchal state, church, and family lose their control over women's bodies as the most basic means of production—the means of reproduction—those structures eventually will be more democratic, and not patriarchal at all. The model and microcosm of authoritarianism in the family will disappear. The nationalistic power to decide how many children and whose they will be; how many workers or soldiers the state wants; and how to keep the ruling racial or class groups recognizable and "pure": all those dominations will gradually melt and dissipate.

No wonder the issue of reproductive freedom faces such fierce opposition. If women seize control of "the means of reproduction," so to speak, the long-term results include the undermining of race, class, and nationalistic divisions—all excellent reasons why we should do it.

Nonetheless, the more immediate and important goal is saving women's health and lives. That personal and natural need is why women—as well as men who care about individual rights, or about women—are beginning to sound the alarm against the so-called human life amendment in its many forms . . . and to work against it. . . .

In all our efforts, it's important to understand that support for reproductive freedom is not necessarily predictable by old political labels. Some lefists and liberals may not take it seriously, or may even oppose it. Classic conservatives who are *not* authoritarians may well agree that the power of the state stops at our bodies, and support reproductive rights *against* government control. Some of the right-wing forces most devoted to restricting or outlawing abortion have internal disagreements on the tactics and the form.

Most important, we must understand that neither confidence nor ambivalence is a luxury we can now afford.

CONCERNING ABORTION: AN ATTEMPT AT A RATIONAL VIEW

Charles Hartshorne

My onetime colleague T.V. Smith once wrote a book called *Beyond Conscience*, in which he waxed eloquent in showing "the harm that good men do." To live according to one's conscience may be a fine thing, but what if A's conscience leads A to try to compel B and C to live, not according to B's or C's conscience, but according to A's? That is what many opponents of abortion are trying to do. To propose a constitutional amendment to this effect is one of the most outrageous attempts to tyrannize over others that I can recall in my long lifetime as an American citizen. Proponents of the antiabortion amendment make their case, if possible, even worse when they defend themselves with the contention "It isn't my con-science only—it is a commandment of religion." For now one particular form of religion (certainly not the only form) is being used in an attempt to tyrannize over other forms of religious or philosophical belief. The separation of church and state evidently means little to such people.

Ours is a country that has many diverse religious groups, and many people who cannot find truth in any organized religious body. It is a country that has great difficulty in effectively opposing forms of killing that *everyone* admits to be wrong. Those who would saddle the legal system with matters about which consciences sincerely and strongly differ show a disregard of the country's primary needs. (The same is to be said about crusades to make things difficult for homosexuals.) There can be little freedom if we lose sight of the vital distinction between moral questions and legal ones. The law compels and coerces, with the implicit threat of violence; morals seek to persuade. It is a poor society that forgets this difference.

What is the *moral* question regarding abortion? We are told that the fetus is alive and that therefore killing it is wrong. Since mosquitoes, bacteria, apes and whales are also alive, the argument is less than clear. Even plants are alive. I am not impressed by the rebuttal "But plants, mosquitoes, bacteria and whales are not human, and the fetus is." For the issue now becomes, *in what sense* is the fetus human? No one denies that its origin is human, as is its *possible* destiny. But the same is true of every unfertilized egg in the body of a nun. Is it wrong that some such eggs are not made or allowed to become human individuals?

Granted that a fetus is human in origin and possible destiny, in what further sense is it human? The entire problem lies here. If there are pro-life activists who have thrown much light on this question, I do not know their names.

One theologian who writes on the subject—Paul Ramsey—thinks that a human egg cell becomes a human individual with a moral claim to survive if it has been

Charles Hartshorne, "Concerning Abortion: An Attempt at a Rational View," *The Christian Century* 98 (1981). Hartshorne is professor emeritus at the University of Texas. His books include *A Natural Philosophy for our Time* (1967) and *Acquinas to Whitehead: Seven Centuries of Metaphysics of Religion* (1976). *The Christian Century* describes itself as an "ecumenical" Christian journal.

fertilized. Yet this egg cell has none of the qualities that we have in mind when we proclaim our superior worth to the chimpanzees or dolphins. It cannot speak, reason or judge between right and wrong. It cannot have personal relations, without which a person is not functionally a person at all, until months—and not, except minimally, until years—have passed. And even then, it will not be a person in the normal sense unless some who are already fully persons have taken pains to help it become a human being in the full value sense, functioning as such. The antiabortionist is commanding some person or persons to undertake this effort. For without it, the fetus will *never* be human in the relevant sense. It will be human only in origin, but otherwise a subhuman animal.

The fertilized egg is an individual egg, but not an individual human being. For such a being is, in its body, a multicellular organism, a *metazoan*—to use the scientific Greek—and the egg is a single cell. The first thing the egg cell does is to begin dividing into many cells. For some weeks the fetus is not a single individual at all, but a colony of cells. During its first weeks there seems to be no ground for regarding the fetus as comparable to an individual animal. Only in possible or probable destiny is it an individual. Otherwise it is an organized society of single-celled individuals.

A possible individual person is one thing; an actual person is another. If this difference is not important, what is? There is in the long run no room in the solar system, or even in the known universe, for all human eggs—even all fertilized eggs, as things now stand—to become human persons. Indeed, it is mathematically demonstrable that the present rate of population growth must be lowered somehow. It is not a moral imperative that all possibilities of human persons become actual persons.

Of course, some may say that the fertilized egg already has a human soul, but on what evidence? The evidence of soul in the relevant sense is the capacity to reason, judge right and wrong, and the like.

One may also say that since the fertilized egg has a combination of genes (the units of physical inheritance) from both parents, in this sense it is already a human individual. There are two objections, either one in my opinion conclusive but only one of which is taken into account by Ramsey. The one he does mention is that identical twins have the same gene combination. The theologian does not see this as decisive, but I do.

The other objection is that it amounts to a very crude form of materialism to identify individuality with the gene-combination. Genes are the chemical bearers of inherited traits. This chemical basis of inheritance presumably influences everything about the development of the individual—*influences*, but does not fully determine. To say that the entire life of the person is determined by heredity is a theory of unfreedom that my religious conviction can only regard as monstrous. And there are biophysicists and neurophysiologists who agree with me.

From the gene-determined chemistry to a human person is a long, long step. As soon as the nervous system forming in the embryo begins to function as a whole—and not before—the cell colony begins to turn into a genuinely individual animal. One may reasonably suppose that this change is accompanied by some extremely primitive individual animal feelings. They cannot be recognizably human feelings, much less human thoughts, and cannot compare with the feelings of a porpoise or chimpanzee in level of consciousness. That much seems as certain as anything about the fetus except its origin and possible destiny. The nervous system of a very premature baby has been compared by an expert to that of a pig. And we know, if we know anything about this matter, that it is the nervous system that counts where individuality is concerned.

Identical twins are different individuals, each unique in consciousness. Though having the same genetic makeup, they will have been differently situated in the womb and hence will have received different stimuli. For that reason, if for no other, they will have developed differently, especially in their brains and nervous systems.

But there are additional reasons for the difference in development. One is the role of chance, which takes many forms. We are passing through a great cultural change in which the idea, long dominant in science, that chance is "only a word for our ignorance of causes" is being replaced by the view that the real laws of nature are probabilistic and allow for aspects of genuine chance.

Another reason is that it is reasonable to admit a reverse influence of the developing life of feelings in the fetus on the nervous system, as well as of the system upon the feelings. And since I, along with some famous philosophers and scientists, believe in freedom (not solely of mature human beings but—in some slight degree—of all individuals in nature, down to the atoms and farther), I hold that even in the fetus the incipient individual is unconsciously making what on higher levels we call "decisions." These decisions influence the developing nervous system. Thus to a certain extent we *make our own bodies* by our feelings and thoughts. An English poet with Platonic ideas expressed this concept as follows:

The body from the soul its form doth take,
For soul is form and doth the body make.

The word soul is, for me, incidental. The point is that feelings, thoughts, experiences react on the body and partly mold its development.

Paul Ramsey argues (as does William Buckley in a letter to me) that if a fetus is not fully human, then neither is an infant. Of course an infant is not fully human. No one thinks it can, while an infant, be taught to speak, reason or judge right and wrong. But it is much closer to that stage than is a three-month fetus. It is beginning to have primitive social relations not open to a fetus; and since there is no sharp line anywhere between an infant and a child able to speak a few words, or between the latter and a child able to speak very many words, we have to regard the infant as significantly different from a three-month or four-month fetus. Nevertheless, I have little sympathy with the idea that infanticide is just another form of murder. Persons who are already functionally persons in the full sense have more important rights even than infants. Infanticide can be wrong without being fully comparable to the killing of persons in the full sense.

Does this distinction apply to the killing of a hopelessly senile person (or one in a permanent coma)? For me it does. I hope that no one will think that if, God forbid, I ever reach that stage, it must be for my sake that I should be treated with the respect due to normal human beings. Rather, it is for the sake of others that such respect may be imperative. Symbolically, one who has been a person may have to be treated as a person. There are difficulties and hazards in not so treating such individuals.

Religious people (I would so describe myself) may argue that once a fetus starts to develop, it is for God, not human beings, to decide whether the fetus survives and how long it lives. This argument assumes, against all evidence, that human life-spans are independent of human decisions. Our medical hygiene has radically altered the original "balance of nature." Hence the population explosion. Our technology makes pregnancy more and more a matter of human decision; more and more our choices are influencing the weal and woe of the animals on this earth. It is an awesome responsibility, but one that we cannot avoid. And, after all, the book of Genesis essentially predicted our dominion over terrestrial life. In addition, no one is proposing to make abortion compulsory for those morally opposed to it. I add that everyone who smokes is taking a hand in deciding how long he or she will live. Also everyone who, by failing to exercise reasonably, allows his or her heart to lose its vigor. Our destinies are not simply "acts of God."

I may be told that if I value my life I must be glad that I was not aborted in the fetus stage. Yes, I am glad, but this expression does not constitute a claim to having already had a "right," against which no other right could prevail, to the life I have enjoyed. I feel no indignation or horror at contemplating the idea that the world might have had to do without me. The world could have managed, and as for what I would have missed, there would have been no such "I" to miss it.

With almost everything they say, the fanatics against abortion show that they will not, or cannot, face the known facts of this matter. The inability of a fetus to say "I" is not merely a lack of skill; there is nothing there to which the pronoun could properly refer. A fetus is not a person but a *potential* person. The "life" to which "pro-life" refers is nonpersonal, by any criterion that makes sense to some of us. It is subpersonal animal life only. The mother, however, *is* a person.

I resent strongly the way many males tend to dictate to females their behavior, even though many females encourage them in this. Of course, the male parent of a fetus also has certain rights, but it remains true that the female parent is the one most directly and vitally concerned.

I shall not forget talking about this whole matter to a wonderful woman, the widow of a philosopher known for his idealism. She was doing social work with young women and had come to the conclusion that abortion is, in some cases, the lesser evil. She told me that her late husband had said, when she broached the subject to him, "But you can't do that." "My darling," she replied, "we *are* doing it." I see no reason to rate the consciences of the pro-lifers higher than this woman's conscience. She knew what the problem was for certain mothers. In a society that flaunts sex (its pleasures more than its serious hazards, problems and spiritual values) in all the media, makes it difficult for the young to avoid unwanted pregnancy, and does little to help them with the most difficult of all problems of self-discipline, we tell young persons that they are murderers if they resort to abortion. And so we should not be surprised that Margaret Mead, that clearsighted observer of our society (and of other societies), should say, "Abortion is a nasty thing, but our society deserves it." Alas, it is too true.

I share something of the disgust of hard-core opponents of abortion that contraceptives, combined with the availability of abortion, may deprive sexual intercourse of spiritual meaning. For me the sacramental view of marriage has always had appeal, and my life has been lived accordingly. Abortion is indeed a nasty thing, but unfortunately there are in our society many even nastier things, like the fact that some children are growing up unwanted. This for my conscience is a great deal nastier, and truly horrible. An overcrowded world is also nasty, and could in a few decades become truly catastrophic.

The argument against abortion (used, I am sorry to say, by Pearl Buck) that the fetus may be a potential genius has to be balanced against the much more probable chance of its being a mediocrity, or a destructive enemy of society. Every egg cell is a possible genius and also a possible monster in human form. Where do we stop in calculating such possibilities?

If some who object to abortion work to diminish the number of unwanted, inappropriate pregnancies, or to make bearing a child for adoption by persons able to be its loving foster parents more attractive than it now is, and do this with a minimum of coercion, all honor to them. In view of the population problem, the first of these remedies should have high priority.

Above all, the coercive power of our legal system, already stretched thin, must be used with caution and chiefly against evils about which there is something like universal consensus. That persons have rights is a universal belief in our society, but that a fetus is already an actual person—about that there is and there can be no consensus. Coercion in such matters is tyranny. Alas for our dangerously fragmented and alienated society if we persist in such tyranny.

SECULAR INFALLIBILITY
Frank Zepezauer

He performs the ritual every minute. A blur of spinning ball enters a mystic zone for an instant, and an instant later he raises his right hand to announce, solemnly, "Strike three!" The batter may hurl his bat down and kick dust, may scowl, plead, argue, or threaten. His manager may flame out of the dugout and leap like Baryshnikov around the stolid figure at the plate. Fifty thousand fans may shake the heavens as they scream for his blood. But, with or without protest, amidst the fury of indignation or the passivity of stunned silence, the decision of the man behind the plate will stand.

I regard the umpire's irrevocable decision as a handy example of secular infallibility, the voice of absolute command in liberal and liberated democracies. Similar examples of ultimate decision confront us daily in our economic and political as well as our sporting lives. At a time when absolutes annoy us, why does secular infallibility, our contemporary secret, provide so much comfort, and papal infallibility, our contemporary embarrassment, provoke so much outrage?

Let's look further at the tranquilizing power of the umpire's decision. It puts our minds at rest because it stabilizes a game constantly threatening to fly apart over issues beyond precise resolution. A ball sailing over the center-field wall excites no quarrel. One slithering along the foul line may throw two cities into ferocious battle. Thus, we turn to human judgment and invest it with final authority. At a legendary moment, for example, in the bottom of the ninth, with home-team runners filling the bases in hopes of bringing in a tying run, and the count at 3 and 2, the pitcher throws a fast-breaking curve to the outside corner which the batter lets pass. Two possibilities compete: ball four, and the batter becomes a hero whose steel nerves pushed in a tying run; or strike three, and he retires in ignominy, a member of a defeated team.

In that mini-second of tense possibility, as the ball streaks through that problematic corner, not obviously over or beyond the plate, the umpire decides—instantly, assertively, inflexibly—and then we relax even if we hate the decision. It could have been a ball or a strike. He calls it a strike. The scorekeeper scratches his mark; the sportswriter completes his sentence; the players abandon the field; the groundkeepers roll out the tarpaulins; the fans glumly depart. Years hence we will read about the local stalwart who watched a ball sail past him at a moment when he could have pummeled it to glory, a fact inscribed indelibly in the records, as indisputable as an earthquake, even though it depended on one man's judgment, perhaps only his arbitrary will.

For practical purposes we grant his judgment a secular infallibility even as we recognize its limitations. He might deliver too many controversial calls and find

Frank Zepezauer, "Secular Infallibility," *National Review* 31 (1981). Zepezauer is the chairman of the English Department at Menlo-Atherton High School in Atherton, California.

himself back in the minors, but his decision will remain untouched, part of an accomplished past. In baseball not even winning or losing counts as much as reaching a decision. So it must be. The logos which carved order out of chaos began with a command; and will, divine or human, maintains it.

We often run across umpires in our out-of-ballpark lives. Every day some decision-maker affixes a grade to a paper, a seal to a warrant, a signature to an order. Each, we assume, follows a rubric shaped by custom, law, politics, and logic, and also, as with the umpire, by the warring intangibles which influence human judgment. As a ball whizzes past a problematic corner, decisions are made that will redirect lives—blocking a student's entry to medical school, or sending a man to jail, or a soldier to his death. We know that mortal uncertainty surrounds the voice of immortal decision; yet we cling to the myth of perfect judgment when we elevate error-prone men and women to Platonic ideas called Professor, Judge, and General. Even when we prolong painful tension through appeal, we affirm an ultimate where the buck will stop.

We have for that reason instituted a Supreme Court of nine men. We know they are merely men, not necessarily the best men or the best judges. We could all name better candidates. But none of that matters, nor even the gossip about infighting in the austere chambers. What matters is that they resolve political tension, even by a vote of 5 to 4, even if the four articulate a better case. And because, for most of us, that's *all* that matters, we bypass the complexity of the deciding process and hurry to the simplicity of its result. They decide. They speak. We accept.

With due reverence we grant that acceptance to the Supreme Court, tolerating, out of republican principle, their magisterial robes and their judicial temple, and yet many of us, Catholics included, do not grant as much to the pope. Of course I strain the comparison. Obvious differences leap up. The Supreme Court determines the laws of a temporal polity even though we hear from time to time that not only civil but natural law governs its thinking. The pope, on the other hand, determines moral law and presumes to speak to all men and women for all time.

But that's not what bothers us. We could defend his presumption as a practical way to resolve theological tension where the alternative is chaos. And we could argue that he defers to a binding rubric: scripture, philosophy, tradition, the lively dialectic of the faithful, the discipline of his prayer and meditation, and the constraints of his holy vows. What bothers us, however, is that in those moments where the rubrics provide no clear direction, sending him and the faithful into spiritual crisis, he asserts that divine will informs human will, transforming his decision into the absolute Voice of God.

We could accept even that much, for in America we once cherished an analogous conviction of a divine will revealing Itself ultimately through the push and pull of democratic debate and election. Although even in more religious times it took a leap of faith to hear the Voice of God in the Voice of the People, and the Voice of the People in the Voice of the President or the Congress or the Supreme Court, we still affirm the sanctity of the God-touched individual even when we doubt the existence of God. Thus, we could accept a pope who claimed to speak for the majority of the faithful, or even the majority of the clergy or the College of Cardinals or the Curia, and spoke in humble democratic language about a decision distilled from the minds of his fellow believers rather than imparted directly from the Mind of God.

It is the monarchical image that distresses our democratic and modernist nerves, the image and the candor it provokes, for we really don't mind the idea or the application of infallibility as long as we don't use the word itself. The pope, however, strains our tolerance by asserting that in certain moments he *is* "infallible." He says it out loud, wearing a silly-looking, triple-decker crown in the midst of medieval pomp, says it again and again, to believing Catholics as well as to free-thinkers in Jordache jeans.

Yet these free souls have themselves created a secular individualism where infallibility has assumed a new, but still secret, form, as we see in the decision to abort a human fetus, my final example. According to present abortion law, the individual as decider enjoys ultimate power, for we do not require a potential mother to justify the assertion of her will by any rubric, law, custom, or principle. We would prefer sober deliberation; we urge it upon her, along with counsel and instruction; but she remains free to listen to us or go her own way, answerable to no one, not the father, nor the unborn child, nor her parents, nor the anguished opponents of her act. We venerate that freedom, and we give it primary value: for we don't insist that she decide according to good reasons, only that she determine her own wants, asserting her "right to choose." Many of us find in her choice a tranquilizing resolution of painful ethical tension. She decides. She speaks. We accept.

And by our acceptance of the arbitrary assertion of her will, we also resolve a crucial question: who is and who is not human. We claim the question remains open, beyond ultimate resolution, entangled in intransigent religious opinion. The Supreme Court itself disclaims the power and wisdom to settle it. Yet, we actually resolve the question every moment of the day, a million times a year.

Consider. Every pregnant woman must now decide her child's fate. Should she decide to keep it, we protect it and treat it, *from the moment of decision*, as a human being. A recent article, for example, tells how physicians can now help unborn babies. They can alter their nourishing amniotic fluid, inject medication directly into their veins, even operate on their internal organs. But the language of the article tells even more. We learn that in one case this awesome technology was activated because "religious convictions prevented an abortion." Thus informed by the mother's choice about the kind of being they were working with, the physicians began speaking of the fetus as a "little patient," an "unborn infant," a "baby," a "kid." The baby who was the object of the article had gotten sick, and medical science fussed over her problem and eventually cured her, and today the child goes to kindergarten.

But medical science would have remained inert, powerless to save her, had some other conviction governed the mother's choice. Had she chosen to abort, she would immediately have denied the humanity of her unborn child, and, *from the moment of decision*, declared it a non-being—a fertilized egg, a blob of protoplasm, a congeries of fetal matter, an intruder usurping the mother's life-support system—and medical science so informed would have just as efficiently destroyed it.

Thus to the supposedly unresolvable question, "Who can really say when human life begins?" we have an unassailable answer: "The mother says." According to the implications of a decision of the Supreme Court, every child born since January 1973, even those carried by mothers who opposed abortion, owes its humanness to the will of the individual who, at a critical moment of her own life, chose to let it live. We grant the exercise of that will final, irrevocable, and absolute authority. It is, in fact, infallible.

PREGNANCY OR ABORTION: A WRENCHING CHOICE
Sydney J. Harris

My dinner partner was a lady who for many years has been a guidance counselor at a small Eastern college that has gone coeducational. The subject of sex came up, and she mentioned that about a dozen or fifteen students become pregnant at the school each year. "At least those are the ones I know about," she said.

"How many decide to drop out of school and have their babies?" I asked.

"None," she answered, "or practically none. Virtually all of them opt for an abortion—and, of course, they can get them legally here."

"Does this bother some of them?"

She nodded. "Terribly. In one case recently, a pregnant girl brought along her best friend, who was so upset at seeing the fetus that she had an emotional breakdown and had to enter the infirmary for a couple of days."

"After so many years, what is your opinion on this?" I inquired.

"My opinion is that anyone who takes a black-or-white position on the subject of abortion is either a fool or a fanatic. It is the grayest moral area I can imagine, and I myself am torn in two each time it happens. Having the baby would be a disaster for most of these children—that's what they still are—and having an abortion is the most traumatic experience they can go through."

"Why don't these presumably educated girls employ birth control methods?" I wondered.

"That's the psychologically interesting part," she reflected. "You see, the ones who get pregnant are not the tramps, as some might call them, but girls with good moral standards. They won't use birth control methods because they feel that by doing so they are tacitly encouraging sex. To be prepared for it is in a way, they feel, to invite it. This way, if sex occurs, it is spontaneous or unexpected, and not calculated on their part."

"So in a sense," I ventured, "it's their moral posture itself that prevents them from being prudent. It seems rather ironic that a high moral code can lead to more downfalls than frank promiscuity."

"That's what is so heartbreaking in my job." She sighed. "It's really the 'nicer' girls who have to come to me with this problem—the more innocent ones, the more naive ones, the girls who denied their vulnerability. The hardened cases are too shrewd and systematic to get pregnant."

"It's a muddied picture, isn't it?" I said. "There seems to be no good answer anywhere between total abstinence and marriage—and sometimes marriage is the worst possible answer."

"There are only bad answers"—she shrugged—"and I've come to the view that the best a guidance counselor can do is offer a choice of evils."

Sydney J. Harris, "Pregnancy or Abortion: A Wrenching Choice," *Pieces of Eight* (Boston: Houghton Mifflin, 1982). Harris is a nationally syndicated columnist ("Strictly Personal") for the *Chicago Sun-Times*. *Pieces of Eight* is a collection of his columns.

THE ARGUMENTS IN FAVOR OF ABORTION ARE STRONG IF YOU ACCEPT ONE IMPORTANT ASSUMPTION
Lewis B. Smedes

Sometimes I like to list the strongest arguments I can find to support a point of view I think is wrong. When I have them before me, I am up against a real opponent rather than a hypothetical one that is an easy target for me to hit.

I tried my hand recently at listing the best arguments I have heard for freedom of abortion in a democratic society. They have been offered as reasons for keeping abortion a wholly private matter, out of the reach of law. Each of them embodies a general principle most of us support. The question is whether any of them, or all of them together, makes a clear case for freedom of abortion. Here they are for the reader to evaluate.

1. *A pluralistic society should not prevent individuals from doing what their religious principles allow.*

Our society is pluralistic. We who accept the privilege of membership in that society agree to respect the people's right to live by their own religious precepts. Some people believe in their hearts that abortion is morally permissible, and they also believe that God gives each woman the responsibility of controlling her own pregnancies. So, in the name of pluralism, people who believe abortion is wrong should not force their beliefs on others.

2. *A free society should not invade the privacy of a woman's body.*

The right to personal privacy is precious. Without it we are all potential victims for a prying secret police. Nothing is more private than a woman's body; it is her physical, emotional, and moral citadel. She cannot be free at all if she is not free to decide for herself, in private, what to do with her body. No law can be good that sends the tentacles of a prying bureaucracy into the holy of holies of a woman's womb.

3. *A just society should not pass laws whose execution inevitably creates unfairness.*

Laws against abortion are always unfair to poor people. Rich women who want abortions can always find a clean clinic to break the law for them. Poor women have to depend upon amateur "doctors" for abortions or bear children they cannot afford to care for. God, the Bible says, is on the side of the poor; antiabortionists are on the side of the rich.

4. *A merciful society should not make laws that force terrible handicaps on children.*

Blanket prohibition of abortion coerces children to exist and bear burdens no child should be forced to carry. Some will have to live with a mother who does not want them. Others will have to endure enormous physical or grievous mental hand-

Lewis B. Smedes, "The Arguments in Favor of Abortion Are Strong if You Accept One Important Assumption," *Christianity Today* 15 July 1983. Smedes is professor of theology and ethics at Fuller Theological Seminary. Among his books is *Mere Morality: What God Expects of Ordinary People* (1983). *Christianity Today* is a "magazine of evangelical conviction."

icaps. It is not righteousness, but brutality, that forces women to bear children whose life will be a misery.

5. *A wise society will not pass laws that it cannot, and perhaps does not have the will to, enforce.*

Nothing erodes the self-respect of a society like making laws it does not have the stomach to enforce or the will to punish offenders for breaking. Few people believe we have the will to add a detail of abortion detectives to already shrunken police forces. Fewer still believe we have the will to prosecute for murder a doctor who aborts a fetus he knows has Tay Sachs disease, or to arrest a teen-age girl for murder because she aborted a fetus she knew she could not care for.

Good arguments? Of course—as long as you accept one all-important assumption. The assumption is that a fetus is definitely not a human being and therefore not entitled to protection against an assault on its life. If, however, you believe a fetus is a human being, or at least deserves to be given the legal status of a human being, none of the arguments is convincing.

A *pluralist* society does not allow people to follow their consciences if their consciences lead them to kill an innocent human being. A *free* society will invade a person's privacy if it is certain that she is privately about to kill an innocent human being. A *just* society may well pass laws whose execution leads to unfairness to some people if not to pass them causes a greater unfairness, the killing of innocent human beings. A *merciful* society may well make laws that burden children if not to make them encourages the killing of innocent, unborn children. A *wise* society may well make laws it does not have the will to enforce if not to pass them makes killing human beings legal. In sum, all of the arguments that are based on what a good society will or will not do fail at the frontier of the rights of a fetus to live.

I have here only tried to show that the best arguments for freedom of abortion run aground on one crucial question: What is a fetus and what rights does it have? Every argument assumes that the fetus's life is at best an issue secondary to every other issue, but it is precisely here that the final decision rests. And it is here that our society is at agonizing odds with itself. Does human fetal life have a value only secondary to every other social value? It is with this question that the conscience of our society must ultimately come to terms.

THE MEDICAL QUANDARY
Jean Seligmann

The ultimate Hippocratic dilemma, the nightmare that unsettles a good doctor's sleep: a pregnant patient, after much agony, has chosen an abortion and the doctor performs the procedure by injecting prostaglandins (hormonelike substances that induce labor) into her amniotic sac. But when, some hours later, the fetus is expelled from the woman's uterus, it is not the 22-week-old creature he had anticipated. It is 26 weeks old—and alive.

This is an unlikely scenario; 90 percent of abortions in the United States are performed before the 13th week of pregnancy, and only 1 percent, or about 13,000 procedures a year, take place after the 20th week (the start of gestation is calculated from the onset of the last menstrual period). But the branch of medicine known as neonatology—the special care of newborns—now routinely saves the lives of preemies who would have died a decade ago. Today, a premature delivery can lead to heroic—and sometimes successful—attempts to save mid-trimester babies. Increasingly, survival is possible for fetuses that can legally be aborted. At the same time, the growing ability to treat fetuses *in utero*—shunts to correct hydrocephalus or bladder blockage, drugs to alter metabolism—deepen the quandary. "When you do things to a child in the womb, you're acknowledging that you're dealing with a patient," says medical ethicist Thomas Murray of the University of Texas Medical School at Galveston. "It's hard to do that and then turn around and abort a child of the same developmental age."

While the numbers of late abortions are relatively small, the moral implications are substantial. As a result, physicians and hospitals are taking new and searching looks at their policies on abortion. Across the United States, many hospitals skirt the issue by simply refusing to perform most abortions after 20 weeks; some physicians have adopted an even earlier "personal cutoff" of 10 or 12 weeks. And when doctors do administer late abortions, they are much more likely to employ the techniques certain to kill the developing child before it leaves the womb—anything to forestall the possibility of a live birth in the operating room.

Dr. Sherwood Lynn, an obstetrician and gynecologist at Houston's Hermann Hospital, used to perform many more abortions that he does now. Today, he refers most requests to area clinics set up expressly for abortions. He does them himself only when a clear-cut medical problem jeopardizes the fetus or mother—for example, if the woman has been taking potent cancer drugs that could cause a fatal maternal hemorrhage during labor and would almost certainly kill the baby. Still, he says, "I don't like to do abortions. It's not a moral question—I just have a bad feeling about it. It's always a strain." One reason for the strain, says Dr. Paul Blumenthal, director of ambulatory care at Chicago's Michael Reese Hospital, is that one of the most widely used techniques for late abortions, dilatation and evacuation (D&E) requires the physician to crush and kill the fetus while it is still

Jean Seligmann, "The Medical Quandary," *Newsweek* 14 January 1985.

in the womb. It's one thing when a physician injects a drug to induce labor and walks away, says Blumenthal, "and another thing to actively take part in the procedure. The physician can't see what he's doing in the uterus. It's bloody and a little frightening."

No woman deliberately plans a late abortion, and most of those who end up having them belong to well-recognized categories. Forty-four per cent of abortions done after the 21st week of gestation are performed on teen-agers, who may not realize that they are pregnant until they feel the baby kicking. Or they may deny the evidence of their own bodies. In states like Massachusetts, where a minor must have the consent of both parents for an abortion, "a young girl may be well into her second trimester before she gets the nerve to tell her momma, who may in turn hesitate to tell daddy," explains Dr. Phillip Stubblefield, chief of obstetrics and gynecology at Mount Auburn Hospital in Cambridge. Or, refusing to confess at all, a teen-ager may shop for a friendlier jurisdiction, delaying the procedure still further.

Other typical recipients of late abortions include poor women, who may find it difficult to scrape up $200 for the procedure or do not know how to find out where to go for the operation; women with histories of irregular menses, and women approaching menopause who attribute missed periods to their impending change of life.

Perhaps the most agonizing late abortions, however, are those that result from yet another product of modern technology. Amniocentesis, the withdrawal and analysis of amniotic fluid to identify possible genetic abnormalities like Down's syndrome in an unborn child, cannot be done until the 14th to 17th week of pregnancy. Moreover, the results of the test may not be ready until the 21st week or even later. Thus, most abortions performed because of amniocentesis findings necessarily take place in the gestation period's problematic zone. But Dr. John Carpenter, director of the prenatal diagnostic center at the Baylor College of Medicine in Houston, says he has no reservations about abortions under such circumstances. However, "I don't do it as a cold-blooded killer," he explains. "I have a great deal of empathy and sympathy for these families. They suffer grief and I suffer grief, too. But I have no qualms because I've seen the impact a seriously impaired child can have on a family."

Within the next five years, amniocentesis and its unsatisfactory timetable may be supplemented by a newer research tool: chorionic villus biopsy. This procedure, in which a small sample of the tissue lining the amniotic sac is removed and analyzed for abnormalities, can be done as early as eight weeks into pregnancy, with results at 12 weeks. In an abortion at that stage, of course, fetal viability is out of the question. But chorionic villus biopsy is more risky to the fetus than amniocentesis, and some researchers doubt that it will ever be safe enough for routine screening.

The most disturbing late abortions, of course, are those that result in live births. Although rare, they sometimes occur because the age of the fetus has been underestimated. The woman may not remember the date of her last menstrual period— or she may deliberately lie about it if she is determined to get an abortion despite an advanced pregnancy. Relying on a physical examination alone, explains Dr. Michael Burnhill, an obstetrician and gynecologist at the College of Medicine and

Dentistry of New Jersey, a doctor can miscalculate fetal age by more than a month. For that reason, many physicians routinely perform an ultrasound scan for abortions after the 12th week of pregnancy. This visual image of the fetus enables a skilled practitioner to estimate its age with a high degree of accuracy.

But even when the age can be determined precisely, doctors don't always agree on when the fetus should be considered "viable," or indeed on exactly what viability means. In neonatal intensive-care units, doctors treat 24- to 26-week-old fetuses weighing as little as 1 pound 10 ounces, and 28-week preemies stand a good chance of surviving to lead healthy lives. But these are babies whose births are intended, and for whom major life-sustaining efforts are made during both labor and delivery. By contrast, observes Dr. Richard Stavis, director of the neonatal unit at Bryn Mawr Hospital in Bryn Mawr, Pa., "when you do an abortion, you're obviously not doing it in the interest of the baby's viability." Stavis considers that viability begins "in the range of 24 weeks," noting that the likelihood of survival before that point is close to zero. But even at 26 weeks, he explains, survival rates are low because the baby is born with immature lungs, skin so fragile it can be torn by surgical tape, and blood vessels that may be too minuscule for the introduction of needles and tubes necessary for monitoring and nutrition.

New Jersey's Burnhill, who has performed abortions at 26 weeks in cases of severe birth defects, believes it is unrealistic to speak of viability before that point, when the baby still weighs less than two pounds. "I don't think a 24-week fetus can ever have an independent existence," he observes, "though you can keep some of them alive on assisted ventilation for a while." Fetuses weighing less than 35 ounces, he notes, are often born with serious defects: learning disabilities, poor vision and impaired hearing. "Technological advances have been keeping them alive, not keeping them intact," says Burnhill, "and the heartbreak for the parents later is staggering."

In most cases of late abortion, physicians try to prevent such tragedies by using one of the two methods that nearly always result in fetal death. One is the relatively new D&E, in which the fetus is literally dismembered by a forceps within the uterus, limb by limb, and the "pieces" are withdrawn through the vagina. Although a D&E is safe for the mother, it can be devastating for the hospital staff; many doctors simply won't do advanced D&E's. Burnhill refuses to perform them later than 14 or 15 weeks into pregnancy, at least in part, he says, because "I have trouble getting nurses and anesthesiologists to work with me." (It may have been this technique that President Reagan was referring to when he asserted last winter that the fetus experiences pain during an abortion. However, while even a 10-week-old embryo will shrink from an instrument poked into the uterus, researchers argue that the neurological pathways necessary for pain perception are not well developed until very late in pregnancy and perhaps not until after birth.)

In the other method, the physician administers substances that first kill the fetus, then induce the labor that will expel it. Saline solution, for example, injected in small quantities into the amniotic sac, usually performs both functions. However, this procedure carries some risk to the woman; the saline may find its way into her bloodstream, causing hemorrhage or lung and kidney damage. Another procedure calls for introducing a small amount of urea into the sac, or injecting it directly into the fetus itself. At some medical centers, the heart drug digoxin is administered to the fetus before labor is induced, resulting in a fatal cardiac arrhythmia.

One of the safest methods for inducing labor in a late abortion is the "instillation" of prostaglandins, which cut off the fetus's oxygen supply. Still, there are occasional live births. Some states and hospitals require doctors to treat such a baby like any other "live" birth from premature labor, but this does not mean that extraordinary, "heroic" efforts are necessarily made to save its life. "If we had an aborted baby below the age of viability that was technically live-born," says Stavis of Bryn Mawr, "we'd put it in an Isolette [incubator], keep it warm, give it oxygen and observe it. But we would not actively intervene to protect that baby from dying." To place tubes in a fetus that has no chance of survival, Stavis believes, is abusive. "It is subjecting the fetus to an experiment," he declares. "To me, that is cruel."

"Nobody who provides abortions wants to kill babies," adds Stubblefield. "Nobody is in favor of infanticide. The question is, where do you draw the line? In my morality, an abortion prior to 24 weeks is a reasonable thing to do; after that it is not." And if a fetus should survive an abortion attempt, Stubblefield says, "if it looks as if it might have a chance—not just for an hour or two, but for survival to leave the hospital—then you give it everything you've got."

SUGGESTIONS FOR WRITING

Informal Essays

1. If you have known a person who has either considered or has had an abortion, use what you know of her experiences to write an essay defending or attacking abortion. Before you begin, read a few selections from this chapter.
2. Write an essay that reflects your philosophy concerning either the sanctity of life or a woman's right to control her own body.

Short Documented Papers

1. Write a paper in which you argue one or two points that support either the pro-choice position or the pro-life position on abortion.
2. Write a report in which you contrast the pro-choice and pro-life positions on a single point related to the general abortion issue.
3. Write a report in which you discuss what you consider to be the weakest of the pro-choice or pro-life arguments.

Longer Documented Papers

1. Argue at length either the pro-choice or pro-life position on abortion.
2. Write a report in which you contrast the pro-choice and the pro-life positions on two or three points in the general abortion issue.
3. Write a report in which you discuss the weaknesses evident in both the pro-life and the pro-choice arguments.
4. Write a report in which you evaluate the most convincing points in both the pro-choice and the pro-life arguments.

· 4 ·

Advertising:
Is It More Than Harmless
Puffery?

A single page of advertising in a national magazine costs a company about $60,000. A single minute of advertising during the Super Bowl telecast costs about $1 million.

With so much at stake, advertisers are naturally going to use all of the resources of art and language to influence our buying habits. In fact, the air seems thick at times with a barrage of commercially seductive images and manipulative language. Sometimes advertisers even hire psychologists to explain the deep urges that drive a consumer to purchase Corn Crispies rather than Crispie Corns.

We are being seduced, the critics of advertising say. With all of that money to spend for artists, copywriters, producers, models, and motivational researchers, advertisers have got us where they want us, and we are almost powerless to resist their pleas.

Those who defend advertising say that the effectiveness of motivational research in advertising is vastly overrated and that consumers are not so weak-willed as the critics of advertising would have people believe. Besides, the defenders add, in a free society advertisers should be able to use language in the same ways that the rest of us use it. The use of a rhetorical technique in advertising, they say, is as fair as its use in novels, essays, and newspaper columns.

Sometimes the issue of fairness comes down to this crucial question: Does a particular ad *intend* to deceive? Unfortunately, it's not always easy to tell. For one thing, an ad can be untruthful without being deceptive. Do you remember those television ads with the little happy-faced brushes that scrubbed a sink clean? That ad was untruthful, but it wasn't deceptive. That is, the soap company obviously wasn't trying to persuade us that cute little living brushes helped their soap do its job; they were trying to say that their soap worked *as if* little brushes were at work. Unfortunately, it's not always so clear when an image is used to illustrate a point; images used as metaphors (like little brushes) can easily blur into deception.

But if we consumers have little difficulty recognizing visual metaphors, we have a harder time recognizing puffery (those exaggerated claims that advertisers make). In fact, it's sometimes next to impossible to tell where hyperbole ends and deception begins. What about the restaurant that claims that its pizza is the best in town? Or the mattress company that claims that you'll sleep like a baby on its individually wrapped springs? Is puffery deceptive? Or is it instead a part of the conventional language of advertisers that no one takes seriously—that never was meant to be taken seriously?

A more serious question is this: Is advertising a healthy or unhealthy influence on society? The charges and countercharges are familiar enough. Advertising, the critics say, encourages a materialistic life-style. (Advertising keeps the economy healthy, the defenders reply.) Advertising, the critics contend, warps our sense of reality, because no one can live up to the handsome people and happy faces of advertisements. (Ads encourage our wish fulfillment fantasies, the defenders reply, and thus help make life more bearable.)

A final question is this: Even if we do find advertising misleading and unhealthy, do we want to regulate it more that it is now? Blatant deception in advertising is now illegal. Should the Federal Trade Commission step in to regulate the language of advertising even further? Should it police puffery, for instance?

Thomas Wolfe once described advertising as "fat, juicy, sugar-coated lies for our great Boob public to swallow." That effectively sums up the feelings of the critics. Advertising's defenders would no doubt agree with Robert Lewis Stevenson's comment that "Everyone lives by selling something."

. . . AND THE HOOKS ARE LOWERED
Vance Packard

The techniques used for probing the subconscious were derived straight from the clinics of psychiatry, for the most part. As Dr. [George Horsley] Smith advised marketers in his book on motivation research, "Different levels of depth are achieved by different approaches" [*Motivational Research in Advertising and Marketing*].

I shall summarize here some of the more picturesque probing techniques put to use by the depth probers of merchandising. For this Dr. Smith's authoritative book has been a helpful guide.

One of the most widely used techniques for probing in depth is what is called the "depth interview." When 1,100 of the nation's top management men met at a conference in New York in early 1956 (sponsored by the American Management Association), they were treated to a closed-circuit TV demonstration of an actual depth interview, with psychologists doing the probing.

These interviews in depth are conducted very much as the psychiatrist conducts his interviews, except that there is no couch since a couch might make the chosen consumer-guinea pig wary. (Many of these consumers are induced to co-operate by the offer of free samples of merchandise. Others apparently just enjoy the attention of being "tested.") Typically the psychologist, psychiatrist, or other expert doing the probing tries, with casualness and patience, to get the consumer into a reverie of talking, to get him or her musing absent-mindedly about all the "pleasures, joys, enthusiasms, agonies, nightmares, deceptions, apprehensions the product recalls to them," to use Dr. Smith's phrase.

Sometimes these depth interviews take place with whole groups of people because, oddly, the group reverie often is more productive. Many people tend to become less inhibited in a group than when they are alone with the interviewer in the same way that some people can only warm up at a party. As Dr. Smith explains it, "What happens is that one member makes a 'daring,' selfish, or even intolerant statement. This encourages someone else to speak in the same vein. Others tend to sense that the atmosphere has become more permissive and proceed accordingly. Thus we have been able to get highly personalized discussions of laxatives, cold tablets, deodorants, weight reducers, athlete's foot remedies, alcohol, and sanitary napkins. On the doorstep, or in the living room, a respondent might be reluctant to discuss his personal habits with a stranger."

Much of the depth probing by marketers is done with what Professor Smith calls "disguised," or indirect, tests. The person tested is given the impression he is being tested for some other reason than the real one. Most are what psychiatrists call "projective" tests. In this the subject is presented with a drawing or other stimulus

Vance Packard, ". . . And the Hooks Are Lowered," *The Hidden Persuaders* (New York: David McKay, 1957). *The Hidden Persuaders* describes and criticizes advertisers' use of motivational research. Packard's other books include *The Waste Makers* (1960), *The Sexual Wilderness* (1968), and *The People Shapers* (1977).

that doesn't quite make sense. Something must be filled in to complete the picture, and the subject is asked to do that. In doing this he projects a part of himself into the picture.

One of the most widely used is the famed ink-blot test developed by the Swiss psychiatrist Hermann Rorschach. Here a series of ten cards on which are printed bisymmetrical ink blots is used. They are ambiguous forms representing nothing whatever. The subject sees in the picture what he "needs" to see, and thus projects himself into it—his anxieties, inadequacies, conflicts.

Many of the depth probers of merchandising however prefer the so-called TAT to the Rorschach. The TAT (Thematic Apperception Test) in its pure clinical form consists of a series of printed pictures chosen carefully from magazine illustrations, paintings, etc. Merchandisers, however, make adaptations by including pictures of their own, pictures they are thinking of using in ad copy.

Again the subject is encouraged to project himself into the picture so that the probers can assess his impulses, anxieties, wishes, ill feelings. Suppose that in a series of pictures every single one shows some fellow in an embarrassing jam with some obvious figure of authority, such as boss, teacher, cop, parent. The testee is asked to tell a story about each picture. If in his stories the underling usually kills or beats up or humiliates the authority figure, we have one kind of character; if he builds a secure and comfortable dependence with the authority figure, we have quite a different story.

A variation is the cartoon-type test where the testee can write in words in a "balloon" of the cartoon left empty. In the Rosenzweig picture-frustration test, for example, one of the figures says something that is obviously frustrating to the other person pictured, and the subject is invited to fill in the frustrated person's response. In one cited by Dr. Smith a man and woman were standing near their parked car as the man hunted through his pockets for his keys. The wife exclaimed, "This is a fine time to have lost the keys!" What would the man reply?

One of the most startling of the picture tests used by market probers is the Szondi test. It is, as one research director of an advertising agency told me, "a real cutie." He has used it with whisky drinkers. The assumption of this test is that we're all a little crazy. The subject being probed is shown a series of cards bearing the portraits of people and is asked to pick out of them the one person he would most like to sit beside if he were on a train trip, and the person pictured that he would least like to sit beside. What he is not told is that the people shown on the cards are all thoroughly disordered. Each suffers severely from one of eight psychiatric disorders (is homosexual, sadist, epileptic, hysterical, catatonic, paranoid, depressed, or manic). It is assumed that we will sense a rapport with some more than others, and that in choosing a riding companion we will choose the person suffering acutely from the same emotional state that affects us mildly.

The ad agency in question used this Szondi to try to find why people really drink whisky. Among its ad accounts are major whisky distillers. The agency was interested in diagnosing the personality of the heavy drinker for a thoroughly practical reason: heavy drinkers account for most of the whisky consumed (85 percent of the volume is consumed by 22 percent of the drinkers). In using the Szondi on heavy whisky drinkers, it tested the subjects before they had a drink and then tested them after they had had three drinks. The research director relates: "A change takes place that would make your hair stand on end!"

Why does a man drink heavily? Here is his conclusion: "He wouldn't drink unless he got a change in personality that was satisfying to him." Some of these people undergo extremely surprising changes of personality. Meek men become belligerent, and so on.

In other tests instruments are used to gauge the subjects' physiological responses as clues to their emotional states. The galvanometer, better known as lie detector, has been used by the Color Research Institute and *The Chicago Tribune*, to cite just two examples. A subject's physiological reactions are clocked while he sees images and hears sounds that may be used in trying to promote the sale of products. James Vicary, on the other hand, employs a special hidden camera that photographs the eye-blink rate of people under varying test situations. Our eye-blink rate is a clue to our emotional tension or lack of tension.

Hypnosis also is being used in attempts to probe our subconscious to find why we buy or do not buy certain products. Ruthrauff and Ryan, the New York ad agency, has been employing a prominent hypnotist and a panel of psychologists and psychiatrists in its effect to get past our mental blockages, which are so bothersome to probers when we are conscious. The agency has found that hypnosis sharpens our power to recall. We can remember things that we couldn't otherwise remember. One place they've been using it is to try to find why we use the brand of product we do. An official cited the case of a man who under hypnosis told why he preferred a certain make of car and always bought it. This man, under hypnosis, was able to repeat word for word an ad he had read more than twenty years before that had struck his fancy. The agency is vague as to whether it is at this moment using a hypnotist. However, it does uphold the fact that the results to date have been "successful" to the degree that "we believe in years to come it may be employed as a method."

One ad man I talked with revealed he had often speculated on the possibility of using TV announcers who had been trained in hypnotism, for deeper impact.

The London Sunday Times front-paged a report in mid-1956 that certain United States advertisers were experimenting with "subthreshold effects" in seeking to insinuate sales messages to people past their conscious guard. It cited the case of a cinema in New Jersey that it said was flashing ice-cream ads onto the screen during regular showings of film. The flashes of message were split-second, too short for people in the audience to recognize them consciously but still long enough to be absorbed unconsciously.

A result, it reported, was a clear and otherwise unaccountable boost in ice-cream sales. "Subthreshold effects, both in vision and sound, have been known for some years to experimental psychologists," the paper explained. It speculated that political indoctrination might be possible without the subject being conscious of any influence being brought to bear on him.

When I queried Dr. Smith about the alleged ice-cream experiment he said he had not heard of it before and expressed skepticism. "There is evidence," he agreed, "that people can be affected by subthreshold stimulation; for example, a person can be conditioned to odors and sounds that are just outside the range of conscious awareness. However, this is rarely done in one instantaneous flash. . . ." When I questioned *The London Sunday Times* about its sources a spokesman reported: ". . . Although the facts we published are well attested, the authorities in question are unwilling to come any further into the open." Then he added: "There have, since publication of this article, been two programmes dealing with the subject on the B.B.C. Television, when experiments of a similar nature were tried on the viewing public; but although some success was claimed, it is generally agreed that such forms of advertising are more suitable for the cinema than for the slower television screen."

Although each depth-probing group has its own favorite techniques, it may use many others when appropriate. The research director at Young and Rubicam, for example, states: "In research at Y.&R. we like to think we practice 'eclectism,' a frightening word which simply means 'selecting the best.' We are willing to experiment with depth interview, word association, sentence completion, Minnesota multiphasic personality inventories (which incidentally turn up things like inward and outward hostility) and even Rorschach and Thematic Appercepion Tests. . . ."

Our subconscious attitudes, of course, are far from being the whole explanation of our buying behavior, even the depth probers are quick to acknowledge. A sale may result from a mixture of factors. Dr. Wulfeck, of the Advertising Research Foundation, points out: "A consumer may have an internal hostility toward a product, and he may still buy it because of other facts such as advertising, distribution, dislike of competing brand, and so on."

Even the advertising agencies most devoted to motivation research still carry on exhaustively the two mainstay kinds of research: market research (study of products, income levels, price, dealers, etc.) and copy research (the testing of specific layouts, phrases, etc.).

There appears to be abundant evidence, however, that by 1957 a very large number of influential marketers were trying to use this new depth approach in some of their work. It was here to stay.

When in the chapters that follow we enter into the wilderness of the depth manipulators by getting down to cases, you may occasionally find yourself exclaiming that only the maverick and extremist fringe of business would embrace such tactics. Here, briefly, is the evidence to the contrary, showing that the depth approach—despite the fact that it still has admitted limitations and fallibilities—has become a very substantial movement in American business. Some of the journals most respected by America's leading marketers had this to say during the mid-fifties:

Printer's Ink: "Overwhelmingly a group of top-drawer advertising agencies and advertising executives, representing many of the nation's outstanding advertisers, favor the increased use of social sciences and social scientists in . . . campaign planning." (February 27, 1953)

Tide: "Some of the nation's most respected companies have sunk millions of dollars into ad campaigns shaped at least in part by analysis of consumer motivations." (February 26, 1955) It reported making a study that found that 33 per cent of the top merchandisers on its "Leadership Panel" were getting M.R. surveys from their ad agencies. (October 22, 1955)

Wall Street Journal: "More and more advertising and marketing strategists are adapting their sales campaigns to the psychologists' findings and advice." It said Goodyear Tire and Rubber, General Motors, General Foods, Jewel Tea, and Lever Brothers were only a few of the large outfits that had made M.R. studies. (September 13, 1954)

Sales Management printed one estimate that $12,000,000 would be spent by marketers in 1956 for research in motivations. (February 1, 15, 1955)

Advertising Age: "The big news in research during 1955 was M.R., its advocates and critics." (January 2, 1956)

Fortune: "Of the $260,000,000,000 spent on consumer products last year (1955) a full half probably went to industries in which one or more major manufacturers had tried M.R." It is estimated that nearly a billion dollars in ad money spent in 1955 came from the big corporations that had used M.R. directly or through their ad agencies, and added that M.R. had been responsible for some major shifts in advertising appeals. (June, 1956)

ARE ADVERTISING AND MARKETING CORRUPTING SOCIETY? IT'S NOT YOUR WORRY

Theodore Levitt

It's natural enough for people now and then to think about the consequences of their actions. It shows that they have compassion, which is a good thing.

In our more abstracted and contemplative moments we all ask ourselves some pretty basic questions. Even the most self-assured entertain doubts. Is it all worth while? Isn't what we do for our daily bread pretty trite, superficial, banal, or even downright corrosive in its general consequences?

If you happen to sell antibiotics, maybe you feel good about what you do, although it may occasionally bother you that a lot of needy people can't afford your asking price. On the other hand, if you sell switch-blade knives, you need a stronger stomach.

ARE YOU A "HIDDEN PERSUADER," SELLING WHAT PEOPLE DON'T NEED?

But what about the in-between cases? The man who sells mud packs to aging matrons in search of youth? Or, what if you push chemises on ladies who were perfectly satisfied wth the styles they reluctantly bought last year? What if you pay big money to the "hidden persuaders" so you can manipulate people into buying things they don't need, can't afford, and are of doubtful utility? What will your soul-searching ruminations yield then?

Or, suppose you're a solid, devoted, church-going family man in the automobile business. How do you feel, knowing that the car has debased American life and morals, facilitating crime, vice, infidelity, adultery and unchastity?

Whatever your business, it is possible to see its wholesale contribution to decadence, self-indulgence, materialism, cynicism, irresponsibility, selfishness—a swelling galaxy of assorted social, economic, human, cultural, psychological, moral and ethical evils. There is no escape. The more successful the quest of your particular business—whatever it may be—the more evil it generates.

This can be said even if, let's assume, you produce and distribute such an apparently neutral commodity as electric power. Electricity runs the factories that produce all the gadgets that are ruining people's sense of values and the barbaric weapons that will destroy us all. Electricity keeps the night clubs operating, and everybody knows what happens in their opaque illumination.

WHERE IS BUSINESS LEADING US?

On what logical grounds can you say that people who argue this way, who perhaps want to return to a more primeval way of life, have any less legitimate claim to

Theodore Levitt, "Are Advertising and Marketing Corrupting Society? It's Not Your Worry," *Advertising Age* 6 October 1958. At the time he wrote this article, Levitt was a marketing and economic consultant.

truth, wisdom, or common sense than you? Maybe they're right. After all, what is the business man's headlong quest leading to? After you have all the gadgets, all the living space, all the deodorants, all the Bermuda shorts, and all the steaks you can possibly use—what then, little man?

We are discussing the general topic of management's mission in the new society . . . and the specific question of certain dangers that may accompany the success of its marketing effort. To set the stage for our discussion, Professor Bursk has asked these questions:

"Suppose . . . we can succeed in endowing consumers with all the material goods—necessities, conveniences, luxuries—that our factories can produce and our stores can handle? There still are grave questions. What will happen to people as human beings? Will they lose their dignity, their culture, their appreciation of spiritual values? Will their standard of living be higher just because they can afford to obsolete their possessions quicker, continually buying new fancy models at the expense of economic waste? What is the psychology of unbounded satisfaction? What are the effects of manipulation—whether it be blatant persuasion, or subtle motivation like the hidden persuaders? Will we become a nation of robots with mechanical appetites?"

These are vital questions. They show a necessary and commendable feel for the real deep-down juice of life. Society needs always to be asking itself where it is going. Otherwise it won't know what road to take. Somebody must think and do something about these questions. But it is the thesis of my remarks today that whoever that somebody is, it should not be the business man.

DOES THE BUSINESS MAN HAVE THE RIGHT TO DECIDE WHAT'S GOOD FOR US?

The cultural, spiritual, social, moral, etc. consequences of his actions are none of his occupational concern. He is in business for his own personal edification— neither to save nor to ruin souls. His job is perfectly neutral on these matters. Besides, the minute he becomes preoccupied with the deeper purposes and consequences of what he does, he becomes a conscious arbiter of our lives. He will be trying consciously to decide what is good or bad for us; what we should or should not have; should or should not see, hear, read, think, or do. He will have thrown the mighty weight of his great economic power behind the community-wide implementation of his own private values and tastes. And even if these are the highest expression of God's will, I submit the result could be nothing less than evil.

Nobody can know better than the adult individual himself what his values and tastes should be, even if he is a congenital idiot. The fact that we put idiots away is beside the point. The point is this: the business man exists for only one purpose, to create and deliver value satisfactions at a profit to himself. He isn't, and shouldn't be, a theologian, a philosopher, or a sort of Emily Post of commerce. His job is ridiculously simple. The test of whether the things he offers do indeed contain value satisfactions is provided by the completely neutral mechanism of the open market.

If what is offered can be sold at a profit (not even necessarily a long-term profit), then it is legitimate. The consumer has cast a favorable economic ballot. He wants it. If enough other consumers don't agree and cast their more powerful political ballots against the commodity or practice in question, that is okay, too. That is the veto of democratic politics over democratic economics. And this ranking is precisely the desirable and necessary order of their importance.

If the business man becomes preoccupied with all the involved normative questions that his activities raise, he will fail to perform his greatest responsibility: to succeed as a business man. The business man should pursue his own sense of workmanship with a singular purpose, unburdened by peripheral considerations that drain his vitality or cloud his objectives. He should be free to probe wherever his instincts and talents lead, just as scientists and philosophers should be free to do in their fields. When it comes to the scope and direction of their jobs, they should be true only to the bedrock purposes of their respective functions—as neutral about the outcome as the goddess of justice.

Everything inseparably has good and bad consequences, depending in part on your values. And every thinking person should try to be aware of both. But what we should want is less, not more, concern with the consequences of successful marketing. We should get away from normative considerations entirely. The reason is purely functional. It is the same one as applies when we say that the scientist should leave dogma and personal preference at the door when he enters his lab. Dogma restricts scientific development, just as much as scientific development undermines dogma. Dogma also restricts top marketing development and performance. And for my part, with special reference to business men, their self-conscious preoccupation with elevating the public is potentially very dangerous.

When you consciously use your product to affect the spiritual, cultural, aesthetic, and home lives of your customers, then you are playing God. It is bad enough that you intimately affect our private lives in the random process of doing your job as business man. To affect them intentionally and in a clearly manipulative fashion that has nothing to do with the object of selling as such, to do that is a compounded evil. There are already too many institutions and individuals tyrannizing us with their own special versions of God's will. We don't need any more.

DO LUXURIES REALLY CORRUPT?

If capitalism learns to distribute and sell goods as well as it can produce them, if really hot-shot marketing becomes successful enough to create a sort of commercial Frankenstein loading people up with redundant goods, creating superficial and vulgar wants, and generating the kind of opulence that turns luxuries into necessities and necessities into ceremonial rather than substantive values—if this happens, perhaps we will get soft and decadent and finally drift down into the quagmire of decay that was Rome's fate.

But let's not go overboard in an orgy of moral self-flagellation. A lot of this viewing with alarm is an irrational Puritan reaction against the good life. We shrink from having really uninhibited good times. We still associate virtue with work and idleness with vice. Deep down inside we can't shake off the guilt of Adam's fall. "In the sweat of thy face shalt thou eat bread." Things must not be too easy. That leads to the degradation of the spirit. Spiritual purity is equated with hard work and physical discomfort. . . .

WHAT BREEDS MORE CULTURE—PLUSH LIVING, FRONTIER ADVERSITY?

I ask you, which capitalist society is culturally and technologically more creative—opulent U.S. or hand-to-mouth Spain? Which condition has produced more statesmen, business leaders, writers, poets, scientists, and clergymen—the well-heeled breeding of the Churchills, the Huxleys, the Rockefellers, and the Adamses, or the mountaineer adversity of the Hatfields and the McCoys? Which soldiers fought more successfully during World War II—the pampered, almost undisciplined Americans with their chewing gum and fleece-lined shoes, or the arrogant Germans goose-stepping in ice-cold leather boots after their intoxicating dream of historic mission?

And what is better, for our wives to spend endless drudging hours scrubbing clothes half-clean on corrugated washboards and serving us half-done, half-digestible cakes they proudly made from scratch, or for the hidden persuaders to have banished their Puritan guilt feelings about using automatic washing machines and pre-mixed flour?

Everybody is a hidden persuader of sorts. Every statement addresses itself to a customer. Every act covets an objective. The fact that some people are getting more efficient than they used to be is entirely beside the point.

To get all excited about the social and human consequences of so-called successful marketing is a sort of know-nothing hysteria. It defies the facts. Are things really as bad as seems always to be implied? After all, last year more Americans attended live performances of serious music than went to professional baseball and football games combined. More books—good books—are being read per capita today than 50 years ago. Our taste in furniture is certainly superior to mid-Victorian monstrosities and the overstuffed Grand Rapids eyesores that dominated our living rooms not so long ago. Magazines like *Harper's Bazaar*, *Playboy*, *Esquire*, and *Holiday* that cater to the so-called people of means (the idle rich?) regularly publish some of the best authors writing in the English language today—people like the late Joyce Carey, Kenneth Tynan, William Sansom, A.B. Guthrie Jr., Anthony West, Sylvia Wright, Eudora Welty and others.

And as for conformity, whatever we have today, we've always had it abundantly. The abiding quality of conformity during some of history's most flowering times of creative uniqueness—whether in music, art, literature, science, or business—is illustrated in a brief passage in Aubrey Menen's wonderfully witty and serious book, "The Prevalence of Witches."

It tells about a group of Englishmen living in the mythical jungle colony of Limbo. One of the older men who'd been there since God knows when always carries a whippy stick. A new arrival, fresh from the Home Office, asks why. The answer: "Everybody who knows how to live in the jungle carries a whippy stick." "What for?" "To break the backs of snakes." "Have you ever broken the back of a snake?" "Never. Whenever I see one I run like hell. But if you're going to be accepted here you'll have to carry a whippy stick. It's like swinging a tennis racket in the suburbs of London on a Saturday afternoon. You must do the proper thing. . . ."

MATERIAL GAIN MEANS SPIRITUAL LOSS—OR DOES IT?

The quest for perfection is a nice ideal. But when individuals generalize their own notions of the beautiful and the true, when they turn into inspired spokesmen intent on making converts—then we are treading on dangerous ground, especially when the effort is sustained by the business man's great secular powers.

Who has the right to say so confidently that spiritual values (whatever they are) are so much worth having? If we invented a super tranquilizer that could be given to babies, like smallpox shots, to make them forever lead lives of spiritual contemplation and withdrawal, like St. Augustine, or even Thoreau—if we could do that, should we administer it? Would that produce the best of all possible worlds? I doubt it, as certainly St. Augustine did in his "Confessic: s." It seems to me he wrote particularly nostalgically about his carefree Manichaean days when yielding to the temptations of the flesh provided many happy hours of youthful diversion. And it is well to remember that Thoreau stayed at Walden Pond less than two years. He voluntarily returned to a world we perversely celebrate him for having rejected. . . .

SPIRITUAL VALUES FOR BOARD CHAIRMEN

Once you begin to second guess the non-material consequences of the soundly materialistic functions of business, you get involved in an endless and fruitless rhetoric. If you are at all serious about these bigger issues, they will keep you from doing the workmanlike job that your business demands. Anyone who seriously dabbles with the higher values during business hours inevitably finds that they engulf him. That is why successful operating men generally leave them alone. No wonder this is the province of the chairman of the board—the elder statesman who is tapering off and now cultivates a garden that promises a different, more elevating kind of yield.

It is true, you cannot as business man serve two masters, God and mammon. As a business man I suggest you serve business and yourself. That is your only function. Saving souls, promoting or preserving spiritual values, elevating taste, cultivating human dignity and consumer self-respect—these high-priority objectives are other people's business if that is what they want to do. The business man's job is to do the things that are the pure, undiluted objectives of business—to satisfy the materialistic and related ego objectives of those who run it. . . .

ADVERTISING AND INTENSIONAL ORIENTATION
S. I. Hayakawa

. . . The fundamental purpose of advertising—the announcing of products, prices, new inventions, or special sales—is not to be quarreled with; such announcements deliver needed information, which we are glad to get. But in national advertising directed to the consumer, the techniques of persuasion are rarely informative. . . . The main endeavor is to "poeticize" or glamorize the objects you wish to sell by giving them brand names and investing those names with all sorts of desirable affective connotations suggestive of health, wealth, popularity with the other sex, social prominence, domestic bliss, fashion, and elegance. The process is one of creating intensional orientations toward brand names:

> If you want love interest to thrive, then try this dainty way. . . . For this way is glamorous! It's feminine! It's alluring! . . . Instinctively, you prefer this costly perfume of Verona Soap. . . . It's a fragrance men love. Massage each tiny ripple of your body daily with this delicate, cleansing lather. . . . Thrill as your senses are kissed by Verona's exquisite perfume. Be radiant.

Advertisers further promote intensional habits of mind by playing on words: the "extras" of skill and strength that enable champions to win games are equated with the "extras" of quality that certain products are claimed to have; the "protective blending" that harmonizes wild animals with their environment and makes them invisible to their enemies is equated with the "protective blending" of whiskies.

There is another subtle way in which advertising promotes intensional habits: through the practice of making slogans out of commonplace facts, advertisers make the facts appear to be unique to particular products. Rosser Reeves, head of Ted Bates and Company advertising agency, cites with admiration a number of phenomenally successful campaigns using this technique—the parenthetical comments are his own: "OUR BOTTLES ARE WASHED WITH LIVE STEAM" ("His client protested that every other brewery did the same"); "IT'S TOASTED" ("So, indeed, is every other cigarette"); "GETS RID OF FILM ON TEETH" ("So, indeed, does every other toothpaste"); "STOPS HALITOSIS" ("Dozens of mouth-washes stop halitosis"); "STOPS B.O." ("All soaps stop body odor").* The skill that advertisers and propagandists often display in this kind of slanting reminds us of William Blake's famous warning:

> A truth that's told with bad intent
> Beats all the lies you can invent.

S. I. Hayakawa, "Advertising and Intensional Orientation," *Language in Thought and Action*, 2nd ed. (New York: Harcourt Brace, 1964). Hayakawa has been a linguistics professor, the president of San Francisco University, and a U.S. senator from California. *Language in Thought and Action*, first published in 1941, is a widely read book on semantics, the science of meaning.

*Rosser Reeves, *Reality in Advertising* (1961), pp. 55–57.

When advertising by verbal hypnotism succeeds in producing these intensional orientations, the act of washing with Verona Soap becomes, in our minds, a thrilling experience indeed. Brushing our teeth with Colgate toothpaste becomes a dramatic and timely warding off of terrible personal calamities, like getting fired or losing one's girl friend. The smoking of Marlboros becomes an assertion of masculinity (instead of a possible invitation to lung cancer)—making one a rugged, outdoor, he-man type, like a telephone lineman or a paratrooper—even though in actuality one may be simply a clerk at a necktie counter. The taking of unnecessary (and even dangerous) laxatives becomes "following the advice of a world-renowned Viennese specialist." We are sold daydreams with every bottle of mouthwash and delusions of grandeur with every package of breakfast food.

Advertising, then, has become in large part the art of overcoming us with pleasurable affective connotations. When the consumer demands that, as a step towards guiding himself by facts rather than by affective connotations of brand names, certain products be required by law to have informative labels and verifiable government grading, the advertising industry raises a hue-and-cry about "government interference with business." This is the sort of argument presented against grade-labeling *in spite of the fact that businessmen, both retailers and wholesalers, rely extensively on grading according to federally established standards when they do their own purchasing.*

In other words, many advertisers *prefer* that we be governed by automatic reactions to brand names rather than by thoughtful consideration of the facts about their products. An important reason for this preference lies in the mechanics of present-day retail distribution. Most of the buying of groceries, for example, is done at supermarkets, where the housewife must make choices among huge and dazzling displays of packaged merchandise, with no clerk to explain to her the advantages of one choice over another. Therefore, to use the terminology of the trade, she must be "pre-sold" *before* she gets to the market—and this is done by getting her to remember, through tireless reiteration on radio and televison commercials, a brand name, and by investing that name with nothing but pleasant connotations.

Thoughtful purchasing is the last thing many merchandisers want. Once the customer is hooked on a brand name, all sorts of tricks can be played on him (or her). A currently widespread practice is to reduce the contents of a package without reducing its size or price; many items traditionally bought in one-pound and half-pound packages now come in such sizes as 15 oz., 14½ oz., 7 oz., and 6¾ oz. These figures are usually printed in tiny letters on the package in places where they are least likely to be seen. For the unwary housewife, the costs of "brand loyalty" can be high.

Within recent years, the advertising of brand names has climbed to a higher level of abstraction. In addition to the advertising of specific products by their brand name, there is now *advertising of advertising.* As the pamphlet of the Brand Names Research Foundation urges, "So it's up to you as a salesman for a brand name to keep pushing not only YOUR BRAND, but brands in general. *Get on the Brand Wagon!*" A whisky advertisement says: "AMERICA IS NAMES . . . Seattle, Chicago, Kansas City . . . Elm Street, North Main, Times Square . . . Wrigley, Kellogg, Squibb, Ipana . . . Heinz, Calvert . . . Goodrich . . . Chevrolet. Names [the American has] always known . . . names of things he's bought and used . . . believed in. . . . Yes, America is names. *Good* names. Familiar names that inspire confidence. . . . For America *is* names . . . *good* names for good things to have. . . ." This sort of advertising of advertising has become increasingly common. The assumption is dinned into us that if a brand name even *sounds* familiar, the product it stands for must be good. ("The best in the land if you buy by brand.") *A graver example of systematic public miseducation can hardly be imagined. Intensional orientation is elevated to a guiding principle in the life of the consumer.*

Sometimes it seems as if the conflict between the aims of the advertiser and those of the educator is irreconcilable. When the teacher of home economics says, "Buy wisely," she means careful and reflective purchasing in the light of one's real needs and of accurate information about the product. When the advertiser says, "Buy wisely," he often means, "Buy our brand, regardless of your special situation or special needs, because DUZ DOES EVERYTHING!" The teacher's job is to encourage intellectual and moral self-discipline. The job of the advertiser often seems to be to encourage thoughtlessness ("impulse buying") and self-indulgence, even at the cost of life-long bondage to finance companies.

However, the writer is far from certain that the conflict between the aims of the advertiser and the educator is inevitable. It is inevitable *if* advertising cannot per-form its functions *except* through the promotion of mistaken reactions to words and other symbols. Because advertising is both so powerful and so widespread, it influences more than our choice of products; it also influences our patterns of evaluation. It can either increase or decrease the degree of sanity with which people respond to words. Thus, if advertising is informative, witty, educational, and imaginative, it can perform its necessary commercial function and contribute to our pleasure in life without making us slaves to the tyranny of affective words. If, however, products are sold largely by manipulating affective connotations—"*pin-point* carbonation," "*activated* chlorophyll," "*dualfilter* Tareytons," "contains *RD-119*," "*tired blood*"— the influence of advertising is to deepen the already grave intensional orientations widely prevalent in the public. The schizophrenic is one who attributes a greater reality to words, fantasies, daydreams, and "private worlds" than to the actualities around him. Surely it is possible for advertising to perform its functions without aggravating our all-too-prevalent verbomania! Or is it?

SHOULD ADVERTISING BE ELIMINATED?
Samm Sinclair Baker

In the light of all the flaws and fraudulent aspects of advertising, should it be eliminated? Absolutely not. In spite of its evils, advertising embodies many indispensible benefits. There are lots of bright, able admen who are concerned about the public welfare as well as their own. But there is urgent need to change today's pervading immoral approach to advertising. Preferably this regeneration should be created by admen themselves.

It is most doubtful that such self-reform will be instituted and carried through adequately by the advertising industry. The many failures in the past have proved that self-regulation is almost impossible, as the few representative samples in this book have disclosed. There are hundreds more examples left untold because of space limitations.

In the spirit of self-regulation, the Association of National Advertisers and the American Association of Advertising Agencies jointly set up the Committee for the Improvement of Advertising Content. The purpose was to seek out complaints about ads. In two years, *only ten advertisements* were found to be in bad taste by the committee.

The auto companies knew for years that their cars had safety flaws, whether or not they were actually "unsafe at any speed." They had many warnings to adopt safety devices and regulations. After long delays in needed reforms, they still didn't take unified action. The government finally had to impose laws to *force* manufacturers to incorporate minimum safety features for every car.

Is there undue stress in this book on the reprehensible practices of advertising? Why not emphasize the honest ads? Because ads, like people, *should* be honest and truthful. When ads, like people, are dishonest, they must be criticized and exposed. That, unfortunately, covers a very large percentage of advertising.

Delivering the provost's lecture at Michigan State University, Prof. John W. Crawford said: "Advertising is an instrument in the hands of the people who use it. If evil men use advertising for base purposes, then evil can result. If honest men use advertising to sell an honest product with honest enthusiasm, then positive good for our kind of capitalistic society can result."

It was not until I was away from day-to-day advertising activity for over a year that I could look at Madison Avenue objectively. Then I realized (recognizing fully my own participation in such a course for decades) that the general approach of admen is based on *the permissible lie.*

Often without being specifically conscious of it, most admen tackle the selling of goods from the viewpoint of seeking to get away with whatever they can—*to the boundary of being punished legally.* The usual belief is that this course is necessary and therefore excusable.

Samm Sinclair Baker, "Should Advertising Be Eliminated?" *The Permissible Lie: The Inside Truth About Advertising* (New York: World Publishing, 1968). Sinclair has worked in various advertising agencies as a copy writer, consultant, executive, and president.

Honest, interesting, informative advertising can be the most productive for the advertiser and agency over the long run. The benefits of advertising a good product can be enormous for all, as well as disastrous for an inferior product, as illustrated by a short short story:

Once there was a baker who baked very poor pies. Naturally he sold very few pies. He decided that he could sell more by advertising. So he placed an appealing ad in the local newspaper; he was a very able adman but an inferior baker.

Soon after he opened his shop the next morning, crowds of women attracted by the ad started pouring in for his pies. His wife was delighted. But suddenly the baker yelled, "Lock the door! Don't let in any more customers!"

When the store had been emptied, he placed a sign on the door: "Sold out of pies." His wife complained, "But we still have dozens of unsold pies."

"I know," said the baker, "but I suddenly realized that if so many people find out how bad our pies are, they'll tell their friends. *Nobody* will ever come to our shop again. We'll be ruined. Before I advertise any more, I'll have to learn how to bake better pies."

That's just one of the important benefits of advertising: It tends to raise the quality of products offered for sale. Nothing fails faster than a poor product that has been boosted by heavy advertising.

For good or evil, advertising—as noted in a *Life* editorial—is a vital part of "the engine of the American economy." It's an essential activity of our economic system. Without advertising, our superior forms of manufacturing, marketing, and distribution which contribute to producing the highest average standard of living in the world could not exist.

The Gross National Product—which is the amount paid out annually in the U.S.A. for goods and services—is about $630 billion at this writing. That's about $112 billion gain in the past three years on record, and it's climbing (expected to be $1.2 trillion in 1975). Translated into terms of human consumption, about $90 billion is now spent just on food each year. The average big supermarket offers about 7,500 different food items. In a single market there is a choice of twenty-two kinds of baked beans.

Some critics of advertising and marketing contend that twenty-two different types and labels of baked beans are too many, creating waste. Is it really too wide a choice for the thousands of families shopping in a giant supermarket? Would 220 kinds of baked beans, or 2,200 be too many brands for almost 200 million people?

It has been said that "what critics call the wastefulness of advertising is really the price that has to be paid for freedom of choice." Furthermore there *is* plenty of choice between advertised and unadvertised labels, so the advertiser is not in the driver's seat.

Some social critics, although very much concerned about material gains and comforts for themselves, attack advertising indiscriminately, failing to realize and acknowledge that it is "the showcase of business"—controlled by business. Along with the evils, the benefits of both must be considered.

It is easy to forget that advertising functions on the smallest, most fundamental terms, as well as the largest. Not every ad is on costly TV programs or full color pages in print. This little sign tacked on a factory bulletin board is an ad for safety:

"Girls, if your sweater is too large for you, look out for the machines. If you are too large for your sweater, look out for the machinists."

A simple letter can be a potent ad, such as this one: "Dear Mr. Walker. . . . In case you haven't noticed, we are busy painting at 19 Pine Lane, around the corner from you. We take great pride in our work, and want the finished job to reflect an attractive, well-kept neighborhood. While our men are at hand, we can offer you savings on a paint job that you may have planned for the near future. Why not drive over and see the work we do, then call us. Yours for a friendly handshake. . . . John Baraglia."

Mr. Walker was thinking about a paint job. He looked at Mr. Baraglia's work. He liked it. John's competitive bid won. Both of them gained through timely, honest, informative advertising.

It is fitting to have some leading practicing admen tell you of its benefits. "Art" (not Arthur) Tatham, board chairman of Tatham-Laird and Kudner Agency, said: "Advertising plays one of the most important roles in providing people with the opportunity freely to that right [freedom of choice]. The exercise of choice depends on information. Advertising provides it . . . much of the task of good advertising is to portray as clearly and intimately as possible the way the product fits into the lives of the particular people it can best serve."

In a message addressed to "bright young men and women," the American Association of Advertising Agencies stated:

> The biggest objection to advertising seems to be that it makes people want things they *really don't need* . . . such things as refrigerator-freezers, air conditioners, movie cameras, sports cars, dishwashing machines, clothes dryers, frozen foods, instant foods, vitamins, new synthetic fibers for lightweight clothing, TV sets, stereo, hi-fi, *two* automobiles, more leisure time and the equipment to enjoy it: boats, skis, fishing and hunting equipment, fast travel by jet—just to name a few.
>
> Sure . . . we could get along without most of these "unnecessary" adjuncts to modern living—and we really wouldn't miss them if we turned back the clock to the days *before you were born*. For as you may or may not realize, most of these things came into real distribution *only during your young lifetime*. And *Advertising* helped make them all possible. So, in a broad sense . . . a *good part* of the *good life* you take for granted today has been stimulated by Advertising over the past twenty years. (The italics are the advertiser's.)

Challenged on this point of "unnecessary adjuncts," an adman was asked, "What in the world, for example, would a woman want with ten new dresses?" He answered quickly, "Ten new hats."

Lord Thomson, English newspaper magnate, wrote in *The Advertising Quarterly*: "Advertising is not expendable. It is not a garnishment of business, but an essential ingredient in our economy. . . . It makes jobs; it reduces selling costs; it helps increase our standard of living. Effectively and properly used, it increases productivity and makes possible the only security a company and its labor forces can hope to have in an uncertain world."

Again note the key phrase in the foregoing: Advertising "effectively and properly used." Most of the objections to advertising are on the score of prevailing *improper* usage.

Does advertising lower prices? The cost reduction process generally operates simply in this sequence:

1. Advertising informs you of the product and its availability.
2. If you try the product and like it, you buy more and tell others about it (unless offensive advertising then sells you off the product).
3. With increased sales, production goes up, cost per unit goes down. You get the benefit usually in lower prices.

Contrary to the belief of many, the more money spent on advertising by a company as sales increase, usually the lower the ad cost per unit. With autos, for example, according to Advertising Publications, Incorporated, the five top companies—American Motors, Chrysler, Ford, General Motors, and Studebaker—in one year increased their total advertising expenditures 5.6 percent. In the same year sales climbed 8.7 percent. Ad cost per car dropped 2.8 percent.

Several dozen people were asked how much of the average $3,000 they paid for their cars was advertising expense. Their guesses ranged from $200 to $500. They were influenced by the tremendous total advertising expenditures for cars—about $250 million in advertising in one year for the top five makers alone.

They were astonished to learn that the average advertising cost for the cars they bought was under $35. Chevrolet, which spent the most—about $65 million—sold over 2.1 million cars, with an ad cost of under $30 per car. On the other hand, Studebaker, which spent about $5.5 million sold about 65,000 cars—with an ad cost of about $85 each; this high cost was subsequently an ingredient in its downfall.

Advertisers keep trying to improve products. This is not due to a sense of public service but because each competitor is trying to outperform the other.

The non-advertiser can operate this way: He sells stores his X-label peas, usually by providing a price advantage and possibly (not necessarily) reducing quality. His product quality is more likely to vary since he has no large advertising investment in X-label to protect. He can profit until customers find X-label peas unsatisfactory. He then changes the name only, offering the same product as Y-label peas. He can continue under different labels, serving different stores.

The brand advertiser can't operate this way. If his quality falters, the public stops buying it. His brand dies, and perhaps his business with it.

The retailer in some instances displays and pushes the private label (unadvertised) product because he may make an eight-cent profit on the twenty-five-cent package, compared with a five-cent profit on the advertised brand. Other retailers give best display to the advertised brand because they found that they sell ten packages at a five-cent profit for a total fifty-cent profit. In the same period of time, they sell five packages of the unadvertised label at eight-cents profit each—a total forty-cent profit—ten cents less total profit than on the advertised brand.

How much profit per package the retailer makes doesn't concern you, of course. You choose—you decide. It's so simple: You buy a can of Del Monte peaches for fifty-three cents. You see unadvertised Delbel peaches for forty-nine cents for the same size can. You try both. If you find Delbel as good as Del Monte, you'll keep buying it and saving four cents per can. Not $1 billion spent on advertising could force you to buy Del Monte against your wishes.

The advertised brand has the advantage of familiarity. Henry Slesar, head of Slesar and Kanzer agency, wrote a famous ad for McGraw-Hill magazines. It showed a stony-faced man staring coldly out at the reader. He was saying: "I don't know who you are. I don't know your company. I don't know your company's product. I don't know your company's reputation. Now—what is it you wanted to sell me?"

Advertising makes it easier for you to *sample* a product and decide for yourself. The largest single order to date in the history of the Cedar Rapids, Iowa, post office was from Quaker Oats cereal mill. It consisted of thirty-five boxcars of 5.7 million sample boxes of Cap'n Crunch pre-sweetened corn and oats cereal. The postage alone cost Quaker Oats about $180,000. People liked the samples and bought the big boxes in stores, scoring a quicker success for Quaker.

Many of the big advertised brands—Daffodil Farm Bread, Vicks Formula 44, Baggies, Yuban Instant Coffee, Kraft dressings, and thousands more—owe some of their success to free or cut-price sampling. Is this any way to run a business, spending a half million dollars and more in one shot to give away your advertised product *free*?

You bet it is—if the product is good.

But—like the baker's pies—if the product is bad, each ad dollar added will kill it quicker.

IS PUFFERY FLUMMERY?
Sid Bernstein

I am squarely, unalterably and completely in favor of puffery in advertising. And so, I've just discovered to my pleasure, is our decade-old unabridged Webster's International dictionary, which contains this definition:

> *puffery*: flattering publicity; extravagant commendation esp. for promotional purposes; *specif*: ADVERTISING.

I am not sure that I would go so far as to classify all advertising as puffery, but I certainly visualize advertising as designed to present "a rose colored vision of loveliness," rather than a cataloging of good and bad features. That is advertising's function—to make the best possible case for its sponsor's product or service. It's important that this basic function be understood by everyone—by practitioners, public, legislators, regulators. At the same time:

I am squarely, unalterably and completely opposed to false, deceptive or misleading advertising.

But I think there is a difference between deception and puffery, and that *fact* and *intent* are the really important elements. Plus the application of common sense.

In Wisconsin, no dealer can now headline an ad, "They Don't Call Us the Best Dealer for Nothing," as one did before the new code went into effect. Presumably, he is also forbidden to invite people to visit his "beautiful" showroom, or to talk to his "most courteous" sales people, or to aver that his cars come in "gorgeous" colors, or will "make you feel like a million dollars" if you buy and drive one.

Horse radish.

That's innocent puffery—and not only advertising, but every form of written and spoken communication is going to suffer if it is circumscribed.

On the other hand, it is definitely not innocent puffery if this dealer says, "Our prices are the lowest in the state," or "Nobody will give you as good a trade-in," or "$1,000 off on our brand new models."

Statements like these are subject to strict factual tests, and they should be rigidly applied. If they are true, fine; if they are untrue or only partly true or true only part of the time, zap the advertiser and zap him hard. He's not guilty of puffery; he's lying and cheating.

But let the advertiser—the company whose money is being spent—be the only one who worries seriously about whether "State Farm is all you need to know about life insurance," or "Ford has a better idea" or "The instrument of the immortals" are statements that have meaning or value in their advertising.

Most of us still have far more serious things to worry about than statements like these.

Sid Bernstein, "Is Puffery Flummery?" *Advertising Age* 2 October 1972. At the time Bernstein wrote this article, he was the president of *Advertising Age*, which bills itself as the "National Newspaper of Advertising."

PUFFERY IS DECEPTION
Ivan L. Preston

. . . Puffery deceives less than the maximum, but it still deceives materially and substantially. It implies false facts which affect purchasing decisions detrimentally for a substantial portion of the public. The fact that people don't complain about it does not prove otherwise. . . .

"Blatz is Milwaukee's finest beer" certainly deceives, . . . even though it does not deceive absolutely. No one would think that all the world, including Blatz's competitors, universally affirms that Blatz is Milwaukee's best. But consumers, while not insisting on that ultimate literal meaning, must think the claim means something! They must think it means that more people than just the Blatz owners and employees think Blatz is the best. They must think there is some specific criterion which the product meets in order to merit the claim of "finest." The truth is that Blatz has offered no such criterion, and to the best of my knowledge none exists. Therefore the belief implied by the claim of "finest" is false and deceptive to the public, and materially so because it affects purchasing decisions negatively.

"You'll meet the nicest people on a Honda," I've already conceded, is not interpreted by people as an absolute guarantee that they'll make the greatest friends they could ever hope to make—or their money back. Of course they won't think that, and as a result the advertiser may insist there's no important element of deception in the claim. But why then does the advertiser use that sort of claim? Undoubtedly it's because he thinks the consumer will be inclined to accept *some* aspect of belief about the relationship between social satisfaction and Honda ownership. If the claim doesn't work it won't be used; if it's used it must be thought to be working. And if it works it must be because the consumer believes *to some extent* that the cycle company is guaranteeing to contribute *in some way* to his social life. His belief may be vague—he may not know exactly how he thinks the cycle will contribute— but he believes for a fact that it will.

And when the consumer believes any such thing he has been materially deceived, because the cycle company is guaranteeing no such thing whatever. There is a vast difference between an ad implying "We'll put you on the road" and one implying "We'll put you into the fun." The manufacturer can give you the physical, tangible product which he can guarantee will put you on the road. He can give you nothing which will guarantee you'll get into the fun. Yet he uses the social-psychological type of misrepresentation because the consumer will treat it to some extent as something guaranteed.

An insidious aspect of this sort of claim is that the consumer may never learn the implied guarantee is phony. If he gets on the road today but doesn't get into the fun,

Ivan Preston, "Puffery Is Deception" [our title], *The Great American Blow-up: Puffery in Advertising and Selling* (Madison: University of Wisconsin Press, 1975). Preston has been a journalism professor at the University of Wisconsin and a member of the editorial board of *Journalism Quarterly*.

he figures the fun will come tomorrow. If it doesn't come tomorrow there's always another day. He never reaches the point where he knows it's not to be. Perhaps this explains why people don't complain about deception—they have to find out about it first, and the subtlety of puffery's deception helps prevent discovery. That is the magic in cosmetic advertising, which deals heavily in social guarantees yet probably plays an infinitesimal role in actual satisfactions. Cosmetics promise much, deliver nothing, and sell like hot cakes for years on end with the same customers. The public couldn't have discovered the deception if it keeps on buying like that.

Keeping the truth hidden is more critical to the cosmetics business than the motorcycle business because its sales consist of small purchases repeated frequently. If the consumer becomes disillusioned with his Honda he will already have afforded the company a good profit on an expensive item which was intended to last for quite a while. The company wouldn't have expected to make a re-sale very soon, anyway. In cosmetics, however, the initial purchase is a small matter, and profit expectations depend significantly upon a great volume of repeat purchases by the same individual. Under these conditions the falseness of the implied promise must be kept hidden through the course of its constant failures, or there will be no point in using it in the first place. The cosmetics people need that kind of concealment, and there is every reason to believe they get it.

The conclusion from such illustrations—and many more could be offered—can only be that puffery deceives the public materially and substantially and should be prohibited. If the law has not yet agreed it is probably because the regulators have not yet sufficiently adapted their thinking to encompass deception which is subtle and indirect rather than direct and absolute. The regulators are accustomed to asking what *specific* false claim is stated or implied to the consumer so that he believes it and is therefore deceived. They are accustomed to concluding that if no *specific* falsity can be definitely identified, then there is no deception in a legal sense.

In order to get action on puffery's deception, we must get the regulators out of that habit. With puffery the consumer usually does not believe some specific claim which is false, but he believes that there is *something* specific which must be true. With Blatz, for example, the consumer does not believe any precise claim about what "finest" means, but he believes it must mean something about fineness. He doesn't believe something specifically, but he specifically believes that there's something. And if in truth the term "finest" means nothing about fineness, then the implication that it means *something* should be regarded by the regulators as a specific falsity and charged as such. Admittedly it's a more vague charge than the regulator is accustomed to handling, but surely it's a sound enough criterion to work with.

Startlingly, there occurred in 1972 a solitary regulatory incident which confirms this line of thinking. The National Advertising Review Board found General Motors to be potentially deceptive in its use of a puffery claim consisting of the symbol "GM" and the phrase "Mark of Excellence" superimposed on a square resembling a small plaque. The Review Board felt the claim's use would be acceptable only if restricted to employment as a company signature or trademark in the corner of a print ad or at the end of a broadcast commercial. But using the claim as a primary part of the company's sales story would be deceptive "in view of the recent spate of recalls of cars because of defects constituting possible safety hazards."

This decision amounted to an admission that "Mark of Excellence" meant something to consumers. It was considerably different from the usual ruling about a phrase so vague. For once, the regulators did not insist on knowing precisely what it would imply, but were content with knowing something it wouldn't imply. It wouldn't imply the sloppy workmanship that has resulted in recalls; it wouldn't imply the dangers to life and limb caused by defects not recalled. Whatever "Mark of Excellence" did mean, it certainly didn't mean those things.

The decision was noteworthy because it used subtle means to interpret subtle deception. It's too bad it wasn't made by the FTC. The National Advertising Review Board is an industry self-regulating organization composed of fifty appointees from advertisers, ad agencies, and the public. Its decisions do not have the force of law and do not constitute legal precedents. Still the ruling was a step in a new direction and contributed strongly toward rejecting the idea that puffery's deception is trivial because it is not absolute.

THE LANGUAGE OF ADVERTISING CLAIMS
Jeffrey Schrank

High school students, and many teachers, are notorious believers in their im-munity to advertising. These naive inhabitants of consumerland believe that adver-tising is childish, dumb, a bunch of lies, and influences only the vast hordes of the less sophisticated. Their own purchases are made purely on the basis of value and desire, with advertising playing only a minor supporting role. They know about Vance Packard and his "hidden persuaders" and the adwriter's psychosell and bag of persuasive magic. They are not impressed.

Advertisers know better. Although few people admit to being greatly influenced by ads, surveys and sales figures show that a well-designed advertising campaign has dramatic effects. A logical conclusion is that advertising works below the level of conscious awareness and it works even on those who claim immunity to its message. Ads are designed to have an effect while being laughed at, belittled, and all but ignored.

A person unaware of advertising's claim on him or her is precisely the one most defenseless against the adwriter's attack. Advertisers delight in an audience which believes ads to be harmless nonsense, for such an audience is rendered defenseless by its belief that there is no attack taking place. The purpose of a classroom study of advertising is to raise the level of awareness about the persuasive techniques used in ads. One way to do this is to analyze ads in microscopic detail. Ads can be studied to detect their psychological hooks, they can be used to gauge values and hidden desires of the common person, they can be studied for their use of symbols, color, and imagery. But perhaps the simplest and most direct way to study ads is through an analysis of the language of the advertising claim.

The "claim" is the verbal or print part of an ad that makes some claim of superiority for the product being advertised. After studying claims, students should be able to recognize those that are misleading and accept as useful information those that are true. A few of these claims are downright lies, some are honest statements about a truly superior product, but most fit into the category of neither bold lies nor helpful consumer information. They balance on the narrow line between truth and falsehood by a careful choice of words.

The reason so many ad claims fall into this category of pseudo-information is that they are applied to parity products, products in which all or most of the brands available are nearly identical. Since no one superior product exists, advertising is used to create the illusion of superiority. The largest advertising budgets are devoted to parity products such as gasoline, cigarettes, beer and soft drinks, soaps, and various headache and cold remedies.

Jeffrey Schrank, "The Language of Advertising Claims," *Teaching About Doublespeak* (Urbana, Illinois: National Council of Teachers of English, 1976). Schrank, once a high school English teacher, is the author of *Media in Value Education: A Critical Guide* (1970) and *Understanding Mass Media* (1976). He has been the editor of *Media Mix Newsletter* since 1970.

The first rule of parity involves the Alice in Wonderlandish use of the words "better" and "best." In parity claims, "better" means "best" and "best" means "equal to." If all the brands are identical they must all be equally good, the legal minds have decided. So "best" means that the product is as good as the other superior products in its category. When Bing Crosby declares Minute Maid Orange Juice "the best there is" he means it is as good as the other orange juices you can buy.

The word "better" has been legally interpreted to be a comparative and therefore becomes a clear claim of superiority. Bing could not have said that Minute Maid is "better than any other orange juice." "Better" is a claim of superiority. The only time "better" can be used is when a product does indeed have superiority over other products in its category or when the better is used to compare the product with something other than competing brands. An orange juice could therefore claim to be "better than a vitamin pill," or even "the better breakfast drink."

The second rule of advertising claim analysis is simply that if any product is truly superior, the ad will say so very clearly and will offer some kind of convincing evidence of the superiority. If an ad hedges the least bit about a product's advantage over the competition you can strongly suspect it is not superior—maybe equal to but not better. You will never hear a gasoline company say "we will give you four miles per gallon more in your car than any other brand." They would love to make such a claim, but it would not be true. Gasoline is a parity product, and, in spite of some very clever and deceptive ads of a few years ago, no one has yet claimed one brand of gasoline better than any other brand.

To create the necessary illusion of superiority, advertisers usually resort to one or more of the following ten basic techniques. Each is common and easy to identify.

1. The Weasel Claim

A weasel word is a modifier that practically negates the claim that follows. The expression "weasel word" is aptly named after the egg-eating habits of weasels. A weasel will suck out the inside of an egg, leaving it appear intact to the casual observer. Upon examination, the egg is discovered to be hollow. Words or claims that appear substantial upon first look but disintegrate into hollow meaninglessness on analysis are weasels. Commonly used weasel words include "helps" (the champion weasel); "like" (used in a comparative sense); "virtual" or 'virtually"; "acts" or "works"; "can be"; "up to"; "as much as"; "refreshes"; "comforts"; "tackles"; "fights"; "come on"; "the feel of"; "the look of"; "looks like"; "fortified"; "enriched"; and "strengthened."

Samples of Weasel Claims

"*Helps control* dandruff *symptoms* with *regular use.*" The weasels include "helps control," and possibly even "symptoms," and "regular use." The claim is not "stops dandruff."

"Leaves dishes *virtually* spotless." We have seen so many ad claims that we have learned to tune out weasels. You are supposed to think "spotless," rather than "virtually" spotless.

"Only half the price of *many* color sets." "Many" is the weasel. The claim is
supposed to give the impression that the set is inexpensive.

"Tests confirm one mouthwash *best* against mouth odor."

"Hot Nestlés' cocoa is the very *best*." Remember the "best" and "better"
routine.

"Listerine *fights* bad breath." "Fights" not "stops."

"Lots of things have changed, but Hershey's *goodness* hasn't." This claim does
not say that Hershey's chocolate hasn't changed.

"Bacos, the crispy garnish that tastes just *like* its name."

2. The Unfinished Claim

The unfinished claim is one in which the ad claims the product is better, or has
more of something but does not finish the comparison.

Samples of Unfinished Claims

"Magnavox gives you more." More what?

"Anacin: Twice as much of the pain reliever doctors recommend most." This
claim fits in a number of categories but it does not say twice as much of
what pain reliever.

"Supergloss does it with more color, more shine, more sizzle, more!"

"Coffee-mate gives coffee more body, more flavor." Also note that "body"
and "flavor" are weasels.

"You can be sure if it's Westinghouse." Sure of what?

"Scott makes it better for you."

"Ford LTD—700% quieter."

When the FTC asked Ford to substantiate this claim, Ford revealed that they
meant the inside of the Ford was 700% quieter than the outside.

3. The "We're Different and Unique" Claim

This kind of claim states that there is nothing else quite like the product advertised. For example, if Schlitz would add pink food coloring to its beer they could say
"There's nothing like new pink Schlitz." The uniqueness claim is supposed to be
interpreted by readers as a claim to superiority.

Samples of "We're Different and Unique" Claim

"There's no other mascara like it."

"Only Doral has this unique filter system."

"Cougar is like nobody else's car."

"Either way, liquid or spray, there's nothing else like it."

"If it doesn't say Goodyear, it can't be polyglas." "Polyglas" is a trade name
copyrighted by Goodyear. Goodrich or Firestone could make a tire exactly
identical to the Goodyear one and yet couldn't call it "polyglas"—a name
for fiberglass belts.

"Only Zenith has chromacolor." Same as the "polyglas" gambit. Admiral has solarcolor and RCA has accucolor.

4. The "Water is Wet" Claim

"Water is wet" claims say something about the product that is true for any brand in that product category, (e.g., "Schrank's water is really wet.") The claim is usually a statement of fact, but not a real advantage over the competition.

Samples of "Water is Wet" Claim

"Mobil: the Detergent Gasoline." Any gasoline acts as a cleaning agent.
"Great Lash greatly increases the diameter of every lash."
"Rheingold, the natural beer." Made from grains and water as are other beers.
"SKIN smells differently on everyone." As do many perfumes.

5. The "So What" Claim

This is the kind of claim to which the careful reader will react by saying "So What?" A claim is made which is true but which gives no real advantage to the product. This is similar to the "water is wet" claim except that it claims an advantage which is not shared by most of the other brands in the product category.

Samples of the "So What" Claim

"Geritol has more than twice the iron of ordinary supplements." But is twice
    as much beneficial to the body?
"Campbell's gives you tasty pieces of chicken and not one but two chicken
    stocks." Does the presence of two stocks improve the taste?
"Strong enough for man but made for a woman." This deodorant claim says
    only that the product is aimed at the female market.

6. The Vague Claim

The vague claim is simply not clear. This category often overlaps with others. The key to the vague claim is the use of words that are colorful but meaningless, as well as the use of subjective and emotional opinions that defy verification. Most contain weasels.

Samples of the Vague Claim

"Lips have never looked so luscious." Can you imagine trying to either prove
    or disprove such a claim?
"Lipsavers are fun—they taste good, smell good and feel good."
"Its deep rich lather makes hair feel good again."
"For skin like peaches and cream."
"The end of meatloaf boredom."
"Take a bite and you'll think you're eating on the Champs Elysées."
"Winston tastes good like a cigarette should."

"The perfect little portable for all around viewing with all the features of higher priced sets."

"Fleishman's makes sensible eating delicious."

7. The Endorsement or Testimonial

A celebrity or authority appears in an ad to lend his or her stellar qualities to the product. Sometimes the people will actually claim to use the product, but very often they don't. There are agencies surviving on providing products with testimonials.

Samples of Endorsements or Testimonials

"Joan Fontaine throws a shot-in-the-dark party and her friends learn a thing or two."

"Darling, have you discovered Masterpiece? The most exciting men I know are smoking it." (Eva Gabor)

"Vega is the best handling car in the U.S." This claim was challenged by the FTC, but GM answered that the claim is only a direct quote from *Road and Track* magazine.

8. The Scientific or Statistical Claim

This kind of ad uses some sort of scientific proof or experiment, very specific numbers, or an impressive sounding mystery ingredient.

Samples of Scientific or Statistical Claims

"Wonder Bread helps build strong bodies 12 ways." Even the weasel "helps" did not prevent the FTC from demanding this ad be withdrawn. But note that the use of the number 12 makes the claim far more believable than if it were taken out.

"Easy-Off has 33% more cleaning power than another popular brand." "Another popular brand" often translates as some other kind of oven cleaner sold somewhere. Also the claim does not say Easy-Off works 33% better.

"Special Morning—33% more nutrition." Also an unfinished claim.

"Certs contains a sparkling drop of Retsyn."

"ESSO with HTA."

"Sinarest. Created by a research scientist who actually gets sinus headaches."

9. The "Compliment the Consumer" Claim

This kind of claim butters up the consumer by some form of flattery.

Samples of "Compliment the Consumer" Claim

"We think a cigar smoker is someone special."

"If what you do is right for you, no matter what others do, then RC Cola is right for you."

"You pride yourself on your good home cooking. . . ."

"The lady has taste."
"You've come a long way, baby."

10. The Rhetorical Question

This technique demands a response from the audience. A question is asked and the viewer or listener is supposed to answer in such a way as to affirm the product's goodness.

Samples of the Rhetorical Questions

"Plymouth—isn't that the kind of car America wants?"
"Shouldn't your family be drinking Hawaiian Punch?"
"What do you want most from coffee? That's what you get most from Hills."
"Touch of Sweden: could your hands use a small miracle?"

THE LANGUAGE OF ADVERTISING
Charles A. O'Neill

Some critics and observers view today's advertising industry as something akin to a cranky, unplanned-for child of the American free-enterprise system; a noisy, whining, brash child who must somehow be kept in line, but who can't just yet be cast out of the house.

For every critic who would like to see the advertising industry thrown completely out of business, it seems there are at least a dozen who accept the need for advertising—accept the theory of it—but find its *language* hard to take. Because advertising language mirrors the fears, quirks, and aspirations of the society that creates it (and that, in turn, is sold by it), it is open to parody and ridicule. Who is to be "blamed" for the success of a nonsensical, nonfunctional product like "Pet Rocks"? The people who write the advertisements or design the packaging, or the people who buy it? Many blame the advertiser, the messenger.

Perhaps the strongest, most authoritative critic of advertising language in recent years is Edwin Newman, the journalist who wrote *Strictly Speaking*. In the introduction to his book, he poses the question, "Will America be the death of English?" Newman does not consider the question to be even remotely rhetorical, for his "mature, well-thought-out judgement" is that it *will.* As evidence, he cites a number of examples of fuzzy thinking and careless use of the King's English by people in public life, including politicians, journalists, and government officials. If he has any affection for the language of advertising, he is holding any mention of it for another book:

> The federal government adopted the comic strip character Snoopy as a symbol and showed us Snoopy on top of his doghouse, flat on his back, with a balloon coming out of his mouth, containing the words, "I believe in conserving energy," while below there was this exhortation: savEnergy.
>
> savEnergy. An entire letter e at the end of save was savd. In addition, an entire space was savd. Perhaps the government should say onlYou can prevent forest fires. . . . Spelling has been assaulted by Duz, E-Z Off, Fantastik, Kool, Kleen . . . and by products that make you briter, so that you will not be left hi and dri at a parti, but made welkom. . . . Under this pressure . . . adjectives become adverbs; nouns become adjectives; prepositions disappear; compounds abound.

In this passage, Newman presents three of the charges most often levied against the language of advertising.

1. Advertising debases English.
2. Advertising downgrades the intelligence of the public.

Charles A. O'Neill, "The Language of Advertising," *Exploring Language*, ed. Gary Goshgarian (Boston: Little Brown, 1977). O'Neill has worked as an advertising copy writer. He is currently with Putnam Investments.

3. Advertising warps our vision of reality, implanting in us groundless fears and insecurities. (He cites, as examples of these groundless fears, "tattle-tale grey," "denture breath," "morning mouth," "unsightly bulge," and "ring around the collar.")

Other charges have been made from time to time. They include:

1. Advertising sells daydreams; distracting, purposeless visions of lifestyles beyond the reach of most of the people who are exposed most often to advertising.
2. Advertising feeds upon human weaknesses, exaggerates the importance of material things, encouraging "impure" emotions and vanities.
3. Advertising encourages bad, even unhealthy, habits like smoking and drinking alcoholic beverages.

Some critics do not find fault so much in the language of advertising as in the public, for accepting it so readily. S.I. Hayakawa, for example, finds "The uncritical response to the incantations of advertising . . . a serious symptom of widespread evaluational disorder." He does not find it "beyond the bounds of possibility" that "today's suckers for national advertising will be tomorrow's suckers for the master political propagandist who will, by playing up the 'Jewish Menace,' in the same way as national advertisers play up the 'pink toothbrush menace,' and by promising us national glory and prosperity in the same way as national advertisers promise us personal glory and prosperity, sell fascism in America."

To evaluate this criticism properly, it should be weighed against some of the things that can be said *for* advertising as it is practiced today:

1. Advertising language is only a reflection of the language of the society around it; slaying the messenger would not alter the fact—if it *is* a fact—that America will be the death of English. Similarly, a case can be made for advertising as an acceptable stimulus for the natural evolution of the language. Is "proper English" the English we speak and write, or is it the language we *think we should* speak and write—the language of The Elements of Style or the usage of the Oxford English Dictionary?

2. Advertising attempts to convince us to buy products; however, we are not *forced* to buy something just because it is heavily advertised. In fact, the evidence is that if a product is not advertised, most people will not buy it even if it costs significantly less than its competitors. For example, The Witco Chemical Company attempted to market Active detergent without advertising, hoping that a 20¢/box price advantage, good point-of-sale displays, and word-of-mouth recognition would stimulate sales. However, consumers bypassed Active, buying the heavily advertised "name" brands instead.

3. Advertising stimulates product development, thus helping people to lead more comfortable lives.

4. Advertising carries information to people, helping them to make intelligent purchasing decisions.

As individual consumers and observers, we have to evaluate both sides of the argument. Or perhaps we *don't* have to evaluate both sides of the argument, because advertising is likely to continue to influence us regardless of what we, as individuals, think. The unplanned-for child may be brash; his language may be sloppy, crude, and simplistic; we may resent the power he holds over us. He may even offend us by carelessly tossing out the rules of grammar we have had drummed into our heads. But American companies continue to spend vast amounts of money to keep him going: from about three billion dollars in 1944, total expenditures in advertising climbed to 100 billion dollars in 1986.

It is also certain that whatever we think of the language of advertising, it will continue to have a profound influence on our lives. As research and development groups continue to develop subtler variations in product lines, and as advertising professionals continue to polish their engineering skills, the language of advertising will become ever more powerful.

Speaking one day on a New York City radio station, philosopher Rollo May told his listeners that a line from a Nice 'n Easy ad ("If I've only one life, let me live it as a blonde!") was "the ultimate existential statement." When Shirley Polykoff wrote that line, was she attempting to create an "existential statement"? No, she was simply trying to sell us something. And in that effort she succeeded mightily.

MYTHS ABOUT ADVERTISING
John Crichton

. . . In recent years various occult powers have been imputed to advertising. These are deeply-held concerns about "subliminal" advertising, or "motivational research." The first suggests that advertising can be successful by operating beneath the ordinary level of comprehension; the second suggests that systematic exploration of the psyche can produce advertising which successfully manipulates people because it is directed toward their most susceptible areas of mind and personality.

Alas for the fable! The human mind is remarkable, and eye and memory can be trained to receive and retain and identify messages or objects flicked on for a split-second. The aircraft identification techniques of World War II are a good example. There is no recorded research which testifies in any respect to the successful use of subliminal advertising in selling. It remains in fact one of those hideous nonsense notions which haunt our fear-filled society.

The motivation research story is more complex. Research will reveal that products, services, and institutions have a personality. Their users and non-users have opinions about the products, sometimes from experience, sometimes from conversations with other users (particularly family and friends); there are publications specializing in analysis of products and their performance, like *Consumer Reports*; some magazines and newspapers have analytical columns which test and review new products.

In short, experience with and opinions about products may be formed from many influences other than advertising.

It is, however, a marketing axiom that people buy satisfactions, not products. As Professor Levitt of the Harvard Business School has said, people don't buy quarter-inch drills, they buy quarter-inch holes. By extension, they don't buy soap, they buy cleanliness; they buy not clothing, but appearance. It is both efficient and ethical to study the public's perception of a product, and to try to alter or to reinforce it, and it may frequently lead to product reformulation or improvement in order to effect the desired change in attitude, buying, and satisfaction leading to repurchase.

There remain three areas which are usually items of vehement discussion with regard to advertising, and its morals and ethics.

The first is *advocacy*. Advertising always advocates. It pleads its case in the strongest and most persuasive terms. It is neither objective nor neutral. It makes its case, as dramatically as possible, with the benefit of words, pictures, and music. It asks for attention, absorption, conviction, and action.

This disturbs critics, who feel that advertising ought to be objective, informative, and dispassionate. They wish advertising not to be persuasive, but informative. Their model for advertising is the specification sheet, and they have to some degree

John Crichton, "Myths about Advertising," *Ethics, Morality, and the Media*, ed. Lee Thayer (New York: Hastings House, 1980). Crichton is the past president of the American Association of Advertising Agencies.

confused *advertising*, which must interest large numbers of people, with *labeling*, which is for the instruction of the individual purchaser, and performs a much different function.

If morals and ethics stem from public attitudes, it may be interesting that the public both perceives and appreciates the advocacy of advertising. It understands clearly that "they are trying to sell me something," and their attitude is appropriately intent and skeptical. Typically they are well-informed about the product and its competitors. It is a useful attitude in a democracy.

Research tells us that the public is both interested in and derisive about advertising. It is interested in the products which are being sold. It finds elements of the selling process entertaining. The public is, however, quickly bored and inattentive when the products or the way they are sold are unattractive to them.

The second problem area is *accuracy*, used here instead of "truth" because its elements are somewhat easier to define. Most advertising people believe advertising should be accurate; that is, they believe the product should not be sold as something it is not, nor should promises be made for its performance which it cannot fulfill.

In general, advertising's accuracy is good. The dress one sees advertised in the newspaper is available in the sizes and colors listed, and at the price advertised. The headache remedy will alleviate headache pain. It could hardly have been on the market for five decades if it did not. The orange juice looks and tastes like fresh orange juice. The instant coffee cannot be distinguished in blindfold tests from ground coffee which has been percolated. The anti-perspirant reduces perspiration.

Beyond accuracy, the question is often one of perception. It is true that the dress in the advertisement is available in the sizes, colors and price advertised—but will the dress make the purchaser look like the slim young woman in the ad? Answer, only if the purchaser looks like her already. There is no magic in advertising, and no magic in most products. The satisfaction with that dress cannot be literal, and most research suggests that in the public mind no such literal translation exists. It is not expected that the purchase of the dress will make the purchaser look like the person in the ad.

And while frozen orange juice may look and taste like fresh orange juice, it will not have the pulpy texture of freshly-squeezed juice, and therefore to many people will never be its equivalent. Therefore the purchaser must decide whether the texture means enough to him to squeeze the oranges. But the accuracy is not the question, it is the extended perception of what the words mean, so that accuracy becomes equivalency.

The third area is *acquisitiveness*. It is felt by many critics that advertising is a symbol of the preoccupation of our society with material things, and that preoccupation preempts the most important spiritual values. It is felt by critics that the steady drum-fire of advertising and advertising claims, the constant parade of products and services, serve to bewitch and beguile the viewer and reader, who gradually is corrupted into being either a hedonist or a consumptionist.

Of this criticism, two things should be said. The first is that the more material a society has, the greater its support for matters and institutions of the mind and spirit. It is the affluent societies of history to which one must look for the art, architecture, music, universities, hospitals, and cathedrals.

The second is that man is acquisitive. Plato again, as the Athenian speaks: "Why, Clinias my friend, 'tis but a small section of mankind, a few of exceptional natural parts disciplined by consummate training, who have the resolution to prove true to moderation when they find themselves in the full current of demands and desires; there are not many of us who remain sober when they have the opportunity to grow wealthy, or prefer measure to abundance. The great multitude of men are of a clean contrary temper: what they desire they desire out of all measure; when they have the option of making a reasonable profit, they prefer to make an exorbitant one. . . ."

It is difficult to imagine that without advertising one would have an elevated society, one in which acquisitiveness had gradually disappeared. What one knows about such diverse tribes as the Cheyennes and the Kwakiutl of the Northwest is that both took individual wealth seriously, whether in stolen horses or in gifts to be given ostentatiously in a Potlatch. Acquisitiveness is innate, as Plato suggested; what advertising does is to channel it.

Daniel Bell, in "The Cultural Contradictions of Capitalism," argues that advertising is a sociological innovation, pervasive, the mark of material goods, the exemplar of new styles of life, the herald of new values. It emphasizes glamour, and appearance. While Bell concedes that a society in the process of quick change requires a mediating influence, and that advertising performs that role, he also sees that "selling became the most striking activity of contemporary America. Against frugality, selling emphasized prodigality; against asceticism, the lavish display." It is his judgment that "the seduction of the consumer had become total," and he believes that with the abandonment of Puritanism and the Protestant Ethic, capitalism has no moral or transcendental ethic, and he points to the conflict between the workaday habits which require hard work, career orientation, and delayed gratification, and the private life in which (in products and in advertisements) the corporation promotes pleasure, instant joy, relaxing, and letting go. "Straight by day," and a "swinger by night," in Bell's capsule summary.

But Bell also sees "in Aristotle's terms, *wants* replace *needs*—and wants, by their nature, are unlimited and insatiable."

Probably no more haunting problem exists for society than motivating people. The system of motivation and rewards within a society is critical to the kind of society it will ultimately be, and to the welfare and happiness of the people in it. The drive for material goods which characterizes most Western societies may be less admirable than a different kind of reward and motivation set of goals. The fact is that the system works, and that it does both motivate and reward people. If it appears to critics that the motivations are inferior, and that the rewards are vulgar, it must be remembered that at least the people have their own choice of what those rewards will be, and observation tells us that they spend their money quite differently. It is essentially a democratic system, and the freedom of individual choice makes it valuable to the people who do the choosing. One man's color television set is another man's hi-fidelity system; one man's summer cottage is another man's boat; and one man's succession of glittering automobiles is another man's expensive education of his children. In each case, the choice of the distribution of rewards is individual.

THE DOUR CRITICS OF ADVERTISING
Harold Edwards

With women clinging to his waist like defensive linemen, Joe Namath grins, holds up a bottle of Brut, and says something like, "Girls love the smell of Brut."

Pretty harmless nonsense, isn't it? Or were you taken in? Did your unconscious rise up and whisper to you, "Henry, Henry, if you buy Brut, you too will have diaphanously-dressed women clinging to your waist"? Were you seduced so thoroughly by the ad that you were *forced* to buy a bottle of Brut?

A number of critics of advertising believe that we *are* too weak to resist the appeals of the adman. Jeffrey Schrank, writing for the National Council of Teachers of English, claims that "Advertisers delight in an audience which believes ads to be harmless nonsense, for such an audience is rendered defenseless by its belief that there is no attack taking place."

"Rendered defenseless." Hmm. What a high opinion of the power of advertising. And what a low opinion of mankind. In fact, a patronizing attitude is never far below the surface of the arguments of those who scorn advertising.

They, the aristocrats of reason and clear thinking, can of course see through the manipulative use of advertising language. We, the confused and irresponsible peasants, need to be protected. For our own good, of course. Always for our own good. *Noblesse oblige*, you know. In fact, some of the critics think we're so defenseless that they want the Federal Trade Commission, acting as our big brother, to step up their interventions so that we'll be protected against the sweet nothings that advertisers whisper into our ears.

Of course the language of advertising works on our unconscious desires and fears. So does all language. *Of course* adwriters manipulate language to influence people. So do all people who use language—from government politicians to newspaper columnists. And so do essayists who want to persuade us that the language of advertising is unfair.

At least the motives of advertisers are out in the open. The copywriters for KreamyKurds Soap may imply in their ads that after lathering with their soap, you'll be accosted by strangers on the street who will beg to touch your lovely skin. Some of us may indeed buy a soap dream instead of a soap bar. However, while the language of a soap advertisement may be rhetorically suspicious, the motives of soap sellers are as clear and as pure as a soap bubble: They want to sell soap. We may not always be able to discern the motives of politicians, educators, and newspaper columnists, but no one above the age of five was ever fooled by the motive of a soap company.

The art of persuasion—for that is what the language of advertising really is—goes back at least to the Greeks, who called it rhetoric and made a science out of it.

Harold Edwards, "The Dour Critics of Advertising." This essay appears here for the first time, by permission of the author.

I'm sure that Greek sandal salesmen, after picking up some rhetorical hints from a streetcorner lecture by a famous rhetorician, ran out and shouted in the market-place: "Comfiest shoe in Heathendom! Plato wears 'em!"

Lawyers try to wipe off the fuzziness from language, to make it logical, cold, and unambiguous. Now the critics of advertising want to do the same to the language of advertising.

They would have advertisers make their ads as grey and as unappetizing as a legal document or a page full of bureaucratic prose. Joseph Seldin ("The Language of Advertising") even objects to the "unrelieved cheerfulness" of ads. Apparently he would prefer that the models scowl occasionally—you know, just like people do in real life. People don't smile in real life, do they? Well of course not. Then they shouldn't smile in ads, either.

In fact, the critics of advertising seem to lack a sense of humor. They don't laugh. They get into snits. They take every ad seriously, even when humor and exaggeration are obviously at work. When Joe Namath gets up to sell Brut, those clinging women drinking in his every word, the dour critics can only see a celebrity hawking perfume. Offended because the ad fails to appeal to their Reason and Intellect, the critics pounce, "Ah hah! EMOTIONAL APPEAL #3: CELEBRITY TESTIMONIAL."

Lacking a sense of humor, the critics solemnly construct their long lists of FALSE CLAIMS AND EMOTIONAL APPEALS, where we are told that advertisements not only hoodwink us with testimonials of famous people, but they fool us with weasel words, swindle us with glittering generalities, and cozen us with incomplete comparatives.

One critic of advertising warns us, in MISLEADING TECHNIQUE #6: THE VAGUE CLAIM, that we ought to watch out for these devious uses of language:

> Fleishman's makes sensible eating delicious.
> For skin like peaches and cream.
> Take a bite and you'll think you're eating on the Champs Elysees.
> The end of meatloaf boredom.

Oh my goodness, Hamburger Helper claims that its product is the end of meatloaf boredom. Let's call in the FTC and the NAB to stamp out these outbreaks of advertising nonsense, these assaults on our logic and good sense.

Let's suppose that the critics had their way and that the ad writers for Hamburger Helper were obligated to be more specific about their claim that their product is the end of meatloaf boredom.

They would no doubt begin by calling in a few lawyers to help them write a two or three paragraph definition of "meatloaf boredom." Then they might send out a questionnaire, along with their newly created precise definition, to those who have bought their product. "Was Hamburger Helper," they might ask, "the end of meat-loaf boredom *for you?*" If enough people answered "yes," they could claim in their ads—now strewn with qualifications and precise legal definitions—that Hamburger Helper is "the end of meatloaf boredom."

I suspect, however, that even that kind of dreary ad wouldn't satisfy the critics of advertising. Indeed, after reading a number of these attacks on the advertising industry, I began to get the distinct impression that their hostility toward advertising goes deeper than their dislike of its language—that it really stems from their dislike of the free marketplace. To the critics of advertising, to try to make a profit is, well, not quite a reputable motive.

At any rate, they hold the language of advertising to a standard that doesn't exist anywhere else in our society outside of a legal contract.

Linguists nowadays tell us that language change is not only inevitable, but usually a good thing. Change, they say, refreshes the language. Yet when advertisers use neologisms—or even usages that reflect current usage—we are told that they are wrecking the language. In *Strictly Speaking*, for instance, Edwin Newman fusses (ironically and superciliously, of course) about the "assaults" on our language when products like E-Z Off, Arrid, and Fantastick cleaner use unorthodox spelling. And Winston has caused the critics intense pain over the years with the claim that their cigarettes "taste good like a cigarette should."

When a careful essayist qualifies his statements, we are told he is being logical. When advertisers qualify their statements, we are told that they are using "weasel" words. To the critics of advertising, a rose by another name doesn't smell as sweet. Jeffrey Shrank, for instance, calls it "weaseling" (rather than "qualifying") when an advertiser says that his product "*helps* control dandruff" (Actually, it's rather difficult to see what alternative the advertiser had. If he had said instead that his product "*controls* dandruff," Shrank and his fellow nitpickers would have jumped up to holler, "FALSE CLAIM!")

When we agree with the emotionally-loaded words of a speaker at a dinner, a politician on the stump, a crusading columnist, we admire his command of the resources of the language, his "rhetoric." When advertisers use those same emotionally-loaded words, the critics say that they are being unfair by seducing our unconscious. (I remember a wine company—I've forgotten the brand—that described its wine as being "as pure as the tear that falls on a sister's grave.")

Of course advertisers use the resources of language and rhetoric to persuade us to buy their products. Ads are full of weasel words, nonce words, vague words, celebrity's words, humorous words, and sometimes outrageously exaggerated words. (Look at those great ads for breast enlargement creams in the back pages of the *National Enquirer*.)

Anyone with a sense of humor or a sense of the absurd ought to sit back and enjoy the color and noise—and the occasional absurdity—of the "literature of commerce." (D.H. Lawrence once wrote that "some of the cunningest American literature is to be found in advertisements of soap suds.")

It's probably no coincidence that some of the harshest criticism of the language of advertising comes from members of the educational establishment, who are insulated against the noise—and the risks—of the marketplace. Indeed, one of the most persistent critics is the National Council of Teachers of English. From their lofty position above the hurly-burly, the Council members look down contemptuously on the dirty little business of buying and selling.

Down below, the language of advertising, like the free market itself, is noisy, impudent, and independent. And the critics don't like it. They want the FTC to intervene even more forcefully than they do now to curtail some of this noisy advertising.

To grant the FTC the power to ban advertising puffery would lead to an unworkable tangle of laws, and it would fatten the swarms of lawyers who think their job is to protect us against ourselves. Surely we don't need lawyers who spend their time defending us against misleading metaphors and pernicious personifications. Do things *really* go better with Coke? Is Schlitz *really* the king of beers? Are we *really* flying friendly skies when we fly United?

We ought to worry about the tendency to turn governmental agencies into language police. Once we get into the habit of denying First Amendment rights to advertisers, we are less likely to hesitate the next time we find that people are using language in ways that we don't like.

Aldous Huxley, whose *Brave New World* is a warning against the tendencies of governments to restrict freedom, enjoyed the language of advertising—and its freedom. In fact, he saw a connection between the language of advertising and a free society. "The art of advertisement writing," he wrote "has flowered with democracy. The lords of industry and commerce came gradually to understand that the right way to appeal to the Free Peoples of the World was familiarly, in an honest man-to-man style."

To insist that the language of advertising is unfair and that we need to be protected from it is pure nonsense.

ADVERTISING AS AGITPROP: PUNCTURING THE MYTHS ABOUT HYPE
Robert L. Heilbroner

"Advertising," says Michael Schudson in the most interesting book I have ever read on the subject, is "capitalist realism." The phrase captures the very essence of what he calls "the uneasy persuasion" at the heart of the occupation. Socialist realism is, of course, the poster art of authoritarian socialism, the state-sanctioned aesthetic of the Soviet Union. It depicts strong, kindly, and terribly dedicated men and women driving tractors, exuding heroism, or simply affirming the joy of life for the edification of ordinary people who need to be reminded of what the socialist fatherland means to them. Advertising, in Schudson's brilliant metaphor, is the equivalent art of capitalism—not at all authoritarian in its origins, but also serving a fundamentally political purpose by depicting men and women who embody the virtues of their fatherland as they drive cars, exude allure, snuggle into designer jeans, or experience the pleasures of helpful banks and welcoming airlines.

The idea of advertising as the poster art of capitalism is useful because it puts into intellectual perspective a cultural phenomenon that is, as they say, hard to relate to. Many years ago I wrote a lighthearted piece in *Harper's* in praise of commercial prose. I am not so lighthearted about the effects of advertising as I was then, but I still enjoy the sheer craft of it. Far better than the soggy dramas of TV serials are those dramalets of misplaced American Express traveler's checks—thirty seconds of heart-stopping near disaster followed by floods of relief: "Never mind, M'sieur. At ze next stop . . ." On the other hand, advertising can be the embodiment of vulgarity, manipulation, and cynicism. I can think of no punishment adequate to its crimes other than to condemn its perpetrators forever to watch suffering housewives being advised by their druggists, butchers, and friends (imagine having such friends!) on the virtues of aspirins, liverwursts, and waxes. I believe Dante would have nodded approval.

In the face of such desecrations it is hard to maintain one's critical sang-froid, and I am not certain one *should* maintain it. In 1976, in *Business Civilization in Decline*, I wrote that advertising was the "single most value-destroying activity of a business civilization," words Schudson finds "troubling" although "overblown." I shall come back to the question of how advertising influences our values. But admittedly any serious consideration of the subject must go beyond the indignation advertising arouses, and Schudson's book manages to put the whole problem in a detached, although critical, framework. He begins by making us understand the difficulties faced by the "persuasion"—a word that nicely sidesteps the term "profession," which this unlicensed occupation likes to claim for itself. There are some 28,000 nationally advertised branded products for sale in the United States, a

Robert L. Heilbroner," Advertising as Agitprop: Puncturing the Myths About Hype," *Harper's* January 1985. Heilbroner, a practicing economist in government and business, has been a professor at the New School of Social Research. He has written numerous economics works, including *The Worldly Philosophers* (1953) and *Marxism; For and Against* (1980).

number that may take on added meaning when we recall that only some 3,000 stars are visible to the eye on a clear night. The advertiser's task is to make one of these stars stand out from the others, but since every star has its own advertising campaign, the overall effect is only to make the whole sky a little more luminous.

The uncountable advertising campaigns going on simultaneously make us inescapably aware of advertising, but virtually immune to any given advertisement. A study cited by Stephen Fox in *The Mirror Makers* claims that the average family is "exposed" to 1,600 ads each day. Of course, not all of them are TV commercials; according to the 1984 edition of the *Statistical Abstract of the United States*, the largest single chunk of the $67 billion of advertising expenditures in 1982—27 percent—went for newspaper ads. About 6 percent went for magazine ads, a little more went into radio, 20 percent was spent on "miscellaneous" items (such things as matchbook covers), and only about 21 percent went for TV ads. Just the same, it is as if more than half the stars in the sky entered our field of vision in the course of an ordinary day.

We are protected from this potentially lethal radiation—imagine actually noticing or thinking about 1,600 "messages" a day—by a thick mantle of inattention and indifference. Only eighty of the stars, the association's study goes on to say, are noted, and a mere twelve provoke a "reaction." These numbers seem to indicate that eighty times a day we, or someone in our family, smile or wince, perhaps   ﹡
unknowingly, and that a dozen times a day we experience some kind of genuine contact—we decide to see a given movie or to take advantage of the A&P special or to think about the card on the subway that promises "If U Cn Rd Ths U Cn . . ." These figures prompt the first faint stirrings of sympathy. They help us understand the prevailing mood of the persuasion, which is not one of gloating triumph but one of perplexity and frustration. Schudson cites a 1963 newspaper survey—somewhat suspect, of course, because newspapers have their interests to protect—that found only 23 percent of TV watchers could identify the product in the last commercial they had "seen." And a 1981 study showed that only 7 percent of TV viewers were able to name the last product that had been pitched at them.

So the advertising man's or woman's life is a hard one, made still harder by the reputation from which the persuasion suffers. A survey of 11,000 high school students in 1958—admittedly, another time, another ethos—placed advertising and public relations eighteenth on a list of twenty occupations, and in 1976 a Gallup poll put advertising and PR at the bottom of eleven fields of work, below "business executives," "senators," "congressmen," and, indignity of indignities, "labor leaders." In the face of the intrinsic difficulties of its task and the assaults on its reputation, it is not surprising that the persuasion is touchy about its image and—despite its treatment of people as exploitable objects—near idolatrous in its glorification of that abstraction, the consumer. "Advertising workers sound almost saintly when discussing the consumer, compared to what one can hear when physicians talk about patients, or, for that matter, when university professors talk about students," says Schudson, who is himself a professor at the University of California at San Diego.

The self-doubt of members of the persuasion is exacerbated by the fact that for all their efforts—indeed, because of the self-annulling consequences of those very efforts—consumers don't "believe" advertising any more than they "trust" advertisers. The coefficient of disbelief varies with the medium and the message: few readers would look for a gimmick in an advertisement featuring airline schedules, but few would fail to look for the fine print in an ad announcing New Low-Price Fares. According to the Newspaper Advertising Bureau, only 39 percent of viewers regard TV ads as "believable," compared with 68 percent for newspaper ads. It is not so much that people think they are being hoodwinked or deliberately deceived (although there have been some delicious cases of that, the most publicized being the addition of marbles to Campbell's soup to make it look chunkier in advertisements); it's just that consumers know that the absence of misrepresentation is not the same as the presence of full representation, and that "the truth" is not the same as the truth.

The impression one gets, both from Schudson's analytic study and from Fox's more straightforward history of the industry and its heroes, is that most advertising serves a defensive function and that relatively little of it can boast of unqualified success. Advertising is a kind of trench warfare in which few victories are won, but many defeats are staved off. If all sellers of automobiles canceled their TV ads, it is doubtful that auto sales as a whole would fall (cigarette sales were not affected by the ban on TV ads) and unclear whether the ranking of the top companies would change. On the other hand, if any single seller left his particular salient unguarded, his territory might well be lost by the encroachment of his competitors. So advertising persists, mainly to enable sellers to patrol their own turf. Yet there is always the hope that an ad will open a great hole, like an artillery barrage. *When Advertising Tried Harder* is a collection of such presumably successful ads, some of which are indeed arresting. As the title suggests, there is the Avis series, the wonderful "You don't have to be Jewish to love Levy's real Jewish rye" campaign, and the hiss of the Schweppes effervescence. Many of these ads are brilliant in their use of photos and copy; my favorite shows a Wolfschmidt's vodka bottle next to a tomato. The bottle says, "You're some tomato. We could make beautiful Bloody Marys together. I'm different from those other fellows," and the tomato answers, "I like you, Wolfschmidt. You've got taste."

Did these ads in fact punch great holes in the defenses of their competitors? That is harder to show than it is to demonstrate their brilliance. Perhaps the most widely admired and frequently mentioned example is Volkswagen's first ad campaign in the United States, launched in 1959—naked pictures of The Bug, with captions such as "Think Small" and witty copy: "It doesn't go in one year and out the other." As Fox says, "For years [these ads] exercised incalculable power over the collective unconscious of the business. In 1976 *Ad Age* asked a panel of industry professionals to name the best ads they had ever seen: Volkswagen was listed by sixty of the ninety-seven replies."

What Fox does not mention, however, is the curiously self-admiring nature of this critical "success." As art, as copy, and as a draft of cool air in a stultifying atmosphere, the Doyle Dane Bernbach ads were remarkable. But did they sell cars? Schudson notes that VW was off to a terrific start *before* the campaign got under way. His point is certainly not to denigrate the VW campaign but to emphasize that advertising is not all of selling, by a long shot. The merchandising of a product—

designing and packaging and distributing and servicing it—probably far outweighs the effects of the propaganda that will ultimately be launched on its behalf. Pepsi-Cola, for example, edged out Coca-Cola in supermarket sales because Pepsi pioneered changes in bottling and store displays. While Coke won TV viewers' hearts, Pepsi got their shopping carts.

Techniques aside, the nature of consumers' "wants" remains amorphous, ambiguous, labile, and maddeningly elusive. We do not clearly understand why consumers latch on to products in the first place or what makes them try other products in the second place. It is reassuring, for anyone who can imagine the anxiety of a world of continuous hairline decision-making, that inertia and routine rule the day in the advertising business, and the failure rate of ad campaigns is much, much greater than the success rate: the Gillette Company never could make the public buy Lady Gillette; Procter & Gamble couldn't sell Pringle's, the stackable potato chip; and the John B. Stetson Company and the Hat Corporation of America seem to have hired the King Canute Agency in their efforts to sweep back the tide of hatlessness.

The same difficulties pervade the field of political advertising, lately a subject of increasing concern but—if Edwin Diamond and Stephen Bates, authors of *The Spot*, are correct—of exaggerated importance. For just as the worries of the "advertising can sell us anything" school are easily revealed as unjustified, so the idea that any candidate can be "sold" seems very far from reality. Expensive and extensive television spots can make us familiar with a person and his or her persona—a recent example is Lew Lehrman, the unknown who nearly won the 1982 New York gubernatorial race against Mario Cuomo. But familiarity is a necessary, not a sufficient, condition for victory. The power of television has certainly altered the qualities that make for political success, but it is *television*—television news, televised debates—not *advertising* on television, that has made the difference. Roger Ailes, the media consultant who "packaged" Nixon in 1968, announced on the eve of Nixon's victory that television advertising of political candidates was "the beginning of a whole new concept. This is it. This is the way they'll be elected forevermore." But in 1983 the same Roger Ailes concluded that "the TV public is very smart in the sense that somewhere, somehow, they make a judgment about the candidates they see. Anybody who claims he can figure out that process is full of it."

So when we examine advertising—political or commercial—from the other side of the camera, we come to the curious conclusion that far from being able to sell everything, advertising can't sell anything. There are exceptions—Listerine probably owed its success to the idea of selling it as a cure for "halitosis." But the fact remains that our shelves are not crammed with every conceivable item but are stocked with the coffees, toothpastes, and aspirins that are part of our daily patterns of life. I think most people would admit that it is a rare occurrence for them to be motivated by advertising to change brands of a product they use every day.

If advertising is so ineffective, why do we feel so much in its thrall? The question is not difficult to answer. Whether or not we become immune to advertising's individual messages, we cannot be immune to the cacophony that intrudes into our lives—a kind of commercial white noise audible every time we read a newspaper or magazine, switch on the radio or TV, open a book of matches, or look up at billboards on the sides of buildings. Now even some taxis in New York subject their hapless passengers to a continuous sequence of messages running ticker-tape fashion before their eyes. One would have to be blind or deaf not to feel beset in such an environment.

Fulminations and irritations aside, what is the actual effect of this thunderous barrage? While advertising may be ineffective when it comes to making us change our consumption habits with regard to well-known commodities, it is a potent means of bringing to our attention both new commodities and substantially changed traditional commodities. Thus advertising helps the central economic function of capitalism—product creation. It was advertising (and not TV advertising, either) that made us a nation of picture takers when the Eastman Kodak camera was introduced as a mechanism requiring no skill ("You push the button, we do the rest"); it was advertising (largely TV) that gave Polaroid its day in the sun; it was advertising that persuaded millions of Americans that it was perfectly safe—and more than that, "friendly"—to board a jet; it was advertising that made us a nation of credit card carriers. Advertising is the great information machine of a capitalist economy, and it is this legitimate and indispensable function that the persuasion offers as a defense against its most stubborn and hostile critics.

The problem arises as we pass from advertising that promotes genuinely new, even novel products to advertising about products that differ only marginally from one another. It is one thing when advertising makes us aware of detergents as a new form of cleansing material, another when it tells us of the extraordinary properties possessed by various brands of these virtually identical products. It does not matter whether we "believe" such absurd claims. What matters is that we are exposed to a cannonade that may leave us individually unscathed while bombarding us collectively with information, misinformation, hard sell, soft sell, seduction, and bullying. Although the effect of this bombardment on our buying habits may be small, the impact on our very conceptions of ourselves is pervasive and penetrative.

This brings us back to the idea of advertising as capitalist realism. Socialist realism, Schudson reminds us, has a number of characteristics and purposes: it pictures life in simplified ways; it moralizes about and idealizes lifestyles; it radiates confidence and optimism. As I said at the outset, there are immediately recognizable analogues between the explicit function of these advertisements for Soviet socialism and the implicit political message carried by the advertisements of Western capitalism. Of course there is no hint of political subservience in the latter case. Many advertising agencies would protest vigorously if told that their creations, in addition to promoting a product, were endorsing a sociopolitical system, and I anticipate poor Professor Schudson receiving an inundation of outraged letters. I shall try to curb that flow by quoting him at some length:

> . . . American advertising, like socialist realist art, simplifies and typifies. It does not claim to picture reality as it is but reality as it should be—life and lives worth emulating. It is always photography or drama or discourse with a message—rarely picturing individuals, it shows people only as incarnations of larger social categories. It always assumes that there is progress. It is thoroughly optimistic, providing for any troubles

that it identifies a solution in a particular product or style of life. It focuses, of course, on the new, and if it shows some signs of respect for tradition, this is only to help in the assimilation of some new commercial creation.

What is "capitalist" about many ads, Schudson goes on to say, is not that they invoke the sanctity of private enterprise. It is that the images they project—images that are often pre- or even anti-capitalist in their celebration of kinship, "together-ness," and the like—are fashioned to sell merchandise, not to promote values, and that the appeals and satisfactions are construed in individual, not collective or social, terms. In one final quote:

> The similarity between advertising and socialist realism is that both forms subordinate everything to a message that romanticizes the present or the potential of the present. If the visual aesthetic of socialist realism is designed to dignify the simplicity of human labor in the service of the state, the aesthetic of capitalist realism—without a master-plan of purposes—glorifies the pleasures and freedoms of consumer choice in defense of the virtues of private life and material ambitions.

Advertising, Schudson concludes, is capitalism's way of saying "I love you" to itself.

So? Is that so awful? Stephen Fox titled his book *The Mirror Makers* because he perceives the trade as reflecting the values of society, not creating them. "One may build a compelling case," he writes, "that American culture is—beyond redemp-tion—money-mad, hedonistic, superficial, rushing heedlessly down a railroad track called Progress. To blame advertising for these most basic tendencies in American history is to miss the point. It is too obvious, too easy, a matter of killing the messenger instead of dealing with the bad news."

There is a great deal of truth in Fox's contention that advertising is only the most visible manifestation, good or bad, of American values. But advertising is not only a bearer of messages; it *is* the message. Advertising does more than portray the values of a capitalist society; it shapes and to some degree creates them. If the lackeys who prepare the canned propaganda for the virtues of the socialist fatherland must bear some responsibility for their work, can we exempt from all responsibility the creators of the ballads of capitalist contentment—who cannot even plead the threat of punishment as motivation for their task?

It is true that advertising serves some very useful functions over and above that of celebrating the materialist way of American life. It does purvey information, albeit in a partisan way. It serves to democratize commodities, making it "imagina-ble" for people to widen their range of experience (although it is shameless in touting commodities that are harmful, like cigarettes, or that are apt to end up as expensive junk, like personal computers). It encourages our fantasies of what we might have or might be, fantasies that are mildly intoxicating until they impose on us near pornographic ideals of beauty or success (those jeans again). Most of all, it supports the media, although this proudest boast must be tempered by the realization that there are other ways of underwriting TV (as the Public Broadcasting Service has shown), and that advertising support exerts its own tacit censorship: "Will the company buy *that?*"

These pluses and minuses are difficult to sum. The deeper trouble with advertising is that, rather like its socialist counterpart, it washes over the mind, leaving a residue of unexamined "belief" in the fatherland, on the one hand, mingled with a pervasive sense of disbelief, on the other. Having quoted at length from Schudson's book, I shall conclude in self-defense by repeating those troubling but overblown words of mine that I mentioned earlier. In *Business Civilization in Decline* I wrote:

> Consider advertising, perhaps the single most value-destroying activity of a business civilization. Schumpeter spoke of the cold rationality that was to prove the undoing of the system. He ignored the extraordinary subversive influence of the relentless effort to persuade people to change their lifeways, not out of any knowledge of, or deeply held convictions about, the "good life," but merely to sell whatever article or service is being pandered. I do not think we pay sufficient heed to the power of advertising in making cynics of us all: at a business forum I was once brash enough to say that I thought the main cultural effect of television advertising was to teach children that grown-ups told lies for money. How strong, deep, or sustaining can be the values generated by a civilization that generates a ceaseless flow of half-truths and careful deceptions, in which it is common knowledge that only a fool is taken in by the charades and messages that supposedly tell us "the facts"?

Thus advertising is both a mirror and a lens. Like a great reflective parabola it collects the values of the social universe in which it exists, and then projects onto the skies of that universe constellations that give shape to its inchoate yearnings and imaginings. It has but uncertain success in illumining any given star, but its collective efforts light up the sky. Are the images and constellations projected onto the social heavens worthy of respect? Michael Schudson's subtitle for his book on advertising is "Its Dubious Impact on American Society." "Dubious" is a carefully chosen word, and I think a very good one. It is dubious whether advertising has the power to rearrange our lives that many of its critics fear, but its vision of what a well-arranged life might be is also dubious, in a much less inconsequential sense.

GOVERNMENT INJUNCTION RESTRAINING HARLEM COSMETIC CO.
Josephine Miles

They say La Jac Brite Pink Skin Bleach avails not,
They say its Orange Beauty Glow does not glow.
Nor the face grow five shades lighter nor the heart
Five shades lighter. They say no.

They deny good luck, love, power, romance, and inspiration
From La Jac Brite ointment and incense of all kinds,
And condemn in writing skin brightening and whitening
And whitening of minds.

There is upon the federal trade commission a burden of glory
So to defend the fact, so to impel
The plucking of hope from the hand, honor from the complexion,
Sprite from the spell.

Josephine Miles, "Government Injunction Restraining Harlem Cosmetic Co.," *Poems: 1930–1960* (Bloomington: Indiana University Press, 1960). In addition to her poetry, Miles has written numerous scholarly studies of poetry and poetic diction, including *Style and Proportion: The Language of Prose and Poetry* (1966). She is a former literature professor at the University of California. Her poetry is included in numerous standard college anthologies.

BARBIE DOLL
Marge Piercy

This girlchild was born as usual
and presented dolls that did pee-pee
and miniature GE stoves and irons
and wee lipsticks the color of cherry candy. .
Then in the magic of puberty, a classmate said:
You have a great big nose and fat legs.

She was healthy, tested intelligent,
possessed strong arms and back,
abundant sexual drive and manual dexterity.
She went to and fro apologizing.
Everyone saw a fat nose on thick legs.

She was advised to play coy,
exhorted to come on hearty,
exercise, diet, smile and wheedle.
Her good nature wore out
like a fan belt.
So she cut off her nose and her legs
and offered them up.

In the casket displayed on satin she lay
with the undertaker's cosmetics painted on,
a turned-up putty nose,
dressed in a pink and white nightie.
Doesn't she look pretty? everyone said.
Consummation at last.
To every woman a happy ending.

Marge Piercy, "Barbie Doll," *Circles on the Water* (New York: Knopf, 1982). *Circles on the Water* is a collection of Piercy's poems. Piercy is both a writer of fiction (*Fly Away Home*, 1984) and poetry (*Stone, Paper, Knife*, 1983). In the introduction to *Circles on the Water*, Piercy writes that she wants her work to be "useful" to women whose consciousnesses haven't yet been raised.

SUGGESTIONS FOR WRITING

Informal Essays

1. After reading a few essays from this chapter, write an essay in which you discuss an ad or two that touched you in some way. Perhaps an ad for GI Joe dolls made you want to go out and buy one. Or perhaps an ad for a perfume touched your inner being.
2. After reading Jeffrey Schrank's essay, "The Language of Advertising Claims," write an essay in which you analyze the various rhetorical devices and emotional appeals of a magazine advertisement of your choice.

Short Documented Papers

1. Argue with one of the essays in this chapter, buttressing your argument with examples from at least two other essays that agree with your point of view.
2. Contrast Sid Bernstein's "Is Puffery Flummery?" with Preston's "Puffery is Deception." Keep out of the argument yourself.
3. Analyze what you consider to be the weakest argument on either side of the controversy.
4. Analyze the strongest argument made on either side of the controversy.

Longer Documented Papers

1. Argue that the language of advertising is unfair.
2. Defend the language of advertising.
3. Argue that advertising is a pernicious (or benign or healthy) influence on society. Take into account the opposing side's arguments.
4. Argue that the government should step up its efforts at policing advertising.
5. Argue that the government should keep its hands off of advertising.
6. Write a research report in which you describe both sides of the controversy concerning the healthy or unhealthy influence of advertising on society.
7. Write a research report in which you describe both sides of the controversy over the uses of language in advertising.

· 5 ·

Sex Differences: Innate or Acquired?

Can anyone possibly take the old battle of the sexes seriously in this day of women's liberation, the Equal Opportunity Act, and the Equal Rights Amendment? Can the dispute be anything but a playful cocktail party topic? Apparently so. At any rate, the debate goes on, not just in cocktail-party chatter but in popular journals like *Runner's World* and *Ms.*, as well as in scientific journals.

Sex differences in behavior are, of course, everywhere apparent, as anyone knows who has observed children in action at a birthday party. The differences in ability are equally apparent. Jane, for example, may become exasperated at Dick's ability to unscrew the lid from the peanut-butter jar that foils her best efforts; and Dick may be frustrated by Jane's ability to thread a needle in a fraction of the time that it takes him to do it.

But what has fueled a new sexual controversy is not the dispute over such differences, but instead over contradictory conclusions about what causes them. It's the old nature versus nurture conflict all over again. As feminists have long pointed out, sex differences have usually been explained through the centuries as innate and unalterable. Women, men typically argued, were by nature physically weaker and psychologically more submissive than men (and, some men argued, intellectually feebler). God made them that way.

During this century, by contrast, the "environmentalists" have carried the day, and their argument has become central to the women's liberation movement. Nurture dictates, feminists say; men and women differ only in one significant way— their reproductive functions. Virtually all other differences are merely the result of social conditioning. This argument contributes a compelling logic to the feminist cause. And of course women's current highly visible and successful presence in the

179

gym, the classroom, the laboratory, and the boardroom has contributed an indisputable credibility to the argument that the environment determines our sexual behavior.

The issue has been recently joined, however, by what feminists see as decidedly reactionary arguments. And these arguments are not coming from quarters that feminists might dismiss as chauvinistic; they are coming from the biologists, neurologists, psychologists, and other members of the intellectual community—many of them women. These conclusions, although they are by no means unanimous, suggest that nurture simply doesn't tell the whole story of sex differences—that those old commonsense notions about the differences between Dick and Jane are partially accurate.

Many sociobiologists, for example, after extensive research with other primates, now conclude that different male and female traits have evolved over millennia, and were originally dictated by their reproductive and social roles in primitive societies back along the evolutionary chain. Recent research in other scientific fields corroborates the sociobiologists' claim that the differences between the sexes stem from heredity as well as from the environment. Neurologists, for example, have presented evidence that the male hormone, testosterone, dramatically alters the brain development of the male fetus and thus accounts for some typically male behavioral patterns.

Many feminists view such research as a pretentious new guise for the same old sexism, and they are not impressed by the fact that women seldom come off as the more flawed sex in these studies. Such research, they insist, can have only an insidious effect on the political and social climate of a culture that is just now, they say, emerging from its long history of female subjugation.

This dispute won't likely go away soon. Neither nature nor nurture has had its full day in court, and the echoes reverberating from the controversy sound remarkably like the rallying cries in that centuries-old battle.

THE WEAKER SEX? HAH!

Women playing lacrosse? Hockey? Women tackling each other in rugby and mixing it up in the scrum? Women running marathons? Small wonder that fathers, husbands and friends worry about the physical strains that the supposedly weaker six is undergoing these days. Relax, fellas: there is little to be concerned about. Women are well suited to take part in rugged athletics. Indeed, women hold many long-distance swimming records for both sexes and have run men into the ground during ultra-marathon races 50 miles long. Says Dr. Joan Ullyot, a physiologist at San Francisco's Institute of Health Research and a world-class marathoner herself: "The evidence suggests that women are tougher than men."

Nature certainly designed women better than men for sport in one basic way. "A man's scrotum is much more vulnerable than a woman's ovaries," says Dr. John Marshall, director of sports medicine at Manhattan's Hospital for Special Surgery and the trainer for Billie Jean King. "A woman's ovaries sit inside a great big sac of fluid—beautifully protected." A woman's breasts are also not easily damaged. Scotching an old myth, Marshall says: "There's no evidence that trauma to the breasts is a precursor of cancer."

Such injuries as girls and women do suffer can often be blamed on improper condition or coaching. Girls are more loose-jointed than boys, making them somewhat more susceptible to injuries like dislocated shoulders. Women can also have problems with what is known as the "overload phenomenon"—putting too much force on a muscle, tendon or ligament. But that can be avoided with proper training. Says Dr. C. Harmon Brown, director of Student Health Services at California State University in Hayward: "Four years ago it was not O.K. for girls to participate in sports, and they were forced to be sedentary. Now it's suddenly O.K., but teachers are not equipped to show girls how to gradually improve their physical fitness and cut down on injuries."

A girl's training need not be less vigorous than a boy's. Dr. Barbara Drinkwater, a research physiologist at the University of California's Institute of Environmental Stress, found that prepubertal girls are precisely the same as boys in cardio-respiratory (heart-lung) endurance capacity. Parents who worry about their young daughters overtaxing tender hearts while turning a fast 440 should realize that the human machine is designed to shut down—through leg cramps, side stitches, and dizziness—if the strain is too severe.

Then there is the canard that a woman's menstrual cycle inhibits peak performance. World and Olympic records, however, have been set by women who were having their periods. Nor does exertion disrupt the cycle for most women athletes. Says one world-class runner: "I'm so regular, it's ridiculous." However, some women undergoing hard training do stop menstruating for months at a time. This cessation of the cycle, called amenorrhea, occurs in about 45% of women who run over 65 miles a week—as well as in dancers, ice skaters and gymnasts. Many experts link

"The Weaker Sex? Hah!" *Time* 26 June 1978.

amenorrhea directly to loss of body fat, a result of exercise. A cutback in training, with subsequent weight gain, generally restores the normal cycle.

Even pregnancy should not automatically deter the athletic woman. Most obstetricians advocate exercise, at least during the first and second trimesters. Dr. Marshall calmly watched his wife enter her first ski race when she was eight months pregnant. Says he: 'I didn't mind seeing my wife even take a fall because the baby is very well protected." Last month, Wendy Boglioli, 23, a former Olympic champion, competed in the national A.A.U. 100-yd. freestyle competition while five months pregnant. She failed to place and felt unusually tired, but suffered no damage.

Many women claim that athletics increases their sex drive. "Exercise puts sparkle in a woman's eyes, pink in her cheeks and creates a physical vitality that almost bursts out," says Dr. Ullyot. "She becomes body centered and very sensual."

A serious woman athlete—even one who trains with weights—hardly faces the specter of turning into a Tarzan. The female body composition is only 23% muscle, in contrast to 40% for men. Dr. Jack Wilmore, president of the American College of Sports Medicine, has found that women, because they have low levels of the androgenic hormones that enlarge muscles, can increase their strength 50% to 75% with no increase in muscle bulk. Witness Virginia Wade, sleek and slender, who can serve a tennis ball at 92 m.p.h.

A top woman athlete has legs just as strong of those of a man her size in the same condition, but the man's arms would be twice as strong. Women have trouble throwing a ball as far as a man not only because of weaker muscles, but because their arms are relatively shorter and their shoulders not as broad. The result is less leverage and power.

One thing is certain: women have only just begun to achieve their athletic potential. Since women started to play the game later than men, they have some catching up to do—and they are. Men now run the 800 and 1,500 meters only about 10% faster than women; in the middle-distance swimming events, the difference is about 7%. Top women marathoners now finish about 30 minutes behind the male winners, and their times are improving every year. Yet the International Olympic Committee recently refused to allow women to run more than 1,500 meters in the 1980 Olympics. Ridiculous, says Dr. Wilmore. "You can train women as hard as you can train men, and the records will fall by the wayside."

DO MALES HAVE A MATH GENE?
Dennis A. Williams

Can girls do math as well as boys? All sorts of recent tests have shown that they cannot. Most educators and feminists have blamed this phenomenon on socialization—arguing that because girls are told they can't do well in math, they develop "math anxiety" and don't. But last week a new study appeared that explains the difference mainly in genetic terms. The authors' conclusion: "Sex differences in achievement in and attitude toward mathematics result from superior male mathematical ability."

Johns Hopkins psychologists Camilla Perssons Benbow and Julian C. Stanley set out to examine the notion—advanced by the University of Wisconsin's Elizabeth Fennêma—that boys do better than girls largely because they take more mathematics courses. Benbow and Stanley used a sample of seventh and eighth graders, whose educational background was nearly identical because it is not until high school that girls tend to drop advanced math courses. The students—about 10,000, 43 per cent girls—were participants in a series of mathematical talent searches carried out between 1972 and 1979, and all were among the top 2 to 5 per cent in mathematical reasoning ability according to a standardized achievement test.

The students took the Scholastic Aptitude Test normally given to high-school seniors. In the results on the math portion of the SAT—there was no appreciable difference in verbal scores—the boys, as a group, outperformed the girls; the smallest average difference in ten testings was 32 points. What the authors found even more significant was that the top-scoring boy in each grouping did better than the top girl, with margins ranging up to 190 points. Among eighth-grade subjects in 1976, more than half the boys scored above 600 of a possible 800, but not one of the girls did. "It is therefore obvious that differential course-taking in mathematics cannot alone explain the sex difference we observed," Benbow and Stanley wrote in the new issue of Science magazine.

The researchers admit that their results do not rule out "other environmental explanations," but they do address one commonly held idea: boys are encouraged to like math more than girls. The psychologists used attitude questionnaires which showed, said Benbow, that "our girls like math just as much as boys" and that they did not believe math would be less useful in future careers.

DIFFERENT REWARDS

The study's conclusions have drawn fierce objections from those who believe that environment, not genes, is the culprit. Says Sheila Tobias, the feminist author of "Overcoming Math Anxiety": "If your mother hates math and your father tells you not to worry your pretty little head about it, do you think that a math test would be an accurate measure of your ability?" Stephen Ivens, research director for the College Entrance Examination Board in New York City, agrees that there is a significant difference between boys' and girls' math scores, but he also maintains that environ-

Dennis A. Williams, "Do Males Have a Math Gene?" *Newsweek* 15 December 1980.

ment is a factor. "If we reward girls differently," Ivens says, "the differences will probably decrease."

Some researchers and educators have begun to try just that. In a study published earlier this year, Judy Genshaft of Ohio State and Michael Hirt of Kent State conducted tests with three dozen teen-age girls to see if they could be encouraged to do better in math. Two groups of girls were given extra lessons or counseling to reduce their anxiety about math; both groups improved their interest and understanding of mathematics in the eight-week sessions. Those in a third group, who received no extra help, showed no improvement. "The socialization factors are so major that they represent our greatest opportunity for improving performance," says Hirt. To that end, more than 130 colleges have begun "math anxiety" programs to help women conquer problems of self-image, tension and alienation that some say contribute to their poorer performance.

Yet the dispute continues, because the two sides see the problem differently. Benbow and Stanley contend that scientists should first determine the source of sex differences in math ability. If the differences are environmental, they may be able to be eliminated; if they are genetic, we must learn to accept them. Their critics, on the other hand, insist that it is impossible to learn the true source of the disparity as long as males and females are not treated equally. Patricia Lund Casserly, a senior research associate with the Educational Testing Service, which produces the SAT's, is among those who believe that results are what really count. "The question of genetic differences doesn't matter to me," she says. "The question is, can girls learn math, can girls make fine scientists and engineers? The answer is yes."

JUST HOW THE SEXES DIFFER
David Gelman

Captain to Laura: ". . . If it's true we are descended from the ape, it must have been from two different species. There's no likeness between us, is there?"
— "The Father," by August Strindberg

So it has begun to seem, and not only in the musings of a misogynist Swedish playwright. Research on the structure of the brain, on the effects of hormones, and in animal behavior, child psychology and anthropology is providing new scientific underpinnings for what August Strindberg and his ilk viscerally guessed: men and women *are* different. They show obvious dissimilarities, of course, in size, anatomy and sexual function. But scientists now believe that they are unlike in more fundamental ways. Men and women seem to *experience* the world differently, not merely because of the ways they were brought up in it, but because they feel it with a different sensitivity of touch, hear it with different aural responses, puzzle out its problems with different cells in their brains.

Hormones seem to be the key to the difference—and an emerging body of evidence suggests that they do far more than trigger the external sexual characteristics of males and females. They actually "masculinize" or "feminize" the brain itself. By looking closely at the neurochemical processes involved, investigators are finding biological explanations for why women might think intuitively, why men seem better at problem-solving, why boys play rougher than girls.

Whether these physiological differences destine men and women for separate roles in society is a different and far more delicate question. The particular way male brains are organized may orient them toward visual-spatial perception, explaining—perhaps—why they are superior at math. Women's brains may make them more verbally disposed, explaining—possibly—why they seem better at languages. Males of most species appear to be hormonally primed for aggression, pointing—it may be—to the long evolutionary record of male dominance over women.

But few of these presumed differences go unchallenged. And whether they imply anything more—about leadership capacities, for example, or that men are biologically suited for the workplace and women for the hearth—is another part of the thicket. The notion that biology is destiny is anathema to feminists and to many male researchers as well. It is their position that sexual stereotyping, reinforced by a male-dominated culture, has more bearing on gender behavior than do hormones. "As early as you can show me a sex difference, I can show you the culture at work," insists Michael Lewis, of the Institute for the Study of Exceptional Children.

The new research has thus revived, in all its old intensity, the wrangle over whether "nature" or "nurture" plays the greater part in behavior. At the same time, it has become a fresh battle ground for feminism, a continuation of the sex war by other means. Spurred by the women's movement, large numbers of female scientists

David Gelman, "Just How the Sexes Differ," *Newsweek* 18 May 1981.

have moved into an area of inquiry once largely populated by men and by male ideas of gender roles. Both male and female investigators have been challenging male-fostered notions of female passivity and submissiveness. But because some are also acknowledging the role of biology, they are catching flak from hard-core feminists, who fear such findings will be used—as they have been in the past—to deny women equal rights.

Some researchers now refuse to be interviewed, or carefully hedge their assertions. "I found myself being screamed at—this time by the very people whose cause I had supported," wrote sociologist Alice Rossi, after she landed in hot water for talking about the "innate predisposition" of women for child-rearing. "People are being really hounded," agrees anthropologist Sarah Blaffer Hrdy, who found she could not even hypothesize about men's math abilities without provoking feminist wrath.

The research comes under indictment on another count: since possibilities for experimentation with humans are limited, it leans heavily on animal studies. Complains Stanford psychologist Eleanor Maccoby, who reviewed the literature on sex differences: "People look at this and say it is all biological. They generalize wildly from a little monkey research." But most researchers are cautions about making the leap from lower primates to Homo sapiens. Human evolution involved a huge increase in brain flexibility that gave rise to human culture. And over the long course of that evolution, humans have become much less the creatures of their hormones than are rats or rhesus monkeys.

Even so, the researchers are providing some fascinating new glimpses into the biology of behavior. Among their odd assortment of laboratory subjects are male canaries whose song repertoire is imprinted, like a player-piano roll, in a cluster of brain cells; virginal female rats that go through the motions of nursing when confronted with rat pups, and young girls who turn "tomboyish" because they were exposed to male hormones before birth.

There are also enough anomalies—male marmosets that tenderly nurture their young, female langurs that fight ferociously for turf—to cast doubts on some firmly entrenched beliefs about gender behavior. But these contradictions, too, are providing new insights into the essential nature of the sexes.

The everyday perception of sexual differences is a mélange of fact and assumption. That men, for the most part, are larger and stronger than women is something that anyone can see and physiologists can verify. There are also clear-cut differences in primary sexual functions: menstruation, gestation and lactation in women, ejaculation in men. Beyond that, observes Harvard biologist Richard Lewontin, "we just don't know any differences except the plumbing features that unambiguously separate men from women." Other presumed distinctions provide a continuing source of strife for both sexes. For example, the proposition that men are naturally more competitive than women seems increasingly debatable as women move into male jobs and sports, where they often prove as combative as men. In any case, the average differences that exist between men and women leave plenty of room for individual variations in the sexes. Not all males in a given group are more aggressive or better at math than all females; not all women are more adept at learning languages. "Women and men both fall along the whole continuum of test results," notes neuropsychologist Eran Zaidel of the University of California, Los Angeles.

Like most behavioral traits, competitiveness is hard to measure objectively, harder yet to attribute to innate causes. Scientists have been trying to zero in on those traits that *can* be measured, by way of psychological tests and brain and hormone studies. A few years ago Diane McGuinness, of the University of California at Santa Cruz, made a study of the vast body of technical literature that has sprung up in the field. She concluded that from infancy on, males and females respond in ways that provide significant clues to their later differences in behavior.

McGuinness believes that girl infants are more alert to "social" cues. They respond more to people, read facial expressions better and seem better able to interpret the emotional content of speech even before they can understand words— a clue to the proverbial "women's intuition." Boy infants are more curious about objects and like to take them apart—the beginning, perhaps, of their superior mechanical aptitude. As infants, they are awake longer and more active and exploratory.

Girls, notes McGuinness, have a "superior tactile sensitivity," even in infancy. They excel in fine-motor coordination and manual dexterity, suggesting why they are better at such tasks as typing and needlework—or neurosurgery. This same affinity for precision and detail seems to account for girls' greater verbal ability. They speak earlier and more fluently and, perhaps aided by superior auditory memory, carry a tune better. (McGuinness doubts a connection, but it has been shown in some studies that mothers tend to carry on more "conversations"—talking and singing—with girl infants than with boy babies.)

Boys stutter more than girls, spell worse and are classified far more often as "learning disabled" or "hyperactive"—quite possibly, McGuinness argues, because the early stress on reading and writing favors girls. But boys have a clear advantage in visual-spatial orientation, marked by a lively interest in geometric forms and in manipulating objects. At an early age boys and girls are about equal in arithmetic, but boys pull ahead in higher mathematics. Their faster reaction time and better visual-spatial ability appear to give them an edge in some sports.

Are these differences real and could they be biologically based? Stanford's Maccoby is skeptical. She and an associate, Carol Jacklin, reviewed more than 1,400 studies of sex differences and concluded that only four of them were well established: verbal ability for girls and visual-spatial ability, mathematical excellence and aggression in boys. Maccoby also contends, as many researchers do, that sex typing and the different set of expectations that society thrusts on men and women have far more to do with any differences that exist—with their divergent abilities—than do genes or blood chemistry. Diane McGuinness, on the other hand, believes there is "compelling" evidence that sex differences are a result of biological determinism, and her colleague, Karl Pribram, agrees. Pribram suspects that men and women may be "programed" differently from the beginning. "We don't know why these things are true," says Pribram. "But it's very difficult to say culture is predisposing males to fail at English and females at math."

To get some inkling how this programming might come about, anthropologists turn to evolutionary scenarios derived from the study of primitive cultures. The most familiar accounts center on hunter-gatherer societies, the prototype of human social organization. There was a clear division of labor along sexual lines in these societies. The risky business of hunting and fighting fell to the males, presumably because they were more expendable: it required only one male to impregnate many females. Thus, males may have evolved the larger musculature, faster reactions and greater visual-spatial acuity for combat, for hurling spears, for spotting distant prey. As an evolutionary result, even today they are more competitive, more at risk. They experience more stress, die younger than women in maturity and suffer more accidental deaths in childhood.

Females were the gatherers and the first agriculturalists. Limited to less venturesome roles by successive pregnancies and the need to care for infants, they may have developed close-to-the-nest faculties of touch and hearing, perhaps even a greater facility for speech as they interacted with their offspring and other females. According to Darwinian theory, these adaptively advantageous traits would then be passed on in the gene pool. Anthropologist Donald Symons carried this thinking a controversial step further in a 1979 book contending that males are predisposed to sexual promiscuity, while females are prone to constancy. His reasoning: a male's reproductive success was determined by the number of females he could impregnate. Females, he said, feared the wrath of jealous stronger mates and found monogamy more conducive to raising offspring—their own measure of reproductive efficacy.

Symons's thesis, wrapped in all its sociobiological trappings, impressed some scientists and infuriated others. In addition, the subject is an explosive one for feminists. If men are driven by testicular fortitude, women reject the notion that they are limited by a kind of ovarian docility. Anne Petersen, director of the adolescent laboratory at Chicago's Michael Reese Hospital, supports this view: "When women really needed to keep making babies because so many died and women themselves didn't live very long, their work was of a different nature and needed to be related to reproduction. That's not true anymore."

Evolutionary evidence does suggest that with the advent of weapons, some physical distinctions between males and females became less necessary. Differences in size and strength have greatly diminished over the millennia, perhaps, according to University of Michigan paleoanthropologist Milford Wolpoff, because "the physical requirements of the male and female roles have become more similar." The main anatomical trend, Wolpoff says, "has been for males to become more feminized."

Harvard's Sarah Blaffer Hrdy is one of the new generation of social scientists who are trying to debunk the concept of female passivity. In a forthcoming book, "The Woman That Never Evolved," Hrdy argues that female territoriality—the aggressive protection of turf—has been overlooked by most anthropologists. "The central organizing principle of primate social life is competition between females, and especially female lineages," she writes. In such matrilinear societies, she argues, "the basic dynamics of the mating system depend not so much on male predilection as on the degree to which one female tolerates another."

Hrdy's work has encouraged other researchers to look beyond the evolutionary stereotypes. Until now, she contends, most such studies have focused on males arranging themselves in order to take advantage of females. "We've really been ass-backwards in trying to understand the primate social organization by looking only at males," asserts Hrdy.

By shifting the anthropological focus, the Hrdy breed of researchers hopes to show that gender roles are not unalterably determined by biology; instead, they may be the product of particular cultures. Even so, the evidence for an inborn masculine "aggression factor" seems inescapable. It is widely agreed that in the majority of animal species, males are more prone to fighting than are females. Biologists trace this to the hormone testosterone, secreted in the testes of the male fetus during a critical period in its development. Although the sex of a fetus is basically determined by its genetic coding (XX chromosomes for females, XY for males), any fetus has the chance of developing either male or female characteristics, depending on the hormones it is exposed to. Testosterone and other male hormones "masculinize" a fetus, differentiating its genitalia from the female's. At the same time, the male hormones prevent the development of ovaries, which secrete female hormones that would stimulate the growth of feminine characteristics.

Scientists first got on the trail of testosterone in 1849. Experiments showed that roosters became less aggressive and lost their sexual drive after they were castrated, then regained their "roosterhood" when extracts from the testes were implanted in them. A century later, in 1959, physiologists Robert Goy and William Young conducted a study still considered a landmark in the field. First they injected pregnant female guinea pigs with massive doses of testosterone. The result: the genetically female offspring in the brood had both male genitalia and ovaries. When the ovaries were removed and the aberrant females were given a fresh dose of testosterone, they behaved like males, even "mounting" other females—the gesture of male dominance in many species.

Goy, now with the University of Wisconsin's Primate Research Center, has confirmed the effects of testosterone in experiments with rhesus monkeys over the past decade. Not only is female behavior partly masculinized by prenatal testosterone, he says, but the robustness and vigor of males depend on how long they have been exposed to the hormone. "The different kinds of behavior that you see young male monkeys display," Goy asserts, "are completely, scientifically and uniquely determined by the endocrine conditions that exist before birth."

To see if hormones play a similar role in human behavior, John Money of Johns Hopkins University and Anke Ehrhardt of Columbia studied one of nature's own experiments—children exposed to abnormally high levels of androgens (male hormones) before birth because of adrenal-gland malfunctions. Among other effects discovered, the researchers at Johns Hopkins found that girls born with this disorder exhibited distinctly "tomboyish" behavior, seldom played with dolls and began dating at a later age than other girls.

The much-cited Money-Ehrhardt research has provided a classic context for the nature-nurture debate. Some scientists maintain that the tomboyism was a clear result of the hormone exposure, and they bolster their argument by noting the scores of animal experiments that demonstrate similar effects. But others criticize the study for failing to emphasize that girls with congenital adrenal hyperplasia do not *look* like normal girls at birth; they often require corrective surgery to restore normal female genitals. Thus, the argument goes, they may be treated differently as they grow up, and their behavior could be more the result of an abnormal environment than of abnormal blood chemistry.

The debate rages back and forth. But at least one scientist who has been on both sides, Rutgers psycho-endocrinologist June Reinisch, recently found evidence to buttress the hormonal argument. Over a period of five years Reinisch studied 25 boys and girls born to women who had taken synthetic progestin (a type of androgen) to prevent miscarriages. When the scientist compared them with their unexposed siblings by giving each child a standard aggression test, she found significant differences between the groups. Progestin-exposed males scored twice as high in physical aggression as their normal brothers; twelve of seventeen females scored higher than their unexposed sisters. "This result was so striking," says Reinisch, "that I sat on the data for a year before publishing."

Reinisch has by no means renounced her belief in the importance of environment. Like many of her colleagues, she suspects that hormones act to "flavor" an individual for one kind of gender behavior or another. But how the individual is brought up is still an important factor. As Robert Goy explains, "It looks as though what the hormone is doing is predisposing the animal to learn a particular social role. It isn't insisting that it learn that role; it's just making it easier. The hormone doesn't prevent behavior from being modified by environmental and social conditions."

As to how the initial "flavor" comes about, researchers now believe that hormones change the very structure of the brain. Some variations in the brains of males and females have been observed in animals. They were found mainly in the hypothalamus and pre-optic regions, which are closely connected to the reproductive functions. In those areas males are generally found to have more and larger "neurons"—nerve cells and their connecting processes. Experiments conducted by Dominique Toran-Allerand of Columbia University using cultures of brain cells from newborn mice have shown that neuronal development can be stimulated by hormones, and this suggests a key to the sexual mystery. Says animal physiologist Bruce McEwen of Rockefeller University: "Growth, as the primary event caused by hormones, could account for the observed differences in brains."

The clearest evidence to date of the brain-hormone link is in songbirds. Several years ago Rockefeller researchers Fernando Nottebohm and Arthur Arnold discovered sex differences in certain clusters of brain nuclei that control the singing function in canaries. The nuclei, they found, are almost four times as large in males as in females—apparently explaining why male songbirds sing and females don't. Singing is part of the mating ritual for the birds, and Nottebohm demonstrated that the size of the nuclei waxed and waned with the coming and going of the mating season. When he treated female songbirds with testosterone, the singing nuclei doubled in size and the females produced malelike songs. "This was the first observation of a gross sexual dimorphism in the brain of a vertebrate," Nottebohm told a scientific meeting last November.

Many scientists are now convinced that hormones "imprint" sexuality on the brains of a large number of animal species by changing the nerve-cell structure.

"Even the way dogs urinate—that's a function that is sex different and is determined by hormones," says Roger Gorski, a UCLA neuro-endrocrinologist who has done important experiments with animal brains.

But what about humans? So far, no one has observed structural differences between the brains of males and females in any species more sophisticated than rats. In humans, the best evidence is indirect. For years researchers have known that men's and women's mental functions are organized somewhat differently. Men appear to have more "laterality"—that is, their functions are separately controlled by the left or right hemisphere of the brain, while women's seem diffused through both hemispheres. The first clues to this intriguing disparity came from victims of brain damage. Doctors noticed that male patients were much likelier than females to suffer speech impairment after damage to the left hemisphere and loss of such nonverbal functions as visual-spatial ability when the right hemisphere was damaged. Women showed less functional loss, regardless of the hemisphere involved. Some researchers believe this is because women's brain activity is duplicated in both hemispheres. Women usually mature earlier than men, which means that their hemispheric processes may have less time to draw apart. They retain more nerve-transmission mechanisms in the connective tissue between the two hemispheres (the corpus callosum) and can thus call either or both sides of the brain into play on a given task.

On the whole, women appear to be more dominated by the left, or verbal, hemisphere and men by the right, or visual, side. Researchers McGuinness and Pribram speculate that men generally do better in activities where the two hemispheres don't compete with, and thus hamper, each other, while women may be better able to coordinate the efforts of both hemispheres. This might explain why women seem to think "globally," or intuitively and men concentrate more effectively on specific problem-solving.

A few enterprising researchers have tried to find a direct connection between hormones and human-brain organization. UCLA's Melissa Hines studied 16 pairs of sisters, of whom one in each pair had been prenatally exposed to DES (diethylstilbestrol), a synthetic hormone widely administered to pregnant women during the 1950s to prevent miscarriages. Using audiovisual tests, Hines found what appeared to be striking differences between the exposed and unexposed sisters.

First, Hines played separate nonsense syllables into the women's right and left ears. Normally, the researcher explains, most people—but especially males—report more accurately what they hear with the right ear. In her tests, the hormone-exposed women picked the correct syllable heard with the right ear 20 percent more often than their unexposed sisters. A test of their right and left visual fields produced comparable results. The implication was that the women's brains had been masculinized. "It is compelling evidence that prenatal hormones influence human behavior due to changes in brain organization," says Hines.

Differences in brain organization may have practical implications for education and medicine. Some researchers believe that teaching methods should take note of right-left brain differences, though past attempts at such specialized teaching have been ineffective. Other scientists predict clinical benefits. It is useful to know, for example, that females who are brain-damaged at birth will cope with the defects better than males. Columbia's Toran-Allerand suggests that certain types of infertility might be corrected once scientists understand how hormones mold the reproductive structures of the brain. "I'm interested in clinical applications," she says, "but all these questions get lost in the furor over behavioral differences."

The furor may be inevitable. The very mention of differences in ability between men and women seems to imply superiority and inferiority. Women researchers in the field have had the toughest going at times. Some have found themselves under Lysenkoist pressure to hew to women's-liberation orthodoxy, whatever their data show. University of Chicago psychologist Jerre Levy, a pioneer in studies of brain lateralization, withdrew from public discussion of her work after she was bombarded with hostile letters and phone calls. Harvard's Hrdy recalls sitting on a panel that was cautiously examining the "hypothesis" of male math superiority when a feminist seated next to her whispered, "Don't you know it's evil to do studies like that?" Says Hrdy: "I was just stunned. Of course it's not evil to do studies like that. It's evil to make pronouncements to say they're fact."

From the time women began moving—rather aggresively—into male-female studies, many researchers have grown wary of making such pronouncements. It has become increasingly difficult to find any statement that is not assidously qualified. One reason is that differences among members of the same sex are far greater than average differences *between* sexes. Monte Buchsbaum of the National Institutes of Health conducted tests of electrical activity in the brain showing that women tend to have a larger "evoked potential" than men—an indication of greater sensitivity to certain stimuli. But, he cautions, "individuals can vary over about a fivefold range. The variation between the sexes is only about 20 to 40 percent." Harvard's Richard Lewontin notes that the average male-female differential in math scores is only "half a standard deviation. That's rather small." The math dispute is "just silly," scoffs Lewontin, and assertions about "who's most aggressive or who's most analytical are just the garbage can of barroom speculation presented as science."

Many researchers contend that a child's awareness of gender is more decisive than biology in shaping sexual differences. "The real problem for determining what influences development in men and women is that they are called boys and girls from the day they are born," says biologist Lewontin. He cites the classic "blue, pink, yellow" experiments. When a group of observers was asked to describe newborn infants dressed in blue diapers, they were characterized as "very active." The same babies dressed in pink diapers evoked descriptions of gentleness. When the babies were wearing yellow, says Lewontin, observers "really got upset. They started to peek inside their diapers to see their sex."

It is clear that sex differences are not set in stone. The relationship between hormones and behavior, in fact, is far more intricate than was suspected until recently. There is growing evidence that it is part of a two-way system of cause-and-effect—what Lewontin calls "a complicated feedback loop between thought and action." Studies show that testosterone levels drop in male rhesus monkeys after they suffer a social setback and surge up when they experience a triumph. Other experiments indicate that emotional stress can change hormonal patterns in pregnant females, which in turn may affect the structure of the fetal brain.

By processes still not understood, biology seems susceptible to social stimuli. Ethel Tobach of New York's American Museum of Natural History cites experiments in which a virgin female rat is presented with a five-day-old rat pup. At first, her response is vague, says Tobach. "But by continuing to present the pup, you can get her to start huddling over it and assuming the nursing posture. How did that come about? There's obviously some biochemical factor that changes . . . When you have the olfactory, visual, auditory, tactile input of a five-day-old pup all those days, it can change the blood chemistry."

A more enigmatic example, says Tobach, is found in coral-reef fish: "About six species typically form a group of female fish with a male on the outside. If something happens to remove the male, the largest female becomes a functional male, able to produce sperm and impregnate females. It has been done in the lab as well as observed in the natural habitat."

The human parallels are limited. No one expects men or women to undergo spontaneous sex changes, and millennia of biological evolution aren't going to be undone by a century of social change. But it is now widely recognized that, for people as well as animals, biology and culture continually interact. The differences between men and women have been narrowing over evolutionary time, and in recent decades the gap has closed further.

Perhaps the most arresting implication of the research up to now is not that there are undeniable differences between males and females, but that their differences are so small, relative to the possibilities open to them. Human behavior exhibits a plasticity that has enabled men and women to cope with cultural and environmental extremes and has made them—by some measures—the most successful species in history. Unlike canaries, they can sing when the spirit, rather than testosterone, moves them. "Human beings," says Roger Gorski, "have learned to intervene with their hormones"—which is to say that their behavioral differences are what make them less, not more, like animals.

IN SPORTS, "LIONS VS. TIGERS"
Eric Gelman

When Don Schollander swam the 400-meter freestyle in 4 minutes, 12.2 seconds at the 1964 Olympics, he set a world record and took home a gold medal. Had he clocked the same time against the women racing at the 1980 Moscow Games, he would have come in fifth. In the pool and on the track, women have closed to within 10 percent or less of the best male times, and their impressive gains raise an intriguing question: will men and women ever compete as equals?

Athletics is one area of sex-difference research that generates little scientific controversy. Physiologists, coaches and trainers generally agree that while women will continue to improve their performances, they will never fully overcome inherent disadvantages in size and strength. In sports where power is a key ingredient of success, the best women will remain a stroke behind or a stride slower than the best men.

A man's biggest advantage is his muscle mass. Puberty stokes male bodies with the hormone testosterone, which adds bulk to muscles. A girl's puberty brings her an increase in fat, which shapes her figure but makes for excess baggage on an athlete. When growing ends, an average man is 40 per cent muscle and 15 per cent fat; a woman, 23 per cent muscle, 25 per cent fat. Training reduces fat, but no amount of working out will give a woman the physique of a man. Male and female athletes sometimes try to build bigger muscles by taking anabolic steroids—artificial male hormones that stimulate muscle growth—even though physicians consider them dangerous and all major sports have outlawed them.

Bulging muscles alone can't make a woman as strong as a man. Men have larger hearts and lungs and more hemoglobin in their blood, which enables them to pump oxygen to their muscles more efficiently than women can. A man's wider shoulders and longer arms also increase his leverage, and his longer legs move him farther with each step. "A female gymnast who puts her hands on a balance beam and raises herself up is showing a lot of strength," says Barbara Drinkwater, a physiologist with the University of California at Santa Barbara, Calif. "But a woman won't throw a discus as far as a man." Although highly conditioned women can achieve pound-for-pound parity with men in leg strength, their upper-body power is usually only one-half to two-thirds that of an equally well-conditioned male athlete.

A few sports make a virtue of anatomy for women. Extra body fat gives a female English Channel swimmer better buoyancy and more insulation from the cold, and narrow shoulders reduce her resistance in the water. As a result, women have beaten the fastest male's round-trip Channel crossing by a full three hours. In long-distance running contests, women may also be on equal footing with men. Grete Waitz's time of 2 hours, 25 minutes and 41 seconds in last year's New York City Marathon was good enough to bring her in ahead of all but 73 of the 11,000 men who finished the race. "Women tend to do better relative to men the longer the distance gets,"

Eric Gelman, "In Sports, 'Lions vs. Tigers,'" *Newsweek* 18 May 1981.

says Joan Ullyot, author of "Running Free." "On races 100 kilometers and up, it may turn out that women are more suited to endurance than men." Under the body-draining demands of extended exertion, a woman's fat may provide her with deeper energy reserves. Satisfied that women can take the strain, the International Olympic Committee has authorized a women's marathon for the 1984 Games. In previous years the longest Olympic race for females was 1,500 meters—less than a mile.

Women athletes have dispelled the myths about their susceptibility to injury. The uterus and ovaries are surrounded by shock-absorbing fluids—far better protected than a male's exposed reproductive equipment. And the bouncing of breasts doesn't make them more prone to cancer, or even to sagging. As for psychological toughness, Penn State physiologist and sports psychologist Dorothy Harris says that "if you give a woman a shot at a $100,000 prize, you discover that she can be every bit as aggressive as a man."

Going one-on-one with a man is not the goal of most women in sports. "It's like pitting lions against tigers," declares Ullyot. "Women's achievements should not be downgraded by comparing them to men's." But as organized women's sports grow up, they will have to face up to at least one serious masculine challenge. According to Ann Uhlir, executive director of the Association for Intercollegiate Athletics for Women, when a college starts taking its women's sports program seriously, it tends to put a man in charge.

IT IS DIFFERENT FOR WOMEN
James Lincoln Collier

"Shortly after our culture said to women, 'You may have orgasms,' it began saying, 'You *must*.'"

So states Dr. John Francis Steege, assistant professor of obstetrics-gynecology at Duke University Medical Center. Contrary to current cultural wisdom, he maintains that orgasm is not inevitably a part of sex for women; indeed, for some women it is not even terribly important.

Dr. Steege is one of a growing number of experts who are saying that sex for women should not be judged by male standards. Investigators in universities and clinics around the country have concluded that males and females do not bring all of the same needs to sex, or experience it in the same way. Although it may be true, as some researchers have reported, that there is little physical difference between male and female orgasm, its *meaning* appears to be different for a woman than for a man.

For almost two decades women have been taught that they can and should have orgasms as easily as men—indeed, more easily, because they have the capacity for multiple orgasms which men lack. Despite all this "consciousness raising," however, many women have more difficulty than men do in achieving orgasm in intercourse. According to a study by Michigan clinicians Dana Wilcox and Ruth Hager, "Our findings challenge the theory that it is pathological for a woman to be unable to experience orgasm from intercourse." They say that less than half (41.5 percent) of women regularly experience orgasm through intercourse alone, without additional stimulation. Instead, some women (33 percent) regularly choose to experience orgasm during foreplay, and a smaller percentage after intercourse.

Why *don't* the majority of women achieve orgasm in intercourse as easily as men? A number of researchers, including Wardell Pomeroy, academic dean of the Institute for the Advanced Study of Sexuality, look to evolution for an answer. So far as we know, in no other species of mammal do females experience orgasm. This is probably because male orgasm is necessary for reproduction, while female orgasm is not. According to one theory, human females have begun to evolve the capacity for orgasm for reasons not fully understood. But the development is still uneven, existing in a greater degree in some women than in others.

Whatever the cause, most women do have a higher "threshold" of orgasmic response than men. That is to say, it takes more to trigger it. Unfortunately, many women have come to believe that they could always be orgasmic during sex if they could only relax, or try a different technique, or *something*. As a result, says William Kephart, professor sociology at the University of Pennsylvania, "these women feel inadequate if they don't regularly have orgasms."

All of this makes it sound as if women who have difficulty in achieving orgasm find sex frustrating. In fact, they don't. Surveys have shown repeatedly that such

James Lincoln Collier, "It *Is* Different for Women," *Readers Digest* January 1982.

women can and usually do enjoy sex. One study, made at Pennsylvania State University by psychologist David Shope, discovered that a high percentage of women who didn't have orgasms felt complete relaxation following intercourse anyway.

If orgasm is not the central goal of intercourse for many women, what *is*? One thing, apparently, is a state which has been referred to as "arousal." In a study at the University of California, Prof. Uta Landy concludes that arousal is very important. "Physiologically," says Landy, "arousal seems to be a pulsing, a push, a throbbing throughout the entire pelvic region which means a readiness for intercourse. The feeling is spread much wider throughout the body than it is in men, where it is usually concentrated in the sex organ."

What men fail to understand—and find puzzling when they do—is that for many women this feeling of arousal is not just a stage on the road to orgasm, but an end in itself. For some women it is a pleasant, "tingly" experience; for others it is almost ecstatic. "It's as if I were bursting with sunshine," says one woman.

Moreover, the state of arousal is not merely physical. Feelings of affection and closeness to the sex partner are also involved. Nor does it necessarily lead to orgasm. When most men achieve a certain level of arousal, they are impelled to go to orgasm. This is not always so for women. Says Shope, "It is evident that petting techniques capable of producing a state of high sexual arousal in women do not ensure the continuation of this state in coitus." Indeed, arousal is more commonly experienced by women in petting or foreplay. When the shift to intercourse comes, in many instances the woman's arousal level may actually *drop*, rather than rise.

And yet for most women intromission—the feeling of the male inside her—constitutes an important part of sex. Most women, in fact, do not feel that the sex act is complete until this happens. According to Shope's study, desire for intromission was strong in 85 percent of the women who were orgasmic, and moderate to strong in 90 percent of the non-orgasmic ones. Even when women did not expect to achieve a climax, nearly all of them wanted intromission anyway.

"This is an interesting point," says Landy, "because, as studies show, intercourse is not necessarily the best way for a woman to achieve orgasm. It suggests that intromission has a meaning of its own for women."

Another point, long held by folk wisdom and now supported by the new studies, is that women are less promiscuous than men. With the new freedoms of the past decade, many women have felt that they ought to be as free as men to seek sex wherever they can find it. Yet it turns out that most women aren't all that interested in casual sex. According to studies by Judith Bardwick, professor of psychology at the University of Michigan, females still have fewer sex partners than do males—even though the rate of non-monogamous sexual relations among women is rising.

Researchers like sociobiologist Richard Dawkins of Oxford University in England and anthropologist Donald Symonds of the University of California at Santa Barbara have an intriguing explanation for this phenomenon, based on the different "sexual strategies" generally pursued by male and female animals throughout evolutionary history. For a male, in order to reproduce himself most successfully, and thus win the evolutionary competition with other males, the idea has been to mate with as many females as possible.

This strategy has been possible because, for males, there is little energy involved in reproduction. For females, however, a great deal of time and energy goes into producing an offspring. So the human female strategy has been to make sure that the father is sufficiently attached to her to help protect and feed the child. Therefore, she naturally prefers to have sex with somebody she believes loves and cares for her, rather than with somebody who will depart the next morning.

Whether all women—or men, for that matter—will accept these explanations of male and female sexual behavior, one thing seems abundantly clear: we must begin to rethink a lot of accepted notions about sex. For men and women, it *is* different.

WHO IS REALLY BETTER AT MATH?

It is well known that teen-age boys tend to do better at math than girls, that male high school students are more likely than their female counterparts to tackle advanced math courses like calculus, that virtually all the great mathematicians have been men. But why? Are women born with less mathematical ability? Or does society's sexism slow their progress?

In 1980 two Johns Hopkins University researchers tried to settle the eternal nature/nurture debate. Julian Stanley—who is well respected for his work with precocious math students of both sexes—and Camilla Benbow had tested 10,000 talented seventh- and eighth-graders between 1972 and 1979. Using the Scholastic Aptitude Test, in which math questions are meant to measure ability rather than knowledge, they discovered distinct sex differences. While the verbal abilities of the males and females hardly differed, twice as many boys as girls scored over 500 (on a scale of 200 to 800) on mathematical ability; at the 700 level, the ratio was 14 to 1. The conclusion: males have inherently superior mathematical reasoning ability.

Benbow and Stanley's findings, which were published in *Science*, disturbed some men and not a few women. Now there is comfort for those people in a new study from the University of Chicago that suggests math is not, after all, a natural male domain. With Researcher Sharon Senk, Professor Zalman Usiskin, a specialist in high school mathematics curriculums and an author of several math texts, studied 1,366 tenth-graders. They were selected from geometry classes and tested on their ability to solve geometry proofs, a subject requiring both abstract reasoning and spatial ability. Says Usiskin: "If you're a math whiz or a computer bug, you're going to pick up equations and formulas that will help you with tests like the SAT. But geometry proof is never learned outside of school." The conclusion reached by Usiskin and Senk: there are no sex differences in math ability.

The results of their study will be presented at this week's meeting of the American Educational Research Association in New York City. In a draft that has already been circulated, the Chicago researchers decided to take a few swipes at the recent Johns Hopkins findings. They argued that Benbow and Stanley had measured performance, not ability. Says Usiskin: "To assume that the SAT has no connection with experience is poppycock." Replies Stanley, who now has 50,000 subjects to bolster his conclusion: "People are so eager not to believe that there is a difference in mathematical reasoning ability between boys and girls that all kinds of people are taking potshots."

The Chicago study, says Stanley, is "irrelevant" because it tests knowledge of mathematics rather than raw ability. He points out that the students were receiving geometry instruction at the time of the test. "What they've done," says Stanley, "is to show that when you teach boys and girls together in math classes, the girls learn quite well, and we've known that for 50 years."

"Who Is Really Better at Math?" *Time* 22 March 1982.

While the critical volleys fly between Baltimore and Chicago, some educators believe that both sides are missing the real target. University of Wisconsin Professor Elizabeth Fennema, who has been studying sex-related differences in math for twelve years, maintains that most female mathematical disabilities result from environment. Says she: "Neither study has collected a bit of data on the genetic evidence. Neither is measuring innate ability." She discourages debate over mathematical genetics, since she believes it is insoluble and burdens one sex with an implied deficiency for which there is no remedy. Indeed, the researchers agree on one important fact: if boys and girls are given capable teaching and comparable attention, both will achieve.

THE PERILS OF PAUL, THE PANGS OF PAULINE
Jo Durden-Smith and Diane deSimone

The back pages of the paper contain some amazing items these days: There's almost always something such as "GENE FOUND FOR DEPRESSION"; "CRIMINAL BEHAVIOR THOUGHT TO BE INHERITED"; "MURDERESS AQUITTED: PSYCHIATRIST POINTS TO PREMENSTRUAL TENSION"; "BRAIN CHEMICAL TIED TO SCHIZOPHRENIA." And: "IS THERE A GENE FOR MATH?"

We read the items separately, not seeing how they hang together. And so we fail to realize that, buried in those small headlines, there is a revolution going on—a revolution that will soon change, once and for all, the way we think about human behavior. . . .

What does that mean for men and women? It means that at precisely the time we're most avidly rushing to psychiatrists and other practitioners of the spirit, science is quietly announcing that the game is off, a new die is cast, the rules have changed. We're not the purely "psychological" creatures we thought we were, fraught with psychological problems that, if they are to be cured, demand psychological understanding. Instead, we are the creatures, to an extent not yet fully known, of *biological* forces. Our mood disorders, our madness and, perhaps, even our crime are biological in both origin and expression—in the brain. That goes for not only the major problems that bedevil this society—the one percent of people who suffer from schizophrenia, the five percent who are crippled by illnesses of mood, the two percent who commit almost all of the crime and the billions of dollars such aberrations cost each year. It goes for the minor problems that bedevil our families and our relationships—the mood swings of parents, the hyperactivity and aggressiveness of children, and come-and-go depressions of women and the irritability and instability of men. At the mysterious heart of *all* these things lies biology—set up by the genes, mediated by the sex hormones and expressed in a different chemistry in the ultimate home of our personality, our brain.

For the moment, then, forget psychology—all the assumptions you've learned about a mind that you inhabit and that you alone can control. Ignore the effects of the environment on who you are and the way you behave. Fix your gaze, instead, on the biological and genetic core of yourself, as a member of one sex of the human species—differently made, differently programed, differently wired and with a different chemical design, differently "juiced," as one scientist recently put it. For, if you do, you'll begin to see why the small newspaper headlines combine into a radically new view of men and women. You'll begin to piece together the causes of many of the misunderstandings and tensions between us. And you'll begin to understand, as science is just beginning to, why the bewildering strengths and weaknesses

Jo Durden-Smith and Diane deSimone, "The Perils of Paul, the Pangs of Pauline," *Playboy* May 1982. Durden-Smith and deSimone are also the authors of *Sex and the Brain* (1983).

of each one of us, man and woman, seem to come packaged together. Why a woman's immune system is superior to a man's but more likely to attack the body it's supposed to protect. Why men, in general, are superior in math reasoning but are much more likely to be sexual deviants or psychopaths. Why women are strong in areas of communication but are preferentially attacked by phobias and depression. And why there are more males at both ends of the intellectual spectrum—more retardates but *also* more geniuses.

If you think that psychiatrists, psychologists and all those who've made a professional commitment to the effects of the environment will be horrified by this altered gaze of yours, you're right. But if you think that their spiritual father, Sigmund Freud, would be equally horrified, you're wrong. Freud treated all sorts of personalities and disorders, among them psychosomatic illnesses, schizophrenia, hysteria and depression. And he said many times that despite all his theories, one day a "constitutional predisposition" would be found to be responsible for our problems. "A special chemism," he predicted, would be discovered at their heart. And he was right. By inference and indirection, such a chemism has been found at the core of our nature as men and women. And we are at the beginning of a road through that chemism that will lead us to a full explanation of why we are differently gifted, differently protected and differently at risk. For the complete story, you'll have to wait 20 years or so; 20 years marked—if one can judge by present signs—by controversy, battle, arguments about free will and radical new approaches to education, health and the treatment of violence, mood and madness. In the meantime, here are the landmarks—and the paths that science is tracing between them.

Let's start with heart disease and heart attacks. Forty million Americans have some form of heart disease, and this year, about 1,500,000 will have heart attacks. The majority in both categories are men. "Ah-ha!" the men among you will no doubt say. "That's the environment. That's stress. Just wait until the same number of women go out into the world and start pulling the same weight that we do. They'll soon be dropping like ninepins from the effects of stress, just as *we* are."

Sorry, guys. That's almost certainly untrue. The connections between the stresses of the brain and the problems of the heart aren't well understood—and that's something you'll have to remember throughout this article, that science knows not a lot but very little. From what science *does* know, however, three things stand out. First, working women are healthier, in general, than their nonworking sisters. Second, women are protected against the most common form of heart disease by their primary sex hormones, the estrogens. And, third, they seem to respond to stress—both chemically and behaviorally—quite differently from men.

Human responses to stress are mediated by a group of brain structures known to control emotion and what scientists fondly call "the four Fs"—feeding, fleeing, fighting and . . . sex. Those structures direct the body's immediate responses to danger—the accelerated heartbeat, the heightened senses, the rush of adrenaline, the raised blood pressure, the preparation for a quick burst of energy. During stress, the hormonal mechanisms by which they do this become more or less continuously activated. A little stress isn't bad for you—it's a necessary part of life and it may, indeed, be pleasurable. But, in the long term, it can have several nasty effects. It can make the body less resistant to infections and, conceivably, to certain forms of cancer. (The dim connection between stress and the defensive immune system should be borne in mind for later.) It can cause heart disease, because the heart, among other things, is forced to work too hard. And it can so excite a center high in the brain that the heart is sent by it into a fatal overdrive—a fibrillation, a full-blown attack. Whether or not those things happen seems to depend on the individual's genetic make-up.

But it also depends on gender. So-called Type-A people—who have a chronic urgency about time and are hard-driving, competitive, extroverted and aggressive—are said to be particularly at risk from the damaging effects of stress. But it's now beginning to appear that this is true of only Type-A *males*. Studies in Sweden have recently shown that Type-A females, when solving work-related problems, simply don't show the increase in heart rate, blood pressure and adrenaline flow that Type-A males do. Even when their over-all health picture is the same, they don't have as many heart attacks.

That doesn't mean, of course, that women aren't responsive to stress. It simply means that their chemistry is different in some way. They seem to find different things stressful, and they seem to react in a different way to the stress in their environment. If there is a word that can sum up this difference in their make-up, it's emotion. Women tend to be put into stress by the emotional coloration of their lives—not by paper problems but by people and communication problems. And when they experience setback, failure or emotional pressure, they don't go into overdrive the way men do. They respond emotionally or fall back into depression. You may not like that, ladies, but it's probably a good thing. It certainly doesn't cause as much wear and tear on the body.

The next question is, *Why* should there be that over-all difference? And the answer is really anybody's guess. It probably has to do with the different evolutionary pressures that affected the development of men and women—men, the hunters and competitors for sex, were more likely to need elaborate stress mechanisms in the presence of danger; and women, the nurturers and centers of social groups, were more likely to need fine-tuned emotional responses and skills. Depression and the effects of continuous stress may be the different prices men and women pay for those legacies—an integral part of our maleness and femaleness.

That that is true—at least for poor males—is suggested by a few pieces of evidence. Scientists working with male laboratory animals have shown that dominance (sexual success and the successful maintenance of a large piece of turf) is associated with high blood pressure and hardening of the arteries, telltale signs of the effects of stress. But they've also found that the animals at the top of the heap have high levels of testosterone, the hormone most essential to maleness. The plot thickens. For it's testosterone that makes hardening of the arteries such a problem in *human* males. It causes the production of a liver protein that ties up cholesterol in the arteries' lining, causing the formation of fat deposits called plaques. The bigger those plaques, the more difficulty the heart has in pumping blood. The more difficulty the heart has, the greater the risk of heart disease.

Findings of this sort are, again, only landmarks in an otherwise empty landscape. But they make it plain that in stress, behavior, emotion, genes, sex hormones, the body and the brain are all interlinked. And they point the way toward the discovery of a more general connection between emotion and disease, the brain and the immune system. For the moment, there are only a few curious straws in this area. Laboratory animals, for example, don't get the hardening of the arteries scientists try to inflict on them if they're handled a lot—if they're loved. And married people are generally happier and healthier than unmarried ones. They have less heart disease. So it goes.

Having left the men among you deeply worried about an area in which you seem to be at a disadvantage, let's turn the tables on the women—let's move upstairs to an area in which *women* seem to be at a disadvantage. It, too, involves anxiety, and it involves an ability—mathematical-reasoning ability. Is that, too, part of a special chemism?

"There you go again," you women will no doubt say. "Everyone knows that's the environment. Girls are taught from the beginning that math is for boys. They're given no encouragement. They have no role models, no expectations, no self-confidence and no support. And a lot less is demanded of them. It's no *wonder* that they become anxious about math. And it's no wonder that they seem to be less good at it than boys."

Sorry, ladies. But that, too, is almost certainly untrue—and it surely isn't the end of the story. Do you begin to see how controversial this theorizing about the differences between men and women can get? Johns Hopkins' Camilla Persson Benbow and Julian Stanley most assuredly do. Three months after those scientists merely *suggested* that there might be real, "endogenous" differences in math ability, they were seen at a conference looking pale and haggard—drained by the often-unreasonable attacks launched against them in the wake of their December 1980 report.

"You have to understand," Benbow says softly, with a distant trace of a Scandinavian accent, "that we didn't start out looking for sex differences in mathematical ability. The Johns Hopkins Study of Mathematically Precocious Youth—S.M.P.Y.—simply conducted six talent searches in the mid-Atlantic states between 1972 and 1979. We were looking for gifted seventh and eighth graders who, though they hadn't usually been taught any higher mathematics, could still manage a very high score on the math part of the Scholastic Aptitude Test—a test designed for bright, college-bound high school seniors. What we were looking for, in other words, was a natural aptitude for mathematical reasoning. We found about 10,000 children in those six years.

"But we also found something that rather shocked us: There were more boys than girls among our kids. On the average, the boys scored much higher than the girls. And on no occasion was a girl tops on the test. Well, we were bound to ask why. So we studied the boys and girls on every variable available that could possibly account for the discrepancy—preparation in mathematics, liking for math, the encouragement given them, and so on. And we could find no difference at all—except the one in over-all ability, mathematical-reasoning ability. Since 1979, we've looked at another 24,000 children and have found the same sex difference in ability. And we've conducted a nationwide talent search for children at the top end of the scale. We found 63 boys—and no girls."

Benbow, a striking woman in her mid-20s, is clearly still surprised, a year after the publication of her and Professor Stanley's paper, by the controversy it generated. She's reluctant to say that the chemistry governed by the sex chromosomes is at the root of that sex difference, and she would love, she says, to find an environmental difference that has been overlooked, to find it and correct it. But she quotes a follow-up study completed on a group of girls who were specially taught and specially encouraged. And even *that*, she says, seems to have made no ultimate difference. At the root, still, is the difference in mathematical-reasoning ability. When the time comes for girls to use it formally in class—in calculus, differential equations and analytical geometry, for example—they seem to fall even further behind the boys, even when they're gifted and have no anxiety about the subject.

"All this," says Benbow carefully, "suggests that there may be a biological basis to the difference, after all. And, if so, then it's likely to be connected to the male's right-hemisphere superiority in visual-spatial tasks. You see, females tend to use their stronger *left* hemisphere—their superior verbal skills—in their approach to problems. I know I do. And there's a certain level at which the verbal approach is inefficient in math—look at the way mathematicians are forced to talk to one another, via symbols on a blackboard. Now, that approach may be something that actually *suits* males. From the beginning, they're less verbally oriented than fe-males—more oriented to things, to objects in space. They're less dependent on context. They're more abstract.

"This may help explain, too, I think, why men are overrepresented in certain disciplines in science—something we've also been studying. To be a good physicist or engineer, for example, requires not only mathematical-reasoning ability but also skill in three-dimensional visual imagery. And that probably makes most women unfit. To be a good scientist at all, in fact, seems to require a set of qualities more characteristic of men than of women—spatial ability, independence, a low social interest and an absorption in things. Let's face it, human males like to manipulate *things*—from Tinkertoys to the cosmos." She laughs. "Females are more dependent, more communicative, more sensitive to context and more interested in people. Perhaps that's why there are so many women in psychology. Like me."

How mathematical-reasoning ability and stress are interconnected may not be clear at first sight. There are, however, a number of threads that do, in fact, connect them. One can be seen intuitively, at the level of personality and problem solving: independence versus interdependence; absorption in abstract problems—things—versus absorption in people; fixated men versus emotional, communicative and less stress-prone women. Another can be seen at the level of the sex hormones. For from various bits and pieces of evidence, men's superior visual-spatial—and, hence, math—ability seems to be related to their testosterone, just as are a number of their problems in stress. Chemism lies at the heart of both and, therefore, may explain why there have been many more male composers and painters—not to mention architects and town planners—in history. Hormones, visual-spatial ability, appli-cation, abstraction. *For every strength, there is weakness, though.* Visual-spatial men are better organized on the right side of their brain, verbal women on the left. But they are both comparatively weak on the side where the other is strong.

That fact takes us deeper into the differences between us. It takes us to the embattled core of our civilization. To crime. To mood. To sudden changes in personality. To madness. And to the problems of our children.

If you've ever given a party for four-and-five-year-olds (or even 11-and-12-year-olds), you may remember that you've known instinctively that girls develop faster and are more mature than boys. They're less shy, more verbal and readier to join the group. They have puberty earlier. And, until then—to use a favorite Monty Python phrase—they're "all-round less weedy." The reason, as you probably sensed at the time, has nothing to do with environment or with the circumstances of your party. It is that boys, *from the beginning*, are more precarious—an altogether more iffy proposition—than girls.

To begin at the beginning: Sperm carrying the male sex chromosome seem to swim faster and have more staying power than sperm carrying the female sex chromosome. That's good. And between 120 and 140 males are conceived for every 100 females. Also good. From there on in, though, it's downhill all the way. More males are spontaneously aborted during pregnancy, and althugh they retain a slight edge at the time of birth—106 to 100—the decline continues. More males than females are born dead. Thirty percent more males than females die in the first months of life. And 70 percent of all birth defects are associated mainly with males. The result is that by the time of puberty, the head start achieved by the male sperm has been lost. And the population of men and women has become about equal—at a considerable cost to males.

The reason is, again, anybody's guess. Some sociobiologists say it has to do with the higher value of the male in a polygamous species. Whatever the ultimate cause, though, there is an immediate one much nearer to hand. For the fact is, the male has to go through many more elaborate transformations in the womb than the female. More can go wrong, so more males die in the womb. And, as a result of all the hormonal toings-and-froings to which they're exposed, they are born less mature, less sturdy and less ready for the world than girls. Like all premature babies, they're more at risk after birth—both in the body and in the brain.

For example, the slightest brain damage—occurring during or after birth—has a far more debilitating effect on boys than it does on girls. What's more, it virtually always strikes boys in the hemisphere in which they're less well organized—the left. It's not male visual-spatial abilities, secure in their right hemisphere, that suffer. It's language skills and language controls, in the left. Boys' left hemisphere, in other words, faces a sort of double indemnity. And the result is that they're four or five times as likely to suffer from language disorders and disabilities as any girl. Boys are more likely (five to one) to stutter when the left hemisphere loses control during speech. They're more likely to be austistic (four to one), often with a complete absence of left-hemisphere language. They're more likely to be what's called an *idiot savant* (figures unknown)—language-damaged and incapacitated but with some narrow, brilliant mathematical skill. (Ah-ha!) And boys are more likely to suffer from two so-called developmental disorders: aphasia, or extreme difficulty learning to talk (five to one); and dyslexia—extreme difficulty with reading and writing (up to six to one). Nelson Rockefeller had dyslexia, so we know the company's good. And, recently, Albert Galaburda of Boston's Beth Israel Hospital found direct evidence that at least one type of dyslexia is caused by early language-area brain damage—damage, when it happens in girls, that has less effect on their more developed and better organized left hemisphere.

But hang on, guys—your problems with your left hemisphere only *start* here. And those problems strike, in a very mysterious way, right to the heart of the male personality. Men commit almost all the violent crime, and the so-called antisocial personality at the root of most of it seems to be caused by poor functioning of the left hemisphere. Men are the sexual deviates—the pedophiles, the fetishists, the exhibitionists and the homosexual sadists. Here, too, something has gone wrong with the way the left hemisphere governs behavior. For *all* the other problems that afflict men and boys much more than they do women and girls, it's almost certainly the same old left-hemisphere story. Hyperactivity, alcoholism, mania and early-onset schizophrenia: left hemisphere. And if you think those things don't concern you personally, you're wrong. Hyperactivity, for example, affects more than 2,000,000 boys in this country. It's not a problem that is, by any means, always outgrown—hyperactive children often grow up to become alcoholics or child abusers, hot-tempered, aggressive and unable to keep a job. As for schizophrenia, you should know this: For every full-blown schizophrenic in this society, there are between three and ten more walking around with lesser but related disorders.

Your first reaction to that news may be, "Yes, but that really *is* the environment, isn't it? That's too many toys, too much stimulation. It's diet. It's a terrible home. It's crazy parents. It's a bad upbringing." Unfortunately, it simply isn't that easy. That it isn't brings us right back to the special chemism we've been talking about all along, the chemistry that distinguishes man and woman. First, those largely male disorders can't be cured by psychiatric hand-holding methods—"understanding" the patient's problem or the environment that "caused" it. Second, the only therapy that ultimately works on such disorders is the use of drugs or anti-hormones that alter the chemistry of the brain. And, third, for all those abnormalities, scientists have recently found just what Freud predicted for his "mental" illnesses—a constitutional predisposition, a *genetic* element.

"The genetic studies," says psychiatrist Pierre Flor-Henry, "have looked not just at how much these things run in families. "They've looked at identical twins. And—most important—they've looked at what happens in *adoption*. Is a child, adopted early, more likely to follow the pattern of his real parents than the pattern of his adoptive parents—in crime, hyperactivity, schizophrenia, and so on? The answer is yes, he is. It's not just the environment, then. Nature, a predisposition, is at work in some way we don't yet fully understand. Equally important, there's also a *connection* between some of them, a genetic connection. For example, alcoholism, hysteria and antisocial personality seem to cluster in the same families."

Flor-Henry is a slight, dapper Franco-Hungarian in his 40s: clinical professor at the University of Alberta, director of admission services at the Alberta Hospital and a man who spends much of his research time trying to pull together into one overall picture all that is now being discovered about the two brain hemispheres, the chemistry and the disorders of men and women. "There's not much to go on," he says. "We still know so little. But genes are responsible for the body's chemistry. So the predisposition is a chemical one, perhaps triggered into expression by damage of some kind or by an event or series of events in the world. It's not guaranteed. But the damage or the events, if they happen, may preferentially affect and alter the chemical organization, in males, of their brain's weaker left hemisphere.

"And the genetic defect then comes into its own, resulting in behavior that's deranged or unstable in one way or another. The behavior—and the brain—can then be treated only with drugs that, either directly or indirectly, put the left hemisphere back into balance. In schizophrenia, that involves drugs affecting the supply of a brain chemical called dopamine. In hyperactivity, it involves drugs that affect the dopamine supply in a *reverse* direction. In sexual deviance—and, perhaps, in antisocial personality, violent crime, it involves drugs that block the action of the main male sex hormone."

If you men are thinking that your comparative left-hemisphere weakness makes you a variable, deviant, hit-or-miss sex, then you're right. Nature doesn't seem to have taken out much insurance on you—especially where the social and verbal left hemisphere is concerned. You are less well protected against your own excesses, just as in stress. If it's any consolation, Flor-Henry believes it's because you evolved as the sex-*seeking* gender. He thinks that the human *right* hemisphere developed in such a way that visual-spatial skills were linked in it to mood, movement and sexual fulfillment. And because the male was the one to go after sex—rather than just being able to sit and wait for it—the organization of the male right hemisphere became particularly pronounced. Males became lopsided—they put all their eggs in the right-hemisphere basket. Females evolved in a more balanced way. Because females were the pursued rather than the pursuers, they were able to develop verbal skills and verbal controls in the left hemisphere that were much more stable, secure and efficient. That goes some way toward explaining why women tend not to become psychopaths and violent criminals. Women, remember, don't go into overdrive when under stress. They tend to become depressed. And their pattern of crime is quite different. They don't act out against people. Antisocial males, on the other hand, virtually *always* attack people. And Flor-Henry thinks they're out of control of the verbal and social left hemisphere. Instead, they're exaggerated, out-on-a-limb, right-hemisphere males using all their visual and spatial skills for aggression.

If this evolutionary dispensation seems profoundly unfair to you males, then all we can do is remind you of the delicate balance between strengths and weaknesses. In the words of an old joke, "With a Bernstein diamond comes the Bernstein curse." And the same rule goes for women. This time, though, they're at risk somewhere else—just where males are strong. In the right hemisphere.

There are three things you can say with certainty about depressed people. One, they don't jump around. Two, they tend to lose all sexual interest. And, three, they're mostly women. Every year, 40,000,000 Americans suffer, to one degree or another, from depression. Two thirds of them are women.

Of course, you can sing the old song about the environment. "Girls are taught from the beginning not to express their anger. They turn their anger inward. When they become women, they find themselves in a rotten, male-dominated society. Men don't give them what they want. They stifle and ignore all women's emotional subtlety. No wonder women are depressed."

The last part of the song is probably true. And, of course, there *are* real environmental causes for depression. If you've set your heart on being a concert pianist and can't even manage *Chopsticks*, you're likely to be depressed. And if you've lost a father, mother, husband, wife, child or friend, you shouldn't be expected to be happy. But that still doesn't explain why so many more women than men are afflicted by a disorder that affects mood, movement and sex drive in their right hemisphere. And it certainly doesn't explain why, though nothing on the surface of a woman's life is wrong, she can suddenly be sent into a terrible tail spin. Psychological explanations of that sort of depression are useless, and such psychiatric treatment of it is, at best, a waste of money and of time—women may simply become even more entrenched in their despair. No, the only way to understand so-called *vital* depression (which women have to endure five times more often than men), as well as phobias (which cripple women at least twice as often), is through women's chemism—genes, hormones and brain chemistry. Again, it lies right at the heart of the female personality. And it can tell us a lot about the human female's emotional vulnerability, her more general swings in mood that break up relationships and leave men feeling left out, unsympathetic and confused.

"Depression and the phobias obviously hang together," says Flor-Henry. "They attack the hemisphere in which the organization of the female brain is more precarious—the right hemisphere. The phobias—they should be called the panics—are panics about heights, open and closed spaces, water, and so on. And they obviously have to do with mood, movement and visual-spatial skill—right hemisphere. The same things are affected in vital depression—*plus*, of course, sexual drive. Again, right hemisphere. There are two other things, too, that yoke them together. First, the only *really* effective treatment for both is with antidepressants—not Valium or Librium but two classes of drugs that have no effect at all, except maybe an unpleasant one, on normal people. And, second, both seem to involve a genetic predisposition, just as the predominantly *male* disorders do. Not much is yet known about the phobias. But work done in Belgium has shown that adopted children with depression are more likely to have that depression in common with their *real* parents rather than with their adoptive parents.

"So," says Flor-Henry, spreading his fingers on the table. "Genetic. Biological. Chemical. Right hemisphere. We don't know how those things interconnect. And we don't know how they relate to the milder forms of depression and mood disorder in women. My guess is, though, that all those things are part of one evolutionary package—affecting the weaker right hemisphere and involving the sex hormones."

The sex hormones—here they are again. They're somewhere at the core of a man's response to stress, and they're also at the heart of the chemistry of a woman's moods. The evidence isn't hard to find. It comes from routine parts of ordinary life—from puberty, childbirth, the menstrual cycle, menopause, the pill. And the upshot of it is this: Alter the level of a woman's sex hormones, in large or even in small ways, and she'll be likely to suffer from subtle and not-so-subtle changes in mood and personality. Sometimes, she'll no longer be in control of her own personality—her hormones will be.

We haven't space here to go into the problems of puberty and menopause, but you should know this: About seven percent of new mothers suffer for weeks, even months, from severe depression—complete with loss of sexual interest—at precisely the time when their hormone levels have been abruptly altered by the births of their children. And an unknown percentage of women on the pill report a bewildering variety of side effects, including lowered sex drive, irritability and, yes, depression. Those things are all too often looked on—by lover, husband, doctor, even the woman herself—as psychological in origin. Her responsibility. And they can lead to the breakup of relationships and marriages. How many new mothers have you known whose husbands left them within 15 months of the baby's birth?

Then there's premenstrual tension. Before you guys walk away or chuckle, you should know that you, too, may have your "time of the month"—that's how new this science is—and it may be marked by the same irritability and tension. If it exists, however, it seems also to be unpredictable and irregular. And that means that you'll have to abandon all your old assumptions about "women's problems." Who, after all, would you want doing skilled and responsible jobs—flying a plane, performing brain surgery, and so on? Someone whose switches in mood are predictable or someone whose switches in mood are *unpredictable*?

British psychiatrist Katharina Dalton believes that premenstrual tension affects four out of ten women to some extent, and for eight days—before and during menstruation—it *seriously* affects the life of one of those four. Being on the pill, says Dalton, actually makes the condition worse. Not ony do the symptoms include brooding, lethargy, depression, loss of memory and emotional control; they also include, she says, an increased incidence of quarrels, accidents, suicides, baby battering and crime.

In November 1981, Dalton appeared in court as a witness for the defense of one of her patients, a 29-year-old English barmaid named Sandie Smith. You may have read about that case, for its implications havn't gone unnoticed by the press. Smith had had 30 previous convictions—for arson and assault, among other offenses—and she was already on probation for having stabbed another barmaid to death in 1980. This time, she was charged with threatening to kill a policeman. Dalton, however, was able to demonstrate that all her crimes were connected by a 29-day cycle—and by premenstrual tension. And Smith was given three years' probation.

The very next day, November tenth, the very same defense—premenstrual tension—was brought up by Dalton in the case of another woman, Christine English, who had had an argument with her lover and had run over him with a car. English was discharged—conditional for a year—after pleading guilty to manslaughter. The court ruled that at the time of her crime, she had "diminished responsibility."

Those are examples of where the new discoveries about the chemistry of men and women can lead, and there's no doubt that the same defense will soon be used in a case in the United States. It will call into question, in a public way, everything we now presume about personal responsibility and the effects of the environment.

Is a woman suffering from premenstrual tension responsible for what she does? Is a man responsible for his reaction to stress? Is a male criminal responsible for his crimes or does the responsibility lie with his testosterone level and his lopsided brain organization?

These are revolutionary new questions. Revolutionary in law. Revolutionary in the home. Revolutionary in the way we think about ourselves and about one another. And if we are to find answers for them, we will have to think very carefully, not only about the chemistry of the brain but also about our place in nature and the way in which our biological evolution may now be at odds with our cultural evolution.

Take phobias, for example. They usually appear in women only during the childbearing years. And, you'll notice, they involve fears of everything that might have been dangerous in the environment in which we evolved—heights, open and closed spaces, water, snakes, and so on. Such phobias weren't a bad idea then—especially if you had to protect a child.

What about depression? Well, for most of our evolutionary history, isolated women could not survive. They *had* to be interdependent members of social groups. Indeed, they were the necessary glue that held those groups together. A woman's tendency to depression, then, may have been a mechanism that reinforced her interdependence and accelerated her back into the group by producing the cry for help. In today's society, of course, there aren't many close-knit social groups. There is a cry for help, but no help comes—and we have a major problem with depression.

Each one of the landmarks in this science of men and women brings us nearer to a picture of the whole landscape of ourselves. In 1981, for example, scientists located for the first time an actual gene that they think is involved in depression. And it's in a very odd place: It's either very close to or actually among a group of genes that govern the development of the human immune system—our defense against diseases. And it's the neighbor of a gene that's responsible, when expressed, for masculinizing female fetuses in the womb.

Maleness and femaleness, mental illness, hormones, hemispheres and diseases: This is the final mystery and our final port of call. What is there at the heart of our nature that gives us not only different strengths and weaknesses but a proneness to such different diseases? How can that be added to the picture?

One thing about organic diseases—they're physical, not "environmental." Either you get them or you don't. So there probably will be no complaints about this part of our story—except, perhaps, from you guys. Because here, again, you're at a disadvantage. You're just not as well protected as women. As if dying in the womb, being born "weedy" and maturing more slowly weren't enough, you're more likely to have inherited one of the whole rash of diseases from which the human female is shielded—including diseases in which your immune system doesn't work properly or hardly works at all. You're also generally more at risk from the whole sea of viruses and bacteria in which we swim.

The truth is, the male's immune system is just not as good as the female's. The reason (here we come to chemism again) has something to do with his Y sex chromosome and his main male sex hormone, testosterone. Little is known about this yet—there are few landmarks in this particular part of the landscape. But testosterone, when given from the outside, seems to act in all humans as a depressor of their immune system; estrogen, the female sex hormone, seems to have the reverse effect. Testosterone, too, is probably also responsible for the fact that men don't produce as much immune-globulin M—a blood protein important to the body's defenses—as women do. That is part of the reason men are more likely to contract such illnesses as hepatitis, respiratory ailments and legionnaire's disease. Estrogen seems to beef up production of immune-globulin M—and it seems, in some mysterious way, to be involved in a process by which a woman's immune defenses, like her hormone levels, actually fluctuate during the menstrual cycle.

The question, of course, is, Why should men be worse off—less well defended— than women? Why should the person standing next to you have a superior immune system, modulated and monitored by her sex hormones? The answer is—and she may not like it—babies. When a woman becomes pregnant, she has to do something truly amazing. For nine months, she has to support inside herself, and *not reject*, as she would a graft, a bundle of tissue that is antigenically different from hers, because of the father's contribution to its genetic make-up. At the same time, she has to protect herself *and* this bundle of tissue against any infections. How does she do that amazing thing? No one really knows. But, to do it, she must have inherited something that works for her throughout her life, a much more sophisticated immune system than any man's, one capable of finer tuning. That is likely to be the gift of her two X chromosomes. On them, she has a double set of immune-regulating genes.

End of story? Not quite. Having been evenhanded with men and women throughout this article, we can't quite leave it here. The moral throughout, for men and women, is that for every advantage, there's a disadvantage; for every plus, there's a minus. And the case of the female immune system is no exception. So efficient is it that it sometimes becomes *overefficient* and attacks the body it's supposed to be protecting. Women suffer much more than men from the so-called autoimmune diseases—from such well-known ones as multiple sclerosis, juvenile-onset diabetes and rheumatoid arthritis to even more mysterious ones, such as Graves' disease, in which the glands, the hormones, the brain and behavior are all affected. The most interesting—and most mysterious—disease in this last category is one called systemic lupus erythematosus (S.L.E.). And it's worth looking at S.L.E. just for a moment, because it suggests how intricately intermeshed the chemistry at the heart of personality is. And it shows, in a sense, how men and women can help each other.

"Systemic lupus affects about 500,000 people in this country, more than 450,000 of them women," says Robert Lahita, a leading S.L.E. researcher and assistant professor of immunology at The Rockefeller University in New York. "It's often extremely hard to diagnose. And it produces in a percentage of people many of the symptoms of depression, obsessional neurosis or schizophrenia. One of the few *visible* symptoms—and it doesn't always occur—is a rash on the cheeks, which in the 19th Century was thought to make the face look wolflike. that's why it's called *lupus*— the Latin for wolf. Basically, it's a disease in which the body mounts an attack on the genetic and protein-making machinery inside the cells of its own tissues.

"Now, why is this disease so extraordinarily interesting? Well, first, because it may be brought on by *stress*, and there's some evidence that it flares up after emotional upsets. So stress and the brain are involved from the beginning. Second, males born with *two* X chromosomes, as well as their usual Y, can get it more often than normal males. Third, women who have it are made much worse when on the pill; it usually starts at puberty, with few cases after menopause, and its symptoms are often aggravated during menstruation. So the female sex hormones are obviously involved.

"It's the abnormal female-hormone pattern that we've been investigating at Rockefeller. And what we've found out is that two things seem to have gone profoundly wrong in these S.L.E. patients. Their estrogen is being processed in a very odd way: They're making too many by-products that have strong hormonal effects and too few by-products that don't have hormonal effects but *do* seem to act as chemical messengers in the brain. In a sense, they're making too little brain-active estrogen. At the same time, though, they may have much less active *testosterone* than they should have. And the approach through testosterone looks like it may be the best treatment we can offer for this mysterious disease. Stress, emotion, sex chromosomes, sex hormones, a deranged immune system and mental disorder—who knows what truths about men and women the study of S.L.E. will help uncover? But, for the moment, the irony is that to treat it in women, doctors will soon be borrowing from men something that lies at the root of *their* response to stress, their left-brain weakness and their immune inferiority."

Borrowing. It is this, perhaps, that gives the gathering science of men and women its special interest. What is it, for example, that makes women more sensitive to pain than men? What is it that makes their brains more responsive to stimuli than men's? What is it that makes men's—but not women's—blood coagulate when they're given aspirin? Perhaps these principles can be borrowed from one sex and given to the other. Perhaps, above all, whatever mysterious principle allows women to live longer than men can *also* be borrowed.

As 20th Century men and women, we're at the beginning of a new age. For the first time, science has tools delicate enough to probe the central mysteries of our behavior and our personality. And, in a sense, all the separate disciplines of science are beginning to come together into one—the science of men and women. Already, that science is burrowing at the roots of madness, stress, mood and lethal physical and mental disorders. And, in the process, it is bringing back from the vast continent of its general ignorance news that all too often we don't want to hear. As is usual with science, that news is both good and bad. Good because it promises new treatments and new cures—and a gradual abandonment of the long-haul tinkering of psychiatry. Bad because it will force us to alter radically the way we think about ourselves—about our minds, our personal responsibility, our free will.

It is also bringing back news that we're going to have to face sooner or later about our separate inheritances as men and women. The news is that we're far older than we think we are. And who we are today is simply the current expression of the long history of our coming to this place. We were, and still are, designed by nature for the purposes of that travel, purposes that are still reflected in our strengths and weaknesses alike. Women are still protected for the purpose of motherhood—whether or not, as individuals, they want to have children. Men are still geared to be hunters and sex seekers—whether or not, as individuals, they hunt and seek sex. Men are also less stable and more various than women. "They're the sex through which nature experiments," says Flor-Henry. "In the large scale of things, you see, individual males don't matter very much. They're throwaways. So that has left nature free to experiment with them. That's why there are more sexual deviants among men. That's why there are more mental retardates among men. And that's why there are more *geniuses* among men."

Pluses and minuses—they belong together at the heart of Freud's special chemism in men and women, making us complementary and necessary to each other. Neither is better, neither is worse. It is not a competition, and we have to learn to understand that. "I think it's rather unfair," says Camilla Benbow, "that when men have a problem, everybody's willing to accept the fact that it's genetic, it's brain damage, it's biological. But when women have a problem, oh, no, it can't be any of those things. It's the environment. I think that's unreasonable."

TIRED OF ARGUING ABOUT BIOLOGICAL INFERIORITY?
Naomi Weisstein

In the past 15 years, primatologists, many of them women like Thelma Rowell, Jane Lancaster, Alison Jolly, Dian Fossey, Jane Goodall, and Biruté Galdikas, have found that female status in the primate world is often high, ranging from assertive to clearly dominant.

"By concentrating on prosimians [for instance, lemurs and indri], one can argue that female dominance is the primitive and basic condition, for among all the social lemurs ever studied, this is so," says anthropologist Sarah Blaffer Hrdy in her delightful and brilliant tour through female primate behavior, *The Woman That Never Evolved* (Harvard University Press). Alison Jolly's *Lemur Behavior: A Madagascar Field Study* (University of Chicago Press) describes dominance in a prosimian. Females grab food from males, push them out of the way (to "displace them," they often don't even push—males just get up and leave if a female approaches), and hit them upside the head when they get cranky. Not that males don't play "typical" aggressive games. They wave their tails at each other in "stink fights," establishing a threat hierarchy presumably by who smells the worst. The females couldn't care less. A female will "bound up to the dominant male (established by the stink wars), snatch a tamarind pod from his hand, cuffing him over the ear in the process." Similar female dominance is observed in other more advanced species—from squirrel monkeys in South and Central America (New World monkeys, still fairly primitive) to the talapoin in Africa (an Old World monkey, not very primitive).

Perhaps more interesting than out-and-out female dominance is the peaceable kingdom of the monogamous primates who share child-rearing. Marmoset fathers carry their offspring except when suckling. A siamang father carries his offspring after the first year of their lives. Defense is also usually shared. One of the more fascinating aspects of monogamous primate life is the duetting, or combined territorial calls of the harmonious pair. In the early morning in the forests of Malaysia, a female gibbon will begin her hour's long great call with her mate supplying backup vocals. As distinct from more hierarchical species, fights among mates are rarely observed (although pairs are intensely territorial and do attack invaders). Rather, monogamous primates seem to spend a great deal of time just digging each other, grooming, hugging, and huddling together. Interestingly, sex is relatively infrequent, a corrective to the widespread caveman theory—argued, for instance, by Donald Johanson and Maitland Edey in *Lucy* (Simon & Schuster)—that human females abandoned estrus cycles and developed continuous sexual receptivity in order to keep the male monogamous and faithful.

Monogamy is not infrequent in primates, from some prosimians (for example, indri) all the way up to the lesser apes, gibbons, and siamangs. Many species are

Naomi Weisstein, "Tired of Arguing about Biological Inferiority?" *Ms.* November 1982. Weisstein, a professor of psychology at the State University of New York at Buffalo, is a founding member of the Chicago Women's Liberation Union.

downright romantic. Titi monkey mates will sit for hours pressed close together, their tails entwined; male marmosets will patiently feed their mates (as will 14 species of New World monkeys).

Even among the "classics," the hierarchal species of Old World monkeys like baboons and macaques, the picture has changed. While every male member of a troop of Amboseli baboons outranks every female member, each has a specific social position that depends on the rank of the *mother*. Knowing the rank of the mother, claims Glenn Hausfater (as quoted in Hrdy), allows you to predict much of an Amboseli baboon's daily life: its diet, the amount of spare time spent foraging and resting, even the average number of parasite ova emitted in a stool (an indication of the quality of the food it gets)—as well as its ability to displace other animals, and the amount of time it will be groomed, deferred to, or harassed—all indications of "dominance." With Japanese macaques, the social organization revolves around grandmothers, mothers, daughters, and sisters. The highest-ranking or "alpha" male outranks the highest ranking female in terms of specific behaviors like displacing others, or taking their food, but his power requires acceptance from influential females.

The emerging picture, then, for females in the primate world, is almost diametrically opposed to what is commonly believed. Female primate behavior is tough, assertive, and socially central. But—here is where interpretation comes in—the variations described are *between* species, and it is possible that each species inherits its specific social behavior. If so, humans, by extension, could be argued to have inherited a rare and virulent form of male dominance. What is more interesting, therefore, is to go back over the data and examine the variations *within* species or between closely related ones. Here, variations in social behavior will most likely be environmental, not genetic.

Among a group of Japanese macaques (Arashiyama west) imported to Texas, the original "alpha" female was deposed by a middle-ranking female and her female relations, reported Harold Gouzoules in *Primates*. A new dominance hierarchy was established and the former alpha and her kin were lowered in rank. Similarly, peasant revolt was reported for a troop of savanna baboons, where the once dominant females were pushed to the bottom of the hierarchy. Parallel rebellions have been observed in a variety of other baboon and macaque species.

These are important data. The overthrow of lineages in hierarchical Old World monkeys upsets the sociobiological belief that dominance or other specific behavioral traits are fixed by the genes. What really seems to be inherited is a lot of political acumen plus the specific social structure of rank. When, through politics, this structure is overturned, behavior turns with it. These data indicate that what's in the genes is not a *specific* social behavior like dominance, but a *general* social understanding: an ability to figure out when to strut your stuff, when to rebel, and when to lie low. (Upsets in rank also suggest that among monkeys, submission is not gladly borne. That's a very different message from the idea that an animal is "naturally" submissive, as some sociobiologists want us to believe.)

The rise and fall of lineages within a generation means that dominance *per se* is not inherited. So do the facts of sexual selection, which turn out to be more complex than previously believed. For instance, a stock-in-trade of comic-book biology is the most tyrannical male winning out in the mating season, thereby reproducing his own shady character and eventually making it a species-wide trait. But observations show that among such species as chimps, females often neglect the most dominant male (as established in threat or fight hierarchies) in favor of the more sociable and less disruptive males. Since rape is virtually unknown among nonhuman primates (subadult orangutans appear to be the one exception), this means the most dominant male doesn't necessarily get the breeding advantage.

Dominance would thus appear to be neither a fixed trait (that is, one always expressed because it is "inherited") nor one assured through the process of sexual selection. But this conclusion applies to individual animals. How about whole sexes? Here, too, there is some reason to believe that dominance can depend just as much on the environment as on the genes. Perhaps the most impressive example of a turnabout in male behavior is in a species of monogamous langur on the Mentawei islands off the coast of Sumatra. All other known langurs are polygamous, highly aggressive, and male dominant (although here, too, as with other Old World monkeys, dominant males are transient and females form the coherent social nucleus of the troop). Life for most langurs is hell. Females fight each other; males kill each other. By contrast, however, the Mentawei island langurs appear to exhibit the harmonious relations of monogamous pair bonds.

What has happened? Since they are genetically so close to their warring cousins, something in the environment of these langurs has radically altered their behavior. The speculation is that human hunting pressure drove the Mentawei island langurs into the protection of monogamy. But what is more important than *why* they got there is *that* they got there. If nearly the same genes produce male tyrants in one environment and gentle companions in another, then genes alone don't determine these specific behaviors in primates. What behaviors will be expressed may depend, in much larger part than previously thought, on what primates are faced with, *not* what they're born with.

The evidence is piling up. Females are generally assertive and central to many primate social organizations. Relations between sexes can change radically with changes in the environment. All these observations should figure critically in the contemporary view of male and female "nature"; and yet, they usually don't. The data come in, but much contemporary evolutionary theory doesn't change. Why?

It is important to understand how profoundly, pervasively, and totally, bias can affect something as purportedly "scientific" as biology. You need much more than evidence to bring down as cherished a notion as male dominion. Whenever privilege is at stake, theories justifying privilege will linger on well after the evidence has overturned them.

It isn't necessarily a conscious conspiracy. Rather, the new data are not acknowledged, or they are treated as trivial, or appropriate implications from them are overlooked. The data don't act to influence the theories, and so the theories remain the same.

This is nowhere more comically evident than in the strangely Victorian accounts of the evolution of human female sexuality. The human female orgasm, according to Donald Symons's 1979 book, *The Evolution of Human Sexuality* (Oxford), is a "byproduct of selection for male orgasm." (And Symons's work was hailed by zoologist E.O. Wilson as "the most thorough and persuasive account of human sexual behavior thus far that incorporates a professional understanding of sociobiology.") Symons claims that women have orgasms as a service to men, not because orgasms would be independently pleasurable and useful to women. Furthermore, orgasms are not assumed to be a part of our evolutionary history and thus found in lower primates as well. As David Barash also writes in *Sociobiology and Behavior* (Elsevier), "The female orgasm seems to be unique to humans."

Since females don't ejaculate, orgasm *is* harder to document in them. But since the late 1960s (well before the Symons and Barash works were published), females in a number of species—rhesus monkeys, stumptail macaques (Suzanne Chevalier-Skolnikoff has provided a wealth of data here), Japanese macaques, orangutans, chimps, baboons—have been observed during sexual activity doing something that really could be nothing else. At a certain point they clutch their partners (frequently, other females), freeze, then pant, moan, open their mouths in a particular way, and make involuntary spasmodic body gestures. Maybe they're faking it? Actual physiological measurements in laboratory studies performed by Frances Burton show that rhesus monkeys go through at least three similar stages of the four that Masters and Johnson describe for women.

I would suggest that difficulty in establishing orgasm among lower female primates has nothing to do with the evidence and everything to do with the androcentric bias that can't imagine why females of any species would develop orgasmic capability independent of males. Sexuality still means male-defined sexuality. (After all, it wasn't until Masters and Johnson's pioneering studies of sexuality in the human female that we ourselves went beyond the male-defined notions. It is hardly surprising that behavioral biology hasn't got there yet.)

Perhaps the most telling example of bias concerns the famous juvenile female, Imo, a Japanese macaque living with her troop at Koshima Islet. Scientists provisioned the troop there with sweet potatoes. Imo discovered that washing sweet potatoes got the sand off. Her discovery quickly spread among the other juniors in the troop, who then taught their mothers, who in turn, taught their infants. Adult males never learned it. Next, scientists flung grains of wheat in the sand to see what the troop would do. Rather than laboriously picking the wheat out of the sand grain by grain, Imo discovered how to separate the wheat from the sand in one operation. Again this spread from Imo's peers to mothers and infants, and, again, adult males never learned it. The fact that these Japanese macaques had a rudimentary culture has been widely heralded. But what are we to make of the *way* culture spread in this troop?

If Imo had been male, we would never have heard the end of the "inventive" capacities of primate males, and since generalization spreads like prairie fire when the right sex is involved, no doubt their role in the evolution of tool use and—why not?—language as well. But the urge to grand theory withers when females are the primary actors, and when the task relates to food—at least food without killing. Imo has been described as "precocious" and left at that. (Precocious, indeed! How would you get the sand out of wheat?)

The lesson of Imo's fate is important. Bias is as much a matter of what is put into theory as what is observed in the first place.

So what does primate biology imply—apart from bias—about our human possibilities? When we look at all the data, and try to interpret them without androcentric bias, what do we have?

"Primates live in pairs, harems, unisex bands, multimale troops, as solitaries, as flexible communities that group and split, and as small subunits which attach to and disengage from very large associations. Females can be dominant, subordinate, equal, or not interested. Virtually every known social system except polyandry (one female, several males) is represented," writes Blaffer Hrdy. That means we belong to an order remarkable for its flexibility, its capacity to adapt to changing environments, needs, and ideas. Except for one species of baboon around the horn of Africa, females are not subordinate in the primate world to anything like the degree intimated by mainstream behavioral biology. Indeed if we derive the meaning of the word "natural" from lower primates, we must conclude that human female subjugation is anything but natural. It is an abomination on nature.

This *does* leave us with a problem, however. If biology tells us that female subjugation is unnatural, how did we get into the patriarchal mess we're in?

Enter Man the Hunter. It has been argued that humans evolved in especially murderous, male-dominant ways because of the exigencies of our particular prehistory. "We are uniquely human even in the noblest [sic] sense because for untold millions of years, we alone killed for a living," writes Robert Ardrey in his 1976 apologia for male privilege, *The Hunting Hypothesis* (Atheneum). But, popular as this view is, it is as wrong as the biological view of male domination. Humans started out small, uncoordinated, with crude tools and a rudimentary language. "A more vulnerable state for a hominid, fresh from the boondocks, in competition with the full paid-up carnivores of the grasslands is hard to imagine" writes John Napier in criticizing Ardrey's statement. "There is absolutely no evidence," said Richard Leakey in a recent televison interview, "that we became human through hunting." "Up until very recent times," he explained, "there's no record at all of human aggression. If you can't find [it] in the prehistoric record, why claim it's there?"

In fact, it's more likely that it was Woman the Gatherer who led the procession down the evolutionary pike. The stone tools found with fossil evidence from some 2 million years ago are small and crude. The most damage these could have done would have been to chop roots into small tough salads, and the evidence overwhelmingly points to gritty roots and tubers as our primary diet for the millions of years we ranged over the dry and inhospitable African savannas. Females would have been under most pressure to gather these roots and tubers because they had to provide not only for themselves but for their young. Anthropologist Nancy Tanner, in her book *On Becoming Human* (Cambridge University Press), argued that mothers and young, learning and gathering in a social environment of growing cognitive and communicative proficiency, were the central actors in our evolution. (Suggestive of Imo's talents, chimp females use food-gathering tools with greater frequency than males—as is also described by William McGrew in *The Great Apes*). According to Tanner (and to Adrienne Zihlman in a recent article in *Signs*), socializing, communicating females took us into the present.

It is now thought likely that the subjugation of women did not start until some 12,000 years ago when hunting and gathering were replaced with domesticated plants and animals. Current hunter-gatherer societies (for example, the !Kung and the Mbuti) give us some idea of how we may have lived in much of our human history; and in these societies, women are most fully equal to men and often supply the major portion of food. But as anthropologist Eleanor Leacock has shown in *Myths of Male Dominance* (Monthly Review Press), even where women aren't the main food-getters (for instance, in the hunting-fishing-and-trapping Montagnais-Naskapi of the Labrador Peninsula), equality between the sexes still prevails. Indeed, Leacock has argued that equality persisted well into early horticulture, and anthropologist Connie Sutton dates the subjugation of women to the development of the state.

Wherever women's troubles started, hunter-gatherers are of utmost importance to our understanding of our genetic legacy. They tell us that male dominance is not in our genes. It is not something we inherited in becoming human, along with the big brain and the small canines. It emerged afterward. It is a specific *cultural legacy*.

But culture carries with it a capacity to change it, and this is the really awesome part of our evolutionary story. Male dominance is one kind of cultural legacy. The vision of a just and equal society is another. What biology has bequeathed to us in those millions of years of gathering on the plains is the capacity to choose between specific cultures, to evaluate our lives, to intervene in our own fate. Biology has provided us with the ability to explore our possibilities, to change what is in the present and try something we would like better for the future. Our biological legacy is the ability to choose how we would like to live.

Rather than a curse against women, biology is a promise to us. Biology shows us that the subjugation of women is anything but natural and fixed. It seems to be a late human invention not likely to have been in the transitional ape-human populations, nor evident in what may well have been the social organization of human society for much of the time that we have been human.

Even without our capacities to create and change specific cultures, biology tells us that we belong to an order stunningly flexible in its social arrangements and capable of great change within species. With this cultural capacity, possibilities expand. Biology tells us that there is nothing genetic stopping us from having full sexual and social expression.

Biology tells us, finally, to get to work.

SEX DIFFERENCES IN MATHEMATICAL REASONING ABILITY: MORE FACTS

Camilla Persson Benbow and Julian C. Stanley

In 1980 we reported large sex differences in mean scores on a test of mathematical reasoning ability for 9,927 mathematically talented seventh and eighth graders who entered the Johns Hopkins regional talent search from 1972 through 1979. One prediction from those results was that there would be a preponderance of males at the high end of the distribution of mathematical reasoning ability. In this report we investigate sex differences at the highest levels of that ability. New groups of students under age 13 with exceptional mathematical aptitude were identified by means of two separate procedures. In the first, the Johns Hopkins regional talent searches in 1980, 1981, and 1982, 39,820 seventh graders from the Middle Atlantic region of the United States who were selected for high intellectual ability were given the College Board Scholastic Aptitude Test (SAT). In the second, a nationwide talent search was conducted for which any student under 13 years of age who was willing to take the SAT was eligible. The results of both procedures substantiated our prediction that before age 13 far more males than females would score extremely high on SAT-M, the mathematical part of SAT.

The test items of SAT-M require numerical judgment, relational thinking, or insightful and logical reasoning. This test is designed to measure the developed mathematical reasoning ability of 11th and 12th graders. Most students in our study were in the middle of the seventh grade. Few had had formal opportunities to study algebra and beyond. Our rationale is that most of these students were unfamiliar with mathematics from algebra onward, and that most who scored high did so because of extraordinary reasoning ability.

In 1980, 1981, and 1982, as in the earlier study, participants in the Johns Hopkins talent search were seventh graders, or boys and girls of typical seventh-grade age in a higher grade, in the Middle Atlantic area. Before 1980, applicants had been required to be in the top 3 percent nationally on the mathematics section of any standardized achievement test. Beginning in 1980, students in the top 3 percent in verbal or overall intellectual ability were also eligible. During that and the next 2 years 19,883 boys and 19,937 girls applied and were tested. Even though this sample was more general and had equal representation by sex, the mean sex difference on SAT-M remained constant at 30 points favor males (males' $\overline{X}$ = 416, S.D. = 87; females' $\overline{X}$ = 386, S.D. = 74; t = 37; $P < 0.001$). No important difference in verbal ability as measured by SAT-V was found (males' $\overline{X}$ = 367, females' $\overline{X}$ = 365).

The major point, however, is not the mean difference in SAT-M scores but the ratios of boys to girls among the high scorers. The ratio of boys to girls scoring above

Camilla Persson Benbow and Julian C. Stanley, "Sex Differences in Mathematical Reasoning Ability: More Facts," *Science* 222 (1983). Benbow and Stanley are faculty members in the department of Psychology at Johns Hopkins University.

the mean of talent-search males was 1.5:1. The ratio among those who scored $\geq$ 500 (493 was the mean of 1981–82 college-bound 12th-grade males) was 2.1:1. Among those who scored $\geq$ 600 (600 was the 79th percentile of the 12th-grade males) the ratio was 4.1:1. These ratios are similar to those previously reported but are derived from a broader and much larger data base.

Scoring 700 or more on the SAT-M before age 13 is rare. We estimate that students who reach this criterion (the 95th percentile of college-bound 12th-grade males) before their 13th birthday represent the top one in 10,000 of their age group. It was because of their rarity that the nationwide talent search was created in November 1980 in order to locate such students who were born after 1967 and facilitate their education. In that talent search applicants could take the SAT at any time and place at which it was administered by the Educational Testing Service or through one of five regional talent searches that cover the United States. Extensive nationwide efforts were made to inform school personnel and parents about our search. The new procedure (unrestricted by geography or previous ability) was successful in obtaining a large national sample of this exceedingly rare population. As of September 1983, the number of such boys identified was 260 and the number of girls 20, a ratio of 13.0:1. This ratio is remarkable in view of the fact that the available evidence suggests there was essentially equal participation of boys and girls in the talent searches.

The total number of students tested in the Johns Hopkins regional annual talent searches and reported so far is 49,747 (9,927 in the initial study and 39,820 in the present study). Preliminary reports from the 1983 talent search based on some 15,000 cases yield essentially identical results. In the ten Middle Atlantic regional talent searches from 1972 through 1983 we have therefore tested about 65,000 students. It is abundantly clear that far more boys than girls (chiefly 12-year-olds) scored in the highest ranges on SAT-M, even though girls were matched with boys by intellectual ability, age, grade, and voluntary participation. In the original study students were required to meet a qualifying mathematics criterion. Since we observed the same sex difference then as now, the current results cannot be explained solely on the grounds that the girls may have qualified by the verbal criterion. Moreover, if that were the case, we should expect the girls to have scored higher than the boys on SAT-V. They did not.

Several "environmental" hypotheses have been proposed to account for sex differences in mathematical ability. Fox et al. and Meece et al. have found support for a social-reinforcement hypothesis which, in essence, states that sex-related differences in mathematical achievement are due to differences in social conditioning and expectations for boys and girls. The validity of this hypothesis has been evaluated for the population we studied earlier and for a subsample of the students in this study. Substantial differences between boys' and girls' attitudes or backgrounds were not found. Admittedly, some of the measures used were broadly defined and may not have been able to detect subtle social influences that affect a child from birth. But it is not obvious how social conditioning could affect mathematical reasoning ability so adversely and significantly, yet have little detectable effect on stated interest in mathematics, the taking of mathematics courses during the high school years before the SAT's are normally taken, and mathematics-course grades.

An alternative hypothesis, that sex differences in mathematical reasoning ability arise mainly from differential course-taking, was also not validated, either by the data in our 1980 study or by the data in the present study. In both studies the boys and girls were shown to have had similar formal training in mathematics.

It is also of interest that sex differences in mean SAT-M scores observed in our early talent searches became only slightly larger during high school. In the selected subsample of participants studied, males improved their scores an average of 10 points more than females (the mean difference went from 40 to 50 points). They also increased their scores on the SAT-V by at least 10 points more than females. Previously, other researchers have postulated that profound differences in socialization during adolescence caused the well-documented sex differences in 11th- and 12th-grade SAT-M scores, but that idea is not supported in our data. For socialization to account for our results, it would seem necessary to postulate (ad hoc) that chiefly early socialization pressures significantly influence the sex difference in SAT-M scores—that is, that the intensive social pressures during adolescence have little such effect.

It is important to emphasize that we are dealing with intellectually highly able students and that these findings may not generalize to average students. Moreover, these results are of course not generalizable to particular individuals. Finally, it should be noted that the boys' SAT-M scores had a larger variance than the girls'. This is obviously related to the fact that more mathematically talented boys than girls were found. Nonetheless, the environmental hypotheses outlined above attempted to explain mean differences, not differences in variability. Thus, even if one concludes that our findings result primarily from greater male variability, one must still explain why.

Our principal conclusion is that males dominate the highest ranges of mathematical reasoning ability before they enter adolescence. Reasons for this sex difference are unclear.

BIG THOUGHTS ABOUT SMALL TALK
John Leo

RALPH: Wanda, look at this phone bill! Has A T & T misplaced some zeros, or did you spend all last month jabbering with far-off friends?

WANDA: None of the above, Ralph. But I must admit you have put your finger on yet another important sexual difference. Women spend far more time on the telephone than men do, even when they have relatively little to say.

RALPH: I am a wily husband, dearest. Do not try to get around me by taking my role in this script.

WANDA: I wouldn't think of it, Ralph. Studies show that males are brief, almost abrupt, on the phone. Once in a while you all blab endlessly, telling knock-knock jokes and so forth, but on the whole, men use the phone like a telegram. This may be because you like to make a show of being terribly busy, or because, by female standards, you are all emotionally constricted. Probably some combination of the two.

RALPH: Getting to the point is not a character flaw, dearest. Why is it that the less a woman has to say, the longer she will stay on the phone to say it?

WANDA: Once again there is a rough truth behind your insult, pugnacious one. Researchers Mark Sherman and Adelaide Haas of the State University of New York at New Paltz found that women are almost three times as likely as men to make a phone call when they have nothing special to say. Women use the phone to work at friendship. You shouldn't feel bad when you bluster about this, by the way. In her book *Intimate Strangers*, Therapist Lillian Rubin says the husband's anger about his wife's use of the phone is absolutely standard in the American household. She thinks that men feel so abandoned when their women are on the phone that it reawakens the male's dependence on Mommy. Don't bother to protest, Ralph. I don't believe it either.

RALPH: This conversation is an amazement, Wanda. Do you intend to speak all my lines?

WANDA: Unfeminine, isn't it? Let us plunge on. We know that men hate to talk about emotions and the psyche. That's why psychology is regarded as a low-prestige, "female" occupation at many colleges. We know that males are far more likely than females to talk about sports and politics, and would practically fall silent nine-tenths of the time if those subjects were out of bounds.

RALPH: How about those Cubs? A helluva team.

WANDA: We know that women work harder at conversation. They ask far more questions, partly to keep the conversation going, partly to placate the male, who tends to control the conversation.

RALPH: You mean like I'm controlling this one?

John Leo, "Big Thoughts about Small Talk," *Time* 17 September 1984.

WANDA: A California researcher taped 52 hours of conversation by three middle-class couples and found that women brought up twice as many topics as men but that males controlled the talks by vetoing subjects they didn't want to discuss. The men achieved this, the clever dears, by grunts and long silences. Out of desperation, the females asked three times as many questions as men and started larding their comments with the interjection "you know." For the average woman, having a civil conversation with a male is like playing tennis with a partner who is asleep.

RALPH: Certainly this is harsh, dearest one. Last week when you were puzzled about what went wrong between you and Doris, didn't I pitch right in and suggest that you call her up and confront her?

WANDA: Very manful and direct, Ralph. And all wrong. Sherman and Haas say this is a standard husband-wife conversation that ends with an angry wife. The woman states an emotional problem, and one-tenth of a second later the man says, "Here's what ya do . . ." That's not why wives raise these issues with husbands. They want emotional support and a good listener, not instant advice.

RALPH: Is there no hope for men?

WANDA: Probably not in our lifetime. In her 1981 book, *Women and Men Speaking*, Sociolinguist Cheris Kramarae reports that 466 men and women termed male speech "forceful, dominating, boastful and authoritarian." Female speech was characterized by both sexes as "friendlier, gentler, faster, more emotional, enthusiastic and trivial."

RALPH: We can always try harder to be trivial. How do you like my new socks?

WANDA: Most of the studies conclude that dominance runs through male conversation with women. The kibbutzim of Israel were supposed to embody the ideal of sexual equality. But Anthropologist Lionel Tiger, in research for his book *Women in the Kibbutz*, found that men talked for three-quarters of the total time at town meetings. The only time women talked more than men was when the topic was curtain-making. The point is . . .

RALPH: What else do we do wrong?

WANDA: You interrupt. Studies at the University of California at Santa Barbara show that men interrupt women all the time. When two men or two women are talking, interruptions are about equal. But when a man talks to a woman, he makes 96% of the interruptions. But . . .

RALPH: These people have nothing better to do than study interruptions?

WANDA: . . . but women make "retrievals" about one-third of the time. You know, they pick up where they left off after the man . . .

RALPH: Surely not all men are like that, Wanda.

WANDA: . . . cuts in on what they were saying. It seems . . .

RALPH: Speaking as a staunch supporter of free speech for women, I officially deplore this, Wanda.

WANDA: I know, Ralph. I know.

SUGGESTIONS FOR WRITING

Informal Essays

1. After reading a few selections from this chapter, write an essay in which you describe an athletic confrontation with a member of the opposite sex. Weave a thesis through your essay or include a thesis in your conclusion.
2. Using a single personal experience, show how you were surprised by the behavior of a member of the opposite sex because it failed to conform to your expectations.
3. Argue that the research that indicates that there *are* real differences between males and females is insidious and plays into the hands of chauvinists.

Short Documented Papers

1. Write a report on the gains that women have made in athletics.
2. Develop an argument supporting the claim that women will *never* be able to close the gap between men and women in athletic performance.
3. Develop an argument supporting the claim that women *will* be able to close the gap between men and women in athletic performance.
4. Write a paper in which you argue for or against the conclusion that males have a "math gene."
5. Write an argument in which you attack or defend one of the studies that supports inherent sex differences. Use several additional sources to support your position.

Longer Documented Papers

1. Some researchers conclude that differences between the behavior of males and females are partly due to the fact that each sex is dominated by a different hemisphere of the brain. Explain this theory and describe those male and female strengths and weaknesses that this theory accounts for.
2. Write a research argument in which you dispute the validity (and perhaps even the accuracy) of three or four conclusions made by researchers on sex differences.
3. Contrast two or three male strengths, or weaknesses, with two or three female strengths, or weaknesses, that have been identified in research on sex differences.
4. Write a report on those female (or male) strengths and vulnerabilities that have been identified in research on sex differences.

· 6 ·

Bilingual Education: Does It Work?

The sentiments evoked by the Statue of Liberty are central to our national identity. Indeed, we are flattered by Emma Lazarus's words chiseled on its base, and we have long seen our nation—ideally anyway—as a great melting pot.

Through the years, immigrant parents struggled with the English language in an effort to accommodate themselves to the nation they had determined to call their own, and they were eager to enroll their children in schools, where they would prepare themselves to become Americans through an immersion in their new language.

This melting-pot ideal was questioned during the 1960s. A rediscovered pride in cultural and ethnic roots and a heightened awareness of civil rights led some people to doubt the effectiveness and validity of forcing immigrant children through such an abrupt cultural transformation. At about the same time, studies showed that the dropout rate of immigrant children was significantly higher than that of their English-speaking counterparts. During this same period, a wave of legal and illegal immigrants from Hispanic countries flooded certain American school systems— particularly those in the Southwest.

Finally, in the 1974 *Lau* v *Nichols* decision, the Supreme Court ruled in favor of Chinese immigrant students in San Francisco, who had contended that their civil rights had been violated because, as non-English-speaking students, they were being denied the quality of education received by their English-speaking peers. The High Court made no specific recommendations, but the Department of Health, Education, and Welfare addressed the problem by requiring that immigrant students be taught basic academic subjects in their native languages.

To many observers, this decision seemed to confer on immigrant children the absolute right to be instructed in their native languages—no matter what those languages might be, and no matter how few pupils in the same school system shared those languages. Congress provided funds for the administration of the HEW mandate, but school systems with sizable immigrant enrollments were faced with the burden of the costs of implementing such a program.

Opponents of the federal government's bilingual-education guidelines rankle at the enormous costs of such a program. They also contend that the program dramatically slows immigrant children's mastery of English—and thus impedes their assimilation into their new culture. Indeed, the most pessimistic of the critics see the Southwest becoming a sort of Spanish-speaking Quebec of the U.S.

Most of those in favor of bilingual education don't question the melting-pot ideal. On the contrary, they contend that their opponents underestimate the allure of American culture to immigrants. Most immigrants, the supporters say, are eager to be assimilated into American life—but assimilation is difficult, they add, if the children, forced to sink or swim in a new language, fail in school. Bilingual education, to its supporters, is thus a more efficient and less painful way to see that immigrant children are able to make their way into the American mainstream.

AGAINST BILINGUAL EDUCATION
Tom Bethell

This year the United States government, which I am beginning to think is afflicted with a death wish, is spending $150 million on "bilingual education" programs in American classrooms. There is nothing "bi" about it, however. The languages in which instruction is conducted now include: Central Yup'ik, Aleut, Yup'ik, Gwich'in, Athabascan (the foregoing in Alaska), Navajo, Tagalog, Pima, Plaute (I promise I'm not making this up), Ilocano, Cambodian, Yiddish, Chinese, Vietnamese, Punjabi, Greek, Italian, Korean, Polish, French, Haitian, Haitian-French, Portuguese, Arabic, Crow (yes, Virginia . . .), Cree, Keresian, Tewa, Apache, Mohawk, Japanese, Lakota, Choctaw, Samoan, Chamorro, Carolinian, Creek-Seminole, and Russian.

And there are more, such as Trukese, Palauna, Ulithian, Woleian, Marshalles, Kusaian, Ponapean, and, not least, Yapese. And Spanish—how could I have so nearly forgotten it? The bilingual education program is more or less the Hispanic equivalent of affirmative action, creating jobs for thousands of Spanish teachers; by which I mean teachers who speak Spanish, although not necessarily English, it has turned out. One observer has described the HEW-sponsored program as "affirmative ethnicity." Although Spanish is only one of seventy languages in which instruction is carried on (I seem to have missed a good many of them), it accounts for 80 percent of the program.

Bilingual education is an idea that appeals to teachers of Spanish and other tongues, but also to those who never did think that another idea, the United States of America, was a particularly good one to begin with, and that the sooner it is restored to its component "ethnic" parts the better off we shall all be. Such people have been welcomed with open arms into the upper reaches of the federal government in recent years, giving rise to the suspicion of a death wish.

The bilingual education program began in a small way (the way such programs always begin) in 1968, when the Elementary and Secondary Education Act of 1965 was amended (by what is always referred to as "Title VII") to permit the development of "pilot projects" to help *poor* children who were "educationally disadvantaged because of their inability to speak English," and whose parents were either on welfare or earning less than $3,000 a year. At this germinal stage the program cost a mere $7.5 million, and as its sponsors (among them Sen. Alan Cranston of California) later boasted, it was enacted without any public challenge whatever.

"With practically no one paying heed," Stephen Rosenfeld wrote in the *Washington Post* in 1974 (i.e., six years after the program began),

Tom Bethell, "Against Bilingual Education," *Harper's* February 1979. Bethell, the former editor of *New Orleans* magazine and the *New Orleans Courier*, has been the Washington editor of *Harper's* since 1976.

Congress has radically altered the traditional way by which immigrants become Americanized. No longer will the public schools be expected to serve largely as a "melting pot," assimilating foreigners to a common culture. Rather, under a substantial new program for "bilingual' education, the schools—in addition to teaching English—are to teach the "home" language and culture to children who speak English poorly.

Rosenfeld raised the important point that "it is not clear how educating children in the language and culture of their ancestral homeland will better equip them for the rigors of contemporary life in the United States." But in response, a withering blast of disapproval was directed at the *Post's* "Letters" column. Hadn't he heard? The melting pot had been removed from the stove.

Bureaucratic imperative (and, I would argue, a surreptitious death wish) dictated that the $7.5 million "pilot program" of 1968 grow into something more luxuriant and permanent. As it happened, the U.S. Supreme Court decision *Lau* v. *Nichols*, handed down in 1974, provided the stimulus.

In this case, Legal Services attorneys in Chinatown sued a San Francisco school district on behalf of 1,800 Chinese-speaking students, claiming that they had been denied special instruction in English. The contention that these pupils had a *constitutional* right to such instruction (as was implied by filing suit in federal court) was denied both by the federal district court and the appeals court. The Justice Department entered the case when it was heard before the Supreme Court, arguing that the school district was in violation of a 1970 memorandum issued by HEW's Office for Civil Rights. This memorandum in turn was based on the 1964 Civil Rights Act, which decreed (among other things) that the recipients of federal funds cannot be discriminated against on the basis of national origin. The 1970 memorandum defined language as basic to national origin and required schools to take "affirmative steps" to correct English-language deficiencies.

Evidently intimidated by this rhetorical flourishing of "rights," the Supreme Court unanimously affirmed that federally funded schools must "rectify the language deficiency in order to open instruction to students who had 'linguistic deficiencies.'" In effect, the Office for Civil Rights had taken the position that the immigrant's tongue was to be regarded as a right, not an impediment, and the Supreme Court had meekly gone along with the argument.

Armed now with this judicial mandate, HEW's civil-rights militants went on the offensive, threatening widespread funding cutoffs. No longer would the old method of teaching immigrants be countenanced (throwing them into the English language and allowing them to sink or swim). No longer! Now the righteous activists within government had exactly what they are forever searching for: a huddled mass of yearning . . . victims! Discriminated against the moment they arrive at *these* teeming, wretched, racist, ethnocentric shores!

America the Bad . . . One Nation, Full of Victims . . . Divisible. (I have in my hands an odious document, the "Third Annual Report of the National Council on Bilingual Education," which remarks that "Cubans admitted after Castro; and more recently Vietnamese refugees . . . became citizens unintentionally." No doubt they are yearning to be free to return to Ho Chi Minh City and Havana.) That's about the size of it in the 1970s, and so it came to pass that the Office for Civil Rights "targeted" 334 school districts, which would have to start "bilingual-bicultural" classes promptly or risk having their federal funds cut off.

"The OCR [Office for Civil Rights] policy is difficult to explain," Noel Epstein remarked in a thoughtful survey of bilingual education titled "Language, Ethnicity and the Schools" and published recently by the Institute for Educational Leadership. "There is no federal legal requirement for schools to provide bilingual or bicultural education." The Supreme Court had merely said that *some* remedy was needed— not necessarily bilingual education. For example, the Chinese children in the *Lau* case could have been given extra instruction in English, to bring them up to par. But the Office for Civil Rights took the position that they would have to be taught school subjects—mathematics, geography, history, et cetera—in Chinese. And the Court's ruling had said nothing at all about bi*cultural* instruction. (This turns out to mean teaching that in any transaction with the "home" country, America tends to be in the wrong.)

In any event, the bilingual education program was duly expanded by Congress in 1974. It would no longer be just for poor children; all limited-English speakers would qualify; the experimental nature of the program was played down, and there was the important addition of biculturalism, which is summarized in a revealing paragraph in Epstein's booklet:

> Bicultural instruction was elevated to a required component of Title VII programs. The definition of "bilingual" education now meant such instruction had to be given "with appreciation for the cultural heritage of such children. . . ." This underlined the fact that language and culture were not merely being used as vehicles for the transmission of information but as the central sources of ethnic identity. The U.S. Civil Rights Commission had in fact urged the name of the law be changed to "The Bilingual Bicultural Education Act," but key Senate staff members blocked this idea. They feared it would "flag a potentially dangerous issue that might defeat the overall measure," Dr. Susan Gilbert Schneider reports in a valuable dissertation on the making of the 1974 act. Some lobby groups had expressed discomfort about federally sponsored biculturalism. The National Association of School Boards suggested that the legislation could be read as promoting a divisive, Canadian-style biculturalism.

It certainly could. Notice, however, the strong suggestion here that the objection was not so much to the possibility of cutting up the country, as to being *seen* to promote this possibility, which of course might defeat it. As I say, these things are best kept surreptitious—at the level of anonymous "Senate staff members."

At this stage the bilingual seed had indeed taken root. Congressional appropriations had increased from the beggarly $7.5 million to $85 million in fiscal year 1975. The Office for Civil Rights was on the alert. A potential 3.6 million "victimized" children of "limited English-speaking ability" had been identified, and they would furnish the raw material for an almost endless number of bureaucratic experiments. Militant Chicanos, suddenly sought out to fill ethnic teaching quotas, stood on the sidelines, ready to pour a bucket of guilt over any old-fashioned, demurring Yankee who might raise a voice in protest.

Even so, there was a cloud on the horizon—perhaps only a conceptual cloud, but nevertheless an important one, as follows: the idea behind bilingual education was that children would begin to learn school subjects in their native tongue while they were learning English elsewhere—in special English classes, on the playground, through exposure to American society generally. But while they were in this "stage of transition"—learning English—instruction in the home tongue would ensure that they were not needlessly held back academically. Then, when they had a sufficient grasp of English, they could be removed from the bilingual classes and instructed in the normal way. That, at least, was the idea behind bilingual education originally.

But you see the problem, no doubt. At bottom, this is the same old imperialism. It is a "melting pot" solution. The children learn English after all—perhaps fairly rapidly. And at that point there is no reason to keep them in bilingual programs. Moreover, from the point of view of HEW's civil-rights militants, there is rapid improvement by the "victims"—another unfortunate outcome.

The riposte has been predictable—namely, to keep the children in programs of bilingual instruction long after they know English. This has been justified by redefining the problem in the schools as one of "maintenance" of the home tongue, rather than "transition" to the English tongue. You will hear a lot of talk in and around HEW's numerous office buildings in Washington about the relative merits of maintenance versus transition. Of course, Congress originally had "transition" in mind, but "maintenance" is slowly but steadily winning the day.

The issue was debated this year in Congress when Title VII came up for renewal. Some Congressmen, alerted to the fact that children were still being instructed in Spanish, Aleut, or Yapese in the twelfth grade, tried to argue that bilingual instruction should not last for more than two years. But this proposal was roundly criticized by Messrs. Edward Roybal of California, Baltasar Corrada of Puerto Rico, Phillip Burton of California, Paul Simon of Illinois, and others. In the end the language was left vague, giving school boards the discretion to continue "bilingual maintenance" as long as they desired. Currently, fewer than one-third of the 290,000 students enrolled in various bilingual programs are significantly limited in their English-speaking ability.

Then a new cloud appeared on the horizon. If you put a group of children, let's say children from China, in a classroom together in order to teach them English, that's segregation, right? Watch out, then. Here come the civil-rights militants on the rampage once again, ready to demolish the very program that they had done so much to encourage. But there was a simple remedy that would send them trotting tamely homeward. As follows: Put the "Anglos" in with the ethnics. In case you hadn't heard, "Anglo" is the name given these days to Americans who haven't got a drop of ethnicity to their names—the ones who have already been melted down, so to speak.

Putting Anglos into the bilingual program killed two birds with one stone. It circumvented the "segregation" difficulty, and—far more to the point—it meant that the Anglos (just the ones who needed it!) would be exposed to the kind of cultural revisionism that is the covert purpose behind so much of the bilingual program. Put more simply, Mary Beth and Sue Anne would at last learn the new truth: the Indians, not the cowboys, were the good guys, Texas was an ill-gotten gain, and so on.

As Congressman Simon of Illinois put it so delicately, so *surreptitiously*: "I hope that in the conference committee we can get this thing modified as we had it in subcommittee, to make clear that we ought to encourage our English-language students to be in those classes so that you can have the interplay."

As things worked out, up to 40 percent of the classes may permissibly be "Anglo," Congress decreed. And this year there has been another important change: an expanded definition of students who will be eligible for bilingual instruction. No longer will it be confined to those with limited English-*speaking* ability. Now the program will be open to those with "limited English proficiency in understanding, speaking, reading, and writing." This, of course, could be construed as applying to almost anyone in elementary or high school these days.

To accommodate this expansion, future Congressional appropriations for bilingual education will increase in leaps and bounds: $200 million next year, $250 million the year after, and so on in $50 million jumps, until $400 million is spent in 1983, when the program will once again be reviewed by Congress.

Meanwhile, HEW's Office of Education (that is, the E of HEW) appears to be getting alarmed at this runaway program. It commissioned a study by the American Institutes for Research in Palo Alto, and this study turned out to be highly critical of bilingual education. The Office of Education then drew attention to this by announcing the findings at a press conference. ("They've got it in for us," someone at the Bilingual Office told me. "Whenever there's an unfavorable study, they call a press conference. Whenever there's a favorable study, they keep quiet about it.")

In any event, the Palo Alto study claimed that children in bilingual classes were doing no better academically, and perhaps were doing slightly worse, than children from similar backgrounds in regular English classes. The study also reported that 85 percent of the students were being kept in bilingual classes after they were capable of learning in English.

There has been very little Congressional opposition to the bilingual programs, thus bearing out what the Washington writer Fred Reed has called the Guppy Law: "When outrageous expenditures are divided finely enough, the public will not have enough stake in any one expenditure to squelch it." (Reed adds, in a brilliant analysis of the problem: "A tactic of the politically crafty is to pose questions in terms of rightful virtue. 'What? You oppose a mere $40 million subsidy of codpiece manufacture by the Nez Percé? So! You are against Indians. . . .' The thudding opprobrium of anti-Indianism outweighs the $40 million guppy bite in the legislators' eyes.")

Risking that opprobrium, John Ashbrook of Ohio tried to cut out the bilingual program altogether. Referring to the evidence that the program wasn't working, but the budget for it was increasing annually, Ashbrook said that "when one rewards failure, one buys failure." On the House floor he added: "The program is actually preventing children from learning English. Someday somebody is going to have to teach those young people to speak English or else they are going to become public charges. Our educational system is finding it increasingly difficult today to teach English-speaking children to read their own language. When children come out of the Spanish-language schools or Choctaw-language schools which call themselves bilingual, how is our educational system going to make them literate in what will still be a completely alien tongue . . . ?"

The answer, of course, is that there will be demands not for literacy in English but for public signs in Spanish (or Choctaw, et cetera), laws promulgated in Spanish, courtroom proceedings in Spanish, and so on. These demands are already being felt—and met, in part. As so often happens, the ill effects of one government program result in the demand for another government program, rather than the abolition of the original one.

This was borne out by what happened next. When the amendment abolishing bilingual education was proposed by Ashbrook (who is usually regarded in Washington as one of those curmudgeons who can be safely ignored), *not one* Congressman rose to support it, which says something about the efficacy of the Guppy Law. Instead, the House was treated to some pusillanimous remarks by Congressman Claude Pepper of Florida—a state in which it is, of course, politically unwise to resist the expenditure of federal money "targeted" for Hispanics. Pepper said: "Now there is something like parity between the population of the United States and Latin America. My information is that by the year 2000 there probably will be 600 million people living in Latin America, and about 300 million people living in the United States."

Perhaps, then, it would be in order for the "Anglos" to retreat even further, before they are entirely overwhelmed. This brings to mind a most interesting remark made by Dr. Josue Gonzalez, the director-designate of the Office of Bilingual Education (the head of the program, in other words), in the course of an interview that he granted me. Actually, Dr. Gonzalez said many interesting things. He suggested a possible cause of the rift with the Office of Education. "Bilingual education was hatched in Congress, not in the bureaucracy," he said. "The constituents [i.e., Hispanics, mostly] talked directly to Congress. Most government programs are generated by so-called administrative proposal—that is, from within the bureaucracies themselves."

He said of regular public education in America: "I've plotted it on a graph: by the year 2010, most college graduates will be mutes!" (No *wonder* the Office of Education isn't too wildly enthusiastic.) And he said that, contrary to what one might imagine, many "Anglo" parents are in fact only too anxious for their children to enroll in a bilingual course. (If Johnny doesn't learn anything else, at least he might as well learn Spanish—that at least is my interpretation.)

The melting-pot idea is dead, Dr. Gonzalez kept reassuring me. Why? I asked him. What was his proof of this? He then made what I felt was a revealing observation, and one that is not normally raised at all, although it exists at the subliminal level. "We must allow for diversity . . . ," he began, then, suddenly veering off: "The counterculture of the 1960s showed that. Even the WASP middle-American showed that the monolithic culture doesn't exist. Within the group, even, they were rejecting their own values."

I imagine that Attila or Alaric, in an expansive and explanatory mood, might have said much the same thing to some sodden Roman senators who were trying to figure out how it was that Rome fell, exactly.

Dr. Gonzalez had me there and he knew it, so he promptly resumed the offensive. "There are those who say that to speak whatever language you speak is a human right," he went on. "The Helsinki Agreements and the President's Commission on Foreign Language Study commit us to the study of foreign languages. Why not our own—domestic—languages?"

Later on I decided to repeat this last comment to George Weber, the associate director of the Council for Basic Education, a somewhat lonely group in Washington. The grandson of German immigrants, Mr. Weber speaks perfect English. "Only in America," he said. "Only in America would someone say a stupid thing like that. Can you imagine a Turk arriving in France and complaining that he was being denied his human rights because he was taught at school in French, not Turkish? What do you think the French would say to that?"

WHY SPANISH TRANSLATIONS?
Mauricio Molina

I was naive 20 years ago. I say this because I came here from Central America and readily accepted what my parents told me. What they told me was that if I wanted to thrive here I had better learn English. English, it seems, was the language that people spoke in this country. In my innocence and naivete, however, it never occurred to me that I really didn't have to. I can see now that I could have refused.

Yes, English is the language of the United States. But if it is, why can I take the written part of my driver's license test in Spanish? If it is, why are businesses forced to provide Spanish translations of practically every blank credit application or contract agreement? And not just businesses—government offices must also have quite a number of Spanish translations for those who want them.

Clearly, my old language did not get left behind. Don't misunderstand; this is real nice. It allows me to luxuriate in the knowledge, sweet indeed, that I am privileged. Without a doubt this is the land of opportunity. And I know it. But for those of us whom people call "Hispanics," it's a little bit more. It's the land where opportunity itself is served and seasoned as if this were the old country.

How stupid you must think me for complaining! Should we not simply take the opportunity and run? Why complain? Complaining may only spoil the fun for those among us who don't want to learn English.

But I choose to complain. I do it because questions nag at me. For instance, just who are those people for whom the Spanish translations are provided? It's a good guess that they're not Chinese, or French, or Serbo-Croatian. Of course, we know them already as "Hispanics." But what in the world does this mean?

A Hispanic is someone who came, or whose ancestors came, from a region where Spanish is the only language spoken. Nothing more. Racially, a Hispanic may be anything. It's a mistake to say "Hispanic" and mean by the term a black Cuban just as much as it would puzzle a Chilean named O'Hara.

As to who precisely among Hispanics has a need for the Spanish translations, I can't tell yet for sure. If you'll follow me a bit, though, we may together unravel this puzzle and learn something.

I would divide Hispanics living in the United States into two groups: those who were born in this country and those who came from elsewhere. It is easy to see that a number of individuals in the latter group, people who perhaps knew no English when they arrived, may have linguistic problems here. Logically, some among them may have need of Spanish translations.

The first group I mentioned, made up of people born and reared here, should have no need of any translations, right? Well, not exactly. I'm told that many among them know English very poorly, if at all. So of course they need the help. But here I hope you'll forgive me if I pause to say that I think this is a very strange

Mauricio Molina, "Why Spanish Translations?" *The New York Times* 12 March 1980, sec A. Molina, who moved to the U.S. from El Salvador in 1958, is an executive recruiter.

thing. I mean, isn't it odd in this day and age that people born right here in the United States may not somehow have mastered English?

Who, then, are the translations meant for? Ah, you probably guessed it by now. They're meant for a goodly cross section of Hispanics—average, reasonably healthy and intelligent children and adults.

I regard these translations as a waste of effort and money. To me they constitute a largesse of opportunity totally lacking a logical foundation. And what is the "logic" behind them? The answer I get is that these people are favored so that they may not suffer, because of their handicap, a diminution of their constitutional rights. The thing isn't done out of kindness, but simply out of a sense of fair play.

Fair play? I think not. Unfairness would be to deny these people the opportunity to learn English. But the question is, are they being denied? From where I live I couldn't throw a rock out the window without risking severe injury to a number of English teachers. And at various places nearby—YMCAs, colleges, high schools, grammar schools, convention halls—English courses are available for the foreign-born or anyone else who needs them. That, ladies and gentlemen, is opportunity. It's there, but it won't pull you by the nose.

This country has been, is and, I pray, will continue to be, the land of opportunity. It has never been a place where the lazy came to be coddled. It has never been a haven for those who would not look out for their needs.

What do I think should be done? I think that no Spanish translations should be made of anything. Except for one. Spanish translations should be made, and these distributed widely, detailing the availability of English courses throughout Hispanic communities.

What if people don't bother to attend? Well, it's a free country.

EASING INTO ENGLISH
Stan Luxenberg

Just as they have done for decades, the children of immigrants—from Ecuador, Italy, Vietnam, and dozens of other countries—continue coming into New York's City's already crowded high schools, speaking little English but hoping to receive the education that will enable them to improve their lives.

Battered by budget cuts and short of teachers, the city's educational system must nonetheless integrate the steady flow of new students into the American main-stream. In the past, newcomers were simply dropped into classes and left to struggle through as best they could . . . or could not.

Recently, however, in response to federal mandates, New York City has been increasing its high school bilingual program aimed at easing the transition faced by non-English speakers. Immigrants are given special courses in English—called En-glish as a second language (ESL)—while at the same time they take the regular content area courses in their native language. The idea is to allow students to continue their education by increasing their knowledge of content at their own grade levels at the same time they are acquiring English.

"When students come here they're scared stiff because they can't speak English," says Alan Irgang, principal of Franklin D. Roosevelt High School in Brooklyn. "If you mainstream them into regular classrooms they wouldn't last."

Most of these students pick up English in two or three years and then switch to regular classes. In some schools they can continue studying their native language so that they can graduate from high school truly bilingual. While the students attend special homerooms for bilingual assistance where they feel more comfortable at a time such support is critical, they are also encouraged to mix with other students. From the beginning they take music, art, and physical education with American-born students. As soon as they pick up some English, they are sometimes moved into regular math classes.

Before the students go into regular English and social studies classes, their English must be fairly good. History poses the biggest problem. As their English improves they may be able to understand generally what a teacher is saying, but it is difficult for them to grasp ideas quickly enough to take notes and to place the content in some perspective. "Once the time is right, the students are better off getting into the mainstream," says Irgang. "We don't help them by keeping them in the bilingual program."

To teach basic courses in foreign languages, the schools must find textbooks and devise a curriculum suitable for the newcomers. Locating materials in Chinese and Italian is perhaps the most difficult. But the teachers are helped by the Comprehen-sive High School Bilingual Program's federal funding which provides $563,019 in

Stan Luxenberg, "Easing into English," *American Education* January/February 1981.

Title VII money (under the Bilingual Education Act) to supplement staff for the five high schools. The money makes possible curriculum specialists in Chinese, Spanish, and Italian who can develop curriculum. In addition, resource teachers work in the schools helping the regular teachers, developing courses and advising students.

About 675 students are in this high school bilingual program—180 Chinese, 50 Italian, and the rest Spanish-speaking. The program, begun five years ago, will end this August.

When students first enter the school system, they are tested to determine how much English they know. Those who do poorly have the option of entering the special ESL program, and their parents are notified about the program. If they want their children put into some regular classes, this is possible too.

For Chinese students, learning English is particularly difficult. Accustomed to reading characters rather than an alphabet, the immigrants must make an intense adjustment to master their new language. At Lower East Side Prep, which serves students living in the city's Chinatown, immigrants take special English courses for three periods a day. Although a few more high schools offer courses for Chinese natives, the Chinatown school has a waiting list of over 200 students wanting to enter.

Lower East Side Prep is particularly appealing because it has only 500 students, including 180 Chinese in the special English classes. It is an alternative school designed for recent immigrants and students who have previously dropped out of school. Many of the students are older, ranging from 18 to 21, and are more motivated than younger people.

It is a school with few classrooms. Instead, students meet in large rooms divided only by blackboards. The Chinese youngsters come from a wide range of backgrounds in Hong Kong, Taiwan, and mainland China. More recently have come Vietnamese boat people who speak Chinese. The families—a mixture of poor peasants and sophisticated middle-class families—have left isolated villages and the large cities.

Some arrive knowing virtually no English. Pau Ngok Wan, 19, arrived in the United States in 1979 from Wenchau, a small city in mainland China. He had a ninth grade education. With the help of an interpreter, Wan explains how the special bilingual program is helping him. "My English is very poor," he says. "I wouldn't be able to stay in a regular high school."

The Chinese students who know little English begin with what the school calls ESL level one, basic English vocabulary, with frequent conversation sessions. When they reach level four they take a special transition course, from which most are able to move into regular English classes. "Sometimes students at this level (four) can write better than the average youngster in tenth grade," says Edward Hom, principal at Lower East Side Prep. "The students have been practicing grammar and punctuation. They can find words in the dictionary."

When students first enter the school, they fill out a brief questionnaire telling how long they have been in this country and how much schooling they had in their native countries. Each takes brief math and English exams which the teachers use as an informal basis for placement in the proper levels. Students who advance faster in English than the rest of the class are moved up to another level. Last September, 161 returning students at the school were tested in English to determine if they needed to continue in the special classes. Of these, 67 passed and were mainstreamed into regular classes.

The ESL courses are taught mainly in English, but teachers sometimes use Chinese to make certain everything is understood. "Is a freezer cold or hot?" asked a teacher in a level four class. "Is it freezing today?" Then she began explaining the word "frozen" and, to make certain the class understood, she lapsed into Chinese.

Students, while given credit for courses taken in their native countries, must still take the credits here required for all New York high school graduates. To earn a degree, students must pass required courses and also the New York State Regents competency exams. Students who came to the country after the eighth grade can take the exam in their native language and qualify for the degree. Of the 60 oriental students who graduated last year from the program, 50 went on to colleges and universities—from the city colleges to ivy league schools. . . .

Most students in the bilingual program are Spanish-speaking, and they face less of a problem in mastering English than the Chinese do. At Benjamin Franklin High School in Spanish Harlem there are 120 students from Puerto Rico and other parts of Latin America in ESL classes. They can normally move from the special classes in a year and a half or two, taking two periods a day of English while in the program. The ESL program produces some of the school's best students, said Melvin Taylor, Benjamin Franklin principal. At that high school—as at other comprehensive bilingual schools—attendance by ESL students is 10 to 20 percent higher than that of regular students. A recent valedictorian of the Harlem school started out in bilingual classes. Taylor has found that education holds a special value for those who come from countries where schools are not open to everyone.

Joe Barbarino, who teaches regular and ESL English classes, agrees. "These kids come wanting to learn. Apathy is nonexistent."

Before the current program, immigrant youngsters entering Benjamin Franklin took special language classes but could not take courses in subject areas. Since it would be two years before they could handle regular courses, students would take six years to finish high school—assuming they stayed that long.

Benjamin Franklin is a large inner-city school with 2,000 students and uniformed guards monitoring the halls. Because the ELS pupils are a relatively small group, they have more direct contact with teachers. They know the assistant principal overseeing the program. The school even helps the students get after-school jobs.

Teachers try to run the ESL classes in English as much as possible, but many—as with the Chinese classes at Lower East Side Prep—fall back on Spanish temporarily when the class is having a particularly hard time. "I'd rather have them know what's going on than sitting like zombies," Barbarino says.

In one exercise his students were practicing how to change a sentence from present to past tense. "What is the past tense of can't?" Barbarino asks them.

Someone says "couldn't," but not all the students are sure what that means. "*Pudo?*" one girl questions, wondering if the Spanish verb she understood means the same as the English word. "Right," Barbarino assures her.

By the time the students have finished two years of special classes, their English is far from perfect. But they can keep up in regular English classes. "They feel better about themselves and their ability to cope," explains Barbarino.

Social studies texts present special problems. Resource teachers are constantly searching for appropriate ones. Spanish translations of the standard American text-books are troublesome for students coming from South America. These students have little background in United States history, while American students were exposed to the subject in fourth and seventh grades, notes Jonathan Houston, the resource teacher coordinator at Benjamin Franklin High School. Students who grew up under dictatorships have little conception of what democracy is. Spanish-language volumes on the subject are aimed at mature scholars. To solve the problem, Houston is developing his own materials. One lesson, for example, emphasizes that many colonists came to the New World to escape persecution, just as many students' families had to flee their homelands.

Finding an appropriate American history text for Italian students is not much easier. The only ones published were written in Italy from a European perspective. According to the Italian author of a text used at Roosevelt High School, George Washington was a poor general and had to rely on Lafayette, the European, for assistance. Even given the European perspective, the material is more difficult for young Italian-born students than for American youngsters. Tony Rutigliano, who teaches the course, must move slowly in order to explain concepts that are foreign to the students. Few have heard, for example, about our war between the states. "I cannot cover what a regular history class would," he noted. "I have to spend time introducing examples of things they understand."

Anna Maria Gallo, assistant principal at Roosevelt in charge of foreign lan-guages, underlines the basic problem of locating suitable books. Most texts, she says, are too hard or too easy. One ESL teacher trained in Spanish and teaching ESL translated Spanish exercises into English for beginners in order to teach Italian students English. "The people who write the books are not in classrooms," says Gallo. "Teachers often have to create their own materials. Everybody's feeling their way through."

Yet it is the teachers' willingness to do more than would be asked in a regular classroom that is making the program work. "They really believe in their students," says Pu-Folkes, "and in giving the youngsters the opportunity to learn in their new country."

THE EDUCATION OF RICHARD RODRIGUEZ
Richard Rodriguez

I remember to start with that day in Sacramento—a California now nearly thirty years past—when I first entered a classroom, able to understand some fifty stray English words.

The third of four children, I had been preceded to a neighborhood Roman Catholic school by an older brother and sister. But neither of them had revealed very much about their classroom experiences. Each afternoon they returned, as they left in the morning, always together, speaking in Spanish as they climbed the five steps of the porch. And their mysterious books, wrapped in shopping-bag paper, remained on the table next to the door, closed firmly behind them.

An accident of geography sent me to a school where all my classmates were white, many the children of doctors and lawyers and business executives. All my classmates certainly must have been uneasy on that first day of school—as most children are uneasy—to find themselves apart from their families in the first institution of their lives. But I was astonished.

The nun said, in a friendly but oddly impersonal voice, "Boys and girls, this is Richard Rodriguez." (I heard her sound out: *Rich-heard Road-ree-guess.*) It was the first time I had heard anyone name me in English. "Richard," the nun repeated more slowly, writing my name down in her black leather book. Quickly I turned to see my mother's face dissolve in a watery blur behind the pebbled glass door.

Many years later there is something called bilingual education—a scheme proposed in the late 1960s by Hispanic-American social activists, later endorsed by a congressional vote. It is a program that seeks to permit non-English-speaking children, many from lower-class homes, to use their family language as the language of school. (Such is the goal its supporters announce.) I hear them and am forced to say no: It is not possible for a child—any child—ever to use his family's language in school. Not to understand this is to misunderstand the public uses of schooling and to trivialize the nature of intimate life—a family's "language."

Memory teaches me what I know of these matters; the boy reminds the adult. I was a bilingual child, a certain kind—socially disadvantaged—the son of working-class parents, both Mexican immigrants.

In the early years of my boyhood, my parents coped very well in America. My father had steady work. My mother managed at home. They were nobody's victims. Optimism and ambition led them to a house (our home) many blocks from the Mexican south side of town. We lived among *gringos* and only a block from the

Richard Rodriguez, "The Education of Richard Rodriguez" [our title], *Hunger of Memory: The Education of Richard Rodriguez* (Boston: David R. Godine, 1982). *Hunger of Memory* is an autobiography that deals with Rodriguez's Hispanic background and his assimilation into the American mainstream through his education in U.S. schools. The book also deals with his decision to leave a promising academic career as a reaction against Federal Affirmative Action hiring practices.

biggest, whitest houses. It never occurred to my parents that they couldn't live wherever they chose. Nor was the Sacramento of the fifties bent on teaching them a contrary lesson. My mother and father were more annoyed than intimidated by those two or three neighbors who tried initially to make us unwelcome. ("Keep your brats away from my sidewalk!") But despite all they achieved, perhaps because they had so much to achieve, any deep feeling of ease, the confidence of "belonging" in public was withheld from them both. They regarded the people at work, the faces in crowds, as very distant from us. They were the others, *los gringos*. That term was interchangeable in their speech with another, even more telling, *los america-nos*. . . .

In public, my father and mother spoke a hesitant, accented, not always gram-matical English. And they would have to strain—their bodies tense—to catch the sense of what was rapidly said by *los gringos*. At home they spoke Spanish. The language of their Mexican past sounded in counterpoint to the English of public society. The words would come quickly, with ease. Conveyed through those sounds was the pleasing, soothing, consoling reminder of being at home.

During those years when I was first conscious of hearing, my mother and father addressed me only in Spanish; in Spanish I learned to reply. By contrast, English (*inglés*), rarely heard in the house, was the language I came to associate with *gringos*. I learned my first words of English overhearing my parents speak to strangers. At five years of age, I knew just enough English for my mother to trust me on errands to stores one block away. No more. . . .

. . . The accent of *los gringos* was never pleasing nor was it hard to hear. Crowds at Safeway or at bus stops would be noisy with sound. And I would be forced to edge away from the chirping chatter above me.

I was unable to hear my own sounds, but I knew very well that I spoke English poorly. My words could not stretch far enough to form complete thoughts. And the words I did speak I didn't know well enough to make into distinct sounds. (Listeners would usually lower their heads, better to hear what I was trying to say.) But it was one thing for *me* to speak English with difficulty. It was more troubling for me to hear my parents speak in public: their high-whining vowels and gutteral consonants; their sentences that got stuck with "eh" and "ah" sounds; the confused syntax; the hesitant rhythm of sounds so different from the way *gringos* spoke. I'd notice, moreover, that my parents' voices were softer than those of *gringos* we'd meet.

I am tempted now to say that none of this mattered. In adulthood I am embar-rassed by childhood fears. And, in a way, it didn't matter very much that my parents could not speak English with ease. Their linguistic difficulties had no serious con-sequences. My mother and father made themselves understood at the county hos-pital clinic and at government offices. And yet, in another way, it mattered very much—it was unsettling to hear my parents struggle with English. Hearing them, I'd grow nervous, my clutching trust in their protection and power weakened. . . .

But then there was Spanish. *Español*: my family's language. *Español*: the language that seemed to me a private language. I'd hear strangers on the radio and in the

Mexican Catholic church across town speaking in Spanish, but I couldn't really believe that Spanish was a public language, like English. Spanish speakers, rather, seemed related to me, for I sensed that we shared—through our language—the experience of feeling apart from *los gringos*. It was thus a ghetto Spanish that I heard and I spoke. Like those whose lives are bound by a barrio, I was reminded by Spanish of my separateness from *los otros, los gringos* in power. But more intensely than for most barrio children—because I did not live in a barrio—Spanish seemed to me the language of home. (Most days it was only at home that I'd hear it.) It became the language of joyful return.

A family member would say something to me and I would feel myself specially recognized. My parents would say something to me and I would feel embraced by the sounds of their words. Those sounds said: *I am speaking with ease in Spanish. I am addressing you in words I never use with* los gringos. *I recognize you as someone special, close, like no one outside. You belong with us. In the family.*

(Ricardo.)

At the age of five, six, well past the time when most other children no longer easily notice the difference between sounds uttered at home and words spoken in public, I had a different experience. I lived in a world magically compounded of sounds. I remained a child longer than most; I lingered too long, poised at the edge of language—often frightened by the sounds of *los gringos*, delighted by the sounds of Spanish at home. I shared with my family a language that was startlingly different from that used in the great city around us.

For me there were none of the gradations between public and private society so normal to a maturing child. Outside the house was public society; inside the house was private. Just opening or closing the screen door behind me was an important experience. I'd rarely leave home all alone or without reluctance. Walking down the sidewalk, under the canopy of tall trees, I'd warily notice the—suddenly—silent neighborhood kids who stood warily watching me. Nervously, I'd arrive at the grocery store to hear there the sounds of the *gringo*—foreign to me—reminding me that in this world so big, I was a foreigner. But then I'd return. Walking back toward our house, climbing the steps from the sidewalk, when the front door was open in summer, I'd hear voices beyond the screen door talking in Spanish. For a second or two, I'd stay, linger there, listening. Smiling, I'd hear my mother call out, saying in Spanish (words): "Is that you, Richard?" All the while her sounds would assure me: *You are home now; come closer; inside. With us.*

"*Sí*," I'd reply.

Once more inside the house I would resume (assume) my place in the family. The sounds would dim, grow harder to hear. Once more at home, I would grow less aware of that fact. It required, however, no more than the blurt of the doorbell to alert me to listen to sounds all over again. The house would turn instantly still while my mother went to the door. I'd hear her hard English sounds. I'd wait to hear her voice return to soft-sounding Spanish, which assured me, as surely as did the clicking tongue of the lock on the door, that the stranger was gone.

Plainly, it is not healthy to hear such sounds so often. It is not healthy to distinguish public words from private sounds so easily. I remained cloistered by sounds, timid and shy in public, too dependent on voices at home. And yet it needs to be emphasized: I was an extremely happy child at home. I remember many nights when my father would come back from work, and I'd hear him call out to my mother in Spanish, sounding relieved. In Spanish, he'd sound light and free notes he never could manage in English. Some nights I'd jump up just at hearing his voice. With *mis hermanos* I would come running into the room where he was with my mother. Our laughing (so deep was the pleasure!) became screaming. Like others who know the pain of public alienation, we transformed the knowledge of our public separateness and made it consoling—the reminder of intimacy. Excited, we joined our voices in a celebration of sounds. *We are speaking now the way we never speak out in public. We are alone—together*, voices sounded, surrounded to tell me. Some nights, no one seemed willing to loosen the hold sounds had on us. At dinner, we invented new words. (Ours sounded Spanish, but made sense only to us.) We pieced together new words by taking, say, an English verb and giving it Spanish endings. My mother's instructions at bedtime would be lacquered with mock-urgent tones. Or a word like *sí* would become, in several notes, able to convey added measures of feeling. Tongues explored the edges of words, especially the fat vowels. And we happily sounded that military drum roll, the twirling roar of the Spanish *r*. Family language: my family's sounds. The voices of my parents and sisters and brother. Their voices insisting. *You belong here. We are family members. Related. Special to one another. Listen!* Voices singing and sighing, rising, straining, then surging, teeming with pleasure that burst syllables into fragments of laughter. At times it seemed there was steady quiet only when, from another room, the rustling whispers of my parents faded and I moved closer to sleep.

Supporters of bilingual education today imply that students like me miss a great deal by not being taught in their family's language. What they seem not to recognize is that, as a socially disadvantaged child, I considered Spanish to be a private language. What I needed to learn in school was that I had the right—and the obligation—to speak the public language of *los gringos*. The odd truth is that my first-grade classmates could have become bilingual, in the conventional sense of that word, more easily than I. Had they been taught (as upper-middle-class children are often taught early) a second language like Spanish or French, they could have regarded it simply as that: another public language. In my case such bilingualism could not have been so quickly achieved. What I did not believe was that I could speak a single public language.

Without question, it would have pleased me to hear my teachers address me in Spanish when I entered the classroom. I would have felt much less afraid. I would have trusted them and responded with ease. But I would have delayed—for how long posponed?—having to learn the language of public society. I would have evaded—and for how long could I have afforded to delay?—learning the great lesson of school, that I had a public identity.

Fortunately, my teachers were unsentimental about their responsibility. What they understood was that I needed to speak a public language. So their voices would search me out, asking me questions. Each time I'd hear them, I'd look up in surprise to see a nun's face frowning at me. I'd mumble, not really meaning to answer. The nun would persist, "Richard, stand up. Don't look at the floor. Speak up. Speak to the entire class, not just to me!" But I couldn't believe that the English language was mine to use. (In part, I did not want to believe it.) I continued to mumble. I resisted the teacher's demands. (Did I somehow suspect that once I learned public language my pleasing family life would be changed?) Silent, waiting for the bell to sound, I remained dazed, diffident, afraid.

Because I wrongly imagined that English was intrinsically a public language and Spanish an intrinsically private one, I easily noted the difference between classroom language and the language of home. At school, words were directed to a general audience of listeners. ("Boys and girls.") Words were meaningfully ordered. And the point was not self-expression alone but to make oneself understood by many others. The teacher quizzed: "Boys and girls, why do we use that word in this sentence? Could we think of a better word to use there? Would the sentence change its meaning if the words were differently arranged? And wasn't there a better way of saying much the same thing?" (I couldn't say. I wouldn't try to say.)

Three months. Five. Half a year passed. Unsmiling, ever watchful, my teachers noted my silence. They began to connect my behavior with the difficult progress my older sister and brother were making. Until one Saturday morning three nuns arrived at the house to talk to our parents. Stiffly, they sat on the blue living room sofa. From the doorway of another room, spying the visitors, I noted the incongruity—the clash of two worlds, the faces and voices of school intruding upon the familiar setting of home. I overheard one voice gently wondering, "Do your children speak only Spanish at home, Mrs. Rodriguez?" While another voice added, "That Richard especially seems so timid and shy."

That Rich-heard!

With great tact the visitors continued, "Is it possible for you and your husband to encourage your children to practice their English when they are home?" Of course, my parents complied. What would they not do for their children's well-being? And how could they have questioned the Church's authority which those women represented? In an instant, they agreed to give up the language (the sounds) that had revealed and accentuated our family's closeness. The moment after the visitors left, the change was observed. "*Ahora*, speak to us *en inglés*," my father and mother united to tell us.

At first, it seemed a kind of game. After dinner each night, the family gathered to practice "our" English. (It was still then *inglés*, a language foreign to us, so we felt drawn as strangers to it.) Laughing, we would try to define words we could not pronounce. We played with strange English sounds, often overanglicizing our pronunciations. And we filled the smiling gaps of our sentences with familiar Spanish sounds. But that was cheating, somebody shouted. Everyone laughed. In school, meanwhile, like my brother and sister, I was required to attend a daily tutoring session. I needed a full year of special attention. I also needed my teachers to keep my attention from straying in class by calling out, *Rich-heard*—their English voices slowly prying loose my ties to my other name, its three notes, *Ri-car-do*. Most of all I needed to hear my mother and father speak to me in a moment of seriousness in broken—suddenly heartbreaking—English. The scene was inevitable: One Saturday morning I entered the kitchen where my parents were talking in Spanish. I did not realize that they were talking in Spanish however until, at the moment they saw me, I heard their voices change to speak English. Those *gringo* sounds they uttered startled me. Pushed me away. In that moment of trivial misunderstanding and profound insight, I felt my throat twisted by unsounded grief. I turned quickly and left the room. But I had no place to escape to with Spanish. (The spell was broken.) My brother and sisters were speaking English in another part of the house.

Again and again in the days following, increasingly angry, I was obliged to hear my mother and father: "Speak to us *en inglés.*" (*Speak.*) Only then did I determine to learn classroom English. Weeks after, it happened: One day in school I raised my hand to volunteer an answer. I spoke out in a loud voice. And I did not think it remarkable when the entire class understood. That day, I moved very far from the disadvantaged child I had been only days earlier. The belief, the calming assurance that I belonged in public, had at last taken hold.

Shortly after, I stopped hearing the high and loud sounds of *los gringos.* A more and more confident speaker of English, I didn't trouble to listen to *how* strangers sounded, speaking to me. And there simply were too many English-speaking people in my day for me to hear American accents anymore. Conversations quickened. Listening to persons who sounded eccentrically pitched voices, I usually noted their sounds for an initial few seconds before I concentrated on *what* they were saying. Conversations became content-full. Transparent. Hearing someone's *tone* of voice— angry or questioning or sarcastic or happy or sad—I didn't distinguish it from the words it expressed. Sound and word were thus tightly wedded. At the end of a day, I was often bemused, always relieved, to realize how "silent," though crowded with words, my day in public had been. (This public silence measured and quickened the change in my life.)

At last, seven years old, I came to believe what had been technically true since my birth: I was an American citizen.

But the special feeling of closeness at home was diminished by then. Gone was the desperate, urgent, intense feeling of being at home; rare was the experience of feeling myself individualized by family intimates. We remained a loving family, but one greatly changed. No longer so close; no longer bound tight by the pleasing and troubling knowledge of our public separateness. Neither my older brother nor sister rushed home after school anymore. Nor did I. When I arrived home there would often be neighborhood kids in the house. Or the house would be empty of sounds.

Following the dramatic Americanization of their children, even my parents grew more publicly confident. Especially my mother. She learned the names of all the people on our block. And she decided we needed to have a telephone installed in the house. My father continued to use the word *gringo.* But it was no longer charged with the old bitterness or distrust. (Stripped of any emotional content, the word simply became a name for those Americans not of Hispanic descent.) Hearing him, sometimes, I wasn't sure if he was pronouncing the Spanish word *gringo* or saying gringo in English.

Matching the silence I started hearing in public was a new quiet at home. The family's quiet was partly due to the fact that, as we children learned more and more English, we shared fewer and fewer words with our parents. Sentences needed to be spoken slowly when a child addressed his mother or father. (Often the parent wouldn't understand.) The child would need to repeat himself. (Still the parent misunderstood.) The young voice, frustrated, would end up saying, "Never mind"— the subject was closed. Dinners would be noisy with the clinking of knives and forks against dishes. My mother would smile softly between her remarks; my father at the other end of the table would chew and chew at his food, while he stared over the heads of his children.

My *mother!* My *father!* After English became my primary language, I no longer knew what words to use in addressing my parents. The old Spanish words (those tender accents of sound) I had used earlier—*mamá* and *papá*—I couldn't use anymore. They would have been too painful reminders of how much had changed in my life. On the other hand, the words I heard neighborhood kids call *their* parents seemed equally unsatisfactory. *Mother* and *Father; Ma, Papa, Pa, Dad, Pop* (how I hated the all-American sound of that last word especially)—all these terms I felt were unsuitable, not really terms of address for *my* parents. As a result, I never used them at home. Whenever I'd speak to my parents, I would try to get their attention with eye contact alone. In public conversations, I'd refer to "my parents" or "my mother and father. . . ."

The silence at home, however, was finally more than a literal silence. Fewer words passed between parent and child, but more profound was the silence that resulted from my inattention to sounds. At about the time I no longer bothered to listen with care to the sounds of English in public, I grew careless about listening to the sounds family members made when they spoke. Most of the time I heard someone speaking at home and didn't distinguish his sounds from the words people uttered in public. I didn't even pay much attention to my parents' accented and ungrammatical speech. At least not at home. Only when I was with them in public would I grow alert to their accents. Though, even then, their sounds caused me less and less concern. For I was increasingly confident of my own public identity.

I would have been happier about my public success had I not sometimes recalled what it had been like earlier, when my family had conveyed its intimacy through a set of conveniently private sounds. . . .

Today I hear bilingual educators say that children lose a degree of "individuality" by becoming assimilated into public society. (Bilingual schooling was popularized in the seventies, that decade when middle-class ethnics began to resist the process of assimilation—the American melting pot.) But the bilingualists simplistically scorn the value and necessity of assimilation. They do not seem to realize that there are *two* ways a person is individualized. So they do not realize that while one suffers a diminished sense of *private* individuality by becoming assimilated into public society, such assimilation makes possible the achievement of *public* individuality.

The bilingualists insist that a student should be reminded of his difference from others in mass society, his heritage. But they equate mere separateness with individuality. The fact is that only in private—with intimates—is separateness from the crowd a prerequisite for individuality. (An intimate draws me apart, tells me that I am unique, unlike all others.) In public, by contrast, full individuality is achieved, paradoxically, by those who are able to consider themselves members of the crowd. Thus it happened for me: Only when I was able to think of myself as an American, no longer an alien in *gringo* society, could I seek the rights and opportunities necessary for full public individuality. The social and political advantages I enjoy as a man result from the day that I came to believe that my name, indeed, is *Rich-heard*

Road-ree-guess. It is true that my public society today is often impersonal. (My public society is usually mass society.) Yet despite the anonymity of the crowd and despite the fact that the individuality I achieve in public is often tenuous—because it depends on my being one in a crowd—I celebrate the day I acquired my new name. Those middle-class ethnics who scorn assimilation seem to me filled with decadent self-pity, obsessed by the burden of public life. Dangerously, they romanticize public separateness and they trivialize the dilemma of the socially disadvantaged.

My awkward childhood does not prove the necessity of bilingual education. My story discloses instead an essential myth of childhood—inevitable pain. If I rehearse here the changes in my private life after my Americanization, it is finally to emphasize the public gain. The loss implies the gain: The house I returned to each afternoon was quiet. Intimate sounds no longer rushed to the door to greet me. There were other noises inside. The telephone rang. Neighborhood kids ran past the door of the bedroom where I was reading my schoolbooks—covered with shopping-bag paper. Once I learned public language, it would never again be easy for me to hear intimate family voices. More and more of my day was spent hearing words. But that may only be a way of saying that the day I raised my hand in class and spoke loudly to an entire roomful of faces, my childhood started to end. . . .

. . . Making more and more friends outside my house, I began to distinguish intimate voices speaking through *English.* I'd listen at times to a close friend's confidential tone or secretive whisper. Even more remarkable were those instances when, for no special reason apparently, I'd become conscious of the fact that my companion was speaking only to me. I'd marvel just hearing his voice. It was a stunning event: to be able to break through his words, to be able to hear this voice of the other, to realize that it was directed only to me. After such moments of intimacy outside the house, I began to trust hearing intimacy conveyed through my family's English. Voices at home at last punctured sad confusion. I'd hear myself addressed as an intimate at home once again. Such moments were never as raucous with sound as past times had been when we had had "private" Spanish to use. (Our English-sounding house was never to be as noisy as our Spanish-speaking house had been.) Intimate moments were usually soft moments of sound. My mother was in the dining room while I did my homework nearby. And she looked over at me. Smiled. Said something—her words said nothing very important. But her voice sounded to tell me (*We are together*) I was her son.

(*Richard!*)

Intimacy thus continued at home; intimacy was not stilled by English. It is true that I would never forget the great change of my life, the diminished occasions of intimacy. But there would also be times when I sensed the deepest truth about language and intimacy: *Intimacy is not created by a particular language; it is created by intimates.* The great change in my life was not linguistic but social. If, after becoming a successful student, I no longer heard intimate voices as often as I had earlier, it was not because I spoke English rather than Spanish. It was because I used public language for most of the day. I moved easily at last, a citizen in a crowded city of words.

AGAINST A CONFUSION OF TONGUES
William A. Henry III

"We have room for but one language here, and that is the English language, for we intend to see that the crucible turns our people out as Americans and not as dwellers in a polyglot boarding house."—Theodore Roosevelt

In the store windows of Los Angeles, gathering place of the world's aspiring peoples, the signs today ought to read, "English spoken here." Supermarket price tags are often written in Korean, restaurant menus in Chinese, employment-office signs in Spanish. In the new city of dreams, where gold can be earned if not found on the sidewalk, there are laborers and businessmen who have lived five, ten, 20 years in America without learning to speak English. English is not the common denominator for many of these new Americans. Disturbingly, some of them insist it need not be.

America's image of itself as a melting pot, enriched by every culture yet subsuming all of them, dates back far beyond the huddled yearning masses at the Baja California border and Ellis Island, beyond the passage in steerage of victims of the potato famine and the high-minded Teutonic settlements in the nascent Midwest. Just months after the Revolution was won, in 1782, French-American Writer Michel Guillaume-Jean de Crèvecoeur said of his adopted land: "Individuals of all nations are melted into a new race of men." Americans embittered by the wars of Europe knew that fusing diversity into unity was more than a poetic ideal, it was a practical necessity. In 1820 future Congressman Edward Everett warned, "From the days of the Tower of Babel, confusion of tongues has ever been one of the most active causes of political misunderstanding."

The successive waves of immigrants did not readily embrace the new culture, even when intimidated by the xenophobia of the know-nothing era or two World Wars. Says Historian James Banks: "Each nationality group tried desperately to remake North America in the image of its native land." When the question arose of making the U.S. multilingual or multicultural in public affairs, however, Congress stood firm. In the 1790s, 1840s and 1860s, the lawmakers voted down pleas to print Government documents in German. Predominantly French-speaking Louisiana sought statehood in 1812; the state constitution that it submitted for approval specified that its official language would be English. A century later, New Mexico was welcomed into the union, but only after an influx of settlers from the North and East had made English, not Spanish, the majority tongue.

Occasional concentrations of immigrants were able to win local recognition of their language and thereby enforce an early form of affirmative action: by 1899 nearly 18,000 pupils in Cincinnati divided their school time between courses given in German and in English, thus providing employment for 186 German-speaking teachers. In 1917 San Francisco taught German in eight primary schools, Italian in six, French in four and Spanish in two. Yet when most cities consented to teach

William A. Henry III, "Against a Confusion of Tongues," *Time* 13 June 1983.

immigrant children in their native Chinese or Polish or Yiddish or Gujarati, the clearly stated goal was to transform the students as quickly as possible into speakers of English and full participants in society.

Now, however, a new bilingualism and biculturalism is being promulgated that would deliberately fragment the nation into separate, unassimilated groups. The movement seems to take much of its ideology from the black separatism of the 1960s but derives its political force from the unprecedented raw numbers—15 million or more—of a group linked to a single tongue, Spanish. The new metaphor is not the melting pot but the salad bowl, with each element distinct. The biculturalists seek to use public services, particularly schools, not to Americanize the young but to heighten their consciousness of belonging to another heritage. Contends Tomás A. Arciniega, vice president for academic affairs at California State University at Fresno: "The promotion of cultural differences has to be recognized as a valid and legitimate educational goal." Miguel Gonzalez-Pando, director of the Center for Latino Education at Florida International University in Miami, says: "I speak Spanish at home, my social relations are mostly in Spanish, and I am raising my daughter as a Cuban American. It is a question of freedom of choice." In Gonzalez-Pando's city, where Hispanics outnumber whites, the anti-assimilationist theory has become accepted practice: Miami's youth can take twelve years of bilingual public schooling with no pretense made that the program is transitional toward anything. The potential for separatism is greater in Los Angeles. Philip Hawley, president of the Carter Hawley Hale retail store chain, cautions: "This is the only area in the U.S. that over the next 50 years could have a polarization into two distinct cultures, of the kind that brought about the Quebec situation in Canada." Professor Rodolfo Acuña of California State University at Northridge concurs. Says Acuña: "Talk of secession may come when there are shrinking economic resources and rising expectations among have-not Hispanics."

Already the separatists who resist accepting English have won laws and court cases mandating provision of social services, some government instructions, even election ballots in Spanish. The legitimizing effect of these decisions can be seen in the proliferation of billboards, roadside signs and other public communications posted in Spanish. Acknowledges Professor Ramón Ruiz of the University of California at San Diego: "The separatism question is with us already." The most portentous evidence is in the classrooms. Like its political cousins, equal opportunity and social justice, bilingual education is a catchall term that means what the speaker wishes it to mean.

There are at least four ways for schools to teach students who speak another language at home:

1. Total immersion in English, which relies on the proven ability of children to master new languages. Advocates of bilingual education argue that this approach disorients children and sometimes impedes their progress in other subjects, because those who have already mastered several grades' worth of material in their first language may be compelled to take English-language classes with much younger or slower students.

2. Short-term bilingual education, which may offer a full curriculum but is directed toward moving students into English-language classes as rapidly as possible.

In a report last month by a Twentieth Century Fund task force, members who were disillusioned with the performance of elaborate bilingual programs urged diversion of federal funds to the teaching of English. The panel held: "Schoolchildren will never swim in the American mainstream unless they are fluent in English."

3. Dual curriculum, which permits students to spend several years making the transition. This is the method urged by many moderate Hispanic, Chinese and other ethnic minority leaders. Says Historian Ruiz: "The direct approach destroys children's feelings of security. Bilingual education eases them from something they know to something they do not."

4. Language and cultural maintenance, which seeks to enhance students' mastery of their first language while also teaching them English. In Hispanic communities, the language training is often accompanied by courses in ethnic heritage. Argues Miami Attorney Manuel Díaz, a vice chairman of the Spanish American League Against Discrimination: "Cultural diversity makes this country strong. It is not a disease."

The rhetoric of supporters of bilingualism suggests that theirs may be a political solution to an educational problem. Indeed, some of them acknowledge that they view bilingual programs as a source of jobs for Hispanic administrators, teachers and aides. In cities with large minority enrollments, says a Chicago school principal who requested anonymity, "those of us who consider bilingual education ineffective are afraid that if we say so we will lose our jobs." Lawrence Uzzell, president of Learn Inc., a Washington-based research foundation, contends that Hispanic educational activists are cynically protecting their own careers. Says Uzzell: "The more the Hispanic child grows up isolated, the easier it is for politicians to manipulate him as part of an ethnic voting bloc."

The signal political success for bilingualism has been won at the U.S. Department of Education. After the Supreme Court ruled in 1974 that Chinese-speaking students were entitled to some instruction in a language they could understand, the DOE issued "informal" rules that now bind more than 400 school districts. Immersion in English, even rapid transition to English, does not satisfy the DOE; the rules compel school systems to offer a full curriculum to any group of 20 or more students who share a foreign language. The DOE rules have survived three presidencies, although Jesse Soriano, director of the Reagan Administration's $138 million bilingual program, concedes, "This is money that could be spent more effectively." About half of students from Spanish-speaking homes drop out before the end of high school; of the ones who remain, 30% eventually score two or more years below their age group on standardized tests. But it is hard to demonstrate the value of any bilingual approach in aiding those students. In 1982 Iris Rotberg reported in the *Harvard Education Review*: "Research findings have shown that bilingual programs are neither better or worse than other instructional methods." Indeed, the DOE's review found that of all methods for teaching bilingual students English and mathematics, only total immersion in English clearly worked.

One major problem in assessing the worth of bilingual programs is that they often employ teachers who are less than competent in either English or Spanish, or in the specific subjects they teach. In a 1976 test of 136 teachers and aides in bilingual programs in New Mexico, only 13 could read and write Spanish at third-grade level.

Says former Boston School Superintendent Robert Wood: "Many bilingual teachers do not have a command of English, and after three years of instruction under them, children also emerge without a command of English." Another complicating factor is the inability of researchers to determine whether the problems of Hispanic students stem more from language difficulty or from their economic class. Many Hispanic children who are unable to speak English have parents with little education who hold unskilled jobs; in school performance, these students are much like poor blacks and whites. Notes Harvard's Nathan Glazer: "If these students do poorly in English, they may be doing poorly in a foreign language."

Even if the educational value of bilingual programs were beyond dispute, there would remain questions about their psychic value to children. Among the sharpest critics of bilingualism is Author Richard Rodriguez, who holds a Berkeley Ph.D. in literature and grew up in a Spanish-speaking, working-class household; in his autobiography *Hunger of Memory*, Rodriguez argues that the separation from his family that a Hispanic child feels on becoming fluent in English is necessary to develop a sense of belonging to American society. Writes Rodriguez: "Bilingualists do not seem to realize that there are two ways a person is individualized. While one suffers a diminished sense of private individuality by becoming assimilated into public society, such assimilation makes possible the achievement of public individuality." By Rodriguez's reasoning, the discomfort of giving up the language of home is far less significant that the isolation of being unable to to speak the language of the larger world.

The dubious value of bilingualism to students is only part of America's valid concern about how to absorb the Hispanic minority. The U.S., despite its exceptional diversity, has been spared most of the ethnic tensions that beset even such industrialized nations as Belgium and Spain. The rise of a large group, detached from the main population by language and custom, could affect the social stability of the country. Hispanic leaders, moreover, acknowledge that their constituents have been less inclined to become assimilated than previous foreign-language communities, in part because many of them anticipated that after earning and saving, they would return to Puerto Rico, Mexico, South America or Cuba, Says Historian Doyce Nunis of the University of Southern California: "For the first time in American experience, a large immigrant group may be electing to bypass the processes of acculturation." Miami Mayor Maurice Ferré, a Puerto Rican, claims that in his city a resident can go from birth through school and working life to death without ever having to speak English. But most Hispanic intellectuals claim that their communities, like other immigrant groups before them, cling together only to combat discrimination.

The disruptive potential of bilingualism and biculturalism is still worrisome: millions of voters cut off from the main sources of information, millions of potential draftees inculcated with dual ethnic loyalties, millions of would-be employees ill at ease in the language of their workmates. Former Senator S.I. Hayakawa of California was laughed at for proposing a constitutional amendment to make English the official language of the U.S. It was a gesture of little practical consequence but great symbolic significance: many Americans mistakenly feel there is something racist, or oppressive, in expecting newcomers to share the nation's language and folkways.

   Beyond practical politics and economics, separatism belittles the all-embracing culture that America has embodied for the world. Says Writer Irving Howe, a scholar of literature and the Jewish immigrant experience: "The province, the ethnic nest, remains the point from which everything begins, but it must be transcended." That transcendence does not mean disappearance. It is possible to eat a Mexican meal, dance a Polish polka, sing in a Rumanian choir, preserve one's ethnicity however one wishes, and still share fully in the English-speaking common society. Just as American language, food and popular culture reflect the past groups who landed in the U.S., so future American culture will reflect the Hispanics, Asians and many other groups who are replanting their roots. As Author Rodriguez observes after his journey into the mainstream, "Culture survives whether you want it to or not."

HISPANIC PUPILS' SOLE HOPE
Irma Herrera

In our not too distant past, 80 percent of all Mexican-American children in Texas had to repeat the first grade because they could not speak English. With bilingual education, this waste of human talent would never have occurred. And yet, as Congress begins to consider reauthorization of the Bilingual Education Act of 1968, we hear again the insidious myth that most Hispanic children do not want to learn English and that their parents—as well as advocates of bilingual instruction—want them educated only in their native language. If we adopt bilingual instruction as an educational policy, they say, we will create a bilingual society. Nothing could be farther from the truth.

I have never met a Hispanic parent who proposed delaying the acquisition of English. Parents who labor at deadend jobs because of poor language skills hardly wish this future on their children. Even Mexican grandmothers, illiterate in English and Spanish, will smile a crinkled smile and say: "El saber es poder," or "Knowledge is power."

Non-English-speaking children are eager to learn and are curious, but they cannot participate in education if they do not understand the instruction. Moreover, they cannot be expected to learn English simply by joining an English-speaking class and absorbing the language by osmosis. I could spend three years in a classroom in China, listening to lessons in Cantonese, and not learn Cantonese. Spanish-speaking children need instruction by people trained in second language acquisition.

Yet today many students who don't understand English sit all day in classrooms, their presence required by law, listening to the noise of an unfamiliar language. These are the physically normal, yet deaf-mute children whom many suggest we can no longer "pamper" with bilingual instruction.

Recently, the Twentieth Century Fund recommended that "the Federal Government promote and support proficiency in English for all children in the public schools." As advocates of bilingual education, we support their recommendation. We do not support their statement that the only way to teach non-English speaking students is by immersing them in English instruction.

Those who would curtly dismiss bilingual education as a failure do not understand all the facts. For one thing, fewer than 20 percent of the several million limited-English students are served by bilingual education. The majority go through instruction that ranges from excellent programs in English as a second language to sink or swim methods. If our schools have so miserably failed to educate the non-English speakers, the fault is not with bilingual education. We must look at how we have traditionally served these students and whether English-language instruction, which was the norm prior to passage of the Bilingual Act, was successful. The figures suggest it was not.

Irma Herrera, "Hispanic Pupils' Sole Hope." *The New York Times* 27 July 1983, sec. A. Herrera is Director of Educational Programs for the Mexican Legal Defense and Education Fund.

Before 1968, the dropout rate for Hispanic students was 52 percent nationwide. In 1982, it was slightly below 40 percent—still triple the rate for the white population but a slight improvement. Much of the progress can be traced to the growth of bilingual education.

English-language development is the keystone of bilingual education. Bilingual programs recognize that a second language is not earned overnight or in one semester. It makes sense to begin teaching students math and reading in a language they already know instead of letting them sit in classes comprehending nothing. It does not make sense to penalize students academically as they tackle the difficult task of learning English.

Although it wasn't called that in my South Texas elementary school in 1956, I received bilingual education. Most students in the Mexican-only school came from non-English-speaking families. When we didn't understand something, our teachers explained it to us in Spanish. Eventually all of us learned English; and, along the way, with help from our teachers in Spanish, we learned how to add and subtract and how to diagram sentences.

Most of us are not any dumber or brighter than the rest of the population. But we do come from homes where the main language is not English. No matter how much our parents may want to, they cannot teach us English or help us with our homework. Our only hope is the schools. They must teach us English and educate us. Bilingual education is the best way to accomplish both.

BILINGUAL CLASSES: A BILATERAL CONFLICT
Sally Reed

When 11-year-old Joanna Poniatowski arrived at the Hanson Park Elementary School on [Chicago's] northwest side last year, she had traveled halfway around the world to settle in a country she had never seen at a school where most of the children spoke a language very different from her own. Her parents, who left their native Poland for Austria two days before martial law was declared, ultimately immigrated to Chicago to live in the world's largest Polish community outside of Warsaw.

Hanson Park School, across the street from St. Stanislaus Roman Catholic Church, where mass is said in both Polish and English, and a stone's throw from a Polish bakery where grandmothers converse in their native dialects, is a refuge for Joanna as she makes her transition from one world to another. Here, under the tutelage of Rafaela Mielcarek, a teacher who speaks both English and Polish, Joanna studies English as a second language and until she masters it, pursues science, math and social studies in her native tongue.

"The purpose of the bilingual-education program is to help children who have come from Poland to learn English," Mrs. Mielcarek said, "but they study other subjects in Polish so that they do not lose time acquiring knowledge in those areas."

Joanna's experience is that of many students who enter American schools each year from Poland, Mexico, Vietnam, Haiti, the Dominican Republic and other countries where English is virtually unknown. To assimilate them, the schools resort to two bilingual approaches: the transformational method for transition into English, or the maintenance method, in which students also continue studying their native language. However, a recent national report and proposed Federal legislation have called these strategies into question, with critics charging that students stay in their native languages too long.

The issue has become all the more complex as the largest influx of new immigrants in more than half a century has been accompanied by reduced Federal and state funding for education.

And besides other problems, bilingual programs are hobbled by a shortage of qualified teachers. According to a Department of Education study of teacher-training programs in bilingual education, 56,000 more teachers are currently needed nationwide from kindergarten through the 12th grade, but the current graduation rate of such teachers is only 2,000 a year.

Polish is one of 140 languages now spoken in the nation's schools. Spanish is the most often spoken foreign language, and last year Vietnamese replaced Chinese as the second most frequently spoken in federally supported school programs.

Sally Reed, "Bilingual Classes: A Bilateral Conflict," *New York Times* 21 August 1983, sec. xii. Reed is the former Senior Editor of *Instructor* magazine.

Miss Poniatowski is one of 46 Polish-speaking pupils in her school. She is one of 220,000 students across the nation in the federally financed Title VII bilingual program, one of 660,000 nationwide in state-financed programs and one of an estimated 3.5 million students needing such services nationally.

For the last 17 years, under legislative mandate and a Supreme Court ruling, schools have been required to provide such students as Joanna with "the use of two languages, one of which is English, as a medium of instruction." According to Title VII of the Elementary and Secondary Education Act, when a school has between 10 and 20 students who speak the same foreign language, the school must provide a separate bilingual teacher.

Unlike an immersion program, where students are quickly placed in an English environment, the transformational and maintenance approaches assume that the fastest way to English is through the native tongue and that skills learned in one language can be transferred to another.

Gloria Zamora, president of the National Association for Bilingual Education, is among those who believe that the transformation approach is "the law of the land."

"The underlying philosophy is to use the first language as a bridge for the second," she said. "The objective is to move the child into English, after which he never again concentrates on a native language."

In the Los Angeles Unified School District, for example, there are 118,000 students of limited English ability, and Hispanic students now make up 49 percent of the school population. Students are taught English as a second language and take their basic subjects in Spanish until they are ready to enter regular English classes.

"Our purpose in bilingual education is to move youngsters into the mainstream curriculum as soon as possible," said Ignacio DeCarrillo, director of the bilingual program for the Los Angeles schools.

At Hanson Park School in Chicago, which also has bilingual programs in Spanish and Italian as well as Polish, Joanna Poniatowski will make the transition to English classes in approximately two years. But she will also maintain her language skills in Polish through a special maintenance class taught by Mrs. Mielcarek. "The pressure is on learning English," Mrs. Mielcarek said. "But the concern is that the Polish not be lost."

The maintenance of their native language is a critical priority in many ethnic communities. In New York City's bilingual programs there are 70,000 students and 13 language groups in 684 public schools. Seventy percent of the students are in a Spanish program. At Public School 155, for example, children who have achieved proficiency in English maintain their basic skills in Spanish through a special language-arts class.

"The goal is not to be dominant in Spanish," said Sonia Gulardo, director of bilingual education for Community School District 4 in East Harlem. "Our students are learning English. But this country needs bilingual people."

In Milwaukee, the school system recently began a bilingual program for 100 Vietnamese and 290 Laotians, including 140 Hmong, an ethnically distinct Laotian hill tribe. The bilingual Spanish program is aimed not only at maintaining native language skills but also developing them so that by the 12th grade students are proficient in two languages.

Some critics of bilingual education simply object to teaching any language to the foreign-born other than English. Others, including the American Federation of Teachers, argue that maintaining a native language keeps the child from being assimilated into the school and becoming proficient in English.

Other critics contend that schools cannot cope adequately with the linguistic diversity of its student population and that some test scores indicate that the approaches have been ineffective. They point to the most extensive study to date, conducted in the late 1970's, by the American Institute for Research, which found that students in Title VII Spanish programs performed at a lower level in English language arts than did non-Title VII students.

This concern is expressed in "Making the Grade," a recent report on Federal education policy issued by the 20th Century Fund. The report recommends that schools "emphasize the primacy of English" and suggests that funds earmarked for bilingual education be used solely to teach non-English-speaking students to read and write English.

The Bilingual Education Improvement bill now in Congress also reflects a shift in thinking on the Federal level, where the budget for Title VII last year was $134 million. It in effect eliminates the emphasis on native languages by accepting different teaching methods such as immersion and English-as-a-second-language classes not based on students' native language.

Opponents to this thinking argue that native languages must be maintained in bilingual programs for linguistic as well as political and social reasons. "We do believe in the primacy of English, and teaching English is our primary goal," said Mrs. Zamora of the National Association for Bilingual Education. "But we believe it doesn't have to be done at the sacrifice of other languages.

"There is now a large body of research, particularly in linguistics," she said, "that supports what Unesco articulated 15 years ago: that is, no matter what language one may come to use as an adult, there are definite cognitive advantages to being educated in one's native tongue."

Indeed, Joan Friedenberg, associate professor of bilingual education at Florida International University, studied Spanish-speaking students in the third and fourth grades in Dade County, Florida, and found that those who learned to read simultaneously in English and Spanish scored higher on achievement tests than those taught to read English alone. Her conclusion was that schools should not delay in teaching English but not at the expense of the native language.

There are, however, as many studies and conflicting tests scores as there are opinions as to the effectiveness of bilingual education. "There is no consensus in the research community about the best results," said Louise Terry Wilkinson, head of the educational psychology department at the University of Wisconsin. In an attempt to isolate variables that may determine the success of the bilingual programs, the National Institute of Education is currently conducting a three-year study to examine language acquisition, the impact of parental and teacher attitudes and comparison of teaching practices.

While it appears that Congress, administrators and tax-weary communities are in no mood to expand bilingual programs, schools such as Hanson Park are faced with the increasing influx of new students. "Bilingual programs can hold kids back, perhaps, and keep them from assimilating as quickly as they might," said Frank J. DePaul, the Hanson Park principal. "But at their best the programs encourage children to read and write in English and children who do not understand a subject because they don't know the language are no longer labeled slow.

"We claim that we want students to learn foreign languages," he added. "Well, here we have these children coming to our schools with a capacity for dual languages. Not maintaining these skills is a terrible waste of our human resources."

TEACH IMMIGRANTS IN THEIR OWN LANGUAGE: INTERVIEW WITH RAMON SANTIAGO

Q Mr. Santiago, why do you favor bilingual education—the teaching of academic subjects to immigrant children in their own language while simultaneously giving them English-language instruction?

A Because bilingual education effectively meets the needs of linguistic-minority children. It respects what the children themselves bring to the classroom—their language and culture.

Bilingual-education programs funded by the federal government came into being in 1968 because non-English-speaking children were making little progress in school and were bored. Their dropout rate was tremendously high. In some ethnic groups, fewer than 20 percent of the students were getting through high school.

Q What is the dropout rate now?

A Participants in bilingual-education programs are four times as likely to finish high school, and the number entering college has increased.

Another gain from preserving native languages is that the United States now has more linguistic resources for its diplomatic dealings with other countries—Vietnam, El Salvador and the Middle East, for example.

Q How many children are now studying in bilingual-education programs?

A In grades one through 12, approximately 3.6 million children in this country don't speak English as a native language. But fewer than 10 percent of them—about 330,000—are in bilingual programs.

Q Traditionally, immigrants have had to master English as the first step toward receiving full political and economic benefits from American society. Doesn't bilingual education slow down this process?

A No. Every immigrant who comes to the United States wants to be able to function in the language of the majority. That is the road to success, and, if anything, bilingual education accelerates this process.

There is a mistaken impression that whenever you teach in a language other than English, you're taking away time needed for English instruction. That is not necessarily true. If a child were taught English all day, he'd go stir-crazy. You cannot expose a youngster to too much of a foreign language too soon.

Also, by teaching some subject matter in a child's native language, a child can build a basic store of facts. When he switches to classes in English, he will

"Teach Immigrants in Their Own Language: Interview with Ramón Santiago," *U.S. News and World Report* 3 October 1983. Santiago is the director of the Georgetown University Bilingual Service Center.

then have a fund of knowledge and be better able to concentrate on expressing himself in English.

Q **Opponents of bilingual education say that when a child does not learn basic academic subjects in English, he is at a disadvantage in coping with American ways—**

A Some people assume that immersing a person in a language situation is like immersing him in a bath of water. Unfortunately, languages are not learned by osmosis that quickly. We have to keep in mind that a child cannot learn basic concepts of mathematics, science and other academic subjects in a language the child doesn't understand.

In bilingual education, you attempt to make a child as comfortable as possible by providing him with something he understands—instruction using his native language.

At the same time, you teach English as a second language. Gradually you alter the proportions until a child is getting zero instruction in his native language when he is ready for mainstreaming.

Q **Might not instruction in languages other than English tend to overemphasize ethnic heritage and deepen the alienation of some groups from American society, perhaps even encouraging separatist movements or bilingual states?**

A In the first place, the melting-pot concept has been disavowed by many sociologists as not representative of U.S. society. Instead, the salad-bowl or mosaic concept is preferred. The U.S. is not any one thing, but a combination of many things.

If you try to de-emphasize the contribution made by people of different backgrounds, you do harm to the American fabric. This does not mean that each element of society has to have its own separate identity, government or schools. But groups should be allowed to keep their distinctiveness. Some people imply that diversity causes disunity. Yet the Civil War was fought between states that shared English as a native tongue. People can find many things to fight about other than language.

I often say that the U.S. could do without bilingual education if it were to do several things: Seal off the borders, take down the Statue of Liberty and enclose itself in a cocoon, ignoring the rest of the world.

Q **Some critics of bilingual education say that Hispanics resist assimilation into the mainstream more than other newcomers to the United States—**

A If they mean that Hispanics as a group have retained more of their language and culture, I would say more power to the Hispanics. When the Indo-Chinese came to the United States, they escaped from cities that were being bombed out of existence or they fled from repressive governments. They pretty much burned their bridges behind them. Their choice in the U.S. is total assimilation or failure.

On the other hand, the two main segments of the Hispanic population, the Mexican Americans and the Puerto Ricans, are either American citizens from birth or migrants—they are not exiles.

Also, I don't believe that the U.S. in terms of pure self-interest would want the many Hispanics to lose their language and culture, because the United States is constantly trying to improve relations with Latin America and with countries that have Spanish language and culture.

Americanism is not expressed only in English. It's possible for linguistic minorities to be fully patriotic and American.

LANGUAGE
James Fallows

. . . A national culture is held together by official rules and informal signals. Through their language, dress, taste, and habits of life, immigrants initially violate the rules and confuse the signals. The United States has prided itself on building a nation out of diverse parts. *E Pluribus Unum* originally referred to the act of political union in which separate colonies became one sovereign state. It now seems more fitting as a token of the cultural adjustments through which immigrant strangers have become Americans. Can the assimilative forces still prevail?

The question arises because most of today's immigrants share one trait: their native language is Spanish. . . .

The term "Hispanic" is in many ways deceiving. It refers to those whose origins can be traced back to Spain (*Hispania*) or Spain's former colonies. It makes a bloc out of Spanish-speaking peoples who otherwise have little in common. The Cuban-Americans, concentrated in Florida, are flush with success. Some of them nurse dreams of political revenge against Castro. They demonstrate little solidarity with such other Hispanics as the Mexican-Americans of Texas, who are much less estranged from their homeland and who have been longtime participants in the culture of the Southwest. The Cuban-Americans tend to be Rupublicans; most Mexican-Americans and Puerto Ricans are Democrats. The Puerto Ricans, who are U.S. citizens from birth, and who have several generations of contact with American city life behind them, bear little resemblance to the Salvadorans and Guatemalans now pouring northward to get out of the way of war. Economically, the Puerto Ricans of New York City have more in common with American blacks than with most other Hispanic groups. Such contact as Anglo and black residents of Boston and New York have with Hispanic life comes mainly through Puerto Ricans; they may be misled about what to expect from the Mexicans and Central Americans arriving in ever increasing numbers. Along the southern border, Mexican-American children will razz youngsters just in from Mexico. A newcomer is called a "TJ," for Tijuana; it is the equivalent of "hillbilly" or "rube."

Still, "Hispanic" can be a useful word, because it focuses attention on the major question about this group of immigrants: Will their assimilation into an English-speaking culture be any less successful than that of others in the past?

To answer, we must consider what is different now from the circumstances under which the Germans, Poles, and Italians learned English.

The most important difference is that the host country is right next door. The only other non-English-speaking group for which this is true is the French-Canadians. Proximity has predictable consequences. For as long as the Southwest has been part of the United States, there has been a border culture in which, for

James Fallows, "Language," *The Atlantic Monthly* November 1983. Fallows, the former chief speechwriter for Jimmy Carter from 1976 to 1978, has been the Washington editor of *Atlantic* since 1979.

social and commercial reasons, both languages have been used. There has also been a Mexican-American population accustomed to moving freely across the border, between the cultures, directing its loyalties both ways.

Because it has always been so easy to go home, many Mexicans and Mexican-Americans have displayed the classic sojourner outlook. The more total the break with the mother country, the more pressure immigrants feel to adapt; but for many immigrants from Mexico, whose kin and friends still live across the border and whose dreams center on returning in wealthy splendor to their native villages, the pressure is weak.

Many people have suggested that there is another difference, perhaps more significant than the first. It is a change in the nation's self-confidence. The most familiar critique of bilingual education holds that the nation no longer feels a resolute will to require mastery of the national language. America's most powerful assimilative force, the English language, may therefore be in jeopardy.

It is true that starting in the early 1960s U.S. government policy began to move away from the quick-assimilation approach preferred since the turn of the century. After surveys of Puerto Rican students in New York City and Mexican-Americans in Texas revealed that they were dropping out of school early and generally having a hard time, educational theorists began pushing plans for Spanish-language instruction. The turning point came with *Lau* v. *Nichols*, a case initiated in 1971 by Chinese-speaking students in San Francisco. They sued for "equal protection," on grounds that their unfamiliarity with English denied them an adequate education. In 1974, the Supreme Court ruled in their favor, saying that "those who do not understand English are certain to find their classroom experience wholly incomprehensible and in no way meaningful." The ruling did not say that school systems had to start bilingual programs of the kind that the phrase is now generally understood to mean—that is, classrooms in which both languages are used. The court said that "teaching English to the students . . . who do not speak the language" would be one acceptable solution. But the federal regulations and state laws that implemented the decision obliged many districts to set up the system of "transitional" bilingual education that has since become the focus of furor.

The rules vary from state to state, but they typically require a school district to set up a bilingual program whenever a certain number of students (often twenty) at one grade level are from one language group and do not speak English well. In principle, bilingual programs will enable them to keep up with the content of, say, their math and history courses while preparing them to enter the English-language classroom.

The bilingual system is accused of supporting a cadre of educational consultants while actually retarding the students' progress into the English-speaking mainstream. In this view, bilingual education could even by laying the foundation for a separate Hispanic culture, by extending the students' Spanish-language world from their homes to their schools.

Before I traveled to some of the schools in which bilingual education was applied, I shared the skeptics' view. What good could come of a system that encouraged, to whatever degree, a language other than the national tongue? But after visiting elementary, junior high, and high schools in Miami, Houston, San Antonio, Austin, several parts of Los Angeles, and San Diego, I found little connection between the political debate over bilingual education and what was going on in these schools.

To begin with, one central fact about bilingual education goes largely unreported. It is a *temporary* program. The time a typical student stays in the program varies from place to place—often two years in Miami, three years in Los Angeles—but when that time has passed, the student will normally leave. Why, then, do bilingual programs run through high school? Those classes are usually for students who are new to the district—usually because their parents are new to the country.

There is another fact about bilingual education, more difficult to prove but impressive to me, a hostile observer. Most of the children I saw were unmistakably learning to speak English.

In the elementary schools, where the children have come straight out of all-Spanish environments, the background babble seems to be entirely in Spanish. The kindergarten and first- to third-grade classrooms I saw were festooned with the usual squares and circles cut from colored construction paper, plus posters featuring Big Bird and charts about the weather and the seaons. Most of the schools seemed to keep a rough balance between English and Spanish in the lettering around the room; the most Spanish environment I saw was in one school in East Los Angeles, where about a third of the signs were in English.

The elementary school teachers were mostly Mexican-American women. They prompted the children with a mixture of English and Spanish during the day. While books in both languages are available in the classrooms, most of the first-grade reading drills I saw were in Spanish. In theory, children will learn the phonetic principle of reading more quickly if they are not trying to learn a new language at the same time. Once comfortable as readers, they will theoretically be able to transfer their ability to English.

In a junior high school in Houston, I saw a number of Mexican and Salvadoran students in their "bilingual" biology and math classes. They were drilled entirely in Spanish on the parts of an amoeba and on the difference between a parallelogram and a rhombus. When students enter bilingual programs at this level, the goal is to keep them current with the standard curriculum while introducing them to English. I found my fears of linguistic separatism rekindled by the sight of fourteen-year-olds lectured to in Spanish. I reminded myself that many of the students I was seeing had six months earlier lived in another country.

The usual next stop for students whose time in bilingual education is up is a class in intensive English, lasting one to three hours a day. These students are divided into two or three proficiency levels, from those who speak no English to those nearly ready to forgo special help. In Houston, a teacher drilled two-dozen high-school-age Cambodians, Indians, Cubans, and Mexicans on the crucial difference between the voiced *th* sound of "this" and the voiceless *th* of "thing." In Miami, a class of high school sophomores included youths from Cuba, El Salvador, and Honduras. They listened as their teacher read a Rockwellesque essay about a student with a crush on his teacher, and then set to work writing an essay of their own, working in words like "garrulous" and "sentimentalize."

One of the students in Miami, a sixteen-year-old from Honduras, said that his twelve-year-old brother had already moved into mainstream classes. Linguists say this is the standard pattern for immigrant children. The oldest children hold on to their first language longest, while their younger sisters and brothers swim quickly into the new language culture.

The more I saw of the classes, the more convinced I became that most of the students were learning English. Therefore, I started to wonder what it is about bilingual education that has made it the focus of such bitter disagreement.

For one thing, most immigrant groups other than Hispanics take a comparatively dim view of bilingual education. Haitians, Vietnamese, and Cambodians are eligible for bilingual education, but in general they are unenthusiastic. In Miami, Haitian boys and girls may learn to read in Creole rather than English. Still, their parents push to keep them moving into English. "A large number of [Haitian] parents come to the PTA meetings, and they don't want interpreters," said the principal of Miami's Edison Park Elementary School last spring. "They want to learn English. They don't want notices coming home in three languages. When they come here, unless there is total noncommunicaton, they will try to get through to us in their broken English. The students learn the language *very* quickly."

Bilingual education is inflammatory in large part because of what it symbolizes, not because of the nuts and bolts of its daily operation. In reality, bilingual programs move students into English with greater or lesser success; in reality, most Spanish-speaking parents understand that mastery of English will be their children's key to mobility. But in the political arena, bilingual education presents a different face. To the Hispanic ideologue, it is a symbol of cultural pride and political power. And once it has been presented that way, with full rhetorical flourish, it naturally strikes other Americans as a threat to the operating rules that have bound the country together.

Once during the months I spoke with and about immigrants I felt utterly exasperated. It was while listening to two Chicano activist lawyers in Houston who demanded to know why their people should be required to learn English at all. "It is unrealistic to think people can learn it that quickly," one lawyer said about the law that requires naturalized citizens to pass a test in English. "*Especially when they used to own this part of the country*, and when Spanish was the *historic language* of this region."

There is a historic claim for Spanish—but by the same logic there is a stronger claim for, say, Navajo as the historic language of the Southwest. The truth is that for more than a century the territory has been American and its national language has been English.

I felt the same irritation welling up when I talked with many bilingual instructors and policy-makers. Their arguments boiled down to: What's so special about English? They talked about the richness of the bilingual experience, the importance of maintaining the children's abilities in Spanish—even though when I watched the instructors in the classroom I could see that they were teaching principally English.

In my exasperation, I started to think that if such symbols of the dignity of language were so provocative to me, a comfortable member of the least-aggrieved ethnic group, it might be worth reflecting on the comparable sensitivities that lie behind the sentiments of the Spanish-speaking.

Consider the cases of Gloria Ramirez and Armandina Flores, who taught last year in the bilingual program at the Guerra Elementary School, in the Edgewood Independent School District, west of San Antonio.

San Antonio has evaded questions about the balance between rich and poor in its school system by carving the city up into independent school districts. Alamo Heights is the winner under this approach, and Edgewood is the loser. The Edgewood School District is perennially ranked as one of the poorest in the state. The residents are almost all Mexican-Americans or Mexicans. It is a settled community, without much to attract immigrants, but many stop there briefly on their way somewhere else, enough to give Edgewood a sizable illegal-immigrant enrollment.

In the middle of a bleak, sunbaked stretch of fields abutting a commercial vegetable farm, and within earshot of Kelly Air Force Base, sits Edgewood's Guerra School. It is an ordinary-looking but well-kept one-story structure that was built during the Johnson Administration. Nearly all the students are Mexican or Mexican-American.

Gloria Ramirez, who teaches first grade, is a compact, attractive woman of thirty-three, a no-nonsense veteran of the activist movements of the 1960s. Armandina Flores, a twenty-seven-year-old kindergarten teacher, is a beauty with dark eyes and long hair. During classroom hours, they deliver "Now, children" explanations of what is about to happen in both Spanish and English, although when the message really must get across, it comes in Spanish.

Both are remarkable teachers. They have that spark often thought to be missing in the public schools. There is no hint that for them this is just a job, perhaps because it symbolizes something very different from the worlds in which they were raised.

Gloria Ramirez was born in Austin, in 1950. Both of her parents are native Texans, as were two of her grandparents, but her family, like many other Mexican-American families, "spoke only Spanish when I was growing up," she says. None of her grandparents went to school at all. Her parents did not go past the third grade. Her father works as an auto-body mechanic; her mother raised the six children, and recently went to work at Austin State Hospital as a cleaner.

Ramirez began learning English when she started school; but the school, on Austin's east side, was overwhelmingly Mexican-American, part of the same culture she'd always known. The big change came when she was eleven. Her family moved to a working-class Anglo area in South Austin. She and her brother were virtually the only Mexican-Americans at the school. There was no more Spanish on the playground, or even at home. "My parents requested that we speak more English to them from then on," she says. "Both of them could speak it, but neither was comfortable."

"Before then, I didn't realize I had an accent. I didn't know until a teacher at the new school pointed it out in a ridiculing manner. I began learning English out of revenge." For six years, she took speech classes. "I worked hard so I could sound— like this," she says in standard American. She went to the University of Texas, where she studied history and philosophy and became involved in the Mexican-American political movements of the 1970s. She taught bilingual-education classes in Boston briefly before coming home to Texas.

Armandina Flores was born in Cuidad Acuña, Mexico, across the river from Del Rio, Texas. Her mother, who was born in Houston, was an American citizen, but *her* parents had returned to Mexico a few months after her birth, and she had never learned English. Flores's father was a Mexican citizen. When she reached school age, she began commuting across the river to a small Catholic school in Del Rio, where all the other students were Chicano. When she was twelve and about to begin the sixth grade, her family moved to Del Rio and she entered an American public school.

At that time, the sixth grade was divided into tracks, which ran from 6-1 at the bottom to 6-12. Most of the Anglos were at the top; Armandina Flores was initially placed in 6-4. She showed an aptitude for English and was moved up to 6-8. Meanwhile, her older sister, already held back once, was in 6-2. Her parents were proud of Armandina's progress; they began to depend on her English in the family's dealings in the Anglo world. She finished high school in Del Rio, went to Our Lady of the Lake College in San Antonio, and came to Edgewood as an aide in 1978, when she was twenty-two.

Considered one way, these two stories might seem to confirm every charge made the the opponents of bilingual education. Through the trauma of being plucked from her parents' comfortable Spanish-language culture and plunged into the realm of public language, Gloria Ramirez was strengthened, made a cosmopolitan and accomplished person. Her passage recalls the one Richard Rodriguez describes in *Hunger of Memory*, an autobiography that has become the most eloquent text for opponents of bilingual programs.

"Without question, it would have pleased me to hear my teachers address me in Spanish when I entered the classroom," Rodriguez wrote. "I would have felt much less afraid. . . . But I would have delayed—for how long postponed?—having to learn the language of public society."

Gloria Ramirez concedes that the pain of confused ethnicity and lost loyalties among Mexican-Americans is probably very similar to what every other immigrant group has endured. She even admits that she was drawn to bilingual education for political as well as educational reasons. As for Armandina Flores, hers is a calmer story of successful assimilation, accomplished without the crutch of bilingual education.

Yet both of these women insist, with an edge to their voices, that their students are fortunate not to have the same passage awaiting them.

It a was very wasteful process, they say. They swam; many others sank. "You hear about the people who make it, but not about all the others who dropped out, who never really learned," Ramirez says. According to the Mexican-American Legal Defense and Education Fund, 40 percent of Hispanic students drop out before they finish high school, three times as many as among Anglo students.

"Many people around here don't feel comfortable with themselves in either language," Ramirez says. Flores's older sister never became confident in English;

"she feels like a lower person for it." She has just had a baby and is anxious that he succeed in English. Ramirez's older brother learned most of his English in the Marines. He is married to a Mexican immigrant and thinks that it is very important that their children learn English. And that is more likely to happen, the teachers say, if they have a transitional moment in Spanish.

Otherwise, "a child must make choices that concern his survival," Ramirez says. "He can choose to learn certain words, only to survive; but it can kill his desire to learn, period. Eventually he may be able to deal in the language, but he won't be educated." If the natural-immersion approach worked, why, they ask, would generation after generation of Chicanos, American citizens living throughout the Southwest, have lived and died without ever fully moving into the English-language mainstream?

These two teachers, and a dozen others with parallel experience, might be wrong in their interpretation of how bilingual education works. If so, they are making the same error as German, Polish, and Italian immigrants. According to the historians hired by the Select Commission, "Immigrants argued, when given the opportunity, that the security provided them by their cultures eased rather than hindered the transition." Still, there is room for reasonable disagreement about the most effective techniques for bringing children into English. A former teacher named Robert Rossier, for example, argues from his experience teaching immigrants that intensive courses in English are more effective than a bilingual transition. Others line up on the other side.

But is this not a question for factual resolution rather than for battles about linguistic and ethnic pride? Perhaps one approach will succeed for certain students in certain situations and the other will be best for others. The choice between bilingual programs and intensive-English courses, then, should be a choice between methods, not ideologies. The wars over bilingual education have had a bitter, symbolic quality. Each side has invested the issue with a meaning the other can barely comprehend. To most Mexican-American parents and children, bilingual education is merely a way of learning English; to Hispanic activists, it is a symbol that they are at last taking their place in the sun. But to many other Americans, it sounds like a threat not to assimilate.

"It is easy for Americans to take for granted, or fail to appreciate, the strength of American culture," says Henry Cisneros, the mayor of San Antonio. Cisneros is the first Mexican-American mayor of the country's most heavily Hispanic major city, a tall, grave man of thirty-six who is as clear a demonstration of the possibilities of ethnic assimilation as John Kennedy was. Cisneros gives speeches in Spanish and in English. Over the door that leads to his chambers, gilt letters spell out "Office of the Mayor" and, underneath, "*Oficina del Alcalde.*" "I'm talking about TV programs, McDonald's, automobiles, the Dallas Cowboys. It is very pervasive. Mexican-Americans *like* the American way of life."

"These may sound like just the accouterments," Cisneros says. "I could also have mentioned due process of law; relations with the police; the way supermarkets work; the sense of participation, especially now that more and more Mexican-

Americans are in positions of leadership. All of the things that shape the American way of life are indomitable."

In matters of civic culture, many Mexican-Americans, especially in Texas, act as custodians of the values the nation is said to esteem. They emphasize family, church, and patriotism of the most literal sort, expressed through military service. In the shrinelike position of honor in the sitting room, the same place where black families may have portraits of John F. Kennedy or Martin Luther King, a Mexican-American household in Texas will display a picture of the son or nephew in the Marines. Every time I talked with a Mexican-American about assimilation and separatism, I heard about the Mexican-American heroes and martyrs who have served in the nation's wars.

All the evidence suggests that Hispanics are moving down the path toward assimilation. According to a survey conducted in 1982 by Rodolfo de la Garza and Robert Brischetto for the Southwest Voter Registration Education Project, 11 percent of Chicanos (including a large number of illegal immigrants) were unable to speak English. The younger the people, the more likely they were to speak English. Ninety-four percent of those between the ages of eighteen and twenty-five could speak English, versus 78 percent of those aged sixty-six to eighty-seven. Not surprisingly, the English-speakers were better educated, had better jobs, and were less likely to have two foreign-born parents than the Spanish-speakers.

The details of daily life in Hispanic centers confirm these findings. The first impression of East Los Angeles or Little Havana is of ubiquitous Spanish, on the billboards and in the air. The second glance reveals former Chicano activists, now in their late thirties, bemused that their children have not really learned Spanish, or second-generation Cubans who have lost interest in liberating the motherland or in being Cubans at all.

Ricardo Romo says that when he taught Chicano studies at UCLA, his graduate students would go into the San Antonio *barrio* but could not find their way around, so much had they lost touch with the Spanish language. At a birthday party for a Chicano intellectual in Texas, amid piñatas and plates laden with *fajitas*, a birthday cake from a bakery was unveiled. It said "Happy Birthday" in Spanish—misspelled. There was pathos in that moment, but it was pathos that countless Italians, Poles, and Jews might understand.

With Mexico next door to the United States, the Mexican-American culture will always be different from that of other ethnic groups. Spanish will be a living language in the United States longer than any other alternative to English. But the movement toward English is inescapable.

In only one respect does the Hispanic impulse seem to me to lead in a dangerous direction. Hispanics are more acutely aware than most Anglos that, as a practical reality, English is the national language of commerce, government, and mobility. But some have suggested that, in principle, it should not be this way.

They invoke the long heritage of Mexican-Americans in the Southwest. As "Californios" or "Tejanos," the ancestors of some of these families lived on and owned the territory before the Anglo settlers. Others came across at the turn of the century, at a time of Mexican upheaval; still others came during the forties and fifties, as workers. They have paid taxes, fought in wars, been an inseparable part of the region's culture. Yet they were also subject to a form of discrimination more casual than the segregation of the Old South, but having one of the same effects. Because of poverty or prejudice or gerrymandered school districts, many Mexican-Americans were, in effect, denied education. One result is that many now in their fifties and sixties do not speak English well. Still, they are citizens, with the right of citizens to vote. How are they to exercise their right if to do so requires learning English? Do they not deserve a ballot printed in a language they can understand?

In the early seventies, the issue came before the courts, and several decisions held that if voters otherwise eligible could not understand English, they must have voting materials prepared in a more convenient language. In 1975, the Voting Rights Act amendments said that there must be bilingual ballots if more than 5 percent of the voters in a district were members of a "language minority group." The only "language minority groups" eligible under this ruling were American Indians, Alaskan natives, Asian-Americans (most significantly, Chinese and Filipinos), and Spanish-speakers. A related case extracted from the Sixth Circuit Court of Appeals the judgment that "the national language of the United States is English."

So it is that ballots in parts of the country are printed in Spanish, or Chinese, or Tagalog, along with English. This is true even though anyone applying for natural-ization must still pass an English-proficiency test, which consists of questions such as "What are the three branches of government?" and "How long are the terms of a U.S. Senator and member of Congress?" The apparent inconsistency reflects the linguistic reality that many native-born citizens have not learned the national language.

By most accounts, the bilingual ballot is purely a symbol. The native-born citizens who can't read English often can't read Spanish, either. As a symbol, it points in the wrong direction, away from a single national language in which the public business will be done. Its only justification is the older generation, which was excluded from the schools. In principle, then, it should be phased out in several years.

But there are those who feel that even the present arrangement is too onerous. Rose Matsui Ochi, an assistant to the mayor of Los Angeles, who served on the Select Commission, dissented from the commission's recommendation to keep the English-language requirement for citizenship. She wrote in her minority opinion, "Abolishing the requirement recognizes the inability of certain individuals to learn English." Cruz Reynoso, the first Mexican-American appointee to the California Supreme Court, was also on the Select Commission, and he too dissented. "America is a *political* union—not a cultural, linguistic, religious or racial union," he wrote. "Of course, we as individuals would urge all to learn English, for that is the language used by most Americans, as well as the language of the marketplace. But we should no more demand English-language skills for citizenship than we should demand uniformity of religion. That a person wants to become a citizen and will make a good citizen is more than enough."

Some Chicano activists make the same point in less temperate terms. Twice I found myself in shouting matches with Mexican-Americans who asked me who I thought I was to tell them—after all the homeboys who had died in combat, after all the insults they'd endured on the playground for speaking Spanish—what language they "should" speak.

That these arguments were conducted in English suggests the theoretical nature of the debate. Still, in questions like this, symbolism can be crucial. "I have sympathy for the position that the integrating mechanism of a society is language," Henry Cisneros says. "The U.S. has been able to impose fewer such integrating mechanisms on its people than other countries, but it needs some tie to hold these diverse people, Irish, Jews, Czechs, together as a nation. Therefore, I favor people learning English and being able to conduct business in the official language of the country."

"The *unum* demands only certain things of the *pluribus*," Lawrence Fuchs says. "It demands very little. It demands that we believe in the political ideals of the republic, which allows people to preserve their ethnic identity. Most immigrants come from repressive regimes; we say, we're asking you to believe that government should *not* oppress you. Then it only asks one other thing: that in the wider marketplace and in the civic culture, you use the official language. No other society asks so little.

"English is not just an instrument of mobility. It is a sign that you really are committed. If you've been here five years, which you must to be a citizen, and if you are reasonably young, you should be able to learn English in that time. The rest of us are entitled to that."

Most of the young people I met—the rank and file, not the intellectuals who espouse a bilingual society—seemed fully willing to give what in Fuchs's view the nation asks. I remember in particular one husky Puerto Rican athlete at Miami Senior High School who planned to join the Navy after he got his diploma. I talked to him in a bilingual classroom, heard his story, and asked his name. He told me, and I wrote "*Ramón*." He came around behind me and looked at my pad. "No, no!" he told me. "You should have put R-A-Y-M-O-N-D."

SUGGESTIONS FOR WRITING

Informal Essays

1. If you belong to a family outside the white Anglo-Saxon Protestant main-stream, write an essay on the ease or difficulty of your own cultural assimilation. Use a quote or two from a couple of the essays in this chapter.
2. If you know of the experiences of an immigrant family or student, use those experiences as an example to make a point about bilingualism.

Short Documented Papers

1. Contrast the ideas expressed by those on opposing sides of a single point in the controversy over bilingualism.
2. Contrast the statistical support that the critics and defenders of bilingual education use to support their views.
3. Contrast the historical precedents that each side uses to support its views.
4. After determining two of the weakest points made by either the critics or the defenders of bilingual education, show their vulnerability.
5. Develop two or three of the most convincing points made by either side of the controversy.

Longer Documented Papers

1. In a research argument, make the case for or against bilingual education.
2. In a research report, contrast three or four of the most important points made by both the critics and the defenders of bilingual education.
3. Determine the weakest points made by both sides of the controversy and demonstrate their vulnerability.

· 7 ·

Fairy Tales:
Benign or Pernicious?

Charles Dickens once wrote, "Little Red Riding Hood was my first love. I felt that if I could have married Little Red Riding Hood, I should have known perfect bliss."

Perhaps the story of *Little Red Riding Hood* didn't affect you as deeply as it affected Dickens (whose sentiments about the little girl *are* a bit extravagant). But what about *Billy Goats Gruff*? Who can forget the goat-eating troll that lurks beneath the bridge? For whatever reason, fairy tales, unlike the hundreds of bland children's stories with contemporary settings, stick in the mind. *Dick and Jane Visit the Farm* was only momentarily interesting. *The Pied Piper of Hamelin* has staying power.

Some people say that the values that we absorbed from those ancient, curiously macabre little tales are pernicious. Indeed, there is something a bit worrisome about the harsh world of fairy tales, which teems with gore and violence, including cannibalism ("Stick out your finger, Hansel"), infanticide, poisoned apples, strangulation, and toothy beasts. Children know that the giant isn't kidding when he screams that he'll grind Jack's bones to make his bread.

Those who admire them reply that the dark world of fairy tales helps children come to grips with our own harsh and violent world. According to the child psychologist, Bruno Bettleheim ("Fairy Tales and the Existential Predicament," p. 305), fairy tales teach children an important lesson in their growth toward maturity: the world is not all sweetness and light; there is a dark side as well.

Not everyone, however, appreciates the values that fairy tales transmit. Educators sometimes worry that fairy tales not only confuse the child about the distinction between reality and illusion, but also teach antisocial messages. The intentions of the troll beneath the bridge *are*, after all, foiled because he defers instant gratification for future rewards. Odd moral, that.

Some feminists are also troubled by the values that fairy tales teach. Originating in male-oriented societies, fairy tales *are* filled with sweet young women—Snow White and Cinderella among them—who sweep floors and lie in a swoon while they wait for their prince charming to come along and rescue them through marriage. In

275

fact, feminist critics of fairy tales have rewritten some of the old tales to downplay their simpering heroines. Others have reprinted neglected fairy tales that feature strong, resourceful heroines.

The defenders of fairy tales claim that the stories teach healthy values. If injustice and disorder threaten the child's world, justice and order can at least be found in fairy tales where evil is overthrown and harmony is inevitably and happily restored. Ultimately, witches *are* baked, wolves *are* slaughtered, and wicked stepmothers *are* vanquished. According to Russell Kirk ("Children and the Lex Talionis," p. 303), fairy tales even encourage a child's "philosophical habit of mind."

This is a good chapter in which to use your personal experiences in your writing assignments. You can probably still remember being curled up on your mom's lap listening to the story of Hansel and Gretel's hairbreadth escape from the cannibalistic witch. A few of the suggestions for writing that follow this chapter ask you to dip into those memories.

We have reprinted the Grimm Brothers' version of *Snow White* to begin this chapter so that you might read it first to see what the original was like before it was slightly rewritten by Walt Disney and others. More importantly, when you write about fairy tales in general, you can use the characters and plot from *Snow White* to illustrate your points. Happily, this tale contains all of the elements of the fairy tale that worry and please the critics: a beautiful young heroine to admire (or despise), an ugly witch to vanquish, a dashing hero, a poisoning, a strangulation, a dance of death, and a happy ending with a marriage. Of course, you won't want to use *Snow White* exclusively; many of your examples can come from the stock of fairy tales you carry around in your head and heart.

One of the "comments" on fairy tales in this chapter is put in the form of a parody of Snow White by Garrison Keillor ("My Stepmother, Myself," p. 318). You'll have to read his parody carefully to discern his point of view.

SNOW WHITE
Jakob and Wilhelm Grimm

Once upon a time in the middle of winter, when the flakes of snow were falling like feathers from the sky, a Queen sat at a window sewing, and the frame of the window was made of black ebony. And whilst she was sewing and looking out of the window at the snow, she pricked her finger with the needle, and three drops of blood fell upon the snow. And the red looked pretty upon the white snow, and she thought to herself: "Would that I had a child as white as snow, as red as blood, and as black as the wood of the window-frame."

Soon after that she had a little daughter, who was as white as snow, and as red as blood, and her hair was as black as ebony; and she was therefore called Little Snow-white. And when the child was born, the Queen died.

After a year had passed the King took to himself another wife. She was a beautiful woman, but proud and haughty, and she could not bear that anyone else should surpass her in beauty. She had a wonderful looking-glass, and when she stood in front of it and looked at herself in it, and said:

"Looking-glass, Looking-glass, on the wall,
Who in this land is the fairest of all?"

the looking-glass answered:

"Thou, O Queen, art the fairest of all!"

Then she was satisfied, for she knew that the looking-glass spoke the truth.

But Snow-white was growing up, and grew more and more beautiful; and when she was seven years old she was as beautiful as the day, and more beautiful than the Queen herself. And once when the Queen asked her looking-glass:

"Looking-glass, Looking-glass, on the wall,
Who in this land is the fairest of all?"

it answered:

"Thou art fairer than all who are here, Lady Queen.
But more beautiful still is Snow-white, as I ween."

Then the Queen was shocked, and turned yellow and green with envy. From that hour, whenever she looked at Snow-white, her heart heaved in her breast, she hated the girl so much.

Jakob Grimm and Wilhelm Grimm, "Snow White," *Grimm's Fairy Tales*, translated by Margaret Hunt, revised by James Stern (New York: Pantheon Books, 1944). The Grimm brothers spent their lives collecting folk tales and studying language. Their first collection of German folk tales was *Kinderund Hausmarchen* (1812).

And envy and pride grew higher and higher in her heart like a weed, so that she had no peace day or night. She called a huntsman, and said: "Take the child away into the forest; I will no longer have her in my sight. Kill her, and bring me back her lung and liver as a token." The huntsman obeyed, and took her away; but when he had drawn his knife, and was about to pierce Snow-white's innocent heart, she began to weep, and said: "Ah, dear huntsman, leave me my life! I will run away into the wild forest, and never come home again."

And as she was so beautiful the huntsman had pity on her and said: "Run away, then, you poor child." "The wild beasts will soon have devoured you," thought he, and yet it seemed as if a stone had been rolled from his heart since it was no longer needful for him to kill her. And as a young boar just then came running by he stabbed it, and cut out its lung and liver and took them to the Queen as proof that the child was dead. The cook had to salt them, and the wicked Queen ate them, and thought she had eaten the lung and liver of Snow-white.

But now the poor child was all alone in the great forest, and so terrified that she looked at all the leaves on the trees, and did not know what to do. Then she began to run, and ran over sharp stones and through thorns, and the wild beasts ran past her, but did her no harm.

She ran as long as her feet would go until it was almost evening; then she saw a little cottage and went into it to rest herself. Everything in the cottage was small, but neater and cleaner than can be told. There was a table on which was a white cover, and seven little plates, and on each plate a little spoon; moreover, there were seven little knives and forks, and seven little mugs. Against the wall stood seven little beds side by side, and covered with snow-white counterpanes.

Little Snow-white was so hungry and thirsty that she ate some vegetables and bread from each plate and drank a drop of wine out of each mug, for she did not wish to take all from one only. Then, as she was so tired, she laid herself down on one of the little beds, but none of them suited her; one was too long, another too short, but at last she found that the seventh one was right, and so she remained in it, said a prayer and went to sleep.

When it was quite dark the owners of the cottage came back; they were seven dwarfs who dug and delved in the mountains for ore. They lit their seven candles, and as it was now light within the cottage they saw that someone had been there, for everything was not in the same order in which they had left it.

The first said: "Who has been sitting on my chair?"

The second: "Who has been eating off my plate?"

The third: "Who has been taking some of my bread?"

The fourth: "Who has been eating my vegetables?"

The fifth: "Who has been using my fork?"

The sixth: "Who has been cutting with my knife?"

The seventh: "Who has been drinking out of my mug?"

Then the first looked round and saw that there was a little hollow on his bed, and he said: "Who has been getting into my bed?" The others came up and each called out: "Somebody has been lying in my bed too." But the seventh when he looked at his bed saw little Snow-white, who was lying asleep therein. And he called the others, who came running up, and they cried out with astonishment, and brought their seven little candles and let the light fall on little Snow-white. "Oh, heavens! oh, heavens!" cried they, "what a lovely child!" and they were so glad that they did not wake her up, but let her sleep on in the bed. And the seventh dwarf slept with his companions, one hour with each, and so passed the night.

When it was morning little Snow-white awoke, and was frightened when she saw the seven dwarfs. But they were friendly and asked her what her name was. "My name is Snow-white," she answered. "How have you come to our house?" said the dwarfs. Then she told them that her step-mother had wished to have her killed, but that the huntsman had spared her life, and that she had run for the whole day, until at last she had found their dwelling. The dwarfs said: "If you will take care of our house, cook, make the beds, wash, sew, and knit, and if you will keep everything neat and clean, you can stay with us and you shall want for nothing." "Yes," said Snow-white, "with all my heart," and she stayed with them. She kept the house in order for them; in the mornings they went to the mountains and looked for copper and gold, in the evenings they came back, and then their supper had to be ready. The girl was alone the whole day, so the good dwarfs warned her and said: "Beware of your step-mother, she will soon know that you are here; be sure to let no one come in."

But the Queen, believing that she had eaten Snow-white's lung and liver, could not but think that she was again the first and most beautiful of all; and she went to her looking-glass and said:

> "Looking-glass, Looking-glass, on the wall,
> Who in this land is the fairest of all?"

and the glass answered:

> "Oh, Queen, thou art fairest of all I see,
> But over the hills, where the seven dwarfs dwell,
> Snow-white is still alive and well,
> And none is so fair as she."

Then she was astounded, for she knew that the looking-glass never spoke falsely, and she knew that the huntsman had betrayed her, and that little Snow-white was still alive.

And so she thought and thought again how she might kill her, for so long as she was not the fairest in the whole land, envy let her have no rest. And when she had at last thought of something to do, she painted her face, and dressed herself like an old pedlar-woman, and no one could have known her. In this disguise she went over the seven mountains to the seven dwarfs, and knocked at the door and cried: "Pretty things to sell, very cheap, very cheap." Little Snow-white looked out of the window and called out: "Good-day, my good woman, what have you to sell?" "Good things, pretty things," she answered; "stay-laces of all colors," and she pulled out one which was woven of bright-colored silk. "I may let the worthy old woman in," thought Snow-white, and she unbolted the door and bought the pretty laces. "Child," said the old woman, "what a fright you look; come, I will lace you properly for once." Snow-white had no suspicion, but stood before her, and let herself be laced with the new laces. But the old woman laced so quickly and laced so tightly that Snow-white lost her breath and fell down as if dead. "Now I am the most beautiful," said the Queen to herself, and ran away.

Not long afterwards, in the evening, the seven dwarfs came home, but how shocked they were when they saw their dear little Snow-white lying on the ground, and that she neither stirred nor moved, and seemed to be dead. They lifted her up, and, as they saw that she was laced too tightly, they cut the laces; then she began to breathe a little, and after a while came to life again. When the dwarfs heard what had happened they said: "The old pedlar-woman was no one else than the wicked Queen; take care and let no one come in when we are not with you."

But the wicked woman when she had reached home went in front of the glass and asked:

"Looking-glass, Looking-glass, on the wall,
Who in this land is the fairest of all?"

and it answered as before:

"Oh, Queen, thou art fairest of all I see,
But over the hills, where the seven dwarfs dwell,
Snow-white is still alive and well,
And none is so fair as she."

When she heard that, all her blood rushed to her heart with fear, for she saw plainly that little Snow-white was again alive. "But now," she said, "I will think of something that shall really put an end to you," and by the help of witchcraft, which she understood, she made a poisonous comb. Then she disguised herself and took the shape of another old woman. So she went over the seven mountains to the seven dwarfs, knocked at the door, and cried: "Good things to sell, cheap, cheap!" Little Snow-white looked out and said: "Go away; I cannot let anyone come in." "I suppose you can look," said the old woman, and pulled the poisonous comb out and held it up. It pleased the girl so well that she let herself be beguiled, and opened the door. When they had made a bargain the old woman said: "Now I will comb you properly for once." Poor little Snow-white had no suspicion, and let the old woman do as she pleased, but hardly had she put the comb in her hair than the poison in it took effect, and the girl fell down senseless. "You paragon of beauty," said the wicked woman, "you are done for now," and she went away.

But fortunately it was almost evening, when the seven dwarfs came home. When they saw Snow-white lying as if dead upon the ground they at once suspected the step-mother, and they looked and found the poisoned comb. Scarcely had they taken it out when Snow-white came to herself, and told them what had happened. Then they warned her once more to be upon her guard and to open the door to no one.

The Queen, at home, went in front of the glass and said:

"Looking-glass, Looking-glass, on the wall,
Who in this land is the fairest of all?"

then it answered as before:

> "Oh, Queen, thou art fairest of all I see,
> But over the hills, where the seven dwarfs dwell,
> Snow-white is still alive and well,
> And none is so fair as she."

When she heard the glass speak thus she trembled and shook with rage. "Snow-white shall die," she cried, "even if it costs me my life!"

Thereupon she went into a quite secret, lonely room, where no one ever came, and there she made a very poisonous apple. Outside it looked pretty, white with a red cheek, so that everyone who saw it longed for it; but whoever ate a piece of it must surely die.

When the apple was ready she painted her face, and dressed herself up as a farmer's wife, and so she went over the seven mountains to the seven dwarfs. She knocked at the door. Snow-white put her head out of the window and said: "I cannot let anyone in; the seven dwarfs have forbidden me." "It is all the same to me," answered the woman, "I shall soon get rid of my apples. There, I will give you one."

"No," said Snow-white, "I dare not take anything." "Are you afraid of poison?" said the old woman; "look, I will cut the apple in two pieces; you eat the red cheek, and I will eat the white." The apple was so cunningly made that only the red cheek was poisoned. Snow-white longed for the fine apple, and when she saw that the woman ate part of it she could resist no longer, and stretched out her hand and took the poisonous half. But hardly had she a bit of it in her mouth than she fell down dead. Then the Queen looked at her with a dreadful look, and laughed aloud and said: "White as snow, red as blood, black as ebony-wood! this time the dwarfs cannot wake you up again."

And when she asked of the looking-glass at home:

> "Looking-glass, Looking-glass, on the wall,
> Who in this land is the fairest of all?"

it answered at last:

> "Oh, Queen, in this land thou art fairest of all."

Then her envious heart had rest, so far as an envious heart can have rest.

The dwarfs, when they came home in the evening, found Snow-white lying upon the ground; she breathed no longer and was dead. They lifted her up, looked to see whether they could find anything poisonous, unlaced her, combed her hair, washed her with water and wine, but it was all of no use; the poor child was dead, and remained dead. They laid her upon a bier, and all seven of them sat round it and wept for her, and wept three days long.

Then they were going to bury her, but she still looked as if she were living, and still had her pretty red cheeks. They said: "We could not bury her in the dark ground," and they had a transparent coffin of glass made, so that she could be seen from all sides, and they laid her in it, and wrote her name upon it in golden letters, and that she was a king's daughter. Then they put the coffin out upon the mountain, and one of them always stayed by it and watched it. And birds came too, and wept for Snow-white; first an owl, then a raven, and last a dove.

And now Snow-white lay a long, long time in the coffin, and she did not change, but looked as if she were asleep; for she was as white as snow, as red as blood, and her hair was as black as ebony.

It happened, however, that a king's son came into the forest, and went to the dwarfs' house to spend the night. He saw the coffin on the mountain, and the beautiful Snow-white within it, and read what was written upon it in golden letters. Then he said to the dwarfs: "Let me have the coffin, I will give you whatever you want for it." But the dwarfs answered: "We will not part with it for all the gold in the world." Then he said: "Let me have it as a gift, for I cannot live without seeing Snow-white. I will honor and prize her as my dearest possession." As he spoke in this way the good dwarfs took pity upon him, and gave him the coffin.

And now the King's son had it carried away by his servants on their shoulders. And it happened that they stumbled over a treestump, and with the shock the poisonous piece of apple which Snow-white had bitten off came out of her throat. And before long she opened her eyes, lifted up the lid of the coffin, sat up, and was once more alive. "Oh, heavens, where am I?" she cried. The King's son, full of joy, said: "You are with me," and told her what had happened, and said: "I love you more than everything in the world; come with me to my father's palace, you shall be my wife."

And Snow-white was willing, and went with him, and their wedding was held with great show and splendor. But Snow-white's wicked step-mother was also bidden to the feast. When she had arrayed herself in beautiful clothes she went before the Looking-glass, and said:

> "Looking-glass, Looking-glass, on the wall,
> Who in this land is the fairest of all?"

the glass answered:

> "Oh, Queen, of all here the fairest art thou,
> But the young Queen is fairer by far as I trow."

Then the wicked woman uttered a curse, and was so wretched, so utterly wretched, that she knew not what to do. At first she would not go to the wedding at all, but she had no peace, and had to go to see the young Queen. And when she went in she recognized Snow-white; and she stood still with rage and fear, and could not stir. But iron slippers had already been put upon the fire, and they were brought in with tongs, and set before her. Then she was forced to put on the red-hot shoes, and dance until she dropped down dead.

THE PSYCHOLOGICAL CASE AGAINST THE FAIRY TALE

H. E. Wheeler

Within the past five years more and more material of a factual nature has been made available for children's reading. Before that time it was difficult to find in primary reading books anything but folklore, fairy tale, and other fanciful material. It has often been pointed out (1) that such material is not as interesting to six-year-old children as are familiar experiences, (2) that children of that age are easily confused as to what is real and what is imaginary, (3) that the schools are already oversupplied with fanciful material because it is easy to write, (4) that folklore often depicts cruelty, personified animals eating one another, trickery, deceit, etc., and (5) that most folklore depicts an environment unknown to an American child in 1929.

However, fanciful material has not been entirely eliminated from the schools. Most teachers seem to hesitate to take a decided stand on either side of the question. The arguments advanced against abolishing the fanciful material are principally (1) that it stimulates the imagination, (2) that it is "every child's rightful heritage," and (3) that it adds to the beauty and richness of life and gives happiness.

Therefore, the present situation may be summed up as follows: children are enjoying the benefits of both types of content without being protected from the harmful effects, if any, of either. Recommended book lists for children prepared by various representative bodies, such as the American Library Association and the International Kindergarten Union, show a large preponderance of fanciful material.

Within the last few months two prominent men in the field of psychology have denounced the fairy tale in no uncertain terms. Dr. Harry A. Overstreet, head of the Department of Philosophy of the College of the City of New York, says:

> People have the curious notion that fairy tales build up the imaginative life of children. As a matter of fact, they pervert the imaginative life. Fairy tales are a left-over primitive "science." The savage had no notion, or only the vaguest notion, of cause and effect. His world was largely one of magic. Things happened by miracle. A "presto," an "open sesame," and the trick was turned. It has taken the world uncounted thousands of weary years to get beyond that primitive state of mind. Most of the degrading misconceptions that man has had about his life, here and hereafter, arose out of this inability to detect cause and effect.
>
> And now parents insist on inflicting this primitivism, this pathetic infantilism of the race, on their children, forcing them to think uncausally, magically, miraculously, forcing them to habituate themselves to the technique of dreamy wish-fulfilment rather than guiding them into the noble technique of observation, exploration, experiment, and objective achievement.

H. E. Wheeler, "The Psychological Case Against the Fairy Tale," *Elementary School Journal* June 1929. At the time he wrote this article, Wheeler was the president of his own publishing company, Wheeler Publishing Company.

The mind of the child should be as carefully guarded against the fantasying which cuts itself loose from the objective realities as an adult should be guarded against the morbid daydreaming that may lead to neurosis and insane delusion.

There are more things under heaven and on earth than are dreamed of in any of the fairy tales. The real world is a marvel, as fascinating to the child as to the adult. Introduce the child vividly, interestingly, to that world, and we stir his imagination into life—his real imagination, not that sorry substitute for imagination which cowers in terror of witches and werewolves or gloats with triumphant joy over riches and power achieved without effort.

Some day—when we become psychologically wise—the fairy tale will be ruled out of the child's life as drastically as overindulgent parents, terrorizing nurse maids, and hell-preaching religionists.

Dr. Alfred Adler, of Vienna, takes just as decided a stand against the psychological effect of the fairy tale. In his lectures he has emphasized the fact that thinking about the magical and miraculous paves the way for an escape from reality via useless daydreaming. Under the pressure of discouragements or defeats, the individual may turn to imaginary success as to a drug and thereby be relieved of the necessity of making any further useful efforts.

If these two men are right, children should not be indiscriminately exposed to fanciful material until a competent person has passed on its psychological effect. Apparently the harmful varieties include (1) stories that promote fear (stories of ghosts, witches, goblins, ogres, giants, and other evil supernatural agencies), (2) stories that portray miraculous achievement without commensurate effort (the story of Aladdin, for example), and (3) stories that give uncausal explanations of natural phenomena (myths and legends).

There is a saying to the effect that he who explodes a myth is never popular. Therefore, it can easily be imagined that those who hold to the fanciful will have the more popular side of the argument.

ARE GORY FAIRY TALES AN EVIL?

Looking over the store of Christmas gifts received by children, the modern parent may find a dubious assortment of fairy-tales among the gift-books. Childless uncles and aunts have perhaps not benefited by the lessons of modern psychological research and have sent on the supposedly innocent pabulum of their own childhood. Parents and educators, however, have been troubled by the stories of blood, cruelty, revenge, and murder that are included in our fairy-tales, and will perhaps welcome the answer to their misgivings furnished by two psychologists writing in *Die Umschau* (Frankfort). The tales have come down to us from remote times, and reflect an even remoter period when our ancestors huddled about the embers of a fire in the caves or on the steppes, and related blood-curdling adventures with wolves or fiercer wild animals, or with men of giant stature and of cruel disposition; and even more terrifying stories of the doings of supernatural beings, devils and witches, kobolds and elves. In these stories we find the origin of many of our most popular legends and tales, and these in their turn have given rise to a thousand variations in the literature of all civilized countries, becoming enshrined in poetry, drama, and opera, as well as in fiction. But whether they are the proper meat on which to feed youthful imaginations—the German writers attempt to answer:

"Many stories set forth in grotesque form stories of ill-will, deception, robbery, and murder—even cannibalism.

"Typical, and of great psychological importance in the folk-tale, is the customary fortunate outcome, with the triumph of justice. The 'happy end' exerts an essential influence in the psychological elaboration of the content. . . . Furthermore it will be found that the horrors related mostly represent a primitive phase in the racial history of the development of the human soul.

"This holds true for numerous gruesome events of ancient and medieval origin. Thus the huntsman kills the envious stepmother of *Snow White; Hänsel* and *Gretel* are exposed in the forest by their parents; *Cinderella's* stepsisters subject her to humiliation and suffering.

"Again, the belief in kobolds and witches gives rise to certain folk-tales. Thus the wicked witch wants to roast *Hänsel*, whereas *Snow White* finds a kind reception on the part of the *Seven Dwarfs* in the Seven Mountains.

"As in the sagas, the animal world plays a part in the folk-tale. Herein we find numerous concepts derived from the fear of wild animals felt by prehistoric men. *Red Riding Hood* is devoured by the *Wolf* and goes on living in its maw together with her grandmother; little *Tom Thumb* wanders through the alimentary canals of various animals before he finds his way back home.

"Moreover folk-tales contain traces of primitive psychological mechanism. Dwarfs are cherished on the one hand as kindly elves, and feared on the other as malicious kobolds. Perilously alluring beings are both feared and revered till a

"Are Gory Fairy Tales an Evil?" *The Literary Digest* 5 January 1929.

chosen acquaintance permits a division of the concepts concerning them into pleasant and unpleasant.

"In the stories given us by Grimm, Hans Andersen, etc., a special distinction is usually made between good and bad animals. The kindly pigeons help *Cinderella* to pick up the lentils, and avenge the persecuted girl by pecking out the eyes of the cruel stepsisters at their darling's wedding. So, too, the *Prince* is instructed by them how to choose the rightful bride. The ducklings build a bridge to enable *Hänsel* and *Gretel* to get back to their parents' house, etc.

"A particularly distinctive feature of the folk-tale is its rejection of logic.

"Thus in 'Hänsel and Gretel' the witch resides in a sugar house, in order to lure children; but how could the old witch, otherwise so crafty, be so foolish as to accept the bare bone which *Hänsel* stretches through the bars instead of the little living hand she demands? And why didn't the children run away sooner from the witch, since she was so very short-sighted? Why didn't the *Wolf* gobble up *Red Riding Hood* when he first met her in the forest, and not until after he had put on the cap and spectacles of the *Grandmother* he had eaten up, and lain down in her bed? not to mention the poisoned apple in *Snow White's* throat, after the removal of which the child came back to life; or the hundred years' sleep of *Sleeping Beauty* in the castle."

The authors answer these queries by declaring that the explanation lies in the fact that the folk-tale is purposely and wilfully illogical, since by this evasion of reality terrible events are robbed of their sting. In fact:

"It is precisely these absurdities which relieve the mind of the virus of these horrors; the lack of logic in the folk-tales paralyzes, so to say, the racially conditioned fear of the environment felt by human beings—a fear retained perhaps by means of 'ancestral memory.'

"From the point of view of the development of the mind the following concepts are essential.

"1. The human mind apparently possesses a subconscious ancestral memory; in its depths slumber the images of the struggles undergone by remote ancestors with huge wild beasts, the fear of these creatures, and the terror roused by mysterious natural phenomena.

"Beneath the threshold of consciousness there still peers forth, likewise, the primitive and uncompromising tendency to react in a certain way to unpleasant features of the environment—as for example, by the ruthless removal of hateful neighbors.

"2. This semiconscious spiritual inheritance of the fear and hate of our forefathers still lives and works, even, to some extent, in the souls of civilized men. The significance of the folk-tale lies in its power to dislodge from our burdened spirit such racially historic nightmares. Thus we experience, as it were, a sort of psychological release or absolution.

"3. The horrors incorporated in the folk-tale are not transferred to the human soul. On the contrary, by the act of telling the tale we undergo a sort of confession and absolution by means of which the sting of a racially inherited horror is plucked from the mind. This is why tales of such dubious character, from the view-point of the psychologist, have not long since vanished from the nursery. The very unreality, the faulty logic of the fairy-tale serve the purpose (however unconsciously) of destroying fear, by eliminating rationality, a painless affair."

The authors repeat, too, that the "happy ending" is a very important factor in this purging of the soul from images of dread and terror. In support of this view they turn to the data given by psychoanalysis, pointing out that while many persons reveal injurious and lingering effects upon the mind, which can be traced to painful impressions made by real occurrences in childhood, it is rare that the dreadful events related in fairy-tales and folk-tales have such an influence. They utter a warning, however, not to tell such stories to children already afflicted with a tendency to morbid mental attitudes. In any case, they stress the importance of having these old stories told by a person of intelligence and sympathy instead of by the crude and insensitive. They applaud the modern editions of folk-tales prepared for adults, and the care taken by publishers of such books to soften the more atrocious features. On the whole, they are inclined to recommend that the imagination of the child should be fed and inspired by the "modern fairy-tales," which stress love of men and animals rather than fear.

THE CHILD'S FIRST LITERATURE
Blanche Weekes

Criticism of the fairy tales . . . is directed against the content rather than the form, for the latter is accepted as being so perfect that modern writers do well to imitate it. As yet, few, if any, have equalled the beauty and charm of the old story patterns. It is argued, however, that the old tales were not created for children; that they are a record of primitive philosophy, religion, custom, standards and taboos, all of which are beyond the ability of a child to comprehend. It is feared he will, therefore, be unable to interpret and account for the harshness and the vindictive cruelty, the unethical conduct and the vicious jealousy of the fairy tale people, which may prove a shock to a sensitive child, or a stimulation to one not at all sensitive, or to one who accepts it all as a standard of adult conduct, something which he himself may imitate. That the story is read, told or given to him to read by an adult is likely to strengthen this last conclusion. It is also contended that the most commonly read stories contain fear-inspiring elements, which may yield unfortunate returns especially in the case of emotionally-disturbed children. Stories to come under the ban would include some of the old favorites, those which have long been popular such as "Jack the Giant Killer," "Bluebeard," "Snow White and the Seven Dwarfs," "Hansel and Gretel," "Cinderella," "Puss-in-Boots," and "Jack and the Bean-stalk."

The counter argument is to the effect that undue alarm is expressed over the blood-thirstiness of Jack the Giant Killer, although the blood-thirstiness of Bluebeard is conceded by nearly everyone. Jack, however, is seen as a hero of romance, going forth to battle single-handed against an evil foe in defense of the weak and oppressed. As for "Puss-in-Boots," the unethical person is merely a cat, whom children will be prone to think of as clever rather than anything else. That the master of the cat was also unethical in not disclaiming the rank of Marquis of Carabas is hardly likely to cross their minds, as in the story he is a subordinate character, especially in comparison with Puss. Indeed he is merely a peg on which to hang the story. "Snow White and the Seven Dwarfs," because of the actions of the jealous step-mother, certainly is not a story for young children, some of whom may have step-mothers of their own. "Cinderella" hardly warrants such severe treatment. The story is comparable in a sense to "Puss-in-Boots": the sister's vain and foolish act of mutilation sinks into insignificance beside the many other episodes that make up the story. The same thing might well be said of the episode in "Hansel and Gretel" in which the children, after a series of cruelties and unkindnesses at the hands of the old witch, thrust her into the oven. But this act, too, becomes subordinated in light of the other thrilling episodes of the story. . . .

Those who oppose the "Nursery Rhymes" and the fairy tales as first literature for children, offer a substitute. Their belief is that the child is more interested in the

Blanche Weekes, "The Child's First Literature," *Literature and the Child* (New York: Silver, Burdett, 1935).

world of reality which lies close about him, than he is in an unknown, unseen world far away in time and space, a world of persons and things which have nothing to do with his real and personal world. The assumption is that fairyland is all about the child in the guise of reality. That he is interested and curious about this world is shown by the questions he asks, and the things about which he talks. Selection of story content would be made, then, on the principle that the things about which he talks and asks are the things he will enjoy when he is spoken to through the medium of a story or poem. The value of using such material lies in the setting up by the child of a sense of right relationships, of himself to the world, and of persons and things in the world, so that there results finally, if little by little, an increased ability to interpret his own daily life experiences of which the story content is a counterpart. When the child, by his own adjustment to reality, shows that he has developed ability to discern relationships and see facts as they really are, then will he be ready, say the protagonists of the new approach to literature, to begin adventuring into the realm of the remote and the unfamiliar through the medium of the tale of wonder and magic.

The intent is to postpone the reading of fairy tales until the child has had time to explore the world of reality, and has learned to distinguish between fiction and fact. However, no objection is voiced if the child reads or listens to such a simple innocuous, yet charmingly impossible tale, as "The Pancake" or any of its variants, even at the early age of four years, for by that time he will have had such experiences that he will laugh at the fun and nonsense. The first tales that treat of unreality, however, must be concerned with things which have a personal significance for him; they should be concerned with things of his own little world. In a sense, they should approximate the make-believe experiences of his play life, in which he, himself, creates stories and little dramatic episodes, endowing at will inanimate things with life, and permitting them adventures which in reality they cannot have—as he well knows through experience with them—adventures likely to be those in which he himself finds pleasure.

The first realistic stories would conform in design or pattern to the nursery rhymes and the old folk fairy or household tales. They would be brief and simple of plot. They would reveal characters in action, glow with color as do the old, glamorous tales. The verse would reflect, as far as possible, the rhythmical cadence and the tonal qualities that make the "Nursery Rhymes" a delight to children's ears. Many of these tales and rhymes would center about the child himself, for in his first personal little world he feels himself the central being and talks of "my" dog, "my" father and "my" brother. Little by little the stories would change as to content, as his little world grows and new elements enter it, more people big and little, part of the community into which his first personal little world slowly and imperceptibly merges.

Thoughtful students of the subject will be prone to ask whether realistic content, especially that drawn from the world of industry, can be rendered in a story form which will do what the folk tales do, permit a play of imagination, appeal to the gamut of emotions, providing opportunity for emotional experiencing, and, at the same time, end on a pleasing and happy note. The same students are also prone to ask whether a child, living a well-balanced life from the moment he comes into the world of reality, who, therefore, will have had many and varied experiences with actualities, with people and things all in right relationship, by the time he is three or four years old, will need to relive experiences embodied in realistic stories; whether he is not prepared by reason of his well-balanced life for excursions into unreality or fairyland. The question in summary, seems to be: to what extent will these first years of balanced living contribute to logical thinking?

Margaret W. Curti points out that "the young child is not only illogical in his general manner of thinking but that the special concepts that he has are vague, unanalyzed and contradictory. He does not at first even distinguish between himself and the world, or realize that his thought is merely subjective activity of his own, powerless to affect objects except through action. He thinks at first that his thoughts can influence events, that the sun and moon and the wind, the rivers, trees, and the rain, exist for his benefit. Later, leaving the stage of magic and animism, he believes in an artificialist explanation of the world—that all things were made for men by man." And the writer asks: "How could any child, no matter how gifted, be expected to pass from the infantile stage of thought which is more primitive than that of the lowest savages, into the logical ways of thinking of highly civilized adults, without crude transition stages? Nor should we be surprised that many children never do reach the higher stages." In relation to the effect of adult guidance, the writer says: "Not only the rate at which children pass through the first primitive stages of thought but the degree to which their mature conceptions of the world and human life become rational are susceptible of control by adults."

In light of these findings and conclusions, the question to be raised is: Whether reading and listening to stories—a part of the child's experience which quite definitely comes under adult control—should not contribute to the correcting of inaccuracies of thought and further logical thinking? Whether, in light of the nature of the young child's primitive, imaginative, and crude manner of thinking, it is the wisest thing to let him roam freely in the world of unreality where physical causation plays so little a part, and the supernatural so great a part? Would it not seem that such experiences are likely to retard, rather than promote, logical thinking, and keep thinking on an infantile plane? The findings and conclusions emphasize a point previously made in the text, that guiding children's reading is a matter of guiding the reading of each child as an individual; the variation in growth rate from the imaginative to the logical form of thinking as well as the probable variation of experience makes this necessarily so. Certainly, in this analysis of a child's manner of thinking, there is support for the conclusion that the earliest reading should be more realistic and less fantastic than has been the case in the past. . . .

FAIRY TALES AND NEUROSIS
Sandor Lorand

In a paper entitled The Occurrence in Dreams of Material from Fairy Tales, written in 1913, Freud hints at the relation that exists between fairy tales and neuroses. In that paper, Freud tells of the dreams of a patient and of the fairy tales which were produced as associations to the dreams. He also suggests the relation between fairy tales and early childhood history: "It is not surprising to find that psychoanalysis confirms us in our recognition of how great an influence folk fairy tales have upon the mental life of our children. In some people a recollection of their favorite fairy tales takes the place of memories of their own childhood: they have made the fairy tales into screen memories."

It is obvious that fairy tales have a constructive value; they fulfil children's wishes: they have the same structure as dreams, and their content is really nothing more than the disguised realization of wishes. In addition to their appeal to children we cannot lose sight of the fact that fairy tales may also satisfy an inner need of adult story tellers, and that they may provide adults with an outlet for the tension resulting from conflicts.

It is difficult to take any definite stand concerning the possible harmful influence of fairy tales on the child. To say that fairy tales can be of use in education, that they help to broaden the imagination of the child, that they widen his mental horizon, that they have a play value, that they give the child an opportunity to solve his conflicts with his parents by identification—is all true. But as my case history will show, under certain circumstances the fairy tale may cause harm and produce a traumatic effect. It may become a permanent pattern for escape and may confuse the mental life of a child, leaving permanent injuries that inhibit future adjustment. It should be emphasized, however, that in such a case the effects are bound up with the child's whole environment, with his position in the family, his relation to his parents and siblings, and that the fairy tales may be no more than a strong contributing factor in the causation of the neurosis.

The case which I will present bears witness to the ways in which the structure of a whole neurosis can be based on folklore material, and the ways in which these stories can be a factor in creating and maintaining anxiety in adult life (they are unquestionably a factor in childhood). The same fairy tales which served once in childhood as a wish fulfilment, and which were of use in the solution of the œdipus conflict of the child may become a source of suffering in the adult. They may become objects of fear, keeping the patient in a steady panic, as an ego defense against his instinctive sexual urges.

In the case history to be presented the adult life of the patient was permeated with threads of folk tales which led back to early childhood actualities when stories were told to him by his mother. During childhood the patient had had an infantile

Sandor Lorand, "Fairy Tales and Neurosis," *Psychoanalytic Quarterly* 4 (1935). Lorand was a practicing psychoanalyst at the time he wrote this article. Later, he became the managing editor of the *Yearbook of Psychoanalysis* (1945–55) and the author of *Psychodynamics and Therapy* (1956).

neurosis which disappeared spontaneously. In puberty it was the cause of many neurotic behavior patterns. In his present adult neurosis both the scars of the infantile neurosis and the puberty difficulties became reactivated; and as the layers covering his past life were removed, it was found that the distortion of reality in his adult state was connected with the distortion of reality by fairy tales in childhood. The hidden material of early childhood experiences was concerned with emotional maladjustment to his parents, which centered around his œdipus situation, and was bound up with very strong castration anxiety.

The patient to whom I refer was in his thirties—accomplished in his social and economic status—but the city streets on which he moved, the house where he lived, the meadows and forests where he played golf, and the lakes where he went fishing, were all filled for him with giants, ogres, witches, and strange animals. In his daily routine life he seemed to come across friends whose faces at times appeared bird-like, and whose noses protruded like beaks. In his dreams the fairy-tale structure of early childhood expanded to an even greater degree. Strange, prehistoric animals reaching through the window, big and baby elephants, snakes, the wolf of Little Red Riding Hood, all were present, and gave rise to preoccupation with fear-fantasies during the day. The happenings of his actual daily life became distorted in his mind and suggested unreality when he tried to check fantasies and to hide desires arising in the course of his routine activities. He was forced to escape to a fairy world as a protection against the same instinctive desires which had been present in early childhood and which had been strengthened by his mother who told him those stories. In his childhood he had been fascinated by the strange tales, and the uglier reality which grew upon him had been warded off and made pleasant by the fictitious stories. In his adulthood his craving for that early reality, when he was alone with mother, still persisted, and the strongest desire of his unconscious was to escape back to his childhood. In childhood he was the hero of all fairy tales. His vivid imagination was strengthened by the mother's attitude of belonging solely to him. In manhood, his unconscious strivings were so powerful in the direction of child-hood that they kept him a child in relation to reality. He was still the center of the fairy tales, but as a sufferer.

When he came to analysis he was obsessed with fears. In the office the typewriter keys looked like animals' teeth; in the midst of his work he was afraid his heart would stop beating; in his business dealings he feared he might lose his voice and bark like a dog. When walking on the street he was afraid that people would look like horses or birds. When driving at night the spare tires of the car in front of him, illuminated by the reflector of his car, appeared to be a huge and frightful face. He feared that he would not recognize the members of his family when he arrived home. At other times, he feared that he would forget who he was or that he would become blind, or that he would see people disintegrate. When shaving he felt that the barber might cut his face, or that the vibrating apparatus would look like a human head. All his fears were prominently connected with his eyesight.

The complaints for which he sought treatment had existed for about ten years in a mild degree. They started when his first child, a son, was born, when he experi-enced for the first time a feeling that his heart would stop beating. Later he suffered from almost continually blurred vision. I shall try to give you a short history of the case, and to condense the daily analysis of two years. I wish to remark here that the patient left treatment over three years ago, and since then has been well adjusted.

The only remaining son of wealthy parents, the patient stopped school at the age of seventeen because he wanted to start in business and make a great amount of money, so that he might retire at about the age of thirty-five and from then on live primarily for pleasure. He had had a younger brother who died at the age of four, when the patient himself was six. Our patient used to play with his brother, especially sexual games, which at that age were already being indulged in with other boys and girls. The games usually consisted of sucking each other's breasts and exploring each other's genitalia, especially the girls'. He always wondered that the girls found his but that he did not find theirs.

He remembers that time as having been the happiest of his life, since his father's travels and business used to permit his being alone with the mother. It was particularly the late afternoon hours which were pleasurable, when he sat at dusk by the window with his mother, looking out, and mother would tell him fairy stories. Most of them were about good fairies, but some were about witches who changed themselves or who had the power to change human beings into animals. Naturally, all the fairy stories carried a moral implication. The patient particularly remembered the tale of Pinocchio, and his mother's assurance that good little boys got their reward as Pinocchio did; but there was also the other side of the story, when the cricket would whisper constantly in his ear that "bad boys who rebelled against their parents would never get along in the world."

Beneath the pleasures of these early years ran a current of resentment against both his parents. This current, not recalled by the patient until it was revealed by analysis, was bound up with his peculiar situation with respect to his father and mother. He bore little affection for his father—because he never saw much of him; rather, he felt almost a hatred arising from the fact that his father came between him and his mother, and from the fact that the father was responsible for the birth of his younger brother, of whom the patient had been jealous.

His masturbatory activities with both girls and boys continued from early childhood up to and through adolescence. At the age of ten or eleven he was seduced by, and slept with, a servant girl. She played with his penis and he sucked her breasts. He still adhered to the fantasy, then, that women have only one opening, located in the rear. (The significance of this I shall make clear later). In his adolescence, being well developed and powerful, he began to go out with girls early, but never had sexual intercourse. Usually, on rides or outings, he got them to masturbate him. His apparently strong development along masculine lines so early proved to be a pretense and was a result of a disproportionately rapid libidinal development and slow ego development, both due to his peculiar relationship to his mother. That is why he could never handle his libidinal urges adequately; and that is why his early masculine development did not last.

At the age of eighteen he had his steady girl, whom he felt obliged to marry, though his parents opposed the marriage on account of his age. He finally married her when he was not quite twenty-two; she was somewhat older.

From the beginning of his marriage he was troubled with ejaculatio præcox, and to satisfy his wife he sometimes practiced cunnilingus. Very soon after his marriage he began to be troubled with various mild anxieties, all concerning his health. He constantly went to doctors to be examined. Twice or three times a year he would be laid up with a cold. He was very much concerned with his stomach functions and his bowel movements. All during the time of his married life he did not give up the idea of trying extra-marital sexual relationships, but he never came to the point of actually trying. He did make acquaintances, and received a certain amount of gratification by discussing sexual matters with women, or at times by petting them, but he always stopped there, usually ending by having an emission. As time went on, he became more and more irritated with his wife, and when his first child was born his anxieties broke out in full force. That was the beginning of the period when anxiety connected with the fairy tale material of his childhood began to torment him in his daily life.

It became clear in analysis that the connection between his anxiety attack and the birth of the child was due primarily to his having become a father. Analogous in a way to post partum psychoses in women, or to depressions in men which develop after marriage, or when they become parents, our patient could not bear the realization of his strong early childhood desires to take the father's place, and when in actuality he became a parent, he could not enjoy it. His wife was a real substitute mother to him, not only because she was somewhat older, but also because her attitude was more that of a mother than a wife. He became obsessed with the idea of leaving his wife—an obsession accompanied by a very strong sense of guilt because it involved the unwelcome child as well as the wife. He was jealous and resentful of his child, whom he identified with his dead young brother, whose presence in early childhood he had not wished because it interfered with having mother and mother's affection all to himself.

These fantasies together with his constant sexual tension did not allow him a moment's rest. When walking in the streets he constantly stared at women, even turning to look at them, although he realized that a man in his social position would be an object of much criticism if observed in such activity. Then his vision became blurred, and the fear of going blind developed as a protection against looking and desiring. Whenever under sexual urge he found himself staring at women in the street, the blurred feeling of his eyes turned him away from those drives and preoccupied him with himself.

He disliked coming home from business. The fear of not recognizing the members of his family was indicative of his strong desire to be away from them, and the resentment he felt against them. The same fear concerned his own parents. The elderly business associates whose noses appeared to him changed into birdlike beaks were all father representatives, reminding him of his father's sexual superiority and reviving in him a fear of castration.

An interesting indication of this strong castration fear was the retention even until puberty of the idea that women have but one opening, and that in the back. This idea had served (as proved by analysis) as a defense against his powerful castration anxieties. It is well known that little boys often adhere in their unconscious to the notion that women have a penis—an idea that spares them the fear of castration when they discover the anatomical difference between boys and girls, and find that little girls have no penis. The fear of meeting the same fate as the little girl, who originally had a penis which was cut off, and whose vagina is a wound resulting from that castration, is thus allayed. By denying any kind of genital in the female, our patient eliminated even the slightest possibility of the fear of castration.

During adulthood, the sport diversions of the patient were all more or less sexualized, as childhood games so often are. When he was putting on the golf course—he won many prizes in tournaments—the smoke stacks in the far distance appeared like a huge animal, the little house on the outskirts of the course like a human face, and he was seized with an irresistible diarrhœa so that he had to rush back to the club house. I may mention here that golf was the only field in which he was superior to his father, and that at the root of that anxiety we again see the returning castration anxiety.

His outstanding fear that the faces of people might change found an interesting explanation. It meant that they would change and look angry, since for him normal faces were always smiling ones. It led back to the fairy tale of Little Red Riding Hood where the wolf took the place of the grandmother, and the fear that faces would change had to do primarily with the mother as the original castrator. He must be a good boy to keep mother smiling, to keep her love, and to prevent her from turning into the unfriendly wolf. Back of all these fears there was a strong dread of both parents. The fear that mother's face would change also led to an actual memory: he remembered how sad mother's face was when she was telling him the stories, sitting at the window, and he connected that sadness with waiting for father. His strong distrust of women led back unconsciously to that memory. He was loved by his mother, but it was an incomplete love since she was waiting for another man. As the patient himself put it: "We are sitting at the window at dusk, she telling stories but waiting for father to come back; and when he came both would go out leaving me alone, at the same time comforting me, telling me not to cry, saying that I should be a nice child. I succeeded in making scenes at times to keep them at home."

Advanced in manhood, he was still laboring with the difficulties of his early œdipus situation. The fears connected with his sexual urges, with the desire to possess a woman, were paralleled by his desire of early childhood to possess the mother. In childhood he had to be good if he were to receive the reward of his mother's love, like the hero of the fairy tale. Thus the one real danger in childhood—losing the mother—was warded off. In his present adult life the desire for a woman became prominent once again, and with the desire came the recollection of fairy tale incidents. These in turn brought anxieties which emphasized the dangers of his adult desires. The woman could be, as in the tale, both the good fairy and the cruel witch, and the father could also be a mighty giant, at times benevolent, at other times severe and punishing. The fairy tales in childhood had helped him in the temporary solution of his conflicts and fears, especially because his mother's attitude was always kind and protecting. They had helped him also to be a good boy, and beloved. In his adult life the fear of the fairy tale material resulted in the same correcting of tendencies which he had been taught to consider antisocial.

In childhood the fairy tale served to ease and partly to solve his difficulties concerning his œdipus conflict. At the present his fantasies and fears served the same purpose but without success, because the œdipus situation had originally been solved only in part. The most that they could accomplish was to make him compliant through anxieties, just as in early childhood his castration fear had made him a compliant and dependent child.

The lack of self-confidence was a result of the chaos which his emotions created in his unconscious. The fairy tales in childhood had served to mitigate the conflict between the desires aiming at possession of the mother and the severity of his superego. They could not serve in the same way in his maturity.

In conclusion, I wish to emphasize the fact, which must be clear from the case presented, that fairy tales *per se* do not cause a neurosis. The fertile soil of early childhood conflicts is already present before the fairy tale contributes to the development of the neurosis, effecting an intensification of the conflicts. The fable may then under given circumstances turn into an inhibition. But that fairy tales may help the child in the solution of conflicts which arise from the œdipus situation is also true. The good or ill effect of fairy stories rests largely on the circumstances under which they are related to the child.

The story must obviously be suited to the child's age and condition. Care should be taken that the tale is told in the proper physical and psychological setting. The time of day when the story telling takes place is, of course, important (for example, no ogre story before bed time). Even such a minor detail as voice modulation should be given careful consideration. Above all, the story teller should be certain that the tale is told for the child, and not out of a sense of duty, or merely to relieve certain tensions of his own.

In the case cited, the patient's mother was herself of the timid, apprehensive type. To sit at the window and tell her boy fairy stories while waiting for her husband had a comforting effect and relieved the tension within her. As for our patient, analysis revealed that the circumstances under which the fairy tales were told were equivalent to a seduction, and instead of helping him in the solution of his œdipus conflict, the stories brought him still closer to his mother and provided a secret means of pleasure in common with her every evening before he went to bed. This is why the feeling of guilt in connection with sex became so strong in the patient. Thus we see the lack of caution and necessary consideration for the child may mean that the fairy tale becomes the source of a constant traumatic reaction in his later life.

THE ACID TEST
Marion Garthwaite

There are lemon trees, fine bearers, too, that produce big, juicy lemons so mild they are almost sweet. But to my notion sweet lemons are anomalies, lacking that *raison d'être*, the sharp and acidulous tartness needed to point up the flavor of meat and fish and salad greens.

Children want their witches, their giants and ogres, sour, too. They want them ugly, wicked, and dispatched, as all evil should be. That's what they're there for—the witches, the dragons, the giants, the whole horde of "wizards and wuzzards." They are there to be vanquished by a boy with the courage to face them down, or by a girl with wits enough to fool them and escape across a bridge of a single hair.

Of late years authors have been watering down witches, gentling them until they are well-intentioned creatures who mean no harm. If a child is too high-strung to listen to exciting stories, he shouldn't hear about witches. He needs some comforting stories that keep his world serene and warm and secure. This is right for most preschoolers, for many children up to the third grade. After that, or even before, if the children are conditioned to it, the Baba Yaga can come sailing in, seated in her stone mortar, sweeping away the path behind her with her besom. For children used to this kind of story, witches should have teeth in them, preferably iron and champing.

This applies to pictures of witches, too. The earlier artists, like Arthur Rackham, knew how to limn fearful witches. Henry Pitz doesn't mince matters, either. His witches and ogres, and Tenggren's, too, mean business—dirty work at the crossroads—fearsomely wicked creatures.

When children have been read to at home, progressing by easy stages from Mother Goose through the old accumulative tales, and then three this and three that, and on to the tougher stories, they can face fierce antagonists with equanimity and relish.

There comes a time when children need to realize that the world is not always serene and warm and secure, that it sometimes takes courage and quick wits and a grim hanging on before witches and hobgoblins can be routed. Like the hobbit, children have two sides to them. There's the side that wants to stay close to warmth and security. But there's also the Tookish side that yearns for far places and adventure and derring-do.

We can't let them go off at a tender age on ventures of their own—too much traffic. But we can give them vicarious experiences to fire their imaginations or to condition them to meet the challenges of an age gearing itself for flight into Heaven-knows-what. It doesn't make sense to keep children wrapped in wool while they miss out on a toughening process, with no understanding of the courage it takes to face struggle or the cleverness it takes to outwit a cunning adversary.

Marion Garthwaite, "The Acid Test," *The Horn Book* 39 (1963). Garthwaite has been a children's librarian and the author of numerous children's books, including *Locked Crowns* (1963) and *Twelfth Night* (1965).

Some of our teen-agers realize they have been softened up instead of steeled. The thinking ones don't thank us for having made things too easy. They are scared, scared they aren't really brave, scared they won't know enough in a world that is tightening its standards of knowledge and reasoning, scared that they might not be able to cope. Cope with what? They aren't even sure of that, and their own fears are much worse than any witch or ogre ever invented.

As a storyteller I am convinced that the children who cringe are enjoying the cringing. They feel safe enough on a lap, in front of a fire, or gathered about a storyteller where there is friendly interest and a warmth of tone that says all will be well in the end—just wait—you'll see.

When the wee red man demands the carving knife to cut off the king's head, a boy will groan, *"Oh! No!"*, and then be lost again in the hilarious story. Children find this tale, told by a storyteller like Josephine Gardner of San Francisco, funnier and funnier the gorier it gets.

The cerebral-palsied children at the El Portal School in Hillcrest, California, are good listeners. They started out with an attention span equal to the early nursery tales with which they were familiar. The day they first heard Howard Pyle's "Three Little Pigs and the Ogre" we talked about ogres ahead of time. What was an ogre? The guesses from the children were, "He's a kind of a wolf," or "I think he's a bad giant."

"Yes, he's a kind of a wolf. He's a kind of a giant. He's always bad. And he's nearly always *stupid!*"

That did it. They enjoy hearing about the stupid old ogre being so gaily outwitted by the three little pigs. Children often feel stupid themselves. They want to hear about big, overgrown creatures being stupid.

These handicapped children identified themselves with the smartest of the three little pigs. They learned to take all kinds of stories—a grim fight to the death between Robin Hood and the savage, horse-hided Sir Guy of Gisbourne; the clang of lance against helmet as Arthur, barely healed of his wounds, once more thunders against the Black Knight; the hungry old witch clutching at Stoutheart and the maiden, as the power of the stone that keeps them flying just out of reach grows less with the setting sun.

There's acid in that old witch from South America, gobbling up the hard-shelled turtles that weigh her down to her doom.

If our villains are halfhearted, if our bandits give back the gold, or our witches fly about doing good deeds, our children can always sit glued to television sets—any time they choose in most homes—watching good triumph over evil by the simple and stultifying process of shooting it out.

There was nothing tame about the old stories. Cuchulain got his name because he became a watchdog for the man whose warden hounds the boy had strangled with his bare hands. Beowulf tore the arm of the monster Grendel from its socket and followed the evil creature to his lair beneath the sea where he fought the dragon's mother to her gory end.

Who dragged whom how many times around the walls of what? What boy sent a slung stone from the brook deep into the forehead of a giant whose spear had a shaft like a weaver's beam and a head that weighed six hundred shekels of iron?

These are stout old stories, full of battle, full of mouth-filling words that picture life and death "running beautiful together" and being met with courage and faith.

I am sure that the vivid stories we heard, the ones my mother or my grandmother read to us, were an emotional release for my brother and me. We used the stories for all kinds of creative activities. We acted them out, made all the costumes, provided all the props, and performed them at the slightest encouragement. We re-created the stories geared to our own experience and created fresh drama to meet our own limitations. The more horrendous the villains the easier it was to act them out.

We liked witch stories, but not stories of gentle, friendly witches. No such sissy stuff for Malcolm and me. We wanted witches who ate people. We were pleased when somebody pushed a wicked witch into the oven or ran off with a willy-willy-wag and the old witch's bag of gold.

Children don't want everybody good. H. H. Munro made this point in his story-within-a-story called "The Story-Teller." The children in that poking-of-fun at all tame storytellers were enchanted when the wolf ate up the insufferably good little girl, all except her good conduct medals. Even *he* couldn't swallow those! The children decided it was the most beautiful story they had ever heard.

On the other hand most children want evil vanquished. But they want the wicked bad enough to deserve it. When the old witch orders Hansel to stick out his finger to see if he has been fattened up enough to roast, anybody can see with half an eye that she is cooking up trouble for herself. I have never found a child who minded the dreadful penalties dreamed up for the wicked in the old tales. Barrels full of nails, pits full of vipers—if the wicked ones have earned it, serves 'em right!

Once when I was telling "Snow White and the Seven Dwarfs" I decided to temper the ending. To a man, the children protested. "You forgot the part where she had to dance in the red-hot shoes until she dropped down dead." Justice had not been done.

Children know it's just a story, a lively tale that goes galloping along to a satisfying end. In so many of these old folk and fairy tales the children see themselves in the same situations, where the small and the put-upon, the weak and the simple can match wits with the biggest and the worst, the slyest and most crafty. They can win out, too, if they are brave enough and kind enough and keep their wits about them. In the folk tales kindness and good manners pay off again and again.

We need to tell or read the old tales of witches and ogres with tongue in cheek, twinkle in eye, laughter in heart. In the voice, too, if the children seem to be taking the story too seriously.

But on the whole, pallid witches that don't bewitch, or gentle dragons that fail to drag people off, may lull our children (and of course this has its place with the too young or the insecure), but they won't do much to stimulate them. They won't do much to entice our young people into a creativeness of their own.

If our children are going to sail off into space in capsules, they should be brought up on the old-time witches who made it on broomsticks. There's no telling what they'll meet at the end of the ride. A firsthand acquaintance with a few dragons or Baba Yagas, Difs or wicked witches might not come amiss.

Witches should be sour, like good lemons, and as tart and zestful.

The only good witch is a really bad one. That's the acid test.

ON THREE WAYS OF WRITING FOR CHILDREN
C. S. Lewis

. . . Do fairy tales teach children to retreat into a world of wish-fulfilment—'fantasy' in the technical psychological sense of the word—instead of facing the problems of the real world? Now it is here that the problem becomes subtle. Let us again lay the fairy tale side by side with the school story or any other story which is labelled a 'Boy's Book' or a 'Girl's Book', as distinct from a 'Children's Book'. There is no doubt that both arouse, and imaginatively satisfy, wishes. We long to go through the looking glass, to reach fairy land. We also long to be the immensely popular and successful schoolboy or schoolgirl, or the lucky boy or girl who discovers the spy's plot or rides the horse that none of the cowboys can manage. But the two longings are very different. The second, especially when directed on something so close as school life, is ravenous and deadly serious. Its fulfilment on the level of imagination is in very truth compensatory: we run to it from the disappointments and humiliations of the real world: it sends us back to the real world undivinely discontented. For it is all flattery to the ego. The pleasure consists in picturing oneself the object of admiration. The other longing, that for fairy land, is very different. In a sense a child does not long for fairy land as a boy longs to be the hero of the first eleven. Does anyone suppose that he really and prosaically longs for all the dangers and discomforts of a fairy tale?—really wants dragons in contemporary England? It is not so. It would be much truer to say that fairy land arouses a longing for he knows not what. It stirs and troubles him (to his life-long enrichment) with the dim sense of something beyond his reach and, far from dulling or emptying the actual world, gives it a new dimension of depth. He does not despise real woods because he has read of enchanted woods: the reading makes all real woods a little enchanted. This is a special kind of longing. The boy reading the school story of the type I have in mind desires success and is unhappy (once the book is over) because he can't get it: the boy reading the fairy tale desires and is happy in the very fact of desiring. For his mind has not been concentrated on himself, as it often is in the more realistic story.

I do not mean that school stories for boys and girls ought not to be written. I am only saying that they are far more liable to become 'fantasies' in the clinical sense than fantastic stories are. And this distinction holds for adult reading too. The dangerous fantasy is always superficially realistic. The real victim of wishful reverie does not batten on the *Odyssey*, *The Tempest*, or *The Worm Ouroboros*: he (or she) prefers stories about millionaires, irresistible beauties, posh hotels, palm beaches and bedroom scenes—things that really might happen, that ought to happen,

C. S. Lewis, "On Three Ways of Writing for Children," *Of Other Worlds* (New York: Harcourt Brace, 1966). C. S. Lewis was a literary scholar (*The Allegory of Love: A Study in Medieval Tradition*, 1936), a science fiction/fantasy writer (*Out of the Silent Planet*, 1938), and a Christian apologist (*The Case for Christianity*, 1943).

that would have happened if the reader had had a fair chance. For, as I say, there are two kinds of longing. The one is an *askesis*, a spiritual exercise, and the other is a disease.

A far more serious attack on the fairy tale as children's literature comes from those who do not wish children to be frightened. I suffered too much from night-fears myself in childhood to undervalue this objection. I would not wish to heat the fires of that private hell for any child. On the other hand, none of my fears came from fairy tales. Giant insects were my specialty, with ghosts a bad second. I suppose the ghosts came directly or indirectly from stories, though certainly not from fairy stories, but I don't think the insects did. I don't know anything my parents could have done or left undone which would have saved me from the pincers, mandibles, and eyes of those many-legged abominations. And that, as so many people have pointed out, is the difficulty. We do not know what will or will not frighten a child in this particular way. I say 'in this particular way' for we must here make a distinction. Those who say that children must not be frightened may mean two things. They may mean (1) that we must not do anything likely to give the child those haunting, disabling, pathological fears against which ordinary courage is helpless: in fact, *phobias*. His mind must, if possible, be kept clear of things he can't bear to think of. Or they may mean (2) that we must try to keep out of his mind the knowledge that he is born into a world of death, violence, wounds, adventure, heroism and cowardice, good and evil. If they mean the first I agree with them: but not if they mean the second. The second would indeed be to give children a false impression and feed them on escapism in the bad sense. There is something ludicrous in the idea of so educating a generation which is born to the Ogpu and the atomic bomb. Since it is so likely that they will meet cruel enemies, let them at least have heard of brave knights and heroic courage. Otherwise you are making their destiny not brighter but darker. Nor do most of us find that violence and bloodshed, in a story, produce any haunting dread in the minds of children. As far as that goes, I side impenitently with the human race against the modern reformer. Let there be wicked kings and beheadings, battles and dungeons, giants and dragons, and let villains be soundly killed at the end of the book. Nothing will persuade me that this causes an ordinary child any kind or degree of fear beyond what it wants, and needs, to feel. For, of course, it wants to be a little frightened.

The other fears—the phobias—are a different matter. I do not believe one can control them by literary means. We seem to bring them into the world with us ready made. No doubt the particular image on which the child's terror is fixed can sometimes be traced to a book. But is that the source, or only the occasion, of the fear? If he had been spared that image, would not some other, quite unpredictable by you, have had the same effect? Chesterton has told us of a boy who was more afraid of the Albert Memorial than anything else in the world. I know a man whose great childhood terror was the India paper edition of the *Encyclopaedia Britannica*—for a reason I defy you to guess. And I think it possible that by confining your child to blameless stories of child life in which nothing at all alarming ever happens, you would fail to banish the terrors, and would succeed in banishing all that can ennoble them or make them endurable. For in the fairy tales, side by side with the terrible figures, we find the immemorial comforters and protectors, the radiant ones; and the terrible figures are not merely terrible, but sublime. It would be nice if no little boy in bed, hearing, or thinking he hears, a sound, were ever at all frightened. But if he is going to be frightened, I think it better that he should think of giants and dragons than merely of burglars. And I think St George, or any bright champion in armour, is a better comfort than the idea of the police.

I will even go further. If I could have escaped all my own night-fears at the price of never having known 'faerie', would I now be the gainer by that bargain? I am not speaking carelessly. The fears were very bad. But I think the price would have been too high. . . .

CHILDREN AND THE LEX TALIONIS
Russell Kirk

Ought we to bowdlerize children's folk tales, so as to present the young with a world of gentleness and peace? Ought we to take the grim out of Grimm? That question arose recently at the 1974 meeting of the advisory board of the Open Court Publishing Company.

Open Court publishes the best series of basic readers for children in all this land, or perhaps all the world—combining literary merit with a wondrously successful method of reading instruction. And Open Court now publishes a children's magazine, *Cricket*, charmingly illustrated and containing first-rate old and new stories (and other features) for little boys and girls. In less than a year, *Cricket* has attained a circulation of nearly a quarter of a million.

At Open Court's annual meeting, one of the principal speakers was Dr. Bruno Bettelheim, the eminent psychologist, talking about emotional problems in learning. Someone raised this question of well-intentioned bowdlerizing. Some parents or teachers have complained that *Cricket* publishes folk tales and fairy tales in their old unexpurgated versions: aren't violence and vengeance disturbing to children?

Not at all, said Dr. Bettelheim—who can be winning and mordant simultaneously. For in the folk tales of wonder, it is the wicked who are punished by poetic justice, and the good who are rewarded. This satisfies the child's yearning for order and justice. By nature, Dr. Bettelheim pointed out, children are attracted to the *lex talionis*, the law of retribution. And it ought not to be otherwise.

In "Little Red Riding Hood," the wolf is weighed down by the bodies of his victims, and so his evil deeds cause his dreadful end: sound morality. If punishment does not follow crime (in the violent seventeenth century or the violent twentieth century), order is undone. The child is eager for a pattern of order. And to present twentieth century children with a realm of fancy purged of violence and disorder would be to leave them woefully unprepared for action when they grow up—or, for that matter, would leave them defenseless in the typical primary school nowadays.

A fault of Maurice Maeterlinck's *The Blue Bird*, Dr. Bettelheim suggested, is that this fantasy leaves the child's sense of justice unsatisfied. In that story, the cat has been malicious and treacherous throughout; while the Dog has been heroically faithful. Yet in the end, the Cat goes unpunished and the Dog unrewarded. As I told Dr. Bettelheim afterward, this injustice in *The Blue Bird* worried me for years when I was a little boy. To each his own: that is the fundamental principle of justice. A world without rewards and punishments is a disordered and unjust world, profoundly disturbing to boys and girls.

Children are ethically alert. In my early years, I learned much from Charles Kingsley's *The Water Babies*—especially from those allegorical figures Mrs. Do-as-you-would-be-done-by and Mrs. Be-done-by-as-you-did. The former of these mater-

Russell Kirk, "Children and the Lex Talionis," *National Review* 15 (1974). Kirk is the author of numerous books on American history and political theory, including *The Conservative Mind: from Burke to Eliot* (1960) and *The Roots of American Order* (1974).

nal figures is Charity; the latter is retributory Justice. If Justice is lacking, Charity is ineffectual.

As G. K. Chesterton put it once, all life is an allegory, and we can understand it only in parable. Fantasy for children, like all important literature, has an ethical end. A fearful joy is part and parcel of that introduction, through fantasy, to the reality of the human condition.

There is any amount of slaughter and derring-do in George Macdonald's *The Princess and Curdie*; my three little daughters love it all, as they love the combats in Sidney Lanier's version of Malory's Arthurian tales. They are terrified and they are rejoiced. And they learn a great deal more of moral evil, and of good, than they could in any "vernal wood."

In *The Princess and Curdie* is a monstrous beast called Lina, who really is a woman cast purgatorially into an animal form, that she may work out her salvation with diligence. When two years ago I read that story to Monica, my eldest daughter (then aged four), she was astonished at the sudden end of Lina, who leaps into a purging fire of roses and thereupon vanishes.

"Where did Lina go?" Monica inquired.

"I'm not certain, Monica," I replied. "To Heaven, perhaps."

"Do you mean she's just visiting friends there, Daddy?"

"Well, no, Monica—I suppose she's gone permanently."

"Oh—you mean she's dead."

This dialogue ushered in theological discussions. My immediate point is that most children do have a nascent healthy skepticism and critical sense; such tales rouse and inform their moral imagination. They do not become goblins because they read about goblins, and the imaginary perils of folktale heroes and heroines may prepare them to encounter with some success the hard moral choices which they must make all too soon.

Some time ago, my wife and I overheard Monica telling Cecilia, a year younger, a wolf tale compounded from many and diverse sources: "And Cecilia," Monica concluded, in deliberate and thrilling tones, *"the wolf is everywhere!"* Cecilia shrieked in her bed, but that was a good cautionary tale for little girls in our time.

Introduction to tales of wonder wakes the philosophical habit of mind. Very recently Cecilia said to her mother, "Mama, I can imagine a thing that has no end. But I can't imagine a thing that has no beginning. Now how is it that God has no beginning?" We don't profess to be able to explain readily to our offspring the problem of infinite duration, yet at least we have led them to ask the right questions.

One of the biggest of questions, asked afresh in every generation, is the question of Justice. The sentimentally permissive fantasy world of Dick, Jane, and Spot is an unjust world, in that it leaves children adrift in a boring pseudosecurity. The world of Hans Christian Andersen or George Macdonald, say, is a hard world, sometimes—but also a world of beauty, vigor, and justice. Unless we recognize the existence of Mrs. Do-as-you-would-be-done-by, and of Mrs. Be-done-by-as-you-did, we come to man's estate morally empty.

FAIRY TALES AND THE EXISTENTIAL PREDICAMENT

Bruno Bettelheim

In order to master the psychological problems of growing up—overcoming narcissistic disappointments, oedipal dilemmas, sibling rivalries; becoming able to relinquish childhood dependencies; gaining a feeling of selfhood and of self-worth, and a sense of moral obligation—a child needs to understand what is going on within his conscious self so that he can also cope with that which goes on in his unconscious. He can achieve this understanding, and with it the ability to cope, not through rational comprehension of the nature and content of his unconscious, but by becoming familiar with it through spinning out daydreams—ruminating, rearranging, and fantasizing about suitable story elements in response to unconscious pressures. By doing this, the child fits unconscious content into conscious fantasies, which then enable him to deal with that content. It is here that fairy tales have unequaled value, because they offer new dimensions to the child's imagination which would be impossible for him to discover as truly on his own. Even more important, the form and structure of fairy tales suggest images to the child by which he can structure his daydreams and with them give better direction to his life.

In child or adult, the unconscious is a powerful determinant of behavior. When the unconscious is repressed and its content denied entrance into awareness, then eventually the person's conscious mind will be partially overwhelmed by derivatives of these unconscious elements, or else he is forced to keep such rigid, compulsive control over them that his personality may become severely crippled. But when unconscious material *is* to some degree permitted to come to awareness and worked through in imagination, its potential for causing harm—to ourselves or others—is much reduced; some of its forces can then be made to serve positive purposes. However, the prevalent parental belief is that a child must be diverted from what troubles him most: his formless, nameless anxieties, and his chaotic, angry, and even violent fantasies. Many parents believe that only conscious reality or pleasant and wish-fulfilling images should be presented to the child—that he should be exposed only to the sunny side of things. But such one-sided fare nourishes the mind only in a one-sided way, and real life is not all sunny.

There is a widespread refusal to let children know that the source of much that goes wrong in life is due to our very own natures—the propensity of all men for acting aggressively, asocially, selfishly, out of anger and anxiety. Instead, we want our children to believe that, inherently, all men are good. But children know that

Bruno Bettelheim, "Fairy Tales and the Existential Predicament," *The Uses of Enchantment* (New York: Knopf, 1976). *The Uses of Enchantment* describes how fairy tales help children adjust. Bettelheim, a psychoanalyst, has written extensively on childhood adjustment, including *Love Is Not Enough: The Treatment of Emotionally Disturbed Children* (1950). He is also the author of a book on his experiences as a prisoner of the Gestapo: *The Informed Heart: Autonomy in a Mass Age* (1960).

they are not always good; and often, even when they are, they would prefer not to be. This contradicts what they are told by their parents, and therefore makes the child a monster in his own eyes.

The dominant culture wishes to pretend, particularly where children are concerned, that the dark side of man does not exist, and professes a belief in an optimistic meliorism. Psychoanalysis itself is viewed as having the purpose of making life easy—but this is not what its founder intended. Psychoanalysis was created to enable man to accept the problematic nature of life without being defeated by it, or giving in to escapism. Freud's prescription is that only by struggling courageously against what seem like overwhelming odds can man succeed in wringing meaning out of his existence.

This is exactly the message that fairy tales get across to the child in manifold form: that a struggle against severe difficulties in life is unavoidable, is an intrinsic part of human existence—but that if one does not shy away, but steadfastly meets unexpected and often unjust hardships, one masters all obstacles and at the end emerges victorious.

Modern stories written for young children mainly avoid these existential problems, although they are crucial issues for all of us. The child needs most particularly to be given suggestions in symbolic form about how he may deal with these issues and grow safely into maturity. "Safe" stories mention neither death nor aging, the limits to our existence, nor the wish for eternal life. The fairy tale, by contrast, confronts the child squarely with the basic human predicaments.

For example, many fairy stories begin with the death of a mother or father; in these tales the death of the parent creates the most agonizing problems, as it (or the fear of it) does in real life. Other stories tell about an aging parent who decides that the time has come to let the new generation take over. But before this can happen, the successor has to prove himself capable and worthy. The Brothers Grimm's story "The Three Feathers" begins: "There was once upon a time a king who had three sons. . . . When the king had become old and weak, and was thinking of his end, he did not know which of his sons should inherit the kingdom after him." In order to decide, the king sets all his sons a difficult task; the son who meets it best "shall be king after my death."

It is characteristic of fairy tales to state an existential dilemma briefly and pointedly. This permits the child to come to grips with the problem in its most essential form, where a more complex plot would confuse matters for him. The fairy tale simplifies all situations. Its figures are clearly drawn; and details, unless very important, are eliminated. All characters are typical rather than unique.

Contrary to what takes place in many modern children's stories, in fairy tales evil is as omnipresent as virtue. In practically every fairy tale good and evil are given body in the form of some figures and their actions, as good and evil are omnipresent in life and the propensities for both are present in every man. It is this duality which poses the moral problem, and requires the struggle to solve it.

Evil is not without its attractions—symbolized by the mighty giant or dragon, the power of the witch, the cunning queen in "Snow White"—and often it is temporarily in the ascendancy. In many fairy tales a usurper succeeds for a time in seizing the place which rightfully belongs to the hero—as the wicked sisters do in

"Cinderella." It is not that the evildoer is punished at the story's end which makes immersing oneself in fairy stories an experience in moral education, although this is part of it. In fairy tales, as in life, punishment or fear of it is only a limited deterrent to crime. The conviction that crime does not pay is a much more effective deterrent, and that is why in fairy tales the bad person always loses out. It is not the fact that virtue wins out at the end which promotes morality, but that the hero is most attractive to the child, who identifies with the hero in all his struggles. Because of this identification the child imagines that he suffers with the hero his trials and tribulations, and triumphs with him as virtue is victorious. The child makes such identifications all on his own, and the inner and outer struggles of the hero imprint morality on him.

The figures in fairy tales are not ambivalent—not good and bad at the same time, as we all are in reality. But since polarization dominates the child's mind, it also dominates fairy tales. A person is either good or bad, nothing in between. One brother is stupid, the other is clever. One sister is virtuous and industrious, the others are vile and lazy. One is beautiful, the others are ugly. One parent is all good, the other evil. The juxtaposition of opposite characters is not for the purpose of stressing right behavior, as would be true for cautionary tales. (There are some amoral fairy tales where goodness or badness, beauty or ugliness play no role at all.) Presenting the polarities of character permits the child to comprehend easily the difference between the two, which he could not do as readily were the figures drawn more true to life, with all the complexities that characterize real people. Ambiguities must wait until a relatively firm personality has been established on the basis of positive identifications. Then the child has a basis for understanding that there are great differences between people, and that therefore one has to make choices about who one wants to be. This basic decision, on which all later personality development will build, is facilitated by the polarizations of the fairy tale.

Furthermore, a child's choices are based, not so much on right versus wrong, as on who arouses his sympathy and who his antipathy. The more simple and straightforward a good character, the easier it is for a child to identify with it and to reject the bad other. The child identifies with the good hero not because of his goodness, but because the hero's condition makes a deep positive appeal to him. The question for the child is not "Do I want to be good?" but "Who do I want to be like?" The child decides this on the basis of projecting himself wholeheartedly into one character. If this fairy-tale figure is a very good person, then the child decides that he wants to be good, too.

Amoral fairy tales show no polarization or juxtaposition of good and bad persons; that is because these amoral stories serve an entirely different purpose. Such tales or type figures as "Puss in Boots," who arranges for the hero's success through trickery, and Jack, who steals the giant's treasure, build character not by promoting choices between good and bad, but by giving the child the hope that even the meekest can succeed in life. After all, what's the use of choosing to become a good person when one feels so insignificant that he fears he will never amount to anything? Morality is not the issue in these tales, but rather, assurance that one can succeed. Whether one meets life with a belief in the possibility of mastering its difficulties or with the expectation of defeat is also a very important existential problem.

The deep inner conflicts originating in our primitive drives and our violent emotions are all denied in much of modern children's literature, and so the child is not helped in coping with them. But the child is subject to desperate feelings of loneliness and isolation, and he often experiences mortal anxiety. More often than not, he is unable to express these feelings in words, or he can do so only by indirection: fear of the dark, of some animal, anxiety about his body. Since it creates discomfort in a parent to recognize these emotions in his child, the parent tends to overlook them, or he belittles these spoken fears out of his own anxiety, believing this will cover over the child's fears.

The fairy tale, by contrast, takes these existential anxieties and dilemmas very seriously and addresses itself directly to them: the need to be loved and the fear that one is thought worthless; the love of life, and the fear of death. Further, the fairy tale offers solutions in ways that the child can grasp on his level of understanding. For example, fairy tales pose the dilemma of wishing to live eternally by occasionally concluding: "If they have not died, they are still alive." The other ending—"And they lived happily ever after"—does not for a moment fool the child that eternal life is possible. But it does indicate that which alone can take the sting out of the narrow limits of our time on this earth: forming a truly satisfying bond to another. The tales teach that when one has done this, one has reached the ultimate in emotional security of existence and permanence of relation available to man; and this alone can dissipate the fear of death. If one has found true adult love, the fairy story also tells, one doesn't need to wish for eternal life. This is suggested by another ending found in fairy tales: "They lived for a long time afterward, happy and in pleasure."

An uninformed view of the fairy tale sees in this type of ending an unrealistic wish-fulfillment, missing completely the important message it conveys to the child. These tales tell him that by forming a true interpersonal relation, one escapes the separation anxiety which haunts him (and which sets the stage for many fairy tales, but is always resolved at the story's ending). Furthermore, the story tells, this ending is not made possible, as the child wishes and believes, by holding on to his mother eternally. If we try to escape separation anxiety and death anxiety by desperately keeping our grasp on our parents, we will only be cruelly forced out, like Hansel and Gretel.

Only by going out into the world can the fairy-tale hero (child) find himself there; and as he does, he will also find the other with whom he will be able to live happily ever after; that is, without ever again having to experience separation anxiety. The fairy tale is future-oriented and guides the child—in terms he can understand in both his conscious and his unconscious mind—to relinquish his infantile dependency wishes and achieve a more satisfying independent existence.

Today children no longer grow up within the security of an extended family, or of a well-integrated community. Therefore, even more than at the times fairy tales were invented, it is important to provide the modern child with images of heroes who have to go out into the world all by themselves and who, although originally ignorant of the ultimate things, find secure places in the world by following their right way with deep inner confidence.

The fairy-tale hero proceeds for a time in isolation, as the modern child often feels isolated. The hero is helped by being in touch with primitive things—a tree, an animal, nature—as the child feels more in touch with those things than most adults do. The fate of these heroes convinces the child that, like them, he may feel outcast and abandoned in the world, groping in the dark, but, like them, in the course of his life he will be guided step by step, and given help when it is needed. Today, even more than in past times, the child needs the reassurance offered by the image of the isolated man who nevertheless is capable of achieving meaningful and rewarding relations with the world around him.

FAIRY TALES—WITHOUT APOLOGIES
Leslie Fiedler

Bruno Bettelheim has long been respected as a healer of troubled children as well as a passionate polemicist, so it is good to have him come out so unequivocally on the side of fairy tales. And what makes it even better is that he turns out to read them well, to take them seriously, and quite genuinely to love them. He thinks, perhaps, that they provide ways of going (permanently) sane rather than (temporarily) mad, which seems to me wrong; but maybe he only thinks he thinks so. Besides, the form has many other defenders at the moment, including unreconstructed horror fans like me (in the course of raising my children, I have worn out three copies of the complete Grimm and—now that they are grown—am wearing out a fourth on my own). My children, as a matter of fact, not only still read fairy tales, but write them, too—like other of their contemporaries who, though they may not have been lucky enough to have been exposed to Grimm, have moved on from Walt Disney to J.R.R. Tolkien, blissfully unaware that such fantasy is supposed to be left behind with childhood.

Fairy tales should need no apologists, on Bettelheim's side or ours, since they represent story in its primordial form, and their history is, therefore, coterminous with the history of that story-telling animal, man. Yet something has gone wrong, for there are parents now who need to be argued into reading them to their kids. And there are young people who grew up in households where all fairy tales were banned; so that they had to seek the satisfactions they provide by saving their pennies to buy bootleg comic books, or by switching from the "educational" channel on TV when no adults were watching.

I have a hunch that the invention of the printing press lies at the root of it all. When the old stories were put in print, they became—or at least threatened to become—"literature," and began running into difficulties that they might have avoided if they had continued to "know their place," i.e., stayed in the oral tradition. It was in the late 17th century that the French academician Charles Perrault published a collection of his own favorites, including such hair-raisers as "Little Red Riding Hood" and "Bluebeard," which until then had been enjoyed only by those denied the privilege of literacy. Though he pretended that his book was composed not by himself but by his son, it was clearly intended for full-grown literates, more particularly courtiers with a taste for cultural slumming, or what we now call "camp." So successful was his effort that within a few years the writing down of such stories and the making up of new ones on their model, ever more elaborate and ironical, had become the rage. Indeed, before the century was over, an immense collection called the *Cabinet des Fées* had been put into print, chiefly by the kind of

Leslie Fiedler, "Fairy Tales—Without Apologies," *Saturday Review* 15 May 1976. Fiedler, an English professor and literary critic, is the author of a number of iconoclastic literary/social analyses, including *An End to Innocence: Essays on Culture and Politics* (1955) and *Love and Death in the American Novel* (1960).

court ladies who also considered it chic to play Blind Man's Bluff and go on picnics dressed as shepherdesses.

The aristocratic audience may not have been aware that what they really sought in such stories, and in the longer prose romances based on their themes and motifs, was the primitive, the magical, and the horrific, otherwise denied them by the pattern of their lives. But perhaps that unawareness was a precondition for the re-entry of such material into polite literature, from which it presumably had been exiled, first by Christianity and then by courtly notions of decorum. To be sure, once the *ancien régime* had fallen, the new ruling classes—less frivolous and more pious than their predecessors—turned against all fiction that dealt with the "marvelous" rather than the "real world." But scholarship and nationalism conspired to help smuggle it back into respectability once more. This happened first of all in Germany, where the Grimm brothers thought they had discovered the roots of their own national culture in the naive mythology of the *Volk*, and resolved therefore to reproduce their "household stories" without the literary emendations or condescending asides that characterized Perrault and his followers.

What they succeeded in doing was to encourage a new literary movement, international in its influence, though this time fully Romantic rather than merely pastoral. Soon after their first published stories had appeared, young German writers like Goethe and Novalis began composing *Kunstmärchen* ("artistic fairy tales"), as part of the ongoing campaign to subvert the Age of Reason in the name of Wonder, Ecstasy, and the "Dark Sublime." Obviously their stories were addressed to adults, primarily the "maddies" of the time, which is to say those most experimental, adventurous, and revolutionary in both art and life-style. But the Grimm brothers had called the tales they collected "Children's Stories" as well as "Household Stories," subscribing to a myth of the fairy tale already present in the frontispiece of Perrault's *Tales of My Mother Goose*, which shows an old woman telling tales by the fireside to a group of youngsters. Indeed, the fairy tale was first brought into upper-class houses from the countryside by old servants, who were taken seriously only by the very young.

It was not until later Victorian times, that age of cultural ghettoization, that *Märchen* were totally remanded to the nursery, and adults could enjoy them only by reading them aloud to their children. It was perhaps the sole way a form so essentially subversive of bourgeois morality and high culture could survive in that troubled era—an era characterized on the one hand by an eruption into print of all that was most brutally repressed in the human psyche, yet possessed on the other by a desire to distinguish such material from belles lettres or Great Books. The explicitly erotic was driven deep underground, along with the works of sadomasochistic occultists like Alistair Crowley; while horror tales only implicitly sexual, like *Dracula*, were classified as trash and left to the new demiliterate pop audience. Other profoundly disturbing but encoded works—ranging from Lewis Carroll's *Alice* books, through the nonsense poetry of Edward Lear, to the traditional fairy tale—were redefined as "children's literature": an indulgence for those who did not yet know better but, unlike the subliterate masses, someday might.

The last strategy, however, backfired. Pedagogical notions of what was proper for children changed rapidly throughout the era, culminating in Freud's revelations about infant sexuality and aggression. Even while it was still officially taught that children were "innocent," there were some who argued that the more gruesome fairy tales were an offense against that innocence. Before Dickens's death, in 1865, in fact, a campaign that threatened to censor Grimm and Perrault out of existence had already been mounted. It proved possible to save the genre for the nursery by bowdlerizing, sentimentalizing, and especially Christianizing it. One did not have to go as far as George Cruikshank, who passed from illustrating Grimm to rewriting "Cinderella" as a temperance tract. Indeed, if one were canny enough, he could—like Hans Christian Andersen and George MacDonald—preserve the essential ir-rationality and horror of the form by providing endings to such stories, not neces-sarily happy, but compatible with Christian morality and the sentimental conviction that a good cry cleansed the soul. Meanwhile, folktales from around the world were collected, translated, and published by scholars like Andrew Lang, who helped make now-forgotten stories out of the *Cabinet des Fées* into Victorian house-hold favorites, even as he was founding the English Folklore Society.

Fortunately for him, European fairy tales were not explicitly erotic—as was, for example, *The Thousand and One Nights*. Their basic appeal was to buried fantasies of murder and cannibalism, beheading and evisceration, dreams of bloody revenge against favored siblings, cruel parents, and oppressive rulers. And though Jack the Ripper had shaken up the age, in the late 19th century there did not yet exist a deep physical revulsion from violence equivalent to that felt toward sex. Ironically, it was the teachings of Freud—understood, half-understood, misunderstood—as well as two world wars and the rise and fall of Hitler, that produced a squeamishness about death equal to the Victorian disgust in the face of love. There was a conse-quent desire to control not just its overt expression (about which it proved possible to do very little) but its reflection in the arts (which were much more easily con-trolled). The middle Fifties of this century saw the climax of an unprecedented campaign of total suppression, a cold war on Thanatos, which began by banning horror comic books and ended either by driving fairy tales at long last from the nursery or by expurgating them as the price of remaining.

A generation or two of children grew up, therefore, being told that the Wolf had never swallowed Red Riding Hood and her Grandmother, but that they had taken refuge in a convenient closet; just as earlier those same children had been led to believe that the bough never broke and the cradle never fell, whatever the nursery rhyme claimed. The new censors were not evil-intentioned haters of life.

THE WORLD OF FAIRY TALES
Ethel Johnston Phelps

. . . Active heroines are not common among the folk tales that survived by finding their way into print; and it is the printed survivals that are the main sources of the tales we know today. Since these tales come from the body of folk tale literature that began to be translated into English in the nineteenth century, they reflect a Western European bias. It is therefore not possible to say that the observations made here apply to all folk literature, but only to the published tales we have inherited.

The overwhelming majority of these tales present males as heroes with girls and women in minor or subservient roles; or they feature young women like Cinderella and Sleeping Beauty, who passively await their fate. Only rarely, scattered among the surviving tales, do we find stories of girls and women who are truly heroines, who take the leading part and solve the problems posed by the adventure. It must be remembered, of course, that out of the enormous literature of oral folk tales, including every culture around the globe and reaching back well over a thousand years, many tales were lost during the centuries of verbal transmission. What proportion of these "lost" tales might have featured active heroines can only be a matter of conjecture.

The awakening nationalism of the nineteenth century brought a sudden surge of interest in the oral tales of the common people. Their tales were seen as a vanishing national heritage that should be collected and preserved. The Grimm brothers began this task with the publication of *Nursery and Household Tales* in 1812; other European and British scholars soon followed.

Only a few women published collections of local tales in the nineteenth century. Almost all the folk tale collectors of the period were well-educated males of a different social class from the rural storytellers they solicited. For Europeans collecting in Asia and Africa, the factor of color and race would be additional impediments to securing truly representative tales.

Folklorists Andrew Lang, George W. Dasent, and Stith Thompson, for example, wrote of the difficulties all folklorists experienced in collecting tales. Although women, particularly elderly women, were "the repositories of these national treasures" (a nation's folk tales) and the best sources of fairy and supernatural tales, some rural women were reported as unwilling to divulge their store of tales to the collector, for fear of ridicule. These reports referred to various areas of Europe, but the same note is made by Sarah F. Bourhill and Beatrice L. Drake, who published tales gathered in South Africa around the turn of the century. Among South African blacks, they noted, women were most often the village storytellers; however, the

Ethel Johnston Phelps, "The World of Fairy Tales" [our title], *Tatterhood and Other Tales* (Old Westbury, New York: Feminist Press, 1978). *Tatterhood* is a collection of fairy tales with strong and resourceful heroines. A later book, *Maid of the North: Feminist Folk Tales from Around the World* (1981), is a similar collection.

women told Bourhill and Drake that they feared ridicule if they told their tales to whites.

Many women did, of course, recite their tales to collectors. But the reticence of some suggests, at the very least, that the tales they were willing to recite were probably those they felt would be socially acceptable and pleasing to the collector. Taking such factors into account, it seems likely that although the preservation and oral transmission of folk tales had for centuries been shared by rural women and men, a much smaller proportion of the tales women knew were collected, recorded, and published. The scarcity of heroic women and girls in the folk tales available today may be one consequence.

Nevertheless, women have always been deeply involved in preserving and transmitting this body of marvelously imaginative folk material. They enjoyed and retold the tales while working or at leisure. Their repertory was often large, and they performed with skill as storytellers, passing on the tales to succeeding generations of women. The phrase, "old wives' tales," now used derisively, takes on a new and more positive meaning—for the "old wives' tales" were, indeed, the very rich and varied source of each nation's heritage of folk literature.

A few folk tales were published in the eighteenth century specifically for children, but it was not until the latter half of the nineteenth century that the tales definitely became a part of children's literature. Andrew Lang's many volumes of fairy tales attained great popularity. It is worth noting, in the present context, that although Andrew Lang selected the stories, it was Leonora Alleyne Lang, his wife, who translated, adapted, and retold for young readers the bulk of the collection, which eventually ran to over three hundred stories. Young women relatives and friends contributed the remaining tales. At the end of the preface to each of the books, Andrew Lang made specific acknowledgment of all these contributions. "My part," he wrote, "has been that of Adam . . . in the garden of Eden. Eve worked, Adam superintended. I also superintend. . . . I find out where the stories are and advise." However, Andrew Lang never saw fit to include his wife's name on the title page along with his own.

The Lang fairy tale books, like all collections of this kind, were retold tales. . . . Adult readers are sometimes troubled by the retelling of folk tales, feeling that they should not be "tampered with." But which version of a tale is authentic, and what is meant by "tampering" is not altogether clear.

In fact, the one thing that is certain about traditional folk tales is that they have been constantly retold, with new tellers changing details and emphasis to suit both the times and the local audience. Most of the tales exist in many versions or variants, often appearing in different countries, sometimes in different areas of one country. There is no one "authentic" version of a folk tale. . . .

In the distant past, the art of storytelling was a major source of community and family entertainment; and the tales were used and perceived in certain ways not central to present-day needs. Then as now, they offered a temporary escape from reality into the realm of fancy, distracting the mind and stimulating the imagination. Sometimes the tales served to explain or rationalize the terrors of the inexplicable and the unknown physical world. Because their themes echoed the accumulated experiences and beliefs of a people's past, they were capsules of folk wisdom, teaching and redefining moral and social values. Promoting messages by implication, rather than by obvious moralizing, they provided food for thought and discussion.

Encounters with the supernatural usually provide the action in these adventure tales. But whether the plot deals with supernatural creatures or humans, the problems posed test the character of the protagonists. Even though magic or wise advice may help them, it is their heroic qualities of courage or compassion, or their pluck or daring or wit, that enables them to combat successfully the varied forces of "evil." These forces may be greater or lesser, ranging from the cannibalistic giant in "Mastermaid" to the odious squire in "The Squire's Bride." Characteristically, folk tales imply that goodness will triumph over "evil."

Although the positive traits displayed by the successful protagonist still have meaning today, it is apparent that the social customs in the old tales, as well as some of their values, are outdated. How is it then that they continue to attract and entertain a contemporary audience? One answer is that a good adventure story dealing with the supernatural will always find an audience. The taste for adventures with the irrational and unknown, as well as the need for escape from reality, has not declined, but seems to fulfill a universal need in both adults and children. Some literary qualities of the folk tales, too, are timeless—the impudent humor of "The Legend of Knockmany" or "The Squire's Bride," for example. And in the underlying themes of the tales we find a comment on personal and social questions that still concern us: how couples conduct their relationships; how old women face threatening circumstances; how young men and women set about solving dilemmas perplexing to themselves or to the community. Although the themes are played out in a realm of magic spells, giants, fairies, and hobgoblins, the imaginative experience can be the yeast of creative thought that carries over to a more prosaic world. This, too, may be among the reasons that folk tales are one of the few forms of children's stories enjoyed by "children of all ages."

Folk tales also serve to provide a continuing link with the past, both in the sense of a heritage shared with many, and as a part of the individual's personal past—for it is usually the adult who enjoyed folk tales as a child who is eager to pass on to children the same enjoyment.

The emotional satisfaction children derive from the tales arises not only from the protagonist's achievement of success or good fortune against odds, but in seeing justice meted out to evildoers—as it often is to children themselves when they misbehave. Reassured by the traditional happy endings of fairy tales, children can delight in the perilous adventures.

Not all the tales that survive today exemplify the merits just discussed, nor do they meet with the wholehearted approval of parents and teachers. Cruelty and violence in the tales have been a subject of concern for some time. More recently, feminists have criticized the tales for their overemphasis on physical attractiveness, as well as the predominance of female characters who are meek and passive or heartlessly evil.

The danger—or value—of cruelty and violence in children's fiction is, of course, a controversial subject, encompassing television fare and comic books as well as classic literature. Among folk tale collectors, the Grimm brothers have been singled out most often for criticism of the goriness of their collections. It is useful to remember, however, that folk tales were originally shaped for an adult audience, and one that has long since vanished. Many of the descriptive details of folk tales reflect the period and the attitudes of the societies from which they sprang. These details are not sacred, nor does the alteration of them generally affect the basic theme, plot, and characters of the tale. What is important to a tale's meaning is that justice be done unambiguously—a consideration that does not invariably require adopting all of the retributive details of the source. It is not surprising that changed attitudes toward cruel and unusual punishments should influence choices among the tales and the way they are retold. . . .

While feminist critics have raised objections to the convention of the heroine's surpassing beauty, there is not general agreement on this point. Some commentators suggest that the heroine's beauty is not the surface perfection of eyes, complexion, and hair, but the whole beauty of a joyous and radiant person, a symbol of inner beauty of character and personality. This interpretation of outer beauty, however, is an adult concept that may not be held by the average child; and certainly, for many children, it is discouraging to read that all heroines are extremely beautiful. More important, to be valued primarily for her beauty demeans the other qualities a heroine may possess. Although elements of extraordinary beauty, like those of extraordinary cruelty and violence, are an integral part of some plots, in many tales these are embellishments that can be dropped without affecting the story.

However, while it is possible to revise some elements of folk tales without destroying their integrity, the fact remains that the largest number of them portray girls and women unfavorably. We would not want all fictional images of women to be uniformly—and unrealistically—admirable. What is troubling is that although stereotypes of both sexes are common in folk tales, there is a marked pervasiveness of older women as frightening hags or evil crones, and of young women and girls as helpless or passive creatures. There are too few surviving tales of likable old women and active, resourceful young women to provide a balanced assortment. . . .

Besides objecting to the folk tale conventions mentioned above, some adult readers question the relevance of the omnipresent queens, kings, princes, and princesses to the world of contemporary children. To children, however, as to the country folk who developed the tales, these rulers are symbols of might and wealth. As such, they represent power far beyond a child's command. At the same time, these royal beings move in a fanciful world easily entered by children, as by the rural audience that heard the tales.

For the queens, kings, princes, and princesses of the tales bear little resemblance to any royalty, then or now. Rather, they resemble the well-to-do landowner, farmer, and squire who were in fact the ruling class of the local countryside in Western Europe. Their actions and behavior are those of a prosperous landowner's family. A prince goes to the castle stable to saddle his own horse, a princess hires herself out as a menial servant, another is sent off to buy fresh eggs; a rajah listens to a poor barber's plea and gives him a piece of land—and so on. The "kingdoms" are very small, about the size of a village, and a day's walk often brings the protagonist to another "kingdom." This is a world not only within the grasp of the rural tellers—it is a world that a child's limited experience can comprehend.

The society depicted is usually simple; and in this simple, altogether fictional world, peasants and potentates intermingle and converse, moving apparently with little difficulty from one social level to another. Sometimes high rank or riches are achieved through cleverness, sometimes through an advantageous marriage. Whatever the specific device, it is the virtues and abilities of the protagonist that bring the material rewards so often included in the happy ending.

Marriage is also a traditional happy ending, and one that may appear outmoded measured by the standards of adults who wish to promote respect for the status of single persons of both sexes. Such a progressive view has in fact made headway, supported by the economics of an urban society. The tales, on the other hand, came out of the experience of a rural people concerned with problems of survival and the hopes and fears related to it. Marriage brought the establishment of one's own household and the continuity of offspring, conferring a settled place in the social and economic structure—all of which were necessary for rural survival and prosperity in earlier centuries. Thus, the marrying-and-living-happily-ever-afterward symbolizes all the material, social, and personal rewards achieved by the protagonist, whether male or female; to alter it in such cases would be to rob the tale of its meaning. The marriage ending reflects negatively on women in the general run of folk tales only because the "heroine" does little except sit, wish and wait for this goal, with no power over her fate and no active involvement in choosing or planning the circumstances of her future life. . . .

MY STEPMOTHER, MYSELF
Garrison Keillor

SNOW

The story the press told was that I was in a life-threatening situation as a child and that the primary causal factor was my stepmother's envy. I can see now that there were other factors, and that *I* didn't give *her* much reinforcement—but anyway, the story was that I escaped from her and was taken in by dwarves and she found me and poisoned me with an apple and I was dead and the prince fell in love with me and brought me back to life and we got married, etcetera, etcetera. And that is what *I* believed right up to the day I walked out on him. I felt like I owed my life to Jeff because he had begged the dwarves for my body and carried it away and so the apple was shaken loose from my throat. That's why I married him. Out of gratitude.

As I look back on it, I can see that that was a very poor basis for a relationship. I was traumatized, I had been lying in a coffin under glass for *years*, and I got up and married the first guy I laid eyes on. The big prince. My hero.

Now I can see how sick our marriage was. He was always begging me to lie still and close my eyes and hold my breath. He could only relate to me as a dead person. He couldn't accept me as a living woman with needs and desires of my own. It is terribly hard for a woman to come to terms with the fact that her husband is a necrophiliac, because, of course, when it all starts, you aren't aware of what's going on—you're dead.

In trying to come to terms with myself, I've had to come to terms with my stepmother and her envy of my beauty, which made our relationship so destructive. She was a victim of the male attitude that prizes youth over maturity when it comes to women. Men can't dominate the mature woman, so they equate youth with beauty. In fact, she *was* beautiful, but the mirror (which, of course, reflected that male attitude) presented her with a poor self-image and turned her against me.

But the press never wrote the truth about that.

Or about the dwarves. All I can say is that they should have been named Dopey, Sleepy, Slimy, Sleazy, Dirty, Disgusting, and Sexist. The fact is that I *knew* the apple was poisoned. For me, it was the only way out.

Garrison Keillor, "My Stepmother, Myself," *Atlantic* March 1982. Keillor is the host of Prairie Home Companion, a weekly live radio show, which is broadcast by National Public Radio. Keillor has written a recent best seller, *Lake Wobegone Days* (1985), which is a fictional description of a small town in Minnesota.

SUGGESTIONS FOR WRITING

Informal Essays

1. Write an essay in which you describe your childhood reaction to a particular fairy tale. Certain episodes and images probably stuck in your mind, others disappeared. Try to analyze why those particular images stuck with you.
2. Discuss why you think that fairy tales continue to fascinate children.
3. Explain why you think that gory and violent episodes make up so large a part of fairy tales.
4. If you can remember the Disney version of *Snow White* in some detail, write an essay in which you contrast it with the Grimm version that is reprinted as the first selection in this chapter. Try to explain the differences as well as describe them.
5. Explain what Garrison Keillor is getting at in his parody of *Snow White*.

Short Documented Papers

1. Discuss what you think the effect of fairy tales is on children. Along the way, mention the arguments by Ethel Johnston Phelps and Russell Kirk.
2. After reading a few essays from this chapter, argue with Russell Kirk's view that fairy tales are good for children.
3. Contrast the views of Russell Kirk and Ethel Johnston Phelps.
4. After reading a few of the essays in this chapter, pick out what you see as a particularly weak argument of the effect of fairy tales on children. Discuss its vulnerabilities.

Longer Documented Papers

1. Write a research argument in which you defend the side of those who say that fairy tales have an unhealthy effect on children. As you argue, take into account the arguments of the other sides.
2. In another research argument defend the side of those who say that fairy tales have a healthy effect on children.
3. Write an even-handed research report in which you describe the major points made by critics on both sides of the controversy over whether fairy tales are good or bad for children.

· 8 ·

Obscenity:
To Censor or Not?

The controversy that swirls around the issue of the censorship of obscenity settles on three questions: What is it? (If it is not possible to define obscenity with any precision, we might end up censoring serious literature and art along with hardcore pornography.) What is its effect? (If its effect is baneful, perhaps it should be censored. If its effect is benign or beneficent, perhaps it should be distributed freely.) Should it be protected under the First Amendment to the Constitution?

It's not surprising that such difficult questions often must be debated in U.S. courts. In fact, the essays in this chapter contain so many allusions to famous obscenity trials that the best help we can offer is to describe a few of these trials.

The first trial didn't occur in the United States at all. In the eighteenth and nineteenth centuries, U.S. judges had the habit of going back to English law to look for precedents. One of these precedents was the case known as *Queen* v. *Hicklin* (1868). In Wolverhampton, England, a local magistrate, Justice Benjamin Hicklin, declared that an anti-Catholic pamphlet ("The Confessional Unmasked; shewing the depravity of the Romish priesthood . . .") was legally obscene. The Hicklin decision established two important precedents for U.S. obscenity trials before the early 1930s: tests for obscenity could be based on the possibility that the material would tend to corrupt anyone who might come in contact with it, including children, and obscenity overrides other values, including a book's literary, scientific, or artistic merits.

It wasn't until the 1930s that U.S. courts began to move away from the *Hicklin* definition of what is legally obscene. In a famous 1934 obscenity trial, *United States* v. *One Book Entitled Ulysses*, Judge John Woolsey ignored *Hicklin* entirely when he ruled that James Joyce's novel, *Ulysses*, was not obscene.

Until the *Ulysses* trial, books were banned on the basis of isolated passages; Woolsey ruled that a book could be ruled obscene based only on the effect of the entire book. Before the *Ulysses* trial, the law took into account the effect that obscene materials might have on children; Woolsey declared that a book's effect on adults with "average sex instincts" was what counted, not its effect on children. (He also concluded that *Ulysses* is an "emetic" rather than an "aphrodisiac.")

In *Roth v. United States* (1957), Sam Roth was convicted of sending pornography through the mails. In this case the Supreme Court defined obscene material as that which "deals with sex in a manner appealing to the prurient interest" and offends "the common conscience of the community by present-day standards." The Court also ruled that obscenity is not protected by the "freedom of speech" safeguards in the First Amendment, though Justices Hugo Black and William Douglas dissented. Both argued that the First Amendment protected all published material, including obscenity.

Douglas and Black's literal reading of the First Amendment opened up a hornet's nest of controversy about its applicability to sexually explicit material. Indeed, Medieval Jewish scholars never expended as much intellectual energy on analyzing the Torah as lawyers, judges, civil libertarians, and conservatives have expended— especially in the last couple of decades—on analyzing the few words of the First Amendment. Here, in part, is what it says:

Congress shall make no law . . . abridging the freedom of speech, or of the press.

There are three problems connected with obscenity and the First Amendment: Did Congress intend those words to cover sexually explicit photographs and words as well as political speeches and writing? If Congress did not intend that the First Amendment protect obscenity from censorship, should the Amendment now be used to protect it? Finally, if Congress cannot censor sexually explicit materials, can the individual states do it?

Let's go back to our history. The definition of obscenity that came out of *Memoirs v. Massachusetts* (1966) made it almost impossible for the federal courts to rule that writing (as opposed to photographs and live shows) is obscene. In its consideration of the famous eighteenth century underground novel, *Fanny Hill*, the Supreme Court declared that written material is obscene only if ". . . the dominant theme of the material as a whole appeals to a prurient interest in sex; . . . the material is patently offensive . . . ; . . . the material is utterly without redeeming social value." Using that definition the Supreme Court declared that *Fanny Hill* was not obscene.

In the Supreme Court's most recent consideration of obscenity, *Miller v. California* (1973), the justices determined by a 5–4 vote that the "common conscience of the community" (see *Roth v. United States* above) need not be national. That is, the community of Murray, Kentucky, might find obscene something that New York City does not.

And that is where it stands. Since *Miller v. California*, the Supreme Court has not handed down any significant obscenity rulings. The controversy, however, continues to swirl as localities wrestle with the two latest precedents, *Memoirs v. Massachusetts* and *Miller v. California*.

If you want a broad survey of what the law allows today in sexually explicit materials, you might go first to "The X-Rated Economy" by James Cook. Although the selection was written in 1978, it is a fairly accurate description of what can be sold on the streets in large cities today.

CENSORSHIP AND THE MOVIES
Judith Crist

At the moment, the lady has lots of company and a good share of it is in high places. The lady is the one who, so the oldie goes, has phoned the police to arrest the man across the way standing around stark and staring and naked. An officer arrived but could see no one. "He's right there, officer. Just climb up on this chair, and scrunch around the window frame, and hang over a little, and you can see him."

The lady, bolstered by a Vice-Presidential declaration that "so long as Richard Nixon is President, Main Street is not going to turn into Smut Alley," is now in the forefront of the latest howl for censorship. We are experiencing the thoroughly expected and not unnatural backlash against the changing mores of the last half of the Sixties. Once again we have completed a social cycle and a social circle that has left the unperceptive with present shock. Normal progressions, accelerated beyond the speed of sight in this age of instant communication, have exploded with terrifying force. And unless the voices of sanity are ready with a reply, we may well be on the brink of the censorious Seventies—a period of retrogression that would negate the astonishing advances toward intellectual honesty and creative freedom that we have made in recent years.

These advances are not blatantly evident to the eye. But consider what an exile from this country in the Sixties would note on his return in 1970. Kurt Vonnegut Jr.'s Looseleaf, returning after eight lost years with the Ulysses-like hero of *Happy Birthday, Wanda June*, observes, "You know what gets me—how all the magazines show tits today. Used to be against the law, didn't it? Must have changed the law. . . . You know what gets me—how everybody says *fuck* and *shit* all the time now. I used to be scared shitless I'd say *fuck* or *shit* in public by accident. Now everybody says *fuck* and *shit* all the time. Something very big must have happened while we were out of the country. . . . You know what gets me—how short the skirts are. Something very important about sex must have happened while we were gone . . .'"

What happened about sex in the Sixties was simply a matter of economics and evolution as far as stage and screen and literature were concerned: a coming of age, a realism in understanding our mores, and a new freedom in the arts. There were the landmark court rulings on obscenity, the frenetic fumbling of the film industry at self-regulation, the fading of local censors, the opening of the floodgates for the exploiters, the all-too-human confusion of freedom with license—and then shock at how far we'd come so soon. From the sealed-lips coolth of Hollywood kisses, we were plunged into a wallow of hip and thigh and genitalia; from the over-dressed

Judith Crist, "Censorship and the Movies" [our title], *Censorship: For and Against*, ed. Harold Hart (New York: Hart Publishing, 1971). Crist is the former film critic for the *Today Show* (1963–73) and the past chairman for the New York Film Critics. She has also been a film critic for *T.V. Guide* and *New York Magazine*.

stage extravaganza, we were down to nudes cavorting, to smutty stories and to social statements. From the bang-bang-you're-dead of off-screen sound-effect violence, we were soaking in full-color blood baths on a small screen in our very homes.

Clark Gable's "Frankly, my dear, I don't give a damn," hard-won from the industry's censors by David Selznick in 1939, had in fewer than 30 years faded before a stream of four-, five- and seven-letter obscenities from the lovely lips of Elizabeth Taylor. Though right up to the Sixties Hollywood insisted on stuffing a jewel into the meanest belly dancer's belly button, by the Seventies there hadn't been a part of the human anatomy that had not been fully displayed on the big screen, and the amount of pubic hair on show became the industry's standard for deciding whether a teen-ager could see a film under parental escort or not at all.

At least, the startled homefolks remarked, they would not be seeing this sort of thing in the privacy of their own homes (where nudity, one gathers from the morality mavens, is strictly taboo). But by the 1970–71 television season, those very R-rated films (requiring parental escort) were being shown virtually intact on the telly; and a couple of cause celebres of the early Sixties, *Hurry Sundown* (with a phallic saxophone scene that had deeply upset the Catholics) and *The World of Suzy Wong* (a eulogy to the virtues of a Hong Kong whore from which Grauman's Chinese had barred unescorted sub-sixteeners) were telecast intact—and in prime network time yet!

All of this seems to have happened overnight, particularly in my own medium of film, where the occasional moviegoer, so long wrapped in the cottonwool of the film industry's moral hypocrisy, has experienced a decade of constant trauma. We tend to cling, first, to our peculiar puritanisms: deny the flesh with shame for the beauty of the body and permission only to watch its desecration and destruction as payment for sin. Secondly, we still believe in the mass-entertainment escapism function of the commercial films of 30 and 40 years ago. Many still think of movies as mass-manufactured fodder for the national 12-year-old mentality that filmdom ascribed to all ages. Few are fully aware of the economic revolution that has brought the independent film maker and the auteur to the forefront with personal films for individuals and special interest groups. Thus, sporadic visits to the changing film scene are unnerving even to the sophisticate. And a professional moviegoer like myself is hard put to remember that it was only ten years ago—and not in another lifetime—that we were goosefleshed by the realization that the undulating shadows at the outset of *Hiroshima, Mon Amour* were naked bodies in embrace. Today, the screen-watching workday is a rare one that has not provided a minimum of three orgasms by noon, plus a goodly detailing of sadism, masochism, homosexuality and mayhem by quitting time.

And for the eroticized enthusiast beyond the "respectable" movie houses, there are the mini-movies showing their stag and blue movies, the peep shows, the pornophoto shops, and the so-called movie-making establishments where patrons can watch the alleged filming of skin-flicks. The day of the exploiter is at hand. The bestseller lists are topped by how-to sex books, and the theaters are flooded with how-to sex movies. Much in the manner of the Hollywood Biblical which wallowed in dancing girls and violence and romance with the Good Book as its alibi, so the sexploitation flick pretends to be "documenting" the state of pornography abroad, or "educating" the inept at refinements of erotica for marital bliss, or "telling it how it is"—with a warning, of course, that lechery, like crime, doesn't pay for anyone but the smut-film maker.

Small wonder, then, that the cry for censorship had arisen in the late Sixties, and has come to a scream with the ultimate libertarianism of the President's Commission on Obscenity and Pornography whose findings were made public in October, 1970. The majority finding, that there was "no warrant for continued governmental interference with the full freedom of adults to read, obtain or view" pornographic materials, confirmed the know-nothing suspicion that the fall into the slimepit was indeed at hand.

Well, not quite. A variety of Congressional committees probing sex and violence in films and on television were still to be heard from. And simultaneously, a New York Criminal Courts judge held that *Censorship in Denmark*, a documentary that detailed Copenhagen's pornography fair for those who couldn't take the sightseeing trip for themselves, was "patently offensive to most Americans because it affronts community standards relating to the description or representation of sexual matters," and had, as its dominant theme, "a prurient interest in sex."

But the point, of course, to the consideration of censorship I am edging toward, is simply that "most Americans" are under no obligation to affront themselves by going to see *Censorship in Denmark*. They are free to exercise the only kind of censorship in which I whole-heartedly believe: self-censorship on the part of the public and, hopefully, on the part of the creator. And it is on behalf of the minority of Americans who would only not be affronted but also might be edified, or enlightened, or simply titillated by this movie that we must fight for the freedom of film.

Before we go further into what is essentially a consideration of a film and theater critic's view of censorship, I should note that far more qualified professionals—lawyers, psychologists, behavioralists, sociologists—have explored the field to a fare-thee-well. No layman could hone the legalisms as brilliantly as has Charles Rembar in *The End of Obscenity*, recounting his triumphant defenses of the publications of *Lady Chatterley, Tropic of Cancer* and *Fanny Hill*, nor as Ephraim London has in his various defenses of films, from the 1952 case of *The Miracle* which established the film as a medium rather than an industry, and, most important, as a medium and an art form entitled to the protection of the First Amendment. It was Mr. London who, at the very time the New York City police were picking up *Censorship in Denmark*, won a reversal from the United States Court of Appeals of a judgment by a lower Federal Court approving a Customs confiscation of a Swedish film *Language of Love*. I think the opinion, written for the three-man court by Circuit Judge Leonard Moore, is worth quoting in part, both for its urbanity and its principle. He describes the film as:

> a movie version of the 'marriage manual'—that ubiquitous panacea (in the view of some) for all that ails modern man-woman relations.
>
> Assuming the Masters and Johnson (*Human Sexual Response,* 1966) premise that the path to marital euphoria and social utopia lies in the perfection and practice of

clinically correct and complete sexual technology, this film offers to light that path in a way the masses can understand. It purports to be an animated Little Golden Book of marital relations, or perhaps the *Kama Sutra* of electronic media, although the film is nowhere nearly as rich in the variety of its smorgasbord of delights as comparison with that ancient Hindu classic might suggest. It may be the vulgate scripture, the Popular Mechanics of interpersonal relations, the complete cure for the ailing marriage. Or so goes the theory of its sponsors.

Language of Love stars four of what are apparently leading Scandinavian sexual technocrats, with brilliant cameo roles for the functioning flesh of various unnamed actors. . . . This film, as did *I Am Curious (Yellow)*, contains scenes of oral-genital contact and other heterosexual activity that no actor or actress would ever have confessed knowledge of in bygone days of the silver screen. Nevertheless, the movie-going public has been confronted with all of this before in recent times.

Viewing the film in its "tedious entirety," Judge Moore held it not proscribably obscene on established constitutional tests, but noted frankly that the court found several sequences offensive:

not because they excited predilections to prurience but because they intruded upon areas of interpersonal relations which we consider to be peculiarly private. Our sensibilities were offended, but that is a matter of taste and de gustibus non est disputandum, particularly in matters of sex and constitutional law.

Granted that certain scenes might have erotic appeal to the average person, the court observed, "Indeed erotic appeal has assumed a position of paramount importance, somewhat overemphasized we think, in the affairs of our daily lives," but it is not to be equated with "prurient interest." Simplistic or superficial, tedious or over-clinical though the discussion of sex might be, the film, the court found, had redeeming social value in its advocacy of ideas.

The court asked:

In final analysis is freedom of speech and expression, including exhibition of motion picture films, to be based on the opinions of 51 percent or even 80 percent of our populace? If so, it might well be that on a national plebiscite the *Language of Love, I Am Curious (Yellow), Les Amants, Memoirs of a Woman of Pleasure (Fanny Hill)* and others would all be condemned by a majority vote. Minorities would then read and see what their fellow men would decide to permit them to read and see. The shadow of 1984 would indeed be commencing to darken our horizon. . . .

The court concluded:

Whether these decisions will bring forth a more enlightened people who have lived long under sex taboos or will cause a moral degradation of the race will be for the historian. . . .

Certainly, a film historian will find an enlightened public feasting off any number of fine films of the past decade that were made possible by a relaxation of taboos. *Hiroshima, Mon Amour, The Virgin Spring, The Apartment, Elmer Gantry, The Hustler, Two Women, Divorce—Italian Style, Tom Jones, 8½, Hud, Dr. Strangelove, The Servant, Darling, Mickey One, Georgy Girl, Bonnie and Clyde, Ulysses, The Graduate, The Killing of Sister George, Last Summer, Midnight Cowboy, Women in Love, The Virgin and the Gypsy, Five Easy Pieces, Putney Swope, Going Down the Road, Brewster McCloud, Little Murders* are but a few of the films of quality that would not have been made, let alone shown to us intact, had there not been a steady erosion of censorship.

The idiocies of film censorship up to 1964 are nowhere better documented than by Murray Schumach in *The Face on the Cutting Room Floor.* He ended his chronicle as the industry was preparing for self-regulation, with a certain optimism. Had the industry settled for a simple not-for-children classification, the system might have functioned on less farcical terms than it has. The ratings start with G, which means for general consumption; M, stands for "mature," a rating abandoned (possibly on the realization that few movies could deserve that label) in favor of GP, which stands for general consumption but parental discretion advised; R, which restricts teen-agers to admission with parental or guardian escort, and X. This last designation was intended to signify adult admission only, but of course, is considered the label of the dirty movie—either to be capitalized on by the smut-men or sought out by the prurient or to be ostracized by theater managements and newspaper advertising pages catering to the bluenoses.

The politicking and juggling and bargaining over the gradations of rating has been shocking, with moviegoers misled and children misguided and the independent and minor moviemaker getting short shrift and little consideration in the rating game. In the same way, the little man has suffered from the censor; fighting a case from police precinct to the Supreme Court is a costly process and, as a result, not a democratic one.

Beyond the film historian, the sociologist and the psychologist have endlessly debated in slick magazines and learned journals whether the moral degradation of the race is upon us. There is mountainous material—none of it definitive—to prove that sex and violence are harmless and/or harmful for the young. For my part, I wish there were as much concern about shielding them from the destructive forces of real life as there is about the possible effects a film or a television show may have upon their little psyches. Children, I have found, are particularly resilient in this audio-visual age; they are no longer naive, as my generation was, about the fictional creations of film. My worry, in fact, is that they are so sophisticated about the manufacture of their entertainments that they even suspect the reality of the riots and battles they see on the news shows, half-expecting the skull-smashed demonstrator and the shattered Vietnamese soldier to wash off the makeup and show up on a game show the next day. But children should be protected from the ugliness, the inhumanity, the grostesque distortions of hard-core pornography, just as they should be protected from the sadism, the perversity, and the disregard of human values in the violent entertainments presented to them in the guise of adventure shows. This is, of course, a parental responsibility; but parents—like booksellers, theater owners, producers, and distributors—may well decline their moral responsibilities. The realist must, I fear, demand some legal restrictions where minors are concerned.

But the American adult must take responsibility for himself, with the right to exercise his own standards. The ones who shout the loudest about being "swamped" and "flooded" with filth via the mails—I often wonder why our mailbox is never defiled by even a dribble—seem never to exercise their privilege of throwing brochures away unread, twisting the dial, or heaven help us, turning off the set, or simply not going into a suspect movie. And the ones who worry most about the children are for the most part bachelors or spinsters who haven't done a day's social service in their lives, beyond, perhaps, joining a police action against a film.

I became aware of this state of affairs from the stream of police witnesses in the case against *The Killing of Sister George* in Boston, where witness after witness testified to forcing himself or herself to sit through the whole film to the near-final two-minute breast-nibbling scene between two women—all for the sake of the children they did not have. And nowhere was there anyone to contradict the exhibitor's contention that no one under the age of eighteen had been admitted to the film.

And what possible ill effect, beyond boredom, could the film or scene have had upon children? In this age of bottle-babies, I doubt that a five-year-old would have had even nostalgic yearnings in the course of the scene. Only the most naive or prudish adult might have been "offended"—but he, of course, was not obliged to attend.

Beyond the effects of violence and sex on children, the social scientists have made endless studies of the effects of pornography on crime and other anti-social actions. Again, so long as the Danes' experience has not been totally researched, the findings can be used on either side.

I remain convinced that no female has been raped by text or film and that the triggering of the psychotic mind cannot be predetermined or even pin-pointed.

I do know, however, what censorship accomplishes, creating an unreal and hypocritical mythology, formenting an attraction for forbidden fruit, inhibiting the creative minds among us and fostering an illicit trade. Above all it curtails the right of the individual, be he creator or consumer, to satisfy his intellect and his interest without harm. In our law-rooted society, we are not the keeper of our brother's morals—only of his rights.

In protecting those rights we must be Voltairean, advocating, as Holmes said, "not free thought for those who agree with us, but freedom for the thought that we hate." It's a good principle, but I must confess that I declined to testify on behalf of *I Am Curious (Yellow)* and *Language of Love.* I claimed the critic's privilege, if not the civil libertarian's, of choosing to advocate beyond pure principle on aesthetic grounds. If other critics had not been found to testify, I would have done my service—but one wearies of going to the barricades to fight for trash. I did testify on behalf of *Sister George,* a remarkably fine film, and for *491,* an earlier work by the director of *I Am Curious,* that was distinguished by honest aspiration and artistry. But my irritation with and optional withdrawal from the legalistic battles were directed purely at the censors, at the U.S. Customs officials and petty police (servants, alas, of small-minded bigoted citizens) who were completely negating their avowed purpose. Had Curious (Yellow) not become a cause celebre, it would have opened in a small art house in New York and suffered a quiet death from negative criticism and word-of-mouth. Instead, misguided but well-intentioned critics took up the cause, its ersatz sexuality was highly publicized and its shrewd importers made millions from a voyeuristic public. Even with Sister George the Boston police doubled-crossed themselves. They seized the film but had to release it immediately under an anti-prior-restraint injunction; the film had been doing good business up to then but zoomed into smash-hit status while the publicized censorship battle was fought.

It's not just the censors who publicize smut. The smart exhibitor in recent years has even capitalized on the censorious critic. The banner quote-line exploited at a theater's showing of Ingmar Bergman's The Silence back in 1964 was a lady critic's "This is the dirtiest movie I've ever seen!" and the leather jackets went pouring in, only to find themselves completely frustrated in their attempts to recognize the highly touted masturbation, intercourse, and cunnilingus scenes that the censors had debated but which Bergman's artistry hid from the pornography-minded. But let's not be snobbish. A Michigan State film society recently touted a revival of The Ape Woman by quoting me as deeming it "the depth of unappetizing movie making."

Well, the depths have been plumbed a lot deeper since that 1964 film and moviegoers are now assured that they will tremble, throw up and sweat at the ecstasies and horrors to be seen within. But we are, I suspect, reaching the end of the era of voyeurism. We have seen it all and are ready to put it in perspective. The blue-movie audience (long ago composed of the wealthy dilettante or the frat boys or the fellows at the firehouse) is made up largely of middle-aged businessmen and oldsters. The younger generation has either been there, legitimately, and taken it in stride—or couldn't care less.

One goes back to the days of one's youth, of pouring over pages 723ff in the Modern Library edition of Ulysses, of gulping down snatches of Lady Chatterley in a bootlegged brown-paper-bound edition, and of going from there into the twin-bedded cinematic world of Doris Day's eternal virginity.

The other day I came home to find my fourteen-year-old finishing Tropic of Cancer. "Boy, what a bore!" he remarked, tossing the book aside. And beyond his qualifications as a literary critic, I think him a healthier type than my contemporaries. So much, then, for the moral decline of the race.

PORNOGRAPHY, CENSORSHIP, AND COMMON SENSE
AN INTERVIEW WITH ALEXANDER BICKEL

George Denison

Q   **Professor Bickel, is pornography a serious problem?**

A   Yes, I think so. In some places the live sex act has been advertised and exhibited. New York's Times Square is a case in point—block after block of X-rated movies, peep shows, pornographic bookstores and massage parlors. This sort of thing is a total debasing of any approach to sex; it is brutalizing.

Rampant pornography raises questions about the kind of society we live in. There are those who say we may not regulate pornography or any other conduct of consenting adults. This is absurd. Like all civilized societies we have long had many rules which attempt to set moral standards and regulate sexual conduct. Regulation of pornography is not different. It is more than coincidence that societies that have decayed and collapsed—the Roman Empire is a perfect example—have generally done so in an atmosphere of steeply declining moral standards.

Q   **What about those who maintain there is no evidence that pornography can influence individuals to commit sex crimes?**

A   They are missing the point. I don't believe obscenity regulations should be supported on the basis of supposed evidence that obscenity leads directly to a particular kind of criminal conduct on the part of particular individuals. What it does produce is a moral atmosphere, and the moral atmosphere is the ultimate regulator of conduct. If something can be *said*, if it can be *shown*, if it is obviously *permitted* by society, then that society begins to think it is do-able. Deviance aside, we all tend to act within the range of what we think is tolerated by our society.

Q   **Will the recent Supreme Court decision help solve the pornography problem?**

A   The Court took pains to restrict its decision to "hard-core" pornography. To be found legally obscene under the Court's test, a work must "appeal to a prurient interest in sex" and must "portray sexual conduct in a patently offensive way." Local communities, the Court said, can apply their own standards in determining these questions. But the Court gave some "plain examples" of material that might be considered patently offensive. The examples were all of the hard-core variety.

At the same time, the Court ruled that for a book or film to be considered obscene, it must, when taken as a whole, lack "serious literary, artistic, political

George Denison, "Pornography, Censorship, and Common Sense" [an interview with Alexander Bickel], *Reader's Digest* February 1974. Bickel is Professor of Law and Legal History at Yale Law School and a widely recognized authority on Constitutional law.

or scientific value." The question of serious value, in my view, is not left to local standards or juries. Instead, it is a constitutional question to be decided ultimately by a judge, subject to review in higher courts including the Supreme Court. Therefore, if a local bluenose decides that he wants to censor, say, a novel by Norman Mailer or even *Last Tango in Paris*, he has a long row to hoe. I believe the Court decision draws the line somewhere between a *Last Tango* and an obvious exploitation film like *Deep Throat*.

Q **Some publishers and film makers claim that the Court's guidelines are so confusing that they don't know what they can publish or distribute.**

A Actually, authors and movie producers have always been faced with some uncertainty about the law. The new decision adds little to that uncertainty. The honest artist or writer who knows that his purpose is to say something of social and intellectual value is safe and has no cause for uncertainty. If he is honest with himself about the purpose of his work, the law will not restrict him. If he feels that he has to show a sexual act in detail, he will presumably know why that is part of his artistic purpose. His serious intent will have to be communicable to others; yet he will be judged on his work taken as a whole.

One or more proscribed sexual acts in a book or film will not be sufficient to make a work legally obscene if the complete work has serious value. Thus, I believe that the Georgia supreme court's finding that the film *Carnal Knowledge* is obscene does not conform to the ruling of the Supreme Court of the United States. The movie includes sex and nudity, to be sure; but the Court will judge it as a whole, and I am certain the finding of obscenity will not be upheld.

Q **What is your reaction to the civil libertarians who call the Court ruling a serious infringement on First Amendment rights?**

A It seems to me that these alarms are naïve, and perhaps willfully so. The alarms might be well founded if the Court let all obscenity questions turn on "community standards." But this is certainly not what the Court has done. The decision does not abandon the Supreme Court's role as the ultimate organ of judicial review under the Constitution. The question of the serious value of a work remains a constitutional issue. Moreover, if a jury in Podunk should find, for example, that the female leg is prurient and offensive, the Supreme Court will still have its say about that, and I should think that such outbreaks of prudishness are well beyond the leeway intended for local community standards.

Q **Others have said that the Court is trying to legislate the nation's morality.**

A Such a statement is a misunderstanding of what a judicial decision is capable of doing. The Court has simply said to states and communities, "If you wish to enforce laws against obscenity, here is the sort of thing we will uphold." The decision, by itself, makes nothing whatever happen. It takes a legislature to pass such a law, a prosecutor to enforce it and a judge and jury to find someone guilty of violating it.

The Supreme Court decision will actually have little to do with what is generally seen in movies or printed in books. Far more important is the sense of public morality—what is acceptable to the community—that prevails in our society. In the past ten years, the sense of most communities has changed.

Community standards are now considerably more permissive, and the result will be that most magazines or movies that deal with sex will not be affected in the least by the Court's guidelines. Of course, hard-core pornography such as a *Deep Throat* can be affected as the Court intended, but again only if a given community wants it to be.

Until the past decade there was actually very little constitutional law about censorship. During that state of affairs, both repressive and permissive public moods governed what we saw and heard. Through the 1920s, for example, burlesque and film nudity flourished. In the 1930s the mood changed and, quite without any new court decision, the public accepted much less in the way of explicit sex. Now the mood has changed again.

Q **Why, then, are obscenity laws necessary or desirable?**

A The role of law, in this as in some other areas, is to make a moral statement about the kind of society we wish to live in. This concerns the tone of society, the mode, the style and quality of life, now and in the future. A man may be entitled to read an obscene book in his room or expose himself indecently there. We should protect his privacy. But if he demands a right to obtain the books and pictures he wants in the market and to gather in public with others who share his tastes, then to grant him his right is to affect the world about the rest of us and to impinge on others' privacy.

Laws will not, of course, wipe all pornography off the face of the earth. But the enforcement of obscenity laws in aggravated cases will reiterate the moral statement that the law makes, and render it visible. There comes a time, and I believe we have reached it, when society is threatened by unbridled obscenity. Societies polluted by moral stench are not likely to survive. And that is why the Supreme Court decision—and the moral statement it permits law to make—are important.

WHAT IS THE CIVIL LIBERTARIAN TO DO WHEN PORNOGRAPHY BECOMES SO BOLD?

Walter Goodman

As pornography has proliferated across the land, from centers of sexual technology such as New York and Los Angeles to less advanced communities, a suspicion that something may be awry has begun to nag at even that enlightened vanguard which once strove to save Lady Chatterley from the philistines. Having opened the door to sex for art's sake, they have found that it is no longer possible to close it against sex for profit's sake.

Where does duty lie today for the dutiful civil libertarian confronted by efforts around the country to prosecute the purveyors of porn? One may wish that Al Goldstein, an avant-garde publisher of the stuff, would go away, but no civil libertarian can cheer the efforts by lawmen in Wichita, Kansas, to have him put away. One might doubt that Harry Reems, who has filled many X-rated screens, is contributing much to the art of the cinema, yet no civil libertarian wants the assistant U.S. Attorney in Memphis, Tennessee, to clap him in irons. What to do?

To grapple with this matter, I brought together two figures known to have provocative—and sharply conflicting—views on the subject: author Gay Talese, whose ongoing research for a book about sex in America includes the management of two New York City massage parlors, and psychoanalyst Ernest van den Haag, adjunct professor of social philosophy at New York University and a favorite "expert witness" of pornography prosecutors everywhere.

Our conversation began with an effort by Professor van den Haag to identify the animal which he believes ought to be locked up:

VAN DEN HAAG: I would call pornographic whatever is blatantly offensive to the standards of the community.

TALESE: But does the public have the right to ban *Ulysses* because some people find it offensive?

VAN DEN HAAG: I think anyone who reads *Ulysses* for the sake of pornographic interests ought to get a medal! The characteristic focus of pornography is precisely that it leaves out all human context and reduces the action to interaction between organs and orifices—and that I find obscene, degrading to sex and dehumanizing to its audiences.

TALESE: So if you have a picture of a girl, including the genitals, then that is pornographic.

Walter Goodman, "What Is a Civil Libertarian to Do When Pornography Becomes So Bold?" [a dialogue moderated by Walter Goodman], *New York Times* 21 November 1976, sec. 2. Gay Talese is the author of *Thy Neighbor's Wife* (1980), a description and commentary on sexual attitudes and practices in the U.S. Ernest van den Haag is a professor of social philosophy at New York University and a longtime contributor to *National Review*, a conservative magazine.

VAN DEN HAAG: Not necessarily.

TALESE: But if she's making love it would be?

VAN DEN HAAG: I'm not even opposed to that altogether. But, if the love-making picture focuses on the operation of the genitals . . .

TALESE: You mean if it shows the genitals while the love-making is going on?

VAN DEN HAAG: If the genitals are shown incidentally, that does not greatly disturb me. But if it is clearly focused on the operation of the genitals and the persons are only shown incidentally, then I think the stuff is pornographic.

TALESE: There's no agreement on a definition at all, even by the people who want to ban it. Obscenity is the *one* crime that cannot be defined. Unlike murder, burglary, forgery, the word means different things to different people—to judges, to newspaper editors, to pornographic film-makers.

VAN DEN HAAG: That's why we have courts of law and lawyers.

TALESE: And it means different things to different lawyers—it's the most imprecise of crimes.

VAN DEN HAAG: Gay, if you were to see a man walking down the street, fully clothed except that his genitals were exposed, would you regard that as obscene?

TALESE: On the issue of whether the cop on the beat has the right to stop public behavior that is unseemly and offensive we have no quarrel. But no policeman ought to have the right to stop two homosexuals in a Holiday Inn in Teaneck, New Jersey, from doing whatever they want together. They have that right, and I have the right to see a film or a play even if it is considered offensive by Sidney Baumgarten of the Mayor's Midtown Enforcement Project. I don't want policemen to tell me what is moral or immoral in my private life. I think we have too much government and where sex is concerned, I want next to no government.

VAN DEN HAAG: I certainly agree, Gay, that you or I should be allowed to indulge in sexual acts in our homes. That's our business. I am not in the least disturbed about that. But when anyone can see the spectacle we are no longer dealing with a private matter, but with a public matter.

TALESE: If I want to pay five dollars to go into a theater to go see "Deep Throat," that's a private matter.

VAN DEN HAAG: Then you regard a public spectacle as a private act.

TALESE: How about buying a book?

VAN DEN HAAG: If it is publicly available to anyone who pays the price, it's a public matter.

TALESE: So, according to you, I have the right to read *Ulysses* or *The Story of O* or *The Sex Life of a Cop* in my home—only I shouldn't be allowed to get it into my home in the first place.

VAN DEN HAAG: The police should not come into your home and check what you're reading—but the police can accuse a seller of selling something pornographic. The matter can then be brought up before a jury and if the jury feels that what the seller sold publicly is pornography, then the seller can be convicted.

TALESE: So you'd ban such magazines as *Playboy* or *Oui* or *Screw*?

VAN DEN HAAG: I have testified against *Screw* and I am in favor of banning it. As for *Playboy* and so on, I would leave those to juries in particular communities. If I'm invited as an expert to testify about the effects they will have on a particular community, I will testify that these effects are deleterious, but it is not for me to decide whether they should be prohibited or not.

GOODMAN: Ernest, why should it be any more the business of a jury what Gay likes to read or watch than it is what he likes to do in bed?

VAN DEN HAAG: Gay's view—one that is widespread—is that society consists of individuals, each independent of each other, and that the task of the government is merely to protect one individual from interference by others. That is not my view. My view is that no society can survive unless there are bonds among its members, unless its members identify with each other, recognize each other as humans and do not think of each other simply as sources of pleasure or unpleasure. For once they do, then they may come to think of people as kinds of insects. If one disturbs you, you kill it. Once you no longer recognize that a person is fully human, like yourself, you can do what the Germans did to the Jews—use the gold in their teeth. Human solidarity is based on our ability to think of each other not purely as means, but as ends in ourselves. Now the point of all pornography, in my opinion, is that it invites us to regard the other person purely as a subject of exploitation for sexual pleasure.

GOODMAN: Gay, am I right in assuming that you don't agree that pornography has such dire consequences?

TALESE: Government interference in these areas is usually justified on the grounds that obscenity is harmful to the morals of society, harmful to family life, harmful to juveniles. But in fact there is no proof that exposure to pornography leads to anti-social behavior. There is no proof that watching a pornographic movie leads anybody to go out and commit rape.

VAN DEN HAAG: You're not getting my point. I do not maintain that reading pornography leads to an increase in crime. It may, but I don't think there's conclusive evidence either way. I feel that the main damage pornography does is not to the individual but to the social climate.

TALESE: Tell me how.

VAN DEN HAAG: You and I both write books, and our books are somehow meant to influence what people feel and think. Sexual mores, you certainly will agree, have changed over the past century. Why have they changed? Basically because of the ideas of people who write books, make movies, produce things. The biology of sex hasn't changed. What has changed is our perception of it and our reaction to it. So I don't think it can be denied that books do have an influence. If that is so, we come to the question of whether the government has the right or duty to limit it. Here my point is a very simple one. Every community has a right to protect what it regards as its important shared values. In India, I would vote for the prohibition against the raising of pigs for slaughter. In the United States, where a certain amount of sexual reticence has been a central value of traditional culture, I would vote for the rights of communities to protect their sexual reticence.

TALESE: And I'm saying that the government should not have the right to deal with this "crime" that it cannot define. The Supreme Court has never been able to define what is obscene to the satisfaction of most Americans. If you are going to give government the power to tell us what is obscene and to restrict our freedom to read books, see films or look at pictures, if you give government that kind of power over the individual, you are not going to maintain a democracy.

VAN DEN HAAG: I am for freedom, too, but you ignore the fact that freedom can be used for good or bad. For instance, if the Weimar Republic had banned its political pornographers such as Hitler, then perhaps six million Jews would not have been killed. The dogmatic insistence on freedom as the only value to be protected by the government disregards such things as survival and community traditions which are essential to survival.

TALESE: But you seem to forget that Hitler himself opposed pornography. Almost the first thing he did on taking power was to ban *Ideal Marriage*, a classic work on sex and marriage.

GOODMAN: Would you put any limits at all on individual liberties in this area, Gay?

TALESE: I believe there should be censorship—in the home. I have two daughters, and in my home I do exercise censorship. I subscribe to magazines and newspapers that I do not leave on the coffee table. But I do not want government to tell me what I can have in my house or what I can have my daughters read.

VAN DEN HAAG: I congratulate you on having this family that you describe. Let me point out that many American families are not so structured. Not all parents are able to exercise such parental discipline.

GOODMAN: But isn't Gay's response to government intrusions into family life in accord with your own principles as a conservative?

VAN DEN HAAG: In an ideal society, things that we now regulate by law, would be regulated by custom and by the authority of parents. We don't live in this ideal society. The authority of parents has been undermined by all kinds of things, starting with progressive education. If we could strengthen the hand of parents and integrate families more, that would be much better. I have found no way of doing so for the time being.

TALESE: So you're willing to give this power to a policeman.

VAN DEN HAAG: I am not proposing that we trust the government with the power of censorship. I'm opposed to censorship, opposed to prior restraint which is unconstitutional. I am in favor of traditional American legislation. Whereby each state, and more recently each community, may determine for itself what it wishes and what it does not wish to be publicly sold. In each case, Ralph Ginzburg or Al Goldstein or you or anyone can publish whatever he wishes. Until the bounds have been exceeded . . .

TALESE: What bounds? It's all so hypocritical. One night these people have been at an American Legion smoker enjoying hard-core porn and the next day they are deciding to put a pornographer in jail. What a member of the jury is likely to say in public has nothing to do with the way he behaves in private. That seems to me socially unhealthy. Many of the people who would go on record to have Times Square closed down because it has too many massage parlors patronize the places. We're dealing here with something very private—sexual desires. Very private.

GOODMAN: But is the expression of these desires around an area such as Times Square really all that private? It seems pretty public to me.

TALESE: Sure, Times Square has always been a center of public entertainment. What some people can't stand is that it is today a center of entertainment for the working class instead of for the elite. There are two kinds of pornography. You have the pornography for the working man, like the 42nd Street peep shows, and you have the "legitimate theater," where the elite can see "Let My People Come," "Oh, Calcutta!" or the works of Edward Albee or Arthur Miller or Tennessee Williams. The government does not as readily interfere with the pornography of the elite as it does with the pornography of the man who buys his magazine at the corner newsstand, which is the museum of the man in the street, or the man who pays 25 cents to see copulating couples in a coin-operated machine. Pornography is primarily denied to the blue collar classes. That has always been the case. Strong government tries always to control the masses—just as much in China and Cuba as in Times

	Square. The people who get their pleasure from going to an art gallery to look at Goya's "The Naked Maja" aren't bothered by government.
GOODMAN:	Ernest, under your definition of pornography, is there any difference between a picture of a copulating couple on a museum wall and in the centerfold of a girly magazine?
VAN DEN HAAG:	Yes, effect and intent are different, and I think the courts are correct in taking the context into consideration. That is, if Hugh Hefner had put "The Naked Maja" in Playboy a few years ago, it might have become pornographic in that context though Goya had not intended it that way.
TALESE:	So pornography is all right for the elite, but not for the working man.
VAN DEN HAAG:	It may appear that way, but the reason, as you yourself pointed out, is that the working man gets his pornography in a more public way. A theater at which you've made a reservation and paid $10 is much less public than the 25-cent arcade; therefore, there is more justification, if you are against pornography, to intervene against one than against the other.
GOODMAN:	You don't deny, Gay, that Times Square has in fact become a place of public pornography.
TALESE:	Yes, our sensibilities are assaulted. I wish the 42nd Street pornographer would be more subtle. But people have as much right to put a quarter in a machine as to pay $5 for "Deep Throat" or $10 for "Let My People Come." I do not want to give to law enforcement officials the right to clean up Times Square, to deny pornography to those who want it. If crimes are being committed, people being mugged, that should be prevented. But nobody is forced to go into a peep show or a massage parlor or to pay for sex with a prostitute.
GOODMAN:	I take it you're opposed to laws against prostitution.
TALESE:	I would really like to see prostitution legalized, but I know that would be the worst thing for prostitution, because it would mean that women would have to be fingerprinted.
VAN DEN HAAG:	You would simply decriminalize it.
TALESE:	I would like to see that happen.
GOODMAN:	And you, Ernest?
VAN DEN HAAG:	For call girls yes; for street prostitution no.
GOODMAN:	Isn't that a trifle elitist, as Gay terms it?
VAN DEN HAAG:	No. A call girl is an entirely private proposition. You call her. In the case of the street prostitute, the initiative must come from the soliciting girl, and that makes a difference.
TALESE:	Have you ever been assaulted by a prostitute on the street? All the girls do is ask a question.
VAN DEN HAAG:	There's more to it than that. In the United States, for some reason, prostitution has always been connected with crime.

The sort of thing that exists around Times Square attracts not only prostitutes and their customers, but people who prey on prostitutes and customers and make the whole area unsafe. I believe that crime must not only be prosecuted; it must also be prevented.

TALESE: What offends the white New Yorker, the customer on his way to the bus terminal, about Times Square is that he walks through the neighborhood and sees the great number of blacks there—the black prostitutes and black pimps. That's what makes people fearful. There is more crime all over the country today, but it has nothing to do with prostitutes working Eighth Avenue. You see, I don't think it's a crime to have sex with a person. The prostitutes are there, on the street in great numbers, because men—not the children Ernest is legitimately concerned about but middle class married white men—want them. For some reason, they find prostitutes necessary. That's their private affair. I don't want to have Times Square become acceptable to Franco Spain. I don't want government to clean it up.

VAN DEN HAAG: You're saying that people should be allowed to have what they want. But should people be forced to have what they don't want? Suppose that a town in Ohio votes that it doesn't want prostitutes on its streets or pornographic movies? You are in favor of pornography in principle, regardless of what the majority wants.

TALESE: I am in favor of freedom of expression.

VAN DEN HAAG: The men who wrote Article I of the Bill of Rights intended to make sure that the government would not suppress opposition. They did not intend to include such things as pornography.

TALESE: They wrote that Congress shall make no law abridging freedom of speech or the press; they didn't add, "except when it comes to sexual expression."

GOODMAN: Gentlemen, I am not sure how much light we have shed on pornography but your respective positions are clear as day. And I thank you.

OBSCENITY—FORGET IT
Charles Rembar

There is, rather suddenly, a resurgence of interest in the legal field that goes by the name "obscenity." Not that it ever lacked for interest. The conjunction of sex and politics is irresistible. But now there is more than interest; there is consternation—on the part of those who fear for our morality, on the part of those who fear the First Amendment will founder on the convictions of Harry Reems and Larry Flynt.

I suggest we abandon the word obscenity. I do not mean that the law should ignore all the many and varied things that legislatures and courts have tried to deal with under this rubric. My suggestion rather is that we drop the word and turn our attention to the social interests actually involved. Then, perhaps, some sensible law-making and law enforcement will follow.

The law is verbal art. It depends for its effectiveness on compact, muscular words; overgrown, flabby words are useless in the law, worse than useless—confusing, damaging. "Obscene" as a description of the morally outrageous or the intellectually monstrous continues to be useful (and generally has little to do with sex). "Obscene" for legal purposes should be discarded altogether. It carries an impossible burden of passionate conviction from both sides of the question. And it diverts attention from real issues. The present litigation over what is called obscenity involves serious public concerns which the word obscures and distorts.

Draw back a bit. Exactly eleven years ago a battle against literary censorship came to a close. What had been censored, for three hundred years, was called, in law, obscenity. Obscenity in its traditional sense—impermissible writing about sex, impermissible either because of what it described or because of the words that were used—was at an end. Writers would be able to write as they pleased on the subject of sex, and use whatever language they thought best. They would no longer have to keep a mind's eye on the censor; they could pay full attention to their art and ideas. The field of legal struggle would move to other forms of expression—films, the stage, television, photography.

So much has changed in the last eleven years that one who had not lived through earlier times would find the freedom that writers now enjoy unremarkable. Yet in the few decades just then ended, such works as Dreiser's *An American Tragedy*, Lillian Smith's *Strange Fruit*, and Edmund Wilson's *Memoirs of Hecate County* had been the subjects of successful criminal prosecution. Recently, in contrast, there has been no suppression of books at all. Obscenity prosecutions are now directed at motion pictures and stage performances and magazines (the last not for their words but for their pictures).

The contest concluded in 1966 was essentially between accepted sexual morality (which sought to govern what was expressed as well as what was done) and the

Charles Rembar, "Obscenity—Forget It," *The Atlantic* May 1977. Rembar, a lawyer, is the author of *The End of Obscenity: The Trials of "Lady Chatterley," "Tropic of Cancer" and "Fanny Hill"* (1968); he successfully defended the publication of the three books mentioned in the title.

guaranties of the First Amendment. The books declared obscene had been attacked and suppressed for a double reason: because in the view of the ruling group, they induced immoral behavior, and because their open publication was immoral in itself. The very first brief in the very first case of the series that changed the law— the trial of *Lady Chatterley*—put the question this way: "Should the courts chain creative minds to the dead center of convention at a given moment in time?" Conventional sexual morality was what was meant and understood.

Whether or not you agree with the view of those who sought to preserve morality by limiting speech and writing, obscenity as a legal concept was a fair description of what they objected to. It had been attacked as indefinable, but it was no harder to define, no vaguer, perhaps less vague, than other concepts the law engages every day—"the reasonable person," for example, or "good faith," not to mention "fair trial." Its scope had varied over the years, but that is true of all legal concepts. The important point for present purposes is that however uncertain its boundaries, the legal term "obscenity" served a specific social goal.

The real difficulty—which had not been suggested as a difficulty until the twentieth century was well under way—was that the pursuit of the goal might run afoul of the First Amendment. Among the things settled in the series of cases that culminated in the *Fanny Hill* decision was that the attempt to enforce these moral standards through anti-obscenity laws must yield to the Amendment.

The First Amendment protects speech and press. Not all speech and press; there are some exceptions—information helpful to an enemy in wartime, for example, or fraudulent statements to induce the purchase of stocks and bonds. (And even speech and press protected by the First Amendment remain subject to some regulation. You may not, without municipal permission, choose to hold a meeting in the middle of a busy street and proclaim your thoughts while traffic waits.) But obscenity is no longer an exception to freedom of speech and press in the traditional meaning of those terms. And it ought not be an exception for speech and press more broadly defined—communication in general.

"Suppress," however, means throttle altogether. Even the liberal justices of the present Supreme Court, the dissenters from the Burger view, have allowed that expression can be in certain ways restricted. That is, the citizen who has something he wishes to communicate may not be silenced completely—he can be as obscene about it as he likes—but the flow of his expression can be channeled. These liberal justices have said that the First Amendment is not infringed by anti-obscenity laws that seek to safeguard children or to prevent the infliction of unwanted displays on a captive audience.

Another limitation on expression occurs when expression is mixed with action. Consider the poor soul arrested for indecent exposure. No doubt he has something to communicate, if it is only "look at me," but what he does is also an act, and there is no possibility the Supreme Court would preclude the prosecution of the flasher on the theory that he is only invoking First Amendment rights.

The most libertarian of our justices, Hugo Black and William Douglas, carved out and set aside "action brigaded with expression." Even while they were advancing their thesis that the First Amendment must be given an "absolute" construction—

that speech and the press must be subject to no restraint whatever—they said that when behavior was involved, a different question was presented. The situation must be analyzed to determine which element, action or expression, can be said to dominate. The control of conduct has never been restricted by the First Amendment. Indeed, the control of conduct is the primary business of government. The prosecution of Harry Reems, actor in *Deep Throat*, poses an interesting problem. The film was made in Florida, where the actors performed their acts; Reems was prosecuted in Tennessee, a place where the film was shown. Behavior more than expression? In Florida maybe, it seems to me; in Tennessee, no.

It is in these three fields that legitimate problems remain—the protection of children, the unwilling audience, and action mixed with expression. In each instance, however, we would do better to use legal concepts other than obscenity.

When we are dealing with behavior rather than expression, the only question is what kind of behavior we ought to regulate—whether, for instance, any kind of private sex between (or among) consenting adults should be prohibited. The answer does not involve the First Amendment. Laws controlling conduct rather than communication, as we have seen, do not infringe freedom of speech or press.

The most prominent current topic on which this distinction may help arises from municipal efforts to deal with the ugly sore of commercial sex—Boston's delimitation of its "Combat Zone," Detroit's recently upheld dispersal ordinance, New York's attempt to restore the center of Manhattan to something like what it used to be. Prostitution, with its corollary crimes, is present. So are pornographic book stores. So are hard-core films. We tend to treat them as though they all present a single legal problem. They do not. Prostitution is behavior, not expression. Whether it should be licensed, or simply decriminalized, or continue to be prosecuted, is a troubling question, but it has nothing to do with the First Amendment. Prostitution is clearly on the conduct side of the conduct-expression divide.

But films and books and magazines are on the other side, and here the other concepts enter, and another distinction. We must distinguish between the willing audience and the captive audience. You can say or write or show what you please, but only to those who are willing to listen, or read, or view. *Tropic of Cancer* printed in volume form is one thing; *Tropic of Cancer* blared out by bullhorn in a public square is quite another. The right to express oneself is not the right to intrude expression on those who do not want it.

Privacy has been recognized as a constitutional right. It is actually a cluster of rights, one of which is the right to be let alone. Exhibition inside theaters is in this sense private; no one is compelled to enter. The same for books and magazines; no one is forced to read them. But once the stuff spills onto the streets—on theater marquees or posters, in storefront windows or newsstand displays—the privacy of those outside is assaulted. The liberty of those who like pornography is not inconsistent with the liberty of those who don't. Neither should be constrained by law— the one denied the means to gratify his voyeurism, the other forced to share it. If the people wish to forbid public exhibition of certain kinds—exhibition which dismays some of those who are trying to enjoy their clear right to use the streets and sidewalks free of assault—there is no First Amendment reason that ought to stand in the way. It need not be labeled obscenity. What is thrust upon the passerby can be regulated because the citizens feel it is disagreeable or offensive or unhealthy— that is, if there are enough such citizens so that under our democratic processes they constitute a majority.

Privacy is the modern idea that inheres in this situation. An ancient legal idea reinforces it. It is the traditional and useful and sensible idea of nuisance. In New York, 42nd Street constitutes a public nuisance. No need to cogitate and strain over whether the displays are obscene. Let the movies be shown in the theaters, but restrict, if the voters wish, what appears on their marquees. Let the magazines be sold—let the pimps to masturbators think of themselves as publishers—but keep their product off the front of newsstands.

Finally, child abuse. Although there is disagreement about *how* their cultural environment affects the emotional development of children, there is consensus that the environment is a powerful factor. (If the reader of this piece has a liberal bent, it may help his thinking on the subject to concentrate not on sex but on violence.) A legislative effort to shield the child from certain representations of sex (or violence) does not, in the view of the justices most concerned with freedom, infringe the First Amendment. Nor does the legislature have to prove that ill effects inevitably flow from what it prohibits. Since the First Amendment is not involved, the only constitutional inhibition is the due process clause, and there the test is not whether the legislature is absolutely right, or even sure of the efficacy of its statute. The test is whether there is a rational basis for its concern, and whether what it tries to do about it is not altogether foolish. The established constitutional formula for testing legislation against the due process clause is that it not be "arbitrary and unreasonable."

It is not arbitrary or unreasonable for the legislature to conclude that inducing children to engage in sexual activity can harm them. Nor is it arbitrary or unreasonable to prohibit the photographing of children who have been induced to do so, or to interdict the publication and sale of magazines in which the photographs appear. The publisher and the seller are principals in the abuse. Without them, it would not occur.

There is also abuse of children in another situation—where the child is audience rather than subject. Here television is the prime subject of concern: children are overexposed to what comes through the tube. It will not do to say the family should exercise control. Pious introductions warning of "mature theme" and advice to exercise "parental guidance" are stupid, unless they are cleverly meant to be self-defeating, and in either event they are revolting. If the children are not watching, the caveat has no purpose; if the children are watching, the caveat is a lure. This is obscenity in its larger, nonlegal sense.

Our habits have come to the point where the family in the home is the captive audience par excellence. Neither the child's own judgment nor, as a practical matter, the authority of parents can make effective choices. A legislative attempt to control the content of television programs that had a reasonable basis in the aim to safeguard children would not violate the Constitution.

Our most liberal justices have pointed out that the world of the child is not the world of the adult, and efforts to limit expression have a special place where children are concerned. (Broadcasters who resist control are making a claim to be free in the sense the right wing often uses—freedom to exploit monopolies.) Here again the standard is not obscenity.

Apart from these three fields, the First Amendment demands that we must put up with a lot of what is disagreeable or even damaging. The point made by feminists—that porno films and magazines demean and exploit women—is a strong one. (It is even stronger than they think: the things they object to demean and exploit all people.) But the First Amendment, I believe, requires that we let the material be produced and published. So long as expression is involved and intrusion is not, and there is no question of child abuse, our arguments should be addressed not to the courts but to the producers and sellers of entertainment. That is not an entirely futile effort. The public can be affected by these arguments, and it is the public after all that makes the selling of entertainment a profitable venture. To the extent that these arguments do not prevail, we must accept the fact that the freedoms guaranteed by the First Amendment are costly freedoms. Very costly. Worth the cost, I would say.

The First Amendment has lately had to contend with more than its old enemies. The effectiveness of any law—including our fundamental law, the Constitution—depends on the people's perception of it. The prime example of a law destroyed because too many saw it as fatuous was Prohibition. Freedom of the press has trouble enough as an operating concept—as distinguished from an incantation—without having to defend itself from those who like to call themselves its friends.

The voguish furor about anti-obscenity laws diminishes the public perception of the First Amendment in two ways. One is the silliness—calculated or naive—of so many who rush to grab and wave the First Amendment banner. Lawyers defend topless bars with phrases out of *Areopagitica*. Blind to the fact that all constitutional law is a matter of degree, an actor solemnly proclaims: "Today Harry Reems, tomorrow Helen Hayes." Fatheadedness rarely helps a cause.

The other source of debilitation is a sort of constitutional imperialism. Freedom of expression is not our only liberty. It is, to my mind, our most important liberty, the basis of all others. But it is part of an entire structure. It is entitled to no imperium; it must democratically live with other guaranties and rights.

The First Amendment has serious work to do. Invoked too often and too broadly, it can grow thin and feeble. The restrictions I suggest are minimal, and specific, and—with the anachronistic concept of obscenity discarded—they allow more freedom than the courts have granted up to now. And, I think, they may help to avoid a dangerous dilution of First Amendment guaranties.

POSTSCRIPT

People to whom I have broached the idea submitted in this essay have asked about its evolution. What goes on in the mind of a lawyer who once attacked obscenity laws so hard and now suggests legal restrictions on some of the things that are commonly called "obscene"?

A novelist, speaking from the feminist side, reads me an essay she is doing. It mentions "Charles Rembar, the attorney who escorted Lady Chatterley and Fanny Hill to their triumphant American debuts, thereby unwittingly spreading his cloak—and ours—in the muddy path for a pack of porno hustlers." Not *unwittingly*, I say, and then I quote from *The End of Obscenity:*

> The current uses of the new freedom are not all to the good. There is an acne on our culture. Books enter the best-seller lists distinguished only by the fact that once they would have put their publishers in jail. Advertising plays upon concupiscence in ways that range from foolish to fraudulent. Theatre marquees promise surrogate thrills, and the movies themselves, even some of the good ones, include "daring" scenes— "dare" is a child's word—that have no meaning except at the box office. Television commercials peddle sex with an idiot slyness.

Among the lesser detriments of the new freedom is the deterioration of the television situation comedy, an art form that has not been altogether bad and has had, indeed, high moments. It suffers now from a blue-brown flood of double-meaning jokes, stupidities accompanied by high cackles from the studio audience. (How do they gather those people? Or is it only a Moog synthesizer?) On the other hand, among the more important benefits are the intelligent discussions, on television, of subjects that could not be publicly discussed before; it is difficult to remember, but a documentary on birth control could not have been aired some years ago. Also, just possibly, a new and wonderful trend in journalism: It may no longer be feasible to sustain a bad newspaper by loading it with leers; since sex stories are much less shocking today, the old circulation formula may be hard to work.

Do the suggestions I make jeopardize the freedom won eleven years ago? I think not. In fact, in terms of what may be suppressed, they expand it. The freedom was won for the printed word; for other forms of expression, the decisions carried implications of greater liberty than had theretofore been enjoyed, though not as complete as writers would enjoy. In arguing the cases, I said that not all media were the same, and called attention to the points that underlie the approach outlined above—the protection of children, the problem of action mixed with expression, and one's right not to be compelled to constitute an audience. (Don't pluck my sleeve as I am passing by, stop poking your finger on my chest; freedom includes freedom from your assailing my senses—these are fair demands that books don't interfere with.)

All that is new in my position is the proposal that we come to the end of obscenity in another sense and turn our attention to the things society may rightfully care about.

The proposal is made with the thought that it can make the First Amendment stronger.

FIRST AMENDMENT PIXILLATION
William F. Buckley

Freedom of the press is in mortal peril again, this time out in Kansas, where pseudonymous postal officials tricked New York pornographer Al Goldstein into mailing them his brainchildren, *Screw* and *Smut*. Civil libertarians are swarming to the defense of Goldstein and his former partner, one James Buckley (don't even ask), who are now on trial on federal charges of mailing obscene materials. "*Screw* is a despicable publication," says Harvard's Alan Dershowitz, "but that's what the First Amendment was designed to protect." False. That's what the First Amendment is currently *used* to protect, but . . . well, class, let's have a short review.

Until very recently nobody suggested that the First Amendment had been intended to protect obscenity. Or that it should be *stretched* to protect it. As for the first point, the record is clear: obscenity, like incitement to riot, has traditionally been illegal. And the intentions of the Framers are limned with shocking clarity in Leonard Levy's *Legacy of Suppression*. Judge Wolsey's famous ruling in *Ulysses*, let it be recalled, denied that *Ulysses* was obscene simply as a matter of fact (more emetic than aphrodisiac, he sniffed), without faintly suggesting that nothing was obscene, or that the law should not take cognizance of—and punish—obscene publications. As a matter of fact, the U.S. struggled along for almost two centuries uninundated by the likes of *Screw*, and is it suggested that during those years American thought was stultified? As for the contention that the First Amendment should be stretched, well, that is incompatible with the principle of the rule of law. Let those who want it changed get another Amendment. Of course they can't: their whole case depends heavily on forging a phony constitutional pedigree for their libertarianism, and only deludes people because they have succeeded in intimating that the Constitution has already committed us, whether we like it or not, to . . . *Screw*.

Yet here is Geoffrey Stone of the University of Chicago: "If a publisher wants to play it safe, he has to attempt to figure out what is the most restrictive, conservative notion of obscenity in the country and not publish anything that violates that standard. The net effect is that the rights of citizens in every other location are impaired." And Dershowitz: "Any community can act as the censor of any other community—that's small-town censorship." If *Screw* is illegal in Paw Paw, Michigan, you see, it will be impossible or unprofitable to publish it in New York, and the mind of every American is manacled. One might as well argue that the remaining dry counties in Kansas inexorably will bring Prohibition back to New York. Actually it is the "libertarian" forces who are battling to impose a single rule everywhere—and who, in the name of "individual" rights, would deny citizens the right to act as

William F. Buckley, "First Amendment Pixillation," *National Review* 29 (1977). Buckley is the editor of National Review, a conservative magazine, the moderator of *Firing Line*, a television discussion show, and was a candidate for mayor of New York City (Conservative Party) in 1965.

a community for certain purposes. As usual, their demand for "freedom" is for a kind of freedom that in fact must come at the expense of a structural principle of real freedom: the principle of federalism.

By all means *do* shed a tear for the First Amendment—not because it is threatened in Kansas, but because it is expounded in the nation's top law schools by such minds as those of Messrs. Stone and Dershowitz.

THE X-RATED ECONOMY
James Cook

In an earlier time, the indictment handed up against 55-year-old Michael Zaffarano would have been an open and shut case. Owner and operator of the D.C. Playhouse, a plush "adult" movie house only two blocks from the White House, Zaffarano had shipped in from New York and California six motion pictures bearing such titles as *Anyone But My Husband* and *Linda Lovelace Meets Miss Jones*. The federal government charged that in so doing Zaffarano and two associates had violated the federal statutes forbidding the movement of obscene and pornographic materials in interstate commerce. Zaffarano did not deny he had shipped in the films and government attorneys obviously thought they had a good case. The films themselves showed not only explicit sexual encounters of a conventional kind but also some decidedly unconventional ones involving sadism and bestiality.

At the end of a week-long trial, a Washington, D.C. jury decided last January that two of the films were not obscene and was unable to make up its mind about the others.

The Zaffarano verdict only confirmed what local prosecutors, the police and entrepreneurs in many places around the U.S. have recognized for years: Pornography is in fact, if not in law, no longer an illegal business. The market for pornographic materials, experts agree, is not confined to perverts or other emotional cripples. To the contrary, the largest part of the market is made up of seemingly solid middle-class people who look and act pretty much like their neighbors. "If this is what they want," Zaffarano announced after his trial, "this is what I'll show."

Of course, pornography is still extremely distasteful to a sizable part of the population. But in an increasingly open and permissive society, those who do enjoy pornography are free to revel in it. Just as the prohibition of alcohol eventually did, the prohibition against pornography is fast becoming unenforceable.

Consider this startling statistic: According to the California Department of Justice, the nation's pornographers do a good $4-billion-a-year business, about as much as the conventional motion picture and record industries combined. That estimate may be grossly conservative. "Two or three times that is more like it," says one West Coast police officer, a veteran of many antipornography drives. "If you're not involved in it in some way, you can't imagine how much money goes into the business."

Who gets all these dollars?

The men's magazines to begin with. With a monthly circulation of 16 million, the ten leading sexually oriented titles—so-called "skin" magazines—will generate close to $475 million in revenues this year, nearly $400 million from circulation alone.

James Cook, "The X-Rated Economy," *Forbes* 18 September 1978. Cook is the executive editor of *Forbes*, a national business magazine.

Then there's the "adult" film business: With 2 million admissions a week at an average of $3.50 a ticket, the 780 adult film theaters in the U.S. will gross over $365 million.

Another $100 million goes into what Duane Colglazier, head of the Pleasure Chest chain of sex shops, calls sexual toys: lubricants, creams, vibrators, massagers and other devices. A sizable portion of such goods moves by mail. How big the mail-order pornography business is—films, magazines, books, toys and other devices—even the Postal Service declines to guess, though a 1970 survey indicated the sex merchants pump something like 50 million advertisements into the mails every year.

But by far the biggest component of the U.S. sex business is done in the thousands of adult bookstores and peep shows around the country, which do little in the way of public accounting. How big? Large adult bookstores and peep shows in New York's Times Square area can easily gross $10,000 a day, though they're hardly typical. But even an average-size operation in Hollywood can take in as much as $1,000 a day. Based on a sampling of actual dealer invoices, the Los Angeles Police Department estimates the sex merchants do $125 million a year in the city of Los Angeles alone, which is roughly three times the retail sales of I. Magnin in the Los Angeles area.

In addition to all this, technology is beginning to open up dazzling new prospects: video cassettes that bring X-rated films into the living room; portable video cameras and player-recorders that will enable anyone to produce his or her own—in effect, do-it-yourself—pornography. Polaroid has already put its Polavision instant motion-picture system on the market, Sony will introduce a portable color video camera in the fall. Makers of these devices like to think that they will be used to enable people to watch more cultural and sports events. They are only kidding themselves. It is an open secret that the biggest market is among those for whom visual sex is a turn-on or entertainment or both.

Although pornography is probably as old as civilization, it was, until recently at least, the plaything of the rich and eccentric. What changed all this in the U.S. was a series of Supreme Court decisions that initially applied the protection of the First Amendment to literary works like *Ulysses* and *Lady Chatterley's Lover* and ended up extending the Court's concern about free speech to fairly forthright pornography. In the landmark Roth decision of 1957, the Court maintained that sexual content alone was not enough to distinguish obscenity. What mattered was whether the material *as a whole* appealed to "prurient interests." In 1966, the Court widened the definition to material "utterly without redeeming social value." That single adverb, *utterly*, meant almost anything would go. The 1974 Miller decision threw the burden of definition back on local community standards, which is what got Washington movie exhibitor Zaffarano off the hook. "For the most part," says Beverly Hills lawyer Stanley Fleishman, a prominent member of what might be called the U.S. pornography bar, "if material is distributed to willing adults under discreet circumstances, there is very little prosecution."

"If I were a pornographer," says one U.S. Customs official, "I would not fear any city, state or federal authority. Once you know what the climate of law enforcement is, you can understand how people get into it."

Which is not to suggest that the pornographer's lot, legally speaking, is always, everywhere, an easy one. The federal government continues active in suppressing pornography. It launched 40 obscenity prosecutions last year and won 57, most of them launched in previous years. The U.S. Customs Service made 15,000 seizures of pornographic material and was able to defend its right to destroy all of it. Even the U.S. Postal Service, acting mainly on citizen complaints, won 11 convictions.

But this kind of harassment does not suppress pornography; it only cuts into the profit margins. "It's a high-profit business, pornography," says Al Goldstein, publisher of *Screw*, "but it's also high risk. My lawyers have made as much as I have."

But Goldstein, who started *Screw* magazine just ten years ago, says he has been a millionaire for some time now. And that goes to the heart of the matter. The sex business is precisely that—a business—and one in which a lot of money can be made. The sex business made Hugh Hefner rich, $150-million rich at last count. The magazine he founded, *Playboy*, was in many ways among the prime movers of the sexual revolution that helped legitimize pornography. His success inspired a host of imitators, not only *Penthouse*, whose circulation of 4.6 million is second only to *Playboy*'s 5 million, and *Hustler*, which went from 160,000 to over 2 million circulation in three years, but a host of others: *Gallery*, which had the backing of F. Lee Bailey as *Genesis* had that of Benihana tycoon Rocky Aoki; *Club*, *Oui*, *Chic*; and a group of more recent and unexpectedly raunchy entrants: *High Society*, *Velvet*, *Eros* and *Cheri*.

Playboy and its imitators, expensive-looking and expensive to produce, command the highest prices ever charged by large circulation magazines in publishing history—these days an average of $2 a copy. *Life*, when it expired as a regular periodical, fetched only 50 cents.

The central element in the sex-oriented magazine business is that sky-high cover price. Individual arrangements vary, but in general the publisher retains close to 50% of the cover price. Another 5% or so goes to the national distributor, with the rest split between the regional wholesaler and retailer. These percentages are not appreciably different from what other major magazines offer, but other things being equal, to a retailer, 30% of $2 is twice as nice as 30% of the $1 that *Time*, *Newsweek* or *Sports Illustrated* sell for. So the newsdealers have plenty of incentive to promote these magazines. And they do. Today 30% of *all* newsstand sales come from periodicals that only 20 years ago might not lawfully have been there at all.

The profits are large enough to assuage even the most puritan conscience. Pressmen walked off the job when Iowa's staid old Meredith Corp. (*Better Homes & Gardens*) picked up the *Penthouse* printing contract two years ago, but with a multimillion-dollar contract at stake, Meredith told the pressmen to get back to their job or look for another. They went back.

Corporate America has pretty much shied away from any direct involvement in the skin-magazine business. Most companies with large printing operations live in terror of some outraged stockholder storming into their annual meeting waving a copy of a skin magazine hot off its press. Philadelphia-based ARA Services, the U.S.' largest magazine wholesaler, inevitably handles a large proportion of such publications. In deference to the attitudes of the communities it serves, ARA requires its distributors to enclose most of the magazine titles in opaque plastic wrappers. "One of the reasons we're especially sensitive," says George Epstein, head of ARA's periodical distribution division, "is that we're a public company." Fawcett, which distributes *High Society*, a skin magazine published by porn-movie star Gloria Leonard, is becoming more sensitive now that they're owned by a big public company like CBS.

For the moment, at least, the men's magazine business seems to have peaked out. *Playboy*'s average circulation has been declining for five years—from 7 million in the last half of 1972 to little more than 5 million in 1977. *Viva* and *Playgirl* have been declining since 1974, and in the last half of 1977 sales were off again for all the major titles except *Penthouse* and *Gallery*. *Hustler*'s circulation in particular has taken an ominous slide—from just under 2 million in the last half of 1976 to 1.7 million last year.

But don't conclude from this that pornography is peaking; the evidence is all to the contrary. The business is simply getting more competitive—and more diversified. There are more bidders for the porno patron's dollar. Though filmmakers like Russ Meyer succeeded in distributing soft-core porn to the conventional movie market as far back as the late Fifties, it's only in the last few years that the adult film has emerged as a mass-entertainment medium and as a real competitor to *Playboy* and *Penthouse*. Until a few years ago the business consisted primarily of 16-mm cheapies made on a shoestring by amateurs for as little as $4,000 apiece.

But no more.

What happened was that an upwardly mobile ex-hairdresser from Queens named Gerard Damiano made a 35-mm movie called *Deep Throat* and demonstrated for the first time it was possible to reach a mass audience with a hard-core film. Made in 1972 for something like $25,000, *Deep Throat* has since grossed some $50 million worldwide, with returns still coming in, and, in the process, set the trend that drove the 16-mm cheapies out of the business.

The instant notoriety that *Deep Throat* achieved made it a kind of "media event." It became respectable, or at least chic, for people aspiring to be "with it" to go to an adult film house—if for nothing else, to find out what all the fuss was about. Having gone once, they came back for more. *Deep Throat* not only created a new audience, but a porno-star system (Linda Lovelace, Harry Reems) as well, and put X-rated movies into the big money for the first time.

The profit potential inherent in adult films is awesome. According to David F. Friedman, chairman of the 260-member Adult Film Association of America, it costs an average of $115,000 to bring in a porno film these days, including $40,000 for promotion and prints, and the average film will return $300,000 to the producers within 18 months—for a not-quite-200% return on investment. That's the *average*. Films like *The Devil in Miss Jones, Behind the Green Door* and *Misty Beethoven* have returned millions. And the life expectancy of a hard-core movie is considerably longer than the conventional film, which may die within a few months. Five years after its initial release, a reedited and somewhat less shocking version of *Deep Throat* is still a box office smash.

As head of Entertainment Ventures, the oldest adult film company in the business, Friedman has been turning out pornographic movies for years, including *Seven Into Snowy*, a porn version of *Snow White*, and *Close Call*, a porn version of *A Chorus*

Line. Friedman explains that certain costs—film stock, processing, equipment rentals and so on—are no less for a $200,000-budget adult film like *Misty Beethoven* than they are on a $25-million blockbuster like *Jaws 2*. But where *Jaws 2* took months to film with a lot of expensive talent, it takes only two weeks to make a *Misty Beethoven* with nonunion crews, a writer, director and cast that cost a fraction of what even a second-tier star like *Jaws'* Roy Scheider commands. And the porn director shoots only two feet of film for every one used, as against four, six or eight feet for the conventional feature. Says Friedman, "It's a very hard business to lose money in."

About 125 feature films will be made this year, most of them by independent producers. But there are moguls, of sorts, at large these days. In Los Angeles there's not only Friedman's Entertainment Ventures but also Essex Films, which turns out maybe a dozen a year. In New York there is Mature Pictures, which turns out two or three every year, and Audubon Films, which makes one or two hard-core films a year under the name of Henry Paris, soft-core films under that of Radley Metzger.

As in men's magazines, the profit margins are so wide that everybody cashes in all the way down the line: producer, distributor and exhibitor. "X-rated product," says one southern theater operator, "is probably the only film product you can make a profit on anymore. On regular films, most of the profit comes from the concession business: popcorn, candy. But X-rated customers are very poor on concessions. We're in the X-rated product because it's business, and good business, and in some instances our theaters wouldn't be viable with any other type of product. In our theaters, pornographic movies are like 50% more profitable than regular movies."

As this southerner well knows, the real advantage is that with X-rated movies the theater owner has the upper hand in bargaining with the distributor. Conventional movies are in such short supply that, with a hit film like *Star Wars*, the distributor commands 70%, 80% even 90% of the theater gross (after the overhead is covered). But in adult film there is now more product available than theaters to show it, so more leverage lies with the exhibitor. In the Washington, D.C. area, for example, there are only 5 adult screens out of 200. Nationwide there are 780 out of 16,827. So the result is that in New York the adult film houses reduce the distributors' cut to 50%, and in Los Angeles and in most other parts of the country to 35% and sometimes considerably less than that.

The market for all manner of sexually explicit films seems certain to grow, not least because the line between hard-core and conventional films is beginning to blur. The Hollywood product is getting more explicit—witness Jon Voight's oral sex scene in *Coming Home*, an R not an X-rated film. At the same time, the hardcore product is getting some class, with more emphasis on story and production values. Many producers these days are making their films in two or even three versions—hard core, soft core and R—so that their films can play in a variety of markets.

"It's almost like making three pictures at once," says Mature Pictures' President Robert Sumner, who's just getting his new film, *Take Off*, into release. *Take Off* is symptomatic of what's happening to hard-core films. Stylishly photographed and handsomely produced, it has a fairly well-developed story line, suggested by *The Picture of Dorian Gray*, and it imposes a pastiche of Hollywood films and film actors over the past 60 years—Cagney, Bogart, Brando, Gould—on the usual pornographic confrontations. *Take Off* cost $225,000, and Sumner's confident the film in its three versions will eventually yield him $3 million to $4 million after costs on a box-office gross of $12 million to $20 million. Which would make it the most successful porn film since *Deep Throat*. Producer's hype? Probably. But Sumner has already sold the German rights for $100,000 and the film has grossed $288,000 in its first six weeks at theaters in six cities around the country.

Sumner believes it to be inevitable that the major motion picture companies will themselves start turning out explicit sex films. He may be right. Paramount, a subsidiary of Gulf & Western, did not hesitate to distribute the solf-core *Emmanuelle*. *Penthouse* has a $16-million hard-core version of Gore Vidal's *Caligula* already in the can, with a cast that includes Peter O'Toole, John Gielgud and Malcolm McDowell.

The hottest topic in the movie business these days is videotape, and the hottest thing in videotape is X-rated movies. So far a dozen or so companies have entered the field, including Sumner's Quality X Video Tape and Friedman's TVX tapes, offering X-rated cassettes for showing on home television sets. Sumner got into the business early last spring—at a cost of $75,000—with the only system, he says, that cannot be pirated. With a library of 40 X-rated films (*Xaviera Hollander, Naked Came the Stranger, Bel Ami,* among others), Sumner has been getting 70 inquiries a day since he ran his first ad in *Hustler* and has already recovered his initial investment. The future, Sumner believes, is in video disks rather than tape, but until then he's hoping to clean up—selling, at $110 each, tapes that cost him just $56 to produce.

"At least 10% of the people who buy tapes," David Friedman figures, "will want a collection of hard-core films for their libraries. It's an absolute natural for homes, for parties, when the boys come over for a beer. The man who buys a copy of *Patton* may look at it one or two times, but one who buys *Seven Into Snowy* is going to look at it 10 or 15 times."

Magazines, films, videotapes—all these amount merely to the most visible part of the X-rated economy. The bulk of the sex industry operates underground, where hundreds and even thousands of small producers—print shops, film processors, publishers, filmmakers, photographers—feed a vast distribution system that reaches into thousands of adult bookstores and peep shows across the country. The profitability varies considerably from product to product, and from one point in the marketing system to another. But even at its worst, it's still considerable.

The least profitable product at present is probably the pornographic paperback. The production economics of pornographic publishing are the same as in any other kind of publishing. Because their press runs are relatively small, pornographic paperbacks are generally more costly to produce than mass-market paperbacks. At the same time, competition has eliminated the premium price that paperback publishers used to enjoy, so their margins are painfully squeezed.

Many of the independents have long since been absorbed by the big distributors. One survivor is Midwood Books, an arm of New York-based Tower Publications, which produces the Belmont-Tower and Leisure Books lines of mass-market paperbacks as well as a handful of magazines, and which still manages to make money on them. Midwood operates almost like a paperback magazine. Its writers will grind out a pornographic novel for a flat fee of $1,000 to $1,500. Midwood publishes 16 titles a month—192 a year—bearing titles like *Naked Caller, Teen Tramp* and *Blow by Blow*. Each book runs around 200 pages, costs about 25 cents a copy to produce and sells about 40% of its 20,000-copy pressrun at $2.25 a copy retail.

The really big moneymaker in the sex business is the peep show—a 16-minute loop of 8-mm pornographic film which the customer views in 2-minute segments as he pumps quarter after quarter into the peep machine. The machines are made by outfits like Louisville, Ky.'s Urban Industries. They cost little to produce—maybe $300. They cost less to maintain—an occasional light bulb and a change of film every two weeks. They generally live rent-free in the adult bookstore they occupy. The film loops they use cost maybe $3 to produce.

"There are companies," says Captain Jack Wilson, recently retired commanding officer of the Los Angeles Police Department's Administrative Vice Division, "that will provide the arcade booth, a change of movie and even mop the floors once in a while. You [the store owner] have no capital investment, and you get 50% of the take. It's a cash business." Wilson says there are 945 such machines in the city of Los Angeles that take in on average $75 a week—$120 a week in a good location— or $3.7 million a year.

As legal and community standards have grown more permissive, pornography has been evolving slowly but surely into a more sophisticated and more concentrated business. What began as fairly simple distribution systems have tended to grow into larger integrated enterprises. At the center has been the distributor, with the capital to finance publishers, filmmakers and store owners. Inevitably this had led them forward into retailing and backward into production. In the U.S. market, U.S. entrepreneurs have taken over. "At one point," says a U.S. Customs official, "most of our pornography came from foreign sources. Now the U.S. can outporn any country in the world."

Competition is everywhere now. Says Beverly Hills porn lawyer Elliot Abelson, "Some very sophisticated people who knew how to market, how to package, how to cut costs, came into the business. A small stag movie used to sell for $50. The price went down to $12.95."

The biggest porn entrepreneur in the U.S. was, until recently, Michael G. Thevis, 46, Atlanta millionaire, purported Carter campaign contributor and con-victed pornographer, who walked out of jail in Indiana last April, a day or two before he was indicted for arson and murder, and disappeared. At this writing, he is still at large. A North Carolina boy, Thevis started out with a single newsstand in Atlanta, discovered that his public had an appetite for sexually oriented material, and over the years built a $100-million pornographic empire.

Thevis operated out of a building occupying one square block of downtown Atlanta—a factory devoted to the mass production of pornography, with printing presses, film-processing laboratories, screening rooms, warehousing facilities. By the time he went to jail in 1974, convicted of transporting obscene materials across state lines, Thevis claimed to have sold interests in his pornographic enterprises to a former employee, LaVerne Bowden. Law enforcement officials have never believed him. In any case, his firm, Peachtree Discount Distributors, is still busy as ever. An old girlfriend and former secretary, Patricia McLean, has taken over as president of Global Industries, a holding company for his more legitimate businesses.

Thevis' counterpart on the West Coast was Milton Luros. A onetime art director for a number of skin publications, Luros moved into the big time by pirating the line of literary pornography that French publisher Maurice Girodias (whose Olympia Press first published Nabokov's *Lolita*, Henry Miller's *Tropic of Cancer*) introduced into the U.S. in the late Sixties. At one time, Luros had a printing plant in Chatsworth, Calif. second only to that of the Los Angeles *Times*. When Luros was indicted in 1974 on a pornography charge, he agreed to plead guilty if the government dropped the charges against his wife. (Friends always thought she was the real brains of the business.) Having been given three years' probation and a $5,000 fine, Luros, like Thevis before him, has been liquidating his empire. He sold Parliament News, keystone of his operation, to a former executive, Paul Wisner, but at least one unit—a theater chain called Erotic Words & Pictures—has gone to an outsider, a Cleveland sex merchant named Reuben Sturman.

With Thevis gone underground, and with Luros watching his step, Reuben Sturman now ranks as the number one merchant of sex in the U.S. Having got his start peddling second-hand comic books, Sturman now operates out of a large three-story brick warehouse in Cleveland's black ghetto. Sturman's company, Sovereign News, encompasses distribution operations in most major cities in the East and Midwest. In addition, he operates a chain of peep shows under the name of Western Amusements, manufactures his own peep machines (Automatic Vending), provides lie-detector tests for employee security (National Polygraph), distributes and manufactures marital aids (Doc Johnson Products and Marche Manufacturing), owns one of the more successful new men's magazines (*Eros*), distributes the Lasse Braun films for Dutch pornographer Albert Ferro and runs a chain of 800 retail bookstores in 60 cities, 50 states and 40 foreign countries.

Under Sturman, the adult book shop has become a clean, well-lighted place. "In our stores," he once told a board meeting, "clerks should be upgraded in intelligence, appearance, etc. . . . Our key store in an area will be known as a Doc Johnson store. It will be upgraded as far as interior, etc." He is bullish on the U.S. porn market, and he thinks he knows how to make the most of it. "The future," he says, "is in audiovisual tape."

What worries law-enforcement people these days—state and local police, and the FBI—are the unmistakable signs of organized crime's growing interest in the porn business. What really opened the industry to the godfathers was the increasingly difficult time legitimate operators had in determining what was legally obscene and what was not. Al Goldstein frankly admits he turned to Star Distributors and Astro News, two outfits controlled by organized crime, because he was unable to find a legitimate distributor willing to handle *Screw*. "The mob influence in distribution," Goldstein says, "is there because nobody else wants to be in the business." Goldstein's view was confirmed in the 1976 Report of the Task Force on Organized Crime of the National Advisory Committee on Criminal Justice Standards and Goals. "Because legitimate distributors were reluctant to handle such potentially illegal material," the report said, "organized crime moved in; first, in the distribution of pornography, and then into all aspects of the industry, literature and films of all types and their production, wholesaling and retailing."

The most notorious presence right now is *Screw's* national distributor, New York's Star Distributors, Ltd., which a decade or so ago fell under the domination of Robert (Debe) Di Bernardo, a member of New Jersey's DeCavalcante crime family. Star operates out of a massive warehouse on Lafayette Street on the edge of New York's Little Italy, in a building which it shares with a number of related businesses, including Di Bernardo's local distributing organization, Bonate, Inc., and the New York branch of Thevis' Atlanta operation. As a distributor, Star specializes in hard-core material, while an associated company, Model, handles soft core.

Star started out as a producer of nudie and girlie magazines, according to a report of the State of New York Commission of Investigation, and was headed for bankruptcy when Debe Di Bernardo took over as president of the company.

Though he had run only a wheel-alignment shop until then, Di Bernardo proceeded to revamp the company. Star's cash position mysteriously improved, and it began acquiring adult bookstores in New York and Philadelphia. These stores quickly won a competitive edge by being able to get the newest material ahead of their independent competitors. Today, Star has all the trappings of a pornographic conglomerate, controlling film-processing labs, printing and publishing operations, even filmmaking, as well as distribution.

Police officers in New York, Washington and Los Angeles believe that Di Bernardo controls Thevis' operation in Atlanta. ("Don't forget, Mike," a police wiretap recorded Di Bernardo as saying when Thevis boasted of owning 90% of the peep shows in the country, "you *manage* the machines. The family is in charge.") And Los Angeles Police Department officials are convinced that Di Bernardo has settled in a big way on the West Coast where Milton Luros was once the dominant factor.

Though its influence has waned considerably since 1971, when Joe Colombo was shot, the Colombo family is the other big organized crime influence in New York porn: in peep shows (through Allstate Film Labs), in local periodical distribution (through Astro News) and in filmmaking (through the Perainos, who helped bankroll the spectacularly successful and trend-setting *Deep Throat*).

Holding an uncertain place in the present U.S. porn market is the aforementioned Michael Zaffarano, onetime bodyguard for Mafia chieftain Joe Bonanno, proprietor of the Pussycat Theatre in New York and the D.C. Playhouse in Washington. An associate of Bonanno's East Coast strongman, Carmine Galante, Zaffarano was convicted for assault and robbery but has never been convicted on a pornography charge. He paid $1.35 million for the Pussycat property at 49th Street and Broadway in New York 18 months ago, and has since turned it into a porno amusement center—a hard-core theater, which Zaffarano operates, a bookstore and peep show and a homosexual club. Zaffarano is described by the California Organized Crime Commission as a kingpin in pornography in New York and Los Angeles. Some years ago, he pooled the Bonanno-Galante interests with those of Colombo by taking over the management of the Colombo group's Allstate Film Labs, which produced films for their Times Square peep shows. Among other achievements, he's supposed to have divided the country into regional distributorships, extracted tribute from independents for the privilege of operating. "Zaffarano," the report goes on, "also acts as mediator when disputes arise among the East Coast groups which now control parts of the pornography business in southern California. . . . He's involved in the production and distribution of films and owns theaters. He's also financed the production of films through legitimate fronts." One police officer puts it more bluntly: "He converts money for the mob, puts illegitimate money into legitimate business."

People like Zaffarano, as a rule, don't get involved in operating these businesses. They are usually content just to have a piece of the action. In New York, according to Jeremiah B. McKenna, general counsel to the New York State Select Committee on Crime, the mob's main interest in the sex business is expressed in real estate deals. Organized crime figures lease buildings for ten years from legitimate owners and then sublease them to the fly-by-night operators of massage parlors, adult book shops, peep shows, at $110, $125 a day cash—double what other businesses would pay. "The shops close up and move on, but that lease stays there until the next fly-by-nighter comes along. The property is held for the sex industry," McKenna says. "A guy can't come in and start selling shoes because the money is too great."

Is the U.S., then, about to be engulfed in a great wave of pornography? Don't bet on it. In the end, the pornography business may become the victim of the very permissiveness that helped it flourish. David Friedman of the Adult Film Association, an apologist for pornography, has something significant to say about the audience for pornographic movies: "Our basic audience is still people over the age of 35, and though we are beginning to attract some young marrieds and younger couples in their middle-to-late 20s, the audience is still composed of people who are probably more sexually repressed than people are today." But that may be merely a marketing problem. If so, it is only a matter of time before someone from Hollywood, *Hustler*, or the Harvard Business School gets to work solving it.

PORNOGRAPHY, OBSCENITY, AND THE CASE FOR CENSORSHIP
Irving Kristol

Being frustrated is disagreeable, but the real disasters in life begin when you get what you want. For almost a century now, a great many intelligent, well-meaning, and articulate people—of a kind generally called liberal or intellectual, or both—have argued eloquently against any kind of censorship of art and/or entertainment. And within the past ten years, the courts and the legislatures of most Western nations have found these arguments persuasive—so persuasive that hardly a man is now alive who clearly remembers what the answers to these arguments were. Today, in the United States and other democracies, censorship has to all intents and purposes ceased to exist.

Is there a sense of triumphant exhilaration in the land? Hardly. There is, on the contrary, a rapidly growing unease and disquiet. Somehow, things have not worked out as they were supposed to, and many notable civil libertarians have gone on record as saying this was not what they meant at all. They wanted a world in which *Desire under the Elms* could be produced, or *Ulysses* published, without interference by philistine busybodies holding public office. They have got that, of course; but they have also got a world in which homosexual rape takes place on the stage, in which the public flocks during lunch hours to witness varieties of professional fornication, in which Times Square has become little more than a hideous market for the sale and distribution of printed filth that panders to all known (and some fanciful) sexual perversions.

But disagreeable as this may be, does it really matter? Might not our unease and disquiet be merely a cultural hangover—a "hang-up," as they say? What reason is there to think that anyone was ever corrupted by a book?

This last question, oddly enough, is asked by the very same people who seem convinced that advertisements in magazines or displays of violence on television do indeed have the power to corrupt. It is also asked, incredibly enough and in all sincerity, by people—for example, university professors and schoolteachers—whose very lives provide all the answers one could want. After all, if you believe that no one was ever corrupted by a book, you have also to believe that no one was ever improved by a book (or a play or a movie). You have to believe, in other words, that all art is morally trivial and that, consequently, all education is morally irrelevant. No one, not even a university professor, really believes that.

To be sure, it is extremely difficult, as social scientists tell us, to trace the effects of any single book (or play or movie) on an individual reader or any class of readers. But we all know, and social scientists know it too, that the ways in which we use

Irving Kristol, "Pornography, Obscenity, and the Case for Censorship," *Reflections of a Neoconservative: Looking Back, Looking Ahead* (New York: Basic Books, 1983). Kristol, once a liberal editor of *Commentary* (1947–52), is now one of the U.S.'s leading "neoconservatives." He is the author of *On the Democratic Idea in America* (1972).

our minds and imaginations do shape our characters and help define us as persons. That those who certainly know this are nevertheless moved to deny it merely indicates how a dogmatic resistance to the idea of censorship can—like most dogmatism—result in a mindless insistence on the absurd.

I have used these harsh terms—"dogmatism" and "mindless"—advisedly. I might also have added "hypocritical." For the plain fact is that none of us is a complete civil libertarian. We all believe that there is some point at which the public authorities ought to step in to limit the "self-expression" of an individual or a group, even where this might be seriously intended as a form of artistic expression, and even where the artistic transaction is between consenting adults. A playwright or theatrical director might, in this crazy world of ours, find someone willing to commit suicide on the stage, as called for by the script. We would not allow that— any more than we would permit scenes of real physical torture on the stage, even if the victim were a willing masochist. And I know of no one, no matter how free in spirit, who argues that we ought to permit gladiatorial contests in Yankee Stadium, similar to those once performed in the Colosseum at Rome—even if only consenting adults were involved.

The basic point that emerges is one that Walter Berns has powerfully argued: No society can be utterly indifferent to the ways its citizens publicly entertain themselves. * Bearbaiting and cockfighting are prohibited only in part out of compassion for the suffering animals; the main reason they were abolished was because it was felt that they debased and brutalized the citizenry who flocked to witness such spectacles. And the question we face with regard to pornography and obscenity is whether, now that they have such strong legal protection from the Supreme Court, they can or will brutalize and debase our citizenry. We are, after all, not dealing with one passing incident—one book, or one play, or one movie. We are dealing with a general tendency that is suffusing our entire culture.

I say pornography *and* obscenity because, though they have different dictionary definitions and are frequently distinguishable as "artistic" genres, they are nevertheless in the end identical in effect. Pornography is not objectionable simply because it arouses sexual desire or lust or prurience in the mind of the reader or spectator; this is a silly Victorian notion. A great many nonpornographic works—including some parts of the Bible—excite sexual desire very successfully. What is distinctive about pornography is that, in the words of D. H. Lawrence, it attempts "to do dirt on [sex] . . . [It is an] insult to a vital human relationship."

In other words, pornography differs from erotic art in that its whole purpose is to treat human beings obscenely, to deprive human beings of their specifically human dimension. That is what obscenity is all about. It is light years removed from any kind of carefree sensuality—there is no continuum between Fielding's *Tom Jones* and the Marquis de Sade's *Justine*. These works have quite opposite intentions. To quote Susan Sontag: "What pornographic literature does is precisely to drive a wedge between one's existence as a full human being and one's existence as a sexual

---

* This is as good a place as any to express my profound indebtedness to Walter's Berns's superb essay "Pornography vs. Democracy," in the Winter of 1971 issue of *The Public Interest.*

being—while in ordinary life a healthy person is one who prevents such a gap from opening up." This definition occurs in an essay *defending* pornography—Miss Sontag is a candid as well as gifted critic—so the definition, which I accept, is neither tendentious nor censorious.

Along these same lines, one can point out—as C.S. Lewis pointed out some years back—that it is no accident that in the history of all literatures obscene words, the so-called four-letter words, have always been the vocabulary of farce or vituperation. The reason is clear; they reduce men and women to some of their mere bodily functions—they reduce man to his animal component, and such a reduction is an essential purpose of farce or vituperation.

Similarly, Lewis also suggested that it is not an accident that we have no offhand, colloquial, neutral terms—not in any Western European language at any rate—for our most private parts. The words we do use are either (1) nursery terms, (2) archaisms, (3) scientific terms, or (4) a term from the gutter (i.e., a demeaning term). Here I think the genius of language is telling us something important about man. It is telling us that man is an animal with a difference: He has a unique sense of privacy, and a unique capacity for shame when this privacy is violated. Our "private parts" are indeed private, and not merely because convention prescribes it. This particular convention is indigenous to the human race. In practically all primitive tribes, men and women cover their private parts; and in practically all primitive tribes, men and women do not copulate in public.

It may well be that Western society, in the latter half of the twentieth century, is experiencing a drastic change in sexual mores and sexual relationships. We have had many such "sexual revolutions" in the past—the bourgeois family and bourgeois ideas of sexual propriety were themselves established in the course of a revolution against eighteenth-century "licentiousness"—and we shall doubtless have others in the future. It is, however, highly improbable (to put it mildly) that what we are witnessing is the Final Revolution which will make sexual relations utterly unproblematic, permit us to dispense with any kind of ordered relationships between the sexes, and allow us freely to redefine the human condition. And so long as humanity has not reached that utopia, obscenity will remain a problem.

One of the reasons it will remain a problem is that obscenity is not merely about sex, any more than science fiction is about science. Science fiction, as every student of the genre knows, is a peculiar vision of power: What it is really about is politics. And obscenity is a peculiar vision of humanity: What it is really about is ethics and metaphysics.

Imagine a man—a well-known man, much in the public eye—in a hospital ward, dying an agonizing death. He is not in control of his bodily functions, so that his bladder and his bowels empty themselves of their own accord. His consciousness is overwhelmed and extinguished by pain, so that he cannot communicate with us, nor we with him. Now, it would be, technically, the easiest thing in the world to put a television camera in his hospital room and let the whole world witness this spectacle. We do not do it—at least we do not do it as yet—because we regard this as an *obscene* invasion of privacy. And what would make the spectacle obscene is that we would be witnessing the extinguishing of humanity in a human animal.

Incidentally, in the past our humanitarian crusaders against capital punishment understood this point very well. The abolitionist literature goes into great physical detail about what happens to a man when he is hanged or electrocuted or gassed. And their argument was—and is—that what happens is shockingly obscene, and that no civilized society should be responsible for perpetrating such obscenities, particularly since in the nature of the case there must be spectators to ascertain that this horror was indeed being perpetrated in fulfillment of the law.

Sex—like death—is an activity that is both animal and human. There are human sentiments and human ideals involved in this animal activity. But when sex is public, the viewer does not see—cannot see—the sentiments and the ideals. He can only see the animal coupling. And that is why, when men and women make love, as we say, they prefer to be alone—because it is only when you are alone that you can make love, as distinct from merely copulating in an animal and casual way. And that, too, is why those who are voyeurs, if they are not irredeemably sick, also feel ashamed at what they are witnessing. When sex is a public spectacle, a human relationship has been debased into a mere animal connection.

It is also worth noting that this making of sex into an obscenity is not a mutual and equal transaction but rather an act of exploitation by one of the partners—the male partner. I do not wish to get into the complicated question as to what, if any, are the essential differences—as distinct from conventional and cultural differences—between male and female. I do not claim to know the answer to that. But I do know—and I take it as a sign that has meaning—that pornography is, and always has been, a man's work; that women rarely write pornography; and that women tend to be indifferent consumers of pornography.* My own guess, by way of explanation, is that a woman's sexual experience is ordinarily more suffused with human emotion than is man's, that men are more easily satisfied with autoerotic activities, and that men can therefore more easily take a more "technocratic" view of sex and its pleasures. Perhaps this is not correct. But whatever the explanation, there can be no question that pornography is a form of "sexism," as the women's liberation movement calls it, and that the instinct of women's liberation has been unerring in perceiving that when pornography is perpetrated, it is perpetrated against them, as part of a conspiracy to deprive them of their full humanity.

But even if all this is granted, it might be said—and doubtless will be said—that I really ought not to be unduly concerned. Free competition in the cultural marketplace—it is argued by people who have never otherwise had a kind word to say for laissez-faire—will automatically dispose of the problem. The present fad for pornography and obscenity, it will be asserted, is just that, a fad. It will spend itself in the course of time; people will get bored with it, will be able to take it or leave it alone in a casual way, in a "mature way," and, in sum, I am being unnecessarily distressed about the whole business. The *New York Times*, in an editorial, concludes hopefully in this vein.

*There are, of course, a few exceptions. *L'Histoire d'O*, for instance, was written by a woman. It is unquestionably the most *melancholy* work of pornography ever written. And its theme is precisely the dehumanization accomplished by obscenity.

> In the end . . . the insensate pursuit of the urge to shock, carried from one excess to a more abysmal one, is bound to achieve its own antidote in total boredom. When there is no lower depth to descend to, ennui will erase the problem.

I would like to be able to go along with this line of reasoning, but I cannot. I think it is false, and for two reasons, the first psychological, the second political.

The basic psychological fact about pornography and obscenity is that it appeals to and provokes a kind of sexual regression. The sexual pleasure one gets from pornography and obscenity is autoerotic and infantile; put bluntly, it is a masturbatory exercise of the imagination, when it is not masturbation pure and simple. Now, people who masturbate do not get bored with masturbation, just as sadists do not get bored with sadism, and voyeurs do not get bored with voyeurism.

In other words, infantile sexuality is not only a permanent temptation for the adolescent or even the adult—it can quite easily become a permanent, self-reinforcing neurosis. It is because of an awareness of this possibility of regression toward the infantile condition, a regression which is always open to us, that all the codes of sexual conduct ever devised by the human race take such a dim view of autoerotic activities and try to discourage autoerotic fantasies. Masturbation is indeed a perfectly natural autoerotic activity, as so many sexologists blandly assure us today. And it is precisely because it is so perfectly natural that it can be so dangerous to the mature or maturing person, if it is not controlled or sublimated in some way. That is the true meaning of Portnoy's complaint. Portnoy, you will recall, grows up to be a man who is incapable of having an adult sexual relationship with a woman; his sexuality remains fixed in an infantile mode, the prisoner of his autoerotic fantasies. Inevitably, Portnoy comes to think, in a perfectly *infantile* way, that it was all his mother's fault.

It is true that, in our time, some quite brilliant minds have come to the conclusion that a reversion to infantile sexuality is the ultimate mission and secret destiny of the human race. I am thinking in particular of Norman O. Brown, for whose writings I have the deepest respect. One of the reasons I respect them so deeply is that Mr. Brown is a serious thinker who is unafraid to face up to the radical consequences of his radical theories. Thus, Mr. Brown knows and says that for his kind of salvation to be achieved, humanity must annul the civilization it has created—not merely the civilization we have today, but all civilization—so as to be able to make the long descent backward into animal innocence.

And that is the point. What is at stake is civilization and humanity, nothing less. The idea that "everything is permitted," as Nietzsche put it, rests on the premise of nihilism and has nihilistic implications. I will not pretend that the case against nihilism and for civilization is an easy one to make. We are here confronting the most fundamental of philosophical questions, on the deepest levels. In short, the matter of pornography and obscenity is not a trivial one, and only superficial minds can take a bland and untroubled view of it.

In this connection, I must also point out, those who are primarily against censorship on liberal grounds tell us not to take pornography or obscenity seriously, while those who are for pornography and obscenity on radical grounds take it very seriously indeed. I believe the radicals—writers like Susan Sontag, Herbert Marcuse,

Norman O. Brown, and even Jerry Rubin—are right, and the liberals are wrong. I also believe that those young radicals at Berkeley, some seven years ago, who provoked a major confrontation over the public use of obscene words, showed a brilliant political instinct. And once Mark Rudd could publicly ascribe to the president of Columbia a notoriously obscene relationship to his mother, without provoking any kind of reaction, the SDS [Students for a Democratic Society] had already won the day. The occupation of Columbia's buildings merely ratified their victory. Men who show themselves unwilling to defend civilization against nihilism are not going to be either resolute or effective in defending the university against anything.

I am already touching upon a political aspect of pornography when I suggest that it is inherently and purposefully subversive of civilization and its institutions. But there is another and more specifically political aspect, which has to do with the relationship of pornography and/or obscenity to democracy, and especially to the quality of public life on which democratic government ultimately rests.

Though the phrase "the quality of life" trips easily from so many lips these days, it tends to be one of those clichés with many trivial meanings and no large, serious one. Sometimes it merely refers to such externals as the enjoyment of cleaner air, cleaner water, cleaner streets. At other times it refers to the merely private enjoyment of music, painting, or literature. Rarely does it have anything to do with the way the citizen in a democracy views himself—his obligations, his intentions, his ultimate self-definition.

Instead, what I would call the "managerial" conception of democracy is the predominant opinion among political scientists, sociologists, and economists, and has, through the untiring efforts of these scholars, become the conventional journalistic opinion as well. The root idea behind this managerial conception is that democracy is a "political system" (as they say) which can be adequately defined in terms of—can be fully reduced to—its mechanical arrangements. Democracy is then seen as a set of rules and procedures, and *nothing but* a set of rules and procedures, whereby majority rule and minority rights are reconciled into a state of equilibrium. If everyone follows these rules and procedures, then a democracy is in working order. I think this is a fair description of the democratic idea that currently prevails in academia. One can also fairly say that it is now the liberal idea of democracy par excellence.

I cannot help but feel that there is something ridiculous about being this kind of a democrat, and I must further confess to having a sneaking sympathy for those of our young radicals who also find it ridiculous. The absurdity is the absurdity of idolatry—of taking the symbolic for the real, the means for the end. The purpose of democracy cannot possibly be the endless functioning of its own political machinery. The purpose of any political regime is to achieve some version of the good life and the good society. It is not at all difficult to imagine a perfectly functioning democracy which answers all questions except one—namely, why should anyone of intelligence and spirit care a fig for it?

There is, however, an older idea of democracy—one which was fairly common until about the beginning of this century—for which the conception of the quality of public life is absolutely crucial. This idea starts from the proposition that democracy is a form of self-government, and that if you want it to be a meritorious polity, you have to care about what kind of people govern it. Indeed, it puts the matter more strongly and declares that if you want self-government, you are only entitled to it if that "self" is worthy of governing. There is no inherent right to self-government if it means that such government is vicious, mean, squalid, and debased. Only a dogmatist and a fanatic, an idolater of democratic machinery, could approve of self-government under such conditions.

And because the desirability of self-government depends on the character of the people who govern, the older idea of democracy was very solicitous of the condition of this character. It was solicitous of the individual self, and felt an obligation to educate it into what used to be called "republican virtue." And it was solicitous of that collective self which we call public opinion and which, in a democracy, governs us collectively. Perhaps in some respects it was nervously oversolicitous—that would not be surprising. But the main thing is that it cared, cared not merely about the machinery of democracy but about the quality of life that this machinery might generate.

And because it cared, this older idea of democracy had no problem in principle with pornography and/or obscenity. It censored them—and it did so with a perfect clarity of mind and a perfectly clear conscience. It was not about to permit people capriciously to corrupt themselves. Or, to put it more precisely: In this version of democracy, the people took some care not to let themselves be governed by the more infantile and irrational parts of themselves.

I have, it may be noticed, uttered that dreadful word censorship. And I am not about to back away from it. If you think pornography and/or obscenity is a serious problem, you have to be for censorship. I will go even further and say that if you want to prevent pornography and/or obscenity from becoming a problem, you have to be for censorship. And lest there be any misunderstanding as to what I am saying, I will put it as bluntly as possible: If you care for the quality of life in our American democracy, then you have to be for censorship.

But can a liberal be for censorship? Unless one assumes that being a liberal *must* mean being indifferent to the quality of American life, then the answer has to be yes, a liberal can be for censorship—but he ought to favor a liberal form of censorship.

Is that a contradiction in terms? I do not think so. We have no problem in contrasting *repressive* laws governing alcohol and drugs and tobacco with laws *regulating* (i.e., discouraging the sale of) alcohol and drugs and tobacco. Laws encouraging temperance are not the same thing as laws that have as their goal prohibition or abolition. We have not made the smoking of cigarettes a criminal offense. We have, however, and with good liberal conscience, prohibited cigarette advertising on television, and may yet, again with good liberal conscience, prohibit it in newspapers and magazines. The idea of restricting individual freedom, in a liberal way, is not at all unfamiliar to us.

I therefore see no reason why we should not be able to distinguish repressive censorship from liberal censorship of the written and spoken word. In Britain, until a few years ago, you could perform almost any play you wished, but certain plays, judged to be obscene, had to be performed in private theatrical clubs, which were deemed to have a "serious" interest in theater. In the United States, all of us who grew up using public libraries are familiar with the circumstances under which certain books could be circulated only to adults, while still other books had to be read in the library reading room, under the librarian's skeptical eye. In both cases, a small minority that was willing to make a serious effort to see an obscene play or read an obscene book could do so. But the impact of obscenity was circumscribed and the quality of public life was only marginally affected. *

I am not saying it is easy in practice to sustain a distinction between liberal and repressive censorship, especially in the public realm of a democracy, where popular opinion is so vulnerable to demagoguery. Moreover, an acceptable system of liberal censorship is likely to be exceedingly difficult to devise in the United States today, because our educated classes, upon whose judgment a liberal censorship must rest, are so convinced that there is no such thing as a problem of obscenity, or even that there is no such thing as obscenity at all. But, to counterbalance this, there is the further, fortunate truth that the tolerable margin for error is quite large, and single mistakes or single injustices are not all that important.

This possibility of error, of course, occasions much distress among artists and academics. It is a fact, one that cannot and should not be denied, that any system of censorship is bound, upon occasion, to treat unjustly a particular work of art—to find pornography where there is only gentle eroticism, to find obscenity where none really exists, or to find both where its existence ought to be tolerated because it serves a larger moral purpose. Though most works of art are not obscene, and though most obscenity has nothing to do with art, there are some few works of art that are, at least in part, pornographic and/or obscene. There are also some few works of art that are in the special category of the comic-ironic "bawdy" (Boccaccio, Rabelais). It is such works of art that are likely to suffer at the hands of the censor. That is the price one has to be prepared to pay for censorship—even liberal censorship.

But just how high is this price? If you believe, as so many artists seem to believe today, that art is the only sacrosanct activity in our profane and vulgar world—that any man who designates himself an artist thereby acquires a sacred office—then obviously censorship is an intolerable form of sacrilege. But for those of us who do not subscribe to this religion of art, the costs of censorship do not seem so high at all.

If you look at the history of American or English literature, there is precious little damage you can point to as a consequence of the censorship that prevailed through-out most of that history. Very few works of literature—of real literary merit, I mean—ever were suppressed; and those that were, were not suppressed for long. Nor have I noticed, now that censorship of the written word has to all intents and purposes ceased in this country, that hitherto suppressed or repressed masterpieces

---

* It is fairly predictable that someone is going to object that this point of view is "elitist"—that, under a system of liberal censorship, the rich will have privileged access to pornography and obscenity. Yes, of course, they will—just as, at present, the rich have privileged access to heroin if they want it. But one would have to be an egalitarian maniac to object to this state of affairs on the grounds of equality.

are flooding the market. Yes, we can now read *Fanny Hill* and the Marquis de Sade. Or, to be more exact, we can now openly purchase them, since many people were able to read them even though they were publicly banned, which is as it should be under a liberal censorship. So how much have literature and the arts gained from the fact that we can all now buy them over the counter, that, indeed, we are all now encouraged to buy them over the counter? They have not gained much that I can see.

And one might also ask a question that is almost never raised: How much has literature lost from the fact that everything is now permitted? It has lost quite a bit, I should say. In a free market, Gresham's Law can work for books or theater as efficiently as it does for coinage—driving out the good, establishing the debased. The cultural market in the United States today is being preempted by dirty books, dirty movies, dirty theater. A pornographic novel has a far better chance of being published today than a nonpornographic one, and quite a few pretty good novels are not being published at all simply because they are not pornographic, and are therefore less likely to sell. Our cultural condition has not improved as a result of the new freedom. American cultural life was not much to brag about twenty years ago; today one feels ashamed for it.

Just one last point, which I dare not leave untouched. If we start censoring pornography or obscenity, shall we not inevitably end up censoring political opinion? A lot of people seem to think this would be the case—which only shows the power of doctrinaire thinking over reality. We had censorship of pornography and obscenity for 150 years, until almost yesterday, and I am not aware that freedom of opinion in this country was in any way diminished as a consequence of this fact. Fortunately for those of us who are liberal, freedom is not indivisible. If it were, the case for liberalism would be indistinguishable from the case for anarchy; and they are two very different things.

But I must repeat and emphasize: What kinds of laws we pass governing pornography and obscenity, what kind of censorship—or, since we are still a federal nation, what kinds of censorship—we institute in our various localities may indeed be difficult matters to cope with; nevertheless the real issue is one of principle. I myself subscribe to a liberal view of the enforcement problem: I think that pornography should be illegal *and* available to anyone who wants it so badly as to make a pretty strenuous effort to get it. We have lived with under-the-counter pornography for centuries now, in a fairly comfortable way. But the issue of principle, of whether it should be over or under the counter, has to be settled before we can reflect on the advantages and disadvantages of alternative modes of censorship. I think the settlement we are living under now, in which obscenity and democracy are regarded as equals, is wrong; I believe it is inherently unstable; I think it will, in the long run, be incompatible with any authentic concern for the quality of life in our democracy.

THE PLACE OF PORNOGRAPHY
Lewis H. Lapham

LEWIS H. LAPHAM: In our discussion today, ladies and gentlemen, I would like to take up three questions. First, what is the *place* of pornography in our society? What purpose does it serve? Why is there so much of it?

Second, what is the *nature* of the product? Why, for instance, does pornography so often seem so earnest, so angry, so empty of wit, humor, or sexual feeling?

Third, what, if anything, should we *do* about pornography? Should we pass laws to regulate it? If so, what sort of laws? By first examining the uses of pornography, I hope we can arrive at a clearer understanding of a subject too often hidden under the blankets of ideology.

Maybe we can begin with Al Goldstein, the only pornographer in our midst.

AL GOLDSTEIN: Well, I have been publishing *Screw* magazine for sixteen years now, and I am still not sure what the word "pornography" means. I have been charged with publishing obscenity a number of times—in Wichita, Kansas, for example, in 1977, I was brought to trial and faced a prison sentence of up to sixty years if convicted. But after the members of the jury examined copies of *Screw*, they voted to acquit me. Now if *Screw* is not pornographic and obscene, nothing is. But the citizens of Wichita decided it was not.

But whatever pornography is, I am convinced it serves a useful purpose. Pornography aims for the groin; its function is to turn us on. In publishing *Screw*, I want to turn men and women on, to celebrate sexual pleasure and sexual abandon. I believe sex, whether it is straight sex, gay sex, group sex, or whatever consenting adults wish to do together, is a very positive thing. To me, an erection is its own best defense. I find it repugnant when some women argue that a penis is an instru-

Lewis H. Lapham, "The Place of Pornography" [A symposium moderated by Lewis H. Lapham], *Harper's* November 1984. Lapham is the editor of *Harper's*. Goldstein is the publisher of *Screw* magazine, which has had a number of problems with pornography laws; Decter is the author of *The Liberated Woman and Other Americans*; Jong is the author of the sexually explicit novels *Fear of Flying* and *Fanny*. Brownmiller is the founder of Women Against Pornography and the author of *Against Our Will: Men, Women and Rape*; Eishtain is a professor of political science at the University of Massachusetts and the author of *Public Man, Private Woman; Women in Social and Political Thought*; Neier is the former national executive director of the American Civil Liberties Union.

ment of assault and rape, that women must always be victims in sexual relations.

Pornography helps us free ourselves from the puritanical attitudes about sex that have long dominated our society. Pornography and fantasy are closely related—pornography helps us to fantasize: to look at a woman and strip her, to look at a man and strip him. I do not consider publishing photographs of nude women exploitation, but a celebration of their bodies. And I do not consider masturbation self-abuse, but rather a celebration of sexuality.

Not only does today's pornography serve to liberate us in our attitudes toward sex; it is also shattering the elitism that has traditionally surrounded pornography itself. Once, pornography was acceptable only if it was sold in fancy, expensive editions that claimed to be "erotic art" from India or Japan. To me pornography is what the truck driver wants, what the sanitation man reads, what the bus driver buys. For them, too, pornography can now serve as a celebration of human sexuality and an aid to sexual congress.

MIDGE DECTER: I don't quite see that pornography functions as an "aid to sexual congress." So far as I know, until quite recently sexual congress didn't particularly require any help; people somehow managed it one way or another all by themselves.

The traditional function of pornography was to offer a vision of erotic utopia. Throughout history, pornography—seedy, hidden beneath counters, and very expensive—offered its readers a vision of anonymous, faceless sex, sex without personality and without consequence. I call this vision utopian because it promised what everyone knew to be impossible: sex without the possibility of pregnancy, without the risk of emotional entanglement, without the need to confront another human being. We can trace this utopian vision back very far—we see it, for instance, expressed in the orgies of the ancient Greeks, in which the participants wore masks. And I believe it derives more from men's fantasies than from women's. But not always: in Erica Jong's *Fear of Flying*, the heroine dreams of just this kind of blind sex—her search for it is what drives her.

ERICA JONG: Until she finds it. That's one of the ironies of the book—which of course most of its critics missed.

DECTER: The point is that traditional pornography was inherently masturbatory. For what is masturbation if not having sex with yourself, and thus not risking any entanglement, any consequence?

Today, pornography works in precisely the opposite way, that is, it attempts to make its audience focus their fantasies on specific people. The "Playmate of the Month" is a particular woman about whom the reader is meant to have particular fantasies. In my view, this has a more baneful effect on people—makes them demented, in fact, in a way that earlier pornography didn't. Today's pornography promises them that there exists, somewhere on this earth, a life of endlessly desirable and available women and endlessly potent men. The promise that this life is just around the corner—in Hugh Hefner's mansion, or even just in the next joint or the next snort—is maddening and disorienting. And in its futility, it makes for rage and self-hatred. The traditional argument against censorship—that "no one can be seduced by a book," as I believe Gore Vidal put it—was probably valid when pornography was impersonal and anonymous, purely an aid to fantasizing about sexual utopia. Today, however, there is addiction and seduction in pornography. Thus the power of pornography to do harm is much greater than it used to be.

JONG: To understand the function of pornography we have to distinguish it from erotica. Erotica celebrates the erotic nature of the human creature, attempts to probe what is erotic in the human soul and the human mind, and does so artfully, dramatically. Pornography, on the other hand, serves simply as an aid to masturbation, with no artistic pretensions and no artistic value. I believe the nature of the pornography we have in America today and the enormous quantity in which we have it reflect our country's puritanical attitudes toward sexuality. I think we should look at our pornography to see what it reveals about our society: it's violent, it's pedophilic, it's full of anger toward women. Today's pornography, in other words, shows us in sharp relief the sickness of our society, the twisted attitudes toward sex that persist beneath the facade of gentility. The ugliness we see in it—the joyless, obsessional, humorless quality—is the ugliness and twisted puritanism that exists in America.

But we cannot legislate these attitudes out of existence. Instead we must seek to change them in the hearts and minds of people. Despite the ugliness of a lot of pornography, despite the fact that I don't want to defend pictures of little girls being molested, I believe that censorship only springs back against the givers of culture—against authors, artists, and feminists, against anybody who wants to change society. Should censorship be imposed again, whether through the kind of legislation introduced in Minneapolis and Indianapolis* or through other means, feminists would be the first to suffer. *Leaves of Grass* will go into the garbage before *The Story of O.* The history of censorship is full of hideous examples of great works of art—books like *Ulysses, The Return of the Native,* and *Tropic of Cancer*—being censored while trash has gone free. As the mother of a girl who is not yet six, I am sickened by child pornography; but I would not legislate against it directly. Perhaps the print industry needs to establish a rating system like that of the film industry.

LAPHAM: We'll come later to the question of what to do about pornography. But first, still in the way of definitions, I'm sure Susan Brownmiller has different opinions about the function of pornography. Is it a mask for Eros, a vision of an erotic utopia, a parliamentary speech in a sexual congress, a masturbatory tool?

SUSAN BROWNMILLER: I certainly think pornography is more than just a "masturbatory tool." I do not oppose masturbation, but I oppose pornography. If I can step back from my strong feelings about it—and I find this very difficult to do— I would say the apparent function and intent of pornography is to serve as an aid for people who, for whatever reasons, have difficulty becoming sexually stimulated. Unfortunately, what seems to stimulate these people is, I believe, a dangerously distorted picture of female sexuality, indeed of human sexuality.

I find this extremely troubling, for I believe that beneath pornography's apparent purpose lies a more dangerous one. In my book *Against Our Will* I wrote a few impassioned pages in which I identified the real purpose, the hidden intent, of pornography as anti-female propaganda. Pornography functions quite simi-

---

*Jong is referring to ordinances passed in both cities last spring, with the support of feminists and conservative Republicans, that condemn pornography as a violation of women's civil rights. The Minneapolis legislation was vetoed by the mayor. The Indianapolis law, which is under challenge in federal court, states that "pornography is central in creating and maintaining sex as a basis for discrimination." Both ordinances, drafted with the help of University of Minnesota law professor Catharine MacKinnon and radical feminist writer Andrea Dworkin, define pornography as "the graphic sexually explicit subordination of women, whether in pictures or in words."

larly to anti-Semitic or racist propaganda. The intent of all three is to distort the image of a group or class of people, to deny their humanity, to make them such objects of ridicule and humiliation that acts of aggression against them are viewed less seriously. Also, the aggression is subliminally encouragd by the propaganda itself. In an age when women are putting forward their aspirations toward equality in a healthy, positive way, pornography is working to increase hostility toward women, and therefore to increase tensions between the sexes. I find this unbearable; and I don't think there's any danger that if we limit pornography we will eventually ban *Leaves of Grass* or *Ulysses* or even Henry Miller's *Tropic of Cancer*. Those battles were fought and won a long time ago. The Indianapolis legislation, by the way, states explicitly that libraries cannot be considered "traffickers in pornography," regardless of what books might be on their shelves. Women Against Pornography has never supported unrestrained censorship; but we believe that liberals must try to do something about pornography, which I consider to be a clear and present danger to women and to the health of our society itself.

JEAN BETHKE ELSHTAIN: What is the place of pornography today? Pornography's place changes as a society transforms itself politically, economically, morally, and aesthetically. Pornography has been heavily commercialized and is now readily available to all classes of society, as Al Goldstein pointed out. Porn has become a growth industry—a $7 billion a year business, by most estimates—and a very public vice, available as it once was not on Main Street, on videotapes sold in the corner drugstore. That pornography's place is now anywhere it can gain a toehold points to complex social transformations: social fragmentation has increased over the past decade in our society; there are no longer any widely shared moral rules; the traditional ties of community that once served to guide people in living moral lives have broken down. This fragmentation has allowed a very ancient theme to emerge in a blatantly public way—the theme of absolutely unbridled erotic freedom.

Pornography has obviously been affected by changes in technology—pornographers now use modern equipment such as videotape. Finally, pornography may be encouraged by challenges to the traditional patriarchal prerogative in our society—challenges to male dominance. As Steven Marcus suggested in his book *The Other Victorians*, there is an inverse relationship between the growing number of dominating and sadistic images of masculine sexuality in pornography and the decline of male dominance in everyday life. In a sense, this is the reverse side of Susan Brownmiller's argument.

What is pornography's function? There are several. First, and most blatantly, porn has a commercial function—it's a big moneymaker. Todd Gitlin observed in his essay "The Left and Porno" that "porn occupies the shadow of legitimate culture and extends the boundaries of it. The marginal moral enterprise, like all crime in capitalist society, becomes big business." Second, if pornography is the marketing of fantasies, then we can assume, following Freud, that these fantasies provide something that is missing from real life—perhaps a sense of robust eroticism and joy in the body, perhaps a feeling of possessing crude power to compel others to do one's bidding. Third, as I mentioned, pornography helps reassure those frightened by the waning male prerogatives in our culture.

Why is there so much pornography? Perhaps because our need to celebrate ourselves and to express our dominance is so great. By "our" I mean a collective masculine we: men in a society that remains male dominated, men who live and work according to an intensely competitive performance principle and who evaluate themselves according to that principle. To attempt to eliminate these fantasies of dominance by censoring pornography—and here I agree with Erica Jong—is futile; such efforts only cover up the deeper truths that the fantasies themselves express.

ARYEH NEIER: For a good many years, I confronted the issue of pornography as a civil libertarian, defending the right of anyone to express himself in any way he chose as long as he did not directly infringe on the rights of others. Since I left the American Civil Liberties Union six years ago I've worked for organizations that are concerned with human rights in various repressive countries. In these countries, whether they are in Central America or Africa or Eastern Europe or wherever, there is virtually no pornography; but there is a great deal of the same hostility toward women and the same violence against women that one finds in the United States. In fact, in many of these countries sexual vio-

lence—mass rape or sexual torture or sexual humiliation—is one of the main forms political repression
takes. I conclude from the astounding level of sexual
violence in these countries and the absence of pornography that pornography is really not very important,
that it is no more or less important than the great
variety of images that dominates the media in the
United States and other Western countries: images of
sex and violence and melodrama and ugliness and
beauty.

I suppose there is so much pornography because,
like the nightly melodramas on television, pornography is not very satisfying stuff; one seeks satisfaction by
exposing oneself to more and more and more of it.
Obviously, improvements in the technology involved
in producing and distributing pornography contribute
to the growing quantity of it. But more important is
the fact that no particular pornographic image in Mr.
Goldstein's magazine, or 100 or 1,000 other magazines,
or 1,000 movies or live shows or whatever, means a
great deal to the viewer. Thus he needs more and more
images. In much the same way, one exposes oneself to
a vast number of violent images or a vast number of
melodramatic plots because none of them amount to a
great deal. What is really important about the surfeit
of pornographic images is that it reflects one side of a
society that is spoiled by too much of everything, including violent images of all sorts.

BROWNMILLER: You're implying that we shouldn't pay any attention to
the quantity of pornography. I feel surrounded by it. I
can't go to my corner newsstand without being confronted by pictures of women mutilated, tortured,
spread into ridiculous postures—pictures designed, I
feel, to humiliate my sex and my dignity as a woman.
More important is the link between these pictures and
violence against women. Too many rapes appear to be
"copycat" crimes—that is, the rapists seemed to be
acting out scenes that had been published in pornographic magazines a month or two before. The gang
rape last year of a woman on a pool table in a New
Bedford, Massachusetts, bar may have been inspired by
an eight-page sequence of photographs in *Hustler* magazine in which a woman is spread out on a barroom
pool table and gang raped. Now many of us here are in
the business of writing; we believe books—words and
ideas—*can* seduce people. But pictures seduce even

more. Today's pornography is not delicate Japanese erotica. Go to Forty-second Street, go into one of the peep shows, see the pictures of eels being stuffed up women's vaginas, the obscene images of dogs with women, dogs with men, the whips, the chains, the chain saws. This is not a question of too many images, but a question of violence.

NEIER: I may not go to Forty-second Street peep shows. But two weeks ago, in a displaced-persons camp in El Salvador, I talked to a group of women, every one of whom had been raped; some told me of friends who had been killed after they were raped. Pornography was not a factor. There isn't any pornography in El Salvador.

The fact is that there is violent humiliation of women all over the world. Pornography is almost irrelevant to the question of sexual violence. You may have made yourself vulnerable to pornographic magazines on a newsstand . . .

BROWNMILLER: What do you mean, "made yourself vulnerable"? Is that like getting yourself raped?

NEIER: Only that many women turn a blind eye to these magazines, while other women feel very vulnerable.

DECTER: I agree with Susan Brownmiller that there is much that is degrading to women in contemporary pornography, though I don't know if this is endemic to pornography as such. I certainly feel degraded by it. And I agree with Aryeh Neier that one of the reasons we have so much pornography is that we have so much pornography; that is, there is a progressive deadening to the stuff. Anyone who watches Mr. Goldstein's television program, *Midnight Blue*, eventually reaches the point where he or she needs an extreme escalation of violence or gaudiness to overcome the tedium. People looking for stimulation must keep upping the ante.

Susan Brownmiller spoke of the violence in pornography—of women being whipped and mutilated and chained. Much of this imagery is drawn from the writings of the Marquis de Sade. Many years ago, thanks to the loosening of censorship, I was finally able to read his books. I discovered that de Sade was a philosopher of homosexuality; his work is a celebration of buggery as the highest form of erotic satisfaction.

BROWNMILLER: What you say about de Sade may be true. Nonetheless, according to the 1970 report of the Commission on Obscenity and Pornography, 90 percent of the pornography produced in this country is heterosexual. Homo-sexual pornography frankly troubles me less because it does not reflect the power imbalance in our culture between men and women. When men are doing it to each other, there is no clear victim.

GOLDSTEIN: You said pornography "reflects" the power imbalance, which I think is the right word. But earlier you claimed it was more than a reflection. You said pornography *causes* the degradation of women, and causes violence against them.

BROWNMILLER: It is a contributing factor. Pornography is propaganda against women, and propaganda is a very powerful spur to action—think of the anti-Semitic propaganda in Hitler's Germany. Pornography promotes a climate of opinion in which sexual hostility against women is not only tolerated but ideologically encouraged. Recent studies, in particular those by Malamuth and Donner-stein,* support the first part of that equation, at any rate.

ELSHTAIN: The link that you're suggesting between pornography and violent sexual crimes draws on simplistic behavior-ist psychology. This psychology doesn't enjoy much credibility today because it doesn't take into account the intricacies of human fantasy life—the complex re-lationship between what goes on in our minds and what we do in the world. Most of the studies that assert a direct connection between pornography and sexual vi-olence are done under highly artificial conditions and don't stand up under close scrutiny. Words and ideas certainly influence how people behave, as Susan Brownmiller said; but to try to draw a direct causal line is to oversimplify the relationship between images, fan-tasies, and actions.

LAPHAM: Do we agree that the increase in pornography, the fact that it has become such a growth industry, is a symp-tom of profound unhappiness in our society?

DECTER: I think we can agree that pornography, in the quantity in which we swim today, is doing something bad *to* us as well. In our society we find less and less good humor and cheerfulness about our inevitable human lot. There is so little play—innocent or otherwise—be-tween men and women, and play is one of the things

Pornography and Sexual Aggression, ed. Neil M. Malamuth and Edward Donnerstein (Academic Press, 1984).

that make their life together tolerable. And whatever little is left of the erotic—with due respect to Erica Jong—is being snuffed out.

GOLDSTEIN: I know I'm on the right side of the argument when I hear feminists like Susan Brownmiller tell *me* about the business I've been in for sixteen years. Her idea of the pornography business has nothing to do with reality. I've heard people here talk about eels and mutilation and pedophilia. I don't see eels; I don't see mutilation. Yes, there are photos with S/M connotations, but they represent less than 3 percent of my business. Pedophilia does not exist in what is called the establishment end of the business—the Adult Film Association and magazines like *Playboy* and *Penthouse* and *Hustler* and *Screw*. I personally believe anyone involved in the sexual exploitation of children should go to prison for twenty years—and I have supported legislation to that effect. I realize this may be construed as an inconsistency in my position. But I have come to feel that pornographic photos of children should not be constitutionally protected. After sixteen years of discussion on panels such as this one I can state that my position is this: I am in favor of pictorial depictions of people fucking. That is what pornography is to me. But children must be protected. There is a higher cause here than First Amendment absolutism and it is the protection of innocent people, and the innocent people are children.

Susan Brownmiller finds pornography appalling because she considers it anti-female propaganda—she objects to what she considers the ideology of pornography. My retort to that is—tough. Anti-female propaganda has as much right to exist as anti-Jewish propaganda and anti-American propaganda. If someone hates women, or hates gay men or midgets for that matter, he has a right to express that opinion. The price of living in a free society is putting up with points of view you don't like. I'll be glad to buy Susan Brownmiller a one-way ticket to Cuba, where there's no pornography.

BROWNMILLER: No one in the country is making billions of dollars on anti-Semitic propaganda or on anti-black propaganda. If these traditional forms of propaganda were huge moneymaking activities, no one would tolerate it. You, Aryeh Neier, would not defend the enormous commercial success of virulent hatred directed against Jews or blacks. Only when it is directed against women do we meekly accept such hatred and propaganda, contenting ourselves with philosophic discussions about whether we are or aren't curtailing free speech.

ELSHTAIN: But the fact that women are participants in this form of—to use your term—propaganda makes it rather different from anti-black or anti-Semitic propaganda. Certainly women could end pornography right now if they adopted a strategy like that of the women in *Lysistrata* and simply ceased to participate in it. Women's complicity cannot be ignored.

LAPHAM: The question still remains as to complicity in precisely *what*; maybe we can now turn the discussion to the specific nature of pornography.

BROWNMILLER: I think we have to recognize that advances in technology have not only played a part in the proliferation of pornography, as Jean said; they have increased its power as well. A photograph is infinitely more shocking than a drawing, for example. A photograph makes people think that what they are seeing is the truth; a drawing tells them that what they are seeing is fantasy. When people look at *Penthouse, Hustler,* or *Screw,* they think: "This is the truth about women." I mean, here's the photograph. A woman is actually *doing* this.

JONG: Yes: "That's what women do."

BROWNMILLER: Exactly, and that's who women are.

JONG: That these photographs constitute a campaign of violence against women is a point well taken. And I disagree with Al's statement that it's just too bad women are being shown this way in photographs. I think we should make people understand how this distorts women's sexuality. What Susan has tried to do in her books—to demonstrate how pornography is violence against women, to show the hostility behind it—is certainly all to the good. I think discussion is vital. But I stop short of supporting legislation to censor pornography.

DECTER: Erica Jong said earlier that pornography is a reflection of the puritanism in our society. Societies and historical periods have varied widely in their sexual attitudes: some have been quite licentious, others quite puritanical. But to call the United States today puritanical seems to me to do something very peculiar to that word. Perhaps we should ask ourselves why, when there is supposedly a great deal of sexual activity and no serious social sanction against it, we have more and more pornography.

JONG: The very proliferation of pornography shows that our society is *not* liberated sexually. In Venice in Casanova's time, for example, a married woman who had one or two lovers was considered virtuous. Only if she had six or seven did her behavior become a bit questionable. Sex then was treated as something light and enjoyable, a celebration of the body; sexual desire was associated with humor and laughter and looked upon as a human foible, tolerated as such things are by wise people. Today's attitudes toward sex are quite different, and they are reflected in our pornography's intense, joyless focus on organs. This pornography is not a celebration of sex as one of the pleasures of life, like enjoying a meal or cuddling a baby. The sex in it is a very frantic, fraught, obsessive, and humorless pursuit, and that very obsessiveness is indeed a product of our puritanism.

ELSHTAIN: I think this joylessness and grimness is a reflection of the production process itself—of the joylessness of work in an advanced industrial society. Human beings, diminished within giant factories and giant bureaucracies, feel powerless to affect what's going on. The mechanistic sexuality of pornography is an outgrowth of our mechanistic world, with its productivity goals and all the rest. Perhaps the real puritanism in pornography is the grim work ethic that permeates our culture.

NEIER: Isn't the joylessness also a function of the fact that there are a lot of untalented people producing pornography? Very few of them have any imagination, so they present all these grim images. Perhaps the real difference between erotica and pornography is simply a question of talent.

Consider Helmut Newton's photographs: they treat women as objects, they are violent, they are sexually explicit. Yet they reflect a certain level of talent, more talent, certainly, than is on display in the pornographic magazines one can buy at newsstands. And so Helmut Newton's photographs are called erotica instead of pornography.

BROWNMILLER: I find Helmut Newton's photographs quite offensive, and I think they are part of the fallout from pornography. *Vogue's* fascination with S/M derives from its popularization in hard-core porn. As for its joylessness . . .

GOLDSTEIN: Isn't it possible this so-called joylessness is a manifestation of the elitism of this panel? This joylessness everyone is making so much of—I don't see it around me. *Screw* every week makes fun of sex. We always say, "Fucking is only friction." Pornography is not joyless. But of course the mass media won't deal with the subject unless it's done in a very serious, pedantic, and elitist way. You people are filtering the subject through your own inhibitions, your own intellectual biases. The attitudes you are displaying in this discussion are those that force the person who masturbates to feel a high degree of self-contempt. As Lenny Bruce said, "America makes Americans sexual cripples and then tries to take away their crutches." If all you see in pornography is joylessness and grimness, perhaps it's because you're viewing it through your own pomposity, elitism, and sexual self-hate.

LAPHAM: I don't see any evidence of those qualities here at all . . .

GOLDSTEIN: Well I do. It's as if Jewish intellectuals don't masturbate.

JONG: I think Philip Roth proved they do.

ELSHTAIN: Don't you think a performance principle exists in pornography somewhat analogous to production quotas?

GOLDSTEIN: Quotas imposed by whom? We don't have quotas. We don't have orgasm counts. Who are you talking about? Give me specific examples instead of these general indictments of porn.

I'd like to know the last time anyone here walked into a porno shop or saw a sex film. You people are uptight intellectuals. I think you should examine your own need to make sex boring. I think you're afraid that if sex is too much fun, you must be doing it wrong.

LAPHAM: I don't agree. The crowds in pornographic bookstores strike me as a very unhappy lot. I don't associate pornography with joyful truck drivers.

NEIER: If people really found one copy of *Playboy* so stimulating, they wouldn't need a hundred other copies of *Playboy* or a hundred copies of other magazines.

GOLDSTEIN: That's ridiculous. Look, we're talking about junk food here. Pornography is junk entertainment, that's all. The fact that pornography is so popular—that *Playboy* sells 4 million copies each month and *Penthouse* 3 mil-

LAPHAM:

GOLDSTEIN:

LAPHAM:

NEIER:

LAPHAM:

NEIER:

lion—indicates that it's a success, not a failure, that people *want* the entertainment it provides. Pornography is minutia—a diversion. It's not much different from *The Gong Show* or *Dynasty*.

We've heard pornography defined as a medicine, as an aid to the repressed, as a political vendetta, as a Greek mask, as a grim reflection of the puritanical work ethic, and now as junk food. But nobody has defined it as a form of speech.

Give me two minutes and I will. In 1975, the U.S. Supreme Court ruled that oral sex can be prosecuted as a "crime against nature" in a court of law. Now I would argue that pornographic magazines and films, by offering pictures of men performing oral sex on women and the other way around, and both ways at once, serve as a visual polemic that encourages people to feel more open about their sexuality. In the pages of *Screw*, and in pornography in general, a philosophic argument is being set out that is intended to liberate people sexually. Pornography advocates ideas: swinging, diversity in sexual positions, openness to homosexuality. In our society Nazis have a right to speak, communists have a right to speak, atheists have a right to speak, people against and in favor of abortion have a right to speak. Sexual swingers have the same right to put their views forward.

But to say that pornography has a viewpoint is like saying cigarettes have a viewpoint, or whiskey has a viewpoint.

No, it's not quite the same thing. Remember that pornography is a representation of something, an image in words or in pictures. Pornography is not the sex act, but a representation of the sex act; in protecting freedom of expression, one protects the representation of something, not the thing itself.

Suppose that instead of defining pornography as a form of expression, we define it as a drug, like liquor or tobacco—a product you buy for the specific physical effect it has on you. Perhaps if we were able to distinguish it in this way from other sorts of written expression, we could regulate it without entangling ourselves in the First Amendment.

But your definition is arbitrary; I could define anything as a drug—soap operas, mystery stories, *Good Housekeeping*, anything I might not happen to like.

DECTER: I think Lewis is implying that pornography, like drugs, is having a bad effect on the community, and we seem to be without any means to deal with it. I'm not talking about restricting "anything we don't happen to like." We are able to make meaningful distinctions between *Lady Chatterley's Lover* or *Ulysses* and the pornography sold at newsstands. Indeed, the courts were once able to arrive at such distinctions.

JONG: Yes, but only after those books had been banned and burned for years.

LAPHAM: Is anyone here in favor of laws to limit pornography?

ELSHTAIN: I support the recent efforts of many communities to organize themselves democratically and regulate pornography through "community standards" legislation or through zoning laws designed to "put pornography in its place" without completely suppressing it. In Massachusetts alone, over a dozen towns and cities have discouraged pornographers from opening "adult bookstores" and sexual paraphernalia shops by restricting them to certain areas. I believe this is as far as we can go without imposing actual censorship.

NEIER: I wouldn't attach much significance to communities "organizing democratically." That a majority of the people in a given community say they don't want to hear or see something is no legal basis for suppressing it. You could suppress virtually anything if all you had to do was submit it to a vote. But our Constitution says that "Congress shall make no law"—that is, the democratic process shall not be a basis for prohibiting speech or expression.

The basic legal problem in restricting or penalizing particular forms of expression is that expression is continually changing. It is thus extremely difficult to determine precisely what will be prohibited. The legislators who write the laws are forced to employ vague terms that they hope will accommodate any changes in expression. But the prosecutors and judges, who must determine what those terms actually mean, inevitably apply them to some forms of expression that those who wrote the laws did not intend to be limited.

Another problem is developing a clear standard that would determine when a particular form of expression should be prohibited: what is it that makes it obscene or whatever? For example, do we claim there is a cause-and-effect relationship between this form of expression and some crime? If so, how can we prove it? Suppose someone argues that such a relationship exists between some other kind of speech and a crime. For example, suppose a "human life amendment" is passed making abortion a crime on the grounds that killing a fetus is murder. Now someone might argue that there exists a cause-and-effect relationship between advocating birth control and abortion and killing fetuses, and that the state therefore has a right to prevent the dissemination of information about birth control.

DECTER: In principle I am in favor of laws limiting pornography. But the great problem we have in even considering such laws is that we must first recognize, as even Al Goldstein has been forced to, that we are not in favor of absolute protection of speech. I say this not as a legal argument but as a cultural argument. We have reached a point of extreme confusion in this society—we no longer have any idea what our values are or what they should be. If pornography is not a cause of this confusion it is unquestionably a symptom. We cannot legislate attitudes, as Erica Jong said. But we as a society must do *something* to protect ourselves. If the law cannot involve an assertion of community standards, what is it for? And if we *have* no community standards in this area, we are more than halfway to the abyss. Amid all our talk about First Amendment absolutism, I must point out that at one time in this country—and not all that long ago, either—speech was not absolutely protected; and I don't think American society then was repressive, or that people's rights and freedoms were violated.

NEIER: You are quite wrong. During World War I, 2,000 people were sent to prison for speaking out against the war—speaking against it, nothing more. We were certainly a more repressive society then. Our protection of speech essentially began after World War I, with the development of the "clear and present danger" test.

One has to ask a simple question of those who favor censorship: What do you regard as an intellectually honest method of distinguishing between material you find offensive and other forms of expression? We need a persuasive argument that regulating pornography would not at the same time allow the regulation of other forms of communication.

BROWNMILLER: Clearly it is essential to protect the freedoms we have; no one wants to return to the repression of the Palmer

Raids era. We must protect the right to political dissent. But I think we *can* separate pornography from genuine political expression. And I do not doubt, Al, that we can preserve the right to engage in cunnilingus and fellatio without help from pornographers. Certainly pornographers have not been in the forefront of the battle to strike down laws prohibiting sodomy; nor have they been in the forefront of the struggle for gay liberation and women's liberation.

Perhaps we should examine the pieties that often prevent people from publicly opposing pornography, even though they may admit in private that it has become a major problem. First, no one wants to be considered politically illiberal, an opponent of free speech. Second, and even more important, no one wants to be considered sexually illiberal or repressed. The anti-pornography movement must convince people that they can be good liberals, support the First Amendment, have a terrific sex life—*and* oppose pornography and fight to curtail it.

NEIER: Fighting to curtail it is one thing, imposing your will on others by invoking the authority of the state quite another. If you want to do that, you owe everyone a strong argument for proscribing pornography that would not also allow the state to prevent Margaret Sanger from distributing birth control literature, which many free-speech court battles centered on in the past. On what basis would you proscribe one and not the other?

BROWNMILLER: That it's dangerous. That it incites people to commit violent acts. That it distorts the nature of sex.

NEIER: But the claim that certain kinds of expression are "dangerous" and an "incitement to violence" is used all the time to try to prohibit speech one doesn't like. We evolved the notion of a clear and present danger to deal with that. For pornography to be suppressed under this test, we would have to demonstrate that it is probable that any viewer would be provoked to commit sexual violence immediately upon seeing it. No one claims that pornography has this instantaneous effect.

DECTER: Can we not at the very least distinguish between books and shows that we read and view voluntarily and the pornography displayed at newsstands and on movie marquees, which we are forced to see?

BROWNMILLER: Yes, we can certainly impose restrictions on public displays of pornography without violating the First

Amendment. I want to protect free speech. I would never say, "Smash the presses! Don't let Al Goldstein put out his smut sheet!" I think he has a right to publish it. But I don't think he can claim he has the right to display his magazine on the newsstands because it is protected speech.

NEIER: The legal term generally used when we talk about restricting public displays is "thrusting," that is, large public displays that someone cannot avoid seeing. I agree that we can regulate such displays without interfering with anyone's right to read what he wants, see what he wants, and express himself as he wants. I don't have difficulty with the idea of regulating thrusting. In Stockholm, for example, there are quite a few sex clubs, but they are permitted to have only very small signs.

GOLDSTEIN: Imposing pornography on an unwilling public, the way the marquees on Forty-second Street theaters do, is as repugnant to me as a hooker soliciting a man when he is walking with his wife. But I believe that adults who want to buy pornography have the right to do so. Those who want to limit it in some way have the problem of distinguishing it, as Aryeh Neier said, from other forms of expression.

BROWNMILLER: But I just offered a concrete suggestion that would not conflict with free expression—restricting public displays. Which would mean, Al, that *Screw* could not be featured prominently on the newsstands.

GOLDSTEIN: I would agree to such a restriction, Susan—but only if you agreed to restrict *Ms.* as well. After all, we must consider the feelings of those people who are offended by Gloria Steinem's arguing in favor of killing little children who aren't born yet. If we must be so sensitive to Susan Brownmiller's aesthetics, why should we ignore the strong beliefs of women marching against abortion in Queens?

BROWNMILLER: Our society is able to understand the distinction between pornography and political disagreement. We can support gay rights; we can support the right to abortion; we can strike down all consensual sodomy laws; and we can still restrict pornography.

NEIER: But you do agree that many people are as offended by what they consider propaganda for abortion as you are by pornography? And you don't want those people to be able to suppress propaganda for abortion.

BROWNMILLER: But "propaganda for abortion" is not a huge business in this country. You can protect the pornographer's right to free speech without giving him access to a billion-dollar business. By restricting public displays, pictures that personally offend many people and encourage violence as well would be removed from public view. It is mainly the danger, not the personal offense, that concerns me.

JONG: I don't think we are limiting freedom of speech if we restrict the display of pornographic magazines on the newsstands.

NEIER: As I said, limiting public display—"thrusting"—I have no problem with.

JONG: And I also don't think we're limiting freedom of speech if we say these magazines must be purchased only by subscription.

GOLDSTEIN: Of course you are: you're limiting availability to the public. You'll guarantee my right to publish *Screw* as long as I stay in the closet and don't try to distribute it. My product is valuable only if it can reach the marketplace. And your attempt to prevent that presupposes you know what's best for the man or woman who wants to buy *Playboy* or *Screw*.

JONG: As I said, I oppose any across-the-board law that could be used to inhibit free speech. Perhaps the best course is to take voluntary action: for example, to institute the coding system for books that I mentioned earlier throughout the publishing industry. The Literary Guild forewarns its subscribers that certain books, including my own, may be offensive to some people. That often piques people's interest in the books—though it is supposedly meant to do the reverse. I find all this absurd, since I think my books demonstrate a healthy celebration of sex. I would sooner see violent books about the Mafia, say, published with caveats. But nobody seems to think they're offensive or harmful. Only sexual desire, the oldest of all human drives, needs a caveat. It's mad!

Whenever I read from my novels or my poetry there is inevitably someone in the audience who says, "It's all very well to speak out for the rights of women in our society, but what *action* should we take?" There are always people who believe that writing and other forms of public argument are not enough. I applaud many of the efforts of the members of Women Against Pornography: the slide shows they have produced showing the true nature of pornography, the polemics they have written exposing the sadomasochism that lies at the root of so much of it. We should continue these efforts. But I oppose invoking the authority of the state on one side or another. I don't believe the state is all-knowing, particularly not our state. I think we should be wary of imposing laws such as that in Indianapolis, which allow the "victims" of pornography to sue for damages. Our society is already obsessed with lawsuits and litigation. Litigation is not the key to reforming social attitudes.

ELSHTAIN: While I also oppose across-the-board statutes restricting pornography, I support community efforts to limit it. But pornography is only a symptom, as both Midge Decter and Erica Jong have pointed out. What we really must address is, in the words of Bernard Williams, the "pervasive lying and destructive sexism of popular culture."* To do this we need to develop a more historically and philosophically sophisticated feminist perspective than that offered by the contemporary feminist anti-pornography movement. Such a perspective would help us explore the links between pornography and the political and economic conditions of a particular time, and the relation between pornography and changes in sexual mores.

BROWNMILLER: Over the last ten years or so the anti-pornography movement has been fighting hard to draw attention to a subject that we find extremely distasteful. I don't want to spend my time fighting against pornography. I would much rather be gardening, or writing my books. But someone has to do it, and feminists have brought new ideas to the struggle. Someone has to make society recognize that pornography is a problem—that it is in fact anti-female propaganda that presents a distorted picture of female sexuality. We've got to do something about it. The question is, how do we do it while protecting our important right of free speech? One way to start is by restricting the public display of pornography. And restricting public display obviously means restricting public access.

NEIER: I could have gone along with you until your last statement. Public access means that a person is able to choose freely whether to expose himself to pornogra-

*Bernard Williams, "Pornography and Feminism," *London Review of Books* March 17–31, 1983.

phy. One restricts public display so that people who *don't* choose to subject themselves to pornography do not have it thrust upon them. I would not oppose restricting public display; but I would oppose restricting public access. The First Amendment protects the freedom of choice of the person who disseminates information and images, and the freedom of choice of the person who receives information and images. We want to protect both sides of that equation. When the person who disseminates imposes his images on an unwilling audience, he may be interfering with the freedom of choice of that audience.

One can sympathize with the feminist attack on pornography but remain wholly unsympathetic to what verges on an effort to invoke the power of the state to suppress it. When one invokes that power, one sets in motion forces that, I believe, will damage, first and foremost, those groups that are relatively powerless. To the extent that the feminist movement speaks on behalf of women victimized by those who have more power, it will be the loser in any effort to legitimize the power of the state to restrict expression.

DECTER: I agree that legislation by itself is not the answer. It never is. The genie is now out of the bottle, and those of us who oppose pornography must press our campaign, not through legal means but in the manner we have today—by conducting public argument. Although pornographers like Al Goldstein claim to be liberating us, we should think a little more seriously about what they are doing to our culture. I believe that among other things they are helping to destroy all humane and valuable attitudes about sex: we will be lucky if there is any sex at all twenty-five years from now.

GOLDSTEIN: Pornography is certainly not the death knell for sex, Midge; marriage is a much greater threat. And to Susan Brownmiller, who has been plucked from her garden to fight the good fight against pornography, I must say that being a pornographer is a dirty job, too, but someone has to do it.

The problem with pornography is that no one really knows what it is, no one knows where to draw the line that separates it from other forms of expression. We know only that certain things offend us; and again, my response is—tough. In a democracy, a lot of things offend *someone*. I am an atheist, yet I must listen to the

diatribes of priests and various religious nuts. But I
listen to points of view I disagree with because that's
what living in a democracy *is*. Totalitarian countries
eliminate this problem; people don't have to worry
about choosing between various points of view because
there is no choice. Here there is, and since I don't
know what's best for me, and you people don't know
what's best for you, why don't we assume that the average person doesn't know either, and that he will
stumble along, making his own choices. That's called
living in a free society.

LAPHAM: With Mr. Goldstein's democratic sentiment, I think
we can bring the discussion to an end. I'm grateful to
all of you for the civility as well as the thoughtfulness
of your remarks. Arguments about pornography have a
way of getting lost in the mists of polemic, and I was
glad to see that the range of your agreement was
broader than I would have guessed. The conversation
seemed to suggest a possible balance between the
claims made on behalf of morality and those made on
behalf of freedom. If we could limit the public uses of
pornography (i.e., its egregious display, its pretense to
political statement), then we could more easily preserve its private uses (as a form of expression, as a
stimulus to sexual feeling). It would be ironic if a too
devout reading of the First Amendment proscribed the
chance of a decent and intelligent compromise.

LETTERS

I enjoyed reading the Forum "The Place of Pornography" [*Harper's*, November 1984]. It was most interesting—though not surprising—that the discussion went round and round without even approaching a useful definition of pornography.

As the panelists made clear, there are many people who would like to regulate porn. Anyone presuming to do so must first separate it from other forms of expression, since free expression is protected by the First Amendment. But if pornography isn't free expression, I don't know what is. For all practical purposes, "pornography" is what the censor wants to censor, and "regulate" is a euphemism.

Susan Brownmiller says in the Forum our society is able to distinguish between pornography and politics, but I think she has failed to do just that. Those who would impose their political views on the rest of us—whether they want prayer in school or censorship—often dress their arguments in pious clothes. They claim that their perspective is the one all right-thinking people must share. Well, it ain't necessarily so.

I am an advocate of First Amendment rights. Given a choice between greater governmental control and greater personal freedom, I would choose freedom. This choice reflects what I consider a healthy repulsion toward imposing one's moral choices on everyone else. The antiporn groups, it seems, would rather err on the side of state power, eroding the rights of the individual.

Midge Decter asserts that pornography is "helping to destroy all humane and valuable attitudes about sex; we will be lucky if there is any sex at all twenty-five years from now." Has she even considered the possibility that porn has positive effects? At a recent conference at Columbia University, the eminent psychoanalyst Dr. Otto Kernberg said that inhibition "limits a couple to conventional standards that stifle passion." He said pornography, on the other hand, can stimulate an active fantasy life—can be an antidote to stifled passion. "A rebellious sex life within the bounds of a couple," he concluded, can be "the cement of marriage."

I am an optimist. If we don't forget that there are more serious threats to our future than pornography, I am certain there will be sex twenty-five years from now. I hope to be having some. I hope I won't need to ask for a censor's permission. Time will tell.

Hugh M. Hefner
Los Angeles, Calif.

"It's horrendous and I hate it but I'll fight for your right to . . ." is the respectable defense of pornography. Less respectable is to admit that porn may not be all bad. Even less respectable is to suggest that the objectification of women—one of porn's most "appalling" features—is neither monolithic nor always evil. It may be something we need, something *women* need.

We need it because it's part of play. And, as the Dutch historian Johan Huizinga wrote, play is "an absolutely primary category of life." He described it as "not serious but . . . absorbing the player intensely . . . connected with no material interest . . . the essential feature of it lies in the parading of something out of the ordinary and calculated to arouse admiration . . . ." Play involves "tension, poise, balance, contrast, variation, solution, resolution, etc . . . . Tension means uncertainty; a striving to decide the issue and so end it."

There's no use saying that both parties are subjects in a "feminist" flirtation; one person may be the subject one moment, the other later on (the way people "take turns" in other games), but at any given moment someone must be the object or the game can't be played. And we might as well admit that being the object is flattering and enormous fun. By pretending it's not we only end up knowing less about ourselves.

We may need to be objects in the same way that we need to play. We may need the admiration, pure and simple—the posturing, the dressing up, the poses, the moves, the chanciness and risk, the successful dénouement.

Objectification—like porn, and as the basis of porn—has always been a target of feminism. As chattel, womb, or cunt we get rather a bad deal. Obviously we have to fight all that, but perhaps we'd do better to determine when objectification is demeaning and when it's a lark; when it's the source of contempt, discrimination, or violence and when it's a game, without profit other than its own kick.

Marcia Pally
New York, N.Y.

There is a great difference between sexual oppression in countries like El Salvador—countries where, as Aryeh Neier pointed out, there is little or no pornography—and rape in the United States. In the countries Neier mentioned, rape and sexual humiliation are means of warfare, means of terrorizing women into silence. Repressive governments use sexual humiliation as a weapon against free speech.

In the United States, women are not raped by government soldiers or police. For the most part, they are raped by men they know: men they work with, acquaintances, family members.

Rebecca Seiferle
Bloomfield, N.M.

I support Susan Brownmiller's contention in the Forum that "pornography promotes a climate of opinion in which sexual hostility against women is not only tolerated but ideologically encouraged."

Recent studies have found that exposure to violent pornography makes some men more tolerant of violence against women and causes them to have more callous attitudes toward them. This does not mean, of course, that men who are exposed to large amounts of violent pornography will eventually commit a violent act. But there may be other effects of such exposure. It might influence the judgment of a man serving as a juror in a rape trial, or it might influence the way he responds to a rapist or a rape victim. These reactions help create a social climate that may encourage men to act in a discriminatory or even violent way toward women.

It is important to stress that there is little scientific support for any simple cause-and-effect relationship between exposure to pornography and violent crime. What recent research does show is that, in general, there is a correlation between the amount of pornography consumed in a state and the rape rate in that state.

There are important exceptions to this correlation. Some states and some countries have a high rate of pornography consumption but a low rape rate. These exceptions suggest that even if some complex causal link were discovered, it would often be mitigated by individual and cultural factors.

We can no longer assume that the media, including pornography, only have to do with fantasy. Media messages that eroticize violence or communicate myths about women can contribute to changes in attitudes, perceptions, and even behavior, although these changes in and of themselves may not cause criminal acts.

Neil M. Malamuth
Dept. of Communication Studies
UCLA
Los Angeles, Calif.

Neil M. Malamuth is co-editor, with Edward Donnerstein, of *Pornography and Sexual Aggression* (Academic Press).

A cogent case can be made that Congress should pass a law forbidding interstate commerce in any goods intended for commercial entertainment that visually depict explicit sexual behavior. If the law specified "the visual portrayal or simulation of ultimate sexual acts, including intercourse, sodomy, cunnilingus, fellatio, analingus, and masturbation, where the penetration or ejaculation of the genital organs is visible," it would solve the problem of vagueness that has plagued the enforcers of current antipornography laws.

The new law would leave books, newspapers, magazines, and all forms of entertainment uncensored so long as they didn't carry pictures portraying explicit sexual behavior. Thus the novels of Henry Miller, say, or D. H. Lawrence would not be affected.

The law would eliminate the enforcement roadblocks created by the Supreme Court in *Miller v. California*; pornographers would no longer be able to exploit such phrases as "patently offensive," "appeals to the prurient interest," and "the material taken as a whole" lacks "literary, artistic, political, and scientific value."

Reo M. Christenson
Department of Political Science
Miami University
Oxford, Ohio

Several of the panelists in the Forum mentioned the Indianapolis Anti-Pornography Ordinance. As mayor of Indianapolis and a strong supporter of the ordinance, I would like to make several points about this new legal approach.

The Indianapolis ordinance does not simply define pornography and then attempt to ban it. Rather, it is a civil discrimination law that provides a remedy through the courts to people deemed harmed by pornography. The ordinance identifies the ways people can be victimized by pornography. These ways were brought to the attention of the Indianapolis City-County Council at public hearings in which testimony was given by former models who were coerced to perform in pornographic productions; by victims of sexual abuse; and by the counselors of sex offenders, who testified that a link exists between pornography and sexual violence. With all due respect to Erica Jong, the ordinance does not aim at reforming social attitudes. Rather, it invokes the traditional power of the courts to provide a forum and a remedy—through suit and settlement—for any person who has been harmed by another through pornography.

On November 19, 1984, a federal court judge in Indianapolis issued a decision in a lawsuit that challenged the constitutionality of the ordinance. Although the court struck down the ordinance on First Amendment grounds, we are determined to appeal the decision. This law is an important social statement, the first of its kind in the country.

Further, it presents issues that may ultimately have to be decided by the U.S. Supreme Court. I believe the Indianapolis Anti-Pornography Ordinance is worth fighting for because the framers of our Constitution did not intend the First Amendment to be a shield for dehumanizing pornography.

William H. Hudnut III
Indianapolis, Ind.

SUGGESTIONS FOR WRITING

Informal Essays

1. After reading a few of the essays in this chapter, write a paper in which you discuss a personal experience you have had with censorship. Perhaps you were a member of a high school or college newspaper staff that ran into a censorship problem. As you look back now, do you still feel the same? Is the issue as clear as it was then? Is censorship of a high school newspaper the same as government censorship of a national magazine? In what way is it the same? In what way is it different? Should high school publications be protected by the First Amendment?
2. Write a humorous paper on your first contact with pornography. Devise your own thesis.
3. Write a paper in which you attack or defend the current rating system for movies (G, PG, PG-13, R, and X).

Short Documented Papers

1. Contrast the positions taken by Ernest van den Haag and Gay Talese in the debate transcribed in "What is the Civil Libertarian to Do When Pornography Becomes So Bold?"
2. After reading the summary of the *Miller* v. *California* decision (1973) in the introduction to this chapter and the interview with Alexander Bickel ("Pornography, Censorship, and Common Sense"), attack or defend the Supreme Court's decision that states or localities should be able to decide what is the "common conscience of the community."
3. After reading "The X-Rated Economy" and "Obscenity—Forget It," attack or defend the position that the right to privacy should override the right to publish and show sexually explicit material.
4. After reading a few of the definitions of pornography given in the chapter introduction and in the articles reprinted in this chapter, see if you can come up with a better definition than those that you have read.
5. Sum up the positions of Al Goldstein and Susan Brownmiller in "The Place of Pornography."
6. Categorize the responses of the participants in the forum transcribed in "The Place of Pornography."

Longer Documented Papers

1. Attack or defend the idea that obscene materials should be protected under First Amendment rights. See in particular the articles by Charles

Rembar, William F. Buckley, Irving Kristol, and the dissenting comments by Justices William O. Douglas and Hugo Black in response to *Roth* v. *United States.*

2. Write a report in which you sum up the main arguments on both sides of the censorship controversy.

3. Argue the anti-censorship case.

4. Argue the pro-censorship case.

· 9 ·

Japanese Internment: Wartime Necessity or Tragic Error?

Wartime passions and anti-Japanese sentiment were running high in the United States in 1942, particularly on the West Coast. It was widely assumed, for instance, that the attack on Pearl Harbor in December of 1941 had been aided by a large network of Japanese informers living on the Hawaiian Islands.

Then, early in 1942, the Japanese bombed other Allied bases and cities, including Hong Kong, Manila, and colonies along the Malaysian Peninsula. Fear of an imminent Japanese invasion gripped California citizens, and rumors of resident Japanese complicity with the enemy circulated widely. Such rumors were stoked by a real scare—the shelling of the coast near Santa Barbara by a Japanese submarine—and by a host of false alarms.

Fueled by these fears, West Coast politicians, newspaper editorialists, and civic groups exerted a great deal of pressure on the federal government to round up the Japanese living on the West Coast and send them to internment camps.

It's not surprising that a nation at war would have worried about the inhabitants of Japanese ancestry in their midst, many of whom had not been assimilated into the mainstream of American society. In fact, the Issei, consisting of Japanese immigrants, most of whom were farmers and fishermen, had been prohibited by the 1924 Immigration Act from becoming naturalized citizens. A second group, the Nisei, consisted of the children of the Issei. American citizens by birth and education, the Nisei were sometimes required by their parents to attend Japanese language schools, and many Californians assumed that Nisei family loyalties might well be stronger than their national ties. The third and smallest group, the Kibei, were more worrisome. Like the Nisei, they were American citizens by birth, but they had been sent by their Issei parents to Japan for their education—an education that many Americans believed included heavy political indoctrination.

Rather than try to sort out this culturally diverse group, a process that might have taken years, Franklin D. Roosevelt signed an Executive Order on February 19, 1942, that sent all 110,000 Japanese living on the West Coast to "relocation camps," where most remained for the duration of the war.

At the time, there were many Americans who protested that Roosevelt's Executive Order was unconstitutional, and many Americans today look back at what we did with shame. The internment, the critics say, was simply the result of prejudice heightened by wartime hysteria, and Pearl Harbor merely contributed a veneer of credibility to the longstanding attempts of the Hearst press, the American Legion, and various conservative and agricultural groups to vilify the Japanese living in our midst.

The issue of Japanese internment may well seem less complicated than other issues in this book. With the luxury of historical hindsight, few of us today— especially those of us too young to have experienced the acute, compelling sense of national peril that gripped people in those times—would be inclined to support that 1942 decision in intern the West Coast Japanese. Nevertheless, the essays in this chapter contain ample supporting evidence for a historical justification of the way our government, under crises conditions, chose to handle a difficult problem.

A brief history of the events leading to the internment of the Japanese in 1942 is contained in "The Activation of the Stereotype" by Jacobus ten Broek and others.

HOW TO TELL YOUR FRIENDS
FROM THE JAPS

There is no infallible way of telling them [the Chinese and the Japanese] apart, because the same racial strains are mixed in both. Even an anthropologist, with calipers and plenty of time to measure heads, noses, shoulders, hips, is sometimes stumped. A few rules of thumb—not always reliable:

- Some Chinese are tall (average: 5 ft. 5 in.). Virtually all Japanese are short (average: 5 ft. 2½ in.).
- Japanese are likely to be stockier and broader-hipped than short Chinese.
- Japanese—except for wrestlers—are seldom fat; they often dry up and grow lean as they age. The Chinese often put on weight, particularly if they are prosperous (in China, with its frequent famines, being fat is esteemed as a sign of being a solid citizen).
- Chinese, not as hairy as Japanese, seldom grow an impressive mustache.
- Most Chinese avoid horn-rimmed spectacles.
- Although both have the typical epicanthic fold of the upper eyelid (which makes them look almond-eyed), Japanese eyes are usually set closer together.
- Those who know them best often rely on facial expression to tell them apart: the Chinese expression is likely to be more placid, kindly, open; the Japanese more positive, dogmatic, arrogant.

  In Washington, last week, Correspondent Joseph Chiang made things much easier by pinning on his lapel a large badge reading "Chinese Reporter—NOT Japanese—Please."
- Some aristocratic Japanese have thin, aquiline noses, narrow faces and, except for their eyes, look like Caucasians.
- Japanese are hesitant, nervous in conversation, laugh loudly at the wrong time.
- Japanese walk stiffly erect, hard-heeled. Chinese, more relaxed, have an easy gait, sometimes shuffle.

"How to Tell Your Friends from the Japs," *Time* 22 December 1941.

JAPANESE SABOTEURS IN OUR MIDST
Stanley High

Japan is ready, in case of war, to hit us hard—from the inside. Japanese on the West Coast are well prepared for the event. They have assembled detailed data on our vital Pacific defenses. They possess the bases, the equipment and the disciplined personnel with which to strike either through sabotage or open acts of war.

Evidence of the thoroughness and extent of Japanese machinations has been dug up through six months of hard work by undercover men set upon the trail by Congress. Neither in war nor in peace would any other nation on earth be so careless of its security as to tolerate the situation which exists at the harbor of Los Angeles, for example.

Los Angeles harbor is one of America's vital defense areas. It is one of the nation's six naval operating bases and usually there are important units of the Pacific fleet at anchor inside its breakwater.

Close to the harbor are 150 producing oil wells. Along its shoreline are tank farms estimated to contain 8,000,000 barrels of oil—enough to flood the surface of the harbor with an inflammable blanket eight inches thick.

Near the center of the harbor, Terminal Island bulges with shipyards, drydocks, storage tanks of oil and aviation gasoline, half a billion dollars' worth of defense projects and Reeves Field, naval flying base.

Here in the midst of this naval stronghold the United States keeps open house for its potential enemies.

On the island is a community of 3500 to 5000 Japanese, most of them fishermen or cannery hands. How many of them are aliens, the authorities have not ascertained—not at least with complete accuracy—but one estimate is 3000 in the whole harbor area. "Little Tokyo" is squalid, but it seems to attract Japanese visitors. Japanese consular officers visit it frequently; officers and men from Japanese vessels seek its hospitality. Groups come from San Diego, Bakersfield and San Francisco.

In the Japanese fishing fleet, obligingly allowed to share harbor space here with the U.S. Navy, there are 250 vessels. Many of them, perhaps 90 percent, are manned by reservist officers and sailors of the Japanese navy. Inshore they fly the Stars and Stripes, as required by law. At sea they frequently run up the flag of the Rising Sun, as the government has photographs to prove.

They are extraordinary fishing boats. They are Diesel-powered with engines that give them a 6000-mile cruising range—say to Panama and back. They have short-wave radio capable of working direct with Japan. Some have radio telephones, sonic depth-finders, million candlepower Sperry searchlights, electrically driven air compressors and winches.

Stanley High, "Japanese Saboteurs in Our Midst," *Reader's Digest* January 1942. High worked for years as the senior editor of *Reader's Digest.* He is also the author of several religious books, including *Billy Graham: The Personal Story of the Man, His Message, and His Mission* (1956).

What the Navy thinks of these boats is summed up in the fact that it recently bought 32 of them for conversion into minesweepers and patrol boats. They are likewise convertible on short notice into minelayers and torpedo boats. Bait boxes are built so that they could conceal a pair of surface torpedo tubes with self-propelling torpedoes. Between the bait boxes and the gunwales is room for two more torpedoes. Or the boat could carry 30 mines with anchors, or 90 without anchors. Its winch could handle an 1800-pound mine.

This potentially dangerous fleet still plies unhampered among our naval vessels and defense plants and up and down our coastline. What they would do in case of war, only war will tell, but a strong hint has been revealed.

Last winter two retired Japanese officers—one for the army and one for the navy—toured our West Coast states to stir Japan's agents to renewed activity. They carried with them a secret document entitled *The Triple Alliance and the Japanese-American War*. One copy got into American hands.

This textbook has much to say about Japan's "surprise fleet," with its "minelayers capable of carrying a heavy load of mines for distribution in American sea routes of merchantmen and battleships." "We can then," the booklet continues, "strike the enemy fleet at a most opportune time and cut off communication lines as well as merchantmen."

Meanwhile, wherever the U.S. fleet is maneuvering, fishing must almost always be good, for the Japanese boats turn up—not forgetting their telescopic cameras. Recently they turned up for the Navy's maneuvers in the Caribbean. West Coast fishermen had never fished those waters before.

Japan has already profited from these operations at sea and ashore. Our coast-line—including the remote bays and harbors of Alaska—is more familiar to Japan and to the Japanese reservists in the West Coast fishing fleet, who have painstakingly photographed, mapped and charted it, than to our own sailors. Helped along by our American laxity, they appear to have done the same job on the U.S. Navy.

A few weeks ago, in this defense area, government investigators came into possession of two documents. The first, printed by the Japanese navy, was purloined from a Japanese naval reservist on Terminal Island. It is a several-hundred-page, ship-by-ship description of the important units of the U.S. fleet—complete with photographs and scale drawings for each. It is up to date, including several ships launched last summer.

The second document is a map, likewise printed in Japan—an overall key to our Pacific naval defenses including Hawaii. Most startling item on it is a diagram showing in accurate detail the battle formation of our Pacific fleet, presumably a well-guarded secret.

Almost as important as the fishing fleet are the Japanese farmers. A government investigator pointed out—two years ago—that there was not a single flying field on the entire West Coast which did not have Japanese farmers nearby.

They seem curiously indifferent about soil fertility. The Kettleman Hills area is poor farm land. But it contains one of the nation's most valuable oil fields. In the adjacent San Joaquin Valley plenty of fertile land is available. But Kettleman Hills, nonetheless, has a thriving community of Japanese truck gardeners.

Recently two Japanese rented—for truck gardening—the 1300-acre Conroy Ranch, most of it too dry to be farmed at all. But the ranch is traversed by the huge aqueduct which carries water to the city of Los Angeles. The ranch house is adjacent to the Water Patrol Road and the aqueduct's casually protected inspection gate.

Of the loyalty to the United States of thousands of our West Coast Japanese, particularly the Nisei, or American-born, there is and can be no question. In fact they have supplied much of the information our government has.

But pressure to serve the Emperor is too strong for many to resist, and over the years Japan has made every effort to keep its hold on the Japanese in America.

At birth Japanese parents register their children with the consul. Those who hesitate are subjected by the Japanese organization to various forms of pressure ranging from social cold-shouldering through business boycott to blunt threats—familiar Axis technique. The registration makes the child a citizen of Japan as well as of the United States—and this is the status of more than 60 percent of California's American-born Japanese.

At kindergarten age, Japan reaches for the child again and he is sent—each day after public school—to one of the 248 Japanese-language schools in California. Almost all the teachers are either alien Japanese or educated in Japan. Many of them are Shinto priests, trained in the religion of Japanese nationalism. Until last spring, when a threatened investigation put them momentarily on the shelf, the textbooks used in these schools were published by the Japanese Imperial Board of Education.

Lesson 30 of the Junior High School Reader declares: "The objective of Japanese education, no matter in what country it may be, is to teach the people never to be ashamed of their Japanese citizenship. We must never forget—not even for a moment—that we are Japanese."

Lesson one in Grade Five begins: "Our heavenly ruler has governed our Empire for ages past and we are his subjects . . . . There is no other country with such a royal lineage. Be thankful you are a Japanese and worship the Imperial Family."

"Hawaii is known as a possession of the United States of America," says the eighth grade reader, "but here the Japanese language is spoken just as you hear it in Yokohama . . . . Hawaii's development to its present stage is due to the Japanese."

After this yearly indoctrination, Japan's helping hand is extended into a network of some 60 useful and potentially useful adult organizations. Every Japanese community of any size has Buddhist temples—over the altars, the inscription: "Now let us worship the Emperor every morning." Shinto—even more undisguised in its propagandist teachings—is also well represented. In Los Angeles there are 16 Shinto temples.

Almost every Japanese family in the U.S. is a member of a "Ken," or clan. Headquarters for each Ken is Japan—in the prefecture from which the family originated. The Ken's aim is to maintain the family tie with Japan. There are 57 Kens in Los Angeles alone. They are linked in an association; its hidden control is in the hands of one of Japan's top-flight spies.

Most potent of all organizations among the Japanese is the Japanese Association. Wherever so much as a handful of Japanese are gathered, an Association is forthwith formed. It serves the community in numerous worthy ways. Control of these Associations—according to the testimony of Japanese—is almost wholly in the hands of aliens. Behind the scenes the strings are pulled by the Japanese consul. The Associations enable the consuls to keep a record of comings and goings of every Japanese, to transmit messages, launch propaganda and, when pressure is required, put on the screws.

Thus the Japanese community—more than any other in the United States—is a fertile field for the purposeful machinations of a foreign power. With the generous support of the government of the United States the field is being cultivated.

The book which the two Japanese officers carried on their last winter's tour comes to this conclusion: "Should America become involved in war she would be subjected to gigantic, united attack from Japan, Germany and Italy. Only the flag of the sun would fly in the Pacific. In the Atlantic, the swastika, which also symbolizes the sun and life, will be active with might. In addition, the meaningful flag of Italy would flash. In the face of all this, if America comes against Japan and tries to block her it would be no more than a pin prick."

It is doubtful whether Japan's spies and saboteurs inside the United States were in need of any such sales talk. Driven by their own well-nurtured patriotism and apparently unmolested by the government they are plotting against, their part in the anticipated triumph appears to be well prepared.

THE DIES REPORT

Baron Gen. Giichi Tanaka, Japanese Premier known as the "Machiavelli of Nippon," called on Emperor Hirohito July 25, 1927, with a 10,000 word document. It was his advice to the new Emperor, who had ascended to the throne on Christmas Day, 1926, and it contained a plan for the conquest of Manchuria and the rest of China, India, Asia Minor, Central Asia, and even Europe by the Japanese. But Tanaka pointed out that Japan must first crush the United States before she could carry out the rest of the program.

Excerpts from the famous Tanaka Memorial were published by the Chinese five days after Japan invaded Manchuria in September 1931 and by the Russian newspaper Pravda on Nov. 5, 1931. The Chinese claimed to have got it from a Korean clerk who stole a copy and the Russians from a clerk who photostated it. The Japanese began a barrage of official denials, which were widely accepted.

On Feb. 27 Rep. Martin Dies of Texas, chairman of the House committee to investigate un-American activities, which is seeking a continuing appropriation of $100,000, made public a 285-page report on Japanese plans and plots which he said was based on a mass of evidence, including the Tanaka Memorial. He had planned public hearings on them last September but waited at the request of Attorney General Francis Biddle.

The Dies report included a secret Japanese "invasion map" of the United States as well as a supplement to the Tanaka Memorial by Lt. Gen. Kiyokatsu Sato urging that Japan capture Hawaii, destroy the Panama Canal from the air, and land troops on the West Coast of the United States to destroy cities and ports. Building a line of defense along the Rocky Mountains, the Japanese, according to Sato, would then take the offensive toward the East Coast.

To further plans for conquest of America, the Dies report revealed, the Japanese Government used thousands of Japanese residents of the United States and its possessions to obtain detailed information about the American Fleet, Hawaii, the Panama Canal, and even the Los Angeles water supply. Code devices included necklaces, matches cut at various lengths, dental plates, the notching of postage stamps, and a copy of George Bernard Shaw's "The Devil's Disciple," certain words of which were underlined in invisible ink.

The report was made public a day before the deadline for re-registration of all enemy aliens in the United States and as the Army and Department of Justice were preparing to move all Japanese, citizens as well as aliens, out of Pacific Coast "combat zones." Residents of Coast communities were more anxious than ever to get rid of their aliens after rumors that signal lights were seen before the submarine attack near Santa Barbara on Feb. 23 and the air-raid alarm over Los Angeles on Feb. 25.

"The Dies Report" [our title], *Newsweek* 9 March 1942.

LIFE IN A CALIFORNIA CONCENTRATION CAMP

Dear Sirs: I inclose excerpts from a letter to a member of my household written by a Japanese student, American-born, registered at the University of California in the Department of Home Economics, who for the last year and half has lived in my home.

Since I do not know how the neighboring American citizens would be disposed toward Japanese criticism of their local "Assembly Center" I feel that it might be inadvisable for you to identify the writer or the camp.

MARION RANDALL PARSONS
Berkeley, Cal., May 26

[The excerpts follow.]

We are now in our "apartment" in —— Assembly Center, having arrived here yesterday after a heavy shower. —— is famous for black clayey soil; so you can imagine what the mud was like. Lunch was a horrid affair—one frankfurter, a mess of overboiled cabbage, white bread, pasty rice, and canned cherries. All the workers are volunteers from the camp, and the cooks are quite inexperienced or else rusty with disuse, since many of the farmers from our vicinity were house boys and cooks some thirty years ago. Dinner was better—canned carrots and peas, one slab of canned pork, lettuce salad, apricots, and plenty of milk. There is a great shortage of waiters and common laborers. My brother was asked to help, but upon hearing that they are paid 70 cents a day and that board and room is subtracted from that, he said no!

The "apartments" are rooms with four, six, and eight beds. Usually they assign one "apartment" to a family. The rooms have screened windows, concrete or wooden floors, and a door that may or may not fit. Some doors are at least two inches too small for the doorway. When we first saw our living quarters we were so sick we couldn't eat or talk—couldn't even cry till later. Since they will not allow less than four in one room my two brothers are living with H— and me. We have put up canvas partitions. These things are tolerable, but you should see the latrines! Ten seats lined up; hard, fresh-sawed, unsandpapered wood; automatic flushing about every fifteen minutes.

My parents feel humiliated but are quite resigned. I admire their stoicism or whatever it is that enables them to hold up under so much. P— is in the hospital, one of the many that filled up the temporary wards as soon as they entered. . . .

I have been offered a job as dietician! Was busy till 10 p.m. yesterday. There is no regular dietician we can work under. Another girl and I have had our hands full helping with the mess halls, planning menus, even cooking. There is great need for

"Life in a California Concentration Camp," *The Nation* 154 (1942). *The Nation* is a liberal political journal.

trained nurses and decent hospital equipment. The only fresh fruit we can get is bananas and the only fresh vegetable is cabbage. Many people need special diet— allergies, diabetes, stomach ulcer, high blood pressure. V— and I feel overloaded, especially because we don't know a thing about planning menus from equations, balancing calories, weighing out grams, etc.

Three-fourths of the population loaf all day while the mess-hall boys and girls and the hospital staff work like horses. Right now the nurses are on duty twelve or fourteen hours a day. We greenhorn dieticians on ten hours can't complain.

We are slowly getting adapted to the diet, lack of privacy, etc., but every time we think of the white plastered walls, sunny rooms, and green gardens we left behind we again drop into depression. . . .

Last night it rained—for many people on their beds. Our head nurse says she cries every night when she thinks of the old folks, many of whom will most likely die here very soon, and of the children, who don't understand why they can't leave this horrid place.

Thanks, millions and millions, for those books. They are life-savers, especially for H—, who feels there's hardly anything left to live for except books.

I have been giving you the worst side of life here—the side most obvious. There is another side to the picture too. Some of the boys play all day, stopping only to sleep and eat. Some of the formerly busy mothers have time to look after their babies and chat with the neighbors. For many this is a long vacation in somewhat drab surroundings.

One man says he has a new slogan. Instead of "Remember Pearl Harbor" it is "Remember the Concentration Camp."

Until our dying day we'll not forget.

CONCENTRATION CAMP: U.S. STYLE
Ted Nakashima

Unfortunately in this land of liberty, I was born of Japanese parents; born in Seattle of a mother and father who have been in this country since 1901. Fine parents, who brought up their children in the best American way of life. My mother served with the Volunteer Red Cross Service in the last war—my father, an editor, has spoken and written Americanism for forty years.

Our family is almost typical of the other unfortunates here at the camp. The oldest son, a licensed architect, was educated at the University of Washington, has a master's degree from the Massachusetts Institute of Technology and is a scholarship graduate of the American School of Fine Arts in Fontainebleau, France. He is now in camp in Oregon with his wife and three-months-old child. He had just completed designing a much needed defense housing project at Vancouver, Washington.

The second son is an M.D. He served his internship in a New York hospital, is married and has two fine sons. The folks banked on him, because he was the smartest of us three boys. The army took him a month after he opened his office. He is now a lieutenant in the Medical Corps, somewhere in the South.

I am the third son, the dumbest of the lot, but still smart enough to hold down a job as an architectural draftsman. I have just finished building a new home and had lived in it three weeks. My desk was just cleared of work done for the Army Engineers, another stack of 391 defense houses was waiting (a rush job), when the order came to pack up and leave for this resettlement center called "Camp Harmony."

Mary, the only girl in the family, and her year-old son, "Butch," are with our parents—interned in the stables of the Livestock Exposition Buildings in Portland.

Now that you can picture our thoroughly American background, let me describe our new home.

The resettlement center is actually a penitentiary—armed guards in towers with spotlights and deadly tommy guns, fifteen feet of barbed-wire fences, everyone confined to quarters at nine, lights out at ten o'clock. The guards are ordered to shoot anyone who approaches within twenty feet of the fences. No one is allowed to take the two-block-long hike to the latrines after nine, under any circumstances.

The apartments, as the army calls them, are two-block-long stables, with windows on one side. Floors are shiplaps on two-by-fours laid directly on the mud, which is everywhere. The stalls are about eighteen by twenty-one feet; some contain families of six or seven persons. Partitions are seven feet high, leaving a four-foot opening above. The rooms aren't too bad, almost fit to live in for a short while.

The food and sanitation problems are the worst. We have had absolutely no fresh meat, vegetables or butter since we came here. Mealtime queues extend for blocks; standing in a rainswept line, feet in the mud, waiting for the scant portions of

Ted Nakashima, "Concentration Camp: U.S. Style," *The New Republic* 106 (1942). *The New Republic* is a liberal political journal.

canned wieners and boiled potatoes, hash for breakfast or canned wieners and beans for dinner. Milk only for the kids. Coffee or tea dosed with saltpeter and stale bread are the adults' staples. Dirty, unwiped dishes, greasy silver, a starchy diet, no butter, no milk, bawling kids, mud, wet mud that stinks when it dries, no vegetables—a sad thing for the people who raised them in such abundance. Memories of a crisp head of lettuce with our special olive oil, vinegar, garlic and cheese dressing.

Today one of the surface sewage-disposal pipes broke and the sewage flowed down the streets. Kids play in the water. Shower baths without hot water. Stinking mud and slops everywhere.

Can this be the same America we left a few weeks ago?

As I write, I can remember our little bathroom—light coral walls. My wife painting them, and the spilled paint in her hair. The open towel shelving and the pretty shower curtains which we put up the day before we left. How sanitary and clean we left it for the airlines pilot and his young wife who are now enjoying the fruits of our labor.

It all seems so futile, struggling, trying to live our old lives under this useless, regimented life. The senselessness of all the inactive manpower. Electricians, plumbers, draftsmen, mechanics, carpenters, painters, farmers—every trade—men who are able and willing to do all they can to lick the Axis. Thousands of men and women in these camps, energetic, quick, alert, eager for hard, constructive work, waiting for the army to do something for us, an army that won't give us butter.

I can't take it! I have 391 defense houses to be drawn. I left a fine American home which we built with our own hands. I left a life, highballs with our American friends on week-ends, a carpenter, laundry-truck driver, architect, airlines pilot— good friends, friends who would swear by us. I don't have enough of that Japanese heritage "ga-man"—a code of silent suffering and ability to stand pain.

Oddly enough I still have a bit of faith in army promises of good treatment and Mrs. Roosevelt's pledge of a future worthy of good American citizens. I'm banking another $67 of income tax on the future. Sometimes I want to spend the money I have set aside for income tax on a bit of butter or ice cream or something good that I might have smuggled through the gates, but I can't do it when I think that every dollar I can put into "the fight to lick the Japs," the sooner I will be home again. I must forget my stomach.

What really hurts most is the constant reference to us evacués as "Japs." "Japs" are the guys we are fighting. We're on this side and we want to help.

Why won't America let us?

OUTCAST AMERICANS
William Robinson

Doc was scared. And you couldn't blame him.

There he was, at thirty-nine, an American, born and reared; taxpayer, voter, clubman; honor alumnus of a famous university; authority on intricate phases of surgery. He was dapper, chipper, proud; a well-tailored little man who had lifted himself by his bootstraps.

And his world was crumbling.

Ten days earlier his California-born wife had taken their two sons and fled to friends in Utah. That left Doc where I found him—in San Francisco, disconsolate, bewildered, in the ruins of his life. Now Uncle Sam had given him just 48 hours to wind up his affairs and prepare to get out of town. The notice was nailed to a telephone pole outside his office door. He didn't know where he was going, nor when, nor how.

Doc is a Japanese-American.

He had been caught up in a fantastic backswirl of the maelstrom of war. With 72,000 other American citizens of Japanese ancestry—men, women, children, and infants—he was being evacuated from the Pacific Coast, now become a theater of military operations, to join 42,000 alien Japanese in exile for the duration.

In Doc's office, I sat on the operating table, Doc on a white stool, endlessly toying with a pair of bright forceps. He was trying to bluff it through, laugh it off, but he kept coming back to personal perplexities. Would they keep him behind barbed wire? Would they confiscate his money? Could he practice his profession in camp? That made him think of the patients he was leaving.

"What can I do about Mrs. Tayama? I had her slated for an operation next week. And little Taki, with that infected arm." He named others and their ailments. He looked searchingly at me. "Say, do you suppose the Government would make an exception in my case? I'm needed here!"

"Why don't you ask them?" I suggested.

"By George," he said impulsively, "I will! I'll go see them right now."

We emerged into Japtown's principal business street, already more than half deserted. Doc got into his car and started the motor, and then, leaning out, he said, as though it were an afterthought:

"By the way, I've been wondering whether families will be permitted to live together in the camps . . ." His voice trailed off. Japs usually hide their sentiments. Sometimes you wonder if they have any.

I told him what Army officials had told me—that every effort would be made to keep families together. He nodded absently. "Oh, well, I just wondered. Give me a ring tomorrow and I'll tell you what happens." He drove away.

Five days later I got around to calling Doc's number. "I'm sorry," said the operator impersonally, "that number has been disconnected." . . .

William Robinson, "Outcast Americans," *American Magazine* September 1942. *American Magazine*, now defunct, was a general interest magazine.

As simply, as inexorably as that, Japanese vanished from our Western seaboard. In late March, fifteen weeks after Pearl Harbor, they were still doing business as usual from Vancouver to San Diego. By June 1 they were gone, swallowed up into stockades, reception camps, and resettlement areas established far back from the military emplacements along the coast.

Behind this monstrous mass migration lies a baffling problem in human justice. Doubtless, many of the Japanese are loyal, trustworthy Americans. But strange things have happened on the West Coast. Investigators have picked up irregular radio signals; a wireless set was discovered in a fishermen's truck; in a Jap home, agents found a searchlight cunningly concealed in a chimney; strange lights have flashed out to sea, possibly to pass on information to enemy submarines. The Government is acting generously and kindly toward the Jap thousands along the West Coast; but because this is total war, intelligence authorities are taking no chances. They have no intention of jeopardizing the safety and security of the entire West Coast by allowing a few hundred or even a few dozen Jap fifth columnists to remain and carry out their work of treason and sabotage.

Japanese born in Japan, or elsewhere outside the United States, are forbidden the right to become American citizens. But their children, born in America, are American citizens. Thus, about two thirds of all persons of Japanese ancestry in the United States are Americans by birthright, subject to all the rights, privileges, and duties of any other American. But are they truly Americans? Is their allegiance unquestionable?

Military and civil authorities in California, Washington, and Oregon frankly don't know. Japanese children customarily attended language schools where they learned the mysticism of Nippon. Every Japanese child is taught to obey its parents unswervingly until they die. Since many of the elders to whom American citizenship is denied are bitter about the discrimination, it is reasonable to assume this also rankles in their offspring.

Authorities know, too, that many American-born Japanese have a personal problem of divided citizenship. By birth, they are Americans under our laws. But— and here's the catch—if the birth of a child was registered with a Japanese consul, the child is entitled also to the citizenship of Japan, under Japanese laws.

In the first excitement after Pearl Harbor, some West Coast legislators debated the advisability of amending our law so that a child of foreign parentage would be required at maturity to produce evidence that he had resided most of his life in the United States and conducted himself in a manner that would demonstrate his fitness for citizenship.

The motion was sidetracked and eventually forgotten, on the ground that no Caucasian could hope to plumb the depths of Oriental minds. Also, it was impossible to determine which American-born Japanese had been registered with the consulates; the busy Japs burned all records in the first moments of the war.

Of course, if you wanted to be naïve about it, you could ask each American Japanese to take an oath of allegiance. But authorities had a hunch it wouldn't amount to much. Two California-born and American-educated Japanese—Hideo Okusako and Charles Hiasao Yoshii—had sworn allegiance to the Stars and Stripes during every year of their schooling, and are now blatting Japanese propaganda to America from radio stations in Tokyo.

Today many mature American Japanese don't know where their own sympathies lie. I am convinced of that, after talking with hundreds of them. All their friendships and contacts are in America. Many don't know either the customs or the language of Japan. Yet, so thorough was their home training, they would feel themselves traitors if they aided America in a war against Japan.

America has never assimilated them. During business hours they associated with white Americans, but after dark they lived in huddled colonies. When they moved into a district, whether in a city or a countryside, Caucasians moved away. Their neighbors were other Orientals or dark-skinned peoples.

Their dual nationality was reflected in their homes. The food usually was an eerie blending of East and West. One Jap family proudly served me strawberry shortcake covered with a gooey, dark brown sauce containing chopped almonds. It was good, but hard to eat with chopsticks, which many Japanese families prefer to knives and forks.

Their confusion extended to their religions. About half of all the Japanese in America are Buddhists, according to official surveys. The others are scattered through all the Christian faiths. Denominations never seemed to make much difference to the Japanese themselves; they went where they were welcomed. In an upper-caste Japanese home one evening, I saw a rosary and a copy of Science and Health with Key to the Scriptures, lying on a teakwood table in front of a pot-bellied image of Buddha.

What cast the die against these strange people was the fact that they had, intentionally or by chance, clustered around important military objectives in the West. One Army airfield was surrounded to the depth of a mile or more by Japanese truck gardens. A Navy base near Los Angeles was flanked by a colony of Japanese fishermen. Near Seattle, Japanese populated an island where movements of ships could hardly be missed. Literally scores of miles of strategic highways along which military columns had to roll were fringed by Japanese-held properties. Military men shudder to think what might have happened in an emergency if those highways had been dynamited or blocked by wrecks of Japanese trucks.

Yet it is characteristically American and democratic that, at first, the Japs were given a chance to leave the coast voluntarily. About 1,000 did. Since many of their elders had been quietly gathered in at the outbreak of the war, a fiery little priest, the Rev. F. J. Caffery, of Los Angeles, became their shepherd. He led a grotesque flock that day late in March—a 10-mile-long procession of automobiles in all stages of decrepitude, over 300 weary miles of meadow and mountain and desert, into oblivion. I went along.

We started at dawn from a park in Pasadena. As the ragtag column started chugging forward, soldiers materialized from somewhere and took places in the line. At the end came an army mechanical unit, complete with tins of gasoline and tow car. They hauled more than one of those jallopies up the mountains before the day was over.

Civilians hardly looked up from their chores as the weird parade went by, although one farmer had erected a sign in his front yard: "Good-by, Japs. See you in Hell." Another had rigged up a signpost with an arrow pointing to: "Tokyo, 6,874 miles."

After hours of desert travel, we entered flat, dusty Owens Valley. Gaunt mountains rose in the west; beyond them lay the waste of Death Valley. Eastward, close by, towered the snow-clad Sierra Nevadas. In the last light we passed the foot of Mt. Whitney, highest peak in the continental United States. Just at dark we came to Manzanar. Soldiers stood guard at the gate.

Then the camp consisted of two dozen long, barracklike, low buildings, sheeted with tar paper and slats. Each building was divided into four compartments, and each compartment held 16 steel cots. An enormous ditching machine was roaring and snorting in the middle of the street, cutting a sewer trench. Under floodlights, hundreds of workmen were building new barracks.

Through this bedlam wandered the new arrivals like wan ghosts, each with his bundle of bedding. I watched an old man peering into the rooms. At the first three he shook his head, but he went in the fourth and dropped his bundle on a cot. I went over to see what had attracted him, but couldn't tell; to me, they all looked alike.

Up the line, somebody began hammering lustily on a dishpan. Th crowd surged that way. I found myself wedged against a slender young Japanese in United States Army uniform, except for insignia. He said his name was Iijima, he had enlisted at St. Louis, Mo., in September, and been mustered out with honor in February. "Why?" I asked. He shook his head. "Search me," he said. "I guess they don't want us in the Army."

The dishpan was being hammered at the door of the communal dining hall. When 1,000 of us crowded in, the walls were bulging. I found myself facing a tall, prim young Japanese girl. Her name, it developed, was Oko Murata. A private secretary in Los Angeles, she had volunteered to do office work in the camp. "I knew I'd have to come sooner or later, so I thought it might as well be sooner," she smiled casually. There were 20 other American-born girls in camp, all aiding in organization.

After a time I walked back down the street. Near the ditching machine I came across a wiry, middle-aged Jap crouching and sifting dirt through his fingers.

"Me," he said, "I'm gardener. Damn' good gardener. Best in Beverly Hills, you bet. This, damn' good dirt. Plenty thing grow here. You watch see." He got up and looked up and down the street, measuring with squinted eyes.

"Here I'm go plant begonia," he said. "There, maybe good cineraria. Make nice border lantana. Fix up middle street like parkway, maybe, with plenty nice flower shrub." He fell silent, busy with his plans. Finally he said, "Yes. Very good. I'm make this little bit of heaven. You watch see." . . .

I went back to Manzanar in early summer. More than 10,000 Japanese were there. The snow line had moved far up the mountains and the gullies were chuckling brooks. The tar-paper shacks were still squat and ugly, but no uglier and much more orderly than many Western desert camps.

Kids were playing ball on a diamond at the edge of town. Girls in slacks and gay print dresses were sitting on the side lines, calling shrill advice. Tall, prim Oko was at her desk in the Administration Building, yawning over columns of figures. She had spring fever, she said. She gave me the gossip.

Three of her girl-friends had met and married young evacuees. One was already expecting. Some of the boys had organized a swing band. A mimeograph newspaper, the *Manzanar Free Crest*, had made its appearance, full of good-natured gags. The police—all Japanese evacuees—had raided three prosperous crap games. Almost $1,000 worth of war bonds and stamps had been sold through the camp post office.

The schools were running full time, using the standard California educational system and textbooks. Several nurseries were operating for the convenience of mothers. A town council, called the Advisory Board, had been formed to work on administrative matters with the army-civilian management set up by the Government. Several church services were held weekly and meetings were always crowded. The hospital was going great guns, momentarily expecting a rush of maternity cases. Young Dr. James Goto, its chief, had finished inoculating evacuees for typhoid and smallpox and was busy with $100,000 worth of equipment and supplies.

I couldn't find my ambitious little gardener friend, but I saw his handiwork everywhere. There were "flower shrub" in tidy parkways and clusters of blossoms in gardens. And on the north side, in the lush, warm shade, cinerarias were taking root.

After that first voluntary evacuation in March, the gloved fist of the Army closed down on Japanese who hadn't gone. From the Presidio of San Francisco, Lieut. Gen. John L. DeWitt, commanding all military operations in the western United States, had issued crisp orders.

First, all Japanese still at liberty were "frozen"—prohibited from traveling more than 5 miles from their homes, never after dark. Next, evacuation zones were set up, bounded by streets in cities or township lines in rural areas. Finally, one after another, the zones were evacuated.

Each person was permitted to take bedding and linens, but no mattress; toilet articles, extra clothing, and essential personal effects. No family could take more than its members could carry. No pets could be taken. No personal items or household goods could be shipped to the assembly center. The Government provided for the storage of heavy household effects such as pianos and refrigerators. On the appointed day, fleets of military trucks rolled into the zone. Soldiers supervised the loading of the evacuees and their bundles. At a signal, the caravans rolled away, leaving whole square blocks of cities and square miles of farm land tenantless.

Economically, the departure of the Japs presented no particular problem in the cities, although bank clearances fell off temporarily in some localities and house servants were hard to get. But it was different in the country. Japs had owned or controlled 11,030 farms valued at $70,000,000. They had provided virtually all the artichokes, early cantaloupes, green peppers, and late tomatoes, and most of the early asparagus. They owned or controlled the majority of the wholesale produce markets and thousands of retail vegetable stands.

When they disappeared, the flow of vegetables stopped. Retail prices went up. Many vegetables vanished entirely. There were rumors of a food shortage. Into this situation plunged dynamic Larry Hewes, regional director of the Farm Security Administration and agricultural member of General DeWitt's Wartime Civil Control Administration. He ranged the farms night and day, cajoling the Japs to keep planting up to the final minute and recruiting white farmers to take over their lands when they had gone. He insisted upon fair prices or equitable share-cropping agreements, and by mid-summer the West's agriculture was rolling along as though nothing had happened. . . .

Now that the Japs have been rounded up and tucked away for the duration, what shall we do with them afterward?

There is one answer, although it doesn't take a long-range view.

At four isolated points in the West, workmen are now constructing new camps to be known as Resettlement Areas. One is in western Oregon, in a great flat, treeless sink known as Tule Lake. Another is on the desolate Colorado desert, on the California—Arizona boundary. There will be others later farther inland, in Utah, Colorado, Idaho, and New Mexico, if the Government is able to overcome the vehement protests of the officials and people of those states.

All of the land to be used for resettlement belongs to the Government; most of it is controlled by the Indian Bureau. It is planned—although rather nebulously— to put the Japanese evacuees onto this land and encourage them to develop its latent agricultural resources.

They will be paid for their work. Secretary of War Stimson has set wages for a 44-hour week at from $8 to $16 a month, plus free food, shelter, medical care, and hospitalization. Free clothing will be issued "when and if necessary." In addition, all evacuees will receive coupon books to buy items at the camp canteens. No family may have a total of more than $7.50 in coupons in any month.

"Naturally," a spokesman for the Wartime Civil Control Administration told me, "the land will revert back to the Government after the war, with all improvements."

"But what about the Japs themselves?" I persisted. "What will happen to them?"

He shook his head slowly. "We can't see that far ahead," he replied . . . .

Two things keep recurring to me as I write this report. The first is the well-scrubbed, moon-shaped face of tiny Kiku, who used to be our housemaid. Her father, an immigrant, was my gardener. He brought up a bottle of saki the night she was born and we drank a toast to the new arrival.

Kiku came to my study the other evening to say good-by. Next morning, she said, they'd come for her.

Searching for words and trying to be bluff and hearty, I said, "Well, have a good time. Where will you be?"

She stood in the doorway like a timid little mouse, her face expressionless. "I don't know, sir. They don't tell us."

I cleared my throat. "No, of course not. Well, take care of yourself."

She turned, and with her back to me she said, "I hope you will think of me. I shall think of you all."

I said, still fumbling awkwardly, "Sure; you bet. Well, so long."

She didn't answer. The door closed and she was gone. I don't know where she is now.

The other thing I keep thinking about is the poignant inscription on the Statue of Liberty. You'll find these words down toward the bottom, serenely untouched by the howling storms of more than half a century:

"Give me your tired, your poor, your huddled masses yearning to be free; the wretched refuse of your teeming shores. Send these, the homeless, tempest-tossed, to me. I lift my lamp beside the Golden Door."

CONDITIONS AT CAMP HARMONY

Some months ago *The New Republic* published an article by Ted Nakashima, an American of the Japanese race who was at the time an inmate of an assembly center. Although his article did not say so, it was Camp Harmony, Puyallup, Washington. Mr. Nakashima's main point was that he is a loyal American, who was engaged on important war work (as an architect drawing plans for houses to be occupied by defenseplant workers) and that he strongly resented being obliged to go and live instead in the virtual idleness of an assembly center. Incidentally, he complained of some of the physical conditions at the center.

The United States Army took exception to certain of these statements made by Mr. Nakashima. At the army's request, *The New Republic* sent a special investigator to Camp Harmony to check Mr. Nakashima's statements. We publish herewith summaries of the criticisms and of the facts as reported by our investigator.

Mr. Nakashima said the inmates of Camp Harmony are confined to quarters at nine and that lights must be out at ten.

Comment: The regulations on this matter have varied from time to time and from camp to camp. When our investigator visited Camp Harmony, the curfew was at ten o'clock and lights must be out at ten-thirty. This seems not unreasonable in a camp with many old people and small children.

Mr. Nakashima said there were no fresh meats, vegetables or butter, that the evacués had to stand in line for meals in the rain and mud, that dishes and silverware were dirty, and there was milk only for children.

Comment: For a short time at the beginning, certainly not more than a month, the evacués got the United States Army "B" ration. They had small quantities of fresh meat, green vegetables and butter. Thereafter they got the army "A" ration, with plenty of all these things. Some of the older Japanese Americans objected to the American food, because they wanted rice. There seems no doubt that the conditions of which Mr. Nakashima complains were temporary and unimportant.

If dishes and silverware were dirty, this was a reflection on the evacués, and not on the American authorities, since the evacués were in charge of dishwashing.

The charge was made that a broken sewer was insanitary and unpleasant.

Comment: A sewer line did break, but was repaired as soon as possible and there have been no further accidents of this kind.

Mr. Nakashima complained that the camp was guarded by men armed with machine guns, with orders to shoot if the evacués came too close to the barbed wire.

Comment: It is true there are armed guards and barbed wire. It is also true that the evacués were ordered not to walk on the grass within ten feet of the barbed-wire fences. There are not, however, any orders to shoot, and the rule about keeping off the grass is widely disobeyed without penalty.

In general it may be said that some of Mr. Nakashima's criticisms were exaggerated, and that those that were true referred to temporary conditions which were ameliorated shortly after Mr. Nakashima wrote his article (but not as a result of his writing, so far as we know). Conditions at this camp, except for the first few weeks, have been as good as could reasonably be expected by anyone. While the problem of what to do about the Japanese Americans in the long run remains unsolved, the army's part in setting up and maintaining proper conditions in the camps has been carried out satisfactorily. Certainly there can be no doubt that our treatment of persons of the Japanese race has been infinitely better than has been the case with Americans who have been captured or interned by the Japanese.

ISSEI, NISEI, KIBEI

When the facts about Japanese brutality to the soldier prisoners from Bataan were made known, Americans were more outraged than they had been since December 7, 1941. Instinctively they contrasted that frightfulness with our treatment of Japanese held in this country; and, without being told, Americans knew that prisoners in the U.S. were fed three meals a day and had not been clubbed or kicked or otherwise brutalized. Too few, however, realize what persistent and effective use Japan has been able to make, throughout the entire Far East, of U.S. imprisonment of persons of Japanese descent. This propaganda concerns itself less with how the U.S. treats the people imprisoned than who was imprisoned. By pointing out, again and again, that the U.S. put behind fences well over 100,000 people of Japanese blood, the majority of them citizens of the U.S., Japan describes to her Far Eastern radio audiences one more instance of American racial discrimination. To convince all Orientals that the war in the Pacific is a crusade against the white man's racial oppression, the enemy shrewdly notes every occurrence in the U.S. that suggests injustice to racial minorities, from the Negroes to the Mexicans and Japanese.

The enemy, of course, deliberately refrains from making distinctions among the various kinds of detention we have worked out for those of Japanese blood in this country. Unfortunately, Americans themselves are almost as confused as the Japanese radio about what has happened to the Japanese minority in this country—one-tenth of 1 percent of the nation's total population. There are three different types of barbed-wire enclosures for persons of Japanese ancestry. First there are the Department of Justice camps, which hold 3,000 Japanese aliens considered by the F.B.I. potentially dangerous to the U.S. These alone are true internment camps.

Second, there are ten other barbed-wire enclosed centers in the U.S., into which, in 1942, the government put 110,000 persons of Japanese descent (out of a total population in continental U.S. of 127,000). Two-thirds of them were citizens, born in the U.S.; one-third aliens, forbidden by law to be citizens. No charges were brought against them. When the war broke out, all these 110,000 were resident in the Pacific Coast states—the majority in California. They were put behind fences when the Army decided that for "military necessity" all people of Japanese ancestry, citizen or alien, must be removed from the West Coast military zone.

Within the last year the 110,000 people evicted from the West Coast have been subdivided into two separate groups. Those who have professed loyalty to Japan or an unwillingness to defend the U.S. have been placed, with their children, in one of the ten camps called a "segregation center" (the third type of imprisonment). Of the remainder in the nine "loyal camps," 17,000 have moved to eastern states to take jobs. The rest wait behind the fence, an awkward problem for the U.S. if for no other reason than that the Constitution and the Bill of Rights were severely stretched if not breached when U.S. citizens were put in prison.

Back in December, 1941, there was understandable nervousness over the tight little Japanese communities scattered along the West Coast. The long coast line

"Issei, Nisei, Kibei," *Fortune* April 1944.

seemed naked and undefended. There were colonies of Japanese fishermen in the port areas, farmlands operated by Japanese close to war plants, and little Tokyos in the heart of the big coastal cities. There were suspected spies among the Japanese concentrations and there was fear of sabotage. Californians were urged to keep calm and let the authorities take care of the problem. In the first two weeks the Department of Justice scooped up about 1500 suspects. A few weeks later all enemy aliens and citizens alike were removed from certain strategic areas such as Terminal Islands in Los Angeles harbor, and spots near war plants, power stations, and bridges. But Californians did not completely trust the authorities. While the F.B.I. was picking up its suspects, civilian authorities were besieged with telephone calls from citizens reporting suspicious behavior of their Oriental neighbors. Although California's Attorney General Warren (now governor) stated on February 21, 1942, that "we have had no sabotage and no fifth-column activity since the beginning of the war," hysteria by then had begun to spread all along the coast. Every rumor of Japanese air and naval operations offshore, and every tale of fifth-column activity in Hawaii, helped to raise to panic proportions California's ancient and deep antagonism toward the Japanese Americans.

For decades the Hearst press had campaigned against the Yellow Peril within the state (1 percent of the population) as well as the Yellow Peril across the seas that would one day make war. When that war prophecy came true, the newspapers' campaign of hate and fear broke all bounds. And, when Hearst called for the removal of all people of Japanese ancestry, he had as allies many pressure groups who had for years resented the presence of Japanese in this country.

The American Legion, since its founding in 1919, has never once failed to pass an annual resolution against the Japanese-Americans. The Associated Farmers in California had competitive reasons for wanting to get rid of the Japanese-Americans who grew vegetables at low cost on $70 million worth of California land. California's land laws could not prevent the citizen-son of the Japanese alien from buying or renting the land. In the cities, as the little Tokyos grew, a sizable commercial business came into Japanese-American hands—vegetable commission houses, retail and wholesale enterprises of all kinds. It did not require a war to make the farmers, the Legion, the Native Sons and Daughters of the Golden West, and politicians resent and hate the Japanese-Americans. The records of legislation and press for many years indicate that the antagonism was there and growing. War turned the antagonism into fear, and made possible what California had clearly wanted for decades—to get rid of its minority.

By early February both the Hearst press and the pressure groups were loudly demanding the eviction of all people of Japanese blood—to protect the state from the enemy, and to protect the minority from violence at the hands of Filipinos and other neighbors. A few cases of violence had, indeed, occurred, and spy talk ran up and down the coast. On February 13, a group of Pacific Coast Congressmen urged President Roosevelt to permit an evacuation; a week later the President gave that authority to the Army. On February 23, a Japanese submarine shelled the coast near Santa Barbara. Lieutenant General John I. DeWitt, on March 2, issued the order that all persons of Japanese descent, aliens and citizens, old and young, women and children, be removed from most of California, western Oregon and Washington and southern Arizona. The greatest forced migration in U.S. history resulted.

At first the movement inland of the 110,000 people within the prohibited zone was to be voluntary. The Japanese-Americans were merely told to get out. Within three weeks 8,000 people had packed up, hastily closed out their business affairs, sold their possessions or left them with neighbors, and set forth obediently toward the east. But Arizona remembered all too well how California had turned back the Okies in the past, and many Japanese-Americans were intercepted at this border. Kansas patrolmen stopped them. Nevada and Wyoming protested that they did not want to receive people found too dangerous in California. About 4,000 got as far as Colorado and Utah. It became apparent that the random migration of so many unwanted people could result only in spreading chaos. By March 29 voluntary evacuation was forbidden, and the Army made its own plans to control the movement.

The évacués reported to local control stations where they registered and were given a number and instructions on what they could take (hand luggage only) and when they should proceed to the first camps, called assembly centers. Although they were offered government help in straightening out their property problems, many thousands, in their haste and confusion, and in their understandable distrust of government, quickly did what they could for themselves. They sold, leased, stored, or lent their homes, lands, personal belongings, tractors, and cars. Their financial losses are incalculable.

The Army, in twenty-eight days, rigged up primitive barracks in fifteen assembly centers to provide temporary quarters for 110,000. Each évacué made his own mattress of straw, took his place in the crowded barracks, and tried to adjust to his new life. By August 10 everyone of Japanese descent (except those confined to insane asylums and other safe institutions) was behind a fence in "protective custody." They were held here (still within the forbidden military zone) until a newly created civilian agency, the War Relocation Authority, could establish other refuges farther inland. WRA's job was to hold the people until they could be resettled in orderly fashion.

WRA appealed to the governors of ten nearby western states. With one exception, Colorado's Governor Carr, they protested that they did not want the Japanese-Americans to settle in their domain, nor did they want any relocation center erected within their borders unless it was well guarded by the Army. Finally nine remote inland sites were found, all of them on federally owned land. (One assembly center in eastern California became a relocation camp.) Most of them were located, for lack of better acreage, on desolate, but irrigable desert tracts. More tar-papered barracks were thrown up, more wire fences built, and once more the people moved. By November, 1942, all the évacués had packed up their miserably few possessions, had been herded onto trains and deposited behind WRA's soldier-guarded fences, in crowded barrack villages of between 7,000 and 18,000 people.

They felt bitterness and anger over their loss of land and home and money and freedom. They knew that German and Italian aliens—and indeed, Japanese aliens in other parts of the U.S.—had been interned only when the F.B.I. had reason to suspect them. Second-generation citizens of German and Italian origin were not evacuated from California; nor were the second-generation citizens of Japanese descent elsewhere in the U.S. put behind fences.

Although the *évacués'* resentment at regimentation within WRA's little Tokyos is deep, it is seldom expressed violently. Considering the emotional strains, the uprooting, and the crowding, no one can deny that the record of restraint has been remarkable. Only twice have the soldiers been asked to come within a WRA fence to restore order.

But WRA and its director, Dillon Myer, have been under almost continual attack by congressional committees in Washington and by a whole long list of badgering groups and individuals on the West Coast. The Dies Committee goes after WRA and the Japanese minority at frequent intervals. Even Hedda Hopper, the movie gossip, prattles innuendoes. Not wishing to "imply anything," she noted last December that "we've had more than our share of explosions, train wrecks, fires, and serious accidents" since WRA has released so many of the *évacués*. Actually, not one of the 17,000 has been convicted of anti-American activity.

WRA has usually been criticized for the wrong reasons. It has been accused of turning loose, for resettlement, "dangerous Japs." The implication usually is that no Japanese-American should be released, although from the very beginning WRA's prescribed purpose was to help the *évacués* to find some place to live outside the prohibited zone. Again and again, the pressure groups and California Congressmen have urged that WRA's ten centers be turned over to the Army. (In February the President, instead, dropped WRA intact, with its Director Dillon Myer, into the Department of Interior.) Most frequently Mr. Myer has been charged with pampering the Japanese-Americans. Almost every day the Hearst papers fling the word "coddling," with the clear implication that all persons of Japanese descent, citizen or no, women and infants, should be treated strictly as prisoners of war, which of course they are not.

No one who has visited a relocation center and seen the living space, eaten the food, or merely kept his eyes open could honestly apply the word "coddling" to WRA's administration of the camps. The people are jammed together in frame barracks. A family of six or seven is customarily allotted an "apartment" measuring about twenty by twenty-five feet. It is a bare room, without partitions. The only privacy possible is achieved by hanging flimsy cotton curtains between the crowded beds.

Furniture is improvised from bits of scrap lumber: a box for a table, three short ends of board made into a backless chair. The family's clothing and few personal possessions are somehow stuffed neatly away—on shelves if scrap lumber—a priceless commodity in all camps, is available. Otherwise, they are stuffed away under the beds. The quarters are usually neat. There are no cooking facilities and no running water in the barracks, unless the *évacué* has brought his own electric plate or had a friend "on the outside" send one in. As in Army camps, each block of twelve or fourteen barracks (250 to 300 people) has its central mess hall, laundry building, public latrines, and showers.

With faithful regularity, irresponsible yarns are circulated that the *évacués* are getting more and better food than other Americans. Actually, the food cost per day is held below 45 cents per person. For 15 cents a meal the food is possibly adequate, but close to the edge of decent nutrition. In most camps, located far from dairy districts, milk is provided only for small children, nursing and expectant mothers, and special dietary cases. There are two meatless days a week and a heavy emphasis on starches. Nearly a third of the food requirements are grown on the irrigated fields of the camp itself. This reduces the actual cash outlay for food to 31 cents per person.

Practically everyone who wants a job can work, and most of the able bodied do. They plant and till the camp's vegetable acreage, prepare the food in the mess halls, do stenographic work for the Caucasian staff, work in the cooperative store. In some centers they make furniture for the administration building or cotton mattresses to take the place of the hard straw pallets. Some are barbers and cobblers for the community, doctors in the hospital, scrubwomen in the latrines, garbage collectors. The maximum wage (a doctor, for instance) is $19 a month; the minimum, $12; the average, $16. In addition, those who work get a clothing allowance for themselves and their dependents—at the most, $3.75 a month for an adult in the northern-most center.

Individual enterprise is forbidden. To set up one's own dress-making service within the community, or to sell shell jewelry or anything else to the outside is prohibited. In order to keep the center wage uniform, all economic activities must be conducted through the community cooperative, which pays its barbers and other workers the standard stipend. With their small monthly wage, and by dipping into their prewar savings, most évacués buy extras to eat, but they can get only nonra-tioned food, since they possess no ration books. They send to the mail-order houses for some of their clothes, buy shoes, yard goods, and clothing at the cooperative store. Their children go to school in the barracks village, and when they are sick, to the center hospital.

Thus the pampering and thus the humiliation. A doctor distinguished in his profession, who lived with grace and charm in a decently comfortable home before the war, is today huddled in a small room with all his family. He practices his profession for $19 a month at the center hospital, serving under a Caucasian of lesser accomplishments, hired for considerably more money. A man who spent twenty years building up his own florist business or commission house, or who operated a large vegetable farm in one of California's valleys, is merely "stoop labor" on the center's acreage.

The record of Japanese-Americans during the depression indicated that they did not take to public relief. They were too proud. They stuck together, helped each other, and almost never appeared on WPA or home-relief lists. To virtually all of them it is now galling to be distrusted wards of the nation, their meager lodging and food a scanty handout, the payment for their labor somewhat the same.

They have always been an isolated, discarded, and therefore ingrown people. Today this is more true than ever. The barracks village as a rule is literally isolated. At Manzanar, California, for example, the center is but a tiny square in a vast and lonely desert valley, between two great mountain ranges. Spiritually the people are just as isolated as that. Thrown together in a compact racial island of their own frustrated people, they grow in upon themselves and each other; they become almost completely detached from American life, the war, the world. Their small children speak more Japanese than they would if they competed daily with other American school children. The teen-age boys and girls are ostentatiously American in clothes, slang, and behavior. It is as if they were trying too hard to convince themselves that they *are* Americans. They know that they must and will go out the gate soon.

The adults think about themselves, and about the past they left. With time and distance, California's farm valleys, towns, and cities become more golden-hued than ever to the *évacués*. They brood vaguely and fearfully on the future; the war, sometimes, seems like a vague abstraction, the cause of their troubles. And they think about rumors—which they often trust more than they do printed, official announcements. It may be a rumor that the Army will take over. Or that the *évacués* in this center will all be transported to another. This is the most nightmarish rumor of all to people who have moved so much in the past two years.

They think, too, about the endless details of their camp life. Each group of 250 or so *évacués* has a block manager who gets $16 a month for listening to their complaints and, if possible, straightening out innumerable daily problems. The food in the mess hall is badly prepared; there is no toilet paper in the ladies latrine; the neighbors play the radio too late and too loud; the roof of No. 29 barracks has a small leak.

Finally, there are gossip and politics. The Japanese-Americans back in California went their way without much participation in politics as most American citizens know it. In the barracks village of WRA there is little real self-government. Most of the centers have a Council made up of block representatives or managers. But there is only a slight area within which such a congress can make community decisions. Usually at the meeting of the Council the members do little more than listen to new rules; new plans of WRA, handed down from Washington or the local director. The block representatives are expected to pass on this information to all the people.

Originally WRA ruled that citizens alone could hold office in the centers, but this proved to be unwise. Two-thirds of the *évacués* are citizens but most of these American-born Nisei are from eighteen to twenty-eight years of age—too young to take on such responsible jobs as the block manager's. Beside, among the Japanese-Americans born here are hundreds of Kibei—young men who were sent to Japan for part of their education. Not all—but a large percentage of them—are pro-Japan, particularly those who gained the latter part of their education in Japan. Disliked by the Nisei majority, outnumbered and maladjusted, the Kibei often have become a nuisance, creating little areas of disaffection in the center.

Thus it turned out that the Issei, the aliens, parents of the Nisei and Kibei could best provide the authority, stability, and seasoned wisdom needed in a block manager. They possessed a tradition of family and community leadership, and had commanded respect in the past. Above all they usually have an earnest desire to make the block of 230 or more people in which they live function in an orderly and quiet fashion. They are aliens primarily because U.S. law forbade them to become citizens. Many of them have a real loyalty to the U.S. not because the U.S. has invited their loyalty, but because they look to their children's American future for their own security.

Politics in the centers has nothing to do with office or votes or *apparent* power. But it *is* power, the power of demagoguery, of spreading the infection of bitterness, exaggerating an instance or affront into an issue that may even get to the point of a small strike against WRA. The leaders have not invariably been pro-Japan. Some, both aliens and citizens, who had been good Americans became indignant at their loss of freedom and their right to participate in the life of their nation.

It may be that the administration was not willing to permit a big funeral for a man accidentally killed when a work truck overturned; it may be that three or four of the Caucasian staff displayed signs of race discrimination; it may be a rumor more plausible than fact. The "politicians" take any one of these, or a series, and worry it into a big camp issue. How great an issue it becomes depends most of all on the degree of confidence the center as a whole has in its director and the coolness and fairness with which he customarily handles his people. Too often the administration is out of touch with the main issues and grievances within the camp. WRA suffers, like every other agency, from the manpower shortage. Competent center directors and minor personnel are scarce. Often enough the director finds his Caucasian staff more of a problem than the *évacués*.

The two so-called "riots," which brought the Army over the fence, arose from the accumulation of small grievances, whipped up to a crisis by groups struggling for power and eager to put the administration on the spot. There was, in each instance, a strike. Actually a strike in a relocation center is self-defeating since almost all labor in the community works to provide goods and services for the *évacués* themselves; no more than a handful work in the staff mess and office building. Only when violence occurred, and the director thought he needed help in maintaining order was the Army invited in.

But trouble rarely reaches either the strike stage or violence. The people in the Pacific Coast's little Tokyos rarely appeared on police blotters in the past, and now the crime record of WRA centers compares favorably with that of any small cities of their size, or, indeed, with any Army camp. Most of the policing is done by the *évacués* themselves appointed to the "internal security" staff of each center.

Policing should be simpler than ever from now on. The ideological air has been cleared; the pro-Japan people have been moved out. The process of sifting the communities, separating the loyal and the disloyal, is virtually complete. The "disloyal" have been sent to a segregation center in northeastern California, leaving the other nine centers populated only by the loyal.

To all the *évacués*, the two words, registration and segregation, are almost as charged with emotion as that disturbing term evacuation. Quite simply the two nouns mean that a questionnaire was submitted to all adults in the centers to determine their loyalty or disloyalty. On the basis of this, plus F.B.I. records and in some instances special hearings, WRA granted or denied the *évacués* "leave clearance," the right to go East and find a job. The same information was used as a basis for segregating the "disloyal" in a separate center. About 18,000 (the "disloyal" and all their dependents) will sit out the war at Tule Lake, within a high, manproof, barbed-wire enclosure, unless Japan shows more enthusiasm than she has to date for their repatriation. (These 18,000 must not be confused with the few thousand interned by the Department of Justice.)

But separating the loyal and the disloyal is not so simple a job as it might seem. Loyalty is difficult to measure accurately on any scales, and the sifting of the *évacués* was clumsily handled. The process began in February, 1943, when the Army decided to recruit a combat unit of Japanese-Americans. A registration form was printed containing twenty-eight questions to determine loyalty and willingness to fight. It was to be filled out by all men of military age. Someone realized that it would be well to have just such records on all adults in the centers. Plans were suddenly changed and everyone from seventeen years of age up was given the twenty-eight questions.

Nothing is more disastrous in a rumor-ridden, distrustful, neurotic community like a relocation center than to make one explanation of purpose today and a quite different one tomorrow. The people, newly arrived in the WRA centers, were still stunned by their evacuation, loss of property and freedom, and were acutely conscious of their stigma as "enemy." There was misunderstanding about the purpose of registration at most of the centers. The questionnaire was so carelessly framed, its wording had to be changed during the process of registration. A few thousand refused to fill out the form at all. Others, remembering that they had lost business, home, and their civil rights, wrote angry ("disloyal") answers. They had no enthusiasm for defending a democratic America that had imprisoned them for no crime and without trial.

WRA, in an effort to be fair, has granted hearings in recent months for those who wished to explain the answers they made in anger or confusion. Pride made a few people stick to what they first wrote. There is little question that the majority of adults sent to Tule Lake feel loyalty to Japan, but there are also behind Tule's fences a few thousand who are not disloyal.

Most of the Issei who chose Tule Lake are there because of firm ties of loyalty to Japan or strong ties of family relationships. Some Issei were afraid of bringing reprisals upon their relatives in Japan by affirming loyalty to the U.S. The parents who chose Tule Lake usually have taken all their children with them. Only a few sons and daughters over seventeen, who had the right to choose for themselves, could resist strong family pressure. It is ironic and revealing that at the high school at Tule Lake, civics and American history are popular elected courses.

Japan, however, makes no legal claims of protective interest in the Nisei or Kibei. When the Spanish consul visits Tule to report conditions of Japan, he is legally concerned only with the welfare of Issei, the nationals of Japan. And, under U.S. law, the Nisei and Kibei cannot abrogate their American citizenship during wartime, even if they want to. Their expatriation, and even the repatriation of most of the Issei to Japan, during the war, is unlikely. Negotiations for the exchange of civilian war prisoners have been slow, and the delay is due to Japan, not to the U.S. State Department.

To a minority living at Tule Lake, Japan's unwillingness to arrange frequent exchange of prisoners is not disheartening. This minority does not want to set sail for Japan; it wants to stay in the U.S. People are at Tule Lake for many complicated reasons besides "disloyalty" and family relationships. There is evidence, for example, that some chose this kind of imprisonment for reasons of security and weariness. This is indicated by the percentages of people in the various centers who said they wanted to be segregated. When the decision was made last fall to turn the Tule Lake camp into a segregation center, nearly 6,000 out of 13,000 residents of that center decided to stay put. This high percentage of "disloyal," the highest in any center, is explained in part by unwillingness to be uprooted and moved again. In the Minidoka relocation center in Idaho, only 225 people out of 7,000 chose to go to Tule.

There are a few tired and discouraged people from other WRA centers who went to Tule Lake because they knew that the barbed wire fences in that camp would stand permanently throughout the war. They reasoned that they would have certain refuge for the duration while the other centers, according to *évacué* rumor, might be abruptly closed, and everyone turned loose without resources.

Some chose Tule Lake imprisonment as a gesture against what they consider the broken promises of democracy. For example, there is a young Nisei who enlisted in California early in 1941 because he felt strongly about fascism. He was abruptly thrown out of his country's army after Japan attacked the U.S. and put behind the fences along with all the other *évacués*. In February, 1943, when he was handed a questionnaire on loyalty and his willingness to defend the U.S., he was too angry to prove his "loyalty" that way; he had already amply demonstrated it. He is at Tule Lake, not because of his love for Japan, but as a protest to the government he honestly wanted to serve back in 1941.

There is the Japanese-American who fought in the last war in the U.S. Army, and is a member of the American Legion. When the Japanese struck Pearl Harbor, he offered his services to the Army and to industry in California. He was turned down. Sent to a relocation center he became a "troublemaker," with the slogan, "If you think you are an American, try walking out the gate." He was packed off to an "isolation center," and finally wound up at Tule Lake. Last year the U.S. Treasury received a check from him, mailed from behind Tule's barbed wire. It was a sum in excess of $100 and represented his income tax for the calendar year, 1942, when he had received belated payment for his 1941 services as navigator on a Portuguese ship. He insisted on paying his tax, as usual. He has, of course, no wish to go to Japan. He too sits out the war at Tule Lake in protest against the failure of democracy.

The minority who are in Tule for reasons of weariness or protest are not important numerically. But they show what can happen to people who are confused, discouraged, or justifiably angry. They reveal some ugly scars inflicted by our society. It is too early to speculate about what will happen to these 18,000 prisoners. A few thousand, at the most, may get aboard the *Gripsholm*. Will all the rest be shipped finally to a defeated Japan? Or will they be a postwar U.S. problem?

When the Tule Lake prisoners will end their days is less important to consider than what is to become of those "loyal" *évacués* who are still in the nine other centers. Everyone deemed loyal, by the sifting process of registration and hearings, has been granted "leave clearance." Fortified with a handful of official papers, a numbered identification card bearing his picture and fingerprints, an *évacué* can set forth to the East. He gets his railroad fare, $3 a day travel money, and if he has no savings, $25 in cash.

During the last twelve months, 17,000 *évacués* have had the courage to go "outside." They are with rare exceptions young and single, or married but childless. A Nisei has to master considerable courage to go out into the society that rejected him two years ago. From behind the fence "the outside" has become vague, enormous and fearful. The huddling together, which is resented, is nonetheless a cohesive, protective force, hard to overcome. As he leaves the soldier-guarded gate, the young Nisei is about as lonely as any human being could be; he faces even more prejudice than his father did as immigrant contract labor.

The most powerful magnets to draw him out are letters from friends who have already gone east. Those who have made the plunge usually report back to their friends enthusiastically. The people who have started a new life—most of them from eighteen to thirty years old—are the pioneers. In the factories and in the restaurants and hotels, in the offices and in the kitchens where they work, they are building a future not merely for themselves, but for those who may follow. When they write back, "We can eat in *any* restaurant in New York" they spread a little hope. Or, "I attracted very little attention on the train." Or "In Chicago, nobody seems to care that I have a Japanese face." They tell of the church groups who are almost alone in providing some kind of organized social protection for those who relocate in cities like Chicago.

They are being sent "outside" wherever a not-too-prejudiced community provides opportunity. Seven WRA regional officers have staffs scouting for job prospects, talking to employers and, in general, smoothing the way. Illinois has taken more relocated American Japanese than any other state—4,000. Most of these have found jobs in and around Chicago. Winnetka housewives compete for Nisei servants, and even the Chicago *Tribune* has been calm. Only Hearst howls.

Ohio's industrial cities have taken about 1,500 from the relocation centers. Although special clearances have been needed for the eastern defense area, a few hundred have already gone to New York City, and the stream to the northeastern states will increase steadily. Scattered throughout midwestern states like Wisconsin, Montana, and Iowa are hundreds more.

There are, of course, areas of resistance. Antagonism to WRA's *évacués* is apt to increase not diminish when the European war ends and the casualty lists come only from the Pacific. Utah has taken about 2,000 *évacués*—mostly in Ogden and Salt Lake City where at first they were quietly absorbed. But last month the state A.F. of L. petitioned Salt Lake City authorities to deny business licenses to people of Japanese ancestry. Two thousand have gone to Colorado, but recent campaigns, like Hearst's in the Denver *Post* and proposed new discriminatory legislation keep the state aroused. Wayne W. Hill, a state representative in Colorado, wearing the uniform of a sergeant in the U.S. Army, got emergency leave from his camp last month to beg the Colorado Legislature not to pass a bill barring Japanese aliens from owning land. About to be discharged from the Army, he said, "I am just as willing to die a political death as I am to die in battle to preserve American freedom." He was warmly applauded, but the House passed the bill; the Senate turned it down fifteen to twelve.

Arizona has had such a spree of race hating in the last year that WRA does not try to place people of Japanese ancestry there. A year ago the governor signed a bill making it impossible to sell anything—even a pack of cigarettes—to a person of Japanese descent without first publishing in the newspaper, days in advance, one's intention to do so, and filing documents with the governor. The law was declared unconstitutional after a few months' operation. It was not aimed merely at the new WRA settlers who number fifty-seven. It was intended to strangle Arizona's prewar

Japanese-American population (632), many of whom make a good living in the highly competitive business of vegetable farming.

With only 17,000 young, unencumbered, and fairly bold Nisei out on their own, the biggest and hardest job of resettlement remains. The supply of young people without dependents is not unlimited. Early this year the Army, which had previously accepted only volunteers, decided to draft the Nisei, like Negroes, for segregated units. This new turn of events will draw off a few thousand *évacués*. But the most difficult problems are obviously the large families and the older people. Depending heavily on the well-known tightness of the family unit of its *évacués*, WRA believes that many of the young men and women already relocated will soon bring their parents and small sisters and brothers out. Perhaps these Nisei who are so aggressively American themselves will not want their families held behind the fences.

However, in WRA centers there are hundreds of families with several young children, none old enough to leave alone. He is a courageous father who dares to start a new life with these responsibilities when, at the center, food, shelter, education, medical care, $16 a month, and clothing are provided. Farm families are often afraid to go to the Midwest to try a totally new kind of agriculture. And many feel that they are too old to start again as day laborers. There are the men who had retail, export, import, wholesale, commission businesses. The concentrated little Tokyos in California make possible a whole commercial structure in which the Japanese provided goods and services for each other. Presumably there will be no more little Tokyos to serve.

Even if the *évacués* were allowed back on the Pacific Coast tomorrow, they could not readily establish themselves in the old pattern. Quite apart from race prejudice, the gap they left has closed in two years. Except for the few who own land, they would have to build in California as patiently as they now do in the East. They have been more thoroughly dislocated than they realize as they think nostalgically about California.

No one can gauge how soon the prewar unwillingness to accept charity or government relief deteriorates into a not-unpleasant habit of security. It is too much to expect of any people that their pride be unbreakable. Some of the old farm women who were "stoop labor" all their lives, even after their Nisei sons' landholdings or leased acres became sizable, have had the first rest in their history. Most of the old bachelors who had always been day laborers frankly enjoy the security of the centers.

If the war lasts two more years, and if WRA has succeeded in finding places for 25,000 more Japanese-Americans in the next twenty-four months (and WRA hopes to better that figure), it will be a job well done. That would leave some 45,000 in the relocation centers, as continuing public wards, not to mention over 20,000 at Tule Lake and the Department of Justice internment camps. Whatever the final residue, 25,000 or 45,000, it is certain that the "protective custody" of 1942 and 1943 cannot end otherwise than in a kind of Indian reservation, to plague the conscience of Americans for many years to come.

Meanwhile in the coming months, and perhaps years, a series of cases testing the constitutionality of evacuation and detention, even suits for recovery of property will come before the higher courts. Verdicts of "unconstitutional," or even eventual settlement of property claims cannot undo the record. It is written not only in military orders, in American Legion resolutions, Hearst headlines, and Supreme Court archives. It is written into the lives of thousands of human beings, most of them citizens of the U.S.

When future historians review the record, they may have difficulty reconciling the Army's policy in California with that pursued in Hawaii. People of Japanese blood make up more than one-third of the Hawaiian Islands' population, yet no large-scale evacuation was ordered after Pearl Harbor and Hickam Field became a shambles. Martial law was declared; certain important constitutional rights of everyone were suspended. The Department of Justice and the military authorities went about their business, rounded up a few thousand suspects. In Hawaii, unlike California, there was no strong political or economic pressure demanding evacuation of the Japanese-Americans. Indeed, had they been removed, the very foundation of peacetime Hawaiian life, sugar and pineapple growing, would have been wrecked. General Delos C. Emmons, who commanded the Hawaiian district in 1942, has said of the Japanese-Americans there: "They added materially to the strength of the area."

For two full years the West Coast "military necessity" order of March, 1942, has remained in force—and unprecedented quasi-martial law, suspending a small minority's constitutional rights of personal liberty and freedom of action. Those loyal *évacués* who can take jobs in war plants in the East have reason to ask why they are forbidden to return to California to plant cabbages. Mr. Stimson and Mr. Knox have assured the nation that the Japanese enemy is *not* coming to our shores. The Pacific Coast is now a "defense command," no longer "a theatre of operations," in the Army's own terminology. Each month the March, 1942, order seems more unreasonable.

Perhaps the Army forbids the *évacués* to return home less for military reasons than because of strong California pressures and threats. The Hearst papers on the Pacific Coast promise pogroms, if any Japanese citizen of alien descent is permitted to come home. New groups like the Home Front Commandos of Sacramento have risen to cry: "They must stay out—or else." The Associated Farmers and the California Grange, the American Legion and the Sons and Daughters of the Golden West reiterate the theme of *or else*. Politicians listen and publicly urge that the despised minority be kept out of California for the duration.

There are Californians who care about civil liberties and human justice and see the grave danger of continued quasi-martial law, but they have difficulty getting their side heard. The California C.I.O., the League of Women Voters, and segments of the church are all putting up a fight against continued "protective security." They work side by side with the Committee on American Principles and Fair Play, a group that includes such distinguished Californians as President Robert G. Sproul of the University of California, Ray Lyman Wilbur, and Maurice E. Harrison.

Lieutenant General John L. DeWitt, who ordered the evacuation of 1942, encouraged California's racist pressure groups when he said, "I don't care what they do with the Japs as long as they don't send them back here. A Jap is a Jap." General

Delos C. Emmons, who succeeded DeWitt on the West Coast last September, says very little. He is the same General Emmons who decided *not* to order wholesale evacuation of the Japanese from Hawaii.

The longer the Army permits California and the rest of the Pacific Coast to be closed to everyone of Japanese descent, the more time is given the Hearst papers and their allies to convince Californians that they will indeed yield to lawlessness if the unwanted minority is permitted to return. By continuing to keep American citizens in "protective custody," the U.S. is holding to a policy as ominous as it is new. The American custom in the past has been to lock up the citizen who commits violence, not the victims of his threats and blows. The doctrine of "protective custody" could prove altogether too convenient a weapon in many other situations. In California, a state with a long history of race hatred and vigilanteism, antagonism is already building against the Negroes who have come in for war jobs. What is to prevent their removal to jails, to "protect them" from riots? Or Negroes in Detroit, Jews in Boston, Mexicans in Texas? The possibilities of "protective custody" are endless, as the Nazis have amply proved.

THE JAPANESE-AMERICANS
Homer A. Harris

To the Editors:

The April issue of *Fortune* [on Japan and the Japanese] is most interesting and despite the handicaps of wartime you have surpassed the September, 1936 issue. . . .

It is most regrettable that the same commendation cannot be extended to the article "Issei, Nisei, Kibei," which has treated this extremely vital, though controversial subject, from a rather superficial and sentimental viewpoint.

The article shows only the Japanese side of the problem, and fails to inquire into the reasons for "a policy as ominous as it is new." It must have occurred to you that the entire West Coast population and the U.S. Army had not become hysterical over the war or were so prejudiced as to waive every consideration except to remove the Japanese from the Pacific Coast. . . .

No other government has ever attempted to control its nationals in this country to the same degree. Every Japanese who came to this country was registered with the consulate, their children were registered at birth, retaining their Japanese citizenship along with their American citizenship. As [the child] grew up he made daily obeisance to the picture of the Emperor. After attendance at the public school each day he was bundled off to a Japanese language school, where under the tutelage of an alien-born teacher, usually a Shinto priest, he was taught the Japanese Language and the worship of the Emperor of Japan. Then at the age of twelve or thereabouts, he was sent in shiploads to Japan to be educated, indoctrined, and trained as a Japanese, body, heart, and soul. Incidentally he put in his compulsory three years' service in the Army or Navy and returned to this country to claim his American citizenship.

More than two-thirds of the Japanese boys were given this training, according to a well-known Japanese American, who has been accepted by agencies of our government as representative of the Japanese citizens. Yet your article speaks of the Kibei as a noisy but unimportant minority among the Nisei. . . .

We know that there were some loyal citizens among the Nisei, knew that they were a minority, but not even the Japanese could or would distinguish between loyal and disloyal.

The coast was under military attack, the details of which probably will not be disclosed until after the war. We knew that submarines were being sunk off the coast long before the shelling of the Santa Barbara coast. The air raid in March, 1942 was not a false alarm as officially reported but a bombing raid with bombs dropped and enemy planes shot down.

Homer A. Harris, "The Japanese-Americans," *Fortune* July 1944. Harris was the secretary-manager of the Associated Produce Dealers and Brokers of Los Angeles when he wrote this reply to the *Fortune* essay, "Issei, Nisei, Kibei," which had appeared in April 1944.

The citizens expected a hit-and-run raid on war plants and then, and only then, did they expect sabotage and aid to the enemy from the disloyal Japanese. After such a raid it is probable that reprisal en masse against all Japanese would have followed. These were the reasons the citizens of the Coast petitioned for the removal of the Japanese. . . .

I cannot overlook the inference in your article that the opposition to the Japanese on the Coast from farmers is based on the fact that the white growers cannot meet Japanese competition. This is true but not in the way you infer. The competition from the Japanese was distinctly unfair and contrary to American principles and law. Japanese control of vegetable production was based on a vertical-trust idea. The Japanese grower employed Japanese truckmen to haul to market to Japanese commission merchants, who sold to Japanese retailers. Preference was given at all times to fellow countrymen. If control of an area was desired, the elaborate series of associations, all stemming back into the Japanese Consulate, were put on the job. The white growers were crowded out of the Santa Maria Valley by Japanese paying landowners more rent than anyone, even themselves, could recover from the production of crops. If a commission merchant were to be eliminated it was easy for the Japanese competitor to pay the growers more than the merchandise sold for. In the case of the retailer the Japanese would undersell him regardless of losses. Through the associations their competitive losses were spread over all the members of a group, or passed on to another group or in some cases subsidized from an outside source. Only a few months before Pearl Harbor the State Department of Agriculture required eighteen Japanese commission merchants to disgorge thousands of dollars they had withheld from growers in one district and overpaid to growers in another district where there was keen competition with Caucasian merchants.

All things considered, the people on the Coast have shown surprisingly little prejudice on the Japanese question. They realize that we have citizens of Japanese extraction, a majority of whom are citizens in name only, and that when the military need has passed these citizens must be given the same privileges as any other. Yet they know that if the Japanese in this country continue to be dominated by the Japanese Government after the war as in the past it will only mean that within a generation we will be at war again.

*   *   *   *   *

Fortune thanks Mr. Harris, secretary manager of the Associated Produce Dealers and Brokers of Los Angeles, for an earnest statement of his viewpoint. The editors, however, can find no verification of the March, 1942 "bombing," and they cannot accept Mr. Harris's interpretation of Japanese-American citizenships. According to the Department of Justice (director of Alien Enemy Control Unit), registering American-born children as dual citizens is a common practice by aliens from all countries. But many American-born children of Japanese later renounced their unsought Japanese citizenship; and many more refused to take such action because they refused to dignify the notion of supposed allegiance to Japan. As for the Kibei, best government figures available indicate that no more than 20,000 out of 70,000 American-born Japanese have ever visited Japan. How many of the 20,000 became indoctrinated as servants of the Emperor, no man can say. *Fortune* rests on its estimate that they are a minority among the 70,000, and more of a nuisance than a menace. In conclusion, *Fortune* gladly meets Mr. Harris on a basic area of agreement: that loyal U.S. citizens, of Japanese or any other extraction, "must be given the same privileges as any other."

The Editors

RACISM ON THE WEST COAST
Carey McWilliams

The West Coast's new campaign to prevent the release of any persons of Japanese ancestry from relocation centers for the duration of the war began in December, 1942, with the appointment by the American Legion, California Department, of a five-man committee to conduct "an impartial investigation of all Japanese Relocation Areas in the State of California." Among the members of this impartial committee were Harper L. Knowles (of La Follette Committee fame); H. J. McClatchy of the California Joint Immigration Committee; and State Senator Jack Tenney of Los Angeles County. Tenney heads the "Little Dies Committee" of the state legislature. Shortly after the committee had been appointed, Tenney announced that it would take over the investigation for the American Legion.

Within the next two months, literally hundreds of West Coast organizations "went on record" by the adoption of a series of stock resolutions on the "Japanese question." I have examined scores of these resolutions and have yet to see one that by its form or content would indicate that it had been offered *by the members* of the particular organization; invariably these resolutions were presented *for concurrence* by one or another of the groups mentioned. With the newspapers featuring this organized activity, feeling began to mount throughout California. The city of Gardena omitted from its honor roll of citizens in the service the names of seventeen Japanese Americans; the American Legion summarily revoked the charters of the Townsend Harris and Commodore Perry Posts (made up of Japanese American veterans of the First World War). In Portland, Oregon, the Legion protested when local citizens sought to provide some volunteer care for a Japanese cemetery. Vigilante groups were formed in Salinas "to prevent the return of the Japanese." The California Federation of Women's Clubs expressed grave concern for their "sisters" in the East and Middle West whose safety, and presumably whose virtue, were being endangered by the release of evacuees from the centers.

The moment the legislature convened in January, 1943, a spate of anti-evacuee bills, resolutions and memorials were introduced. In debating these measures, mass evacuation was cited *as proof* of the disloyal character of the evacuees by the very individuals who had urged mass evacuation *for the protection* of the evacuees against mob violence. Statements and chants were hurled at the evacuees that no one had dreamed of during the period immediately after Pearl Harbor. Throughout the year legislative investigations, state and federal, were carefully spaced in such a manner as to provide an endless stream of newspaper headlines. First the Tenney investigation; then the farcical investigation conducted by Senator Chandler of Kentucky (which was really directed by Ray Richards of The Los Angeles Examiner); then the Dies Committee investigation in June, 1943; then an investigation by still another

Carey McWilliams, "Racism on the West Coast," *The New Republic* 110 (1944). McWilliams, editor of *The New Republic* from 1955 until 1975, was often in the forefront of the radical social causes of his day. He is the author of *Prejudice: Japanese Americans, Symbol of Racial Intolerance* (1944).

committee of the California Assembly; and, finally, yet another investigation by the Dies Committee.

Before the Dies Committee had conducted any investigation whatever, Representative J. Parnell Thomas, from a room in the Biltmore Hotel in Los Angeles, began to release a barrage of sensational stories about the War Relocation Authority and the evacuees. Calling "smear" witnesses to the stand, the committee tried its best to prevent the WRA from refuting their baseless charges. Some 35 factual misstatements were pointed out in the testimony of one witness. At these hearings, witnesses were openly encouraged to threaten the evacuees with mob violence. Public officials charged with the duty of law enforcement were given a pat on the back when they predicted "free murder," "violence" and "bloodshed" if a single evacuee were permitted to return to the West Coast.

At the hearings of the Gannon Committee (of the state legislature), Mrs. Maynard Force Thayer of Pasadena—stanch Republican, an outstanding clubwoman, a pillar of the community—was browbeaten by the chairman of the committee in a manner that finally evoked a murmur of protest from The Los Angeles Times. Mrs. Thayer was asked, for example, if she had ever "smelled the inside of a Japanese home"; she was asked if she wanted the government "to protect a people who farm their wives out to another man to procreate his name"; and she was queried as to her opinion about a "people where different sexes do nude bathing together." When Mrs. Thayer tried to get in a word about the Bill of Rights, she was rebuked by Mr. Gannon as follows: "The Bill of Rights is not such a sacred thing . . . don't you know that at the time the Bill of Rights was written we had 150,000 slaves in the United States? What did the Bill of Rights do about that?" While this fantastic and obscene circus was being conducted, The Los Angeles Examiner, in one day, devoted 62 inches of space to the hearings. In being haled before these committees, I was questioned, not about the evacuees of the WRA program, but about my views on "racial integrity," "mongrelization," "mixed marriages," "miscegenation statutes" and similar fancy topics.

At the time of the so-called "riot" at Tule Lake, the real riot occurred, not in the center, but in the pages of the California newspapers. Newspaper stories appeared charging that "bombs, knives, guns and various lethal weapons" had been found among the evacuees; that a Japanese evacuee had "pushed his way into" the bedchamber of a "white woman"; that the personnel of the center was "intermingling" with the evacuees; that the evacuees were being "coddled" and "pampered" (on a food allowance of 43 cents per person per day). Mr. Ray Richards of the Hearst press even suggested that Dillon Myer had knowingly failed to confiscate "lethal weapons" and that he had been a party to the "manufacture" of such weapons (see The San Francisco Call-Bulletin, December 21, 1943). With unblushing mendacity, The Los Angeles Herald-Express carried a headline reading: "Bare Deadly Peril as Armed Japanese Stream into California." Representative John Costello went so far as to announce, on December 9, 1943, that "hundreds of Japanese Americans and alien Japanese" were being permitted to return to California. Needless to say, there was no semblance of truth in these charges. Later The Los Angeles Times, in fancy headlines, charges that "450 Cases of Whiskey Go to Tule Lake" and, again, "Whiskey Flows to Tule Lake." The whiskey in question was consigned to the *town* of Tule Lake, not to the relocation center. "These Japs," wrote a columnist in The Times (referring not to the Japanese in Japan but to some 70,000 American citizens of Japanese ancestry), "are a depraved breed who can't be dealt with like mischievous boys . . . . We should wake up to the fact that protection of Americans from these degraded brutes is of more importance than the Little Tokyo Knitting and Brotherly Love Club." Only the fact that the Japanese government, in November, 1943, canceled further negotiations for the exchange of nationals, finally brought about some moderation in this frenzied campaign.

A section of the West Coast press systematically deflects hatred of Japan against the evacuees and uses hatred of the evacuees to justify its contention that the war in the Pacific is primarily racial in character. The consistent theme of the Hearst press is that "the war in the Pacific is the World War, the War of Oriental Races against Occidental Races for the Domination of the World" (The Los Angeles Examiner, March 23, 1943). Here is another characteristic statement from The San Francisco Examiner of January 25, 1943 (italics mine):

> Bad as the situation is in Europe, the war there is between European Occidental nations, *between white races.* Antagonisms, hatreds and jealousies, no matter how violent, cannot obscure the fact that the warring nations of Europe stem from common *racial,* cultural, linguistic and social roots. *It is a family affair,* in which the possibility of ultimate agreement and constructive harmony has not been dismissed even by the most determined opponents.

There can be no question but that anti-evacuee agitation in California is being cultivated for partisan political purposes. The hearings mentioned were, in large part, aimed at "smearing" the administration and building up a wall of reactionary feeling by stimulating racial hatred. To some extent this agitation has unquestionably been effective. Political officials in California have been cowed into silence; even those who are inclined to be fair do not dare to speak out on this issue. Just as Senators Hill and Pepper have been forced to disavow any interest in racial equality, so even the fair-minded members of the California delegation in Congress have been coerced on this thoroughly bogus "Japanese problem." Not one of these men dares to state publicly his real views on the evacuee problem.

No more serious mistake could be made than to encourage the belief that these groups can be handled quietly or that, by tactful diplomacy, they can be induced to forget the "Japanese issue." The aggressions of race bigots in California are of the same character as the insulting attacks made in Congress on the Negro minority by the white-supremacy advocates from the Deep South. Race bigotry in California can never be appeased. Every concession made to bigotry on the West Coast (and mass evacuation was such a concession) only encourages bolder aggression. As Representative Eberharter said, in his courageous minority report as a member of the Dies Committee, these recurrent investigations in California have "fostered a type of racial thinking which is already producing ugly manifestations and which seems to be growing in intensity. Unless this trend is checked, it may eventually lead to ill advised actions that will constitute an everlastingly shameful blot on our national record." Recent flare-ups against the evacuees in other sections of the country show that, in the absence of a strong affirmative federal policy and program on the race question, California bigots stand a good chance of spreading their particular version of the white-supremacy doctrine throughout the nation.

The military situation in the Pacific has changed since mass evacuation was ordered. The Japanese have been forced out of the Aleutians; Hawaii has been converted into one of the great fortresses of the world (and martial law has been modified); the Japanese are on the defensive throughout the Pacific. Various emergency measures adopted after Pearl Harbor have been relaxed on the West Coast and the general situation has so changed in our favor as to warrant the military in lifting the ban against the return of the evacuees. As long as the ban exists, race bigots in California will have an issue about which they will continue to conduct ever more fantastic and increasingly violent campaigns. If the ban is lifted, there will be no mass return of the evacuees and the freely predicted "murder" and "bloodshed" will not occur. There is a respectable opinion in California today that favors lifting the ban. The organizations I have mentioned create, rather than reflect, public opinion on the West Coast.

Issues of great importance are involved in this question. In default of an affirmative federal policy and program on race relations, race-minded groups in California will continue, in effect, to dictate our policy as a nation toward the peoples of the Orient. By taking advantage of this latent weakness in the federal government, California since 1882 has forced the Washington authorities to adopt a series of measures each of which has seriously jeopardized our national interests in the Far East: the exclusion of Chinese immigration; the passage of the 1924 immigration law; the mass evacuation of the resident Japanese. It requires no insight to predict that this same situation will continue until the American people realize that local areas should not be permitted to force the federal government into the position of having to adopt their particular attitudes on race relations.

AMERICAN FAIR PLAY?

For 13 weeks the Hood River (Ore.) Post of the American Legion persisted in its shameful pre-eminence—its members had struck the names of 16 Japanese-American soldiers from a public honor roll, had steadfastly refused to restore them. The Legion's embarrassed national commander had sent a "recommendation" which sounded like an order: put the names back. Some 500 of Hood River County's 11,580 citizens signed a full-page newspaper advertisement headed: "So Sorry Please. Japs Are Not Wanted in Hood River." Hood River's Legion Post replied to the national organization: ". . . inadvisable at this time. . . ."

But last week, after digesting some strong hints that their charter might be in danger, Hood River's legionnaires finally voted to restore 15 of the 16 names.

Relieved, National Commander Edward N. Scheiberling whipped out a press release: ". . . source of gratification to the American Legion everywhere . . . sound sense of American fair play. . . ." Said the New York *Times*, "The Hood River Post is to be congratulated on having the courage to admit its mistake."

But racial intolerance on the West Coast had abated not a whit:

- Hood River, still as anti-Japanese as ever, mouthed a rumor—white servicemen would demand the removal of their names if those of the Japanese-Americans went back. At week's end the honor roll was still bare of Nisei names.

- In Seattle, Tetel Takayoshi, graduate of the University of Washington and prewar teaching supervisor at King County's Harborview Hospital, returned to her old job. "I'm glad to be back," she reassured her friends. "I was born here—this is my home." But after eleven days of snubs and silences she quietly packed her bags, headed back to Denver.

- In Portland, Ore., R. Tsubota, a truck farmer, brought a truckload of vegetables to the Portland Farmers' Market, found himself virtually boycotted. At nearby Gresham, citizens circulated a petition asking that all persons of Japanese blood be deported to a Pacific island.

- Sam Takeda, a San José, Calif. farmer, awakened with a start one night last week—the front of his house had been soused with gasoline, set afire. After he beat out the flames, someone fired a shot at him.

The Nisei were not friendless on the Pacific Coast—many openly welcomed them and hundreds deplored acts of violence. In Woodinville, Wash., Kametaro Funai, just out of a relocation camp, ran up against the manpower shortage. Promptly, some University of Washington students came out to help him on his farm.

"American Fair Play?" *Time* 19 March 1945.

But whether the nation liked it or not, the Japanese-haters' methods were proving exceedingly effective. Of 33,000 Japanese and Nisei who had left war relocation centers, only 1,640 had returned to the West Coast. Of 60,397 still in WRA camps, only 1,938 had announced any intention of going back to their old homes. The rest, bewildered by the ways of their erstwhile neighbors and friends, made plans to go to other parts of the country, or just waited, wondering what to do.

POSTWAR EXPORTS

They were born in the U.S. and, until Pearl Harbor, had therefore enjoyed all the blessings of citizenship. They had gone to the public schools, voted, earned a living. Some of them had friends or relatives in the U.S. armed forces. But last week these 6,000-odd U.S. Japanese were busy renouncing their citizenship to swear allegiance to Emperor Hirohito.

By & large, they were the fanatical, trouble-making variety of Nisei segregated at Tule Lake, Calif., for disloyalty. Until a year ago change of allegiance was so difficult to achieve that a Nisei had to commit treason or desert from the armed forces to make it. Now, thanks to a recent act of Congress, anybody can renounce his U.S. citizenship if the U.S. Attorney General finds it is not contrary to the national defense.

Some of the Nisei who have got or are getting a chance at renunciation are afraid that to be returned to the hostile Pacific Coast would be worse than being reinterned as aliens. But the majority of them dearly want to go back to Japan—even though they can see from their newspapers how their future homeland is being devastated by the U.S., how close it is to defeat. After the war is over they will be sent back to what is left of the land few of them have ever seen.

"Postwar Exports," *Time* 2 April 1945.

OUR WORST WARTIME MISTAKE
Eugene V. Rostow

Time is often needed for us to recognize the great miscarriages of justice. The Dreyfus case had lasted four years before public opinion was fully aroused. The trials of Sacco and Vanzetti endured six years. As time passes, it becomes more and more plain that our wartime treatment of the Japanese and the Japanese-Americans on the West Coast was a tragic and dangerous mistake. That mistake is a threat to society, and to all men. Its motivation and its impact on our system of law deny every value of democracy.

In the perspective of our legal tradition, the facts are almost incredible.

During the bleak spring of 1942, the Japanese and the Japanese-Americans who lived on the West Coast of the United States were taken into custody and removed to camps in the interior. More than one hundred thousand men, women, and children were thus exiled and imprisoned. More than two-thirds of them were American citizens.

These people were taken into custody as a military measure on the ground that espionage and sabotage were especially to be feared from persons of Japanese blood. The whole group was removed from the West Coast because the military authorities thought it would take too long to conduct individual investigation on the spot. They were arrested without warrants and were held without indictment or a statement of charges, although the courts were open and freely functioning. They were transported to camps far from their homes, and kept there under prison conditions, pending investigations of their "loyalty." Despite the good intentions of the chief relocation officers, the centers were little better than concentration camps.

If the evacuees were found "loyal," they were released only if they could find a job and a place to live, in a community where no hoodlums would come out at night to chalk up anti-Japanese slogans, break windows, or threaten riot. If found "disloyal" in their attitude to the war, they were kept in the camps indefinitely— although sympathy with the enemy is no crime in the United States (for white people at least) so long as it is not translated into deeds or the visible threat of deeds. On May 1, 1945, three years after the program was begun, about 70,000 persons were still in camps. While it is hoped to have all these people either free, or in more orthodox confinement, by January 1, 1946, what is euphemistically called the Japanese "relocation" program will not be a closed book for many years.

The original program of "relocation" was an injustice, in no way required or justified by the circumstances of the war. But the Supreme Court, in three extraordinary decisions, has upheld its main features as constitutional. This fact converts a

Eugene V. Rostow, "Our Worst Wartime Mistake," *Harper's* 191 (1945). Rostow has been a professor and dean at the Yale University Law School and served as Undersecretary of State for Political Affairs in the Johnson Administration. He has written numerous books, including *Planning for Freedom* (1959) and *Law, Power, and the Pursuit of Peace* (1968).

piece of wartime folly into national policy—a permanent part of the law—a doc-trine enlarging the power of the military in relation to civil authority. It is having a sinister impact on the minority problem in every part of the country. It is giving aid to reactionary politicians who use social division and racial prejudice as their tools. The precedent is being used to encourage attacks on the civil rights of both citizens and aliens. As Mr. Justice Jackson has said, the principle of these decisions "lies about like a loaded weapon ready for the hand of any authority that can bring forward a plausible claim of an urgent need." All in all, the case of the Japanese-Americans is the worst blow our liberties have sustained in many years. Unless repudiated, it may support devastating and unforeseen social and political conflicts.

What was done in the name of military precaution on the West Coast was quite different from the security measures taken in Hawaii or on the East Coast, although both places were active theaters of war in 1942.

On the East Coast enemy aliens were controlled without mass arrests or evacua-tions, despite their heavy concentration in and near shipping and manufacturing centers. Aliens had been registered, and the police had compiled information about fascist sympathizers, both aliens and citizens. "On the night of December 7, 1941," Attorney General Biddle reported, "the most dangerous of the persons in this group were taken into custody; in the following weeks a number of others were appre-hended. Each arrest was made on the basis of information concerning the specific alien taken into custody. We have used no dragnet techniques and have conducted no indiscriminate, large-scale raids." General regulations were issued, somewhat restricting the freedom of all enemy aliens over fourteen years of age. They were forbidden to enter military areas; they had to get the District Attorney's permission before traveling; they were forbidden to own or use firearms, cameras, short-wave radio sets, codes, ciphers, or invisible ink. This control plan kept security officers informed, but otherwise allowed the aliens almost their normal share in the work and life of the community.

Enemy aliens under suspicion, and those who violated the regulations, were subject to summary arrest, and were then promptly examined by one of the special Alien Enemy Hearing Boards. These boards could recommend that the individual alien be interned, paroled, or released unconditionally. The examinations were smoothly conducted, and they did nothing to lower prevailing standards of justice. Of the 1,100,000 enemy aliens in the country, 9,080 had been examined by the end of June 1943, about 4,000 of them being then interned. By June 30, 1944, the number interned had been reduced to approximately 2,500.

In Hawaii a different procedure was followed, but one less drastic than the evacuation program pursued on the West Coast, although Hawaii was certainly a more active theater of war. Immediately after Pearl Harbor, martial law was installed in Hawaii, and the commanding general assumed the role of military governor. Yet, although about one-third the population of Hawaii is of Japanese descent, and although the tension was great after the Pearl Harbor raid, there was no mass roundup on the islands. Fewer than 800 Japanese aliens were sent to the mainland for internment, and fewer than 1,000 persons of Japanese ancestry, 912 of them being citizens, were sent to relocation centers on the mainland. Many of the latter group were families of interned aliens, transferred voluntarily. Those arrested in Hawaii were taken into custody on the basis of individual suspicion, resting on previous examination or observed behavior. Even under a regime of martial law, men were arrested as individuals, and not because of the color of their skins. Safety was assured without mass arrests, or needless hardship.

On the West Coast the security program was something else again. Immediately after Pearl Harbor there were no special regulations for persons of Japanese extraction. Known enemy sympathizers among the Japanese, like white traitors and enemy agents, were arrested. There was no sabotage by persons of Japanese ancestry. There was no reason to suppose that the 112,000 persons of Japanese descent on the West Coast, less than 2 per cent of the population, constituted a greater menace than such persons in Hawaii, where they were 32 percent of the population.

After a month's silence, the organized minority whose business it has been to exploit racial tensions on the West Coast went to work. They had strong support in the Hearst press and its equivalents. Politicians, fearful of an unknown public opinion, spoke out for white supremacy. West Coast Congressional delegations led by Senator Hiram Johnson, urged the administration to exclude all persons of Japanese blood from the coast states. Anti-Oriental spokesmen appeared before special hearings of the Tolan Committee, and explained the situation as they conceived it to Lieutenant General J. L. DeWitt, commanding the Western Defense Command. Tension was intensified, and doubters, worried about the risks of another Pearl Harbor, remained silent, preferring too much caution to too little. An opinion crystallized in favor of evacuating the Japanese.

After some hesitation, General DeWitt proposed the policy of exclusion on grounds of military need. The War Department backed him up. No one in the government took the responsibility for opposing or overruling him.

Despite the nature of the emergency, the Army's lawyers wanted more legal authority before action was taken. The President issued an Executive Order in February 1942, and in March Congress passed a statute, authorizing military commanders to designate "military areas" and to prescribe the terms on which any persons could enter, leave, or remain in such areas. A policy of encouraging the Japanese to move away individually had shown signs of producing confusion. It was therefore decided to establish a compulsory system of detention in camps, to simplify the process of resettlement, and to afford the fullest measure of security.

The history of law affords nothing more fantastic than the evidence which is supposed to justify this program. General DeWitt's final recommendation to the Secretary of War, dated February 14, 1942, but not made public until early in 1944, explains the basis of his decision.

"In the war in which we are now engaged," he said, "racial affinities are not severed by migration. The Japanese race is an enemy race and while many second and third generation Japanese born on United States soil, possessed of United States citizenship, have become 'Americanized,' the racial strains are undiluted." From the premise of a war of "races," the general had no difficulty reaching his conclusion. There is "no ground for assuming," he said, that Japanese-Americans will not turn against the United States. So much for the idea that men are presumed innocent until proved guilty, and that American citizens stand on an equal footing before the law without regard for race, color, or previous condition of servitude! "It therefore follows," the general added, "that along the vital Pacific Coast over 112,000 potential enemies, of Japanese extraction, are at large today. There are disturbing indications that these are organized and ready for concerted action at a favorable opportunity. The very fact that no sabotage has taken place to date is a disturbing and confirming indication that such action will be taken."

There was somewhat more evidence than the absence of sabotage to prove its special danger. The Japanese lived closely together, often concentrated around harbors and other strategic areas. Japanese clubs and religious institutions played an important part in their segregated social life. Japanese language schools existed, to preserve for the American born something of the cultural heritage of Japan. The Japanese government, like that of many other countries, asserted a doctrine of nationality different from our own, which gave rise to possible claims of dual citizenship. Thus a long-standing conflict in international law, involving many countries other than Japan, was invoked to cast special doubt on the loyalty of American citizens of Japanese descent.

Much of the suspicion inferentially based on these statements disappears on closer examination. In many instances the concentration of Japanese homes around strategic areas had come about years before, and for entirely innocent reasons. Japanese cannery workers, for example, had had to live on the waterfront in order to be near the plants in which they worked. Japanese truck gardeners had rented land in the industrial outskirts of large cities to be close to their markets. They had rented land for gardening under high tension lines—regarded as a very suspicious circumstance—because the company could not use the land for other purposes; the initiative in starting this practice had come from the utility companies, not from the Japanese.

Despite discrimination against the Japanese, many had done well in America. They were substantial property owners. Their children participated normally and actively in the schools and universities of the West Coast. Their unions and social organizations had passed resolutions of loyalty in great number, before and after Pearl Harbor. It is difficult to find real evidence that either religious or social institutions among the Japanese had successfully fostered Japanese militarism or other dangerous sentiments. The Japanese language schools, which the Japanese-Americans themselves had long sought to put under state control, seem to represent little more than the familiar desire of many immigrant groups to keep alive the language and tradition of the "old country"; in the case of Japanese-Americans, knowledge of the Japanese language was of particular economic importance, since so much of their working life was spent with other Japanese on the West Coast.

Some elements among the Japanese were, of course, suspect. They were known to the authorities, who had for several years been checking on the Japanese-American population. Many had been individually arrested immediately after Pearl Harbor, and the others were under constant surveillance.

It is also true that a considerable percentage of the evacuees later gave negative answers to loyalty questions in the questionnaires they were asked to fill out while in camps. Many of those answers were expressly based upon the treatment the individuals had received; the same shock of evacuation and confinement undoubtedly was responsible indirectly for many more. Basically, however, the issue of abstract loyalty is irrelevant. Disloyalty, even in the aggravated form of enthusiastic verbal support for the Axis cause, is not a crime in the United States. At most, it is a possible ground for interning enemy aliens. Citizens must do more than talk or think disloyal thoughts before being arrested and jailed.

Apart from the members of the group known to be under suspicion, there was no evidence beyond the vaguest fear to connect the Japanese on the West Coast with the unfavorable military events of 1941 and 1942. Both at Pearl Harbor and in sporadic attacks on the West Coast the enemy had shown that he had knowledge of our dispositions. There was some signaling to enemy ships at sea, both by radio and by lights, along the West Coast. There were several episodes of shelling the coast by submarine—although two of the three such cases mentioned by General DeWitt as tending to create suspicion of the Japanese-Americans took place *after* their removal from the coast. (These were the only such items in his report which were not identified by date.) And those subsequently arrested as Japanese agents in the Pearl Harbor area were all white men.

The most striking comment on the quality of the evidence produced by General DeWitt to support his proposal was made by Solicitor General Fahy, whose job it was to defend the general's plan before the Supreme Court. He relied upon the general's report "only to the extent that it relates" statistics and other details concerning the actual evacuation and the events which took place after it. But the briefs that he himself presented were identical in the substance of their argument. The Japanese-Americans were an unknown, unknowable, foreign group, living together, and moving in mysterious ways, inscrutable to puzzled white men. Therefore, let them be imprisoned; let their property be taken into custody, sold off at bargain prices, dissipated, and lost; let their roots be torn up, let their children suffer the irreparable shock of life in a concentration camp; let their relation to society be distorted by the searing memory of humiliation, rejection, and punishment.

The evidence supports one conclusion only: the dominant element in the development of our relocation policy was race prejudice, not a military estimate of a military problem.

By the time the issues raised by this program reached the Supreme Court, the crisis which was supposed to justify it had passed. The first cases came up in June 1943, the second and third in December 1944. The course of the war had changed completely; the Japanese were no longer prowling off California, but fighting defensively among the islands of the Western Pacific.

The problem presented to the Supreme Court was thus completely different from that which confronted worried soldiers, legislators, and executive officials in the melancholy months after Pearl Harbor. Invalidation of the relocation scheme would do no possible harm to the prosecution of the war. The Supreme Court could afford to view the issues in perspective, giving full weight to its own special responsibilities for the development of constitutional law as a whole.

Moreover, the issue for the court was infinitely more complex than that which faced General DeWitt in 1942. The court had to decide not only whether General DeWitt had acted within the scope of his permissible authority, but whether it should validate what had been done. As many episodes in our constitutional history attest, those are different issues. The court could not escape the fact that it was the Supreme Court, arbiter of a vast system of customs, rules, habits, and relationships. Its decision inevitably would have far-reaching effects—on the power of the military, on our developing law of emergencies, on the future of those demagogues and political groups which live by attacking minorities, and on the future decision of cases in lower courts and police stations, involving the rights of citizens and aliens, the availability of habeas corpus, and like questions.

The question of how and on what grounds the Supreme Court should dispose of the cases also was one of broad political policy. Would a repudiation of Congress, the President, and the military in one aspect of their conduct of the war affect the people's will to fight? Would it create a campaign issue for 1944? Would it affect the power and prestige of the Supreme Court as a political institution?

In a bewildering and unimpressive series of opinions, relieved only by the dissents of Justice Roberts and Justice Murphy in one of the three cases—*Korematsu v. United States*—the court chose to assume that the main issues did not exist. In avoiding the risks of overruling the government on an issue of war policy, it weakened society's control over military power—one of the controls on which the whole organization of our society depends. It failed to uphold the most ordinary rights of citizenship, making Japanese-Americans into second-class citizens, who stand before the courts on a different legal footing from other Americans. It accepted and gave the prestige of its support to dangerous racial myths about a minority group, in arguments which can easily be applied to any other minority in our society.

The reasoning of the court was simple and direct. The problem was the scope of the war power of the national government. Both Congress and the executive seemed to have decided that special measures were required because espionage and sabotage were especially to be feared from persons of Japanese descent on the West Coast in the spring of 1942. It was not the job of the Supreme Court to decide such questions for itself. Its task was that of judicial review—to uphold the judgment of the officers directly responsible for fighting the war if, the court said, there was "any substantial basis" in fact for the conclusion that protective measures were necessary.

Two propositions which the court accepted as "facts" were held to afford a sufficiently "rational basis" for military decision. The first was that in time of war "residents having ethnic affiliations with an invading enemy may be a greater source of danger than those of different ancestry"—a doctrine which belongs with the race theories of the Nazis and, moreover, is contrary to the experience of American society in both our World Wars. (The weight of scientific evidence is that the most important driving urge of such minority groups is to conform, not to rebel.) The second was that on the West Coast in 1942 there was no time to isolate and examine the suspected Japanese on an individual basis—although of the 110,000 persons subject to the exclusion orders, 43 percent were over fifty or under fifteen years old; they had lived in California without committing sabotage for five months after Pearl Harbor; in the country as a whole, thousands of aliens were examined individually without substantial delay; and in Britain 74,000 enemy aliens were checked in a few months.

By accepting the military judgment on these two points, without any evidence in the record to back it up, without requiring any testimony from the military, and even without adequate discussion by the court itself, the court has taken "judicial notice" of doubtful and controversial propositions of fact, as if they were as well-established as the census statistics or the tide tables. The court could have sent the cases back for a full trial on the justification for General DeWitt's decision. Instead, it upheld his ruling. Thus it created a profound question as to the position of the military power in our public life. . . .

The Japanese exclusion program rests on five propositions of the utmost potential menace:

1. Protective custody, extending over three or four years, is a permitted form of imprisonment in the United States.
2. Political opinions, not criminal acts, may contain enough danger to justify such imprisonment.
3. Men, women, and children of a given racial group, both Americans and resident aliens, can be presumed to possess the kind of dangerous ideas which require their imprisonment.
4. In time of war or emergency the military—perhaps without even the concurrence of the legislature—can decide what political opinions require imprisonment, and which groups are infected with them.
5. The decision of the military can be carried out without indictment, trial, examination, jury, the confrontation of witnesses, counsel for the defense, the privilege against self-incrimination, or any of the other safeguards of the Bill of Rights.

The idea of punishment only for individual criminal behavior is basic to all systems of civilized law. A great principle was never lost so casually. Mr. Justice Black's comment was weak to the point of impotence: "Hardships are a part of war, and war is an aggregation of hardships." It was an answer in the spirit of cliché: "Don't you know there's a war going on?" It ignores the rights of citizenship, and the safeguards of trial practice which have been the historical attributes of liberty.

We believe that the German people bear a common political responsibility for outrages secretly committed by the Gestapo and the SS. What are we to think of our own part in a program which violates every principle of our common life, yet has been approved by the President, Congress, and the Supreme Court?

Three chief forms of reparation are available, and should be pursued. The first is the inescapable obligation of the federal government to protect the civil rights of Japanese-Americans against organized and unorganized hooliganism. If local law enforcement fails, federal prosecutions under the national Civil Rights Act should be undertaken.

Secondly, generous financial indemnity should be sought. Apart from the sufferings of their imprisonment, the Japanese-Americans have sustained heavy property losses from their evacuation.

Finally, the basic issues should be presented to the Supreme Court again, in an effort to obtain a prompt reversal of these wartime cases. The Supreme Court has often corrected its own errors in the past, especially when that error was occasioned by the excitement of a tense moment. After the end of the Civil War, several earlier decisions were reversed by *Ex Parte Milligan*. The famous flag-salute case of 1940 has recently been overruled in the decision of *West Virginia* v. *Barnett*. Similar public expiation in the case of the Japanese-Americans would be good for the court, and for the country.

THE NISEI COME HOME
Victor Boesen

Yoshimatsu Masuda works two days a week in a fish cannery near Long Beach, California. It is no job for an old fisherman who spent 20 years of his life pulling his livelihood out of the Pacific, but it's the best Masuda can do under the circumstances. California has a law prohibiting alien Japanese from owning commercial fishing licenses.

Some day, Masuda hopes, the law will be revoked and he can go back to his old business. He has faith in his neighbors. "California people all right," he says warmly. "It's state guv'ment causes trouble." As far as California's attitude to its alien Japanese and its citizens of Japanese ancestry is concerned, the old fisherman is correct on both counts.

After many years of persecution because of their race, dating back to the 1890's, the Japanese are beginning to feel they really have a home in California. Returning from wartime relocation centers in other states, they discover that the old hostility has lessened perceptibly and that both Japanese aliens and Nisei (second-generation Japanese born in the US) have been encouraged to take up their old occupations.

Most of the animosity that still persists stems, as old Masuda puts it, from the state government's continued efforts to keep the Nisei in a sort of second-class-citizen category. Discriminatory laws such as the fishing-license ban that beached Masuda and the state's Alien Land Law still remain on the books. An occasional legislator like State Senator Jack Tenney, head of California's "Little Un-American Activities Committee," embarks on anti-Japanese tirades; Attorney General Fred N. Howser has tried, unsuccessfully, to deprive Japanese aliens of their landholdings, but their efforts have evoked little approval from the average Californian. And although the Hearst newspapers and the ultra-conservative Native Sons of the Golden West still bait the Japanese, their antics arouse less and less enthusiasm.

There is nothing miraculous in this change of attitude. Californians have not undergone a sudden spiritual catharsis which has divested them of deep-seated moral prejudices. Moral or anthropological considerations have little to do with it; many Californians have simply learned that the people they used to regard as "interlopers" are actually useful, conscientious citizens—and as such are to be valued highly.

The war decisively banished any doubts as to the courage or patriotism of Japanese Americans. At the very time California businessmen and farmers were taking over the properties of Japanese who had been evacuated to relocation centers, the nation's newspapers were carrying glowing accounts of the heroic 442nd Nisei Infantry Battalion in Italy. And despite the efforts of state officials, various freelance Japanophobes and anti-Japanese sections of the press (Hearst papers and the Sacramento *Bee*) to make it appear otherwise at the time, the Japanese committed no

Victor Boesen, "The Nisei Come Home," *The New Republic* 118 (1948). *The New Republic* is a liberal political journal.

known act of disloyalty to this country, as attested by the FBI, the Army's Western Defense Command and the Navy.

In addition, the war indirectly created a new respect for the multitudes of Japanese truck farmers and gardeners who had to leave the area for alleged security reasons. While these people sweated out the war in relocation centers, the Californians discovered, by trying it themselves, that their erstwhile neighbors had done a superb job in cultivating and reclaiming the land and raising produce for sale at attractive prices.

There are other less utilitarian reasons why Californians are not rallying much to the tom-toms in Sacramento, and why, for instance, townspeople boycotted a barber who put up a "No Japs Wanted" sign in his window. The Nisei are intelligent and well behaved; they have an extremely low crime rate and boast the highest percentage of college graduates of any racial group in the country. The 442nd Infantry's IQ was among the best in the Army.

The feelings of many Californians about the return of the Japanese were expressed by a Negro who had moved into Los Angeles' "Little Tokyo" during the war. "Now that they've returned," he declared, "it's only right they should get their places back, because this is their home." And the Negro moved out.

The Nisei are pleased at the clearing atmosphere. One of them gives the typical report that Japanese are increasingly finding their way into the Caucasian business world, that they are being accepted both as employees and as fellow businessmen. To Nisei war vets, this atones in part for the wartime seizures of Japanese fruit, vegetable and produce industries, which have yet to be regained.

Agents of the War Relocation Authority, who conceived a healthy respect for the Japanese during the internment period, have helped persuade Caucasian employers to give the Nisei a try at office jobs, hitherto closed to them. The results have been excellent. When a presentable, efficient Nisei girl places herself as a typist or secretary, she usually creates a demand for more.

Jimmy Yahiro, proprietor of the Nisei Employment Agency in Los Angeles, says he has "no trouble in placing the girls in all kinds of office jobs"; the pastor of a Japanese church remarks, "The girls and women are getting lots of positions in stores on Broadway, in Beverly Hills and in country and city offices. I placed several in an exclusive Beverly Hills dress shop at $10 a day."

The men who get a chance make good just as quickly as the girls. One 442nd vet was refused a chemist's job. "Try the back door," counseled a Nisei attorney. "Take any kind of work they hire. Show them what kind of fellow you are." The boy followed his advice; today he is a chemist for an oil company.

To help break down dying prejudice, Nisei who are accepted into "white" employment practise a discipline not always found among other workers. Several hundred have gone into the hot, unpleasant work of pressing records in the phonograph-recording industry. One such worker, a college graduate, said, "Many Nisei dropped off as soon as they found they had to go through the training period at low wages. Some of us older men felt that this created a bad impression, and now we have set an unwritten policy that no Nisei is to take a job unless he will stick. . . ."

Many Nisei, discovering the community's growing willingness to accept Japanese, are going into business for the first time. Patronage of a Japanese establishment in a Caucasian neighborhood may be sparse at first, but it soon grows. Take the experience of the Nisei who opened a service station.

"My first Caucasian customers would drive away when they saw I was Japanese," he declared. "Then a few began stopping and found that I gave prewar service. Once they came in, they became regular customers."

Meanwhile, those business and professional men who haven't yet picked up where they left off during the war, are resorting to gardening. Today, in the Los Angeles area alone, more than 3,000 Japanese, a third more than were similarly employed in 1941, are tending the district's yards and estates, grown unkempt while they were away. Angelenos are so happy to have them back that they are paying them up to $600 a month, compared to $125 before the war. Some of the more industrious gardeners, juggling six or seven lawns at a time, have earned as much as $50 a day. What the clients don't know is that very often the little man clipping the hedge is a college graduate in one of the professions or an ex-businessman with more money in the bank than his employer.

For those able immediately to resume operations at their old stands in such Japanese specialties as flower markets, flower farms and wholesale fish markets, business is brisk. Such resistance as Caucasian interlopers put up at the start quickly faded or is working out to the advantage of the Japanese.

The first Nisei to return to Los Angeles, co-owner with his father and two brothers of a flower market on the edge of Little Tokyo which had been operated for them by Caucasian managers, found signs on the wall reading, "No Japs Allowed Between 7th and 8th." He kept out of sight all day, and that evening asked his Caucasian manager about the signs. The next day he found police posted around the market, with a radio car standing by. "You have nothing to be afraid of," they told him.

The only unpleasant incident to occur in the store came when a man proclaimed in loud tones: "I wouldn't spend a dime in a place run by Japs!" No one seemed interested. Some time later, this same man, who runs a flower shop in connection with a funeral home, phoned to ask if he could buy some flowers. The original returnee took the call. His brothers, both back by now, suggested that the man be told to go to hell. This was vetoed, however, and today his monthly account averages $1,400.

Soon after his first order, he came around and apologized for his earlier conduct. "I made a fool of myself," he kept repeating. Now he and his wife exchange dinner invitations with the brothers and their families, and go fishing together.

George Endow, a San Fernando Valley flower grower, who also runs the Sugar Bowl Café in Little Tokyo, estimates that there has been a 60-percent comeback among Japanese flower growers—largely because the Caucasians who took over in their absence were amateurs and unable to compete on the basis of quality production. To offset this disadvantage, the Caucasians boycotted those wholesalers who bought from Japanese growers, which merely drove more wholesalers to the Japanese owners.

Another Japanese comeback has been made in fish wholesaling. A typical example is furnished by Frank Tsuchiya, of the Pacific California Fish Company. His firm, which did a million-dollar-a-year business before the war, not only has all its old customers back but has expanded its operations by 35 percent.

[All of this] is encouraging, but it is only a symptom of something bigger. That something bigger is the growing realization of the people of California that Nisei make good neighbors.

ARGUMENTS IN FAVOR OF EVACUATION
Morton Grodzins

SABOTAGE, ESPIONAGE, AND THE FIFTH COLUMN

The sabotage, espionage, and fifth-column argument started in the largest number of instances from what was believed to have taken place on December 7, 1941. Stories of "what happened at Pearl Harbor" did not begin to circulate generally until the very end of December. Once the style was set, these stories became endless. The form resolution passed by eleven California county boards of supervisors noted that "during the attack on Pearl Harbor . . . the Japanese were aided and abetted by fifth columnists of the Japanese race." The same point about Pearl Harbor was made in Congress at least ten times between January 20 and February 18, 1942. Pearl Harbor was a partial foundation for the first demand of the California Joint Immigration Committee in favor of evacuation and a prominent reason for evacuation advanced by American Legion groups. Pearl Harbor formed the basis of the anonymous chain letters circulated in southern California during January and February and was mentioned frequently, and sometimes hysterically, in letters received by Attorney-General Biddle. Newspaper stories sometimes made the Pearl Harbor stories very precise, and on one occasion the moderate *San Francisco Chronicle* printed drawings by a staff artist illustrating the exact manner in which Japanese blocked roads with overturned trucks and signaled attacking planes with flashlights.

It was a short step between what was alleged to have happened at Pearl Harbor and what might happen on the Pacific Coast. Californians were in general agreement with Attorney-General Earl Warren that the state presented "the most likely objective in the Nation" for sabotage and espionage activities. Mayor Bowron of Los Angeles, the city managers of Oakland and Alameda in the San Francisco region, the governors of Washington and Oregon, and the mayors of the largest cities in those states all expressed similar views.

An important variation of the argument was the thesis of *concerted sabotage.* Attorney-General Warren of California was its chief exponent. On February 2 Mr. Warren asserted it was "significant" that there had been no reports of sabotage and fifth-column activities in the state. This, he said, looked "very much" as if it were "a studied effort not to have any until the zero hour arrives." The California attorney-general made the most elaborate presentation of this argument in his testimony before the Tolan Committee. His remarks at this point were confined to the Japanese alone:

"To assume that the enemy has not planned fifth column activities for us in a wave of sabotage is simply to live in a fool's paradise.

"Unfortunately, however, many of our people and some of our authorities . . . are of the opinion that because we have had no sabotage and no fifth column

Morton Grodzins, "Arguments in Favor of Evacuation," *Americans Betrayed* (Chicago: University of Chicago Press, 1949). Grodzins was a member of the research team that conducted the Japanese American Evacuation and Resettlement Study at the University of California from 1942 to 1948.

activities in this State since the beginning of the war, that means that none have been planned for us. *But I take the view that that is the most ominous sign in our whole situation. It convinces me more than perhaps any other factor that the sabotage that we are to get, the fifth column activities that we are to get, are timed just like Pearl Harbor was timed and just like the invasion of France, and of Denmark, and of Norway, and all of those other countries.*

"*. . . Our day of reckoning is bound to come. . . . When, nobody knows, of course, but we are approaching an invisible deadline.*"

This stand received the widest concurrence. And the argument was used by Congressman Tolan; Mayor Riley of Portland, Oregon; Mayor Millikin of Seattle; Mayor Bowron of Los Angeles; the Korean "espionage agent," Kilsoo K. Haan; columnists Walter Lippmann and Westbrook Pegler; several editorial writers; a number of correspondents of Attorney-General Biddle; and, not least of all, by General DeWitt in his recommendation for mass evacuation.

Direct evidence of sabotage intent or sabotage practice was cited in a number of instances. Immediately after Pearl Harbor it was reported that ground glass had been found in shrimp canned by Japanese workers and that Japanese saboteurs had sprayed overdoses of arsenic poison on vegetables. Japanese residents allegedly set up a number of unusual signaling devices similar to those which had been reported at Hawaii: "A beautiful field of flowers on the property of a Japanese farmer" near Ventura, California, had been plowed up because "it seems the Jap was a fifth columnist and had grown his flowers in a way that when viewed from a plane formed an arrow pointing the direction to the airport. The chief of police of Los Angeles charged that on December 8 and 9 "a large amount of loose hay was piled in the shape of an arrow pointing to one of our major aviation plants." The district attorney of Tulare County said that "Jap truck farmers of the Ivanhoe district had planted tomatoes so they form a crude arrow pointing to an air training field."

By far the most damaging claims of sabotage intent came to the public attention as the result of numerous raids by the Federal Bureau of Investigation. After the promulgation of the contraband orders in January sensational mass raids were made. The newspaper headlines were large and the stories shocking. On February 6, for example, a two-line, eight-column streamer headline on page 1 of the *San Francisco Chronicle* announced raids on what FBI agents "feared to be a deadly nest of saboteurs on the edge of the huge Mare Island Navy Yard." With the searches still continuing, it was revealed that contraband goods had been seized that included a "complete set of US Navy signal flags, at least five illegal radios, at least two guns, at least two illegal cameras." Five days later contraband material seized in the search of a hundred homes and business establishments near Monterey Bay uncovered "more than 60,000 rounds of rifle ammunition, 14,900 rounds of shotgun ammunition, 378 pistol bullets, eleven still cameras," and a large amount of additional contraband material. Revelations of this kind were made at almost daily intervals for more than a month, with pictures of the contraband goods and the arrested aliens appearing frequently.

The cumulative effect of the claims and alleged proofs of the sabotage, espionage, fifth-column dangers showed itself in many of the letters urging evacuation that came to national legislators and administrative officials. The same considerations had a great weight in swinging editorial opinion in favor of evacuation, the statement of the *Stockton Record* of February 21 being typical in this regard:

"In recent days FBI agents have operated in many parts of California and uncovered caches of arms and contraband. . . . The circumstances smack strongly of those which contributed to the tragedy of Pearl Harbor. . . . The United States cannot afford to take chances. . . . The Pacific coast is in danger."

PUBLIC MORALE

Quantitatively of little importance, the public morale argument was put succinctly by Governor Olson of California when he said that if evacuation were carried out "everyone would feel much safer about the alien and the Japanese population." The loss of the sense of security resulting from the continued presence of Japanese Americans was set forth by the State Personnel Board as one justification for suspending all Japanese American employees of California. To the Department of Justice came letters demanding more rapid action on the part of officials in removing Japanese, whose very presence on the coast was described as undermining public morale and hampering the war effort. The following was a representative complaint: "Here on the west coast your snail-like action in dealing with the Japs has come in for much criticism almost to the point of creating a don't give a dam [sic] attitude."

HUMANITARIANISM

Two categories of this argument were differentiated, one dealing with the danger to resident Japanese if they were not taken into custody, the other dwelling upon the humane manner with which the evacuation would be carried out.

a) Vigilantism and race riots.—The statement that evacuation was necessary in order to insure "the safety of the people who are moved as well as the safety of all the rest of the population" became a catch phrase of the pre-evacuation period. Citizens writing to President Roosevelt (whose mail on the subject came to Attorney-General Biddle) set the proposition in its shortest threatening form: "Unless you remove all Japanese, alien and American born, from California, we the people will slaughter them."

As early as January 16 an officer of a powerful agricultural marketing group wrote his congressman that "in the Imperial Valley a group of Filipinos met and were drawing names of individual Japanese out of a box to be 'taken care of' by those drawing the names. . . . It would not take very much of a 'match' to start a terrific conflagration." This fear was echoed on several occasions in the halls of Congress, and Congressman Voorhis, one of the three moderates of the western bloc, based his approval of mass evacuation on his fear of what might happen to the Japanese.

Local law-enforcement officers of California expressed the greatest concern over the possibility of vigilante action, regarding it as a prime reason for the necessity of evacuation. The sheriff of Merced said that he heard "rumblings of vigilante activity"; the chief of police of Huntington Beach described anti-Japanese sentiment "at fever heat"; the police chief of Watsonville wrote that "racial hatred is mounting higher and higher" and that Filipinos were "arming themselves and going out looking for an argument with Japanese." Attorney-General Warren himself expressed a similar view, and the mayor of Olympia, Washington, wrote that unless all Japanese, "irrespective of citizenship," were removed from the entire coastal region, "there will be a recurrence of the old time vigilante action that will effect a removal in its own peculiar way."

b) *Humane evacuation.*—The second type of humanitarian argument not only held that mass evacuation could be carried out without undue economic, physical, and moral hardship but also adduced positive values to that movement. At times the issue was put negatively: "No one wants to see them suffer. I have lots of very nice Japanese friends and I like them." Congressman Leland Ford went one step further and said that mass evacuation was a "very humanitarian" device, since it would avoid separating families, which might occur if only alien enemies were moved. A resolution of the Pacific League, a conservative civic organization of Los Angeles, took exactly the same line.

APPROVAL OF JAPANESE MILITARISM

A large portion of the public argument in favor of evacuation attempted to prove that all Japanese were of particular danger to the nation's safety. The first category of these proofs dwelt upon the active (or passive) approval of Japanese military aggression on the part of American residents of Japanese ancestry.

In some cases this allegation was made in the broadest terms, a correspondent of the *Sacramento Bee* writing: "It is not logical to think that very many are loyal to us. They cannot help but sympathize with their own country." Californians writing to national officials emphasized the same point: "There are no Japs that would do anything for us, even though second generation and American citizens, they all have and are at this moment working for their country."

In its most damaging aspect, this symbol of identification was wielded in a specific fashion. On many occasions the allegation was made that approval of Japanese militarism on the part of Japanese Americans was demonstrated by the fact that no resident Japanese ever gave information to law-enforcement officers about the subversive activities of other members of the group. This declaration was made by Attorney-General Warren and by at least five other persons before the Tolan Committee alone, including two California police chiefs. It was later given credence by a high-ranking military officer.

A similar type of issue was made over the claim that Japanese Americans knew about Pearl Harbor in advance. As one person wrote to President Roosevelt, "Surely some of the many '100% Loyal Japanese Americans' knew what was going to take place there [Hawaii]. Why didn't *one* of them step forward and forewarn us if they are so 'loyal.'" The city manager of Alameda, California, made the same charge, and Mayor Bowron of Los Angeles said that a "large number" of resident Japanese "knew what was coming" and "overplayed their hand" in the year before the war by going "out of their way" to demonstrate American patriotism.

More tangible evidence of the support of Japanese militarism by American Japanese was presented by Attorney-General Warren to the Tolan Committee. The attorney-general put into the record several pages of quotations from vernacular newspapers of the United States describing contributions of tinfoil, clothing, other materials, and cash made to the Japanese government by Japanese residents in the United States between 1938 and 1941. He quoted items to prove the interest of Japanese Americans in the welfare of Japanese military leaders.

INFLUENCE OF THE JAPANESE GOVERNMENT

The second argument designed to prove the special danger of Japanese Americans was based on the influence the Japanese government allegedly wielded over the Japanese American community. It was held that this influence was made effective through propaganda, financial subsidy, or physical coercion (usually by Japanese consular agents) through the media of the prefectoral organizations, the language schools, or the Buddhist (and Shinto) church. The dual-citizenship status of the Nisei was held up as the symbol of the imperial government's power.

The releases issued by the California Joint Immigration Committee emphasized these points. A correspondent of the Attorney-General declared that the Japanese Americans had been "well instructed" by agents of the emperor, while another wrote that "pressure brought to bear on them by the Japanese government" would make it "almost impossible for them to remain loyal to the United States government." Governor Olson stated that the language schools taught allegiance to Japan and asserted that the "schools have been conducted through the aid and abetment of the Japanese consulates." He also said that the consuls had promoted "fifth column activities" by "insisting that the entire Japanese population really belonged to Japan. Attorney-General Warren described at length the "agricultural, commercial, educational, social, religious, and patriotic associations," which blanketed every Japanese community. At the top of the pyramid of the many associations were the Japanese Association of America in northern California and the Japanese Central Association in southern California. The attorney-general pointed out that one or another of the associations had sent gifts to the Japanese government, instilled "the Japanese military code of boshido," encouraged Japanese Americans to return to Japan for their education, and persuaded those educated in Japan to return to America.

The issue of dual citizenship was raised on many occasions. It was the starting point that led to the eventual dismissal of all Americans of Japanese ancestry employed by the state of California and a frequently utilized argument of military officials.

MIGRATION AND DISTRIBUTION

Those who urged the course of mass evacuation pointed to the manner in which resident Japanese were congregated in the vicinity of strategic industrial and military installations. In many cases the attempt was made to show that the distribution was not accidental but rather that it had taken place by means of fraudulent immigration or planned internal migration.

Attorney-General Earl Warren of California made this argument in its most complete form, and his presentation had the greatest influence on the military officers in whom discretion for evacuation rested.

Newspaper correspondents and editorialists took up the geographic issue with enthusiasm. The *San Diego Union*, for example, commented: "Maps showing the strongest concentration of Japanese, both aliens and citizens, along the Pacific Coast reveal that almost without exception they are settled in the vital strategic military points, factories, reservoirs and beachlands. No group of 200,000 or so persons could have completely surrounded such vital areas had they not planned it carefully in advance, which probably is precisely what they did."

THE RACIAL ARGUMENT

Distrust of the Japanese race as such was implicit in a large part of all the arguments in favor of evacuation. That distrust was put explicitly on many occasions, by all types of persons and in a variety of ways.

Congressman Rankin put the racial argument in its most sweeping form when he told the Congress that "once a Jap, always a Jap" and that "you cannot regenerate a Jap, convert him, and make him the same as a white man any more than you can reverse the laws of nature." Persons writing to the Attorney-General developed the same theme: "They are the most cunning and unreliable of any class living. A Jap is a Jap. The only one you can trust is a dead one." Those contributing letters to newspapers were equally inclusive, e.g., "They are treacherous and barbarous by nature."

Officials of the three western states were inclined to admit that some proportion of the resident Japanese were loyal to America but professed a complete inability to distinguish loyal from disloyal. The governor and attorney-general of California, the attorney-general of Washington, and the mayors of Los Angeles, Seattle, and Portland, among many others, took this view. All thought it "difficult" or "impossible" to segregate the good Japanese from the bad, whereas, in the words of Attorney-General Warren, "when we are dealing with the Caucasian race [German and Italian aliens] we have methods that will test the loyalty of them." Mayor Bowron thought many Japanese Americans might "intend to be loyal" but asked, "When the final test comes, who can say but that 'blood will tell'?" Lesser law-enforcement officers of California supported mass evacuation for substantially the same reason.

The racial argument sometimes held that Japanese all looked alike, sometimes that their thought-processes were inscrutable to Caucasians. These themes were occasionally supplemented with the statement (by the Native Sons of the Golden West, for example) that the high birth rate of resident Japanese was a mark of their special danger and, by extension, a reason for evacuation.

CULTURAL FACTORS

The last, and least frequently used, of the arguments purporting to prove the special danger of Japanese Americans was based on the cultural habits of the group. The lag making for nonallegiance was noted in religion, education, language, and familial patterns.

A spokesman for the California Joint Immigration Committee put great emphasis on Japanese cultural patterns making for poor Americanism. Many American citizens of Japanese ancestry, he said, were sent to Japan for an education which "for all intents and purposes" made them Japanese. Language schools in America tended to accomplish the same purpose. The religion of emperor worship similarly led people away from Americanism.

This last point was apparently a reference to Shintoism. An Oregon state senator extended the danger classification to Buddhists, stating that "the Buddhist religion is looked on as a national Japanese custom," and "even among the children there isn't much social mixing between the Buddhist and the Christian children." A California club leader was more absolute: "Persons of Japanese ancestry cannot safely be treated as American citizens until at least three generations have been reared in this country. It takes that long to get a group of nationals who believe in both emperor and ancestor worship, and who are most rigidly bound down by family ties, to really break loose and become Americans."

These allegations received general support from a number of political leaders, and the State Personnel Board of California utilized the cultural patterns of Japanese Americans as one reason for discharging them from state employment.

ECONOMIC ASPECTS

The importance of Japanese Americans to the economic life of the western states became inextricably involved in the determination of evacuation as public policy. Experts were not lacking who testified to the substantial contribution of Japanese Americans to the economy of the country, especially in the production of vegetables. The necessity of meeting the extraordinary quotas of the "Food for Victory" program gave added point to these statements. On the other hand, a chorus of voices affirmed that Japanese Americans were either not important to the nation's economy or actually detrimental to it. A secondary economic argument held that whatever economic losses might be suffered as a result of evacuation would be offset by the useful productive work of Japanese Americans in areas of concentration.

Those most insistent upon the economic unimportance of Japanese American farmers were themselves farmers. The Western Growers Protective Association and its allied organization, the Grower-Shipper Vegetable Association, produced numerous statements to demonstrate that a movement of Japanese would cause "no dislocation of food commodities." In their own publications and in communications to state and national political leaders, these groups pressed home this point. Various units of the California Farm Bureau Federation and a leader of the Associated Farmers took substantially the same stand. Political leaders, including Governor Olson, contributed supporting views.

The principal economic theme dwelt on the small contribution made to total farm production by resident Japanese farm operators. Opinion was more divided with respect to the effect of evacuation on the supply of farm laborers. The farm bureau federations, which were quick to deny the importance of Japanese entrepreneurs, were among the first to suggest that the labor loss could be negated by using Japanese as field hands under Army guard. This idea was also expressed by many others.

A number of persons testified that the only production losses as the result of evacuation would be in so-called nonessential, "specialty" crops. A substantial minority, however, denied the possibility of even this minor loss and saw only positive economic advantages in the movement. The latter viewpoint was expressed by a Seattle lawyer who asserted that "Japanese standards of living and working conditions" had eliminated white gardeners. This had brought about "an unhealthy economic condition," and "no greater service can be rendered the country than to restore the former condition."

THE APPEAL TO PATRIOTISM

One of the earliest and most persistent of the symbols manipulated in favor of evacuation maintained that loyal Japanese should co-operate in the evacuation movement and stamped those who refused to co-operate as disloyal. Congressman Leland Ford wrote in this vein as early as January 16, asserting that a patriotic Japanese could make his contribution to the safety of the country "by permitting himself to be placed in a concentration camp." If American citizens of Japanese ancestry were not "loyal enough" to volunteer for internment, then "they ought to be placed in a camp anyhow." The logic of this point of view apparently appealed to many political leaders, including the governor of California, the mayor of Los Angeles, and the city managers of Oakland and Alameda. Correspondents of Attorney-General Biddle and a number of newspaper editorialists utilized the same argument. A spokesman for the Los Angeles County Defense Council acknowledged that the council's appeal to patriotism was an effort to circumvent the legal obstacles of forced movements. "We have considered and realized the limitation of the committee in dealing with the American citizens of Japanese descent from a constitutional point of view and we are seeking to overcome that by inviting them to participate in the war effort here by joining their relatives outside of the prescribed areas."

NECESSITY FOR DRASTIC MEASURES

Some persons felt so strongly about the Japanese problem that they urged the most extreme action, without regard for legal limitations and without recourse to any specific reason except "something drastic has to be done."

A California congressman put the matter: "Let's move these Japanese out and talk about it afterwards." The mayor of a California City was even more specific when he wrote to Congressman Tolan that "the Constitution can go overboard, if necessary." The same views were held by California law-enforcement officers. The district attorney of Madera County, for example, wrote: "We must forget such things as the writ of habeas corpus, and the prohibition against unreasonable searches and seizures. The right of self-defense, self-preservation . . . is higher than the Bill of Rights."

More intemperate statements were not lacking. Persons writing to the Justice Department seethed: "Francis Biddle and other Washington officials are hypnotized by the constitutional niceties. . . . Like Pegler, I say 'To hell with habeas corpus' "; asserted: "We can't trust them and must take off the kid gloves and play the game the Axis way"; and demanded that the Attorney-General be replaced by "a hard boiled gentleman, one who is not afraid of doubtful constitutional rights of traitors." Others wrote that "a good dose of toughness and not politics is what we and our allies need. . . . It is time to see some drastic action on our part"; that it was necessary to "give these vermin the treatment they deserve"; and that, if injustice were done, "we could smile about it, and, in their own vernacular say 'So sorry.' Let's get tough, for heaven's sake. . . . Let's get tough with everybody."

THE ACTIVATION OF THE STEREOTYPE
Jacobus ten Broek, Edward N. Barnhart,
and Floyd W. Matson

The Japanese attack on Pearl Harbor came as a profound shock, if not a complete surprise, to residents of the Pacific Coast states. Although for many years most citizens had been aware that war was a possibility, many refused to believe the first reports from Honolulu and were convinced only by repeated broadcasts and ubiquitous black headlines. But the full import of the news soon became apparent as all service personnel was ordered to report to stations, as jeeps and convoys in war regalia appeared on the streets, and military aircraft began to roar overhead. By midafternoon of December 7, 1941, thousands of citizens were rushing to recruiting stations to enlist or offering their services in any capacity.

Before they could recover from the initial shock, West Coast residents were confronted with more bad news. Coincident with the Pearl Harbor attack enemy forces had struck with disastrous effect at Hong Kong, Manila, Thailand, Singapore, Midway, Wake, and Guam. Japanese bombers had at a single blow destroyed the air defenses of Hong Kong, and within a few days occupied Kowloon peninsula and placed the British crown colony in jeopardy. On December 10 the "impregnable" British warships *Repulse* and *Prince of Wales* were sunk by Japanese planes, thus upsetting the balance of naval power in the far Pacific. The little kingdom of Thailand had surrendered on December 8, and the enemy began a swift southward movement through the British Malay States toward Singapore. Other Japanese troops landed in the Philippines on December 10 and were converging on Manila. Guam was captured on December 11, the fate of Wake Island appeared sealed (it fell on December 23), and Midway was imperiled by an enemy task force. Meanwhile, dispatches which had filtered through censorship suggested that American losses at Pearl Harbor were far worse than at first indicated. It was freely predicted that Alaska and the Pacific Coast itself were next in line for Japanese attack and even attempted invasion.

People everywhere were frightened, and their fear was heightened by a feeling of helplessness. The threat of bombings and invasion, plus the absence of precise information as to events in Hawaii, quickly bred rumors of total disaster. It was whispered that the entire Pacific fleet had been destroyed; that every reinforcing ship sent out from the mainland had been sunk off the coast by Japanese submarines.

Almost at once rumors about the resident Japanese began. Japanese gardeners were said to be equipped with short-wave transmitters hidden in garden hose; Japanese servants and laborers who failed to appear for work on December 7 (a Sunday)

Jacobus ten Broek, Edward N. Barnhart, and Floyd W. Matson, "The Activation of the Stereotype," *Prejudice, War, and the Constitution* (Berkeley: University of California Press, 1954). Ten Broek, a professor at the University of California, was asked by the directors of the Japanese American Evacuation and Resettlement Study to summarize the voluminous data amassed by the Study. He did so with the help two University of California colleagues, Edward N. Barnhart and Floyd W. Matson.

were accused of prior knowledge of the Hawaii attack. Japanese farmers were charged with smuggling poison into vegetables bound for market, and cans of seafood imported from Japan were said to contain particles of ground glass. Signaling devices similar to those reported found in Hawaii were alleged to have been set up in coastal areas. A number of anxious Californians, according to one report, went so far as to plow up "a beautiful field of flowers on the property of a Japanese farmer," because "it seems the Jap was a fifth columnist and had grown his flowers in a way that when viewed from a plane formed an arrow pointing the direction to the airport."

These rumors and accusations arose largely as a result of the stories of fifth-column activity at Pearl Harbor which were rapidly accumulating in the press. After an inspection of the Pacific base, Secretary of the Navy Knox was quoted as saying that sabotage at Pearl Harbor constituted "the most effective fifth-column work that's come out of this war, except in Norway." Newspaper headlines on the Knox report generally stressed this aspect: "Secretary of Navy Blames Fifth Columnists for the Raid," "Fifth Column Prepared Attack," "Fifth Column Treachery Told." Other stories told of secret signaling and faked air-raid alerts by Hawaiian Japanese at the time of the attack, of arrows cut in the cane fields to aid enemy pilots, and roadblocks improvised to tie up military traffic.

In opposition to the rumors and scare stories was a succession of official assurances that all dangerous enemy aliens had been apprehended, that necessary precautions had already been taken, and that Japanese Americans as a whole were loyal to the United States. This viewpoint was, moreover, echoed in the editorials of most California newspapers during the first days of war. Despite these assurances, however, Americans became increasingly restive as the prospect of Japanese attack or invasion grew more plausible. For half a century they had heard of the treachery and deceitfulness of resident Japanese—of how the "Japs" were concentrated in strategic areas of the state; of how by "peaceful invasion" they hoped to take over first California and ultimately the nation; of how they formed a network of spies and soldiers in disguise, patiently awaiting the Imperial signal to rise against the white man.

The news from the battle-fronts, recording new Allied losses almost daily, made the most alarmist forebodings seem realistic. Charges of fifth-column plots multiplied rapidly and broadened in scope, soon including the mainland as well as Hawaii, and possible future actions as well as past events. It was reported, for example, that a Los Angeles naval sentry had seen signal lights in a Japanese waterfront colony; that the suicide of a Japanese doctor had uncovered a spy ring in the same area; that members of the notorious Black Dragon Society had been planted in cities and fishing communities; that the fifth-column character of Japanese schools in America had been exposed. The halls of Congress echoed with such exposures; Senator Guy Gillette of Iowa warned that "Japanese groups in this country planned sabotage and subversive moves," and Congressman Martin Dies of Texas announced the discovery of a book revealing Japanese plans to attack the United States.

Meanwhile the war was being brought steadily closer to home. On December 20 it was announced that Japanese submarines were attacking West Coast shipping;

and on the same day two tankers were reportedly torpedoed off California. Two days later newspapers told of the shelling of a freighter by an enemy sub near Santa Barbara; the next day two more tankers were said to have been attacked off the California coast. Residents of the coastal states began to feel that their shores were under virtual blockade by enemy submarines.

The refugees from Hawaii, arriving in late December, brought new rumors of sabotage by island Japanese on December 7. It was said that Japanese had placed obstructions on the road to Pearl Harbor to keep reinforcements from getting through; that they had sabotaged the planes on the landing fields; that one group had entered Hickam Field in a milk truck, let down the sides and turned machine guns on American pilots as they ran to their planes.

Impressive "confirmation" of these rumors was contained in a sensational dispatch by a United Press correspondent, Wallace Carroll, who visited Honolulu shortly after the attack. Repeating with an air of authority most of the charges made by Honolulu refugees, the report declared that numbers of Hawaii Japanese had had advance knowledge of the bombing, and that Japanese produce merchants delivering to warships had been able to report on United States fleet movements. Carroll speculated that newspaper advertisements placed by Japanese firms may have been coded messages, and asserted that the enemy raiders had been aided by improvised roadblocks and arrows cut in the cane fields. The hands of Japanese pilots shot down during the assault were, he said, adorned with the rings of Honolulu high schools and of Oregon State University. The dispatch continued:

> Japanese of American nationality infiltrated into the Police Departments and obtained jobs as road supervisors, sanitary inspectors or minor government officials. Many went to work in the postoffice and telephone service, ideal posts for spies. . . .
> An American resident, who had studied Japanese methods in Manchuria and North China, told me that the Japanese fifth column and espionage organizations in the islands were similar to those which had been used to undermine the Chinese.

Accounts such as this, together with reports of new Allied reverses and tales of atrocities in the Philippines, goaded some Filipino Americans into direct retaliation against their Japanese neighbors. On December 23 a Japanese American, honorably discharged from the United States Army, was found stabbed to death on a Los Angeles sidewalk; his assailants were reported to be Filipinos. On Christmas Day in Stockton, windows of numerous Japanese business houses were smashed, assertedly by gangs of Filipinos. The next day in the same city an alien Japanese garage attendant was shot to death by a Filipino; newspapers prominently featured the incident, under such headlines as "Jap, Filipino District Under Guard; 1 Slain," "Stockton Jap Killed by Filipino; Riots Feared; Area Under Guard." By the end of December similar incidents were publicized almost daily. On December 29, a Japanese waiter was shot to death by a Filipino in Chicago. On December 30 an alien Japanese was shot and wounded in Sacramento; on New Year's Day a Japanese and his wife were murdered in the Imperial Valley. Other cases were reported from Gilroy and Livermore, and even from Utah.

Thus, within the first three weeks of war, the familiar Japanese stereotype was again visible on the Pacific Coast, and aroused individuals and groups were militantly reacting to it. The surprise attack of December 7, occurring in the midst of peace negotiations, seemed a definite confirmation of the old remembered tales of Japanese deceitfulness. Although for a time many citizens were reluctant to blame resident Japanese for the actions of Japan, and newspaper comment frequently was on the side of tolerance, the accumulating "evidence" of sabotage and espionage gradually put an end to toleration. Popular anger and apprehension rose in proportion to the continuing successes of the enemy, and by the end of 1941 suspicion and animosity were the most frequently expressed attitudes toward the Japanese Americans.

January was another month of disasters for the Allies and frustrations for the people at home. Manila fell to the Japanese on January 2, and an outnumbered American garrison began its struggle at Bataan and on Corregidor, with little hope of reinforcement. Japanese troops were advancing through Malay jungles to the crucial port of Singapore. Borneo was invaded and the entire East Indies came under attack. The scattered islands of the far Pacific were falling before the enemy with incredible rapidity; there were landings in New Guinea, and Australia was directly menaced. At home, reports continued of West Coast shipping attacked by enemy submarines; and off the eastern coast the Germans were rapidly intensifying their U-boat warfare and had torpedoed several Allied vessels.

In this atmosphere of frustration, fear, and anger, popular sentiment on the West Coast in the first month of 1942 was concentrated more and more against resident Japanese. Although the official restrictions on enemy-alien activity had been directed impartially at Germans, Italians, and Japanese, in the popular mind the Japanese were special targets of suspicion. Their Oriental appearance marked them inescapably in an area whose greatest danger was from the Far Eastern end of the Axis. Acts of violence against Japanese Americans continued to be reported in the press from such widely separate areas as Seattle, Fresno, Sacramento, and Santa Maria. Front-page attention was given FBI raids and arrests of Japanese allegedly possessing contraband. Popular tensions were increased by the charge in the Roberts Committee report that espionage in Hawaii had centered in the Japanese consulate, and that through its intelligence service the Japanese had obtained complete information on Pearl Harbor. The principal effect of such disclosures, however they were intended, was strongly to support the rumors of disloyalty among Japanese in Hawaii and to cast further doubt upon the loyalty of Japanese along the coast.

Early in January prominent voices began to call for more vigorous steps to control the resident Japanese, including their mass removal from the West Coast. News commentators, editorial writers, and public officials expressed displeasure at the "indecision and inaction" of the Department of Justice and urged drastic measures. John B. Hughes, a Los Angeles commentator for the Mutual Broadcasting Company, gained prominence as the first widely heard newsman to press the subject of evacuation. In the first of a month-long series of anti-Japanese broadcasts, Hughes compared the treatment of local Japanese with that of Americans captured by Japanese armies and warned that the failure to adopt strong measures would result in "disaster to the Pacific Coast." In subsequent commentaries he lent his support to rumors of espionage and fifth-column activities, charging that United States Japanese had contributed funds to Japan's war chest and hinting that the control of California's vegetable output was part of the over-all Japanese war plan.

Hughes also entered into a correspondence with Attorney General Biddle in which he urged the internment of both aliens and citizens of Japanese ancestry. "Persons who know the Japanese on the west coast," he wrote, "will estimate that ninety percent or more of American-born Japanese are primarily loyal to Japan." The commentator's justification for this indictment was the old yellow peril thesis of race: "Their organization and patient preparation and obedience to unified control could never be possible among the nationals of any Caucasian people. The Japanese are a far greater menace in our midst than any other axis patriots. They will die joyously for the honor of Japan." As a clincher, a justification was offered which was to be frequently advanced by proponents of evacuation: "There was an old law in the West, the law of the Vigilantes. Its whole code was: Shoot first and argue later. That code will be invoked, I'm afraid, unless authorities formulate a policy, an adequate policy, and put it into effect."

The calculated purpose of the Hughes campaign, like others which followed it in the press and on the air, was to persuade the public to demand a policy of action toward the local Japanese: specifically that of rounding them up and removing them from the coast. This policy of exclusion, frequently urged in conjunction with demands for internment, had a threefold appeal: first, in the light of what the public feared from the Japanese (espionage and sabotage) it seemed a perfect remedy; second, it offered an outlet for the public's antipathy toward the resident Japanese by urging forceful action against them; and finally it offered an opportunity for action, a chance to "do something," to a population fretting to strike back against Japan but so far offered no chance for direct action.

Hughes was not long in finding company among newspapermen. By the end of January a radical shift had taken place in the editorial position of California newspapers. During the first month of war these journals had for the most part been tolerant if not sympathetic toward the Japanese in America; but in the following three weeks unfavorable comment gradually increased to the point where it equalled expressions of tolerance. In the last days of January the trend suddenly accelerated and pro-Japanese utterances were lost in a barrage of denunciation—which centered on charges of Japanese disloyalty, demands for strict control measures, and growing sentiment for mass evacuation.

The keynote of the evacuation demands was sounded by the San Diego *Union*, one of the first major journals to press the issue, which opened a sustained editorial campaign on January 20 with arguments drawn largely from fifth-column rumors:

In Hawaii and in the Philippines treachery by residents, who although of Japanese ancestry had been regarded as loyal, has played an important part in the success of Japanese attacks. . . .

Every Japanese—for the protection of those who are loyal to us and for our protection against those who are not—should be moved out of the coastal area and to a point of safety far enough inland to nullify any inclinations they may have to tamper with our safety here.

In subsequent editorials the *Union* dwelt on the evils of Japanese citizenship, maintained that there was no way of determining the loyalty of "our so-called American citizens of Japanese ancestry," and exclaimed: "We are confronted on both sides by enemies who have devoted their entire careers to development of treachery, deceit, and sabotage. We can afford to be neither soft-headed nor soft-hearted in dealing with them or their agents."

The Hearst newspapers on the Pacific Coast, which in earlier years had led in the agitation against resident Japanese, did not conspicuously join the editorial clamor for evacuation—although news articles frequently were slanted against the Japanese. But it was in the Hearst press that the first of numerous syndicated columns condemning the Japanese minority was published. On January 29, Henry McLemore, a former sports reporter, wrote from Los Angeles:

> The only Japanese apprehended have been the ones the FBI actually had something on. The rest of them, so help me, are free as birds. There isn't an airport in California that isn't flanked by Japanese farms. There is hardly an air field where the same situation doesn't exist. . . .
>
> I know this is the melting pot of the world and all men are created equal and there must be no such thing as race or creed hatred, but do those things go when a country is fighting for its life? Not in my book. No country has ever won a war because of courtesy and I trust and pray we won't be the first because of the lovely, gracious spirit. . . .
>
> I am for immediate removal of every Japanese on the West Coast to a point deep in the interior. I don't mean a nice part of the interior either. Herd 'em up, pack 'em off and give 'em the inside room in the badlands. Let 'em be pinched, hurt, hungry and dead up against it. . . .
>
> Personally, I hate the Japanese. And that goes for all of them.

The mood of the McLemore attack was not widely evident in editorial comment prior to February. But the "Letters to the Editor" columns of many newspapers in the last weeks of January showed a rising tide of anti-Japanese feeling along the coast. In these informal communications, more graphically than elsewhere, the myths and slanders of bygone years were dusted off and put on display. The Sacramento *Bee* printed a letter from one of its readers who invoked the ancient battle-cry "America for Americans," and complained that Japanese were "forcing other races off the land, including whites from pioneer families." A letter in the Santa Rosa *Press Democrat* asked: "Biologically and economically, is the Jap fitted to mingle in American life?" and asserted that "when our trouble is over they must be returned to their rising sun." Another Sacramento reader declared that Japanese American citizens would "betray the land of their birth . . . simply because they are treacherous and barbarous by nature." A Native Daughter of the Golden West asked: "Did God make the Jap as He did the snake, did you hear the hiss before the words left his mouth? Were his eyes made slanting and the hiss put between his lips to warn us to be on our guard?" A San Francisco reader urged the authorities to "put all the Japs in camps . . . . First thing you know they will be pulling another surprise on us."

On January 17, the California senate also passed without dissent a measure aimed at Japanese employees of the state. Claiming that numbers of state workers appeared to "possess dual citizenship," the bill called upon the State Personnel Board to prevent the employment of anyone "who is not loyal to the United States and to . . . provide for the dismissal from the [state civil] service of such persons as may be proved to be disloyal to the United States." Although Japanese were not directly named in the bill, all the lawmakers who spoke on the proposal referred openly to the need for examining the loyalty of Japanese American employees. Senators Jack Metzger and John Harold Swan, coauthors of the bill, produced a photostatic copy of a payroll sheet of the State Motor Vehicle Department which contained only Japanese names, and Senator Swan purported to see in this "a systematic plot to get Japanese on the state payroll and allow them to bore from within." Senator Metzger contributed to the fifth-column rumors by charging that "Japanese fifth columnists in milk wagons drew machine guns instead of milk bottles out of twenty-one wagons in Honolulu the morning of December 7 and turned them on Pearl Harbor barracks." Later the same senator was reported as saying: "I don't believe there is a single Japanese in the world who is not pulling for Japan. They will spy, commit sabotage, or die if necessary."

In the national capital, outcries against the Japanese Americans began to be heard from West Coast congressmen late in January. As in other circles, congressional discussion during the first six weeks of war had generally shown confidence in the loyalty and integrity of resident Japanese. An early harbinger of changing attitudes among West Coast congressmen was the insertion into the *Congressional Record* by Congressman Leland Ford of Los Angeles of an anti-Japanese telegram from movie actor Leo Carillo, which read in part: "Why wait until [the Japanese] pull something before we act. . . . Let's get them off the coast into the interior. . . . May I urge you in behalf of the safety of the people of California to start action at once."

The decision to evacuate all Japanese Americans from the West Coast, which came during February, was reached in a context of gathering fear, suspicion, and anger on the part of the American public—a mood occasioned by the unanticipated disasters in the Pacific. Had the United States fleet not been decimated at Pearl Harbor, but steamed off intact to meet and destroy the Japanese navy, as most Americans had been certain it would; had the Japanese armies been turned back at Singapore by the land and sea defenses which had been thought invincible; in short, had the Allies taken the initiative at the outset and shown promise of checking the Japanese advance, it is doubtful that American opinion—public and private, official and unofficial—could have been mobilized in support of evacuation. Assured of ultimate victory and sustained by a diet of war successes, a secure and confident America might well have fulfilled its democratic ideal of tolerance and hospitality toward the Japanese minority in its midst.

But the war did not go that way, and Americans were given no prospect of security or gleam of optimism. In mid-February, only seventy days after the first attack on Malaya, "impregnable" Singapore surrendered unconditionally to the Japanese, in what Winston Churchill was to call "the greatest disaster to British arms which history records." The capitulation forced an Allied withdrawal to the Dutch East Indies, and the way not lay open for an enemy attack upon Burma and India. The Japanese, in fact, had entered Burma a week before to cut the Burma Road and isolate China. The Indies were sealed off and their fate ordained by the fall of Sumatra, Borneo, and Celebes; and in a series of sea engagements during February the Japanese first split and then methodically destroyed American and Allied naval forces. Enemy penetration of the southwest Pacific was equally rapid and decisive. In January Japanese forces had leveled the centers of defense in the Solomons; from these positions they now struck west at New Guinea, bombing Salamaua and Port Moresby and even neutralizing Port Darwin on the Australian coast. By the end of February an invasion of Australia seemed imminent; the final fall of the beleaguered Philippine garrison was virtually assured; the surrender of Java and the complete conquest of the rich Indies was only days away; and the great subcontinent of India was threatened with assault. Nothing had occurred to indicate that the bewildering tide of conquest might soon be stemmed, and not a few Americans wondered when their turn would come in the Japanese schedule of invasion.

Early in the month, meanwhile, in conjunction with its program of alien evacuation from prohibited areas, the Justice Department began a series of "spot raids" to uncover contraband and counter anticipated sabotage. FBI agents, together with state and local officers, descended without warning or warrant upon a number of localities and searched the homes of Japanese. Large amounts of "contraband" were found, and numbers of alien Japanese were apprehended. Each of these surprise raids received attention from California newspapers, usually beneath black banner headlines. Particular stress was placed upon the lists of contraband seized. One search, for example, was reported to have uncovered "11 cameras, 14 short wave radio sets, 12 binoculars, a telescope, nine rifles, six revolvers, many thousands of rounds of ammunition, 84 knives, a large searchlight, four floodlights, four telescope gun sights, a box of sulphuric acid, Japanese maps and three sets of maps and charts of the Monterey Bay area." The Japanese operator of a sporting goods store was said to possess "70,000 rounds of rifle and shotgun ammunition, 12 rifles and shotguns, a public address system, cameras and film, books of Japanese propaganda and a radio operator's handbook."

The effect of these accounts in augmenting public suspicions may be glimpsed in a letter to Attorney General Biddle from a San Diego resident: "How much longer are we going to let these traitorous barbarians strut among us seeking every means of destroying us, storing arms and ammunition right under our noses and within stone's throw of our war industries, just because hasty action on our part might be impolite or offend the one out of every hundred Japs who is not conspiring against us?" Editorial writers also were influenced by the apparent findings of the anti-Japanese raids. A typical comment in the Stockton Record declared that "in recent days FBI agents have operated in many parts of California and uncovered caches of arms and contraband. . . . The circumstances smack strongly of those who contributed to the tragedy of Pearl Harbor. . . . The Pacific Coast is in danger."

The inevitable effect of the arrests and spot raids, dramatically pointed up by the press, was to confirm the traditional image of the Japanese handed down from earlier generations and revived upon the outbreak of war. The rising tide of popular feeling is shown by the frequent appeals of the Department of Justice—and especially of Attorney General Francis Biddle—asking the public to forego vigilantism and maintain tolerance toward the Japanese Americans. But such appeals did little to check the rise of anti-Japanese sentiment. In fact, the control measures adopted by the Department of Justice seemed to many only a further confirmation of their fears: the creation of prohibited and restricted zones, the establishment of a curfew, the dramatic searches and seizures—all appeared to justify the deepening public suspicions of the Japanese, both citizens and aliens, as actually or potentially disloyal and dangerous.

The aggravated state of public opinion was also reflected during February in the words and actions of prominent politicians and political bodies. The boards of supervisors of eleven California counties joined in a solemn declaration that "during the attack on Pearl Harbor . . . the Japanese were aided and abetted by fifth columnists of the Japanese." State Attorney General Earl Warren had first proclaimed his attitude on January 30, when a press dispatch quoted him as saying that the Japanese situation in the state "may well be the Achilles heel of the entire civilian defense effort. Unless something is done it may bring about a repetition of Pearl Harbor." On February 2, Warren revealed to a private conference of sheriffs and district attorneys his intense suspicion of resident Japanese—which was so profound that the very absence of sabotage seemed to him a sure sign of its future occurrence: "It seems to me that it is quite significant that in this great state of ours we have had no fifth column activities and no sabotage reported. It looks very much to me as though it is a studied effort not to have any until the zero hour arrives." He concluded that "every alien Japanese should be considered in the light of a potential fifth columnist," and urged that the Alien Land Law be enforced to remove all Japanese from areas near vital installations. (It should be emphasized, however, that the public report of the conference called only for removal of enemy aliens—*not* of all Japanese Americans.)

In subsequent days Attorney General Warren produced a variety of arguments purporting to show that resident Japanese were not only dangerous but much more of a threat than resident Germans or Italians. His arguments constitute a resumé of anti-Japanese cliches which had been accumulating for over half a century. There was, he said, no way to determine the loyalty of Japanese Americans. It was impossible for Americans to comprehend Oriental ways; the alien culture was diffused through religion, language schools, and the practice of sending children to Japan for education. In Japan "they are indoctrinated with the idea of Japanese imperialism. They receive their religious instruction which tied up their religion with their Emperor, and they come back here imbued with the ideas and policies of Imperial Japan." Warren alleged that Japanese in America generally approved of Japan's military conquests, implying that they would also favor the conquest of America; and he declared that the Japanese government exerted a broad control over the activities of all Japanese in this country.

Equally vigorous in his opposition to the Japanese, and in his contributions to the stereotype, was Mayor Fletcher Bowron of Los Angeles. In a radio address of

February 5, Bowron warned of the danger of leaving the California Japanese at liberty. Among the Nisei there were "a number who are doubtless loyal to Japan, waiting probably, with full instructions as to what to do, to play their part when the time comes." The next day the mayor was quoted as denouncing the "sickly sentimentality" of Americans who feared injustices to the Japanese. The control "measures taken so far are so ineffectual as to be ridiculous." On Lincoln's birthday he again devoted his weekly radio address to the Japanese problem, arguing that if Lincoln were living he would round up "the people born on American soil who have secret loyalty to the Japanese Emperor." On still another occasion he disclaimed "any racial or other prejudice," but declared that "I know of no rule, no way to separate those who say they are patriotic and are, in fact, loyal at heart, and those who say they are patriotic and in fact at heart are loyal to Japan."

The shift in public sentiment, visible in late January, from comparative tolerance to general hostility toward the Japanese minority, was accurately mirrored in the Pacific Coast press. The ratio of unfavorable to favorable editorials was nineteen to one in the five days between January 22 and 26; hostile letters to the editor, chiefly demands for mass evacuation, attained their peak between February 1 and 5. By February, also, news stories favorable to the Japanese Americans were reduced from a December high of 22 percent to less than 3 percent, and during the thirty-day period from January 12 to February 10, fifteen times more news space was given to unfriendly items than to favorable copy. News stories devoted to evacuation demands reached their peak in the five days from February 6 to 10; these stories alone occupied seven times the space taken by all favorable news copy in the month from January 12 to February 10.

Editorial pressure in early February centered chiefly on the danger of a West Coast "Pearl Harbor." There was general agreement with the opinion of the Sacramento *Bee* that "the experience with the fifth column in Hawaii is overwhelming evidence that . . . the authorities must take no chances with possible Jap or Axis sympathizers." Newspapers pointed frequently to contraband seized by the FBI as sufficient evidence of Japanese disloyalty, and much attention was given to the growing number of evacuation demands by politicians, officials, and organizations. The activities of the Western congressional bloc were widely featured, often with speculation that federal action approving Japanese removal was soon to be taken.

Editorial writers voiced increasing opposition during February to the nonevacuation policy of the Department of Justice. Equally noteworthy were the exhortations of several widely syndicated columnists who added their voices to the cry for mass removal. Henry McLemore, whose personal campaign had begun late in January, continued to press his attack against the Department of Justice. Observing that aliens had been allowed weeks in which to evacuate the prohibited zones and would have "time to perfect their time bombs, complete their infernal machines," McLemore charged the Attorney General with handling the Japanese threat "with all the severity of Lord Fauntleroy playing squat tag with his maiden aunt."

Walter Lippmann, one of the most influential political columnists, added his name in mid-February to the list of those opposing federal policy and urging stronger measures. Subsequently Westbrook Pegler, then a Scripps-Howard columnist, translated the Lippmann argument into his own idiom, declaring on February 16 that "the Japanese in California should be under guard to the last man and woman right now and to hell with *habeas corpus* until the danger is over." Pegler went on:

> Do you get what [Lippmann] says? . . . The enemy has been scouting our coast . . . . The Japs ashore are communicating with the enemy offshore and . . . on the basis of "what is known to be taking place" there are signs that a well-organized blow is being withheld only until it can do the most damage. . . .
>   We are so dumb and considerate of the minute constitutional rights and even of the political feelings and influence of people whom we have every reason to anticipate with preventive action!

Under the prodding of public opinion and the press, members of Congress from the West Coast states intensified their efforts toward the formulation of a severe control program aimed at the Japanese. On February 10 a committee set up by the joint Pacific Coast delegation approved a resolution recommending total evacuation of all Japanese from the coastal area. The recommendation was made despite advice from Army and Navy authorities that a sustained Japanese attack on the coast was "impossible" and that even enemy raids, although possible, "would be sporadic and would have little, if any, bearing on the course of the war." The reasons for disregarding this advice, as given in a letter to the President from the joint delegation, were plainly the exploded myth of sabotage at Pearl Harbor and the stereotyped belief in disloyalty and treachery among Japanese Americans. The letter pointed to "the seriousness of the Japanese menace along the entire Pacific Coast" which had evoked "insistent demands for prompt action," and asserted that "the critical nature of the situation and its latent subversive potentialities are so compelling as to justify the taking of extreme and drastic measures."

The mounting anger and suspicion of many citizens was expressed during February in the demands of various officials that the government act against the Japanese Americans without regard to legal or constitutional restraints. The mayor of one California city advised Congressman Tolan that "the Constitution can go overboard, if necessary"; should evacuation prove awkward in constitutional terms, "then we must win the war by dictatorship methods." A California congressman put the case more succinctly: "Let's move these Japanese out and talk about it afterwards." And the district attorney of Madera County declared that "we must forget such things as the right of *habeas corpus* and the prohibition against unreasonable searches and seizures. The right of self-defense, self-preservation . . . is higher than the Bill of Rights."

The opening days of March found the Japanese ordered away from the coast in the so-called "voluntary evacuation" program instituted by General DeWitt and the Western Defense Command. At the end of the month is "voluntary" program gave way to forced evacuation and internment. But public hostility remained; although newspaper columnists and editorialists turned most of their attention to other issues and policies, attacks against the Japanese continued. For the most part the trouble centered in Tulare and Fresno counties, where open vigilante action continued as the weeks passed and local Japanese still remained in residence. During March an attempt was made to burn down a Japanese-owned hotel at Sultana. On April 13 at Del Ray five evacuees were involved in a brawl with the local constable—following which a crowd of white residents, some armed with shotguns, threatened violence to a nearby camp of Japanese Americans. On succeeding nights the windows of four Japanese stores were smashed, and similar incidents occurred in Fresno. In northern Tulare County, a group known as the "Bald Eagles"—described by one observer as "a guerilla army of nearly 1,000 farmers"—armed themselves for the announced purpose of "guarding" the Japanese in case of emergency. A similar organization was formed in the southeast part of the county, where a large number of evacuees were concentrated.

SUGGESTIONS FOR WRITING

Informal Essays

1. Do you think that the U.S. government's decision to relocate West Coast Japanese-Americans was heavily influenced by wartime hysteria? Write a short essay on this topic. Use two or three examples from the readings to support your thesis.
2. Discuss the implications that Franklin D. Roosevelt's Executive Order to intern Japanese-Americans has for Americans who are fully convinced that the human folly they see elsewhere couldn't happen here.

Short Documented Papers

1. Discuss and analyze the reactions of individual Japanese-Americans to their incarceration and internment.
2. Argue the case that Roosevelt's Executive Order to intern Japanese-Americans had little or nothing to do with national security.
3. Write a report on anti-Japanese hysteria in the months following the Pearl Harbor attack within one of the following groups: California newspapers, California politicians, or California civic and agricultural organizations.
4. Discuss the extent to which the rumors of an imminent Japanese invasion were substantiated by fact, and the extent to which such rumors were groundless.

Longer Documented Papers

1. Write an argument in which you justify the federal government's decision to evacuate Japanese-Americans from the West Coast and intern them in camps during most of World War II.
2. Write a report on the federal government's decision to evacuate Japanese-Americans from the West Coast and intern them in camps during most of World War II.
3. Argue that Roosevelt's Executive Order was a mistake.
4. Write a report on anti-Japanese sentiment in the U.S. from 1941 to 1945.
5. Write a report on Japanese-American relocation camps during World War II. Try to include the point of view of both the War Relocation Authority and the Japanese-Americans. Remember, this is a report, not an argument, so you'll have to remain objective and disinterested—which may not be easy.

· 10 ·

Putting It Together: A Research Writer's Handbook

WHAT IS A RESEARCH PAPER?

Ideally, a research paper begins when you are curious or angry about something. You might, for instance, wish to learn how the statues on Easter Island were constructed. Or you might want to marshal your ideas—and the ideas of others—to convince your readers that we should keep gory fairy tales out of the hands of small children.

To support your ideas, you search out books, articles, and other writings. Then, using the facts and ideas you find in them, you write an original work. We call this a source, or research, paper because it includes a record of the books, articles, and newspapers—your sources—that you used to write it. It is an original work because no one has combined the ideas and evidence from those diverse sources in such a way before you did.

The Research Report

One kind of research paper is called the research report. The research report is an impartial presentation of an idea. In a research report you illustrate rather than argue an idea.

Naturally, when you write a report about a controversial issue your main purpose is simply to explain and describe the controversy; you are not trying to persuade the reader that one or the other side is correct.

The Research Argument

Another kind of research paper is the research argument in which you try to persuade your readers that one side of an issue—your side, of course—is the right one.

In writing a research argument, you are taking a side; as you go along, you tell your readers what the controversy is about, but your real purpose is to show why your position is the right one.

You aren't detached. Indeed, you may argue your side vigorously. But you remain reasonable and fair in your presentation.

Stages in the Writing of a Research Paper

If your source material is limited to the selections in this book, here is an easy way to write a simple research paper.

1. Begin your reading in an assigned chapter with a selection that presents a balanced overview of the issue. Then, even if you've already decided what side of an argument you're going to take, read several more selections with an open mind. You might find that the arguments on the other side of the issue are so good that you'll want to switch sides.

2. Choose a topic from the suggestions for writing. A list follows each chapter.

3. Prepare a preliminary outline. If you're going to argue an issue, then you already have some reasons for your position. If you're going to write a report, no doubt you probably have ideas about how it can be broken down into segments. Take the time to list these on a sheet of paper. While you're doing this, see if you can think of any more. The more detailed your outline is, the more efficient your research will be.

4. Now begin your serious reading, taking notes as you go. An easy way to take notes is to use 4- by 6-inch notecards. In the upper right-hand corner, write the subject of each notecard, using the headings from your preliminary outline. In the upper left-hand corner, write down bibliographic information. (See "Formats" later in this chapter for the information you'll need to document your sources.) On subsequent cards based on that same source, simply write the author's last name in the upper left-hand corner.

Most of your notecards will be made up of paraphrases, but quote your source every time he or she is especially forceful. You won't use all the quotes you copy, but at this stage you don't know exactly what you'll be quoting, so it's better to have more material available than you'll eventually need.

Following each paraphrase or quotation, record the page number where you found it. You'll need those page numbers when you write your paper.

Each notecard is filled only with evidence from a particular essay. A notecard deals with a single idea, not with entire essays. In other words, take only one note per card.

As you read more deeply into your subject, you will probably have to revise your outline. In fact, you may want to spend some time at this point in constructing a revised outline, making it as detailed as you can. The new outline will help when you move to the next step, writing a first draft.

5. Write a first draft. Arrange the notecards according to your outline, and write the first draft from the material you have on your notecards. As you write, record the author's last name and the page number of the quotation or paraphrase in a parenthesis following each quotation or paraphrase. (See "Special Problems" for a further description of how to document sources within the text.) By the way, it's a good idea to leave plenty of white space in this first draft to allow for later revisions.

If you can, let your first draft cool for a day or two. Then go back and reread it, making as many improvements as needed by writing over, under, and through your words.

At this point you might find that you need to go back to your sources—or even find new sources—to be able to further develop certain ideas that are sketchy in your first draft.

6. Write a second draft, based on the revisions made to the first draft. Continue to revise. Work hard at making your prose clear and concise. Make sure that all paraphrases and quotations are introduced properly. (We discuss how to introduce borrowings later in this chapter.)

7. If your second draft is in good shape, polish it, proofread it, and then type a final version of your paper.

8. Finally, prepare a title page, a final outline, a note page (if you need one) and a page of works cited. (The formats for all of these are described later in this chapter.)

LIBRARY RESEARCH

If your instructor assigns a source paper that requires library research, this section can serve as a useful guide.

1. If you are beginning with a general subject, go to the library and do some preliminary reading. You might, for instance, go to an encyclopedia and read the entry on your subject, or you can find a relevant book in the card catalogue and read the introductory chapter. For more help, go to the *Reader's Guide to Periodical Literature* (more about that later) and read a couple of articles that seem to be overviews of your subject.

2. Now that you know more about your subject, begin to narrow it. It's just not possible to write a research paper on topics that are as broad as, let's say, censorship or bilingual education.

To narrow a subject, then, begin with something you're interested in and keep narrowing until you have a topic that you can deal with adequately in a short research paper. Let's begin with the subject of architecture and narrow that general subject down to an acceptable topic for a research paper.

1. architecture
2. monuments
3. ancient monuments
4. South Sea Islands monuments
5. Easter Island statues

You have arrived at an adequately narrowed topic, but you still need a thesis—a sentence or two that express a specific attitude or idea *about* that topic. So your next step is to turn the topic into a thesis by coming up with an idea about those statues.

6. There are three conflicting theories about how the Easter Island statues were constructed.

Now you have it.

2. Prepare a working outline. Break your topic down into the subtopics that occur to you at this point. The more detailed the preliminary outline is at this point, the more time you can save during the next step.

3. Go to the library and begin your research. To make this discussion more specific, we'll illustrate it with a thesis tied closely to a historical event—an analysis of the initial public reaction to the stock market crash of 1929, and with a thesis not tied to any particular date—the conflicting theories about how the Easter Island statues were constructed. Here, then, is how to find information in the library about these two research topics.

The Card Catalog

The card catalog is an index to books, and contains author cards, book title cards, and subject cards. Because you probably don't know any authors or titles that can be of use in your research yet, you'll be using only the subject cards to lead you to books about the Easter Island statues or about the stock market crash.

This is where your preliminary reading comes in handy. Because you have already learned something about your topic, you should know some key words that will lead you to a subject card that lists a book on the Easter Island statues. Try terms such as "archaeology," "South Sea islands," and "Easter Island." Keep looking and keep thinking of new key words until you have several likely sources.

For the stock market crash, look up key words like "business," "stock market," "economic depression," and other similar terms.

But if you find a book that covers your topic too thoroughly, you may have to find a new thesis. A research paper can be justified only if it requires evidence from a variety of sources. If the information you need can be found in a single work, you're not writing a true research paper.

In many modern libraries the card catalogue has been replaced by a microfilm catalogue or a computer catalogue. Do not be intimidated by this new technology. When you arrive at the microfilm viewer or computer station, there will be directions or a friendly librarian to help you learn how to use the machines.

The Reader's Guide to Periodical Literature

The Reader's Guide to Periodical Literature, located in the reference room, will likely be your handiest source of information. This multi-volumed set contains bibliographic information that will lead you to articles that were published in over one hundred of the most widely circulated magazines in the U.S.

The *RGPL* is easy to use. The volumes are arranged by years. (The first volume is dated 1900–1904.) In each volume, you can find entries under an author's name, the title of an article, or the subject of an article.

For your research on the Easter Island statues, it might be best to work backward, starting with the most recent year. Once again, look under key words that you think might lead you to magazine articles.

For your paper on the initial reaction to the stock market crash, begin with the 1929 volume—the year of the crash—and work your way forward for a year to two. Because you are writing about the initial reaction to the crash, there's no sense in going much further.

When you find an article listed, you will also find information specifying when and where the article was published. Before you go to the stacks to try to locate the magazine, check the index of the periodicals that are available in your library. This index is sometimes called a circular file.

New York Times Index

The volumes in this index are also arranged by year. Thus, you would consult the 1929 volume for the stock market crash. There you would find bibliographic information that will lead you to news articles and editorials on the crash of the market that appeared in the *New York Times*. Because the *New York Times* is on microfilm, you'll have to learn to use the microfilm reader.

Unless you know a particular date when the Easter Island statues were in the news, you're better off skipping the *New York Times Index* in your search for articles on the statues. Use your time wisely. You can come back to this index when you have a date or two.

Specialized Indexes

There are hundreds of other indexes to periodicals in addition to *The Reader's Guide to Periodical Literature*. For instance, if you need articles on art, applied science, biology, business, political science, and many other subjects, your library is likely to have an index that lists articles within those fields. If, for example, you were researching Picasso's Blue Period, you would certainly want to consult the *Art Index*, which lists articles in art journals from 1929 to the present. For our topic of the stock market crash, you might want to consult the *Business Periodicals Index*.

There isn't a specialized index for the Easter Island statues topic, but you might try the *Humanities Index*. It contains articles on fields as diverse as archeology and semantics.

Other Reference Works

In addition to the four main sources of information discussed above, you might want to use the other reference books that are usually located in the library's reference room. There are, for instance, specialized dictionaries. If you wanted to begin your paper with a quotation, you can find one on your subject in the *Oxford Dictionary of Quotations* or some other dictionary of quotations. To see how a word was used in 1856, you can look up the word in the thirteen-volume *Oxford English Dictionary*.

General encyclopedias like the *Encyclopaedia Britannica* and the *Encyclopedia Americana* can be useful, especially at the beginning of your research when you want an overview of the subject. The articles in these encyclopedias are usually followed by short bibliographies. Later on in your research you may need to consult a specialized encyclopedia. If you were writing on the origin of existentialism in France, for instance, you might want to consult the *Encyclopedia of Philosophy*.

Finally, there are atlases, year books, almanacs, who's whos, plot digests, and hundreds of other reference works to help you write a documented paper.

From this point on, complete your library paper by following the steps that we have described for writing a research paper based on the essays in this book (pp. 474–75). That is, you take notes, write a first draft, write a second draft, proofread your manuscript, and type a final version.

We have one more suggestion: when all else fails, talk to the research librarian. The research librarian can help you find the materials you need quickly and efficiently.

SPECIAL PROBLEMS IN RESEARCH WRITING

Handling Quotations

1. **Documenting Quotations.** Except for famous quotations used incidentally, all quoted material must be documented. That is, when you use a quotation, you also have to tell the reader where you found it.

2. Introducing Quotations. When you use a quotation, you should, at the very least, tell whom you are quoting and how the quotation is related to the idea that you just presented.

If you think it pertinent, include even more information, such as the writer's claim to expertise and the journal in which the article appeared. In this text, you can usually find information about an author in a note at the bottom of the page on which his or her work begins.

Do not simply add a quotation without some kind of introduction as in this example:

> Artists are sometimes delighted by the disruptive nature of art. "Art upsets, science reassures."

In order to write effectively, you must incorporate the quotation into the flow of your writing as in this example (note the bridge in italics):

> Artists are sometimes delighted by the disruptive nature of art. *The early 20th-century French expressionist, George Braque, for instance, once said, apparently with a great deal of satisfaction,* "Art upsets, science reassures."

All bridges into quotations needn't be quite so involved as this, but you do need to build some kind of a bridge into every quotation.

Handling Paraphrases and Summaries

Unlike quotations, which are the *exact* words of someone else's writing, summaries and paraphrases are *your* versions of someone else's writing.

Summaries and paraphrases differ only in their length. A summary is a very brief version of the original. You could, for instance, summarize an entire chapter with a single sentence. A paraphrase is much longer. In fact, a paraphrase is sometimes a sentence-by-sentence rewriting of the original, often approaching it in length.

1. Documenting Summaries and Paraphrases. In a research paper, summaries and paraphrases (like quotations) have to be documented. That is, you have to tell the reader, in a citation located at the back of your paper, exactly where you found your borrowing, right down to the page number.

You don't, however, have to document common facts. For instance, you wouldn't have to tell your reader where you found the fact that the stock market crashed in 1929. That fact is not arguable, and it can be found in all books that have to do with the stock market crash. As you might expect, much of the information found in a general encyclopedia doesn't need to be documented. Encyclopedias generally deal with information about ideas, people, and events that is neither arguable nor unique. (Remember that you should not rely too heavily on encyclopedias as sources in a research paper.)

Most of the information in your research paper, however, will be followed by documentation. But you don't need to stop after every sentence to document the information in that sentence. Think in terms of paragraphs. That is, if you are writing a paragraph that is a paraphrase of someone else's paragraph, wait until you get to its end before you stop to document it. The reader knows, then, that the entire paragraph is indebted to the source that is found documented at its end. If, however, you add a quotation in the middle of a paragraph—either from the source you're paraphrasing or from another source—you'll have to stop to document it. Readers expect each quotation to be followed by its source. Of course, if your paragraph is composed from a variety of sources, you'll have to stop to document each one.

2. Summaries and paraphrases need adequate introductions. Of course, you needn't put quotation marks around summaries and paraphrases, but you do have to prepare the reader for the summary or paraphrase by constructing the same kind of bridge or words that you use to introduce quotations. At the very least, you should inform the reader who wrote the original. It is even better to provide your reader with the author's claim to expertise. You can do this by introducing your quotation with a statement like this: "Jamie Larson, a Smithsonian historian, says that . . ."

You will often need to include, within that introduction, transitional words such as "for instance" and "according to." ("*According to* James Johnson, a Harvard psychologist, . . .") If you think it significant, include even more information, like the writer's century and country.

Let us reiterate: don't move from your prose into that of someone else without telling your reader, in a clear introduction, something about the source you're using. And when you change sources, stop to inform your reader of that change. Don't allow the reader, even for a second, to confuse your statements with those of your sources.

3. While you're paraphrasing, frequently remind your reader that these are not your ideas. We have italicized those little reminders in the following paraphrase.

> In "Cruel Lib," Keith Mano says that it's a hard truth for many people to face, but most people are not very talented, pretty, or "charismatic." When they discover their real self, *Mano says*, they usually find that there's not much there. *Mano concludes* by saying that it's sometimes better for people to be limited—and thus protected from life's harsher realities—by the roles that society expects them to play than to have their inadequacies constantly exposed to the world.

Without these constant reminders, it's hard for a reader to keep track of the point of view within a paragraph.

How to Paraphrase Effectively

Because you should only use quoted material when it is especially effective, much of your research paper will be made up of paraphrases. Therefore, it's vital to learn how to paraphrase well. To illustrate the techniques of this skill, let's look at an original passage from a short review of a play, *The Diary of Anne Frank*, followed by three paraphrases of parts of that review. First the original:

> The intent of <u>The Diary of Anne Frank</u> is to communicate the fear and claustrophobia of the characters, who are hiding from the Gestapo. If we did not share the feelings of these Jewish fugitives in the overcrowded loft of an Amsterdam office building, we should soon tire of what is, after all, only another picture of life in a tenement. But the authors have done their work so well that there is no evading the special tension inherent in the situation.
>
> The play gives a vivid picture of the stresses and strains on the tempers and characters of the two families huddled into the same cramped refuge. And when the good and bad qualities of the refugees have been sufficiently exposed, the developing characters of the young diarist and her shy lover emerge to give the play shape and force.

And here are three paraphrases, each followed by a brief analysis.

> **Paraphrase 1:** This play communicates the fear of hiding from the Gestapo. We share the feelings of the Jewish fugitives in the overcrowded loft; if we did not we should soon tire of just another picture of life in a tenement. But there is no evading the special tension in the situation.
>
> The play gives a vivid picture of the two families huddled into the cramped refuge. The developing characters of the young diarist and her shy lover emerge to give the play shape and force.

This paraphrase is weak—indeed, it approaches plagiarism—because it uses too much of the original passage's diction and sentence structure. For instance, the original contains the phrase, "to communicate the fear and claustrophobia of the characters, who are hiding from the Gestapo." The paraphraser's version ("communicates the fear of the people who are hiding from the Gestapo") is not only too close in diction ("communicates the fear" and "hiding from the Gestapo"), but it is also obvious that the syntax of the paraphrase is modeled on the syntax of the source. Later in the paraphrase the writer again picks up too much of the original's diction. He uses, for instance, these words from his source: "families huddled," "cramped refuge," "shy lovers," "emerge," and "shape."

Of course, you have to use many of the common words that your source uses, but you shouldn't use too many words that seem a part of the source's idiom, or style. It's not enough to merely leave out a word or two and change a word here and there. A paraphrase has to be in *your* idiom, not in that of the original author. If you have problems with this, you might have to read a passage carefully, set it aside, and then try to get the gist of it down on paper without referring back to the original until you're finished.

A paraphrase also has to be an *accurate* representation of an original passage. It shouldn't mislead the reader into thinking that the original says something that it doesn't. Here's an example of that:

> **Paraphrase 2:** The play explains what it is like to hide from the Gestapo. However, we soon tire of this, because it is just another picture of slum life.

As you can see, the reviewer doesn't say that we soon tire of the play because it is just another picture of slum life. The reviewer says that *if* we didn't share their feelings, we would soon tire of the play. That is a big difference. The paraphraser misread the original—and therefore misrepresented it to us.

And finally, here is a good paraphrase of the original:

> **Paraphrase 3:** This play shows us, quite forcibly, the strains of two Jewish families who are hiding in a loft from the German Gestapo. The authors infuse their play with a special emotional quality that lifts it above other plays about tenement families.
>
> The strain of living under such conditions brings out, very clearly, both the virtues and the vices of the characters. But it is a growing love between Anne Frank and a young boy that, finally, lends shape and emotional impact to the play.

In summary, a paraphrase must be put into the paraphraser's own idiom, and it must be faithful to the original.

FORMAT

Here are the five parts of a research paper that most instructors normally emphasize.

1. title page
2. outline (optional, especially in short papers)
3. text, with citations
4. a page for notes (if you use any)
5. a page for a list of the works you've cited in your text (roughly equivalent to the old bibliography page)

Format for the Title Page

For a title page, one picture *is* worth a thousand words. So here is what one looks like. Use it as your model.

The Controversy over the Language of Advertising
by
Shirley Donahue

English 101, Section 4
Mr. Phillips
November 3, 1986

Outline Format

The outline of your research paper comes next. It serves as your table of contents and begins on a new page. Here is the way it looks:

```
                         Outline

Thesis: The controversy surrounding the language of ad-
        vertising centers around the issue of fairness.
  I. Many critics believe that the language of advertis-
     ing is unfair.
           A. One critic believes that advertisers used
              too many "weasel" words.
           B. Another critic believes that advertisers
              pander to our base emotions.
           C. Yet another critic believes that advertis-
              ers make false claims.

 II. Many supporters argue that the language of adver-
     tising is not unfair.
           A. One writer says that the language of adver-
              tising simply reflects a society's values
              and shouldn't be singled out for blame.
           B. Another writer says that some critics mis-
              understand the intent of advertising.
           C. Another defender claims that advertising is
              similar to poetry in its manipulation of
              language.
```

Text Format, Including Format for In-Text Citation

On the first page of the text, repeat the paper's title about ten lines from the top of the page. Don't number the first page, but do number all pages thereafter, including the "Notes" page and the "Works Cited" page. Page numbers appear in the upper right-hand corner.

You may be happy to know that there's a new and easier way for you to acknowledge information that you have borrowed. The Modern Language Association has recently simplified the whole process of citing sources.

Footnotes are no longer used to document material that you have borrowed from secondary sources. Now when you borrow someone else's ideas, you need only to follow the borrowing with the page number of the article or book that you have borrowed from. (Use the page numbers in this text as if they were the page numbers of the original sources.) These brief acknowledgments direct your reader to a separate page called "Works Cited," which is located at the end of your paper. There the reader can find the complete bibliographic information about your sources. Here then is what a citation within the text looks like:

```
A cardiologist, Gregory Wallace, claims that too much aerobic ex-
ercise actually damages the heart (59).
```

Now your reader knows to look up "Wallace" in the alphabetized list of works that you've used to write your paper, and that this information was taken from page 59 of the Wallace work.

Of course, if you don't mention the author's name within your text, you'll need to include his or her name in the parenthesis. Otherwise your reader wouldn't know which of the entries in your "Works Cited" list that page number in your text belongs to. Here, then, is the way a citation should look if you don't use the author's name in the text:

```
One cardiologist claims that too much aerobic exercise actually
damages the heart (Wallace 59).
```

OTHER EXCEPTIONS

1. If you use more than one work by Wallace in your paper, you'll have to add the name of the article you are referring to: ("Is Too Much Exercise Bad for You?" 67).
2. If you are referring to an anonymous work, put the name of the article in parenthesis: (*Annual Report* 23).
3. If a title is long, use a shortened version, but be certain that the shortened version begins with the same word in the title that is alphabetized in your "Works Cited."
4. When your borrowing comes from a work that consists of more than one volume, you'll have to include the volume number and page number within the parenthesis: (Hibbard 3:   12). Now the reader knows to go to page 12 of the third volume of Hibbard's work.
5. When you refer to a play, put in the act and scene: (*Macbeth* III,i). Of course, if you mention the play in your text, you needn't repeat the title in the parenthesis.

And that's about it. This revised style eliminates footnote format problems. You no longer need to worry about running out of room at the bottom of the page before you can type your footnote in. In most cases all you have to do is put a page number in parenthesis immediately following your quotation or paraphrase.

Note Page Format

There is a separate "Notes" page for supplementary information that might be helpful to your reader. Of course, if you don't feel the need to make these supplementary comments, you don't need a note page at all. But if you do, merely put a superscript number where you want the reader to leave the text and go to your page called "Notes." (To put in a superscript number, roll up your paper half a notch and type in the number.) Here's the way your text will look when you use a note number:

```
Of course, not all Hispanics are eager to have their children go
through a bilingual program.¹
```

The number "1" directs your reader to a "Notes" page, which is located between the last page of the text and the "Works Cited" page. Here's the format for that "Notes" page:

```
                            Notes

        ¹Richard Rodriguez's autobiography tells of his
   schoolboy experiences as a Hispanic in a school in
   which the vast majority of teachers and students were
   Anglos.  He concludes that his immersion in English—
   as painful as it might have been—was the best thing
   that could have happened to him (13).

        ²For a further discussion of Hispanic parents' am-
   bivalence concerning their children's education, see
   Smyth 24—35.
```

As you see, each item is indented five spaces and begins with a superscript number. The author's name, Smyth, mentioned in note 2, refers your reader to the alphabetical listing in "Works Cited." Note 1 needs only a page number because the author's name, Rodriguez, is mentioned in the note itself. The reader thus knows to look up "Rodriguez" in the "Works Cited" page.

Works Cited Page Format

The "Works Cited" page located in the rear of a paper contains an alphabetized list of every work that is mentioned in the parentheses scattered throughout the research paper.

Before we get to the format for those entries, here's what a small "Works Cited" page looks like. Note that the entries are alphabetized by the author's last name. When an article has an anonymous author, alphabetize by the name of the article, disregarding the words "a," "an," and "the."

```
                          Works Cited

    Anderson, George M.  "American Imprisonment Today."
         American 46 (1982): 354-56.
    Baugh, Albert C., and others  A Literary History of En-
         gland.  New York: Appleton-Century, 1948.
    Hendin, David.  Death as a Fact of Life.  New York:
         Norton, 1973.
    "I Pulled the Plug."  Family Health July-Aug. 1980.
    Ivins, Molly.  "New Environmental Fight Looms over De-
         veloping Coal-Rich Utah Area."  New York Times
         12 March 1979, A14.
    Sandburg, Carl.  Abraham Lincoln: The War Years.
         4 vols. New York: Harcourt Brace, 1939.
```

Now we can go on to the formats for the individual entries in that "Works Cited" page. If none of the following model entries matches the kind of entry you've come up with, either use the model that is closest to your entry or combine formats from different entries. For example, let's say you need to acknowledge an idea from a pamphlet that has two editors. First, follow the general format for pamphlets. Then follow the format for authors with two or more books (under "Books"). Finally, add the word "eds." (plural of ed.) in the proper location. That proper spot can be found by looking under the heading "Book with an Editor." It's very simple, and sometimes you'll need to be creative. Here's what you've come up with:

> George, Marie and Joe Fulsome, eds. <u>Saving the Tigers</u>. Pam-
> phlet. Los Angeles: Save the Beasts Association, 1985.

BOOKS

Book with a Single Author

Hendin, David. <u>Death as a Fact of Life</u>. New York: Norton, 1973.

Book with Two Authors

Funk, Wilfred, and Norman Lewis. <u>30 Days to a More Powerful Vocabu-
lary</u>. New York: Pocket Books, 1970.

Book with More Than Two Authors

Baugh, Albert C., and others. <u>A Literary History of England</u>. New
York: Appleton-Century Crofts, 1948.

Book with Corporate Author

American Health Society. <u>Heart Disease</u>. Garden City, New York:
American Health Society, 1981.

A Work in More Than One Volume

Sandburg, Carl. <u>Abraham Lincoln: The War Years</u>. 4 vols. New York:
Harcourt Brace, 1939.

An Edition of a Book After the First Edition

McCrimmon, James M., <u>Writing with a Purpose</u>. 3rd ed. New York:
Houghton Mifflin, 1963.

An Article or Story in an Edited Book

Kramer, Samuel. "Sumerian Literature and the Bible." In <u>The Bible in
Its Literary Milieu</u>. Eds. John Maier and Vincent Tollers.
Grand Rapids: William B. Eerdmans, 1979. 272-84.

MAGAZINES AND NEWSPAPERS

Signed Article in a Magazine with Separate Pagination in Each Issue

Lambert, Darwin. "We Can Have Wilderness Wherever We Choose." <u>The
Reader's Digest</u>. May 1972: 125-28.

Unsigned Article in a Magazine with Separate Pagination in Each Issue

"I Pulled the Plug." <u>Family Health</u> July-Aug. 1980: 30-33.

Article in a Magazine with Continuous Pagination Throughout a Volume of Issues

Anderson, George M. "American Imprisonment Today." <u>America</u> 46
    (1982): 354—56.

Newspaper

Ivins, Molly.   "New Environmental Fight Looms over Developing Coal-
    Rich Utah Area." <u>New</u> <u>York</u> <u>Times</u> 12 March 1979, sec. A: 14.

Book Review

Goatley, David.   "Saving the Waves."   Rev. of <u>Golden</u> <u>Caves</u>, by Angie
    Davis.   <u>West</u> <u>Coast</u> <u>Review</u> 3 March 1979: 41—42.

ENCYCLOPEDIAS, PAMPHLETS, AND OTHERS

Encyclopedia

Goedicke, Hans.   "Sphinx in Art and Mythology." <u>Encyclopedia</u> <u>Ameri-</u>
    <u>cana</u>.   1971 ed.

Almanac

"Nobel Prize Winners."   <u>Reader's</u> <u>Digest</u> <u>Almanac</u> <u>and</u> <u>Yearbook</u>.
    1980 ed.

Pamphlet

<u>Automobile</u> <u>Safety</u>.   Pamphlet.   Detroit: National Consumer's Associa-
    tion, 1972.

Radio or Television Newscast

News story on NBC Nightly News.   NBC, 12 March 1985.

Copyrights
and Acknowledgments

The authors are grateful to the following publishers and copyright holders for permission to use the selections reprinted in this book.

AMERICAN ASSOCIATION FOR THE ADVANCEMENT OF SCIENCE   "Sex Differences in Mathematical Reasoning Ability: More Facts" by Camilla Persson Benbow and Julian C. Stanley from *Science*, December 2, 1983. Copyright © 1983 by the American Association for the Advancement of Science.

BASIC BOOKS   "Pornography, Obscenity, and the Case for Censorship," excerpt from *Reflections of a Neoconservative: Looking Back, Looking Ahead* by Irving Kristol. Copyright © 1983 by Basic Books, Inc., Publishers. Reprinted by permission of the publisher.

CHICAGO TRIBUNE   "A Forest of Manmade Threats Descends on Yellowstone" by James Coates from *The Chicago Tribune*, May 19, 1985. Copyright © 1985 by *The Chicago Tribune*. Reprinted by permission of *The Chicago Tribune*.

CHRISTIANITY TODAY   "The Arguments in Favor of Abortion Are Strong if You Accept One Important Assumption" by Dr. Lewis B. Smedes from *Christianity Today*, July 15, 1983. Copyright © 1983 by *Christianity Today*. Reprinted by permission. "Does Life Begin Before Birth?" by John R. W. Stott from *Christianity Today*, September 5, 1980. Copyright © 1980 by *Christianity Today*. Reprinted by permission.

THE CHRISTIAN CENTURY   "Concerning Abortion: An Attempt at a Rational View" by Charles Hartshorne from *The Christianity Century*, January 21, 1981. Copyright © 1981 by The Christian Century Foundation. Reprinted by permission of *The Christian Century*.

JAMES LINCOLN COLLIER   "It *Is* Different for Women" by James Lincoln Collier from *Reader's Digest*, January 1982. Reprinted by permission of the author.

JUDITH CRIST   "Censorship and the Movies" (our title) by Judith Crist from *Censorship: For and Against*, ed. Harold Hart. Reprinted by permission of the author.

DON CONGDON ASSOCIATES   "The Damnation of a Canyon" from *Beyond the Wall* by Edward Abbey. Copyright © 1984 by Edward Abbey. Reprinted by permission of Don Congdon Associates, Inc.

Author-Title Index

N

Nakashima, Ted, "Concentration Camp: U.S. Style," 405

Nathanson, Bernard N., "Deeper into Abortion," 96

Nation, "Life in a California Concentration Camp," 403

"New Environmental Fight Looms over Developing Coal-Rich Utah Area," Molly Ivins, 37

New Republic, "Conditions at Camp Harmony," 414

Newsweek, "The Dies Report," 402

"Nisei Come Home, The," Victor Boesen, 447

O

Obscenity—Forget It," Charles Rembar, 340

"Of Two Minds about Abortion," Andrew Hacker, 99

O'Neill, Charles A., "The Language of Advertising," 159

"On Three Ways of Writing for Children," C. S. Lewis, 300

"Outcast Americans," William Robinson, 407

"Our Worst Wartime Mistake," Eugene V. Rostow, 439

P

Packard, Vance, ". . . And the Hooks Are Lowered," 131

Park, Charles F., Jr., "Conservation and the Environmental Crisis," 32

"Perils of Paul, the Pangs of Pauline, The," Jo Durden-Smith and Diane deSimone, 201

Phelps, Ethel Johnston, "The World of Fairy Tales," 313

Piercy, Marge, "Barbie Doll," 177

"Place of Pornography, The," Lewis H. Lapham, 367

"Pornography, Censorship, and Common Sense" (an interview with Alexander Bickel), George Denison, 330

"Pornography, Obscenity, and the Case for Censorship," Irving Kristol, 358

"Postwar Exports," *Time*, 438

"Pregnancy or Abortion: A Wrenching Choice," Sydney J. Harris, 121

Preston, Ivan L., "Puffery Is Deception," 150

"Psychological Case Against the Fairy Tale, The," H. E. Wheeler, 283

"Puffery Is Deception," Ivan L. Preston, 150

R

"Racism on the West Coast," Carey McWilliams, 432

Reed, Sally, "Bilingual Classes: A Bilateral Conflict," 257

Rembar, Charles, "Obscenity—Forget It," 340

Riggs, Cynthia, "Access to Public Lands: A National Necessity," 68

Robinson, William, "Outcast Americans," 407

Rodriguez, Richard, "The Education of Richard Rodriguez," 242

Rostow, Eugene V., "Our Worst Wartime Mistake," 439

S

Sandza, Richard, "'Boomers' vs. 'Sniffers,'" 66

Schrank, Jeffrey, "The Language of Advertising Claims," 153

"Secular Infallibility," Frank Zepezauer, 117

Seligmann, Jean, "The Medical Quandary," 124

"Sex Differences in Mathematical Reasoning Ability: More Facts," Camilla Perrson Benbow and Julian C. Stanley, 221

"Should Advertising Be Eliminated?" Samm Sinclair Baker, 144

Smedes, Lewis, B., "The Arguments in Favor of Abortion Are Strong if You Accept One Important Assumption," 122

"Snow White," Jakob Grimm and Wilhelm Grimm, 277

Stanley, Julian C. *See* Benbow, Camilla Perrson

Stegner, Wallace, "Wilderness Letter," 24

Steinem, Gloria, "The Ultimate Invasion of Privacy," 109

Stott, John R., "Does Life Begin Before Birth?" 106